Introducing Christianity

What is Christianity? How did it begin? What do Christians believe? What are their customs and history? How has Christianity developed though the centuries, and how diverse is Christianity today? *Introducing Christianity* is an essential introduction to one of the world's great religious traditions.

James Adair narrates the history of Christianity, the intellectual and historical context of its origins, its triumph under the Romans, the upheavals of the Crusades, the Protestant and Catholic Reformations and the challenges of the Enlightenment and of the modern age. He explores the intriguing new forms Christianity took in the nineteenth century, the evolution of sects such as Mormonism and Jehovah's Witnesses, and its mission to Africa. Taking a historical and phenomenological approach, Adair interrogates Christianity's role in the modern world, as he surveys liturgical, geographical and denominational perspectives of contemporary Christianity, as well as how Christians interact with modern culture, particularly science, the arts, ethics, political and other religions.

Written in a vivid and lively style, by an experienced teacher, *Introducing Christianity* is the ideal resource for students beginning their studies of Christianity. Richly illustrated, it also includes quotations from original sources, learning goals, summary boxes, questions for discussion, and suggestions for further reading, and a comprehensive glossary, to aid study and revision.

James R. Adair is Assistant Professor at Baptist University of the Américas in San Antonio, Texas. He was the editor of the *Society of Biblical Literature Text-Critical monograph series* from 1997–2004 and is the general editor of *TC: A Journal of Biblical Textual Criticism*.

World Religions series

Edited by Damien Keown and Charles S. Prebish

This exciting series introduces students to the major world religious traditions. Each religion is explored in a lively and clear fashion by experienced teachers and leading scholars in the field of world religion. Up-to-date scholarship is presented in a student-friendly fashion, covering history, core beliefs, sacred texts, key figures, religious practice and culture, and key contemporary issues. To aid learning and revision, each text includes illustrations, summaries, explanations of key terms, and further reading.

Introducing Buddhism
Charles S. Prebish and Damien Keown

Introducing Christianity
James R. Adair

Introducing Hinduism
Hillary P. Rodrigues

Introducing Japanese Religion
Robert Ellwood

Forthcoming:

Introducing American Religions
Introducing Chinese Religions
Introducing Daoism
Introducing Islam
Introducing Judaism
Introducing New Religious Movements
Introducing Tibetan Buddhism

Introducing Christianity

James R. Adair

Routledge
Taylor & Francis Group

NEW YORK AND LONDON

First published 2008
by Routledge
270 Madison Ave, New York, NY 10016

Simultaneously published in the UK
by Routledge
2 Park Square, Milton Park, Abingdon, Oxon OX14 4RN

Routledge is an imprint of the Taylor & Francis Group, an informa business

© 2008 James R. Adair

Typeset in Jenson and Tahoma by
HWA Text and Data Management, Tunbridge Wells
Printed and bound in Great Britain by
TJ International Ltd, Padstow, Cornwall

Library of Congress Cataloging-in-Publication Data
A catalog record for this book has been applied for

ISBN10: 0–415–77211–7 (hbk)
ISBN10: 0–415–77212–5 (pbk)

ISBN13: 978–0-415–77211–2 (hbk)
ISBN13: 978–0–415–77212–9 (pbk)

Contents

Illustrations

Figures

Charts

Maps

Acknowledgments

We are indebted to the people and archives listed below for permission to reproduce photographs or original illustrative material. Every effort has been made to trace copyright-holders. Any omissions brought to our attention will be remedied in future editions.

Figure 1.1 Illustration from John Bunyan's *The Pilgrim's Progress* © CORBIS.

Figure 1.2 Page from a Gutenberg Bible © Annebique Bernard/CORBIS SYGMA

Figure 2.1 Floorplan of St Peter's Basilica, Rome from Carlo Fontana, *Il Tempio Vaticano e sua origene* (Rome: Francesco Buagni, 1694), p. 381

Figure 2.4 Detail showing figures' faces from *Pieta* by Michelangelo Buonarroti © David Lees/CORBIS

Figure 4.1 Detail of *Deesis* mosaic in Hagia Sophia © Hanan Isachar/CORBIS

Figure 5.1 Detail of *Disputation with Simon Magus and Crucifixion of Saint Peter* by Filippino Lippi © Atlantide Phototravel/CORBIS

Figure 5.2 *The School of Athens* by Raphael, Alinari Archives/CORBIS

Figure 6.1 Statue of Diocletian © Bettmann/CORBIS

Figure 7.1 Gold medallion with Constantine and Alexander the Great © Krause, Johansen/Archivo Iconografico, SA/

Figure 7.2 St Catherine's Monastery near Mt Sinai © Hanan Isachar/CORBIS

Figure 8.1 The Court of Theodora © Archivo Iconografico, S.A./CORBIS

Figure 9.1 Exterior view of Hagia Sophia © Francesco Venturi/CORBIS

Figure 10.1 *David* by Michelangelo Buonarroti © Todd Gipstein/CORBIS

Figure 10.2 *The Ecstasy of Saint Catherine of Siena* by Agostino Carracci © Alinari Archives/CORBIS

Figure 10.3 *Virgin of Guadalupe* by Isidro Escamilla © Brooklyn Museum/CORBIS

Figure 11.1 Exterior of St Peter's Basilica, Rome from Carlo Fontana, *Il Tempio Vaticano e sua origene* (Rome: Francesco Buagni, 1694), p. 417

Figure 11.2 Portrait of Martin Luther by Lucas Cranach the Elder © Bettmann/CORBIS

Figure 12.1 Jean-Jacques Rousseau by La Tour © Bettmann/CORBIS

Figure 13.1 Allan Pinkerton, Abraham Lincoln, and John A. McClernand © Bettmann/ CORBIS

Figure 13.2 Aquatint portrait of Simón Bolívar © Bettmann/CORBIS

Figure 14.1 Pope Pius XI © Bettmann/CORBIS

Figure 15.1 Ecumenical Patriarch Bartholomew I, the website of the Ecumenical Patriarch

Figure 15.2 Baker Mushroom Cloud © CORBIS

Figure 15.3 The World Council of Churches © Igor Sperotto/WCC

Figure 16.1 Dome of St Paul's Cathedral © Construction Photography/CORBIS

Figure 18.1 Lyndon Johnson and Martin Luther King © Bettmann/CORBIS

Figure 19.1 Luis Palau © Brooks Kraft/CORBIS

Figure 20.1 16th-century miniature painting depicting Noah's Ark © Archivo Icono-grafico, S.A./CORBIS

Figure 20.2 "Mr Bergh to the Rescue," cartoon by Thomas Nast © CORBIS

Figure 21.1 Detail of the *Ecstasy of Saint Teresa* by Gianlorenzo Bernini © Bettmann/ CORBIS

Figure 21.2 St Basil's Cathedral, Moscow © Barry Lewis/CORBIS

Figure 21.3 Interior of The Crystal Cathedral © G.E. Kidder Smith/CORBIS

Figure 22.1 Robinson smiles as he takes seat in bishop's chair in New Hampshire © Brian Snyder/Reuters/CORBIS

Figure 22.2 Archbishop Oscar Romero © Leif Skoogfors/CORBIS

Figure 23.1 Hurba Synagogue © Hanan Isachar/CORBIS

Figure 23.2 Rio de Janeiro and Christ the Redeemer © Imageplus/CORBIS

Abbreviations of the books of the Bible

Gen	Genesis	Amos	Amos
Exod	Exodus	Obad	Obadiah
Lev	Leviticus	Jon	Jonah
Num	Numbers	Mic	Micah
Deut	Deuteronomy	Nah	Nahum
Josh	Joshua	Hab	Habakkuk
Jdg	Judges	Zeph	Zephaniah
Ruth	Ruth	Hag	Haggai
1 Sam	1 Samuel	Zech	Zechariah
2 Sam	2 Samuel	Mal	Malachi
1 Kgs	1 Kings	1 Esd	1 Esdras
2 Kgs	2 Kings	Tob	Tobit
1 Chron	1 Chronicles	Jdt	Judith
2 Chron	2 Chronicles	1 Macc	1 Maccabees
Ezra	Ezra	2 Macc	2 Maccabees
Neh	Nehemiah	3 Macc	3 Maccabees
Est	Esther	Wisd	Wisdom of Solomon
Job	Job	Ecclus	Ecclesiasticus
Ps(s)	Psalm(s)	PrMan	Prayer of Manasseh
Prov	Proverbs	Bar	Baruch
Eccl	Ecclesiastes	Matt	Matthew
Song	Song of Solomon	Mark	Mark
Isa	Isaiah	Luke	Luke
Jer	Jeremiah	John	John
Lam	Lamentations	Acts	Acts
Ezek	Ezekiel	Rom	Romans
Dan	Daniel	1 Cor	1 Corinthians
Hos	Hosea	2 Cor	2 Corinthians
Joel	Joel	Gal	Galatians

Eph	Ephesians	Jas	James
Phil	Philippians	1 Pet	1 Peter
Col	Colossians	2 Pet	2 Peter
1 Thess	1 Thessalonians	1 John	1 John
2 Thess	2 Thessalonians	2 John	2 John
1 Tim	1 Timothy	3 John	3 John
2 Tim	2 Timothy	Jude	Jude
Titus	Titus	Rev	Revelation
Phlm	Philemon		
Heb	Hebrews		

Other abbreviations

Ign *Eph* Ignatius, *Epistle to the Ephesians*
1 Clem   1 Clement

Part I

Introduction to Christianity

1   *Basic questions*

And it was in Antioch that the disciples were first called Christians.

(Acts 11:26)

In this chapter

What is religion? What is myth? What are sin, salvation, and faith? What is the Bible? How is Christianity related to other religions? These are some of the basic questions that students need to ask as they start their study of Christianity. This chapter answers these questions, or, in most cases, offers entrées into the discussion of answers to these questions, for many of them defy a simple answer.

Main topics covered

- Definition and discussion of religion
- Definition and discussion of myth
- Definition and discussion of sin
- Definition and discussion of salvation
- Definition and discussion of faith
- Contents and overview of the Christian scripture
- Relationship between Christianity and other religions

Christianity came into being in a distant corner of the Roman Empire during the reign of the emperor Tiberius, about 30 C.E. Like another great world religion, Buddhism, Christianity drew its name not from the personal name of its founder, Jesus of Nazareth, but from his title, "the Christ." The earliest adherents of Christianity were Jews from the region of Galilee, north of Jerusalem, but followers of "The Way," as many early Christians called their movement, were soon to be found throughout the Roman Empire and beyond. Although most of the earliest Christians were Jews, Christianity became a predominantly Gentile (i.e. non-Jewish) movement within 100 years of Jesus' death. The Christian church grew through times of peace and persecution over the next two centuries, eventually becoming the official religion of the Roman Empire (as well as other, smaller states to the east and south). Christianity has continued to grow, and to develop, over the centuries, and today it claims more than 2 billion followers worldwide, comprising almost one-third of the earth's population.

What is Christianity? What are its origins? What do Christians believe? What are their customs and history? How has Christianity developed through the centuries, and how diverse is Christianity today? These and many other questions will be addressed in subsequent sections of this study. First, however, it is important to discuss briefly the overall approach that this book will take as it presents Christianity to the reader. In this book, Christianity will be discussed from the perspectives of history and phenomenology rather than theology. The distinction is important. The historical, phenomenological approach to Christianity adopted here will describe the origins and growth of the Christian movement in relation to the surrounding culture and competing ideas, not in an attempt to demonstrate the superiority of Christianity to other religions, nor to describe in intricate detail the doctrines and dogmas of one branch of Christianity or another (for significant differences, as well an important similarities, do exist), but rather to paint a picture of Christianity as it has manifested itself through the two millennia of its development, up to the present day. Approximately two-thirds of the book will describe the history of Christianity, from its origins to the present day, and the other third will describe what Christianity looks like today and how its adherents interact with various aspects of the modern world, including science, the arts, ethics, politics, spirituality, and other religions.

Some theologians in the 1960s and 1970s proclaimed that God is dead, and others today have proclaimed the modern era a "post-Christian" age. There is no doubt that the challenges of both modernism and postmodernism are changing the way that many people view Christianity, but it must also be said that Christianity remains a vibrant religion in which untold millions of people continue to find comfort, strength, guidance, and meaning – albeit in many different ways! As you get ready to dive into the study of this fascinating religion, prepare to discover in Christianity a movement whose roots predate Jesus but extend into the present, churches that – for the most part – share a core set of beliefs but vary widely in other matters of faith and practice, and individuals who have been inspired to do great and sometimes terrible things in the name of Christ.

Before delving into the historical origins of Christianity, it is helpful first to address some fundamental questions about religion in general and Christianity as a particular manifestation of religion. We will then offer a brief, factual overview of Christianity in comparison with other religions, as well as various forms of Christianity in comparison with one another. Finally, although our primary focus in this study will not be theology, we will discuss briefly the concept of the divine, or sacred, as it is treated in Christianity.

What is religion?

When we say that Christianity is one of the major world religions, what exactly do we mean by the term *religion*? Although this question might appear to be easy to answer, it is not. *Religion* is notoriously hard to define. Consider, for example, the following two definitions.

> Action or conduct indicating a belief in, reverence for, and desire to please a divine ruling power, the exercise or practice of rites or observances implying this ... a particular system of faith worship.
>
> (*Oxford English Dictionary*)

> A religion is a unified system of beliefs and practices relative to sacred things, that is to say, things set apart and forbidden – beliefs and practices which unite into one single moral community called a Church, all those who adhere to them.
>
> (Durkheim 1915: 62)

Both definitions indicate that both belief and practice help define religion, but neither covers even every major world religion, much less the smaller religious traditions. Not all religions are concerned with pleasing a divine ruling power, nor are the beliefs and practices which characterize some religions particularly unified or systematic. In his classic work on world religions, *The Religions of Man*, Huston Smith says,

> Religion alone confronts the individual with the most momentous option this world can present. It calls the soul to the highest adventure it can undertake, a proposed journey across the jungles, peaks, and deserts of the human spirit.
>
> (Smith 1958: 11)

Again, however, this description of religion fails to cover every instance of religious expression, since not all religions include the concept of the soul.

All of the previous attempts to define religion do so in terms of groups of adherents. William James, in his study *The Varieties of Religious Experience*, opts for a more individualistic definition:

> The feelings, acts, and experiences of individual men in their solitude, so far as they apprehend themselves to stand in relation to whatever they may consider the divine.
>
> (James 1902: 31)

Similarly, Friedrich Schleiermacher says,

> Religion is for you at one time a way of thinking, a faith, a peculiar way of contemplating the world, and of combining what meets us in the world: at another, it is a way of acting, a peculiar desire and love, a special kind of conduct and character.
>
> (Schleiermacher 1958: 27)

However, can *religion* really be defined on so narrow a basis as individual faith and practice? If so, then there are probably millions, or even billions, of different religions in the world today.

To return to a more "corporate" definition, Rudolph Otto, in *The Idea of the Holy*, describes the sacred, or divine, with the Latin phrase *mysterium tremendum et fascinans*, "terrifying and fascinating mystery" (Otto 1958: 12, 35; the composite phrase expresses Otto's view, although he never uses it himself). Ninian Smart likes this definition of the Holy within religion, but he notes that not all religions refer to an external source of inspiration or fear, so he advocates adding the idea of inner enlightenment, or mysticism, to Otto's definition (Smart 1977: 21). Timothy Fitzgerald warns that all attempts to define religion run the risk of imposing one set of cultural assumptions and values (e.g. the Western worldview) on people whose beliefs and practices might be quite different from one's own.

> The term "religion" is meant to be neutral and apply to all cases, leaving out a faith commitment in the method of study. However, it still imports a host of assumptions that can distort the object of study; chief among them the assumption that "religion" is about human responses to the divine.
>
> (Fitzgerald 2000: 10)

In the light of this proliferation of attempts to define *religion*, it is apparent that a single definition is unlikely to cover every distinct system of religious beliefs and practices adequately. However, there is enough commonality among them to give the reader a general idea of some necessary components of any religion: adherents, beliefs, practices, and some concept of a reality or realities beyond ordinary human experience. Christianity, of course, does explicitly include the concept of the divine, and one can arrive at a set of core beliefs with which most, though not all, people who identify themselves as Christians would agree. But is the very idea of religion still valid in the modern world, and, if so, is Christianity, as some Christians claim, the very antithesis of religion?

Karl Barth, one of the most influential theologians of the twentieth century, denied that Christianity was a religion, for he saw a qualitative difference between the two. For Barth, religion is the human attempt to reach God, whereas Christianity is God's attempt to reach humankind: "The revelation of God denies that any religion is true. … No religion can stand before the grace of God as true religion" (Barth 1936–1977: 1.2: 325–6). Barth's distinction between religion and Christianity, however, is based on his idiosyncratic definition of religion, a definition that followers of other religions would not necessarily accept. (Nor would they accept his claims that Christianity is uniquely revealed by God, an idea common to many religious traditions.) Dietrich Bonhoeffer borrowed Barth's terminology concerning the distinction between Christianity and religion, but he critiqued Barth's view as "a positivism of revelation" (Bonhoeffer 1967: 140), preferring instead to go beyond Barth and question whether it was possible to envision a "religionless" or secular form of Christianity, one in which traditional understandings of God were no longer important (140–1). Bonhoeffer's musings about religionless Christianity, along with more recent forays in this direction, such as the "Death of God" and "Non-theistic" approaches to Christianity, are interesting, but they are ultimately theological questions that take us too far afield at this point in our discussion. Suffice it to say that although we may be unable to define the elusive term *religion* precisely, the general parameters of its definition are clear enough, and Christianity is indeed an example.

What is myth?

When the word *myth* is used in common parlance, it often means a story that involves one of the Greek gods, like Zeus, or perhaps one of the Norse gods, like Thor. A secondary meaning associated with the term is something that is unreal or untrue, as in the sentence, "The unicorn is a mythical beast" (Thurber 1940: 66). In the context of the academic study of religion, however, the word *myth* means something entirely different.

For scholars of religion, *myth* is a narrative that recounts sacred history, usually related to (semi-)divine beings or cultural heroes (Eliade 1959: 95). This concept of myth presupposes the existence of a reality beyond ordinary experience, one whose essence can be described as sacred, as opposed to common (or profane). In his book *Religion und Kultus*, Sigmund Mowinckel discusses the relationship between ancient Israel's sacred story (its myth) and its worship practices (its *cult*). Mowinckel sees in ancient Israel's worship practices a re-enactment of Israel's sacred history. For example, the cultic ritual of the paschal meal (Passover) is a retelling of the exodus, the story of God's deliverance of Israel from slavery in Egypt. Similarly, religion scholars see the Eucharistic meal, or *Eucharist*, in Christianity (also called Communion or the Lord's Supper) as a retelling of the story of Jesus' crucifixion, one of the sacred stories (myths) of Christianity.

If sacred history is described as myth, is it thereby untrue? On the contrary, for practitioners of religion, sacred history deals with ultimate, essential truths, whereas ordinary history deals with less important, existential truths. For Christians, the narrative and meaning behind Jesus' birth, public ministry, crucifixion, and resurrection are the heart of the Christian story. They may be described as Christian myth not because they are untrue (the common meaning of *myth*) but precisely because they are the essence of truth itself. To describe sacred history as true, however, is not necessarily the same as saying that it is historical, and one of the great debates within Christianity over the past century has revolved around the question of the relationship between history and myth.

In the wake of the Enlightenment's emphasis on the triumph of reason over ignorance, some Christian thinkers saw the need to make the sacred stories of Christianity correspond more closely to the rational world. One somewhat crude, early attempt in this vein was Thomas Jefferson's *The Life and Morals of Jesus of Nazareth*, also known as the Jefferson Bible, which was a harmony of the four canonical gospels with all references to the miraculous omitted. For Jefferson, the mythological portions of the gospel story were no longer relevant to people living in an enlightened age and so should be discarded.

The twentieth-century theologian Rudolf Bultmann also saw problems with the mythological nature of the New Testament, but rather than simply omitting those portions of the sacred story that do not seem consistent with a rationalistic worldview, Bultmann said Christians must learn to "demythologize" the stories. The purpose of myth in the Christian story, Bultmann said, was to communicate the Christian understanding of the place of humanity in the world in which we live. If the mythological language of the New Testament no longer communicated the Christian viewpoint clearly, it was necessary to reinterpret the myth to make it understandable in the present day. "The purpose of demythologizing is not to make religion more acceptable to modern man by trimming the traditional Biblical texts, but to make clearer to modern man what the Christian faith is" (Bultmann 1953: 182).

In contrast to the perceived need to remove or reduce the amount of mythological content in a religion's sacred stories, some more recent scholars emphasize the necessity of mythology for expressing religious ideas. Rationalism alone is an insufficient basis for knowledge, for it cannot reach beyond the mundane into the sacred. Rather than myth being something that modern adherents of Christianity and other religions must shed, myth is something that we cannot live without, at least if we want to say anything meaningful about the divine and its connection to contemporary humanity (Griffith-Dickson 2005: 80–1). Postmodern reevaluations of the Enlightenment worldview highlight the inadequacy of its exclusive emphasis on reason as the means by which one can attain knowledge, and while the discussions are ongoing, it seems likely that modern Christians will continue to use mythological language to assert the deepest truths of their faith.

What is sin?

> For the wages of sin is death, but the free gift of God is eternal life in Christ Jesus our Lord.
>
> (Rom 6:23)

Sin may be defined as separation from God, either as the result of an explicit act or as the result of the metaphysical state in which one finds oneself. In ancient Judaism, as in other religious traditions of the ancient Near East, sin could take the form of violating an ethical norm of some sort (e.g. theft), or it could involve violating a taboo (e.g. touching a dead body), either accidentally or otherwise. The modern distinction between transgressions of a ritual or of a moral nature does not seem to have been made in the legal code found in the Hebrew Bible. However, Jesus' de-emphasis on the severity of ritual transgressions (e.g. eating grain on the Sabbath, Mark 2:23–28) and corresponding emphasis on the severity of moral transgressions (e.g. the Sermon on the

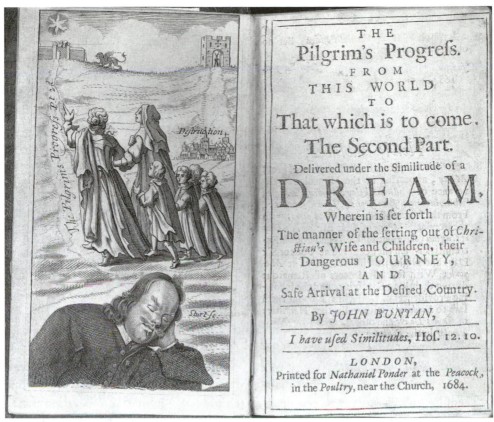

Figure 1.1 Frontispiece and title page from The Second Part of *The Pilgrim's Progress*, John Bunyan's 1678 allegory of the Christian life.

Mount, Matt 5–7), coupled with the destruction of the Jewish Temple in 70 C.E., ending the offering of sacrifices, and the shift in the demographic of the early church from majority Jewish to majority Gentile, led to Christianity's exclusive emphasis on moral transgression as the quintessential act of sin.

In the gospels, Jesus talks quite a bit about specific examples of sin (e.g. hypocrisy, judging others, mistreating the poor), but Paul's treatment of sin is somewhat different, for Paul speaks of people as existing in a state of sin, whose origin can be traced back to Adam, the progenitor of the human race (Rom 5:12–14). Similarly, the Gospel of John suggests the idea that at least some people are born in a state of sin (John 9:34). The idea that people are born in a state of sin, and particularly Paul's words in Rom 5:12, led to the development of the doctrine of original sin, which states that all humans are born with the taint of sin already affecting them. This position was affirmed by the Catholic and Orthodox churches, but it was rejected by the Protestant churches, which argued that only specific, intentional acts of sin could put a person in a state of sin.

For those who find themselves separated from God, whether through some overt act, through a failure to act, or because of a state of sin – and the list includes everyone, for "all have sinned" (Rom 3:23) – the gulf between the holy God and the sinful human must be bridged. For Christians, Jesus Christ is the means by which sin can be overcome and humanity can be reconciled to God, attaining salvation.

What is salvation?

Jesus' name is related to the Hebrew word for salvation, as an early Christian tradition explicitly notes ("You shall name him Jesus, for he will save his people from their sins," Matt 1:21). The word *salvation* in English carries with it an otherworldly connotation, but the equivalent word in Hebrew, the language in which the Hebrew Bible (Old Testament) was written, generally conveys the meaning *deliverance*, usually of a temporal sort. In the Hebrew Bible, the act of deliverance *par excellence* is the exodus, which gives birth to the nation of Israel. The prophets frequently use the word, sometimes in a historical setting referring to God's past acts of deliverance, and sometimes in reference to the future (e.g. Isa 52:7), almost (?) always in a temporal (even if eschatological) context.

By contrast, the concept of salvation in the New Testament moves from the temporal to the eternal. Whereas Jesus' disciples are reported to have expected political deliverance from the Roman Empire in the near future, even after the resurrection (Acts 1:6), the New Testament as a whole presents salvation in metaphysical, or even eternal, terms. "For the wages of sin is death, but the free gift of God is eternal life, through Jesus Christ our Lord" (Rom 6:23); "The Son of Man (Jesus) came not to be served, but to serve, and to give his life as a ransom for many" (Mark 8:45); "But as many as received him, to them he gave the power to become children of God" (John 1:12). Salvation means reconciliation with God, from whom sin had estranged the human race (Col 1:13–14), and the result of salvation is both a real, abundant, eternal life with God (John 10:10) and a metaphorical place in heaven, even while one remains on earth (Eph 2:4–7).

If Jesus is the means of salvation for the human race, how can people appropriate the salvation that he offers? Christians have offered three different answers to this question: faith, works, and knowledge. Of these three, the dominant answer historically has been faith, and the classic expression of this viewpoint is found in Eph 2:8: "For by grace have you been saved, through faith, and that not of yourselves, it is the gift of God, and not of works, lest anyone should boast." This statement presents the position associated with Paul clearly and unequivocally. However, it is not the only answer found in the New Testament.

James 2:14–26 offers a different answer to the question of what people must do to attain salvation. While not denying the importance of faith, James says that faith that is unaccompanied by works is useless. He does not say that salvation can be obtained by works alone, but he does seem to suggest that salvation in the absence of works is impossible. The debate over the efficacy of faith alone versus faith accompanied by works has been an ongoing debate throughout the centuries of Christian history. Augustine in the fifth century advocated faith alone, while his contemporary Pelagius emphasized the necessity of works as well. Martin Luther was so attached to Paul's ideal of salvation by grace through faith *alone* that he proposed removing the book of James from the New

Testament canon. In response, the Roman Catholic Church, at the Council of Trent (1545–1563), declared that good works can aid the believer (i.e. one who already has faith) in attaining salvation. The Second Vatican Council (1962–1965), however, while not contradicting the statement of the Council of Trent, put more emphasis on faith than on works in its statements, and it explicitly acknowledged the validity of other Christian churches, including, presumably, those churches that deny that works have any role to play in salvation.

As we will discuss more fully below, the early Christian community was quite diverse in its beliefs and practices, and forms of Christianity that differed significantly from what later became known as the Great Church (i.e. that segment of Christianity that held positions later declared to be orthodox) abounded. One group of people who considered themselves Christians were known as Gnostics. The word Gnostic comes from a Greek word meaning *knowledge*, and Gnostics believed that salvation could only be attained through esoteric knowledge. Gnostic traditions predate Christianity, and there were Gnostic movements associated with paganism and Judaism as well as Christianity. Nevertheless, full-blown Christian Gnosticism probably did not arise until the second century C.E. These Gnostic Christian groups, which otherwise were quite diverse, all believed that people could attain salvation only by means of obtaining certain bits of knowledge, passed down by Jesus to one or more of his disciples. The contents of this knowledge are generally unknown today, since they were closely guarded secrets, and the very esoteric nature of Gnosticism doomed it to nonviability, at least on a large scale. Nevertheless, Christian groups whose view of salvation included an emphasis on knowledge flourished for several centuries, and remnants of some of these Gnostic groups are still extant today.

In addition to faith, works, and knowledge, some Christian groups over the centuries have seen certain sacred rituals, or sacraments, as essential for salvation, though not sufficient in themselves apart from faith (and possibly works). The most common ritual considered necessary for salvation by some Christians is baptism, which serves as an initiation into the body of Christ, the church. The Roman Catholic Church for centuries taught that baptism was necessary to wash away the stain of original sin, but in the post-Vatican II Church, the absolute necessity of baptism for salvation is denied, though infant baptism is still encouraged in areas where the Church is firmly established. At the same time, a renewed emphasis on the training (catechism) of older children and adults prior to baptism is increasing in the Roman Catholic Church, as evidenced by the growth in Rite of Christian Initiation of Adults (RCIA) programs. To the extent that the RCIA program represents a de-emphasis on infant baptism and a move toward baptism of older children and adults after a period of training, at least in certain circumstances, the Roman Catholic Church is emulating the common practice in most churches in the first few centuries, some of which required a training period of up to three years before a candidate could receive baptism and become a full-fledged member of the church. Some Protestant churches, for example the Church of Christ, also teach that baptism is a necessary component of salvation.

What is faith?

> Now faith is the assurance of things hoped for, the conviction of things not seen.
>
> (Heb 11:1)

As we have seen, the strongest streams of Christian tradition have held that faith is central to attaining salvation, or perhaps to establishing a relationship with God that leads to salvation. Faith is described variously as an initial act of the acceptance of Jesus as Lord (Paul), as a motivation for acts that demonstrate one's faithfulness to God (James), or as a journey along which one travels throughout a lifetime (John). The author of the book of Hebrews offers a concise definition of faith: "Faith is the assurance of things hoped for, the conviction of things not seen" (Heb 11:1). After giving this definition, the author proceeds to give numerous examples, primarily from the Hebrew Bible, of people who have lived lives of faith. In every case offered, the man or woman of faith demonstrates faith by acting in accordance with his or her understanding of God's will. It appears then, that this definition of faith accords most closely with James's description, but perhaps this is a matter of emphasis rather than preference for one description of faith over another. In the gospels, Jesus often uses the word in a context that emphasizes temporal rather than eternal salvation. For example, in Mark 5:34, after healing a woman, Jesus tells her, "Your faith has saved you" (i.e. "healed you"; the word in Greek can be translated in both ways). Most Christians would agree that faith as it relates to salvation is connected in some way with faith as it relates to healing and other temporal forms of deliverance. The problem comes in achieving a single, simple definition of faith.

Modern Christians use the word faith in different, sometimes ambiguous ways, and the debate over the true nature of faith continues among Christians today. In answering the question "what is faith?" it is helpful to examine various ways in which the term is defined and used. In Greek, the noun translated into English as "faith" and the verb translated "to believe" are closely related to one another, derived from the same root. Faith is an active concept that requires an object, something to be believed. Marcus Borg offers four possible meanings for the word faith, all of which are used in the context of Christianity by practicing Christians today (Borg 2003: 28–37). These various meanings of the word differ primarily in their object.

The first way in which faith is defined is as *assent*, the acceptance of a set of propositions about God, Jesus, Christianity, and so forth. The object of this type of faith is a body of doctrines, and a Christian who assents to these doctrines is said to be *orthodox* (i.e. having correct doctrine). The delineation of the specific set of doctrines that comprise orthodoxy varies, depending on the group of Christians being described, but the importance of adhering to a set of standards is central to this view of faith.

The second way in which faith is defined is as *trust in God*. Rather than a set of beliefs, this type of faith has as its object the divine personage of God. Christians who exercise this sort of faith trust God to care for their needs, to guide them in important decisions, and to support them throughout the vicissitudes of life. Truly trusting God, according to Christian philosopher Søren Kierkegaard, requires infinite resignation on the part of an individual (that is, the total elimination of self-will), so that that person can put complete trust in God (Kierkegaard 1954: 57).

Faith may also be defined as *faithfulness to God*. In this type of faith, the object of faith is God's decrees, in a general sense, or God's will, in a personal sense. The Christian exercising this kind of faith says, "What God commands, I will do." So, for example, Augustine, an early Christian bishop and theologian, prays, "Give what you command, and command what you will" (*Confessions* 10.29). Augustine sees faithfulness as obedience to God, but he also believes that faithfulness is impossible unless God grants a person the ability to be faithful.

A fourth way to define faith is as *seeing the world around us as the gracious gift of God*. This type of faith is similar to trust in that it is directed in part to God, but the true object of this sort of faith is the totality of existence, including God. People practicing this kind of faith are not necessarily oblivious to the evils and suffering that are a part of life. They just believe that God is ultimately at work even in the worst of situations to bring grace to God's creation.

These four types of faith are not mutually exclusive, and Christians who use the term *faith* are not always precise in their usage. It is helpful to be aware of the different possible meanings of the term when examining stated Christian beliefs, for changing the definition of faith may change the meaning of certain Christian doctrines in radical ways.

What is the Bible?

Christianity – along with two other great Western religious traditions, Judaism and Islam – is sometimes called a "religion of the book." The sacred text of Christianity is the Bible, a collection of many shorter works written by different authors over a period of perhaps a thousand years. The Christian Bible is divided into two parts. Traditionally, these parts are called Old Testament and New Testament. However, these traditional terms have some difficulties. The phrase Old Testament might imply something that is incomplete or that has been superseded by the New Testament. That is certainly not the meaning inherent in the term, since the Old Testament was sacred scripture for Jesus and for all the New Testament writers, and it is the "scripture" referred to in 2 Tim 3:16.

Several alternative names have been proposed to Old Testament. *Hebrew Bible* is perhaps the most common alternative, and it is often used by both Jews and Christians to express the facts that (1) it was written primarily in Hebrew and that (2) it is complete in and of itself as the scripture of Judaism. Another alternative is *Tanakh*, an acrostic based on the first letters of the three-fold Jewish division of the Hebrew Bible into Law (*torah*), Prophets (*nevi'im*), and Writings (*ketuvim*). Tanakh is equivalent to the phrase "Jewish scriptures." Some scholars refer to this portion of scripture as the *First Testament*, a phrase which replaces the negative connotations of *Old* with the more positive *First*.

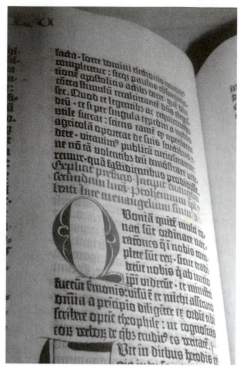

Figure 1.2   The first extensive book to be printed on Johannes Gutenberg's printing press, about 1450, was a Latin version of the Bible. Several Gutenberg Bibles are still in existence.

There are problems with each of these alternatives, however. *Hebrew Bible* suggests not only a dominant language but also a canon of books written in Hebrew, omitting some of the books accepted as scripture by Catholic and Orthodox Christians (the deuterocanonicals or apocrypha). *Tanakh* shares this difficulty. Furthermore, *Hebrew Bible* seems to privilege a particular language-version of the Bible, but many Christians are not willing to concede priority to the Hebrew version of the text in all places. In particular, the Latin Vulgate and the Greek Septuagint continue to wield significant influence in the Roman Catholic and Orthodox churches, respectively, particularly in regard to the liturgy, although most modern scholars use the Hebrew version extensively. Finally, *First Testament* seems to be a logical alternative, but it is not yet widely used outside a fairly small scholarly circle.

The term *New Testament* is not as problematic, but the term itself almost requires the corresponding phrase *Old Testament*. The term Christian Bible cannot be used, of course, because the Christian Bible includes the Old Testament/Hebrew Bible/Tanakh/First Testament as well. This book will use the various terms for the Old Testament more or less interchangeably, but readers should be aware of both the problematic nature of all the current terms and the inherent ambiguity that surrounds the terms, especially in light of the discussion of the canon that follows.

Most of the Old Testament was originally written in Hebrew; Aramaic portions are Dan 2:4–7:28; Ezra 4:28–6:18; 7:12–26; Jer 10:11; Gen 31:47 (two words). Other isolated Aramaic words appear sporadically, especially in the younger books. Among the books accepted by Catholics but not Protestants, some were originally written in Hebrew or Aramaic, and others were written in Greek. The New Testament was written entirely in Greek, but here and there it preserves words and phrases in Aramaic, the language spoken by Jesus and other early Christians, for example, *Eloi, Eloi, lema sabachthani* (Mark 15:34); *Talitha, cum* (Mark 5:41); *Ephphatha* (Mark 7:34); *Marana tha* (1 Cor 16:22). Unlike in the Hebrew Bible, which preserves Aramaic in its original script, in the New Testament, Aramaic words are transliterated into Greek.

As Jews and Christians spread out in the ancient world, they carried their sacred texts with them. Soon they needed translations of the Bible into other language, both for proselytization/evangelism and for their own use. The earliest extensive written translation of the Hebrew Bible was the Septuagint, or Old Greek version of the Pentateuch (usually abbreviated as LXX, because of a legend involving 70 or 72 translators). The earliest translations of the New Testament were into Latin and Syriac.

The earliest portions of the Old Testament are probably the poems called the Song of Deborah (Jdg 5) and the Songs of Miriam and Moses (Exod 15), and the latest portion is probably the book of Daniel. In the New Testament, the earliest book is probably 1 Thessalonians, and the latest is perhaps the Gospel of John or, according to other scholars, the Pastoral Epistles (1–2 Timothy and Titus) or 2 Peter.

Many books in the Bible are named after particular people, but readers should not assume that the title of the book accurately indicates the author. In the Old Testament, books are typically named for the main character rather than the author (e.g. Joshua, Esther, Jonah). There are references to the authorial activity of Moses, David, Solomon, Jeremiah, and Nehemiah, among others, but none of them is probably the final author of the books associated with them.

For example, the Pentateuch is traditionally ascribed to Moses, but since it describes his death, Moses can hardly be the author, at least of the final form of the book. There are many indications that the Pentateuch was written by several people over a long period of time. Stylistic differences among different sections and the repetition of similar material suggest multiple authorship (e.g. the two creation stories in Gen 1 and Gen 2, the two versions of the Ten Commandments in Exod 20 and Deut 5). Historical anachronisms (historical data true when the Pentateuch was written but not in Moses' day) suggest a long period of time over which the Pentateuch was written (e.g. Gen 12:6: "The Canaanites were then in the land," suggesting that when the verse was written, they were no longer in the land; Deut 1:1: "beyond the Jordan" as a reference to the east side of the Jordan, a perspective that implies residence on the west side of the Jordan; Deut 17:14–20: references to a king, when kings were apparently not anticipated so early in Israel's history).

In the New Testament, the authors of letters are usually named, though scholars debate the attribution of some of the letters (e.g. the Pastoral Epistles or 2 Peter). The letter to the Hebrews is an exception, because no author is mentioned; though it is traditionally associated with Paul, the differences in style from other Pauline writings and the lack of Paul's name in the text itself argue against Pauline authorship.

Unlike the letters, the gospels and Acts do not name their authors, although Luke and Acts have similar dedications to Theophilus at the beginning and thus presumably the same author. Early Christian traditions associated the canonical gospels with Matthew, Mark, Luke, and John. However, it is interesting to note that Papias, a prominent Christian writer from the early second century, said that he trusted oral reports from people who had known the apostles more than any written word, so he, at least, seems to have had some doubts about the apostolic authorship of the gospels.

When people today see a book, they tend to think that a single author probably wrote it, but that is a modern assumption. Ancient writers tended to reuse older, traditional material, changing it as necessary to meet their needs, and the Bible is no exception. The biblical text itself refers to several sources, now lost, such as the Book of Jashar, the Annals of the Kings of Israel, the Records of the Prophet Nathan, and the Records of the Seer Gad. In addition to these named sources, it is clear that the author of the books of Chronicles used Samuel and Kings as a source, and many other examples of literary dependence are evident as well. In the New Testament, most scholars believe that the authors of Matthew and Luke used Mark and another, lost source called Q (from the German *Quelle*, "source"). 2 Peter and Jude also give evidence of literary dependence on one another, and some scholars believe that Colossians and Ephesians do as well. It is clear from a careful reading of the Bible that biblical authors frequently used earlier sources, some of which are included in the Bible and some not.

Scribes also played an important role in the development of the Bible. We tend to think of scribes as people who simply copied the text that lay before them, but scribes were often much more involved in the development of the text, particularly, but not exclusively, when the text being copied had not yet achieved canonical status. In some ways, when a text was considered authoritative, it was more liable to certain types of scribal modification, such as explanatory additions, harmonizations, and theological corrections.

Scribes involved in transmitting the Hebrew Bible often inserted traditional material into the text they were transcribing. For example, there are two accounts in 1 Samuel 16 and 17 of David being introduced to Saul in the traditional Hebrew text (known as the Masoretic Text, or MT). The LXX omits 1 Sam 17:12–31, 55–18:5. The MT probably contains additional traditional material that was added at some point after the original composition began to circulate (it was not present in the Hebrew version that the LXX translators used).

Scribes sometimes added material intended to clarify something for the contemporary audience. For example, the explanation "prophets were called seers in those days" (1 Sam 9:9) is such a clarification.

As the text began to be considered authoritative, passages that the scribes considered theologically difficult were sometimes modified. For example, in Jdg 18:30, the name "Moses" is changed to "Manasseh" in order to protect the memory of one of Israel's most important personalities (this correction is marked in many Hebrew manuscripts by a raised letter "n" in the text, an indication that something unusual has happened to the text at that point). Another example is Job 2:9, where Job's wife urges him to "bless God and die" in the MT, but the LXX retains the original "curse God and die." A third example is found in 1 Sam 3:13, where Eli's sons are criticized for "blaspheming themselves," which makes no sense; the original read "blaspheming God," a difference of one letter in Hebrew. Jewish scribal tradition preserves a record of many such scribal corrections, but by no means have records of all changes been kept.

In the New Testament, extensive material (i.e. one sentence or more) is added most frequently in the gospels. The ending of the Lord's Prayer in Matt 6:13, "for yours is the kingdom and the power and the glory forever, amen," is such an addition to the original. Luke's version of the Lord's Prayer (Luke 11:2–4) is shorter than Matthew's, but many manuscripts add material to make it conform more closely to Matthew's version. A third example is the story of the Woman Caught in Adultery (John 7:53–8:11), a bit of oral tradition that was added to the Gospel of John (and in some manuscripts, to Luke!).

Theologically-based modifications also occur occasionally in the New Testament. In John 1:18, the phrase "only begotten God," which appears in several manuscripts and modern translations, is probably a theological modification to the original "only begotten Son" that was intended to emphasize the divinity of Christ. In Mark 1:41, most manuscripts say that Jesus looked "with compassion" on a leper before cleansing him, but it is possible that the original reading said that Jesus looked "with anger," a reading preserved in several witnesses. If the latter reading is original, it was changed to preserve a gentler image of Jesus.

One of the most obvious and commonly attested types of modification of the scriptural text was the addition of material at the end of a book. Examples of appended material abound in the Bible. For example, the first 16 chapters of the book of Judges deal with various charismatic rulers (traditionally called judges) of the tribes of Israel, but the book ends with two sections of material (Jdg 17–18 and Jdg 19–21) that, though set in the same general time period, have nothing to do with charismatic rulers, but deal with incidents involving isolated tribes. Another example involves the book of Samuel (1–2 Samuel are one book in Hebrew) and accounts of David's adventures. The logical end of the book comes in 2 Sam 20, after David's kingdom has been restored to him following Absalom's rebellion. 1 Kgs 1, the story of David's old age and his appointment of Solomon, follow logically at this point, but someone has added Chapters 21–24 at the end of Samuel, a collection of words and deeds of David that were apparently too good to omit from the book.

Additions at the end of prophetic books are common as well. A short, one-verse addition appears in Hos 14:9, where a wisdom saying has been appended to the book. A much longer addition appears in the book of Isaiah, where the material related to the eighth-century prophet Isaiah the son of Amoz ends in Chapter 39 and material from more than a century later appears in Chapters 40–66 (see, for example, contemporary references to Cyrus the Great, king of Persia, who lived in the sixth century B.C.E., in Isa 44:28; 45:1). Other Old Testament examples of additional material added to the end of a book include Prov 30–31; Eccl 12:9–14; Jer 52; Zech 9–14; and the entire book of Malachi, which appears to be an appendix to the Book of the Twelve (i.e. the twelve Minor Prophets).

In the New Testament, scribes confronted with the ending of Mark in 16:8 added a longer ending (Mark 16:9–20), supplementing the surprisingly short original ending with traditional material, much of it taken from the other gospels. The Gospel of John originally ended at 20:31, but after the author's death his followers added chapter 21.

Once the books of the Bible achieved essentially their final forms, following their composition and sometimes extensive periods of transmission, how were they chosen for inclusion in the canon? In other words, who made the decision to include certain books in the Bible and to exclude other books, and how were those decisions made? These questions will be discussed in the next chapter, under the heading "The Christian scriptures."

How is Christianity related to other religions?

Jesus, his disciples, and most other early followers during the first two generations of Christianity were Jews. They worshiped in synagogues on the Sabbath, the Jewish holy day, and those living in or around Jerusalem continued to participate in worship in the temple, until its destruction by the Romans in 70 C.E. Jesus and early Christian leaders accepted authoritative Jewish writings as authoritative for themselves as well, designating them as "scripture" (e.g. "All scripture is inspired by God," 2 Tim 3:16). As Gentiles (i.e. non-Jews) joined the church in increasing numbers throughout the first century, Christianity began to move away from typical Rabbinic Judaism in doctrine (especially in their identification of Jesus as Messiah and Son of God), practice (e.g. the discontinuation of circumcision and the Jewish dietary rules), and self-identity (i.e. Christians saw themselves as Christians rather than Jews, as opposed to seeing themselves as Jews who were also Christians). The church in Jerusalem was forced to deal with the question of large numbers of Gentiles outside Judea joining the church as early as 49 C.E. (see Acts 15), and by the end of the first century, the separation of Christianity from Judaism was apparently complete, from the standpoint of both Jews and Christians. Even the Roman government acknowledged the existence of Christianity as a religion distinct from Judaism.

Despite the separation of Christianity from Judaism, most Christians, even Gentile Christians, continued to acknowledge the Jewish roots of their faith. Christian leaders continued to quote the sacred literature of Jews as scripture, even though they now had several original Christian writings to which they also gave that designation (the New Testament). Christians looked favorably upon such exemplars of faith as Abraham,

Christianity compared with other religions

Since the earliest days of Christianity, different beliefs and practices have separated Christian groups from one another, and members of one group have often denied the term "Christian" to members of other groups with whom they disagreed on some fundamental tenet of religion. The practice continues today, with the result that some denominations (associations of churches sharing common beliefs and practices) see themselves as the only true Christians, believing that others are apostates or heretics (i.e. people who have left the true faith). Other Christians have a more expansive view of Christianity, acknowledging that true Christians can belong to any of a number of denominations, but they identify as Christian only those who have had a specific, personal religious experience (e.g. a "crisis conversion") or who have undergone a specific Christian ritual (e.g. baptism). Still others identify as Christian any who belong to a wide range of "traditional" denominations or groups of denominations (e.g. Roman Catholic, Eastern Orthodox, Protestant), but they express reservations about groups outside this mainstream. In this book, we will accept as Christian all those individuals and groups that are self-identified as Christians, whether in the traditional mainstream or not, and whether practicing or not. Our discussion will necessarily focus on the largest and historically most influential of these groups, but we will also have occasion to mention some of the smaller, more recent, and more doctrinally distinct groups along the way.

According to adherents.com, a Web site that tracks many different statistics concerning religions, Christianity (in the broad sense defined above) is followed by 2.1 billion people, approximately 33 percent of the current world population. The ten largest religions, with the number of adherents, are as follows:

1 Christianity: 2.1 billion
2 Islam: 1.3 billion
3 Secular/nonreligious/agnostic/atheist: 1.1 billion
4 Hinduism: 900 million
5 Chinese traditional religion (including Taoism and Confucianism): 394 million
6 Buddhism: 376 million
7 Primal-indigenous: 300 million
8 African Traditional and Diasporic: 100 million
9 Sikhism: 23 million
10 Juche: 19 million

Other major religious traditions with connections to Christianity include Judaism (14 million; rank: 12), Bahá'í (7 million; rank: 13), and Rastafari (600,000; rank: 21).

Sarah, Moses, David, and the prophets, and they named their children after heroes and heroines of the Hebrew Bible.

The other major religious tradition closely associated with Christianity is Islam. A group of Arabs called Nabateans, who lived in the region between Syria and Arabia, east of Galilee and Judea, converted to Judaism in large numbers in the first century C.E. By the fourth century the Nabateans, along with other Arabs, had become Christians, and Christianity was prevalent among some Arab groups by the sixth century, though traditional Arabian religion also flourished. It was into this mixed context of Judaism, Christianity, and traditional religion that Muhammad came in the early seventh century, preaching a message of strict monotheism – something with which both Jews and Christians would agree. Muhammad saw himself as a prophet sent by God to complete and correct the teachings of Judaism and Christianity. Islam considers Muhammad to be the greatest prophet, but it also reveres Jesus (called Isa in the Qur'an) and other Jewish prophets and patriarchs as well.

Although Judaism and Islam are the largest religious traditions with direct historical connections to Christianity, other religions have also drawn from, or in one case contributed to, Christianity. Zoroastrianism, which predates Christianity, contributed ideas to Christianity, primarily through its contact with Judaism during the Second Temple period (516 B.C.E–70 C.E.; the contributions of Zoroastrianism to Christianity will be considered in the next chapter). Christianity, in turn, has influenced many younger religious traditions, in addition to Islam, including Bahá'í, Santería, Haitian Vodou, and Rastafari.

Different types of Christianity

The traditional division of Christianity into three large subgroups – Catholicism, Orthodoxy, and Protestantism – has the advantage of identifying the three largest groups of Christian denominations, but it lumps together many people who would not identify themselves closely with others in the group (particularly within the Protestant designation), and it masks a large diversity of opinion regarding faith and practice (again, largely within the Protestant group). Nevertheless, the division is helpful from a historical perspective, since the groups classified under Catholicism and Orthodoxy are much older than those classed together as Protestant, which emerged in the early sixteenth century.

If Christians classified as Protestant in a broad sense are broken down further into groups of related denominations, the ten largest Christian groups are as follows (according to adherents.com):

1 Catholic (including Old Catholics and other non-Roman churches): 1.05 billion
2 Orthodox/Eastern Christian (including Eastern churches not in communion with Constantinople, e.g. Coptic Orthodox): 240 million
3 African indigenous sects: 110 million
4 Pentecostal: 105 million
5 Reformed/Presbyterian: 75 million
6 Anglican/Episcopalian: 73 million
7 Baptist: 70 million
8 Methodist: 70 million
9 Lutheran: 64 million
10 Jehovah's Witnesses: 14.8 million

These distinctions among Christians based on denominational affiliation mask the extensive transdenominational nature of modern Christianity, especially within, but not limited to, Protestantism. For example, Christians who see themselves as Evangelical (theologically conservative, with an emphasis on personal conversion) share many beliefs and values with segments of the Roman Catholic and Anglican traditions, while differing sharply on many issues with so-called Mainline Protestants (e.g. Methodists, Lutherans, Presbyterians). Similarly, Christians who would classify themselves as Ecumenical (desiring unity within the church on the basis of historical beliefs and widespread practices) transcend traditional denominational barriers, sometimes dividing Christians who share a common historical heritage (e.g. Baptists).

As the previous discussion demonstrates, Christianity is a diverse religious movement that is characterized by both commitment to tradition and a continuing search for truth. The description of Christianity that follows should be seen as descriptive rather than normative, and as befits an introductory text, it is necessarily limited in scope, though representative of large segments of Christianity both historically and in the present.

Key points you need to know

- Christianity derives its name from the title given to its founder, Jesus of Nazareth, who came to be called "the Christ," that is, "the one anointed (by God)."
- Christianity is a large and diverse religion, numbering about 2 billion members from every continent.
- Though hard to define in a way that is fully satisfactory, religion may be thought of as a system of beliefs and practices, including some concept of a reality or realities beyond ordinary human experience, that is observed by adherents.
- In the academic study of religion, myth may be defined as a narrative that recounts sacred history, usually related to (semi-)divine beings or cultural heroes. This technical definition of myth is different from the more common understanding of myth as something entirely fanciful.
- The central Christian stories (myths, in the sense defined above) include Jesus' birth, public ministry, crucifixion, and resurrection.
- In Christian thought, sin is separation from God that results either from an explicit act or from a metaphysical state in which one finds oneself.
- Salvation is another word for deliverance, and it is typically used to refer to deliverance of an individual from a state of sin and restoration to communion with God.
- Throughout the centuries of Christian history, different Christians have taught that salvation may be attained through one or more of the following: faith, good works, or knowledge.
- Faith is variously defined as assent to a set of beliefs about God, trust in God, faithfulness to God, or seeing the world as the gracious gift of God.
- The sacred scripture of Christianity, the Bible, is divided into two sections, the Old Testament (sometimes called the Hebrew Bible) and the New Testament. The Old Testament contains works written by Jews before the birth of Jesus, and the New Testament contains works written by Christians (some Jews and some Gentiles) after the death and resurrection of Jesus.
- Christianity originated as a reform movement within Judaism, but Christianity was considered a distinct religion by most Jews and Christians, as well as by the Roman Empire, by about 100 C.E.
- Islam, which was founded by Muhammad in the seventh century C.E., was influenced by both Judaism and Christianity. Christianity has also had an impact on many younger religions, such as Bahá'í and Rastafari.

Discussion questions

1. In what ways is Christianity similar to and different from other modern religions?
2. How does the question of the historicity of central Christian myths affect your evaluation of Christianity?
3. How important is the issue of salvation in the modern world? From what sorts of things do modern people desire to be saved?
4. Which of the four definitions of faith offered is the most relevant for Christians today?
5. If the two religions with which Christianity is most closely related, from a historical standpoint, are Judaism and Islam, why is it that Christians have had more difficult relationships with Jews and Muslims over the centuries than with followers of other religions, such as Hindus or Buddhists?

Further reading

Adherents.com. http://www.adherents.com.

Augustine. *The Confessions.*

Bonhoeffer, Dietrich 1967. *Letters and Papers from Prison.* Revised edn. Edited by Eberhard Bethge. Translated by Reginald Fuller. New York: Macmillan.

Borg, Marcus J. 2003. *The Heart of Christianity: Rediscovering a Life of Faith.* New York: HarperSanFrancisco.

Bultmann, Rudolf 1953. "The Case for Demythologizing: A Reply." Chapter in *Kerygma and Myth: A Theological Debate,* vol. 2. Edited by Hans Werner Bartsch. London: SPCK.

Durkheim, Émile 1915. *The Elementary Forms of Religious Life: A Study in Religious Sociology.* Translated by Joseph Ward Swain. London: Allen & Unwin.

Eliade, Mircea 1959. *The Sacred and the Profane: The Nature of Religion.* Translated by Willard R. Trask. New York: Harcourt, Brace & World.

Eliade, Mircea 1963. *Myth and Reality.* Translated by Willard R. Trask. New York: Harper & Row.

Fitzgerald, Timothy 2000. *The Ideology of Religious Studies.* Oxford: Oxford University Press.

Griffith-Dickson, Gwen 2005. *The Philosophy of Religion.* London: SCM.

James, William 1902. *The Varieties of Religious Experience.* New York: Longmans, Green.

Kierkegaard, Søren 1954. *Fear and Trembling and Sickness unto Death.* Translated by Walter Lowrie. Princeton, NJ: Princeton University Press.

Mowinckel, Sigmund 1953. *Religion und Kultus.* Translated by Albrecht Schauer. Göttingen: Vandenhoeck & Ruprecht.

Otto, Rudolf 1958. *The Idea of the Holy.* Translated by John W. Harvey. New York: Oxford University Press.

Schleiermacher, Friedrich 1958. *On Religion: Speeches to Its Cultured Despisers.* Translated by John Oman. New York: Harper & Row.

Smart, Ninian 1977. *The Long Search.* Boston, MA: Little, Brown.

Smith, Huston 1958. *The Religions of Man.* New York: Harper & Row.

2 Christianity and the divine

In [God] we live and move and have our being.
(Epimenides, quoted in Acts 17:28)

In this chapter

This chapter begins by discussing the contrast between the sacred and the profane in religion in general and in Christianity in particular. The sacred (or holy) plays a major role in Christianity, and the role of the sacred in several aspects of the Christian experience is surveyed.

Main topics covered

- Definition and distinction between the sacred and the profane
- Sacred time
- Sacred space
- Sacred symbols and artefacts
- Sacred interactions (i.e. interactions between God and humans)
- Sacred personages
- Sacred metatime (the time beyond time)

Sacred and profane

Like most other world religions, Christianity recognizes a distinction between the world of ordinary experience and the divine realm. This difference is illustrated by a variety of word-pairs that are frequently employed: physical and metaphysical, human and divine, temporal and eternal, natural and supernatural, finite and infinite, imminent and transcendent, normal and paranormal, profane and sacred. At the root of this fundamental distinction, for Christians at least, is the belief in God. Almost all Christians would affirm their belief in God, but the Christian understanding of God varies considerably, depending on the individual person or group.

For many Christians, God is a discrete being of immense power (omnipotence) and knowledge (omniscience). In this view, God stands outside of creation and is separate from it. For some, God is intimately involved in the day to day operation of the universe. For others, God has set up the universe with physical laws (e.g. the laws of motion, the four fundamental forces, general and special relativity, quantum mechanics) and with a set of universal constants (e.g. Planck's constant, the mass of a resting electron or quark, the speed of light), which God has designed to bring about the world as we know it. In this view, God has designed the universe so well that intervention is rarely required. (While some Christians insist on continuing to use traditional masculine titles (e.g. Father, King, Lord) and pronouns when referring to God, most acknowledge that this practice is conventional rather than an accurate description of God as a male being. In this book, outside of direct quotations, references to God will avoid male pronouns such as "he," "him," "himself," etc. Instead, words such as "God" or even "Godself" will be used.)

Other Christians see God not as *a being* but as *being itself*, or as theologian Paul Tillich put it, *the Ground of being*. God is the source of all matter, life, and thought, but is not composed of these materials. God is not so much separate from creation as beneath it; the acts of creating and sustaining are essentially the same. One common way of describing God that is consistent with this approach is as *Wholly Other*.

The distinction between the sacred and the profane is discussed at length by Rudolf Otto, in *The Idea of the Holy*. Otto describes the Holy (or Sacred) as that mysterious something which makes rational humans tremble in fear when they encounter it. Paradoxically, not only does the Holy make rational humans tremble, and thus strive to avoid contact, it also fascinates and attracts them to itself. Otto describes the Holy as non-rational, or perhaps supra-rational, using human rationality as a standard of comparison. This description is interesting in the light of classical portraits of God, drawing on Greek philosophical traditions, as ultimate Reason (*logos*).

Christian scripture and tradition identify the sacred, present to a greater or lesser extent, in many different areas of human experience. Over the remainder of this chapter we will discuss the concepts of sacred time, sacred space, sacred symbols, sacred interactions, and sacred personages. We will conclude with a section on sacred meta-times, unique events that are beyond ordinary human history.

Sacred time

The apostle Paul wrote, "Some judge one day to be better than another, while others judge all days to be alike" (Rom 14:5). Already in the first decades after Jesus, Christians debated the holiness of certain days of the week or year. Some early Christians apparently followed the Jewish custom of fasting on Monday and Thursday, but soon Wednesday and Friday became the days designated each week as days set aside for fasting.

Most of the earliest Christians were Jews, and they observed the Sabbath (sundown Friday to sundown Saturday) as a day of rest and worship. By the beginning of the second century, however, when Christianity had become largely Gentile, Sunday was the more common day of worship, in commemoration of Jesus' resurrection "on the first day of the week" (Matt 28:1).

The idea of a Christian liturgical year developed gradually, perhaps influenced in part by a similar practice in Judaism. The first event to be commemorated annually by many Christians was the Feast of the Resurrection, or Easter. Although Sunday was celebrated on a weekly basis in memorial of the resurrection, a larger, more elaborate annual celebration had developed by the second century. After the emperor Constantine legalized Christianity in 313 c.e., he called the first ecumenical council at Nicaea in 325, and one of the items on the agenda was a discussion of the proper day to celebrate Easter: some celebrated it always on Sunday, while others observed Easter on whatever day of the week the anniversary of Christ's resurrection happened to fall. Like the Jewish feast of Passover, whose celebration coincided with the crucifixion and resurrection, the date of Easter was based on a lunar calendar, so its exact date (on the solar calendar) varied considerably from year to year. The Christians meeting at Nicaea decided that Easter should always be celebrated on Sunday, so to the present day Easter is celebrated on the Sunday following the first full moon after the vernal equinox, which corresponds to the first month in the traditional Jewish calendar. Western (Roman Catholic and Protestant) and Eastern Christians have slightly different methods of calculating the date of Easter, so it is common for Catholic/Protestant Easter to fall on a different date than Orthodox Easter.

Other important events in the life of Jesus came to be celebrated on certain days of the year as well. No one knew the date of Jesus' birth, but the church eventually chose December 25 as the date to celebrate the birth of Christ (Christmas), probably because of that date's association with the Roman feast of Saturnalia, the birth of the new year. Jesus' baptism and the visit of the Magi came to be celebrated on January 6, popularly called Epiphany. Other important events on the Christian Calendar (or Liturgical Calendar) include Pentecost (50 days after Easter), a celebration of the gift of the Holy Spirit as described in Acts 2, and the seasons of Advent (the four weeks prior to Christmas) and Lent (the seven weeks prior to Easter).

3–24 December 2006	Season of Advent
25 December 2006	Christmas Day
25 December 2006–5 January 2007	Season of Christmas
6 January 2007	Epiphany
6 January–20 February 2007	Season of Epiphany
21 February 2007	Ash Wednesday
21 February–7 April 2007	Season of Lent
8 April 2007	Easter
8 April–26 May 2007	Season of Easter
27 May 2007	Pentecost
27 May–1 December 2007	Season after Pentecost

Not all Christians observe the Liturgical Calendar, and Catholics, Protestants, and Orthodox who do follow it do so with some variations in tradition. For those who do observe it, the following table shows a typical year in the church. Note that the Christian Calendar begins with the season of Advent, which anticipates the coming of Christ.

Many other days are recognized on the Christian Calendar, such as Good Friday, Ascension Sunday, Trinity Sunday, and the Reign of Christ, also known as Christ the King Sunday. In some Christian traditions various days on the calendar are associated with Christian saints (e.g. Mary the Mother of God, St. Francis of Assisi, or St. Catherine of Siena), are set aside for special observances (e.g. rogation days), or are associated with local events or personalities of importance (e.g. the Virgin of Guadalupe in Mexico and elsewhere).

Special days on the calendar often call for special worship services, at which particular prayers may be cited or scriptures read. The Season of Lent, which commemorates the suffering and death of Jesus, is often observed with fasting or voluntary abstinence from certain foods or activities for the duration of Lent. Even Christian groups that do not follow the Liturgical Calendar usually observe at least Christmas and Easter to a greater or lesser extent. All Christians who celebrate such holidays, whether many or only a few, see them as "holy-days," times not just for rest from labor but for celebration, introspection, and spiritual renewal.

Sacred space

The Lord is in his holy temple;
>   let all the earth keep silence before him! (Hab 2:20)

For many Christians, particular locations, whether geographical or relative, have great spiritual meaning. Jerusalem is often referred to as the Holy City by Christians, and the land that today falls within the nation of Israel and the Palestinian territories is called the Holy Land. These places, as well as specific sites within them, such as the Church of the Holy Sepulcher in Jerusalem or the Cave of the Nativity in Bethlehem, are considered sacred by many Christians, because of their association with the earthly life and death of Jesus, and they are popular travel destinations for many Christians from around the world. Despite the importance that they attach to these sacred sites, Christians do not see a visit to the city of Jerusalem in the same way that Muslims might see a visit to the city of Mecca, as a sacred obligation. It is rather a place where events of great spiritual importance occurred, and many Christians hope that a visit to such a sacred site might impart a meaningful spiritual experience.

In the Middle Ages, the symbolic importance of the city of Jerusalem was evident not only in the numerous campaigns (the Crusades) that were fought to "liberate" it from its Muslim conquerors, but also in a series of maps that were drawn called Mappae Mundi (maps of the world). These maps were not drawn with correct proportions or accurate representations of land masses or water in mind. They were rather ideological representations of the world known to Europeans. Many of these maps, such as the

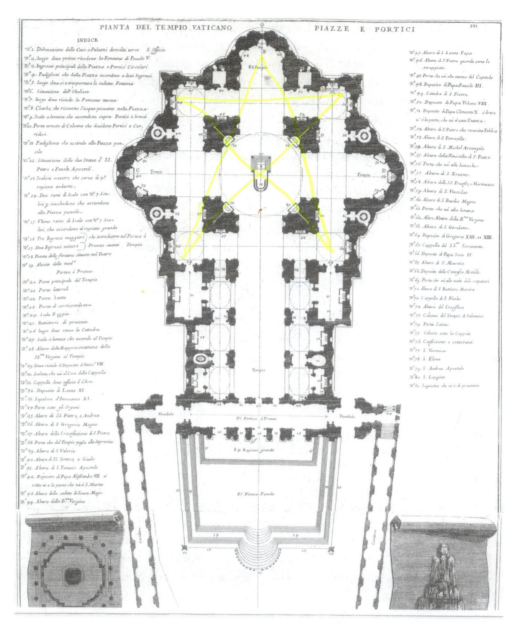

Figure 2.1 The floor plan for St. Peter's Basilica in Rome is typical of many churches, although on a larger scale than most. The central aisle (vertical) and the transept (horizontal) form the shape of a cross.

Mappa Mundi in Hereford Cathedral in England, locate Jerusalem in the very center of the map, where it represents the center of the world, the source of divine guidance and blessing.

Relatively early in the history of Christianity other sites of special religious significance, or associated with Christian saints and especially martyrs, became destinations of pilgrimage for many Christians (the word *martyr* comes from a Greek word meaning "witness"). Chaucer's *Canterbury Tales* is set against the backdrop of a pilgrimage to

Canterbury Cathedral undertaken by various travelers, who tell stories along the way to keep themselves entertained. Other great European churches were also frequented by Christian travelers on pilgrimages: Chartres Cathedral in France, St. Peter's Basilica in Rome, and Cologne Cathedral in Germany, to name a few. In modern times many Christians continue to flock to sites associated with apparitions of the Virgin Mary, including the Virgin of Guadalupe in Mexico City, Our Lady of Fatima in Portugal, and the Virgin of Medjugorje in Bosnia. Many Christians report receiving special blessings associated with these sites.

When travel to the holy lands became too dangerous during the Middle Ages, Christian leaders in various cathedrals laid out a "virtual" pilgrimage trail, or labyrinth. The most famous labyrinth was at the cathedral in Chartres. Pilgrims walked the intricate maze, laid out in a circle divided into four quadrants, praying or meditating. If the purpose of their visit to the labyrinth was repentance, they often traversed it on their knees. The center of the labyrinth represented the goal of their journey and was sometimes equated with Jerusalem.

Church architecture itself is often designed with the concept of sacred space in mind. The high ceilings and tall towers of many church buildings symbolize the vertical relationship that Christians have with God – vaulted ceilings are a way of capturing a little bit of the sky, which is associated with the holy realm of heaven. Some cathedral ceilings are even painted to resemble the starry night sky, as was the ceiling of the Sistine Chapel, before Michelangelo was commissioned to produce the famous frescoes that are there now. Other churches are built with high, vertically oriented windows that serve the dual purpose of admitting light and making the sky seem part of the sanctuary itself.

Many churches, particularly among more liturgical denominations, are laid out in the form of a cross, reminiscent of the cross on which Jesus was crucified, and the interior of the sanctuary is divided into areas of varying holiness. Many of the medieval cathedrals of Europe also follow the cruciform pattern. In these churches, the long, central portion of the church where the congregation stands or sits is called the nave. The nave may be

When April with his showers sweet with fruit
The drought of March has pierced unto the root
And bathed each vein with liquor that has power
To generate therein and sire the flower; ...
Then do folk long to go on pilgrimage,
And palmers to go seeking out strange strands,
To distant shrines well known in sundry lands.
And specially from every shire's end
Of England they to Canterbury wend,
The holy blessed martyr there to seek
Who helped them when they lay so ill and weak.

(Chaucer, *Canterbury Tales*, Prologue)

Figure 2.2 The fish is an ancient symbol used by Christians. It may have been chosen because several of Jesus' earliest followers were fishermen or because the letters of the Greek word for fish are an acronym for "Jesus Christ, God's Son, Savior."

surrounded by one or more pairs of aisles. Together, the nave and the aisles are in the part of the building that corresponds to the longer, vertical portion of the cross. The transept is in that part of the church that corresponds to the horizontal portion of the cross, and it is intended for the clergy who will participate in the service. Beyond the transept, in line with the nave, is the sanctuary, the holiest part of the church, where the altar is located. Located underneath the altar in many, particularly older, churches is a crypt; many early churches were built on top of Christian holy sites, especially the graves of saints and martyrs. Twentieth-century excavations under the altar of St. Peter's Basilica in Rome confirmed ancient legends that the earliest church built on that spot (the present structure was built between the sixteenth and seventeenth centuries) was constructed on top of the grave of the apostle Simon Peter, one of Jesus' original disciples. In most Protestant churches the place of honor which is accorded to the altar in Roman Catholic and Orthodox traditions is assigned instead to the pulpit, the lectern or cabinet from which the sermon (from a Latin word meaning "word" of God) is proclaimed.

Sacred symbols and artefacts

From almost the beginning of the Christian movement, followers of Jesus made use of symbols to represent who they were and what they believed. Although the most widely recognized symbol in use today by Christians is the cross, the earliest Christian symbol was probably not the cross, but rather the fish. The fish may seem an unusual symbol for the religious movement that became Christianity, but early Christians recognized a number of significant parallels between the simple fish symbol and the origins of their faith. Several of Jesus' earliest disciples, including Simon Peter, had been fishermen. Stories that related how Jesus called his first disciples said that he called them from being fishermen to being "fishers of men." Several of the narratives that circulated in the early church involved fishing: Jesus' miracle of the loaves and fishes, the miraculous catch of fish, Peter's catching of a fish with a coin in its mouth, and others. Finally, the Greek word for fish, *ichthys* (ιχθυς), was used as an acronym that expressed the essence of the Christian proclamation about Jesus. The five Greek letters are the first letters of the words "Jesus Christ, God's Son, Savior." The fish symbol is attested from the last decades of the first century and may be even earlier. In settings where the observance of the Christian religion was prohibited, Christians may have identified themselves to one another by means of the simple, dual-arc fish: one Christian would draw an arc in

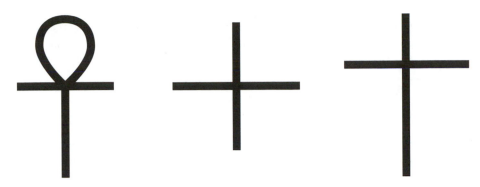

Figure 2.3   In ancient Egypt, the *ankh*, a looped cross, was a symbol for life, and this meaning, together with its resemblance to other types of crosses, led to its adoption as a symbol used by Egyptian Christians. The Greek cross, with its vertical and horizontal pieces of equal length, is the version of the Christian symbol that came to be favored by the Eastern Church. The Latin cross, whose vertical segment is longer than its horizontal piece, was favored by the Western Church.

the dirt, and if the other person was a Christian, he or she would draw the second arc and complete the diagram. The fish symbol fell out of widespread use among Christians for centuries but has been revived in recent decades – usually in the form of the simple dual-arc fish, also known as the Jesus fish – so that it is once again a popular Christian symbol.

Jesus' sayings were passed down orally among the earliest Christians, decades before the current gospels were composed. One group of sayings, many of which are recorded in the Gospel of John, are the so-called "I am" sayings, in which Jesus compares himself metaphorically to a number of things. "I am the door." "I am the light of the world." "I am the way, the truth, and the life." Perhaps the most popular "I am" statement, at least as reflected in early Christian art, was "I am the Good Shepherd." Images of Jesus as the Good Shepherd are frequently found on or near early Christian graves, which were often placed in underground burial grounds (catacombs).

Without a doubt the most important Christian symbol throughout time has been the cross. The cross symbolizes the instrument of Jesus' death, but it also alludes to the redemptive value that Christians see in Jesus' death, and to Jesus' resurrection from the dead. Although the cross on which Jesus was crucified likely took the shape of a capital T, the shape that came to predominate in Christian symbolism more closely resembles a simple, lowercase t (Roman cross), or even a plus sign (equilateral cross), though variants abound. For example, an Egyptian variant of the cross has a loop at the top; Egyptian Christians apparently borrowed the hieroglyphic symbol for life (*ankh*) for this cross. One form of the cross used frequently by Orthodox Churches resembles a large plus sign, with smaller equilateral crosses in the four quadrants of the larger cross. Another variant of the cross, commonly associated with Roman Catholicism, is the crucifix, a Roman cross on which is placed the body of the crucified Jesus.

Other Christian symbols in general use today include the steeple, a vertical spire on church buildings pointing to the heavens, the communion cup, the fleur-de-lis (also a symbol of the Virgin Mary), and the Greek letters Alpha (A) and Omega (Ω). Many symbols are associated with particular sacred times of the Christian year, such as the following.

Christmas/Epiphany:	Star
	Crèche
	Angel
	Holly
	Pomegranate
	Dove
Lent/Easter:	Crown of thorns
	INRI (Latin acronym for Jesus of Nazareth, King of the Jews)
	Lamb
	Palm branches
	Spear
Pentecost:	Fire
	Clover or shamrock
	Dove

Whereas symbols are abstract representations of particular aspects of the Christian faith that can be replicated at will, sacred artefacts – often called relics – are concrete objects that many Christians associate with a manifestation of the divine. Such artefacts are usually associated with a Christian saint, particularly a martyr, and they may be divided into two groups: body parts and other items (e.g, articles of clothing). As already noted, graves of Christian martyrs became places of pilgrimage in the early history of Christianity, and shrines and churches were frequently built over the tombs. Other churches acquired relics of the martyrs – locks of hair, fragments of bone, or teeth – and became pilgrimage destinations as well. A church's desire to attain such relics was based both on the miracles frequently attributed to the relics by the faithful and on the economic benefits that pilgrimage destinations enjoyed.

One of the most famous examples of the quest for relics was the search undertaken by Helen, the mother of the first Christian emperor Constantine, for the true cross of Jesus. After her son became emperor, she traveled to the Holy Land in search of the cross upon which Jesus was crucified. Legend says that she located three crosses in Jerusalem and identified the true cross by its healing power. Pieces of the true cross, along with nails from that cross, are alleged to exist in a number of different places.

The sacred artefact that has most occupied the imagination of Christians for the past several hundred years, primarily through fictionalized accounts of its quest in literature and film, is the Holy Grail, or the cup (or dish) from which Jesus drank at the Last Supper on the night before his crucifixion. Despite the popularity of the legend, it is apparently quite late; the first reference to the Grail is found in the medieval story of Percival, one of King Arthur's knights, written by Crétien de Troyes in the late twelfth century. Another artefact, real but apparently late medieval in origin, is the Shroud of Turin, which some identify as the burial cloth of Jesus.

Although many Christians continue to view sacred artefacts as containing some sort of spiritual power, deriving from their association with Christian saints or martyrs, other Christians see the attention paid to sacred objects as misguided, even if they are authentic relics, or even idolatrous. Another approach to such artefacts, prevalent especially among Orthodox Christians, but not limited to the Orthodox, sees them as legitimate objects of veneration, alongside works of art such as icons.

Orthodox worship often includes the veneration of icons, or sacred images. Icons are painted depictions of Jesus, Mary, the saints, or angels, usually painted in accordance with certain stylistic conventions. The difference between an icon and a painting that is a work of art is largely a matter of intent. Icons are generally produced to be used in worship, whereas typical paintings, even of religious scenes, are not. Although Christian critics of the veneration of icons often refer to the practice as worship of the images, the Orthodox make a distinction between worship, which is properly directed toward God, and veneration, which uses an icon as an aid to worship or honor the figure represented in the icon. The veneration of images, including statues of Jesus, Mary, and the saints, is also practiced in the Roman Catholic Church, though it is not as prevalent as in the Orthodox Church, particularly since the Second Vatican Council (1962–1965). However, the veneration of images continues to be popular among Catholics in many countries.

Sacred interactions

For Christians, the primary way in which humanity encounters God is through worship. Although Christians believe that God is omnipresent (present everywhere), they believe that people come into contact with God in an especially profound way through worship. Thus, it is preferable to speak of sacred interactions between God and humans than of sacred human acts, as though humans could conjure up the divine of their own volition. Sacred acts, properly speaking, are the exclusive domain of God.

According to Matthew's gospel, Jesus told his disciples, "Wherever two or three of you are gathered together in my name, there I am in the midst of you" (Matt 18:20). While the original context of this saying indicates that it was mainly intended as a statement concerning ecclesiastical authority, the idea of Jesus' presence with Christians when they gathered for worship was generally acknowledged. Specific acts of worship such as prayer, singing, and confession of sins are directed toward God and are seen as part of the divine–human interaction that occurs in worship, especially corporate worship. The exposition of God's word, called the sermon or homily, is considered a divine–human interaction that flows in the opposite direction, from God, through the messenger, to the people of God.

For many Christians, the divine–human interaction is crystallized in a series of symbolic acts called sacraments in some traditions, ordinances in others. As the name implies, those who consider these acts sacraments (Catholics and Orthodox) see a more direct contact with the divine than do those who view them as ordinances (most Protestants). For Catholics and Orthodox, the sacraments are means through which divine grace is transmitted in a mystical way to worshipers.

The initial sacrament/ordinance which Christians receive is usually baptism, an initiation into the body of Christ. Baptism is performed only on adults and older children in some traditions and on infants in other traditions. It may consist of the sprinkling of water on the head, pouring water over the head, or total immersion. Baptism represents the new birth into the Christian life, the washing away of sins, and the believer's identity with the death, burial, and resurrection of Jesus.

The most frequently practiced sacrament/ordinance is variously called Holy Communion, the Eucharist (from a Greek word meaning "thanksgiving"), or the Lord's Supper. It consists of a symbolic meal of bread and wine, representing the body and blood of Jesus and commemorating Jesus' final meal with his disciples prior to his crucifixion. Some churches substitute wafers or another starchy food for bread, and others use non-alcoholic alternatives to wine. While most Christians who regularly attend public worship receive communion once a week, others receive it daily, while members of other traditions receive it only monthly or less frequently. In the sacramental traditions, the Eucharist is believed to impart divine grace to the recipient. The early second century bishop Ignatius of Antioch referred to it as "the medicine of immortality" (Ignatius *Eph.* 20). The Eucharist is a meal that believers in Christ share with one another and with God. For many Christians, however, it is not only a meal but also a reenactment of Jesus' sacrifice on the cross. For Roman Catholics, the bread and wine are literally transformed into the body and blood of Christ, hence their healing power. For other Christians, particularly many Protestants, the Eucharist is a memorial meal that symbolizes communion with God.

While baptism and communion are the two most commonly observed sacraments or ordinances, some Christians recognize others as well. Marriage is considered a sacrament in the Roman Catholic and Orthodox traditions, as are Holy Orders (the commitment to full-time Christian ministry), Penance/Confession, Confirmation/Chrismation, and Anointing of the Sick. Whether these sacred interactions are considered to impart grace directly, as in the sacramental traditions, or are seen as symbols of spiritual truths or mysteries, all Christians see great value in observing them.

Sacred personages

According to the New Testament, Jesus' disciples commonly addressed him as *Lord*. Since they spoke Aramaic, the word they would have used was probably *Mar*, which is equivalent to the Hebrew *Adon*, "lord" or "master." Although God is often referred to in the Hebrew Bible as *Adon*, the word most commonly rendered "Lord" in English translations (often printed in small capitals as LORD) is the proper name for God, *YHWH*, often rendered "Yahweh" in modern discussions. However, Greek translations of the Old Testament regularly rendered both *YHWH* and *Adon* as *kyrios*, "Lord," and this word is used as well in the New Testament as an appellation for Jesus (and

Figure 2.4 Detail from Michelangelo's *Pietà* located in St. Peter's Basilica in Rome, which represents two of Christianity's most sacred personages, Jesus and the Virgin Mary.

occasionally for other people as well). Regardless of whether the practice of using the Greek *kyrios* to render both Hebrew words originated with Jews or Christians (scholars debate this point), it is clear that the early church referred to both God and Jesus as Lord, an indication that Jesus was considered to have a special relationship with God – at the very least – from the beginning.

Paul's letter to the Christians of Galatia, one of the earliest preserved Christian documents, refers to Jesus as the *Son of God*, and this appellation undoubtedly goes back to the earliest days of Christianity, although Jesus apparently did not use the term of himself (he called himself *Son of Man*, an Aramaic phrase meaning "human being," though some scholars posit a more nuanced meaning). The term Son of God could properly be applied to anyone in covenant relationship with God (e.g. Gal 3:26; John 1:12); however, referring to Jesus as *the* Son of God quickly became popular in early Christianity (cf. Mark 1:1; 15:39), and it is clear that Jesus was seen by early Christians as God's son in a unique way. In the Hebrew Bible, the term *Son of God* is often used to refer to the Davidic king (e.g. Ps 2:7), and it was used in reference to the messiah in the Second Temple period, including by the Qumran community. For Paul, the title Son of God presented Jesus' claim to be the Jewish messiah, which is equivalent to the Greek word *Christ*, another title associated with Jesus. It did not directly imply Jesus' divinity. However, other Pauline language, including his application of Old Testament references to Yahweh as applying to Jesus (e.g. Rom 10:13; Phil 2:10–11), show that Paul

Saints in Christian tradition

The list of people considered saints is long, and differences of opinion exist among the various Christian traditions that recognize saints. All would consider Mary, the 11 disciples (minus Judas Iscariot), the Apostle Paul, and James and Jude the "brothers" of Jesus as saints. There is general agreement about many other people as well, but Catholics recognize many people not recognized by the Orthodox, and vice versa. Anglicans mostly follow the Catholics in their recognition of saints, at least those who were recognized prior to the Reformation. Some of the more interesting figures who are recognized as saints by one or more traditions are the angels Gabriel (Orthodox, Catholic) and Michael (Anglican, Orthodox, Catholic), Czar Nicholas II (Orthodox), King Charles I of England (Anglican), and Pope Pius X (Catholic), the most recent Roman Catholic Pontiff to be canonized. One Oriental Orthodox communion, the Ethiopian Orthodox Church, recognizes Pontius Pilate, the Roman governor who sentenced Jesus to death, as a saint, based on a local tradition that Pilate later converted and was martyred for his faith.

understood Jesus to be intimately and uniquely associated with God. If the letter to the Colossians was written by Paul (scholars debate this point), then the comment in Col 2:9, that in Christ the whole fullness of deity dwells in bodily form, supports Paul's view of Jesus' unique relationship with God (Hurtado 2003: 101–8).

As Christianity developed in the Gentile world as the first century drew to a close, terms like *Son of God* and *Lord* lost the more nuanced meanings that they usually have in the New Testament writings themselves and became understood as direct claims of divinity. Son of God meant God, and Lord also meant God. The most explicit statements in the New Testament itself concerning the equation Jesus = God are found in the Gospel of John, the latest canonical gospel, probably written at the very end of the century. John 1:1–18 contains a hymn celebrating Jesus as the *Word* (*Logos*) of God, a Greek philosophical term that can also be rendered the *Reason* of God. The very first verse of this passage equates the Word with God. Near the end of the same gospel, the apostle Thomas, upon seeing the resurrected Jesus, cries out, "My Lord and my God!" (John 20:28). This statement is the most explicit statement in the New Testament concerning Jesus' divinity, but the idea that Jesus was somehow equal to, or part of, God was quickly established as the dominant Christian view. Although for centuries after this the church debated the exact nature of the relationship between the Son of God and God the Father, Jesus' status as a divine figure was firmly established as the official position of Christianity from this time.

If Jesus is the most important divine personage in Christian thinking and worship, the second most important figure for many Christians through the ages has been his mother Mary. The gospels of Matthew and Luke present Mary as a virgin, God's chosen vessel who gave birth to Jesus. Although the New Testament doesn't make any claims about Mary's Perpetual Virginity, the tradition that she remained a chaste virgin throughout her life was popular by the second century (Jesus' brothers and sisters, referred to in the New Testament, were assigned to Joseph and a previous wife, who died prior to his betrothal to Mary, or else they were considered cousins rather than siblings). Other traditions about Mary, including her immaculate conception (i.e. her sinlessness from the point of her own conception) and her bodily assumption into heaven, arose relatively early in the history of Christianity and are commonly accepted by many Christians today, especially Roman Catholics. The Orthodox often refer to Mary as *Theotokos*, a Greek term meaning "God bearer," roughly equivalent to "Mother of God," a term used by Catholics. Protestants, though assigning great honor to Mary as the mother of Jesus, generally reject the doctrines of Mary's perpetual virginity, immaculate conception, and bodily assumption as being unscriptural, since they arose in Christian tradition after the close of the New Testament.

In addition to Jesus and Mary, many others who lived lives of great piety, who were martyred for their faith, or who are believed to have performed miracles are identified as saints by many Christians. Saints may be defined as ordinary people who lived extraordinary lives or had extraordinary faith in God. In Catholic and Orthodox traditions, they are often treated as intercessors on behalf of living Christians, passing the requests of the faithful on to God. Although they certainly recognize the superior lives of certain believers throughout history, most Protestants do not recognize the special status of any deceased believers as saints. To be more precise, they believe that all Christians are saints, by virtue of God's grace and their relationship with God through faith in Christ. Anglicans and Lutherans, however, join Catholics and Orthodox in recognizing specific people as saints.

In addition to human men and women, Christians traditionally recognize as sacred personages the class of semi-divine beings known collectively as angels and demons. Earlier parts of the Old Testament sometimes refer to beings called "the sons of God" (Ps 29:1; Job 1:6) or even "the gods" (Pss 82:1; 138:1), among whom is "the Satan," (i.e. the Accuser; Job 1:6). By the late Second Temple period, Jewish thought had developed to the extent where leading heavenly beings allied with God (angels) were sometimes given names – Gabriel, Michael, Raphael, Uriel – as were leading evil beings (demons) – Satan, Asmodeus, Beelzebub. Gabriel, Michael, and Satan are all mentioned in the New Testament, which also includes numerous references to unnamed angels and demons, as well as other spiritual powers (see, e.g. 1 Cor 15:24; Eph 1:21). Christian art and literature is full of references to angels and demons, and many Christians today from all traditions continue to accept these beings as playing a part in life on this planet, albeit usually behind the scenes. Other Christians see these beings as mythological expressions of supernatural power, good and evil.

Sacred metatime

> Abandon all hope, you who enter here.
>
> (Words over the gate to hell in Dante's *Inferno*)

Our earlier discussion of sacred time focused on recurring days of special significance throughout the week (Sunday) or within the Christian year (e.g. Advent, Christmas, Easter). These sacred times are based on the cycle of the seasons and the rhythm of the earth as it journeys around the sun once a year. Despite recognizing these cyclical events, however, Christianity has a profoundly linear view of history, with a distinct beginning and end. These events are, strictly speaking, considered to be outside of time, so they may be referred to as sacred metatime.

The Christian doctrine of the beginning of the earth and/or universe is often called *cosmogony*, from Greek words that mean "beginning of the world." Both the Old and the New Testaments refer to the beginning as a unique act of God, but it is the first chapter of Genesis that most fully describes the events of creation. Though many Christians take this passage in a more or less literal sense, most Christians recognize the mythological character of the language. The creation of the universe, and specifically of the earth and its inhabitants, is described as taking place over six days. The basic structures of the universe, as seen from the perspective of earth, are described: heaven and earth; sun, moon, and stars; waters above the vault of the sky (i.e. the source of rain) and waters below (i.e. rivers, seas, etc.). The immovable boundaries of the earth are similarly detailed: light and dark; dry land and sea; individual species of animals. A modern, scientific understanding of the origins of the universe and of life on earth does not match a literal reading of the first chapter of Genesis, but they present no difficulty to a mythological reading. From this perspective, the God who is responsible for the creation of the world and its inhabitants is the same God who called Abraham out of Ur, spoke to Moses in the burning bush, and was the Father of Jesus Christ. Creation is not self-sufficient or self-organizing. It owes its very existence to God.

Just as the beginning of the universe falls outside the scope of normal time, so too does the end of the world. The Christian doctrine of the end of the world, or *eschatology* ("the study of last things"), is described in the New Testament in various ways: kingdom of God, end of the age, Parousia (Second Coming of Christ), new heaven and new earth. At some point in history, God will intervene in the natural course of events and bring them to an end. This intervention is not the result of the natural development of history, so it cannot be predicted by futurologists. Though some Christians believe that they recognize in certain current events signs that the end of the world is coming soon, most understand that Christians throughout history have thought the same thing, so the eschaton is completely unpredictable. As is the case with biblical descriptions of the beginning of the world, so biblical descriptions of the end of the world are couched in mythological language. The book of Revelation is the classic example of the use of complex imagery and figurative language to describe the events leading to the end of the age. Other parts of the New Testament that describe the end include 1 Thes 5:1–11; Mark 13 (and parallels in Matthew and Luke); and 2 Pet 3:8–10. Events leading up to the end of the world include war, earthquakes, and unusual meteorological phenomena, though at other times the end is projected to come suddenly, "like a thief in the night." The end itself is described as including the total destruction of the earth by fire, the resurrection of the dead, a final judgment, the physical return of Jesus, and the creation of a new heaven and a new earth. That these descriptions are not totally consistent with one another is a reminder that the biblical writers used conventional, sometimes mythological, language to describe the expected end of history.

In addition to creation and the eschaton, another type of sacred metatime involves the disposition of the souls of the dead in the interim between the present and the end of the age. The predominant view in the Hebrew Bible concerning the state of the departed was that they occupied a place called *Sheol*, a place of darkness and lack of knowledge, isolated from God, similar to the Greek concept of Hades. At some point in the Second Temple period, however, the idea of a differentiated judgment arose. The dead would ultimately be raised and judged according to their deeds, with the good taken to be with God and the wicked forever separated from God (see Dan 12:1–2). By New Testament times, the predominant Jewish position was that the righteous dead would eventually be raised to eternal life in *heaven* with God, while the wicked would be cast into a place of eternal torment, *hell*, along with Satan and his demons. This, at least, was the view of the Pharisees, as well as of Jesus and his disciples. Since the Pharisaic party formed the basis for Rabbinic Judaism, which survived the fall of Jerusalem (70 c.e.) and two Jewish rebellions against Rome (66–73 c.e. and 132–135 c.e.), a common belief in heaven and hell as the destination of the dead was shared by Jews and Christians. Some Christians believed that departed believers entered a state of unconsciousness, or sleep, until they were awakened for the final judgment. Others believed that souls were sent immediately to either heaven or hell, and the final judgment was merely a confirmation of their reward or punishment.

As Christianity developed in the second and subsequent centuries, the concept of *soul-sleep* was set aside by the vast majority of Christians, who believed that the dead went immediately to their place of reward or punishment, according to their faith and their deeds. By the beginning of the third century, many Christian scholars posited a third possible destination for the souls of the dead: *purgatory*. The word purgatory comes from a Latin word meaning "cleansing," and purgatory came to be seen as the destination of the majority of Christians, those who died with unconfessed venial (minor) sins or who had not experienced the full punishment for their sins while on earth. Those Christians who accepted the doctrine of purgatory believed that the wicked went directly to hell, the saints directly to heaven, and the vast majority of Christians to purgatory for a varying period of time, where they would suffer punishment in accordance with their sins, before eventually being allowed to enter heaven. In the early fourteenth century, Dante Alighieri, a native of Florence, wrote an imaginative description of hell, purgatory, and heaven that has shaped the view of many people since that time: *The Divine Comedy*. Today the doctrine of purgatory is accepted primarily by Roman Catholics. It is rejected by Orthodox and Protestant Christians. The doctrine of soul-sleep has been revived in relatively modern times by some groups of Anabaptists and by Seventh-day Adventists.

Some Christians subscribe to the idea of *annihilationism*, in which the righteous dead live forever in heaven, while the souls of the unrighteous are destroyed, rather than condemned to an eternity of torture in hell. Still others are *universalists*, who believe that all people, regardless of their deeds while on earth, will eventually be reunited with God. In regard to the exact nature of existence in the afterlife, Christians are divided between those who look for a resurrection of the physical body (the traditional view) and those who do not.

Key points you need to know

- Christian perspectives on God vary from seeing God as a supernatural being to seeing God as the ground of being.
- Rudolf Otto described the Holy (or Sacred) as something that is at the same time terrifying and fascinating, a description that fits well with Christians' views of God.
- Most Christians recognize different seasons of the Christian year, beginning with Advent (in late autumn) and proceeding through seasons such as Christmas, Epiphany, Lent, and Eastertide. Other Christians only recognize Sunday, or in some cases Saturday, as a day that is special.
- Many Christians consider places such as sites associated with Jesus (e.g. the Cave of the Nativity in Bethlehem or the Church of the Holy Sepulcher in Jerusalem) as sacred. Others consider some of the great cathedrals around the world to be sacred. Church buildings themselves, or parts of the buildings such as the altar, are often considered sacred as well.
- Although the most important symbol of Christianity throughout history has been the cross, the earliest sacred symbol was probably the fish.
- Relics of the saints, icons, and other objects like the Shroud of Turin are considered sacred by many Christians.
- Although Christians believe that God is everywhere, they most frequently experience encounters with God in worship, especially corporate worship. In many Christian traditions, sacred rituals knows as sacraments or mysteries are important ways in which Christians may encounter the divine.
- For Christians, the most important and universally acknowledged sacred personage is Jesus Christ. Many Christians also acknowledge the holiness of specific saints, particularly Mary the mother of Jesus, and of angels.
- Christians have a linear view of time, so they believe it has a definite beginning (the act of creation) and end (the eschaton). Beyond these boundaries is eternity, which encompasses heaven, hell, and, for Roman Catholics, purgatory. Some Christians, however, deny the existence of hell as a place of permanent torment for the wicked.

Discussion questions

1.   Why is the distinction between sacred and profane necessary in Christianity?
2.   What makes a place sacred? Can sacred places be moved elsewhere and retain their holiness (e.g. moving a cathedral stone by stone or moving the ground upon which an important event occurred)?
3.   What is the difference between veneration and worship of an object?
4.   Why is the sacrament of communion so important for many Christians?
5.   How does the concept of sacred metatime fit into the scientific worldview, which proposes both a Big Bang at the beginning of the universe and an eventual dissipation of the universe's energy as the stars burn out?

Further reading

Bradner, John 1977. *Symbols of Church Seasons and Days*. Harrisburg, PA: Morehouse.

Bruyneel, Sally and Alan G. Padgett 2003. *Introducing Christianity*. Maryknoll, NY: Orbis.

Eliade, Mircea 1959. *The Sacred and the Profane: The Nature of Religion*. Translated by Willard R. Trask. New York: Harcourt, Brace & World.

Hurtado, Larry W. 2003. *Lord Jesus Christ: Devotion to Jesus in Earliest Christianity*. Grand Rapids, MI: Eerdmans.

Otto, Rudolf 1958. *The Idea of the Holy*. Translated by John W. Harvey. New York: Oxford University Press.

Part II

Historical overview of Christianity

3 *The historical and intellectual context of Christianity*

And the Lord spoke to Moses saying, "You have heard the voice of the words of this people, which they spoke to you. All they have said is right. If only it were the case that they had this heart to fear me and to keep all my precepts always, so that it might go well for them and for their children forever! I would raise up a prophet for them like you from among their brothers, and I would put my words in his mouth, and he would speak to them all that I command him.

(4QTestimonia 1–6)

In this chapter

Christianity did not arise in a vacuum. It developed out of the soil of Judaism, under the banner of the Roman Empire. Both Judaism and Greco-Roman history and thought affected the origin and influenced the earliest development of Christianity. This chapter examines the history of Israel, with special emphasis on the Babylonian exile and the Second Temple period, the times most important for the development of ideas that would influence Christianity. The Zoroastrian and Greco-Roman influences on both Judaism and Christianity are also examined.

Main topics covered

- History of Israel (including Judah) from its emergence in Canaan through the fall of the northern kingdom (Israel), the Babylonian exile, and the Persian, Greek, Maccabean/Hasmonean, and early Roman periods
- Development of Jewish theology and perspectives during the late monarchic, exilic, and Second Temple periods that would have a profound impact on Christianity
- Social setting of Judaism during the time of Jesus

Judaism

> The grass withers, the flower fades;
>> but the word of our God will stand forever. (Isa 40:8)

Christianity began as a reform movement within Judaism, and all of the earliest Christians, including Jesus, were Jews, so an understanding of the Jewish context in which Christianity was born and flourished is essential to understanding Christianity itself. The nation of Israel emerged in the land of Canaan – where the modern nations of Israel, Jordan, and the Palestinian Territories are – in about the thirteenth century B.C.E. As Israel moved into the land from the east, another group of people, the Philistines (who would bequeath their name to Palestine) moved in from the west, part of the vast movement of people from the eastern Mediterranean region, the Sea Peoples, who invaded, or attempted to invade, the lands of the ancient Near East, including Egypt, Anatolia, Mesopotamia, and Canaan. At first Israel consisted of a number of disparate groups, or tribes, loosely united by a common language (Hebrew, a dialect of Canaanite) and the common worship of the god named Yahweh. By the end of the eleventh century, Israel had come into contact with the Philistines, as well as with some of the powerful Canaanite city-states, and many groups of Israelites joined forces under the early kings Saul, David, and Solomon to fight their enemies and establish a nation-state. (This description of Israel's early history is disputed by some historians and archaeologists, but since it continues to be accepted by many scholars, and since it formed part of the Jewish self-understanding during the Second Temple period, the period during which Christianity arose, it is unnecessary to consider alternative hypotheses.)

When Israel emerged as a nation in the land of Canaan between the thirteenth and eleventh centuries, the ancient Near East was engulfed in a political power vacuum that lasted from the end of the thirteenth to the middle of the eighth century B.C.E. Prior to this time, the powerful empires of Egypt and Hatti (peopled by the Hittites, based in Anatolia, modern day Turkey) struggled with one another over control of Canaan. Further to the north and east, Assyria and Babylonia had been great powers for centuries. About the time that the Sea Peoples invaded, however, all of these empires were greatly reduced in strength, to a large extent as a direct result of the invasion. The Hittite Empire in Anatolia was completely overrun and ceased to exist. Egypt, Assyria, and Babylonia lost much of their power and were forced to confine their activities to within their own historical borders. Aside from sporadic exhibitions of power, such as Egyptian Pharaoh Sheshonk's raid of Israel in the tenth century and Assyria's abortive attempt to invade Syria and Canaan in the ninth century, these former empires left the lands of Canaan, the Transjordan, Phoenicia, and Syria alone. As a result, small states arose and flourished in these areas. Two of the most important states were Israel and Judah.

Although the traditional understanding of the history of the Israelite kingdoms is that a single, unified kingdom existed under Saul, David, and Solomon before it was divided following Solomon's death, a closer reading of the biblical text indicates that

Israel (the northern tribes) and Judah (the southern tribes) had their own self-identities even during the reigns of the earliest kings. In fact, according to the Bible, David reigned over Judah by itself before being invited to take the throne of Israel as well after the death of Eshbaal, Saul's son. This merger of northern and southern tribes began to unravel during the reign of Solomon, and it fell apart completely after his death, when the northern tribes selected their own king, Jeroboam, rejecting Solomon's son Rehoboam. After this point the states of Israel and Judah followed their own courses, sometimes fighting one another in border disputes, sometimes joining forces to fight common adversaries.

The 450 year regional power vacuum came to an end in 745 B.C.E., with the ascension of the Assyrian king Tiglath-pileser III to the throne. Assyria began its incursions into territories outside its borders over the next few years, including Israel and Judah. Neither nation could stand against the superior military might of Assyria. Israel fell to Assyria in 722 B.C.E., its leading citizens were exiled to other Assyrian controlled territories, and its land became an Assyrian province. The northern kingdom of Israel never recovered from exile. The vast majority of its citizens either became absorbed into the Assyrian Empire and its culture or fled south into the territory of Judah. A small number preserved the worship of Yahweh and other Israelite traditions and became the ancestors of the Samaritans, adversaries of the Jews during the Second Temple period. Judah survived total annihilation by submitting to Assyrian rule, but its territory was greatly reduced in size. After a brief revival of Judah's fortunes when the Assyrian Empire fell to the Neo-Babylonian Empire and its allies, Judah itself was conquered by the Babylonians in 587 B.C.E. The Babylonians under king Nebuchadnezzar destroyed the city of Jerusalem, burned down the temple, and carried the leading citizens of Judah into exile.

Despite its high profile in the Hebrew Bible as the destroyer of the kingdom of Judah, the Neo-Babylonian Empire was a mere flash in the pan on the world stage, retaining power for only seventy years. A new power from the east, the Persian Empire, under the leadership of Cyrus the Great, conquered Babylonia in 539 B.C.E., and the Jews who had been exiled in Babylonia for fifty years were allowed to return to their homeland. Many Jews returned, but many more chose to remain behind, because they had established homes and businesses in Babylonia during their time in exile. Since the Jews who returned from Babylonia to Jerusalem belonged to families that had been the most powerful and educated in preexilic Judah, they naturally assumed leadership roles in the newly constituted Persian territory of Judah. Not surprisingly, the returnees' assumption of power put them at odds with some who had remained in the land during the period of Babylonian hegemony, and with the Samaritans to the north as well. Nevertheless, the returnees set the pace for the religion of the Jews, and their interpretations and innovations ultimately prevailed, at least in Judah. During two centuries of Persian rule, the Jews were allowed to rebuild both the city of Jerusalem and the temple of Yahweh (the Second Temple), and they were also allowed to practice their faith without hindrance. They were not allowed to rule themselves, however, and they remained citizens of the Persian province called "Beyond the River" (i.e. the Euphrates River).

A number of significant developments within Judaism took place during the late monarchic period, the Babylonian exile, and the Persian period which had an impact on the development of Christianity. One development that changed the course of Jewish history was the rise of the prophetic movement in the eighth century B.C.E. in both Israel and Judah. Although prophets were not unknown in earlier times, their lasting influence was assured when the words of Amos and Hosea, Micah and Isaiah began to be recorded and preserved for posterity. Prophets were primarily concerned with the moral and religious state of the nation, and they had few qualms about criticizing the leading citizens of Israel and Judah, including the kings. Some prophets operated largely within the official power structure, maintaining close connections to the royal court, while others worked on the periphery of power. Not surprisingly, those outside the structures of power, such as Amos and Jeremiah, tended to be more pointed in their criticisms of their political leaders, but their messages were often echoed by prophets closer to the centers of power. The preexilic prophets urged their contemporaries to repent of their evil ways and return to faithfulness toward both God and their neighbors. Although they were unsuccessful in preventing the calamitous devastations that the Assyrians wrought on Israel and the Babylonians on Judah, their words made a tremendous impact on many, particularly the Jewish community that was transplanted to Babylonia.

One of the highlights of the prophetic message that emerged during the exilic period and became a centerpiece of Judaism from that time forward was the proclamation that Yahweh was not merely the tribal god of the Jews but was in fact the God of all humankind. Even the official religion of preexilic Israel and Judah might best be described as *henotheistic* rather than *monotheistic*. That is, Yahweh was the only god worthy of Jewish worship, but it was tacitly acknowledged that other nations had their own gods as well. Outside official circles, the inhabitants of Israel and Judah often worshiped other deities alongside Yahweh, such as Baal and Asherah. The situation changed dramatically with the exile, however. The exilic prophets, particularly the anonymous prophet called Second Isaiah, preached that the gods of the nations were not really gods at all, and they ridiculed those who made idols and worshiped them as gods. "Yahweh is the everlasting God, the creator of the ends of the earth!" proclaimed the prophet (Isa 40:28). This belief that the God whom the Jews worshiped was the only God is true monotheism, and it became the official position of Judaism – and of Christianity and Islam later – through the influence of the prophets. When combined with the ethical emphasis of most of the prophets, their overall message is often characterized as *ethical monotheism*.

During the Babylonian exile, prophets like Ezekiel and Second Isaiah encouraged the exiles to retain their hope in God. Yes, God had punished the people for their sins, but their fortunes would one day be restored, and a righteous remnant would persevere through the toughest times. When the Persians conquered Babylon and Cyrus the Great allowed the Jews to return to their homeland, many believed that God would immediately restore the fortunes of the Jewish people. When the Jewish state was not reestablished during the Persian period, however, many Jews began to look again at the promises of the prophets, to see if they had misunderstood. Some looked to the postexilic prophets, such as Haggai and Malachi, who pointed out moral laxness and religious aberrations that continued to prevent God from establishing a renewed kingdom for the Jews. Others re-read the earlier prophets and saw a common thread of hope that permeated many of the earlier writings. This hope was based on God's promise to David that he would always have a descendant (literally, a son) on the throne of Israel. The prophets spoke of a future king, whom they sometimes called the Branch, or the Root of Jesse (David's father). Many Jews in the postexilic period began to focus their hopes for the complete restoration of the community on a coming king, whom they called the *messiah*, or "anointed one." The Greek equivalent of *messiah* is *christos*, or Christ.

During the Second Temple period, certain elements of the prophetic movement began moving in a new direction. Whereas most previous prophets had focused on the moral and religious lapses of the Jewish people and their need for repentance, some prophets now began to focus their attention on the suffering of the Jewish people under foreign domination, and they predicted radical changes ahead. Even the classical, preexilic prophets had spoken on occasion of the last days, when God would establish and rule over an eschatological kingdom. However, those prophets had imagined that the kingdom would be established gradually, as the nations turned to Yahweh in worship and praise (see, e.g. Mic 4:1–4). Some of the postexilic prophets who spoke of the future reign of God envisioned a dramatic intervention on the part of God, replete with signs and wonders that would dismay the nations and give hope to the Jews. This type of prophecy is called apocalyptic, from a Greek word meaning a secret that has been revealed. Some scholars believe that apocalyptic prophecy has roots in Israel's wisdom traditions as well as in prophecy, and if so, that connection may explain the elaborate symbolism that often characterizes apocalyptic material. Although the prophecies associated with Zechariah, Second Zechariah, and Third Isaiah show tendencies in the direction of apocalyptic prophecy, the only full-blown apocalyptic work in the Hebrew Bible is the book of Daniel. Written in the context of the abuses of the Jewish population by the Greek (Seleucid) king Antiochus Epiphanes in the second century B.C.E., the book uses dreams, visions, and intricate symbols to spell out the coming deliverance of Israel from its enemies.

Old Testament passages traditionally seen as messianic prophecies by Christians (1)

The original promise

Your [David's] house and your kingdom shall be made sure forever before me; your throne shall be established forever. (2 Sam 7:16)

Many other Jewish apocalypses were written over the next few centuries, and Christians wrote them as well. The most important Christian work in this vein is called the Apocalypse in Greek but is usually referred to as Revelation in English. Many Jews during Jesus' day, apparently including the Jewish community associated with Qumran (i.e. the authors of the Dead Sea Scrolls), were heavily influenced by apocalyptic thinking and prepared themselves for God's direct intervention in the affairs of the Jewish people in the near future. Jesus and his followers seem to have been influenced by the apocalyptic movements of the day as well, as witnessed in Jesus' statement, "The time is fulfilled, and the kingdom of God has come near. Repent and believe in the good news!" (Mark 1:15). Apocalyptic fervor among Christians probably reached its peak during the First Jewish War, which culminated in the destruction of the Second Temple in 70 c.e., but the sporadic Roman persecution of Christians over the next two and a half centuries also led Christians to think in apocalyptic terms about God's intervention in the world. Throughout the history of the church, including today, groups of Christians have continued to believe that they were living in the last days and that God was on the verge of acting directly to bring an end to the normal course of world history.

In response to the prophetic call for people to examine their own lives, and the life of the community, for moral and religious transgressions, the Jewish community in Babylonia put a new emphasis on studying and observing the law. Jewish tradition saw Moses as the lawgiver, but in fact the law had developed over a period of several centuries, first orally and then in written form. The book of 2 Kings describes the discovery of a book of the law during the reign of King Josiah, in the late seventh century b.c.e., and a reform movement based on this book, probably an early form of Deuteronomy, began in Judah. After the destruction of Jerusalem, the Jews in exile looked to the law with even more ardor, to the extent that it became perhaps the most important unifying force for Jews in the Second Temple period. The person most often identified with the postexilic emphasis on the importance of the law is Ezra, a legal scholar who is traditionally dated to the middle of the fifth century b.c.e. Some traditions have Ezra re-creating the entire Mosaic law, which had been destroyed by the Babylonians, but it is more likely that he was merely an important advocate for the centrality of the law for the Jewish people. The law gave the common people instructions on how to live their lives: what to eat, what to wear, how to observe the Sabbath, how to conduct business with neighbors, and so forth. It also gave the priests and other community leaders instructions on maintaining ritual purity, offering sacrifices, and dealing with crimes of various sorts, among other things. The law became a rallying point for many Jews during and after the exile, and it provided a glue that held the community together against difficult odds.

The institutions that were most closely associated with the emerging importance of the law were the temple – rebuilt in 516 b.c.e. – and the synagogue. Both of these institutions would play a prominent role in the development of early Christianity as well. The precise origins of the synagogue are obscure, but it is probable that it originated among the Jews in exile in Babylonia. The synagogue was a place where Jews could assemble to study the law and worship God. Unlike the temple, which, according to the law, was unique and could only be built in Jerusalem, synagogues could be built anywhere a community of Jews lived. In fact, a separate building was not necessary, and Jews starting a new synagogue often began meeting in the home of one of the members. The study that took place in the synagogues focused at first on the law, which was codified by the fifth century B.C.E. in the five books of Moses, but over time the prophets and other writings, such as the Psalms, were studied and used in worship. Oral traditions involving the proper interpretation of the law were also developed and transmitted in synagogues, and in schools associated with the synagogues. In many ways the synagogue was the center of Jewish community life, and it provided a forum for creative thinking about God and the future of the Jews. A typical synagogue service during the Second Temple period included prayer, the singing of psalms, scripture reading, and exposition of the scripture. This pattern of worship was adopted and adapted by early Christians.

When the foundation for the restored temple was laid after the return from exile, some who saw it wept for joy because the temple would be rebuilt, and others wept for sorrow because they saw that it would be only a modest replica of Solomon's magnificent temple (Ezra 3:10–13). What began as a rather small building, however, grew over time, as subsequent Jews added onto the building itself and the surrounding temple complex. If the synagogue was the place where the law was studied, the temple was the place where the law was practiced, or at least those parts of the law dealing with sacrifice and ritual purity. The altar of burnt offerings in the Jerusalem temple was the only place authorized by the law for Jews to offer sacrifices. (Rival temples were constructed in Elephantine and Heliopolis, Egypt, but they never attracted anything other than a local following; the first was destroyed by the Egyptian people in 410 B.C.E., and the second was shut down by the Romans in 74 C.E.) The sacrificial system was important in Jewish theology as the primary means by which sin could be removed, both for individuals and for the community as a whole. Priests in the temple performed daily sacrifices, and three major festivals every year – Unleavened Bread (Passover), Weeks, and Booths – brought thousands of visitors to Jerusalem with their own offerings. The most important single ceremony was the annual Day of Atonement (Yom Kippur), when the high priest would enter the innermost sanctuary (the holy of holies) and sprinkle the blood of a sacrificed goat inside. At the same time, after the high priest laid his hands on its head, a second goat would be released into the wilderness. These two rituals symbolized the removal of the nation's sin.

About 19 B.C.E. Herod the Great began a major overhaul and rebuilding of the temple, and the end result was a truly magnificent set of buildings. The renovations and expansion begun by Herod took several decades to complete, and only a few years after its completion, the Roman army destroyed the temple during the First Jewish War, in 70 C.E. The New Testament indicates that Jesus and his disciples worshiped in the Jerusalem temple, and Jesus' death took place during the Feast of Unleavened Bread. The book of Acts records that the disciples continued to worship in the temple following Jesus' death and resurrection. Both Jews and Christians reacted to the destruction of the temple in 70 C.E. The Jews put more emphasis on the study of the law, which they

Some important dates in the history of Israel and Judah

c. 1000 B.C.E.	Traditional date for the start of King David's reign
922 B.C.E.	Division of the kingdom into Israel (North) and Judah (South)
722 B.C.E.	Fall of Israel to the Assyrian king Sargon II
587 B.C.E.	Fall of Judah to the Babylonian king Nebuchadnezzar, destruction of the First Temple, and beginning of the Babylonian exile for many Jewish leaders
539 B.C.E.	Conquest of Babylonia by Persian king Cyrus the Great
538 B.C.E.	Cyrus's decree allowing exiled Jews to return to their homeland
516 B.C.E.	Foundation laid for the Second Temple
332 B.C.E.	Alexander the Great conquers Judah and surrounding territories from the Persians, incorporating it into the Greek Empire
323 B.C.E.	Death of Alexander the Great divides Greek Empire among rival generals, with Judah eventually falling under the control of the Ptolemaic Empire, based in Egypt
198 B.C.E.	After a series of wars, Judah transferred to Seleucid Empire, based in Syria
167 B.C.E.	Maccabean revolt against Seleucid King Antiochus Epiphanes begins, eventually establishing an independent Jewish state
63 B.C.E.	Roman general Pompey captures Judah and annexes it to the Roman Empire
70 C.E.	Destruction of the Second Temple in Jerusalem as a result of the First Jewish War against Rome
70 C.E.	Johanan ben Zakai and his followers, who opposed the War, move to Jabneh and found a school, which becomes an important center for the study of Rabbinic Judaism
73 or 74 C.E.	Jewish fortress at Masada captured by the Romans
135 C.E.	Simon bar Kokhba, leader of the Second Jewish War against Rome, defeated, and Jews expelled from Jerusalem

came to view as a valid substitute for animal sacrifice. Christians came to understand the death of Jesus as a sacrifice like that performed in the temple, especially on the Day of Atonement, but superior to those sacrifices in that it only needed to be performed once (Heb 9:11–14).

Another important change that began during the exilic period and continued throughout the Second Temple period was the adoption of Aramaic rather than Hebrew as the dominant spoken language of the Jews. Aramaic, like Hebrew, was a Semitic language, but it was distinct enough that the two languages were mutually unintelligible. Aramaic became the *lingua franca* of the region under the Assyrians, and it continued to

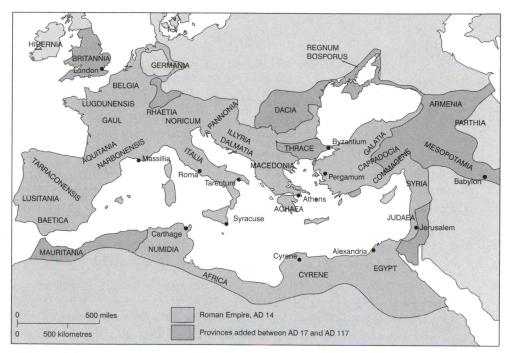

Map 3.1 Map of the Roman Empire. At its greatest extent in the first and second centuries C.E., the Roman Empire encompassed the Mediterranean world, reaching north to Britain and East to Syria. The Jewish homeland, where Christianity originated, was in the Roman province of Palestine (called Judea during Jesus' day), on the eastern edge of the empire.

be the predominant language under the Babylonians and Persians, even though all three of those nations had their own languages as well. Although many Jews, particularly those whose ancestors had remained in the land during the Babylonian exile, continued to speak Hebrew, Aramaic became more and more important over time. Large portions of two of the latest books in the Old Testament, Ezra and Daniel, were written in Aramaic rather than Hebrew. As more and more Jews spoke Aramaic rather than Hebrew, synagogue worship became problematic, because many could no longer understand the biblical text when it was read. Jews in Aramaic-speaking synagogues began providing an Aramaic translation of the Hebrew text, and over time standard Aramaic translations, or *targums*, were developed. At first these translations were transmitted orally, but they were eventually written down. Aramaic was the language spoken by Jesus and his disciples, and several Aramaic words occur in the New Testament. Even though all the New Testament books were apparently written originally in Greek, some scholars assert that a knowledge of Aramaic can help clarify certain problematic passages, which they suggest may be mistranslations into Greek of originally Aramaic sayings or narratives.

Although the spiritual center of Judaism after the return from exile and the rebuilding of the temple was Jerusalem and the surrounding region, an increasing number of Jews chose to live outside Palestine. The Jews who were scattered throughout much of the world came to be known as the *Diaspora*, or "scattered" Judaism. When Cyrus the Great allowed the Jews in Babylonia to return to their homeland, he did not force them to do so, and many Jews elected to stay in the land that they had made their home for 50 years. Babylonia became one of the chief intellectual centers of Judaism, and centuries later it shared with Palestine the honor of being one of the places associated with the development of the Talmud, the codified oral tradition that guided the daily lives of many Jews throughout the world. Egypt was also a center of Jewish thought and culture. The first translation of a portion of the Old Testament into another language was made in Alexandria, Egypt, when the Greek translation of the Pentateuch, the Septuagint, was created. Alexandria was also the home of the influential Jewish scholar Philo, an older contemporary of Jesus, whose allegorical interpretations of the Jewish scripture strongly influenced later Christian thought. In addition to Babylonia and Egypt, other major concentrations of Jews could be found in Asia Minor, Greece, Italy, and Syria. The dispersal of the Jews, who were so familiar with Jewish scripture, law, and customs, paved the way for the spread of Christianity, especially in its early decades, when it was still a largely Jewish religious movement.

The official religion of the Persian Empire was Zoroastrianism, a monotheistic religion founded by Zoroaster (also called Zarathustra) around 1000 B.C.E., or perhaps earlier. The Jews came into contact with adherents of the religion when the Persians defeated Babylonia and became overlords of the Jews and other regions of the ancient Near East. While many of the developments in Jewish theology and practice that occurred during and after the exile were undoubtedly the result of organic growth from earlier forms of Israelite religion, Jewish contact with Zoroastrian ideas is the probable explanation for other ideas that arose during the Second Temple period.

In contrast to the traditional Jewish view of the afterlife, in which all people go to Sheol after death, Zoroastrians believed in a dramatic final judgment. They believed that God (whom they called Ahura Mazda) would weigh every person's deeds, both good and evil, and would send people either to a place of reward or a place of punishment. It is probably not coincidental that many Jews in the Second Temple period abandoned the notion of Sheol and adopted belief in separate destinations for the good and the wicked, heaven and hell. One attractive feature of belief in a differentiated judgment was that it helped to resolve the dispute about *theodicy*, or the justice of God. The book of Job, which still assumes the doctrine of Sheol, raises the question of why the righteous often suffer while the wicked often prosper. A final judgment based on one's deeds followed by assignment to either heaven or hell provides an answer to Job's question that was not available to the author when the book was written. As noted in the previous chapter, early Christians followed the lead of the Pharisees in accepting the idea of a final judgment, followed by consignment of individuals to heaven or hell. For Christians, however, one's faith in Christ, or lack thereof, was of equal or greater importance than the mere excess of good deeds in comparison with bad deeds in determining one's ultimate fate.

One idea that the Jews shared with Zoroastrians, absolute monotheism, apparently arose independently in Judaism, prior to extensive Jewish-Zoroastrian contact, during the Babylonian exile. However, the idea that God has an evil counterpart, albeit an inferior one, seems to have been taken from Zoroastrianism's teachings about Angra Mainyu, the evil spirit. In earlier parts of the Old Testament, God is sometimes said to have influenced a person to commit evil deeds, as when God hardened Pharaoh's heart so that he would not release his Israelite slaves from Egypt. In later writings, however, the figure of Satan emerges as a counterpoint to God, although having lesser powers. Satan appears only three times in the Hebrew Bible: as Job's accuser in Job 1–2, as the high priest Joshua's accuser in Zech 3, and as David's tempter in 1 Chron 21. The last example is the most telling, for an earlier, parallel account of David's decision to take a census of the Israelite nation also appears in 2 Sam 24. In Samuel, written before the idea of Satan had permeated Jewish thought, the scripture says that "God incited David to take a census of the people," an act that resulted in the deaths of thousands at the hands of God. In Chronicles, on the other hand, the author says that "Satan incited David to take a census of the people." Satan is not particularly evil in the Old Testament accounts, but may almost be seen as performing a useful, if distasteful, function for the benefit of God. However, later Jewish writings transform Satan into a creature of pure evil, a fallen angel in rebellion against God. This is the picture of Satan that appears in the New Testament as well.

Related to the development of the idea of Satan as a sort of evil alter-ego to God is the emergence in the Second Temple period of belief in angels and demons. Earlier parts of the Hebrew Bible sometimes mention *the* angel of God, a visible manifestation of God who interacts with humans, but the idea that there are numerous angels and demons at work in the world first appears in rudimentary form in Daniel and Tobit. More developed ideas about angels and demons can be found in 1 Enoch, a non-canonical Jewish document, and in writings found among the Dead Sea Scrolls. These works elaborate on the idea of angels and demons further, assigning many of them distinct names and functions. The New Testament adopted this contemporary Jewish view about angels and demons, although without the detailed elaboration of some of the Jewish writings.

The Greco-Roman world

After living under Persian rule for about two centuries, the Jews became subjects of a new empire in 332 b.c.e. Alexander the Great swept out of Macedonia into Asia Minor in 334 b.c.e., defeating the Persian army in battle after battle over the next two years. After his death in 323, several years of infighting among Greek generals and their troops occurred. When the dust settled about 20 years later, the Jews in Palestine were subject to the Ptolemaic Empire, based in Egypt. However, the neighboring Seleucid Empire, based in Syria and Mesopotamia, coveted Palestine, and they fought several wars with the Ptolemys over control of the land, finally culminating in a complete Seleucid victory by 198 b.c.e. Both the Ptolemaic and the Seleucid empires were Greek in many respects: their rulers were descendants of leading Greek and Macedonian families, the upper classes adopted both the Greek language and culture (Hellenism), and Greek increasingly became the language of the common people as well. Though many Jews resisted the encroachment of Hellenism, others embraced it as necessary for the sake of prosperity in their new circumstances. Still others saw Greek accomplishments in philosophy, mathematics, science, and rhetoric as cultural advances, and they embraced Hellenism eagerly.

Under the Ptolemys, the Jews of Palestine were allowed to practice their religion without serious encumbrances, but the situation changed under the Seleucids. In 175 B.C.E., Antiochus Epiphanes ascended the throne of the Seleucid Empire. At the same time, Jewish Hellenists assumed political control in Jerusalem, contrary to the wishes of the majority of the population. Tensions between the majority of the Palestinian Jews and Antiochus rose as the latter instituted a number of reforms designed to weaken the influence of Judaism. He established a gymnasium in Jerusalem, an attempt to further the spread of Hellenism and to ensure the political success of the Hellenistic party. He built a fortress in the middle of Jerusalem, so that the city became, in effect, an occupied city. He opened the temple up to the public, in violation of Jewish law. Finally, he desecrated the sacred altar of burnt offerings by erecting an altar to the Greek gods on top of it, destroyed copies of the Hebrew scriptures, and rededicated the Jerusalem temple to Zeus. The desecration of the altar is referred to in the book of Daniel as the "abomination of desolation," a term used again 250 years later in the book of Revelation. In response to all these assaults on their religion and culture, many Jews banded together and began fighting a guerrilla war against the Seleucids in 167 B.C.E. Initially led by the priest Mattathias and his son Judas Maccabeus ("the Hammer"), the rebellion continued for several decades, and the Jews managed to create a small, independent state, ruled by the descendants of Mattathias, called the Hasmoneans. The events of these days, told from the Jewish perspective, are recorded in the First and Second books of Maccabees.

Altogether, the Maccabean revolt and the Jewish state ruled by the Hasmonean dynasty lasted only about 100 years, and in 63 B.C.E., Jewish hopes for a viable, independent state came to an end when the Roman general Pompey captured Jerusalem in the name of the Roman Republic. With Pompey's conquest, Judea became a Roman province ruled by a governor (along with Samaria and Galilee). The Hasmonean family continued as high priests until the time of Herod the Great (37–4 B.C.E.). The most notable Roman ruler of this period was Julius Caesar, who ruled as dictator of Rome from 49 to 44 B.C.E., when he was assassinated on the Senate floor. Civil War broke out across the empire and continued until the time of Augustus, the first emperor, in 27 B.C.E. Augustus ruled for more than 40 years. He was noted for building great highways, expanding Rome's borders, increasing the wealth of the empire, and establishing the famous *Pax Romana*, the "Roman peace." Augustus was emperor at the time of Jesus' birth, and his successor Tiberius was emperor during Jesus' active public ministry.

Herod the Great was an Idumean by ancestry but Jewish by religion (Idumea was a province that bordered Judea). He won the support of Pompey and later Mark Antony, and he was appointed first governor of Galilee and then King of Judea. The territories over which he ruled eventually included Idumea, Galilee, Samaria, and Perea, in

Early Roman emperors important for their impact on Christianity

Augustus (27 B.C.E.–14 C.E.)

Tiberius (14–37)

Claudius (41–54)

Nero (54–68)

Vespasian (69–79)

Titus (79–81)

Domitian (81–96)

Trajan (98–117)

Hadrian (117–138)

addition to Judea. Through the Roman civil wars he managed to win the support of the current Roman leader, eventually including Augustus. Herod was a successful but ruthless ruler, killing all his enemies and suspected enemies, including several members of his own family. He instituted numerous building projects, including the expansion and refurbishing of the Second Temple and the fortress of Masada. The ruler of Judea when Jesus was born, according to the gospels of Matthew and Luke, he died in 4 B.C.E. Several of Herod's descendants ruled parts of Palestine for years, but Judea itself came under direct Roman control after 6 C.E., when the people petitioned Augustus to remove Herod's son Archelaus from power. Augustus responded by placing Judea under direct Roman control and appointing a Roman governor. Another of Herod's sons, Herod Antipas (the Herod mentioned in the gospels as living during Jesus' public ministry), was ruler of Galilee. Pontius Pilate, Roman governor of Judea from 26 to 36 C.E., was governor at the time of Jesus' crucifixion. After a brief respite from the Roman governors from 41 to 44 C.E. under Herod Agrippa I, a grandson of Herod the Great, Roman governors were appointed again in 44 over Judea.

A series of incidents led to Jewish unrest and revolt against Rome in 66 (the First Jewish War), led by the Zealots. After several early victories, the Jews were defeated by the armies of Vespasian and his son Titus. Titus captured Jerusalem and destroyed the temple in 70. The First Jewish War ended with the capture of the fortress of Masada in 73 or 74, following the suicide of 960 defenders of the fortress. Judaism survived when Johanan ben Zakkai, leader of the Pharisees and opposed to the revolt, was granted permission to move with his followers to the city of Jabneh in Galilee. Jabneh became an important center for Rabbinic Judaism. The Second Jewish War (132–135) was led by Simon bar Kokhba, thought by many to be the messiah. The defeat of the Jews and the death of bar Kokhba resulted in the execution of many Jewish leaders and the expulsion of all Jews from Jerusalem, which had been renamed Aelia Capitolina just before the war started. Although many Christians also suffered alongside the Jews during the First Jewish War, by the time of the Second War Rome recognized them as members of a

Old Testament passages traditionally seen as messianic prophecies by Christians (2)

The wonderful child

Then Isaiah said: "Hear then, O house of David! Is it too little for you to weary mortals, that you weary my God also? Therefore the Lord himself will give you a sign. Look, the young woman is with child and shall bear a son, and shall name him Immanuel". (Isa 7:13–14)

The people who walked in darkness
  have seen a great light;
 those who lived in a land of deep darkness –
  on them light has shined.
You have multiplied the nation,
  you have increased its joy;
 they rejoice before you
  as with joy at the harvest,
  as people exult when dividing plunder.
For the yoke of their burden,
  and the bar across their shoulders,
  the rod of their oppressor,
  you have broken as on the day of Midian.
For all the boots of the tramping warriors
  and all the garments rolled in blood
  shall be burned as fuel for the fire.
For a child has been born for us,
  a son given to us;
 authority rests upon his shoulders;
  and he is named
  Wonderful Counselor, Mighty God,
  Everlasting Father, Prince of Peace.
His authority shall grow continually,
  and there shall be endless peace
 for the throne of David and his kingdom.
  He will establish and uphold it
 with justice and with righteousness
 from this time onward and forevermore.
 The zeal of the Lord of hosts will do this. (Isa 9:2–7)

A shoot shall come out from the stump of Jesse,
  and a branch shall grow out of his roots.

> The spirit of the Lord shall rest on him,
> 　the spirit of wisdom and understanding,
> 　the spirit of counsel and might,
> 　the spirit of knowledge and the fear of the Lord.
> His delight shall be in the fear of the Lord.
> 　He shall not judge by what his eyes see,
> 　or decide by what his ears hear;
> but with righteousness he shall judge the poor,
> 　and decide with equity for the meek of the earth;
> 　he shall strike the earth with the rod of his mouth,
> 　and with the breath of his lips he shall kill the wicked.
> Righteousness shall be the belt around his waist,
> 　and faithfulness the belt around his loins.
> The wolf shall live with the lamb,
> 　the leopard shall lie down with the kid,
> 　the calf and the lion and the fatling together,
> 　and a little child shall lead them.
> The cow and the bear shall graze,
> 　their young shall lie down together;
> 　and the lion shall eat straw like the ox.
> The nursing child shall play over the hole of the asp,
> 　and the weaned child shall put its hand on the adder's den.
> They will not hurt or destroy
> 　on all my holy mountain;
> 　for the earth will be full of the knowledge of the Lord
> 　as the waters cover the sea. (Isa 11:1–9)

separate religion, and they were allowed to remain in Jerusalem when the Jews were expelled. The two Jewish wars and their aftermaths led to drastic upheavals in Judaism, and in Christianity as well. Partially as a result of these events, both Jews and Christians in Palestine and elsewhere saw themselves as members of two distinct, incompatible religious groups.

The period of Greek and Roman hegemony over Palestine and other parts of the western Mediterranean world from about 300 B.C.E. to 100 C.E. saw several developments within Judaism that influenced nascent Christianity. At the same time, Greco-Roman culture impacted Christianity directly, without the mediation of Judaism.

One of the characteristics of late Second Temple Judaism was the emergence of what might be called political parties, although religious parties or sects might be a more accurate term. Some of these groups arose in the aftermath of the Maccabean Revolt, as Jews with different opinions about religious matters and relations with foreign rulers coalesced around charismatic leaders.

The Pharisees, whose name probably comes from the Hebrew word meaning "separated," were the biggest of the Jewish sects by the first century c.e. They stressed the study of and obedience to the law, both the written law and oral tradition (the *Mishna*). Based in the synagogues, they accepted the books of the prophets as authoritative alongside the law. They also accepted the Psalms and other selected books. The Pharisees were the most popular sect with the common people, and they shared a common belief in some of the more recent development within Judaism, including the resurrection of the dead, heaven and hell, and angels and demons. At one time during the Hasmonean kingdom, the Pharisees were fierce opponents of the Hasmonean dynasty, and thousands of Pharisees and their allies were killed by the king Alexander Jannaeus, a supporter of the Sadducees. During the next century, the Pharisees opposed the Roman rule over the Jews, but most were opposed to open rebellion. A few, however, openly sided with Jewish rebels. The most notable Pharisee to actively oppose the Romans was Rabbi Akiba, who supported the Jewish rebel leader Simon bar Kokhba during the Second Jewish War (132–135 c.e.), believing him to be the messiah. After the rebellion failed, Akiba was taken by the Romans and executed. Despite Akiba's connection to the revolt, the Pharisees were the party in the best position to lay the foundation for a new Judaism, built on the ashes of the destruction of Jerusalem, the temple, and the expulsion of the Jews from Jerusalem. Both medieval rabbinic Judaism and all forms of modern Judaism owe their existence to the Pharisaic party. Despite Jesus' sometimes harsh remarks about the failure of some Pharisees to live up to their own high standards, it is clear that Jesus himself agreed with the Pharisees against their opponents on many matters of doctrine and interpretation.

The Sadducees – whose name is probably derived from Zadok, David's high priest – were primarily the party of priests and temple functionaries. Based in the temple rather than the synagogues, they stressed proper temple observance and championed the sacrificial system. Their scripture apparently encompassed only the five books of Moses, the Torah or Pentateuch. They rejected the belief in the resurrection of the dead, heaven and hell, and angels and demons as recent innovations. Whereas the Pharisees had their strongest support among the common people, the Sadducees' chief supporters were the ruling classes, supporters of both the Hasmonean and Roman rulers. The Sadducees ceased to exist as a distinct group after the Roman destruction of the temple in 70 c.e. Like the Pharisees, they are mentioned frequently in the New Testament as opponents of Jesus. Along with leading Pharisees, leading members of the Sadducean party comprised the *Sanhedrin*, the Jewish supreme court and chief legislative body, which met to resolve weighty matters of law and debate important matters, such as the decision to go to war.

Another Jewish faction that arose in the late Second Temple period was a group called the Essenes. The origin of the Essenes is somewhat obscure, but they seem to have emerged from the same movement of *Hasidim* ("pious ones") that gave birth to the Pharisees after the Maccabean Revolt. At some point, however, the Essenes, whose name perhaps means "the holy," separated from the Pharisees, probably over doctrinal matters. The first century C.E. Jewish historian Josephus says that many Essenes led a celibate but communal life, while others married and lived in Palestinian cities and towns near non-Essenes. The Essenes seem to have been outsiders, both theologically and socially, even when they lived near other Jews. They had different ideas about temple worship and the religious calendar, and they enforced a strict observance of the law, according to their own understanding. Although the Essenes are not mentioned in the New Testament, many scholars believe that one large Essene community lived at Qumran, on the shores of the Dead Sea, and produced the Dead Sea Scrolls. If this surmise is accurate, this group of Essenes was an apocalyptic group, expecting the imminent end of the world and the establishment of the kingdom of God. Like the Pharisees, they rejected any kind of political alliance with Rome, and they may have participated in the First Jewish War against Rome. Because of their presence in the Judean desert and their ascetic practices, some scholars have suggested that John the Baptist, and maybe even Jesus, had some connection with the Qumran community. However, recent scholars have tended to downplay the similarities between John and Jesus on the one hand and the Essenes/Qumran community on the other.

While most scholars believe that the group that produced the Dead Sea Scrolls was a semi-monastic community, probably Essene, living at Qumran, a minority believe that the scrolls that were deposited in the caves near Qumran may represent the views of a larger and more diverse group of Jews, perhaps collected from the Jerusalem temple and deposited in the caves at the time of the Roman invasion of Judea about 66 C.E. Regardless of their specific origins, the Dead Sea Scrolls provide valuable information about the Judaism of the day, information that informs the study of Christianity. The apocalyptic nature of some of the writings has already been mentioned. One work in particular, the War Scroll, describes a battle between the "sons of light" (the faithful Jews) and the "sons of darkness" (the Romans) that will usher in the eschatological kingdom of God. Some of the biblical commentaries from Qumran, such as the commentary on the book of Habakkuk, show how Jews more or less contemporary to Jesus understood the words of the prophets to apply to themselves and their particular situations. Since early Christians did much the same thing, these Jewish parallels are instructive.

Josephus identified the Pharisees, Sadducees, and Essenes as the three "philosophical sects" among the Jews, but another group, the Zealots, was also active in the region during Roman times. The Zealots were more a political than a religious group, whose primary goal was to wrest control of Judea and surrounding Jewish territories from Roman hands. Theologically aligned with the Pharisees, they backed up their opposition to Rome with action, taking the lead in the First Jewish War. Because of their strong support for Jewish nationalism, they had the support of many of the common people, who also chafed under Roman rule. One of Jesus' disciples, Simon, is identified as a Zealot in the Gospel of Luke. A few scholars have suggested that Jesus himself might have been a Zealot, whose call to arms was toned down after his death, but Jesus' apparently authentic teaching about peacemaking and loving one's enemies militates against this view.

Key points you need to know

- After emerging as a nation during the thirteenth century B.C.E., Israel and Judah formed small kingdoms, alongside several others, in the land bordering the easternmost part of the Mediterranean Sea, during a regional power vacuum that lasted about 450 years.
- The Assyrian Empire destroyed Israel (the northern kingdom), and the Babylonian Empire forced the leaders and ruling class of Judah (the southern kingdom) into exile.
- Many important theological and social developments occurred during the late monarchic, exilic, and Second Temple periods in Judah, including the rise of the prophetic movement, the idea of ethical monotheism, the messianic hope, apocalyptic expectation of God's intervention in history, the composition of the scripture, the study of the Law, the emergence of the synagogue as an important institution, the growth of the importance of Aramaic as the language of many Jews, the Jewish Diaspora in Greek-speaking lands, the idea of separate destinations for the good and the wicked in the afterlife, the idea of Satan, and the idea of angels and demons.
- After successfully rebelling against their Seleucid (Greek) overlords, Judah established an independent state as a result of the Maccabean Revolt, which lasted about 100 years. This state in turn was conquered by the Romans.
- Several distinct sects, or religious parties, arose in late Second Temple Judaism: the Pharisees, Sadducees, Essenes, and Zealots. The only one to survive the destruction of the Second Temple in 70 C.E. was the Pharisees, whose leaders laid the groundwork for the emergence of Rabbinic Judaism.

Discussion questions

1. Why did the Jews survive the Babylonian exile as a distinct socio-religious group, while the descendants of the northern kingdom of Israel did not emerge from the Assyrian exile as a distinct group?
2. What were the three most far-reaching theological developments within Judaism during the exile and Second Temple periods?
3. Of the theological developments that occurred within Judaism from the time of the Babylonian exile, how many were adopted into Christianity?
4. How important an influence was Zoroastrianism on Judaism during the Persian period? Would Judaism likely have developed some of the same theological ideas independently of Zoroastrian influence?
5. How did the success of the Maccabean Revolt affect the history of the Jews under the Romans?

Further reading

Ahlström, Gösta W. and Gary O. Rollefson 1993. *The History of Ancient Palestine*. Edited by Diana Edelman. Minneapolis, MN: Fortress.

Hanson, Paul D. 1979. *The Dawn of Apocalyptic: The Historical and Sociological Roots of Jewish Apocalyptic Eschatology*. Revised ed. Philadelphia, PA: Fortress.

Hayes, John H. and J. Maxwell Miller, eds. 1977. *Israelite and Judaean History*. London: SCM.

Mowinckel, Sigmund 1954. *He That Cometh: The Messiah Concept in the Old Testament and Later Judaism*. Translated by G. W. Anderson. New York: Abingdon.

Neusner, Jacob 1988. *The Mishnah: A New Translation*. New Haven, CT: Yale University Press.

Sanders, E. P. 1992. *Judaism: Practice and Belief 63* B.C.E.–*66* C.E. London: SCM.

Whiston, William 1980. *The Works of Josephus*. Lynn, MA: Hendrickson.

4 The founder and foundational documents

In those days Jesus came from Nazareth of Galilee and was baptized by John in the
Jordan. (Mark 1:9)

In this chapter

Christianity derives its name from Jesus Christ, the founder of the faith. The earliest
surviving Christian documents, the New Testament, describe Jesus in a variety of
ways – messiah, teacher, rabbi, Son of God, Son of Man, *logos* – all of which reflect
the perspective of faith. However, different New Testament writers understood Jesus
in different ways. Modern historians draw on a critical reading of the New Testament
and other materials to reconstruct the life of the "historical Jesus," which differs in some
details from the picture found in the New Testament. In addition to discussing what it
is possible to know about Jesus, this chapter also treats the development of the Christian
canon, both Old Testament and New Testament.

Main topics covered

- Portraits of Jesus in the New Testament writings attributed to Paul, Mark, Matthew,
  Luke, John, and others
- Survey of the examination of the life of Jesus by historians
- Brief overview of the life of Jesus
- Idea of the canon in early Judaism and Christianity
- Development of the Old Testament canon in Judaism and Christianity
- Development of the New Testament canon in Christianity
- Differences of opinion among various Christian groups concerning the extent of the
  canon

Jesus Christ

The Jesus of the New Testament

> But when the fullness of time had come, God sent his Son, born of a woman, born under the law, in order to redeem those who were under the law, so that we might receive adoption as children.
>
> (Gal 4:4)

The New Testament tells the story of Jesus and his earliest followers, but despite the fact that Jesus is mentioned on almost every page, it is impossible to construct a single, consistent picture of Jesus on the basis of New Testament writings. One reason for this state of affairs is that the books of the New Testament were written over a period of 50 to 75 years, and the church's perspective about Jesus developed over that time. Another reason is that the various New Testament authors, even authors who were contemporaries, had different ideas about who Jesus was and what was significant about his life. A third reason is that no one, even the authors of the four gospels, undertook to write a biography of Jesus, at least in the way that modern people understand the term. Modern biographies are usually fairly comprehensive in their coverage of a person's upbringing, and they present the story of a person's life chronologically. The New Testament writings do neither. When discussing Jesus as the New Testament portrays him, it is important to keep these facts in mind.

Although people today most frequently use the term *gospel* to refer to an account of Jesus' life – and in particular one of the canonical gospels: Matthew, Mark, Luke, or John – the earliest Christians used the word in an entirely different manner. The word translated *gospel* in English meant "good news" in Greek, the language of the New Testament. For Christians, the good news *par excellence* was the story about Jesus. But what exactly was included in the gospel?

The earliest New Testament books to describe the life of Jesus were the letters of Paul. Paul was a Jew who was transformed from a persecutor of the church into a staunch defender of the cause of Christ, after undergoing a life-altering experience on the road from Jerusalem to Damascus, sometime around the year 36 C.E. About ten years after his conversion to Christianity, Paul set out with his colleague Barnabas to establish new churches in the eastern Mediterranean region. Over the next several years, according to his own preserved writings, Paul and his coworkers planted many churches in western Asia, Macedonia, and Achaia (Greece). He was eventually taken to Rome as a prisoner, and church tradition says that he was released and subsequently carried the gospel as far as Spain, though the New Testament provides no evidence to support this tradition. He was apparently executed by the Romans, probably under the Emperor Nero about 64 C.E.

Paul made it a practice to write letters to churches he had either founded or worked with, and in one case, he wrote a letter to the church in a city he planned to visit: Rome (although he didn't originally plan to visit the city in chains!). In these letters, Paul addresses specific needs of the congregations, answers questions about which the churches had written him, presents his theological beliefs, and offers advice on proper behavior. He refers frequently to Jesus in his letters, but it is noteworthy that he almost always refers to his death, resurrection, ascension into heaven, and imminent return. Only very rarely does he mention anything that Jesus said or did prior to his death on the cross (he mentions Jesus' words at the Last Supper in 1 Cor 11:23–25, the meal he shared with his disciples the night before his crucifixion). He does not quote any of Jesus' sayings, describe any miracles attributed to Jesus, or discuss any significant events in Jesus' life. All that he says about Jesus' birth is that he was "born of a woman, born under the law" (Gal 4:4).

For Paul, Jesus was God's Son, the Christ (i.e. the messiah). Paul offers a succinct statement of his understanding of Jesus in Rom 1:3–4: "The gospel concerning his [God's] Son, who was descended from David according to the flesh and was declared to be Son of God with power according to the spirit of holiness by resurrection from the dead, Jesus Christ our Lord." The title "Son of God," as used in the New Testament, primarily refers to Jesus' identity as the messiah, the descendant of David to whom Jews looked to restore the kingdom. It did not originally carry with it any association with divinity. On the other hand, Paul clearly understood Jesus to be more than an ordinary human, as witnessed by his statements about Jesus' exaltation to the right hand of God (Rom 8:34), his sinlessness (2 Cor 5:21), his identity as Lord (Rom 10:9), and his imminent return to summon the faithful, both living and dead (1 Thess 4:15–17). Perhaps the most exalted language about Jesus that appears in a genuine Pauline epistle is found in Phil 2:6–11:

Though he was in the form of God,
   he did not regard equality with God
   as something to be exploited,
but emptied himself,
   taking the form of a slave,
   being born in human likeness.
And being found in human form,
   he humbled himself
   and became obedient to the point of death –
   even death on a cross.
Therefore God also highly exalted him
   and gave him the name
   that is above every name,
so that at the name of Jesus
   every knee should bend,
   in heaven and on earth and under the earth,
and every tongue should confess
   that Jesus Christ is Lord,
   to the glory of God the Father.

Most scholars believe that Paul incorporated an early Christian hymn into his letter to the church at Philippi, but if so, this hymn still reflected Paul's own understanding of Jesus. Does this hymn refer to Jesus as a preexistent part of the Godhead, or does it present Jesus as a Second Adam who chose the path of obedience (cf. Rom 5:12–21)? Scholars are divided on the issue.

The clearest presentations of Jesus appear in the gospels: Matthew, Mark, Luke, and John. Because Matthew and Luke closely follow Mark's outline of Jesus' public ministry, these three gospels are called the Synoptic Gospels, that is, gospels that present the story of Jesus from a similar viewpoint. The Gospel of John presents a view of Jesus that is considerably different both in narrative structure and in theology.

Shortly after Paul's death, the first canonical gospel, the Gospel according to Mark, was written. Unlike Paul, who focused exclusively on Jesus' death and resurrection, Mark (the canonical gospels contain no statements concerning authorship, so we will use the traditional names of the evangelists, or gospel writers, for the sake of convenience) begins his gospel at the beginning of Jesus' public ministry, which he associates with Jesus' baptism at the hands of John the Baptist. The Gospel of Mark starts, "The beginning of the gospel of Jesus Christ." Many witnesses add the phrase "the Son of God" immediately after this. Regardless of whether the phrase belongs there, the presentation of Jesus as the Son of God (i.e. the Messiah) is central to Mark's message. In fact, after Jesus dies on the cross, a Roman centurion at the foot of the cross remarks, "Truly this man was God's Son" (Mark 15:39). For Mark, the most important part of the gospel message is Jesus' death and resurrection, but he does spend about two-thirds of the book describing Jesus' ministry of teaching, healing, casting out demons, and performing miracles. Yes, Jesus' death and resurrection are singularly significant, but Jesus revealed himself as Son of God from the beginning of his public ministry, according to Mark. For Mark, calling Jesus the Son of God implies not that Jesus was divine but rather that Jesus was uniquely chosen to be God's anointed servant, whose suffering and death would reconcile humankind with God (Mark 10:45; see above on Paul's use of the term).

The Gospel of Mark is not a biography of Jesus, for it neither treats his origin and early experiences nor lays out his life chronologically. The question of Jesus' origin is developed further in the other gospels, but Mark's outline of Jesus' life forms the basis for both Matthew's and Luke's presentation of Jesus. Mark gives few indications about the time at which different events in Jesus' ministry occurred. Individual *pericopes* (individual, well-defined sections of text) are joined together with words like "and," "again," "then," "in those days," "after he went out," and so forth. It is probable that Mark makes use of material that had been passed down orally for many years, and Mark was the first one to connect many of them together in a narrative framework. Only with Jesus' entry into Jerusalem during the last week of his life does Mark begin specifying that certain events occurred on particular days of the week (traditionally called Passion Week). The overall impression one gets from reading the Gospel of Mark is that the entirety of Jesus' public ministry took place over the course of about one year, though this impression may not be historically accurate.

Old Testament passages traditionally seen as messianic prophecies by Christians (3)

The suffering servant

Here is my servant, whom I uphold,
my chosen, in whom my soul delights;
I have put my spirit upon him;
he will bring forth justice to the nations.
He will not cry or lift up his voice,
or make it heard in the street;
a bruised reed he will not break,
and a dimly burning wick he will not quench;
he will faithfully bring forth justice.
He will not grow faint or be crushed
until he has established justice in the earth;
and the coastlands wait for his teaching.
Thus says God, the Lord,
who created the heavens and stretched them out,
who spread out the earth and what comes from it,
who gives breath to the people upon it
and spirit to those who walk in it:
I am the Lord, I have called you in righteousness,
I have taken you by the hand and kept you;
I have given you as a covenant to the people,
a light to the nations,
to open the eyes that are blind,
to bring out the prisoners from the dungeon,
from the prison those who sit in darkness.
I am the Lord, that is my name;
my glory I give to no other,
nor my praise to idols.
See, the former things have come to pass,
and new things I now declare;
before they spring forth,
I tell you of them. (Isa 42:1–9)

See, my servant shall prosper;
he shall be exalted and lifted up,
and shall be very high.
Just as there were many who were astonished at him

– so marred was his appearance, beyond human semblance,
   and his form beyond that of mortals –
so he shall startle many nations;
   kings shall shut their mouths because of him;
  for that which had not been told them they shall see,
   and that which they had not heard they shall contemplate.
Who has believed what we have heard?
   And to whom has the arm of the Lord been revealed?
For he grew up before him like a young plant,
   and like a root out of dry ground;
  he had no form or majesty that we should look at him,
   nothing in his appearance that we should desire him.
He was despised and rejected by others;
   a man of suffering and acquainted with infirmity;
  and as one from whom others hide their faces
   he was despised, and we held him of no account.
Surely he has borne our infirmities
   and carried our diseases;
  yet we accounted him stricken,
   struck down by God, and afflicted.
But he was wounded for our transgressions,
   crushed for our iniquities;
  upon him was the punishment that made us whole,
   and by his bruises we are healed.
All we like sheep have gone astray;
   we have all turned to our own way,
   and the Lord has laid on him
   the iniquity of us all.
He was oppressed, and he was afflicted,
   yet he did not open his mouth;
  like a lamb that is led to the slaughter,
   and like a sheep that before its shearers is silent,
   so he did not open his mouth.
By a perversion of justice he was taken away.
   Who could have imagined his future?
  For he was cut off from the land of the living,
   stricken for the transgression of my people.
They made his grave with the wicked
   and his tomb with the rich,

although he had done no violence,
  and there was no deceit in his mouth.
Yet it was the will of the Lord to crush him with pain.
  When you make his life an offering for sin,
   he shall see his offspring, and shall prolong his days;
  through him the will of the Lord shall prosper.
  Out of his anguish he shall see light;
  he shall find satisfaction through his knowledge.
   The righteous one, my servant, shall make many righteous,
  and he shall bear their iniquities.
Therefore I will allot him a portion with the great,
  and he shall divide the spoil with the strong;
  because he poured out himself to death,
  and was numbered with the transgressors;
  yet he bore the sin of many,
  and made intercession for the transgressors. (Isa 52:13–53:12)

My God, my God, why have you forsaken me?
  Why are you so far from helping me, from the words of my groaning?
O my God, I cry by day, but you do not answer;
  and by night, but find no rest.
Yet you are holy,
  enthroned on the praises of Israel.
In you our ancestors trusted;
  they trusted, and you delivered them.
To you they cried, and were saved;
  in you they trusted, and were not put to shame.
But I am a worm, and not human;
  scorned by others, and despised by the people.
All who see me mock at me;
  they make mouths at me, they shake their heads;
"Commit your cause to the Lord; let him deliver –
  let him rescue the one in whom he delights!"
Yet it was you who took me from the womb;
  you kept me safe on my mother's breast.
On you I was cast from my birth,
  and since my mother bore me you have been my God.
Do not be far from me,
  for trouble is near

> and there is no one to help.
> Many bulls encircle me,
>   strong bulls of Bashan surround me;
> they open wide their mouths at me,
>   like a ravening and roaring lion.
> I am poured out like water,
>   and all my bones are out of joint;
>   my heart is like wax;
>   it is melted within my breast;
> my mouth is dried up like a potsherd,
>   and my tongue sticks to my jaws;
>   you lay me in the dust of death.
> For dogs are all around me;
>   a company of evildoers encircles me.
>   My hands and feet have shriveled;
> I can count all my bones.
>   They stare and gloat over me;
> they divide my clothes among themselves,
>   and for my clothing they cast lots.
> But you, O Lord, do not be far away!
>   O my help, come quickly to my aid!
> Deliver my soul from the sword,
>   my life from the power of the dog!
>   Save me from the mouth of the lion! (Psalm 22:1–21a)

If Mark is vague about the temporal aspects of Jesus' ministry, he is somewhat more specific in presenting the geographical aspects. After Jesus' baptism by John in the Jordan River, in the wilderness of Judea, Jesus returns to his home region of Galilee and begins proclaiming his message, which Mark summarizes in this way: "The time is fulfilled, and the kingdom of God has come near; repent, and believe in the good news." In addition to preaching, Jesus calls people to follow him, teaches in the synagogues and elsewhere, casts unclean spirits out of people, heals people, tells parables, disputes with religious leaders, and performs miracles. In the Gospel of Mark, Jesus begins his ministry in Galilee. After a while, he occasionally journeys with his disciples into predominantly Gentile regions (e.g. Tyre, Sidon, Decapolis). At a certain point in his ministry, he begins telling his disciples that he is destined to be killed in Jerusalem (Mark 8:31), and eventually he makes his way through the Transjordan region into Judea, where he spends the last week of his life in and around Jerusalem teaching his disciples and engaged in disputes with the Jewish religious authorities. On Thursday evening of Passion Week, Jesus eats the Passover meal with his disciples, as Jews all over the city, and indeed all over the world, are doing that night. After finishing the meal, Jesus leads his disciples to a place called Gethsemane, where he spends time in prayer. One of his disciples, Judas Iscariot, leads a group of armed men loyal to the Jewish religious authorities to Gethsemane, where he identifies Jesus by greeting him with a kiss. The guards arrest Jesus and take him before the Jewish council, the Sanhedrin, where various accusations against Jesus are raised. Finally, the high priest asks Jesus directly if he is the Messiah, the Son of God, and Jesus replies that he is. The Sanhedrin condemns Jesus, and the next morning they take him to the Roman governor Pilate, who alone has the authority to execute a prisoner. After a brief interview with Pilate, in which Jesus says very little, Pilate offers to release a prisoner for the crowd, but the crowd, at the instigation of the religious authorities, calls for Jesus to be crucified. Pilate assents, and after having Jesus flogged, orders him to be crucified. The crucifixion begins almost immediately, and Jesus carries his cross (with the assistance of Simon, a traveler visiting Jerusalem) to Golgotha, the place of execution. From the cross, Jesus utters only a single cry, as recorded by Mark: "My God, my God, why have you forsaken me?" After a few hours on the cross, Jesus dies, and his body is taken by Joseph of Arimathea and deposited in his own tomb. Jesus dies on Friday before sunset, and because the next day is the Sabbath, Jesus' followers are unable to prepare the body in any way for burial. On Sunday morning, when the Sabbath is over, Mary Magdalene and two other women take spices to the tomb in order to anoint the body properly for burial, but they find the stone rolled away from the entrance to the tomb. Furthermore, they encounter a young man in a white robe, apparently an angel, who says that Jesus has been raised from the dead and has returned to Galilee to meet his disciples. The Gospel of Mark ends with the women leaving the tomb in confusion, afraid to tell Jesus' disciples what had happened. The abrupt ending of Mark's gospel has caused great consternation over the years, and at a very early point – probably by the second century – an ending that includes several appearances of the risen Jesus was added to the gospel. Whether the original ending of the gospel was lost or whether the author intentionally ended the gospel as he did is a matter of continued scholarly discussion.

The Gospel of Matthew, written perhaps two decades after Mark, follows the general outline of Mark, and in fact the author uses Mark as one of his sources. He also apparently uses another document, called Q, which consisted primarily of Jesus' sayings but also included some narrative material, such as the account of Jesus' temptation by the devil in the wilderness (Matt 4:1–11). (Q is a hypothetical document reconstructed by scholars; no copy of it has yet been found.) Matthew also uses material that is unique to his gospel, such as the stories of Jesus' birth and infancy. He does not simply copy the stories he got from Mark and Q into his own gospel, but he often changes certain aspects of the stories to reflect his own understanding of Jesus and his mission. Matthew's gospel seems to be directed to an audience that consisted largely of Jewish Christians, and he shapes the story of Jesus to demonstrate that he was the Jewish messiah who had been foretold by scripture. One way in which Matthew does this is by quoting scripture that was "fulfilled" by events connected with Jesus' life. Several of these so-called "formula quotations" appear in Matthew's infancy narrative, such as his quotation of Isa 7:14, "They shall call his name Emmanuel," in connection with Jesus' miraculous virgin birth (Matt 1:23).

Matthew, who was writing primarily for a Jewish-Christian audience, presents Jesus as the long-expected Jewish messiah, or Son of David, an emphasis found particularly in the formula quotations (in addition to Matt 1:23, see also Matt 2:6, 15; 4:15–16; 13:35), but also in Matthew's genealogy of Jesus (Matt 1:2–17). Unlike Mark, who frequently mentions Jesus' expression of emotions, Matthew generally tones down or eliminates Jesus' emotional displays (for example, compare Mark 1:41 with Matt 8:3; and Mark 10:14 with Matt 19:14). He also modifies passages in Mark that suggest that Jesus' power was limited (compare Mark 6:5 with Matt 13:58). The probable reason for these changes to Mark's presentation of Jesus in Matthew's gospel is that both Matthew and the community to which he was writing had come to view Jesus as something more than just God's specially chosen Son. He was conceived through God's power (that is, the Holy Spirit; Matt 1:18) and was able to draw on the power of God in a way that other people did not. This is probably the reason why, in the story of the Rich Young Ruler, Jesus asks the man in Mark's recounting of the story, "Why do you call me good? No one is good but God alone," whereas in Matthew's version, Jesus asks, "Why do you ask me about what is good? There is only one who is good" (God or Jesus? The passage is ambiguous). Matthew understood that Mark's version of the story could be read as a denial of Jesus' special connection to God, so he modified his portrayal of Jesus to remove the potential offense.

Matthew emphasizes Jesus' role as a great teacher and purveyor of a new understanding of the Jewish law, like a second Moses. Thus, Jesus offers new interpretations of the Mosaic law in the Sermon on the Mount (Matt 5–7), a collection of Jesus' sayings delivered on a mountaintop to his disciples and the crowds that followed him. In Matthew, Jesus emphasizes the importance of being "perfect," fully in compliance with the divine law, as interpreted by Jesus (Matt 5:48; 19:21), or "righteous," living uprightly in accordance with God's will (Matt 3:15; 5:20; 13:43). Jesus himself provides the ideal model for his followers of perfection and righteousness. Despite Matthew's portrayal of Jesus as the law-fulfilling, righteous messiah whose association with God is unique, he does not portray Jesus as fully divine. Jesus does not know when the final judgment will come upon the earth (Matt 24:36), and his solitary cry from the cross mirrors the portrayal of the scene in Mark's gospel (Matt 27:46).

Luke's gospel was composed at approximately the same time as Matthew's, and like Matthew, he uses both Mark and Q as sources. Also like Matthew, he begins his story of Jesus with his birth from the Virgin Mary in Bethlehem. However, Luke's portrayal of Jesus differs in significant ways from both Mark and Matthew. Luke's audience was probably composed primarily of Gentile converts to Christianity, so although Luke does identify Jesus as the Jewish messiah (like all the other evangelists), he lacks Matthew's emphasis on Jesus as the perfect fulfillment of the Jewish law or as the new lawgiver. Instead, he presents Jesus as the savior of the world (Luke 2:11; cf. also Luke's genealogy of Jesus, Luke 3:23–38, which traces Jesus' lineage not just back to Abraham, the ancestor of the Jews, as Matthew does, but to Adam, the progenitor of the entire human race, and ultimately to God). It is true that Jesus' ministry prior to his death is exclusively to the Jews in Luke's gospel, but Luke understands that God's plan for the salvation of the Gentiles required that the message first be presented to the Jews. Salvation for the Gentiles begins with the descent of the Holy Spirit (which Luke sees as the power of God for ministry and evangelism) on the Day of Pentecost (Acts 2:1–4) and continues throughout the early decades of the Christian movement, as described in Acts (written by the same author as the Gospel of Luke).

To an even greater extent than Matthew, Luke downplays the emotions (compare Mark 3:5 and Luke 6:10; Mark 10:21 and Luke 18:22) and limitations of Jesus (Mark 13:32, which says that the Son does not know when the end of the world will come, though present in Matthew, is omitted in Luke). Furthermore, Jesus does not cry out from the cross, "My God! My God! Why have you forsaken me?" Instead, Luke portrays Jesus as offering forgiveness to the repentant thief who is crucified beside him (Luke 23:39–43) and willingly offering up his spirit to God (Luke 23:46). (Another saying of Jesus from the cross, found in many manuscripts in Luke 23:34, is probably not original to the gospel.)

Luke portrays Jesus as a great prophet, like Elijah or Elisha (Luke 4:24–27; 24:19). As a prophet, he has access to the power conveyed by the Holy Spirit (Luke 1:76; 7:39), and he is destined to suffer the fate of other prophets: death in Jerusalem (Luke 13:33). Like many of the prophets in the Jewish scriptures, Luke presents Jesus as especially interested in the welfare of the poor and marginalized in society, including "sinners" (i.e. those considered outcasts by many; Luke 7:36–50), Samaritans (Luke 10:30–37), and women (Luke 7:11–15; 8:1–3). Like the prophets, Jesus is especially critical of those who hoard wealth (Luke 12:15–21; 16:19–31). On the other hand, he praises those who use their wealth to help others (Luke 19:1–9).

The book of Colossians is attributed to Paul, but many scholars believe that it was written by someone else in Paul's name, sometime after Paul's death. (See below for more discussion on genuine vs. disputed Pauline letters.) This letter presents a view of Jesus that is somewhat more exalted (i.e. it portrays Jesus as having more divine qualities) than either the universally acknowledged genuine Pauline letters or the Synoptic Gospels. Col 1:15–20 presents Jesus this way:

He is the image of the invisible God,
the firstborn of all creation …
All things have been created through him and for him.
He himself is before all things,
and in him all things hold together.

The author says that Jesus was preexistent, that is, he was alive prior to his birth in the days of Herod the Great. Furthermore, he is uniquely related to God and instrumental in the creation of the world. In the understanding of the author, Jesus plays a role in creation similar to that played by divine Wisdom in Prov 8:22–31, which says in part:

The Lord created me [i.e. Wisdom] at the beginning of his work,
　　the first of his acts of long ago.
Ages ago I was set up,
　　at the first, before the beginning of the earth …
When he marked out the foundations of the earth,
　　then I was beside him, like a master worker.

The anonymous book of Hebrews similarly portrays Jesus as uniquely related to God and involved in creation (Heb 1:1–3a). He is superior to both humans and angels (Heb 1:4–14). The author uses Plato's Theory of Ideas to present Jesus as the ideal high priest (or rather, the Idea of the high priest), whose sacrifice for sins is eternally efficacious because it takes place in heaven, the realm of Ideas, rather than on earth, the realm of shadowy copies (Heb 9:1–28).

The most exalted portrayal of Jesus in the New Testament is undoubtedly found in the Gospel of John. Unlike Mark, who begins his gospel with Jesus' appearance in Galilee at the start of his public ministry, or Matthew and Luke, who begin their accounts with the birth of Jesus in Bethlehem, John starts at the beginning of creation: "In the beginning was the Word, and the Word was with God, and the Word was God" (John 1:1). The word translated "Word" is the Greek word *logos*, which can be translated as "word," "deed," or "reason." In certain Greek philosophical writings, especially those of the Stoics, the *logos* is the divine reason behind the creation of the world. John associates Jesus with this divine *logos*, but he deviates from the Greek philosophers by positing the doctrine of the Incarnation, the taking on of a human body by the divine *logos*: "The Word became flesh and lived among us" (John 1:14).

The Gospel of John, the last of the canonical gospels to be written, portrays Jesus as a divine being whose human body can barely contain the deity within. John presents Jesus as performing seven signs, or miracles, events in which Jesus' true divine nature breaks through his human flesh and does something miraculous: turning water into wine, feeding a crowd of five thousand, healing a blind man, raising a dead man, and so forth. Jesus in John's gospel also passes along special truths about himself by means of various "I am" statements. For example:

I am the living bread, which came down from heaven. (John 6:51)

I am the light of the world. (John 8:12)

I am the door. (John 10:9)

I am the good shepherd. (John 10:11)

I am the resurrection and the life. (John 11:25)

I am the way, the truth, and the life. (John 14:6)

The Gospel of John follows the public ministry of Jesus with an extended section of Jesus' instructions for his disciples on the last evening of his life (John 13–17). In these chapters, Jesus explains in detail why he must depart from them (through his crucifixion) and how God will provide for them (through the gift of the Holy Spirit).

Even John's description of the arrest and crucifixion of Jesus are significantly different from that found in the Synoptic Gospels. In the latter, prior to his arrest Jesus prays ardently in the garden that God will give him the strength to do God's will. In John, Jesus awaits his arrest calmly. With complete foreknowledge of what will transpire, Jesus exhibits his innate power, so that the soldiers sent to arrest him fall down on the ground (John 18:4–8). On the cross, Jesus utters no cry of desperation as in Matthew and Mark. Instead, he makes arrangements for the care of his mother, asks for a drink of sour wine, and utters a triumphant cry: "It is finished!" After his resurrection, Jesus appears to his disciples and confers on them the gift of the Holy Spirit (John 20:19–23). His disciple Thomas, who was not present at Jesus' first appearance to his disciples, is present at Jesus' second appearance, and he offers the most explicit statement concerning the divinity of Jesus in the entire New Testament, calling him "My Lord and my God" (John 20:28).

It is clear from this overview of the New Testament testimony concerning Jesus that a wide diversity of opinion existed concerning the founder of the faith. Nevertheless, it is also evident from this more or less chronological survey that early Christians' view of Jesus changed over the course of the first century, in at least two different ways. First, those events in Jesus' life that were considered important for his followers' understanding of who he was shifted back in time during the earliest decades of the faith. For Paul, Jesus' death and resurrection were paramount. For Mark, Jesus' important activity began with his public ministry in Galilee. For Matthew and Luke, the first important event in Jesus' life was his miraculous birth. Finally, for Colossians, Hebrews, and John, Jesus was involved in some way with God's work of creation.

The second way in which the early Christian view of Jesus changed as the first century passed involves the identification of Jesus as human and/or divine. That Jesus was the Jewish messiah, the fulfillment of scripture, was a universal view among early Christians. What exactly was his relationship with God was debated. Some early Christians saw Jesus as predominantly human, and they found New Testament support in the Synoptic Gospels, particularly in Mark, which frequently describes Jesus as an emotional being who feels compassion, love, anger, and fatigue, as well as in Paul's description of Jesus as one who was "declared to be Son of God" (Rom 1:4). Other early Christians saw Jesus as primarily divine, and they found New Testament support in the exalted descriptions of Jesus in Colossians, Hebrews, and John. These two ideas, Jesus' humanity and his divinity, were in tension with one another from the earliest days of Christianity, and Christians struggled to reconcile these divergent ideas about Jesus for several centuries, before arriving at what would become the official position of the church in 451 C.E. at the Council of Chalcedon: Jesus is both fully God and fully Man.

Portions of Jesus' life considered noteworthy by New Testament authors

Paul, the earliest Christian author whose works are preserved in the New Testament, focused almost exclusively on Jesus death, resurrection, and ascension in his letters, rarely mentioning anything about Jesus' life or teaching. As the first century wore on, subsequent writers would take an interest in progressively earlier parts of Jesus' life, as the following table indicates.

Book/Author	First noteworthy event in Jesus' Life
Paul (letters date *c.* 50–64)	Jesus' death on the cross
Gospel of Mark (*c.* 65–75)	Jesus' baptism at the beginning of his ministry
Gospels of Matthew and Luke (*c.* 80–90)	Jesus' miraculous, virgin birth
Gospel of John (*c.* 90–100)	Jesus as God's agent in creation

The historical Jesus and the Christ of faith

Jesus the pioneer and perfecter of our faith, who for the sake of the joy that was set before him endured the cross, disregarding its shame, and has taken his seat at the right hand of the throne of God.

(Heb 12:2)

In 1906 Albert Schweitzer, who would later gain fame and the Nobel Peace Prize for his medical work in Africa, published a book entitled (in German) *From Reimarus to Wrede: A History of Research on the Life of Jesus*. The book was translated into English four years later with the title *The Quest of the Historical Jesus*. Schweitzer began by observing that the earliest Christian writer, Paul, expressed no interest in knowing the historical Jesus, but only the crucified and risen Christ (2 Cor 5:16). Although the Synoptic Gospels subsequently gave some emphasis to Jesus' human side, both the Gospel of John and early Christian tradition put more emphasis on the divine, upon which the great medieval systems of dogma were built. Even the Protestant Reformation was unable to penetrate beyond the veil of the Christ to peer into the life of the historical Jesus. Not until the Enlightenment, Schweitzer said, when people began to reject the dogmatic proclamations of Christian orthodoxy, did people begin to consider the life of the man Jesus, apart from later theological accretions.

Schweitzer examined previous efforts to write historical biographies of Jesus, beginning with Hermann Samuel Reimarus, whose "Wolfenbüttel Fragments" were

Figure 4.1 Jesus Christ the all-powerful ruler of the universe stares out at viewers in this thirteenth-century mosaic from the Hagia Sophia church (later a mosque, now a museum) in Istanbul.

published posthumously in 1778. Reimarus stressed the distinction between the proclamation of Jesus by his early followers and the message of Jesus himself. According to Reimarus, Jesus was a Jew who fully accepted the messianic expectation of his contemporary Jews. His innovation was in proclaiming that the messianic kingdom (i.e. the kingdom of God) was about to be realized. As a Deist, Reimarus denied the reality of miracles – that is, events contrary to the laws of nature – but he acknowledged that Jesus performed healings that his contemporaries took to be miraculous. Jesus saw himself as the promised messiah, but few of the Jews of either Galilee or Jerusalem believed in him, and his death on the cross marked the tragic end of his mission. After his death, his disciples decided to continue living the life Jesus had taught them, so they stole Jesus' body, invented stories about his resurrection, and announced that Jesus would return soon to the earth to save the faithful. Reimarus's portrait of Jesus was a radical departure from the traditional Jesus accepted by the vast majority of Christians in the eighteenth century, so it is not surprising that his work was roundly renounced by many. Nevertheless, Reimarus's work had raised many questions regarding the historicity of the gospel accounts, questions that were to influence future scholars.

In the wake of the publication of the Wolfenbüttel Fragments, many people over the next century undertook to write "lives of Jesus," either historical reconstructions or fictional recastings. One of the most influential was that of David Friedrich Strauss, *The Life of Jesus Critically Examined*. Strauss was a university student in Berlin when he came under the spell of the famous theologian F. D. E. Schleiermacher. He was particularly fascinated by Schleiermacher's lectures on the life of Jesus. He soon realized, however, that the Jesus that Schleiermacher painted in his lectures was not so much historical as the idealized Jesus that fit into his own theological system, a Jesus who reflected the concerns and ideals of early nineteenth century liberal Christianity. Determined to develop a more historically accurate picture of Jesus, Strauss devoted himself to writing a historical life of Jesus, which he published in 1835. In response to his many critics, he issued several more editions over the next 30 years, and he also wrote other books on the subject. Despite the disciples whose names were associated with the gospels of Matthew and John, Strauss denied that any of the gospels were written by eyewitnesses. He characterized the stories of Jesus' birth and resurrection as myth, detracting from the more historical events of Jesus' actual life. Strauss, a devoted student of the philosopher G. W. F. Hegel, took the traditional Christian doctrine of Jesus as God and man and reinterpreted it in light of Hegelian philosophy. For Strauss, Jesus could only be understood by combining the supernatural portrayals (thesis) with the naturalistic ones (antithesis) into a new, historical understanding (synthesis). Strauss used the same method to investigate the specific events mentioned in the gospels, calling into question the historicity of many of them.

Strauss's work generated a great deal of controversy, and he had ardent supporters as well as opponents. One of the most important of those who valued the work of Strauss was Ernest Renan, whose *Life of Jesus* was innovative in its narrative artistry. Unlike the dense, scholarly prose of Strauss, Renan wrote his biography of Jesus in a florid, attractive style meant for the masses rather than the elite. Renan saw more of historical value in the gospels than Strauss did, though like the latter he denied the possibility of a straightforward literal reading. Renan's *Life of Jesus* was important not just for its artistic rendition of Jesus' life but also because it was the first investigation of the historical Jesus written by a Catholic. Despite Renan's artistry, he was a dedicated historian as well. Although skeptical of miracles, he did not reject the possibility of the miraculous outright; he simply questioned whether a miracle had ever been satisfactorily, historically authenticated.

The last person whom Schweitzer discussed in his *Quest* was Wilhelm Wrede, a contemporary of Schweitzer. Historians of Christianity prior to Wrede had come to the conclusion that Mark, as the first gospel written, was also the most historically based, and they consequently based their analyses of the life of Jesus primarily on Mark. Wrede's study of the Gospel of Mark, however, led him to propose the idea of the *messianic secret*. He noted that Jesus repeatedly told people throughout the gospel not to proclaim his miraculous deeds, that is, not to announce him as messiah. Rather than a historical reminiscence, Wrede suggested, the messianic secret was a literary device that was used to explain why people during Jesus' public ministry did not accept him as the messiah. Wrede suggested that Jesus did not believe himself to be the messiah. It was only after his death that his disciples understood him to be the messiah, and Mark used the device of the messianic secret to project the idea back into the mouth of Jesus himself. For Wrede, Jesus was a teacher and miracle worker, whose liberal attitudes toward the law were opposed by the Jewish authorities, who conspired with the Romans to put him to death.

In contrast to Wrede's view, Schweitzer himself thought that Jesus both believed himself to be the Jewish messiah and taught his disciples the same. For Schweitzer, Jesus was an apocalyptic messiah, one who believed he was the key player in bringing about the eschatological kingdom of God on earth. When Jesus saw that the crowds were not flocking to him in large enough numbers to precipitate a national movement, he purposefully set the events in motion that led to his death, fully expecting divine intervention, either immediately or in the near future. After his death, the Christian community, in the wake of their experiences of the risen Lord, still expected God's quick intervention into human affairs. Only later, as the hope of an imminent Parousia faded, did Christians begin to write gospels and reinterpret Jesus as the founder of the church. Schweitzer admitted that his understanding of Jesus might not be correct, but he noted that both he and Wrede shared a common conclusion, that the historical Jesus was largely unknowable. Still, he said, both the historical Jesus and the Christ of faith bid others to follow him, as Schweitzer did by spending the rest of his life as a medical missionary in Africa. Schweitzer ended his book with a lyrical passage that illustrated the compulsion he felt in his own life.

> He comes to us as One unknown, without a name, as of old, by the lake–side, He came to those men who knew Him not. He speaks to us the same word: "Follow thou me!" and sets us to the tasks which He has to fulfil for our time. He commands. And to those who obey Him, whether they be wise or simple, He will reveal Himself in the toils, the conflicts, the sufferings which they shall pass through in His fellowship, and, as an ineffable mystery, they shall learn in their own experience Who He is. (403)

Schweitzer's work brought an end to the quest for the historical Jesus, at least for several decades. Many scholars were convinced that he had demonstrated the impossibility of using the gospels as historical sources, yet not all were satisfied by his apocalyptic interpretation of Jesus. New developments in biblical scholarship in the twentieth century, especially the advent of form criticism and redaction criticism, led to the so-called New Quest for the Historical Jesus (also called the Second Quest), beginning in the 1950s. Scholars such as Gunther Bornkamm and James M. Robinson reevaluated the historicity of the gospel accounts, and while agreeing that the gospels do not contain straightforward, purely objective history, they concluded that much of historical value, relating to both the time of Jesus and the time of the gospel authors, could be gleaned from a careful study of the material. The discovery of the Gospel of Thomas, an extracanonical gospel found in the sands of Egypt in 1945, spurred new interest in the historical investigation of the life of Jesus as well. The New Quest has continued to the present day, and scholars offer many different pictures of the historical Jesus. For John Dominic Crossan, Jesus was a Jewish, Mediterranean peasant who was nevertheless possessed of great wisdom and who taught his disciples a gospel of radical egalitarianism. For Marcus Borg, Jesus was "a Jewish mystic ... a healer and exorcist ...

a wisdom teacher … a prophet … and a movement initiator" (Borg 2006: 163). For N. T. Wright, Jesus was an eschatological prophet who believed God had commissioned him to announce liberation to his contemporaries. Many recent works on the historical Jesus have emphasized Jesus' self-identity as a Jew, including John P. Meier's *A Marginal Jew: Rethinking the Historical Jesus* and Amy-Jill Levine's *The Misunderstood Jew: The Church and the Scandal of the Jewish Jesus*.

The diverse understandings of who Jesus was historically is mirrored by the various ways in which Christians over the past two millennia have viewed the Christ of faith. Historian Jaroslav Pelikan's masterful book *Jesus through the Centuries* traces different portraits of Jesus in different periods of Christian history. For early Jewish Christians, Jesus was a rabbi. For early Christians struggling to define the relationship between the divine and human in Jesus, he was the cosmic Christ, the divine Reason of God. For mystics throughout Christian history, Jesus was the bridegroom of the soul. For the Protestant Reformers, he was the mirror of the eternal. For those who reveled in the Enlightenment, he was the teacher of common sense. For those suffering from oppression, he was the liberator. These are just a few of the ways in which Jesus has been viewed by his followers over the centuries.

Despite their different historical and theological understandings of Jesus, Christians affirm him as a prophet, a teacher, and the founder of the Christian religion. Most also see him as messiah and divine Son of God. The religion itself bears his title – Christ – and adherents of Christianity strive to conform to Jesus' examples and teachings, as they understand them, through the power of the Spirit of God.

A brief overview of the life of Jesus

> When he came to Nazareth, where he had been brought up, he went to the synagogue on the sabbath day, as was his custom. He stood up to read, and the scroll of the prophet Isaiah was given to him. He unrolled the scroll and found the place where it was written:

"The Spirit of the Lord is upon me,
    because he has anointed me
        to bring good news to the poor.
He has sent me to proclaim release to the captives
    and recovery of sight to the blind,
        to let the oppressed go free,
to proclaim the year of the Lord's favor."

> And he rolled up the scroll, gave it back to the attendant, and sat down. The eyes of all in the synagogue were fixed on him. Then he began to say to them, "Today this scripture has been fulfilled in your hearing."
>   (Luke 4:16–21) (Jesus' inaugural words in his public ministry, according to the Gospel of Luke.)

Although scholars continue to debate many details of Jesus' life, mission, and self-understanding, a plausible, widely-accepted historical reconstruction of at least the major events in his life is possible. According to the gospels of Matthew and Luke, Jesus was born in Bethlehem of Judea during the reign of Caesar Augustus (27 B.C.E.–14 C.E.). Matthew says that Jesus was born before the death of Herod the Great (4 B.C.E.), whereas Luke places his birth during the time when Quirinius was governor of Syria (6 or 7 B.C.E.). Some scholars attempt to reconcile the two dates by proposing a second, earlier tenure as governor of Syria for Quirinius, while others believe that Matthew's placement of the birth of Jesus during Herod's reign is not historically accurate. Despite the concurrence of both Matthew and Luke that Jesus was born in Bethlehem of Judea, many scholars suggest that he was actually born in or around Nazareth in Galilee instead. In any case, all agree that Jesus was born with a few years of the turn of the common era and that he was raised by his parents, Joseph and Mary, in Nazareth of Galilee.

Although the third-century Christian scholar Origen denied it in his refutation of the pagan scholar Celsus's critique of Christianity, Jesus seems to have been trained as a carpenter or other type of craftsman, following in the footsteps of his father. It is likely that Jesus, like the vast majority of other peasants of his day, was illiterate. It is certain, at any rate, that he did not write anything that has been preserved. At some point in the late 20s Jesus abandoned his previous line of work and traveled to the wilderness of Judea to become one of the multitudes being baptized by John "the Baptist" (or "the Baptizer") in or around the Jordan River. He embarked upon an itinerant ministry based in Galilee that included teaching and healing. He was particularly renowned for using parables and commonplace illustrations in his instruction, and his association with the poor and the outcasts of society made him popular with many of the common people. On the other hand, his criticism of the rich and powerful, including some of the religious elite, won him opposition as well. He became known as a healer, often performing exorcisms ("casting out demons," which were seen as the cause of certain types of maladies) in order to effect a cure.

Although the length of his public ministry is unknown – the narrative structure used in the Synoptic Gospels suggests one year, while the Gospel of John suggests about three years – he gained a certain amount of fame over this time, gathering around himself many followers, both men and women. Twelve of the men who followed him were designated "his disciples," or simply "the Twelve": Peter and his brother Andrew, James and John the sons of Zebedee, Philip, Thomas, Bartholomew, Matthew, James the son of Alphaeus, Simon the Zealot, Thaddaeus, and Judas Iscariot (Luke substitutes Judas the son of James for Thaddaeus, while John, who does not provide a list of the Twelve, includes Nathaniel among Jesus' disciples). At some point he decided to travel to Jerusalem for the Feast of Unleavened Bread (Passover). While in Jerusalem, one of his disciples, Judas Iscariot, betrayed him to his enemies, and Jesus was arrested and crucified by the Roman governor Pontius Pilate, apparently with the approval of at least some of the Jewish ruling elite. The exact charges against Jesus are unclear, though in light of the contentious history between the Jews and the Romans during the first century C.E., it is likely that Jesus was accused of threatening to lead a revolt against Rome. The story of Jesus might have ended with his death on a cross, but within a few weeks of his death, some of his followers startled their contemporaries by announcing that they had seen the resurrected Jesus in the days and weeks immediately following his crucifixion. Jesus' death did not put an end to the Jesus movement (or "the Way," as some early believers called it), but it transformed it into a reform movement within Judaism, and soon into a separate religion that welcomed Gentiles as well. This movement, whose followers came to be called Christians, was based not only on the teachings and example of Jesus but also upon an understanding that his death and resurrection were confirmation from God that Jesus was, in a unique sense, God's son.

The Christian scriptures

Although independent attestation from non-Christian sources for Jesus' life is scant – the first-century historians Josephus (a Jew) and Tacitus (a Roman) both briefly mention Jesus and indicate that he was executed during the reign of Pontius Pilate – unanimous Christian testimony affirms his public ministry, crucifixion, and resurrection during the reign of the Roman emperor Tiberius and the governorship in Judea of Pontius Pilate, probably around 30 C.E. Like Jesus, early Christians, who were primarily Jews, accepted the Jewish scriptures as their own sacred literature, though they read them in the light of their understanding of Jesus as Jewish messiah. The earliest extant Christian writings come from Paul and consist of letters he wrote to churches and individuals in Asia Minor and Europe. The gospels, which tell the story of Jesus, were written between 65 (the earliest probable date for Mark) and 95 (the latest probable date for John). The history of the church in the first century may be gleaned from the letters of Paul and others (the so-called catholic or general epistles), plus the letter of Clement of Rome to the Corinthian church (1 Clement), from the book of Acts (probably written in the 80s), from post-Jesus traditions extracted from the gospels, from contemporary Jewish and Roman sources, and from later Christian writings that refer to traditions from the first century. The most extensive and important of these sources are the writings that were eventually collected by Christians and called the New Testament, so an investigation of the formation of the Christian scriptures is important for a good understanding of Christianity in the first century and beyond. A look at the canonical process for the Hebrew Bible within Judaism also provides useful information for an understanding of the collection and selection of the Christian scriptures.

Canon

The term *canon* comes from a Greek word meaning a reed or measuring stick. It is used today to refer to a list of authoritative writings. In the case of the Bible, we can really only speak of a canon of scripture when the list becomes fixed (i.e. no other books may

Chart 4.1   The Old Testament canon

Catholic	Orthodox	Protestant	Jewish
Law (Pentateuch)	*Law (Pentateuch)*	*Law (Pentateuch)*	*Law (Torah)*
Genesis	Genesis	Genesis	Genesis
Exodus	Exodus	Exodus	Exodus
Leviticus	Leviticus	Leviticus	Leviticus
Numbers	Numbers	Numbers	Numbers
Deuteronomy	Deuteronomy	Deuteronomy	Deuteronomy
History	*History*	*History*	*Prophets (Nevi'im)*
Joshua	Joshua	Joshua	Joshua
Judges	Judges	Judges	Judges
Ruth	Ruth	Ruth	Samuel
1–2 Samuel	1–2 Samuel	1–2 Samuel	Kings
1–2 Kings	1–2 Kings	1–2 Kings	Isaiah
1–2 Chronicles	1–2 Chronicles	1–2 Chronicles	Jeremiah
Ezra	Ezra	Ezra	Ezekiel
Nehemiah	Nehemiah	Nehemiah	Book of the Twelve
Tobit	1 Esdras	Esther	
Judith	Tobit		*Writings (Ketuvim)*
Esther (+ additions)	Judith	*Poetry*	Psalms
1–2 Maccabees	Esther (+ additions)	Job	Proverbs
	1–3 Maccabees	Psalms	Job
Poetry		Proverbs	Song of Songs
Job	*Poetry*	Ecclesiastes	Ruth
Psalms	Job	Song of Songs	Lamentations
Proverbs	Psalms (+ Psalm 151)		Ecclesiastes
Ecclesiastes	Proverbs	*Major Prophets*	Esther
Song of Songs	Ecclesiastes	Isaiah	Daniel
Wisdom of Solomon	Song of Songs	Jeremiah	Ezra–Nehemiah
Ecclesiasticus	Wisdom of Solomon	Lamentations	Chronicles
	Ecclesiasticus	Ezekiel	
Major Prophets	Prayer of Manasseh	Daniel	
Isaiah			
Jeremiah	*Major Prophets*	*Minor Prophets*	
Lamentations	Isaiah	Hosea	
Baruch	Jeremiah	Joel	
Ezekiel	Lamentations	Amos	
Daniel (+ additions)	Baruch	Obadiah	
	Ezekiel	Jonah	
Minor Prophets	Daniel (+ additions)	Micah	
Hosea		Nahum	
Joel	*Minor Prophets*	Habakkuk	
Amos	Hosea	Zephaniah	
Obadiah	Joel	Haggai	
Jonah	Amos	Zechariah	
Micah	Obadiah	Malachi	
Nahum	Jonah		
Habakkuk	Micah		
Zephaniah	Nahum		
Haggai	Habakkuk		
Zechariah	Zephaniah		
Malachi	Haggai		
	Zechariah		
	Malachi		

be added or taken away), although, within Judaism, canonization of the Hebrew Bible occurred in stages. In Christianity, on the other hand, the process of canonization dealt with either the entire Old Testament or the entire New Testament as complete sets of documents.

The canon of scripture developed in both Judaism and Christianity over a long period of time before becoming fixed in the specific books included today by Jews and Christians. In general, a three-fold process was involved in books coming to be considered canonical. First, a book was considered useful. Second, it was considered authoritative. Third, it was considered canonical (i.e. part of a fixed list). Within Christianity, the canonical process proceeded differently for the Old and New Testaments, so we will consider the canonization of these two sets of books separately.

The Old Testament

For Protestants, the Old Testament consists of 39 books. Roman Catholics include 46 books in their Old Testament canon, including all of the books considered scriptural by Protestants plus several additional books or parts of books. The canon of Eastern Orthodox Christians is similar to the Roman Catholic canon, with a few variations. Jews accept exactly the same books as Protestants (Martin Luther based his revision of the Catholic canon on Jewish practice), but they number the books differently, so that Jews only count 24 books. Chart 4.1 shows the Old Testament books accepted by Catholics, Orthodox, and Protestants, divided into traditional divisions. For the purposes of comparison, the Jewish canon, with the traditional Jewish divisions, appears in the fourth column.

The books listed in the Orthodox column are those accepted by the Greek Orthodox Church. Other Orthodox traditions may vary slightly from this list. The Ethiopian Orthodox Church has the most idiosyncratic canon of the Old Testament, including all those books in the Greek Orthodox Canon, but adding the books of Enoch, Jubilees, and 2 Esdras (4 Ezra).

The variations in the Old Testament canon among different Christian traditions result from the fact that the Jewish canon itself was not completely settled when the church came into being. A brief explanation of the formation of the Jewish canon will help clarify some of the differences among Christian traditions regarding the Old Testament. The Jewish concept of canon began developing after their return from Babylonian exile in the sixth century B.C.E., but the canon was not absolutely established in its present form until the second or third century C.E. The destruction of the Temple in 70 C.E. and the expulsion of the Jews from Jerusalem in 135 C.E. spurred the development of the canon, although by that time the boundaries were almost fixed. The three sections – Law, Prophets, and Writings – were accepted as authoritative in the order presented. The Law was probably accepted as authoritative by the fourth century B.C.E., and the Greek translation of the Law was probably created in the third century B.C.E. (the LXX). The Prophets were fixed in their present form and accepted as authoritative by the second century B.C.E. The book of Sirach (also called Ecclesiasticus), written in Hebrew about 180 B.C.E., lists notable heroes of the Bible from the Law and Prophets, but the only one it mentions from the Writings section is Nehemiah. Most notably, he omits Daniel. Sirach's grandson, writing a prologue to his Greek translation of the book about 117 B.C.E., speaks of "the Law, the Prophets, and the others that followed them," suggesting that although the Law and the Prophets were fixed by this time, the Writings were not. This view is confirmed by the New Testament, where Jesus speaks of "the Law, the Prophets, and the Psalms" (Luke 24:44; elsewhere he speaks only of "the Law and the Prophets": Matt 5:17; 7:12; 22:40; Luke 16:16; cf. also Acts 13:15; 2 Macc 15:9; 4 Macc 18:10). There is evidence that the Jews continued to discuss the authority of books like the Song of Songs and Esther until perhaps the second or third century C.E. (The Samaritans, who permanently split from the Jews in about the fifth century B.C.E., continue to accept only the Law as canonical.)

If the Jews fixed their canon of scripture by the third century C.E. or so, Christians continued to debate which books in their Old Testament were authoritative. Since few Christians after the second century read Hebrew, they read the Old Testament in Greek, and several additional Greek works of Jewish origin were available to them. When the Latin Vulgate was produced in the fifth century, it included Latin translations of several of these Greek works, over the objections of the principal translator, Jerome, who advocated an Old Testament that matched the books of the Jewish canon. His voice was a minority position, however, and his contemporary Augustine and others argued successfully for including books such as Tobit, Judith, Sirach, and the books of the Maccabees. These books continued to be used by most Christian writers throughout the Middle Ages, but it was not until Martin Luther advocated a return to the Jewish canon of the Old Testament that the Roman Catholic Church officially established the present list of Old Testament books used by Catholics at the Council of Trent in 1546. The Eastern Orthodox Church acted even later, accepting an Old Testament canon that was similar, though not identical, to the Catholic canon at the Synod of Jerusalem in 1672. Protestants mostly followed Luther's recommendation to revert to the Jewish canon, though many (including Luther) continued to read the "Apocrypha" and value it highly. Today, the term "Apocrypha" is considered somewhat pejorative, so many Christians call the books deuterocanonical instead (i.e. belonging to a second canon).

The New Testament

The canon of the New Testament had a separate and equally interesting development. Churches began copying and collecting the letters of Paul and perhaps one or two gospels, as they became available, in the late first and early second centuries. Since many Christians of the first and second generations believed that Christ would return quickly, they felt no need for a fixed list of authoritative Christian books. By the middle of the second century the situation had changed, both because of the perceived delay of the Parousia (the return of Christ to the earth) and because of historical developments within the church. An educated and wealthy Christian named Marcion began to preach that the God of the Old Testament was a God of war, while the God of the New Testament, the father of Jesus Christ, was a God of love, and the two were not the same. Marcion thus rejected the entire Old Testament, and he accepted as authoritative only the Gospel of Luke (in an abridged form) and ten of the letters of Paul (not including the Pastoral Epistles). Another Christian, Montanus, who lived at about the same time, began to teach that he and his female associates were in direct contact with the Holy Spirit and that their words had the authority of the written word found in the Law and the Gospels. Most Christians rejected the canon of Marcion as too restricted and the

Chart 4.2   The New Testament canon

Gospels	*Pauline Letters*	*General (or Catholic)*
Matthew	Romans	*Epistles*
Mark	1 Corinthians	Hebrews
Luke	2 Corinthians	James
John	Galatians	1 Peter
	Ephesians	2 Peter
History	Philippians	1 John
Acts	Colossians	2 John
	1 Thessalonians	3 John
	2 Thessalonians	Jude
	1 Timothy	
	2 Timothy	*Apocalyptic*
	Titus	Revelation
	Philemon	

Who wrote the books of the New Testament?

Many modern Christian scholars doubt that the authors traditionally associated with some of the books of the New Testament actually wrote them. The four gospels are all anonymous, despite their attribution to Matthew, Mark, Luke, and John, so the identity of the authors is debatable. Similarly, many doubt that Peter is responsible for both 1 Peter and 2 Peter, which are quite different in terms of style and vocabulary – and many would suggest that neither was written by the apostle. The greatest debate, however, centers on the letters attributed to Paul. Whereas 13 letters were traditionally attributed to Paul (14 if Hebrews is included), most modern scholars believe that the Pastoral Epistles – 1 and 2 Timothy and Titus – were written long after Paul's death, perhaps in the second century. Many also dispute whether Colossians, Ephesians, and 2 Thessalonians are genuinely Pauline.

Eusebius's view of the New Testament canon

Since we are dealing with this subject it is proper to sum up the writings of the New Testament which have been already mentioned. First then must be put the holy quaternion of the Gospels; following them the Acts of the Apostles. After this must be reckoned the epistles of Paul; next in order the extant former epistle of John, and likewise the epistle of Peter, must be maintained. After them is to be placed, if it really seem proper, the Apocalypse of John, concerning which we shall give the different opinions at the proper time. These then belong among the accepted writings. Among the disputed writings, which are nevertheless recognized by many, are extant the so-called epistle of James and that of Jude, also the second epistle of Peter, and those that are called the second and third of John, whether they belong to the evangelist or to another person of the same name. Among the rejected writings must be reckoned also the Acts of Paul, and the so-called Shepherd, and the Apocalypse of Peter, and in addition to these the extant epistle of Barnabas, and the so-called Teachings of the Apostles; and besides, as I said, the Apocalypse of John, if it seem proper, which some, as I said, reject, but which others class with the accepted books. And among these some have placed also the Gospel according to the Hebrews, with which those of the Hebrews that have accepted Christ are especially delighted. And all these may be reckoned among the disputed books. (*Church History* 3.25)

"canon" of Montanus as too broad, and prominent Christian leaders began to offer their opinions on which Christian books were authoritative.

As early Christians debated which books should be considered authoritative, a number of criteria appear to have been important:

1. *Apostolicity.* Was the work written by an apostle or by one of the associates of the apostles? (For example, Matthew and John were attributed to apostles, while Luke was associated with Paul and Mark with Peter.)
2. *Antiquity.* Did the work date from the earliest time (before the end of the first century, more or less)? (For example, many other gospels were available by the second and third centuries, but they were rejected by most Christians as of recent vintage.)
3. *Orthodoxy.* Regardless of the date, did the work reflect the opinion of the leaders of the churches in leading Christian centers such as Jerusalem, Alexandria, Rome, Antioch, and, later, Constantinople? (The opinion of the bishop of Rome was especially important to Christians in the West after the third or fourth century.)
4. *Spiritual value.* Was the work useful for Christian doctrine or devotion? (2 and 3 John were challenged by some early churches, probably because of their brevity.)

5. *Acceptance by the Churches.* This is ultimately the most important criterion, and it encompasses the others. If a work was widely accepted, it was sure to be counted as authoritative.

The four gospels, Acts, and the 13 letters of Paul were quickly adopted by the majority of Christians as authoritative. 1 Peter, 1 John, 2 John (?), and Jude were also widely accepted by the third century, but Hebrews, Revelation, and a book called the Apocalypse of Peter were disputed. Other books which had brief local support, such as 1 Clement, the Didache, and the Shepherd of Hermas, were no longer in contention as authoritative books by the middle of the third century, though they were still read. The books of James, 2 Peter, and perhaps 3 John were largely unknown to most churches of the time.

By the early fourth century, the churches in the eastern part of the Roman Empire accepted 21 books without question – the four gospels, Acts, 14 letters of Paul (including Hebrews), 1 John, and 1 Peter – and they used the other six books of the modern New Testament canon widely. In the West, 24 books, including Revelation, were generally accepted, and only Hebrews, James, and Jude were questioned. In 367 Athanasius, bishop of Alexandria, wrote a letter in which he listed the New Testament books he considered authoritative, and it is the first list that exactly matches the modern New Testament (though the order of the books varies). Athanasius' opinion was not immediately accepted by the rest of the church, but gradually over the next century or two both the Eastern and the Western churches moved toward a 27-book canon. By the middle of the fifth century, the Western church firmly accepted all 27 books, though some Eastern churches still disputed Revelation, but by the year 600 the canon was settled throughout the majority of Christendom.

The books included in the modern New Testament canon are listed in Chart 4.2. Note that the book of Hebrews is sometimes considered one of the Pauline letters (the traditional view) and sometimes one of the General or Catholic letters (the modern view). (Catholic letters are letters to the churches in general and are not named after the Roman Catholic Church.)

An interesting exception to this description of the development of the Christian canon is found in the churches of eastern Syria (a region whose dominant language was Syriac, a form of Aramaic), which accepted a harmony of the gospels known as the Diatessaron, created by Tatian in the second century, rather than the four separate gospels. It was not until the fifth century, under the influence of a certain forceful bishop named Rabbula, that the four separate gospels replaced the Diatessaron in most Syriac churches. The Syriac church also resisted the four minor catholic epistles (2 Peter, 2–3 John, Jude) and Revelation, so they had a 22-book canon for several centuries; they apparently also substituted a book called 3 Corinthians for Philemon. Eventually, under the influence of the churches to the West, most Syriac Christians moved in the direction of a 27-book canon, though the 22-book canon remained truer to their nationalistic feelings for some time.

Although the vast majority of contemporary Christians agree on the content of the New Testament canon, some Christians from small, eastern traditions add books such as the letters of Clement and the Apostolic Constitutions. The Ethiopian Orthodox Church has both a "narrow canon," whose New Testament is the same as that of most other Christians, and a "broad canon," which adds several additional books.

Key points you need to know

- The earliest description of Jesus is found not in the four gospels but in the letters of Paul.
- The word "gospel" was used with somewhat different meanings by different New Testament writers.
- The earliest of the four gospels in the New Testament was Mark, and the gospels of Matthew and Luke used Mark as one of their sources when composing their gospels.
- The story of Jesus' virgin birth was not found in the earliest witnesses to the life of Jesus, Paul and Mark, but was included in both Matthew and Luke.
- Mark, the earliest gospel, begins the story of Jesus with his baptism by John the Baptist, whereas Matthew and Luke begin with Jesus' birth.
- The Gospel of John, the latest of the four canonical gospels, equates Jesus with the preexistent, divine *logos* (Word or Reason) that was God's agent in creation.
- Whereas the Synoptic Gospels (Matthew, Mark, Luke) generally present Jesus as a human specially chosen and empowered by God, John presents Jesus as a divine being inhabiting a human body. The question of the relationship of the human and the divine in Jesus arose already in the first few decades after Jesus' death.
- Most historians view the canonical gospels as important sources for reconstructing the life of Jesus, but since they detect both discrepancies in the gospel accounts and evidence that the evangelists were more concerned with theological presentations of the life of Christ than with creating biographies in the modern sense, they read these accounts critically.
- The canon of the Hebrew Bible developed within Judaism over a period of several centuries. Modern disagreements among Christians over the inclusion of several books are a direct result of the fact that the canon of the Hebrew Bible (Old Testament) was not yet settled at the time of Jesus.
- The canon of the New Testament developed within Christianity over a period of several centuries. Its development was spurred by the failure of Christ to return to earth quickly, as many early Christians expected, as well as by historical events in the second century revolving around Marcion and Montanus.

Discussion questions

1. What is the difference between Paul's use of the term *gospel* and the use of the same term in the canonical gospels themselves, and in the present day?
2. What is the significance of the different starting points of the four gospels?
3. How does the Jesus reconstructed by the historians compare with the Christ of faith? Is the difference important?
4. How important for faith and practice are the different Old Testament canons accepted by Catholics, Orthodox, and Protestants?

Further reading

Ackroyd, P. E., and C. F. Evans, eds 1970. *The Cambridge History of the Bible*. Vol. 1: *From the Beginnings to Jerome*. Cambridge: Cambridge University Press.

Borg, Marcus J. 2006. *Jesus: Uncovering the Life, Teachings, and Relevance of a Religious Revolutionary*. New York: HarperSanFrancisco.

Bruce, F. F. 1988. *The Canon of Scripture*. Downers Grove, IL: InterVarsity.

Crossan, John Dominic 1991. *The Historical Jesus: The Life of a Mediterranean Jewish Peasant*. New York: HarperSanFrancisco.

Ehrman, Bart D. 2004. *The New Testament: A Historical Introduction to the Early Christian Writings*, 3rd edn. New York: Oxford University Press.

Levine, Amy-Jill 2006. *The Misunderstood Jew: The Church and the Scandal of the Jewish Jesus*. New York: HarperSanFrancisco.

Meier, John P. 1991–2001. *A Marginal Jew: Rethinking the Historical Jesus*, 3 vols. Anchor Bible Reference Library. New York: Doubleday.

Meyer, Marvin 1992. *The Gospel of Thomas*. New York: HarperSanFrancisco.

Pelikan, Jaroslav 1999. *Jesus through the Centuries: His Place in the History of Culture*, 2nd edn. New Haven, CT: Yale University Press.

Schweitzer, Albert 1968. *The Quest of the Historical Jesus*. Translated by W. Montgomery, with an Introduction by James M. Robinson. New York: Macmillan.

Westcott, Brooke Foss 1896. *A General Survey of the History of the Canon of the New Testament*. London: Macmillan.

Wright, N. T. 1996. "The Historical Jesus and Christian Theology." *Sewanee Theological Review* 39: 404–12.

5 Defining Christianity

As the Jews were making constant disturbances at the instigation of Chrestus, [Claudius] expelled them from Rome.

(Suetonius, *Life of Claudius* 25.4)

In this chapter

Although Jesus and all of his earliest followers were Jews, Christianity began to spread rapidly among the Gentiles (non-Jews) within the first few decades of the Church's existence. The exact relationship between Judaism and the new religion called Christianity was a matter of vociferous debate during this time, but by the end of the first century C.E. Christianity had separated permanently from Judaism. Even after that time, however, the extent to which Christianity should be anchored to its Jewish base and the extent to which it could borrow from Greco-Roman philosophy and scholarly traditions was disputed. In the end, Christianity retained its Jewish roots, while at the same time borrowing heavily from the great Greek and Roman thinkers of antiquity.

Main topics covered

- Different overall approaches to the history of the Church
- The mission of early Christianity to the Jews
- The mission of early Christianity to the Gentiles
- The break with Judaism
- Extreme Jewish and Gentile forms of Christianity in the first century
- Tertullian's perspective on the question of Christianity's relationship with Greco-Roman philosophy
- The perspective of Justin Martyr and Clement of Alexandria on the question of Christianity's relationship with Greco-Roman philosophy, and the influence of Philo of Alexandria on both these men
- Origen's perspective on the question of Christianity's relationship with Greco-Roman philosophy

Approaches to the history of the Church

Christians who have written histories of the church over the past several centuries, especially prior to the twentieth century, have often relied upon one of two traditional views of the overall history of Christianity. For Catholics, the traditional view went something like this:

1 The church in the first century was pure and orthodox.
2 Major heresies arose in the second century and threatened the orthodox church.
3 Constantine, who legalized Christianity and was the first Christian Roman emperor, was a largely positive factor in the history of the church.
4 Many giants of the faith lived and worked throughout the Middle Ages.
5 The Protestant Reformation was a negative factor in the history of the church.
6 The Catholic Reformation was a positive factor in the history of the church.

The Protestant view was similar up until the time of Constantine, after which it differed sharply from the traditional Catholic view:

1 The church in the first century was pure and orthodox.
2 Major heresies arose in the second century and threatened the orthodox church.
3 Constantine, who legalized Christianity and was the first Christian Roman emperor, was a largely negative factor in the history of the church.
4 Although many giants of the faith lived and worked during the Middle Ages, they were primarily early, and by the end of the Middle Ages the Roman Catholic Church was in drastic need of reform.
5 The Protestant Reformation was a positive factor in the history of the church.
6 The Catholic Reformation (which Protestants often call the Counter-Reformation) had some positive effects, but it did not go far enough in the direction of needed reform, especially doctrinal and ecclesiastical reform.

Some Anabaptists and Evangelicals modified the traditional Protestant model to say that the Protestant Reformation was inadequate, while the Radical Reformation took reform to its logical conclusion. The traditional Orthodox view was similar to the Catholic view, but it blamed the Great Schism between the Catholics and the Orthodox that occurred in 1054 on the Catholics, and it was critical of many subsequent developments within Catholicism.

Modern scholars – Catholic, Orthodox, and Protestant alike – view these traditional outlines of church history as simplistic and based on highly selective readings of history. For example, the idea that the first century was a golden age of purity and orthodoxy in the church ignores the harsh critiques of fellow Christians that are found within the New Testament itself, and it also begs the question of what orthodoxy means at such an early period in the history of Christianity. Similarly, the claim that heresy invaded previously orthodox areas in the second century has been called into serious question by modern historians, who assert that forms of Christianity that would not be recognized as orthodox today were sometimes the first type of Christianity in a particular region. The history of the church is complex. It is a story, from the very beginning, that involved strong personalities, differences of opinion, and accusations that one's adversaries had abandoned the true faith. On the other hand, it is also a story that involved courageous individuals and communities, acts of great faith and love, brilliant thinkers, and a willingness to engage in discussion with those whose views differed. It is a story, in other words, of saints and sinners, of the proud and the humble, of ordinary people who shared a devotion to God based on their common commitment to Jesus Christ.

The first century

Peter, James, and other leaders of the Jewish mission

The earliest narrative of the history of the church is the book of Acts in the New Testament. Although it was clearly written as an apology for Christianity in a Roman context and structured to trace the movement of the gospel message from Jerusalem to Rome, its sketch of the growth of the church is probably broadly historical. According to Acts, the followers of Jesus had several encounters with the risen Lord in the days following Easter, and after 40 days several of them observed him ascend into heaven. By this time the ranks of his followers had swelled to about 120 people (Acts 1:15), including Jesus' mother and brothers. Ten days later, on the Jewish Feast of Pentecost, the Holy Spirit descended on the followers of Jesus and filled them with the extraordinary ability to speak in languages which they did not know, so that visitors to Jerusalem were miraculously able to hear the gospel proclaimed in whatever language they happened to speak. Although the gospels other than Luke suggest that Jesus' disciples returned to Galilee after the resurrection, the tradition that the church was born on Pentecost quickly became the dominant testimony of the Christian community, and the church in Jerusalem was considered the mother church of Christianity.

Whenever Jesus' 12 disciples are listed, Simon Peter is always mentioned first. He is also the disciple most often mentioned by name in the gospels; his name appears more than four times more frequently than that of any other disciple. Along with James and John, the sons of Zebedee, Peter is portrayed in the Synoptic Gospels as one of Jesus' closest confidants. Whatever Peter's position was among the disciples when Jesus was alive, he clearly emerged in the post-Easter period as the leading figure in the fledgling church. Peter's position of leadership is confirmed by Paul's allusions to him as leader of the church in Jerusalem (Gal 1:18; 2:7; 1 Cor 1:12; Paul consistently calls him *Cephas*, the Aramaic equivalent of the Greek *Peter*). Both Paul and the gospels indicate that the resurrected Jesus appeared personally to Peter, in addition to appearing to the disciples as a group. In Acts, Peter is the chief spokesperson for Christianity, presiding over the choice of Matthias to replace the traitor Judas Iscariot, preaching the inaugural sermon to the multitudes on Pentecost, and speaking out boldly for the faith in the face of persecution from the Jewish elders. Peter was reportedly imprisoned on more than one occasion but was miraculously delivered. Despite his identity as Apostle to the Jews, Peter is also described in Acts as the first to bring the gospel to the Gentiles, in the person of the Roman centurion Cornelius. After the author of Acts shifts his focus to Paul, Peter, who played such a prominent role in the early chapters, no longer figures into the story. Nevertheless, at some point Peter apparently traveled to Rome, where several early Christian writers (e.g. Clement of Rome, Dionysius of Corinth, Tertullian) describe him as being martyred. Peter was probably killed when Nero began persecuting Christians in the summer of 64, blaming them for the fire that destroyed much of the city of Rome, a fire which some suspected Nero himself of ordering. Several traditions identify Peter as the first bishop (pastor) of the church of Rome, although the Roman church undoubtedly predates Peter's time there. The great Basilica of St. Peter's in the Vatican was built on the foundation of earlier structures, all of which were erected over a grave thought to be that of Peter. The most direct claim for Peter's authority in the New Testament is found in the Gospel of Matthew. In Matt 16:18–19, Jesus tells Peter, "You are Peter [Greek: *petros*], and upon this rock [Greek: *petra*] I will build my church, and the gates of Hades will not prevail against it." Whether or not Jesus uttered these words (the other Synoptic Gospels do not contain them), it is clear that the author of Matthew – along with many other early Christians – considered Peter the obvious leader of the church, the rock on which it was founded. Peter's presence and martyrdom in Rome may indicate that his early focus on the mission to the Jews changed as time passed, for the church of Rome undoubtedly contained many Gentiles, as well as Jews.

Peter was not the only Christian leader associated with the Jewish mission. After Peter, the most prominent member of the church in Jerusalem was James, the brother of Jesus. James does not appear to have been a follower of Jesus during his lifetime, but Paul says that Jesus appeared to him after his resurrection (1 Cor 15:7), and Jesus' brothers are listed in Acts 1 as present in Jerusalem on the day of Pentecost. Paul lists him as a "pillar" of the Jerusalem church (Gal 2:9), along with Peter and John the son of Zebedee. In Acts 15:12–21, James is portrayed as the person who makes the ultimate decision at the Jerusalem Council (cf. Acts 15:19, "I have reached the decision"), even though Peter is also present. Perhaps this indicates that James was considered the leader of the church in Jerusalem, while Peter focused his attention on the wider Jewish (and later Gentile?) mission. According to Josephus, James and some of his companions were stoned to death in Jerusalem in about 62 c.e. (Did Peter leave Jerusalem for Rome at this time to avoid the same fate?).

It is likely that many of the other disciples of Jesus continued to be leaders in the Jesus movement, both in Jerusalem and beyond, but reliable history contains no record of their activities. Various traditions provide stories of miracles performed, churches planted, and martyrdoms suffered, but most are of extremely doubtful historical value. Two exceptions to this generalization are the sons of Zebedee, James and John. Acts says that James the son of Zebedee was killed by King Herod Agrippa I (Acts 12:1–2), a statement that seems quite likely to be historically accurate. His brother John is mentioned by Paul as one of the pillars of the church, but several traditions associate him with the city of Ephesus, where he reportedly died of old age toward the end of the first century. If John the son of Zebedee may be identified with "the disciple whom Jesus loved" in the Gospel of John (neither James nor John are ever mentioned by name in the gospel), John 21 was probably added to the original Gospel of John as an appendix shortly after the death of the Apostle John. The Jerusalem church included seven deacons (ministers), who were chosen to minister to the Greek-speaking Jewish widows. One of these, Stephen, is described in Acts 7 as the first Christian martyr.

Paul and other leaders of the Gentile mission

But all human efforts, all the lavish gifts of the emperor, and the propitiations of the gods, did not banish the sinister belief that the conflagration [the Great Fire of Rome] was the result of an order. Consequently, to get rid of the report, Nero fastened the guilt and inflicted the most exquisite tortures on a class hated for their abominations, called Christians by the populace. Christus, from whom the name had its origin, suffered the extreme penalty during the reign of Tiberius at the hands of one of our procurators, Pontius Pilatus, and a most mischievous superstition, thus checked for the moment, again broke out not only in Judaea, the first source of the evil, but even in Rome, where all things hideous and shameful from every part of the world find their centre and become popular. Accordingly, an arrest was first made of all who pleaded guilty; then, upon their information, an immense multitude was convicted, not so much of the crime of firing the city, as of hatred against mankind. Mockery of every sort was added to their deaths. Covered with the skins of beasts, they were torn by dogs and perished, or were nailed to crosses, or were doomed to the flames and burnt, to serve as a nightly illumination, when daylight had expired.

Nero offered his gardens for the spectacle, and was exhibiting a show in the circus, while he mingled with the people in the dress of a charioteer or stood aloft on a car. Hence, even for criminals who deserved extreme and exemplary punishment, there arose a feeling of compassion; for it was not, as it seemed, for the public good, but to glut one man's cruelty, that they were being destroyed.

Tacitus, *Annals* 15

The most important figure in first-century Christianity, after Jesus, was Saul, a Jew from Tarsus in Asia Minor, who also went by the name Paul. The words of Paul are preserved in several undoubtedly authentic letters that he wrote to Christians in Asia Minor and Europe, and other letters, whose authenticity is questioned by many scholars (if not by Paul, they may have been written by associates of Paul), are also preserved in the New Testament. In his letters, Paul often gives biographical information about

Figure 5.1 Fifteenth-century painter Filippino Lippi depicted Peter and Paul in a dispute with their detractor Simon Magus before the emperor Nero.

himself. In addition, about three-fifths of the book of Acts is devoted to the life of Paul. From these sources, it is apparent that Paul at one time was a Pharisee, a group of Jews who advocated strict observance of the law, according to their own interpretation (the interpretation that ultimately became normative for Rabbinic Judaism). During the earliest days of Christianity, Paul was a strong opponent of the Christian movement, believing it to be a threat to traditional Judaism. Paul himself says that he was "violently persecuting the church of God" (Gal 1:13). Although none of Paul's extant letters describe the dramatic experience that led him to become a Christian, Acts says that Paul had a miraculous encounter with the risen Christ while on the road from Jerusalem to Damascus. Paul calls it "a revelation of Jesus Christ" (Gal 1:13).

After about ten years, Paul, a tent-maker by training, embarked on a series of journeys throughout western Asia and Greece, establishing churches and preaching the gospel to both Jews and Gentiles. His greatest success was among Gentiles, perhaps initially among those God-fearers who were associated with Jewish synagogues and who were therefore familiar with the scripture in the LXX version. As noted above, Paul's understanding of the *gospel* revolved around the death, resurrection, ascension, and imminent return of Christ. Although it is impossible to say for certain how many converts to Christianity Paul and his associates won, by the time of his death about 64 C.E. he had founded many churches throughout the eastern Mediterranean region, and it is likely that the number of Christians in these churches, or in churches started as a direct result of his work, numbered in the hundreds. Since most of these Christians were Gentiles, Paul became known as the Apostle to the Gentiles, a title by which he also referred to himself (Rom 11:13).

One of the earliest controversies that arose within Christianity revolved around Paul and his mission to the Gentiles. Since Christianity began as a movement within Judaism, and since the leaders of the early church in Jerusalem were Jews, Paul's efforts to reach out to the Gentiles, and the methods he employed, raised questions. Were Gentile converts to Christianity required to conform to the traditional norms of Judaism, including male circumcision and observing Jewish dietary regulations? About 49 c.e. Paul traveled to Jerusalem to meet the leaders of the Jewish mission, Peter, John, and James the brother of Jesus. The record of this meeting preserved in Acts, written at least 30 years after the fact, suggests that Paul agreed to require that Gentile converts to Christianity conform to a limited set of regulations: to abstain from eating food that had been offered to idols (pagan gods), from sexual immorality (perhaps relating to certain pagan religious practices), from meat taken from animals that had been strangled (contrary to Jewish regulations concerning the slaughter of animals), and from eating food from which the blood had not been properly drained. Paul's record of the agreement in Gal 2:1–10, written within about five years after the Jerusalem Council, is radically different. After noting that the leaders of the Jewish mission did not even require his Gentile convert Titus to be circumcised, Paul says that the only requirement laid upon him in his Gentile mission was to remember the poor, perhaps especially the Christian poor of Judea. Paul's failure to mention any restrictions regarding dietary rules suggests that their inclusion in Acts may have been intended to play down the heated nature of the controversy, a controversy that would have been largely moot when Acts was written. Paul's dispute with the leaders of the Jerusalem church over the question of whether Christians should be required to conform to the customs of Judaism came to a head in Antioch, when Paul opposed Peter to his face and accused him of hypocrisy for failing to share a meal with Gentile Christians (Gal 2:11–14). Although the rift between Paul and Peter may have been settled, the vehemence of the controversy between Paul and his detractors, the Judaizers (Christian Jews who advocated a stricter observance of traditional Jewish custom) can be seen in Paul's wish that they might castrate themselves (i.e. by taking their insistence on circumcision to an extreme; Gal 5:12).

While on a visit to Jerusalem in about 58, Paul was arrested and held by the Romans, because of accusations that he had brought a Gentile into the temple area, a region restricted to observant Jews. After being held in custody in Caesarea, the provincial capital, for two years, Paul eventually appealed his case to the emperor, as was his right as a Roman citizen. He arrived in Rome in about 60 and was placed under house arrest, according to Acts. Acts ends before Paul's case is resolved, probably because one purpose of the book is to emphasize the fact that Christianity represents no threat to the Roman Empire, and a description of Paul's execution at the hands of Nero a few years later might be seen as inflammatory. Although some traditions claim that Paul journeyed as far west as Spain in order to preach the gospel, the most reliable evidence suggests that he remained in Rome after being brought there as a prisoner. It is possible that he was released for a short time, but if so, he did not remain free for long. Paul died in the same Neronian persecution that took Peter's life, in the wake of the conflagration that burned the city of Rome.

Paul's importance for shaping Christianity can hardly be overemphasized. While the majority of Jesus' original disciples – along with Jesus' brother James, who joined the Christians shortly after Jesus' death – seem to have remained in Jerusalem for many years, Paul and his associates Barnabas, Silas, and Timothy took the message of Christ to Cyprus, Asia Minor, Greece, and beyond. They were not the first to take the gospel outside the boundaries of the Holy Land – Christians were in Rome long before Paul first visited – but they were the among the most purposeful in doing so. As the church became predominantly Gentile by the end of the first century, its center of gravity shifted from Jerusalem to Asia Minor and Greece, and many of its most influential churches were those associated with Paul, such as Antioch (in northwest Syria), Ephesus and Corinth. Early Christians collected and made copies of Paul's letters, sharing them with churches in neighboring cities, so Paul's ideas spread beyond those churches to which he had originally written. At the end of the first century, when Clement, the bishop of Rome, writes to the church at Corinth, he mentions some of the things that Paul had said to the Corinthians in his letters, an indication that the church in Rome had copies.

Paul, who had once been an advocate of a rather strict form of Judaism, came to believe that Christianity should be characterized by a radical freedom from human rules and customs, whether Jewish or otherwise. It was not that he advocated libertinism (cf. Rom 6:1–2), but he believed that it was sufficient for Christians to be obedient to the spirit of Christ that dwelt within them (Rom 8:1–8), vitiating the need for other rules and regulations. "For freedom Christ has set us free. Stand firm, therefore, and do not submit again to a yoke of slavery" (Gal 5:1). Paul also saw Christianity as radically egalitarian, eliminating the distinctions between Jew and Gentile, slave and free, male and female (Gal 3:28). In fact, one of the characteristics of early Christianity that distinguished it from Judaism was its admission of women to the ranks of leadership within the church (e.g. Rom 16:1–15, which mentions several women who were leaders in various capacities). Paul believed that the Christian's relationship with God was based on the grace of God and accepted by faith in Jesus Christ. There was no way, Paul said, to achieve righteousness by observance of the law (Rom 1:16; 3:28). Instead, Christians benefit from the death of Christ, which alone is capable of reconciling people to God (Rom 5:8–9).

Paul's importance to the development of Christianity is evident from the fact that more than one-third of the New Testament is comprised of letters attributed to Paul and those chapters of Acts (9, 13–28) devoted to tracing Paul's ministry from the Damascus road to Rome. Only Jesus himself receives wider coverage. The Roman Catholic Church considers Paul to have been the co-founder, with Peter, of the church in Rome, even though it clearly existed prior to his arrival there.

Though Paul was the most prominent Apostle to the Gentiles, many other people worked to bring the gospel to the Gentiles, some in association with Paul and others independently. On Paul's first venture as a Christian missionary at the behest of the church of Antioch, he was accompanied by Barnabas, a native of Cyprus. After Paul and Barnabas parted ways, ostensibly over a disagreement concerning the fitness of a young man named John Mark to accompany them on their next planned journey, Paul chose Silas as a traveling companion. Others whom Paul identifies as companions in the work of the gospel include Timothy, Titus, and Luke. Paul sometimes worked with the husband and wife team of Priscilla and Aquila. Apollos, a native of Alexandria, Egypt, also worked with Gentile Christians in some of the same churches that Paul did (Ephesus, Corinth), though apparently at different times.

Independently of Paul, Philip, one of the deacons chosen by the Jerusalem church (different from Jesus' disciple Philip), is pictured in Acts preaching in Samaria and delivering the gospel message to an Ethiopian eunuch on the road from Jerusalem to Gaza. In addition to John's work in Ephesus, other traditions of questionable historical value associate other disciples and "apostolic men" with the spread of the gospel to far-flung lands: Mark is associated with the mission to Egypt, Thomas with India, and Andrew with Scythia, just to name a few of the traditions. There is a tendency for the names of famous people to become associated with events such as the founding of the first church in a region, but in many cases the fact is that Christians whose names have long been forgotten took the message of Christ with them as they traveled throughout the Roman Empire and even beyond its borders, winning converts and establishing churches wherever they went. By the end of the first century, Christianity had roots in many places throughout western Eurasia and North Africa, including Judea, Samaria, Galilee, Syria, Phoenicia, Arabia, Asia Minor, Macedonia, Achaia, Crete, Cyprus, Dalmatia, Italy, Gaul, Egypt, and possibly Spain.

The break with Judaism

The earliest followers of Jesus, like Jesus himself, were Jews. Although they considered Jesus to have been the Jewish messiah, they remained within the synagogue for several decades, and they also continued to worship as Jews in the Jerusalem temple, until it was destroyed by the Romans in 70 C.E., during the First Jewish Revolt against Rome. Contention between Christian and non-Christian Jews in the first century grew as the number of Christians grew and as increasing numbers of Gentiles joined the movement. The primary point of contention, of course, revolved around the fact that Christians believed Jesus to be the promised messiah, while most Jews rejected that assessment of Jesus. Christianity grew most rapidly in the first century among the Greek-speaking Jews and the Gentile "God-fearers" who frequented the synagogues throughout the Roman Empire. They used the LXX as their scripture, like their fellow Greek-speaking Jews, but they interpreted it in the light of their understanding of Jesus. Although the LXX was a Greek translation of the Hebrew Bible, early Christians emphasized certain points of difference between the Greek and Hebrew versions that were advantageous to the Christian interpretation. For example, Christians pointed to the reading of Isa 7:14 in the LXX, which says, "The virgin shall conceive and bear a son, and you shall call his name Immanuel," as being a prophecy of Jesus' birth; the Hebrew version of that passage simply says "the young woman" rather than "the virgin." Christians, of course, identified Immanuel, Hebrew for "God with us," with Jesus. Christian use of the LXX eventually led Greek-speaking Jews to abandon it in favor of more recent Greek translations of the Tanakh that more closely reflected their Hebrew texts. By the end of the first century, Christian Jews had largely abandoned, or been expelled from, the synagogues of non-Christian Jews. Christians instead gathered together for worship and fellowship exclusively in churches, communities of Christian believers.

The conflict between Paul and the Judaizers was an intra-Christian conflict, but it paralleled a growing conflict between the increasingly Gentile Christian church and traditional Judaism. It also foreshadowed anti-Judaic feelings that would soon become all too prevalent in Christianity as a whole. The roots of the conflict date to the time when Christianity was a minority position in Judea and other Jewish enclaves. Sporadic persecution of Christians by the Jewish hierarchy in Jerusalem, and eventually the ousting of Christian Jews from the synagogue, led some early Christians to do what other oppressed minorities often do: lash out at those in the majority, whom they view as oppressors. Anti-Jewish feelings can be found in the gospels themselves, especially in the accounts concerning the death of Jesus. Although Pilate is clearly the person who had ultimate responsibility for the death of Jesus – crucifixion was strictly a Roman form of execution, not a Jewish one – all four gospels emphasize the complicity of the *Sanhedrin*, the Jewish ruling council in Jerusalem. Moreover, they all accuse the Jewish leaders of insisting that Pilate execute Jesus, even though Pilate himself is not convinced that he deserves death. Modern historians debate the role that the Jewish leaders played in the death of Jesus, with many suggesting a greater role for the Romans throughout the process than the gospels indicate. Regardless of the culpability of the Jewish leaders in Jesus' death – and it is probable that at least some leading Jews were strong opponents of Jesus – the transfer of guilt from individual Jews to the Jewish people as a whole was as unwarranted in the first century as it is today. The most blatant passage indicating the blame that some Christians put on the Jews for the death of Jesus occurs in Matt 27:24–25. After Pilate washes his hands before the Jewish people and declares to them his innocence of Jesus' blood, the crowd replies, "His blood be on us and on our children!" In its historical context, this statement of Jewish corporate responsibility is most likely a reference to the Roman destruction of Jerusalem in 70 c.e., which some Christians understood as God's judgment on the Jews for their role in Jesus' death. Nevertheless, passages such as this and others (e.g. Luke 23:1, 18; John 16:2; Acts 19:9), which were originally expressions of frustration by a religious minority, most of whom were Jews (Jewish Christians) themselves, were transformed after Christianity became largely Gentile into animosity between the Church and the Synagogue. Over the centuries, after Christianity grew to be much larger than Judaism, this anti-Jewish sentiment manifested itself from time to time in increasingly intemperate writing (e.g. the second-century Epistle of Barnabas or the sermons of the fourth-century bishop John Chrysostom of Constantinople *Against the Jews*), laws that discriminated against Jews (e.g. the law codes of the Christian emperors Constantine, Theodosius, and Justinian), attacks on Jews during the Crusades and in pogroms, and, most recently, in virulent anti-Semitism, manifested most clearly in the Holocaust during World War II. By the end of the first century, the break between Christians and Jews was complete. Christians now saw themselves, and other people saw them, no longer as Jews but as adherents of a new religion: Christianity.

Developments within Christianity

As more people became convinced of the truth and value of the Christian movement, Christianity grew, and with growth came diversity of opinion and practice. Many scholars believe it is more accurate to speak of early *Christianities* at the end of the first century and beyond than to speak of early *Christianity*. Certainly the variety of ways in which those who saw themselves as followers of Christ in the earliest period of Christian history was large, and the concept of *orthodoxy* (right belief) was not settled.

One of the movements that emerged in the first century was probably related to the early controversies between Paul and the Judaizers. Some Jewish Christians – perhaps a large number – did not believe that Jesus had come to establish a separate religion. While accepting Jesus as the Jewish messiah, they refused to abandon many of the traditions that their ancestors had been practicing for centuries. Dietary laws, rituals involving washing, observance of the Sabbath – despite Paul's denigration of these customs as aspects of the law that could now be discarded, many Jewish Christians continued to see value in them. Even the Christians' expulsion from the synagogue could not convince some to turn against the beliefs and customs that had sustained the Jews through times of persecution and desperation. One such group of Jewish Christians was known as the Ebionites, a name that comes from the Hebrew word for "poor." The Ebionites believed that Christians should continue to follow many regulations of the Jewish law, and they rejected Paul as an apostate (one who has left the true faith). At least some of the Ebionites also rejected the Virgin Birth and any notion that Jesus was divine. The Ebionites, and other groups of Jewish Christians with similar beliefs, continued to exist for several centuries, primarily in Palestine and further east.

At the other end of the theological spectrum from the Ebionites were the Docetists, a group of Gentile Christians who stressed the divinity of Christ to the exclusion of his humanity. The Docetists, whose name derives from the Greek word meaning "to seem," believed that Jesus only *seemed* to have a physical body and to suffer and die on the cross. It is likely that the introductory sentence of 1 John, which refers in explicit terms to the disciples' physical encounters with Jesus, was written in order to counteract a Docetic tendency in the Christian community to which the letter was addressed. It is clear that first-century Christians held a wide diversity of opinion concerning the identity of Jesus

Christ, ranging from the Ebionites' belief that Jesus was a fully human messiah, through the emphases on Jesus' humanity in the Synoptic Gospels, through Paul's portrayal of the exalted Christ, through the stress on Jesus' divinity in the Gospel of John, to the complete denial of Jesus' humanity by the Docetists. This range of choices for ways of understanding Jesus would begin to be narrowed down over the next few centuries, as the concept of orthodoxy began to emerge.

One development within Christianity that has little to do with doctrinal differences involved the organization of the church, sometimes referred to as *polity*. Jesus apparently left no instructions for the organization of the church after his death. In fact, the church is only mentioned twice in the gospels, both times in Matthew (Matt 16:18; 18:17), neither of which mentions church organization, although both imply a hierarchical structure of some kind. There are several Greek words used in the New Testament that apply to people in the church who hold a leadership position of some sort: *elder* (also transliterated as *presbyter*, a reference to the wisdom and respect that comes with

The Apostolic Fathers

Aside from the New Testament, some of the earliest Christian writings that have been preserved form a collection known as the Apostolic Fathers. These works date from about 96 to the mid-second century. Although total unanimity does not exist on the precise extent of the works that should be included in this group, here is a typical list, taken from the work of renowned scholar J. B. Lightfoot:

1 Clement (Letter of Clement, bishop of Rome to the church at Corinth)
2 Clement (An ancient, anonymous Christian sermon)
Letters of Ignatius, bishop of Antioch

>> To the Ephesians
>> To the Magnesians
>> To the Trallians
>> To the Romans
>> To the Philadelphians
>> To the Smyrnaeans
>> To Polycarp

Letter of Polycarp, bishop of Smyrna, to the Philippians
Martyrdom of Polycarp
Didache (also called the Teaching of the Twelve Apostles)
Epistle of Barnabas
Shepherd of Hermas
Epistle to Diognetus
Fragments of Papias

age), *bishop* (supervisor or overseer), *deacon* (minister or servant), *pastor* (shepherd), and *teacher*. *Prophets* and *evangelists* are also mentioned, as are *apostles*, a term usually, but not always, reserved for the 12 disciples of Jesus and for Paul. These last three terms seem to refer to people whose ministry is not focused in a single church. Most scholars see no sharp distinction among the terms elder, bishop, and pastor, as least as they were used in most first-century churches. Deacons, on the other hand, seem to have filled a different role from an early period (cf. Acts 6:1–6; Phil 1:1), serving as assistants to more senior ministers. For very small churches, of course, one minister (elder/bishop) probably sufficed to do the work, perhaps assisted by a deacon. As churches in some areas began to grow, however, particularly in the cities, the need for a more developed structure was felt. The Pastoral Epistles, written perhaps in the first or second decade of the second century, reflect two tiers of clergy (ministers): elders and deacons, as does the *Epistle of Polycarp*, written before 140. In contrast, Ignatius's letters to six churches and one individual (Polycarp) assume a three-tiered structure in which the bishop presides over a group of elders, both of which are assisted by deacons. Over time, the three-tiered structure came to predominate, at least in larger churches. Eventually, after the church in one city became too large to meet in a single building, the congregation split into smaller groups, each led by an elder/presbyter (also called a priest), while the whole church was presided over by a bishop.

A Jewish or Greco-Roman religion?

> Then after fourteen years I went up again to Jerusalem with Barnabas, taking Titus along with me. I went up in response to a revelation. Then I laid before them (though only in a private meeting with the acknowledged leaders) the gospel that I proclaim among the Gentiles, in order to make sure that I was not running, or had not run, in vain. But even Titus, who was with me, was not compelled to be circumcised, though he was a Greek.
>
> (Gal 2:1–3)

The break between the Church and the Synagogue in the late first century transformed Christianity from a reform movement within Judaism into a full-fledged religion. The Roman historian Suetonius, in his *Life of Claudius*, describes the emperor Claudius's command to expel the Jews from Rome because they were "continually making disturbances at the instigation of Chrestus," probably a reference to disputes between Jews and Christians. If Claudius was unable to distinguish Christians from Jews in the fifth or sixth decade of the first century, his successor Nero had no such trouble in the seventh decade. By the early 60s, Christians in Rome had distinguished themselves from Jews, not only in their own eyes but also in the eyes of their Roman overlords. The separation of Christians from Jews probably took a little longer in Judea and Galilee

Old Testament passages traditionally seen as messianic prophecies by Christians (4)

The ruling king

I see him, but not now;

  I behold him, but not near –

  a star shall come out of Jacob,

   and a scepter shall rise out of Israel;

  it shall crush the borderlands of Moab,

   and the territory of all the Shethites.

Edom will become a possession,

  Seir a possession of its enemies,

  while Israel does valiantly.

One out of Jacob shall rule,

  and destroy the survivors of Ir. (Num 24:17–19)

I will tell of the decree of the Lord:

  He said to me, "You are my son;

  today I have begotten you.

Ask of me, and I will make the nations your heritage,

  and the ends of the earth your possession.

You shall break them with a rod of iron,

  and dash them in pieces like a potter's vessel". (Psalm 2:7–9)

The Lord says to my lord,

  "Sit at my right hand

  until I make your enemies your footstool."

The Lord sends out from Zion

  your mighty scepter.

  Rule in the midst of your foes.

Your people will offer themselves willingly

  on the day you lead your forces

  on the holy mountains.

 From the womb of the morning,

  like dew, your youth will come to you.

The Lord has sworn and will not change his mind,

  You are a priest forever according to the order of Melchizedek. (Psalm 110:1–4)

But you, O Bethlehem of Ephrathah,
  who are one of the little clans of Judah,
  from you shall come forth for me
  one who is to rule in Israel,
  whose origin is from of old,
  from ancient days.
Therefore he shall give them up until the time
  when she who is in labor has brought forth;
  then the rest of his kindred shall return
  to the people of Israel.
And he shall stand and feed his flock in the strength of the Lord,
  in the majesty of the name of the Lord his God.
  And they shall live secure, for now he shall be great
  to the ends of the earth;
and he shall be the one of peace. (Mic 5:2–5a)

The days are surely coming, says the Lord, when I will raise up for David a righteous Branch, and he shall reign as king and deal wisely, and shall execute justice and righteousness in the land. In his days Judah will be saved and Israel will live in safety. And this is the name by which he will be called: "The Lord is our righteousness." (Jer 23:5–6)

Rejoice greatly, O daughter Zion!
  Shout aloud, O daughter Jerusalem!
  Lo, your king comes to you;
  triumphant and victorious is he,
  humble and riding on a donkey,
  on a colt, the foal of a donkey.
He will cut off the chariot from Ephraim
  and the war-horse from Jerusalem;
  and the battle bow shall be cut off,
  and he shall command peace to the nations;
  his dominion shall be from sea to sea,
  and from the River to the ends of the earth. (Zech 9:9–10)

than in areas of larger Gentile concentration, but it was probably complete even in the Holy Land by the end of the first century, some 70 years after Jesus' death.

The emergence of Christianity as a separate religion did not, however, put an end to its connection with Judaism. On the contrary, Christians of the second and third centuries – most of whom were Gentiles – debated among themselves the question of the relationship between Christianity and Judaism on the one hand, and Christianity and the dominant Greco-Roman culture on the other. All Christians acknowledged the Jewish origins of Christianity – after all, Jesus himself was a Jew – and most saw Jesus as the Jewish messiah. Furthermore, they continued to read the sacred scripture of the Jews, seeing it as a testimony to Christ, even as they produced distinctively Christian writings as well. The fact that Christianity was made up primarily of Gentiles rather than Jews, however, raised questions in the minds of many. Was the Greco-Roman background of most Christians something to be cast aside and abandoned as inferior to the Jewish heritage of the early church? Did the philosophical traditions of the Greeks and Romans have anything to contribute to the new religion? How the majority of Christians answered these questions did much to shape the fledgling church.

Tertullian

Toward the end of the second century a lawyer and orator named Quintus Septimius Florens Tertullianus, a native of Carthage, became a convert to Christianity. A man of tremendous rhetorical abilities, a keen intellect, and a fierce commitment to his beliefs, Tertullian quickly became one of the leading spokespeople for Christianity in the Roman Empire. Widely acknowledged as the first great Latin theologian, Tertullian wrote many treatises in support of Christianity, most of them polemical in nature. He placed great value in the traditions handed down by the apostles of Jesus, both in written form (the scriptures) and through the teaching of the churches that they established. He applied his legal acumen to resolve the apparent discrepancies that he observed in the traditions about the description of the divine and the human in Christ and about the relationship between Jesus and God. On the basis of his analyses of the gospels, the letters of Paul, and other Christian writings (the canon was not yet settled), he came up with the concept of "three persons but one substance" to describe the relationship between Father, Son, and Holy Spirit. He was also the first to use the term "Trinity" to refer to the three-fold nature of God.

Tertullian was a harsh critic of those he deemed "heretics," that is, those whose beliefs deviated from what he considered the norm of Christian faith. He seems to have written treatises in opposition to every individual or group with whom he disagreed, sometimes individually (e.g. his treatises *Against Marcion*, *Against Hermogenes*, *Against the Valentinians*, *Against Praxeas*, *Against the Jews*) and sometimes as a whole (the *Prescription of Heretics*). In the *Prescription of Heretics*, he is critical of the heretics' use of scripture, stating that since they do not belong to the mainstream of Christianity, they cannot make any valid claim to use scripture in making their case. He also condemns

Greek philosophy as the source of many of the heretical ideas used by his opponents. In fact, he says, almost every wicked idea used by the heretics can be traced to Greek philosophy: Valentinus's doctrine of emanation of aeons to Plato, Marcion's "better God" to the Stoics, the idea that the soul perishes to the Epicureans, the equation of matter with God to Zeno, and ideas relating God to Fire to Heraclitus. He continues:

> Wretched Aristotle! who taught them dialectic, that art of building up and demolishing, so protean in statement, so far-fetched in conjecture, so unyielding in controversy, so productive of disputes; self-stultifying, since it is ever handling questions but never settling anything … What is there in common between Athens and Jerusalem? What between the Academy [of Plato] and the Church? What between heretics and Christians? … Away with all projects for a "Stoic," a "Platonic," or a "dialectic" Christianity! After Christ Jesus we desire no subtle theories, no acute enquiries after the gospel.
>
> (*Prescription of Heretics* 7)

For Tertullian, scripture and apostolic tradition are sufficient to demonstrate all the truths of Christianity, and they are also sufficient to refute all false doctrines. One of

Figure 5.2   Renaissance artist Raphael painted *The School of Athens*, which includes such notable ancient philosophers as Socrates, Plato, Aristotle, and Pythagoras. Unlike Tertullian and some other early Christians, Renaissance scholars were happy to claim inspiration from the great philosophical minds of the past.

Tertullian's favorite words in his treatises is "truth," and he was convinced that apostolic Christianity had a monopoly on it, while the heretics and pagan philosophers had none at all. It is precisely in Tertullian's railing against philosophy that his training as a lawyer comes most clearly to the fore. Tertullian views Christianity as his client, for whom he is an advocate. His role as advocate is to win the case by demolishing the opposition; there is no question of compromise in the courtroom. Despite his excited rhetoric, however, he is not completely convincing. His descriptions of the Trinity as three persons but one substance owe more to Greek philosophy, and even Greek theater, than to scripture. Tertullian was trained in the philosophy of the Greeks and Romans, and he was not above using ideas gleaned from philosophy to make his points.

It is ironic that Tertullian's strict interpretation of Christianity eventually led him to join a splinter group called the Montanists (more on this group below), a sect that was later viewed by the Great Church (i.e. the group that eventually came to dominate) as heretical. Despite his membership in this heretical group, however, Tertullian's writings continued to be valued for their ingenuity and their forcefulness, if not for their subtlety. Some two centuries after his death, another famous North African theologian, Augustine of Hippo, attempted to rehabilitate Tertullian's orthodoxy, claiming that he recanted his Montanist beliefs on his deathbed and returned to the arms of the orthodox church. No evidence of such a recantation exists, however, and it would have been contrary to Tertullian's personality to have admitted such a gross error on his part. Tertullian's association with the Montanists, like Origen's adoption of ideas later considered heterodox some 50 years later, only serves to demonstrate the impossibility of using the term *orthodox* at this early stage of Christian history. The church was still struggling with many ideas, trying some on for size. Tertullian's rejection of philosophy as contrary to the needs and benefit of the church was one idea that ultimately did not fit.

Justin Martyr, Philo, and Clement of Alexandria

Justin Martyr was born in Palestine in about 100. A son of pagan parents, he was attracted to various schools of Greek philosophy at points in his life, including Stoicism, Pythagoreanism, and Platonism. One day while walking along the seashore, a Christian challenged him to read the Hebrew prophets, whom he said would satisfy Justin's longing for a true knowledge of God. Justin became convinced that Christ was the fulfillment of the words of the prophets and the source of divine truth, so from that point on he traveled from place to place as an itinerant Christian teacher, having concluded that Christianity was the true philosophy. Justin was convinced that all those who live according to reason are Christians, including such pre-Christian Greek philosophers as Socrates and Heraclitus (*Apology* 1.46). Even though he had not found the answers he sought in Greek philosophy – and he was convinced that they were not there – he saw value in philosophy. The problem with philosophy was not that it was contrary to the teachings of Christ but that it fell short of Christ's teaching. Thus Plato, for example, could enlighten a person and assist him on the road to true knowledge, but the highest form of wisdom was found only in Christ (*Apology* 2.13). Justin set up philosophical schools in Ephesus and Rome to teach Christianity, and he was martyred for his faith in 165.

While Tertullian was busy in Carthage churning out polemical treatises, in Alexandria, Egypt, some 2,000 kilometers to the east, another Christian scholar was doing his part to promote Christianity, but in a very different way. Clement was the leader of a catechetical school in Alexandria (i.e. a school for Christian training). In addition to studying with Pantaenus, the previous master of the school, Clement had traveled widely and studied with many other teachers as well, some Christian, some not. In fact, he was converted to Christianity in the course of his studies, which took him to Greece, Mesopotamia, and Palestine. Clement valued the Hebrew legacy of Christianity, but he valued Greek philosophy even more highly, especially the teachings of Plato. His attraction to Plato also led him to study the works of Philo, an Alexandrian Jew who was a contemporary of Jesus. Platonists in the first century advocated reading the legends of the Greek gods allegorically rather than literally, in order to find a deeper meaning in the stories than a superficial reading might produce. Philo, a Platonist himself (he was also influenced by other Greek philosophies, including Stoicism), applied the allegorical method to his study of the Jewish scriptures, and he discovered in the Hebrew Bible (in the LXX version) many of the teachings of Plato. However, Platonic doctrine in the Hebrew Bible predated Plato himself, Philo said, being found on the lips of Moses. According to Philo, Plato learned his philosophy by studying the works of Moses, so by implication, reading the scripture through Platonic eyes was bound to produce a greater understanding of the sacred text.

One particular way in which Philo anticipated certain later Christian emphases was his discussion of the *logos*. The word *logos* was used by the Stoics and other Greek philosophers to denote the divine mind or the rational principle that lay behind the universe. From a Platonic perspective, as Philo described it, the *logos* was the Form of Forms, or the Idea of Ideas, that is, the principle that lay behind all of reality. Philo was not just a student of Greek philosophy, however. He was also a student of the Hebrew Bible, so he also described the *logos* in terms more amenable to the Jewish scriptures, such as the spoken, creative word of God. The *logos* is also the first-born of the Father (God), a clear parallel to later Christian thought about Christ. It is possible, perhaps probable, that Philo's idea of the *logos* lies behind the pronouncements about the *logos* in the first chapter of the Gospel of John. It was certainly influential in the later Christian understanding of John's *logos* passage. Philo was so influential among Christians, in fact, that Jerome, the fifth-century translator of the Latin Vulgate, considered Philo to be one of the "ecclesiastical writers," despite being a Jew who never converted to Christianity (*On Famous Men* 11)!

Though Clement was born about 100 years after Philo's death, Philo's influence on him is unmistakable, but Clement was a creative thinker in his own right as well. In addition to incorporating Philo's doctrine of the *logos* into Christianity by explicitly identifying the *logos* as Christ, Clement had a positive attitude about the value of Greek philosophy in general. In fact, Clement said that philosophy for the Greeks played the same role that the Law (*torah*) did for the Jews.

> For philosophy was a "schoolmaster" to bring the Greek mind to Christ, as the Law brought the Hebrews. Thus philosophy was a preparation, paving the way towards perfection in Christ.
>
> (*Stromateis* 1.5.28)

Clement's approach to philosophy was even more positive than Justin's, although he agreed with Justin that philosophy by itself was incomplete.

Clement's affection for Platonism led him to regard certain forms of Christian Gnosticism with greater favor than any other early Christian writer now considered orthodox. Gnosticism will be described in greater detail below, but for now it suffices to say that its name was derived from *gnosis*, the Greek word meaning *knowledge*, and Gnostics believed that they knew certain truths that ordinary Christians did not know, truths that were beneficial in furthering their relationship with God. For many Gnostics, Plato's philosophy – particularly his theory of Forms and his description of the *demiurge*, or creator god – were foundational to their thinking about the relationship between God and Christ, on the one hand, and humanity, on the other. Clement sometimes used the word *Gnostic* to refer to Christians who made up a sort of spiritual elite. Faith was the starting point for Christians, Clement believed, but *gnosis* was the goal of the Christian life. In the process of moving from faith to knowledge, the believer would become more like God, experiencing freedom from the passions that interfered with the soul's ascent toward God. Despite some similarities between Clement's understanding of Christianity and that of the Gnostics, he objected to Gnosticism on two grounds: first, that it lay outside the historical, apostolic church, and second, that it was offensive to freedom of the will and common sense. Nevertheless, he found discussions with Gnostics to be both stimulating and beneficial.

Clement, like Tertullian, was well-read and knowledgeable about Greek philosophy, but his irenic temperament led him in a different direction. Whereas Tertullian saw the totality of Greek learning as an impediment to Christianity, Clement used the poets and philosophers to build bridges between the Christians and the Greeks, in order to bring them to Christianity. He was particularly interested in presenting Christianity in a positive way to those inquirers who had a solid background in the classics of the Greco-Roman educational system. Most Christians found Tertullian's approach toward philosophy too dismissive of an important part of Greco-Roman intellectual and cultural heritage, yet they also found Clement's attitude toward philosophy a little too close for comfort to the Gnostics. What was needed was a viable mediating position that could provide a way forward.

Origen

> The scriptures were written by the Spirit of God, and have a meaning, not such only
> as is apparent at first sight, but also another, which escapes the notice of most.
>
> (Origen, *On First Principles* 1.8)

Origen succeeded Clement as head of the Alexandrian catechetical school in 203, when he was only 18 years old. He was a brilliant student, hence his appointment as head of the school, but his personality was quite different from Clement's. Whereas Clement had a natural inclination toward reconciling opposing viewpoints, Origen – particularly as a young man – was more of a rigorist. He had even reportedly castrated himself in accordance with his understanding of Jesus' teachings, making himself a eunuch for the sake of the kingdom of heaven (Matt 19:12), though some scholars think this story was circulated by his enemies, who wanted to discredit him. He was certainly more critical of the Gnostics than Clement had been, refusing to pray with them (i.e. refusing to acknowledge them as true Christians). Although he studied philosophy and considered it valuable, he never accorded it the same weight that Clement did. In a letter he wrote to his former student Gregory (the Wonderworker), Origen says,

> And I would wish that you should take with you on the one hand those parts of the
> philosophy of the Greeks which are fit, as it were, to serve as general or preparatory
> studies for Christianity, and on the other hand so much of Geometry and Astronomy
> as may be helpful for the interpretation of the Holy Scriptures. The children of the
> philosophers speak of geometry and music and grammar and rhetoric and astronomy
> as being ancillary to philosophy; and in the same way we might speak of philosophy
> itself as being ancillary to Christianity.
>
> (*To Gregory* 1)

One of Origen's primary interests was evangelism, and he engaged in debates with both Gnostics and Jews in attempts to persuade them of the truth of the Christian faith, as he understood it. He wrote many commentaries on books of the Bible, both Old Testament and New Testament (although the New Testament had not yet achieved its final shape), and many letters and treatises as well. His greatest single scholarly undertaking, however, was the creation of the *Hexapla*, a six-columned Old Testament containing the Jewish scripture in Hebrew, in Greek transliteration of Hebrew (for the purposes of pronunciation), and in several different Greek translations, including the LXX. Origen employed many scribes to create his masterpiece, and he worked on it over a period of perhaps 40 years. His primary purpose in creating the Hexapla was to create an evangelistic tool that Christians could use in their discussions with the Jews, since Origen had noticed, like others before him, that the Hebrew Bible of the Jews differed in significant ways from the Greek LXX of the Christians. He even employed a converted Jew to teach him Hebrew, so that he could work with the Hebrew column of the Hexapla as well as with the Greek columns.

It is clear from Origen's work on the Hexapla, as well as from his other writings, that his approach to Christianity was more "biblical" than Clement's, whose approach might be called "philosophical." It is not true, however, that Origen eschewed classical learning, even in his approach to interpreting the Bible. Origen agreed with some critics of more mainstream Christianity, like the Gnostics and Marcion, that the Bible, if read literally, contained impossibilities and absurdities. For example, Origen said, God was not a farmer who planted a literal garden in the east (Gen 2:8). Jesus' command for Christians to have only one coat or pair of shoes (Matt 10:10) was absurd for those who lived in cold climates. The inclusion of griffins among the list of unclean animals (Lev 11:13 LXX) did not imply the existence of these mythical animals. Origen distinguished three senses in which the scripture could be understood: the literal, moral, and spiritual senses. Of these, the literal understanding of a passage was the least important. Far more important was the ability of Christians to delve into the deep meaning of every passage through intense study and meditation.

The clearest example of Origen's use of philosophy, particularly Neo-Platonism, to interpret scripture is evident in his attempt to explain the relationship between Father, Son, and Holy Spirit – the Trinity. Taking up the language from the Gospel of John that the Son was begotten by the Father (e.g. John 3:16), Origen borrowed from Platonic philosophy to equate the divine *logos*, which for Platonists was the only-begotten Son of the divine Father, with Christ as the divine *logos* in John. Christ was eternally begotten from the Father, just like rays of light that eternally radiate from the sun. Origen's early attempt to explain the Trinity was very influential for Christianity, particularly in the Greek-speaking east.

For reasons not entirely clear, Origen ran into trouble with his bishop Demetrius, perhaps because of Demetrius's jealousy over Origen's growing reputation throughout the entire eastern Mediterranean region, among pagans as well as Christians. Another possible reason for the rift was that Demetrius believed that Origen did not pay him due deference. When Origen was invited to speak in Caesarea and Jerusalem in 215, he accepted without consulting Demetrius. Demetrius responded by condemning Origen's actions. Although the two were reconciled within a few years, a similar incident in 229 led Demetrius to write letters to fellow bishops denigrating Origen. Origen left the catechetical school in Alexandria and established a new school in Caesarea, where he completed work on the Hexapla and was in great demand as a speaker throughout the east.

Around 250, Origen was arrested and tortured during the Decian persecution, the greatest general persecution of Christians by the Romans to that point in time. Although he survived his imprisonment and was eventually released, the harsh treatment he received led to his death in 254. Origen was the greatest theologian of the third century, and he was recognized as the dominant theologian in the East for more than 100 years after his death. As orthodoxy developed in the centuries following Origen, some of his writings were held up to later standards of the Christian doctrinal norm and were found wanting, and 300 years after his death, the church declared certain aspects of his teaching to be heretical. Nevertheless, Origen's influence continued, especially in the East, and today Origen is acknowledged as one of the most important writers and scholars in the early church. His voluminous writings illustrate the viability of integrating a strong commitment to the Bible with the best aspects of Greek philosophy, and for the next 1,250 years or more the church followed Origen's lead.

Key points you need to know

- The earliest Christians were Jews who continued to worship in the temple and in the synagogues for many years, while also worshiping with fellow Christians separately.
- Some early Christians believed that it was necessary for Gentile converts to Christianity to obey Jewish laws and customs, such as circumcision and the observance of Jewish dietary laws, just as the Jewish Christians did.
- Other early Christians, most notably Paul, believed that Gentile converts were under no obligation to follow Jewish laws and customs when they became Christians.
- By the end of the first century C.E., Christianity and Judaism had separated permanently, and Christianity had become a predominantly Gentile religion.
- Tertullian was the leading opponent of using Greco-Roman philosophy as a tool for understanding and interpreting Christianity.
- Justin Martyr and Clement of Alexandria believed that Christianity was the greatest philosophy but that it could be understood better by studying Greco-Roman philosophy.
- Philo of Alexandria, a Jewish scholar who was an older contemporary of Jesus, read the Hebrew Bible allegorically, an approach that was borrowed by later Christian scholars such as Clement and Origen. These Christians, as well as Justin Martyr, also accepted Philo's appreciation for the best elements of Greco-Roman philosophy.
- Origen forged a middle ground between the extremes of Tertullian and Clement of Alexandria, accepting the value of some aspects of Greco-Roman philosophy but grounding his understanding of Christianity in scripture rather than philosophy.

Discussion questions

1. Why did Christianity's demographic shift from being predominantly Jewish to predominantly Gentile push it in the direction of becoming a distinct religion? What historical factors were involved in the split?
2. What factors led to Paul, rather than one of Jesus' original disciples, being the leader of the Gentile mission?
3. Which aspects of Greco-Roman philosophy are most compatible with Christianity? Which are least compatible?
4. How did Christianity's eventual acceptance of many aspects of Greco-Roman philosophy affect the development of Christian doctrine?

Further reading

Clement of Alexandria, *Exhortation to the Heathen*.

Clement of Alexandria, *Stromateis*.

Frend, W. H. C. 1984. *The Rise of Christianity*. Philadelphia, PA: Fortress.

González, Justo 1984–1985. *The Story of Christianity*. 2 vols. New York: HarperSanFrancisco.

González, Justo 1987. *A History of Christian Thought*. Revised edn, 3 vols. Nashville, TN: Abingdon.

Holmes, Michael W. ed. 1999. *The Apostolic Fathers*. Revised edn, Grand Rapids, MI: Baker.

Jerome, *On Famous Men* 11.

Justin Martyr, *Apology*.

Latourette, Kenneth Scott 1975. *A History of Christianity*. Revised edn, 2 vols. New York: Harper & Row.

Origen, *To Gregory* 1.

Pelikan, Jaroslav 1971–1989. *The Christian Tradition: A History of the Development of Doctrine*. 5 vols. Chicago, IL: University of Chicago Press.

Quasten, Johannes and Angelo Di Berardino. 1950–1986. *Patrology*. 4 vols. Vol. 4 translated by Placid Solari. Allen, TX: Christian Classics.

Tertullian, *Against Marcion*.

Tertullian, *Prescription of Heretics*.

Tillich, Paul 1968. *A History of Christian Thought*. Edited by Carl E. Braaten. New York: Simon and Schuster.

6 Conflict and persecution

> But when the magistrate persisted and said, "Swear the oath, and I will release you; revile Christ," Polycarp replied, "For eighty-six years I have been his servant, and he has done me no wrong. How can I blaspheme my King who saved me?"
>
> *(Martyrdom of Polycarp)*

In this chapter

Christianity was not a legally recognized religion in the Roman Empire for almost 300 years after its inception, and Christians suffered sporadic persecutions from the Roman government that grew more intense and widespread beginning about the middle of the third century. As Christianity struggled to present itself as a religion worthy of respect to the Romans, Christians disagreed among themselves concerning some of their core beliefs and practices. The terms orthodoxy and heresy, which could be defined with some precision in later centuries, were not easily distinguished in the earliest centuries of Christianity, as the Church struggled to define itself doctrinally.

Main topics covered

- Definition and discussion of the terms *orthodoxy* and *heresy*
- Dominant early forms of Christianity in several locales
- Marcion, Montanus, and the problem of revelation
- The Apologists and the Great Church
- Early Roman persecutions of Christians
- The first widespread, imperial persecutions
- The Great Persecution

Internal struggles

The use of the term *orthodoxy* to refer to beliefs held before the Council of Nicaea in 325 is an anachronism. The word implies a recognized, at least quasi-official standard, and in the years in which Christianity was an illicit religion within the Roman Empire, such a standard did not exist. It is probably more accurate to say that rather than a single standard, several different standards existed, which differed from one another in detail. In fact, the primary reason that the Emperor Constantine called the Council of Nicaea was to address matters of disagreement among Christians, so that a recognized standard could be created. Of course, some Christians did espouse views during the pre-Constantinian period that agreed well with later official church positions (i.e. orthodoxy), but it was unclear in the earliest period of church history exactly which views would gain approval of the majority of the church and which would not. This conundrum helps explain why renowned Christian scholars like Tertullian and Origen, some of whose ideas formed the basis of later, orthodox Christian thought, had some of their teachings condemned years after their deaths. Both Tertullian and Origen saw themselves as fully within the mainstream of Christian thought, even though their ideas were quite different from one another in some respects. The question of what was orthodox and what was not was a matter that many early Christians discussed, without always reaching consensus. What constituted orthodoxy, and what constituted heresy in the first three centuries of Christianity, and who decided which was which?

Orthodoxy and heresy

In his seminal 1934 book *Orthodoxy and Heresy in Earliest Christianity* (original German title *Rechtgläubigkeit und Ketzerei im ältesten Christentum*), Walter Bauer proposed the provocative idea that the earliest form of Christianity that was established in many areas was a form that in later times would have been considered heretical. The traditional understanding of the rise of heresy – that is, that it developed in various areas out of orthodox congregations when a heretical teacher caused some to deviate from the norms of Christianity – was historically inaccurate for many geographical regions, Bauer claimed. Instead, the very earliest form of Christianity itself deviated from the later norm in many places.

Independent from the time of the dissolution of the Seleucid Empire (*c.* 132 B.C.E.) until it was annexed by Rome and became a Roman province in 214 C.E., Osroene was a small state on the border between the Roman and Parthian Empires. The capital city was Edessa, the center of culture and linguistic production in the region, both before and after the Romans gained control of it. One tradition says that King Abgar V of Edessa exchanged letters with Jesus, who promised to send one of his disciples to heal him of a disease. After Jesus' resurrection, Thaddaeus, one of 70 apostles commissioned by Jesus prior to his death, came to Edessa and cured Abgar. Historians attribute no historical value to the legend of Jesus and Abgar, but it is clear that people who identified themselves as Christians were living in Edessa by the middle of the second century. In fact, a number of different Christian groups, with quite different points of view, could be found in Edessa by the late second century. Included in this number were followers of Marcion, Bar Daisan (or Bardesanes), and Tatian. These teachers held beliefs that differed from later orthodoxy in different ways. Marcion rejected the Old Testament, because he believed that the God found there was different from the God described in the New Testament as the Father of Jesus Christ. Bar Daisan preached a version of Christianity that was influenced by Gnosticism. Tatian practiced an extremely ascetic form of Christianity that forbade marriage and the begetting of children. At the end of the third century yet another important figure associated with Edessa, Mani, combined aspects of Gnosticism with Christian teachings. It is unclear when those Christians whose views corresponded most closely with later orthodoxy – they might be called proto-orthodox – appeared in Edessa, but if they were present in the second and third centuries, they were apparently a small minority. Not until the fourth century did noteworthy "orthodox" Christians, such as the bishop Kune and the poet and scholar Ephrem Syrus, arise in Edessa. Evidence of the prominence of "heterodox" Christianity in the earlier period is the fact that the first Christian king, Abgar IX, was a convert of Bar Daisan's, and the preferred gospel of Syriac Christians from the second century and for several centuries thereafter was Tatian's *Diatessaron*, a gospel harmony. In the fifth century the bishop Rabbula established orthodoxy by force in Edessa, removing copies of the *Diatessaron* from the churches and replacing them with translations of the four separate gospels.

The situation of Christianity in Egypt in the pre-Constantinian era was similar to that in Edessa. Later tradition says that Christianity was introduced into Egypt by Mark, the author of the gospel and an associate of Peter and Paul, but the exact manner in which Christianity entered Egypt is unknown. What is known is that by the late second and early third centuries, when Clement and Origen were leading the catechetical school in Alexandria, a wide variety of people who saw themselves as Christians were in Egypt, including followers of Marcion and several Gnostic Christian groups associated with Basilides, Carpocrates, and Valentinus. An early document called the Gospel of the Egyptians was Gnostic, and another called the Gospel of the Hebrews (i.e. Jewish Christians; there was a large Jewish community in Alexandria) was also influenced by Gnosticism. Among the cache of ancient Christian writings found in Nag Hammadi, Egypt, in 1945, most of the writings were Gnostic, and none was exclusively "orthodox" in nature. Writings associated with Peter, including the canonical 2 Peter and the noncanonical Preaching of Peter and Apocalypse of Peter, were also associated with Egypt, perhaps testifying to now-lost traditions involving Peter's association with Egypt. Though proto-orthodox Christians were present in Egypt from at least the second century, and probably in the first as well (was Apollos an "orthodox" Christian when he was in Alexandria? cf. Acts 18:24–26), they were not clearly the dominant group until at least the third, and probably the fourth century.

One type of Christianity which Bauer mentions in passing but which probably deserves greater attention is the Jewish Christianity that is evident in Egypt, Asia Minor, Palestine, and elsewhere. Jewish Christians, as noted above, continued for several decades to associate themselves with the temple and synagogue, and even after their ultimate separation from mainstream Rabbinic Judaism toward the end of the first century, many Jewish Christians continued to put an emphasis on the importance of the law. They often had their own gospels – such as the Gospel of the Hebrews, the Gospel of the Nazoreans, and the Gospel of the Ebionites (though these may not have been three separate works) – while some groups apparently preferred the Gospel of Matthew, the most Jewish of the gospels in some ways. Paul combated Jewish Christianity in Asia Minor already in the first century, and diatribes against the Jews, such as a section in the Epistle of Barnabas, were probably inspired by conflicts between mainstream, Gentile Christianity and Jewish Christianity. Jewish Christianity was undoubtedly the dominant form of Christianity in Palestine until at least the early part of the second century, though it is impossible to determine exactly what its beliefs were. It is probable, however, that many Jewish Christians continued to insist on at least a modified adherence to the Law of Moses, even for Gentile converts (Acts 15:1–31). Some Jewish Christians also questioned the Virgin Birth and the divinity of Christ.

With the large number of Christianities available to people, how could one strain rise to the top and establish itself as the preferred version? Such a Christianity would require an ancient pedigree, a sizeable following, persuasive communication tools, and an effective enforcement mechanism. All four of these desiderata were present in Rome. By the time Christianity reached the Eternal City, as it is sometimes called, Rome had risen from a small hamlet almost 800 years earlier to become the capital of the greatest empire in the world. The largest city in the empire, it was a magnet for people of every ethnic and national background and creed, including nascent Christianity. Christianity arrived in Rome without fanfare, probably sometime in the first two decades after Jesus' death. As is the case with most other large cities in the Roman Empire, the person who first brought Christianity to Rome is unknown, but the Roman church has traditionally looked back to the two leading figures in first-century Christianity as its founders: Peter and Paul. Although neither apostle was the literal founder of the church in Rome, both Peter and Paul made their way to Rome sometime before the mid-60s, and both perished during the Neronian persecution of Christians. Peter was widely recognized as the leader of the original 12 disciples, and some saw him in a sense as Christ's successor. Despite being a Jew himself, Paul was the leading protagonist of Gentile Christianity, the Apostle to the Gentiles. Having these two men associated with the earliest days of the church in Rome gave the church there great authority in its debates with its rivals over the right to assert the correct form of Christianity. This authority was recognized outside Rome as well; for example, Irenaeus of Gaul, one of the leading apologists for Christianity (see below), writes in his book *Against Heresies*, "It is a matter of necessity that every Church should agree with this Church [Rome], on account of its pre-eminent authority, that is, the faithful everywhere …" (*Against Heresies* 3.3.2).

Because Rome was the largest city in the empire, its church quickly became the largest in the empire as well. It was also the richest, as the Roman church attracted increasing numbers of merchants and upper class members to supplement the members of the lower class who made up the bulk of the church in the city. Marcion, for example, was a wealthy shipbuilder from Pontus in Asia Minor who joined the Roman church around 140 and donated a large amount of money. When leaders of the Roman church discovered that Marcion's teachings concerning Christianity were significantly different from their own, they returned his donation and excommunicated him from the church. The fact that the church could so easily refund a large donation several years later indicates the level of wealth that the church had attained. With wealth, a large membership, and association with the capital city came influence, and the church in Rome from an early time asserted its authority without compunction. Already at the end of the first century, Clement, the bishop of the Roman church (or perhaps one of a handful of influential leaders), wrote a letter to the church in Corinth, giving advice and admonishing the church to follow his instructions. Subsequent bishops of Rome were no less shy about asserting their authority over other churches, particularly in smaller cities and towns. In the following century Victor, bishop of Rome, claimed the authority to excommunicate the churches of the Roman province of Asia for their improper observance of Easter (Eusebius, *Church History* 5.24.9); although his efforts were ultimately unsuccessful, it is clear that he believed he had the authority to act unilaterally in the matter on behalf of the majority of the church. At the Council of Nicaea in 325, Rome was declared to be one of the primary seats of Christianity, along with Alexandria and Antioch, an official recognition of an authority that had long existed, so its voice in questions of orthodoxy was a dominant one.

One of the most important tools for communicating the content of the Christian message in encapsulated form was the creed. The word *creed* comes from the Latin word *credo*, meaning "I believe." New believers were taught the creed, and they were expected to say it when they were initiated into the church through baptism. The New Testament speaks frequently of traditions passed down from the earliest days of the church (e.g. 1 Cor 11:23–25; 2 Thess 2:15; Jude 3), but only in 1 Cor 15:3–7 does it approach anything close to the creed as it was recited in the later church:

> For I handed on to you as of first importance what I in turn had received: that Christ died for our sins in accordance with the scriptures, and that he was buried, and that he was raised on the third day in accordance with the scriptures, and that he appeared to Cephas [Peter], then to the twelve. Then he appeared to more than five hundred brothers and sisters at one time, most of whom are still alive, though some have died. Then he appeared to James, then to all the apostles.

Creeds were also called *symbols* or *rules of the faith*. They developed rapidly in the second century, with different but similar forms used in different places. Ignatius, Justin Martyr, Irenaeus, and Tertullian all bear witness to a common, though not yet fixed,

The Apostles' Creed

I believe in God the Father almighty, creator of heaven and earth;

    And in Jesus Christ, his only Son, our Lord, who was conceived by the Holy Spirit, born from the Virgin Mary, suffered under Pontius Pilate, was crucified, dead and buried, descended to hell, on the third day rose again from the dead, ascended to heaven, sits at the right hand of God the Father almighty, thence he will come to judge the living and the dead;

    I believe in the Holy Spirit, the holy catholic Church, the communion of saints, the remission of sins, the resurrection of the flesh, and eternal life. Amen

(Kelly 1972: 369)

testimony of the faith, in which Christ was born of the Virgin, crucified under Pontius Pilate, raised from the dead, and ascended into heaven. It is significant that all these witnesses to early forms of the creed come from the west, that is, from churches that were likely to recognize the primacy of Rome – and of course, Justin himself was in Rome, so his version of the creed probably reflects that in common use there. The creed used in Rome became the dominant creed used in the west by the third century. Eastern Christians undoubtedly had similar formulations – Origen alludes to them – but no early version of an eastern creed has been preserved. When the Council of Nicaea adopted an official creed in 325, though it was probably based on an eastern creed, such as that used in Caesarea, it closely resembled that used in Rome. The Apostles' Creed, which came to be the standard creed in the west, was based on the traditional creed of Rome. (See Boxes in this chapter for the full text of the Apostles' Creed and in Chapter 7 for the text of the Nicene Creed.)

    Creeds were used to teach the basics of the faith to new believers, but they also served to distinguish those who accepted the creed from others who called themselves Christians but had a very different understanding of the faith, such as the Ebionites, Marcionites, and Gnostics. The clauses of the creed were developed over time to teach certain very specific ("orthodox") doctrines, or to counteract certain teachings considered false ("heretical"). For example, the clause that says Jesus suffered and died under Pontius Pilate combats the Gnostic idea that the Christ was a spirit and did not suffer. The clause proclaiming the virgin birth counteracts the Ebionite teaching that Jesus was born through natural sexual reproduction. Clauses in the later creeds about God as creator of heaven and earth stress the continuity of the God of the Old Testament with the God of the New Testament, countering Marcionism. Clauses that specified that Jesus was begotten, not made, and of one substance with the Father were added by the Council of Nicaea to counteract Arianism (see below). Creeds were concise expressions of the faith that could easily be learned and transmitted by the faithful. They proved to be effective tools for communicating what many held to be the essence of the Christian faith. The fact that the creed used in Rome came to dominate the west and influence the east was an important step in establishing the Roman church as the standard for orthodox teaching.

The church in Rome had all the prerequisites for establishing its understanding of Christianity as the standard for others to follow. Its claim to an ancient origin and founders without peer was unmatched by a church in any other locale. Its status as the church in the largest city in the Roman Empire, the capital, ensured that large numbers of people, both in and out of Rome, would recognize its authority. Its development of a creed that was widely accepted guaranteed that its message would be promulgated widely, and the creed was soon supplemented by two other tools that helped it communicate and define its faith: the canon and apostolic succession. All that the Roman church lacked to establish itself as the champion of orthodoxy was the means to enforce its decisions. As noted above, when Victor of Rome tried to excommunicate the churches of Asia in the second century, he was unsuccessful, being opposed even by other Christians in the West. As the years went on, however, the authority of Rome in the West became almost absolute, and its influence in the East was also considerable. In the fourth and fifth centuries, as the Germanic tribes encroached on Roman territory in the West and eventually conquered the entire western part of the empire, the only position of power from Roman times that remained standing was the bishop of Rome, also known as the pope. When Alexandria, Antioch, and Jerusalem fell to the Muslims in the sixth century, the authority of the Roman church was further increased. Rome, which had been a standard-bearer for what became the orthodox position from earliest times emerged as the primary champion of the proto-orthodox cause in the West as early as the third century, and its influence even in the East continued to grow over the next few centuries. Heresy – that is, visions of Christianity that differed markedly from the view of the majority in Rome from at least the early second century and from the view of the majority in Alexandria and Antioch from at least the fourth century – faced a formidable opponent in an orthodoxy that was recognized in both the East and the West. The struggle between orthodoxy and heresy was one that orthodoxy was destined to win, but only after a tremendous struggle to define the faith.

Marcion, Montanus, and the problem of revelation

> Marcion is more savage than even the beasts of that barbarous region [Pontus]. For what beaver was ever a greater emasculator than he who has abolished the nuptial bond? What Pontic mouse ever had such gnawing powers as he who has gnawed the Gospels to pieces?
>
> (Tertullian, *Against Marcion* 1.1)

Christianity's center of gravity in the second century was Asia Minor, a primarily Greek-speaking region that was home to important cities such as Ephesus, Pergamum, Smyrna, Hieropolis, and Sardis. All of these cities, and many others, were home to sizeable Christian populations, and Asia Minor was the part of the Roman Empire where Christians were the most heavily represented among the general population. It is not surprising, then, that two of the most important and controversial figures in the early church, Marcion and Montanus, were both born in this region. Both men advocated understandings of Christianity that were radically different than the forms of Christianity that were practiced by the majority of believers in Christ, and both were charismatic individuals who attracted large followings. In their own ways, both claimed to understand better than their contemporaries the true nature of the Christian message, and the churches they established rivaled the proto-orthodox churches for ascendancy for 100 years or more.

Marcion's historical impact on Christianity can hardly be overemphasized, and twentieth- century historian Adolf von Harnack called him the founder of a new religion. Marcion was the son of the Christian bishop of Sinope in Pontus, Asia Minor, and he became rich as a shipbuilder. He traveled to Rome about 140, joined the church, and donated a large sum of money, but as his ideas about Christianity developed, his contemporaries in Rome, including Justin Martyr, became increasingly opposed to his teachings. In the middle of the second century, the term "scripture" was still used by Christians to refer to the Old Testament, and while collections of Christian writings existed, no fixed list of books was widely accepted. Indeed, the importance of creating an authoritative list of Christian writings was not yet acknowledged. When Marcion read the Old Testament, he saw a god who was jealous and vindictive, who loved one group of people and hated others, who was capricious and mean-spirited, ordering his followers to kill the women and children in the land of Canaan when they captured it. In contrast, when Marcion read the Christian writings, he saw Jesus as someone who preached peace, love, and reconciliation for all people. Jesus had no favorites, and he had no enemies. Jesus was the messenger of a god who was quite different from the warrior god of the Old Testament. Yes, that god was powerful enough to create the world (Marcion called him the *demiurge*, or creator-god), but he was morally and intellectually deficient. For Marcion, Jesus represented a "foreign god," one who, far from being revealed in the Jewish scriptures, was unknown prior to the advent of Jesus Christ.

Marcion advocated a break between Judaism and Christianity that was far more radical than the rejection of the law. Instead of interpreting passages from the Hebrew Bible as pointing to Jesus as the Christ, Marcion discarded the Hebrew Bible in its entirety, along with any connection between Judaism and Christianity. Marcion believed that Jesus was a spiritual being whose association with the Jews was purely coincidental and completely unimportant. He founded churches in Rome and Asia Minor, and Marcionite churches grew and expanded rapidly over the next century. As scripture, Marcion modified the Gospel of Luke, removing the first two chapters, which describe Jesus' birth, and also "correcting" the rest of the gospel in places where Marcion believed it had been corrupted by Judaizing influences (i.e. those passages that spoke positively of the creative activities of God or that associated Jesus' teachings with the Old Testament). Marcion saw Paul as the ultimate interpreter of Christianity, so he also included ten letters of Paul (omitting the Pastoral Epistles) in his list of authoritative Christian writings. Marcion has often been classified as a Gnostic, and indeed his Docetic understanding of Jesus, his rejection of the creator god of the Old Testament, and his tendency toward dualism are features shared with the Gnostics (see below for a more extensive description of Gnosticism), but certain features of Marcion's interpretation of the Christian message differ from that of the Gnostics. Chief among these is the fact that Marcion claimed no secret knowledge (*gnosis*); on the contrary, he believed himself to be expounding the pure form of Christianity previously proclaimed by Paul, and based on the truth of Jesus' own teachings. Furthermore, Marcion's Christianity was based on traditional Christian writings – scripture – that were also accepted by other Christians, albeit in an altered form, especially in the case of the Gospel of Luke.

Some of the greatest scholars of the proto-orthodox church – Justin Martyr, Irenaeus, Tertullian, Clement of Alexandria, and Origen, among others – wrote against Marcion and his followers. Nevertheless, Marcionism flourished for several centuries, especially in the East. The form of Christianity that Marcion advocated was attractive to many people, and it proved powerful enough to its followers that Marcionite Christians suffered alongside proto-orthodox Christians in the great Roman persecutions of the second, third, and fourth centuries (Eusebius, *Church History* 4.15.46; 5.16.21; 7.12.1). After orthodox Christianity was accepted as the official religion of the Roman Empire in the late fourth century, some Marcionites were persecuted and forcibly converted, while others either turned to orthodox Christianity or drifted into other religions, such as Manichaeism. The heyday of Marcionite Christianity was over by the fifth century, though groups of Marcionites probably continued in existence for some time thereafter.

Montanus was a contemporary of Marcion and also from Asia Minor, probably from the province of Phrygia, where the movement was centered. Montanus was raised as a pagan, and only in 155 or so was he converted to Christianity. Unlike Marcion, Montanus embraced the Old Testament, and he was particularly impressed with the writings of the prophets. He saw himself as a prophet who received direct revelations from the Holy Spirit, and he even sometimes referred to himself as the *Paraclete*, a word used in the Gospel of John to refer to the Holy Spirit. He was accompanied by two women, Priscilla and Maximilla, who proclaimed themselves to be prophetesses who also heard the Spirit of God. Montanus taught that Christians were living in the last days, in the Age of the Spirit, and he advocated a rigorous moral life, in anticipation of the imminent return of Christ to earth in Pepuza, a city in Asia Minor.

Montanus claimed that the prophecies of himself and his associates – "The Three," as they were sometimes called – had the same authority as the Old Testament and the writings of Christian authors that were beginning to be gathered into authoritative collections. In fact, they said that their prophecies were the final revelation of God. They often purported to speak under the immediate influence of the Holy Spirit, prophesying in ecstatic utterances – that is, unintelligible words – as they were directed by the Spirit. The church of Montanism spread throughout Asia Minor, to Rome, and to North Africa, where Montanism won its most famous convert, Tertullian, early in the third century. Tertullian was attracted to Montanism because of the rigorous discipline that it imposed upon its followers, since he, too, was critical of the lax behavior of many Christians and the pollution of Christianity by paganism, for example, through its contacts with Greek philosophy. Theologically, Montanism was quite similar to proto-orthodox Christianity, but it differed in having a stricter moral code: celibacy was encouraged, widows and widowers were not allowed to remarry, and Christians who had committed a grave sin would not be forgiven. It also differed from proto-orthodox Christianity in the authority it assigned to the prophecies of Montanus, Priscilla, and Maximilla.

Despite their significant differences, Marcionism and Montanism shared an emphasis on the importance of Christians living chaste, moral lives. Another similarity was that they both based their belief systems on the interpretation of a single charismatic leader, rather than following the judgment of the Great Church, as the proto-orthodox sometimes called themselves, a church that was widespread geographically and could claim important teachers from the beginning of the second century and even earlier. The differences between the teachings of Marcion and Montanus on the one hand and the proto-orthodox church on the other revolved around the question of *revelation*. In what ways had God communicated, and in what ways did God continue to communicate, with Christians? Marcion restricted God's revelation to a modified form of Luke and ten letters of Paul, discarding both the Old Testament and other Christian writings that were widely accepted in many Christian communities. In contrast, Montanus accepted as authoritative both the Old Testament and a wide range of Christian writings in current circulation, including the gospels of Matthew, Mark, and John, the book of Acts, and the other three Pauline epistles, but he also ranked the prophecies which he and his female associates received as equivalent in value and authority with those other writings.

The proto-orthodox church disagreed with the claims about revelation that both the Marcionites and the Montanists made. They deemed the canon of Marcion to be too restricted, and they considered that of Montanus to be too expansive. In comparison with the view of contemporary proto-orthodox Christians, Marcion's canon was "orthodox *minus*," while Montanus's was "orthodox *plus*." As noted in the previous chapter, one way in which the Great Church responded to Marcion and Montanus was by beginning to assemble a canon of their own. Already in the second century the majority of Christians in many locations in both the East and the West accepted the four gospels of modern Christianity, the book of Acts, 13 letters of Paul, and at least three of the so-called catholic epistles, along with the entirety of the Old Testament. Like the creed, the canon was a tool that helped to define the beliefs of the church, and it also helped to distinguish the proto-orthodox from those whose canons were substantially different. In addition to the Marcionites and Montanists, this group included all those Christians who accepted gospels other than Matthew, Mark, Luke, and John, and it also included the Gnostics, who had their own set of sacred writings. By adopting a canon, the church proclaimed that while God might continue to be revealed to people in the contemporary era, these purported revelations could be checked against a set standard: the canon of scripture.

The Apologists and the Great Church

> We have come, not to flatter you by this writing, nor please you by our address, but to beg that you pass judgment, after an accurate and searching investigation, not flattered by prejudice or by a desire of pleasing superstitious men, nor induced by irrational impulse or evil rumors which have long been prevalent, to give a decision which will prove to be against yourselves. For as for us, we reckon that no evil can be done us, unless we be convicted as evil-doers, or be proved to be wicked men; and you, you can kill, but not hurt us.
>
> (Justin Martyr, *First Apology* 2)

If such a large number of different version of Christianity existed in the second and third centuries, how did one version – the proto-orthodox – manage to achieve its status as the authoritative, or orthodox, form of Christianity? Tools such as the creed and the canon, which were developed in different locations but through collaboration among Christians from many areas, were important factors in the emergence of orthodoxy. However, neither the creed nor the canon in and of themselves had the power to convince people of the correctness of the Great Church. What was needed were persuasive writers who could both champion the proto-orthodox position and combat other points of view. The Great Church produced several such writers, or *Apologists*, and over the course of about two centuries their writings laid the groundwork for the triumph of what Christians today now call orthodoxy. Although the word *apology* in modern parlance usually means to express sorrow and ask forgiveness for a wrong done to another, the Greek word *apologia* means something entirely different. An apology in the Greek sense means a defense of one's beliefs, and the early Apologists were adept at expressing their Christian faith in persuasive and disarming ways. The Apologists fought their literary battles on two fronts. On the one hand, they opposed others who called themselves Christians but whose views differed significantly from their own. On the other hand, they presented the case to the Roman government that Christianity was reasonable, that Christians made good Roman citizens, and that outlandish accusations made against Christians were false.

As noted above, Justin Martyr was a Christian teacher who set up philosophical schools in Ephesus and Rome to teach what he believed to be the highest philosophy, Christianity. Two of his writings that have been preserved are apologies addressed to the Roman emperor Hadrian on behalf of Christianity. Justin notes that Christians are sometimes accused of being atheists, and it is true that, like Socrates, Christians reject the Greek gods as false. However, since they worship the true God, "the Father of righteousness and temperance and the other virtues, who is free from all impurity" (*Apol.* 1.6), as well as Jesus Christ, the divine Reason (*logos*) sent from God, they cannot honestly be called atheists. It is true that Christians talk about establishing the kingdom of God, Justin says, but the kingdom of which they speak is not an earthly kingdom, so it is no threat to Rome. On the contrary, since Christians follow Jesus' commands to live honorable lives, pray for their enemies, eschew violence, and obey the lawful civil government, they are model citizens. In many ways, Justin says, even though the word "Christian" is new, the religion itself is not new, for all who have lived according to the principles of reason (*logos*), whether Greek or barbarian (i.e. non-Greek), were Christians, though their knowledge was incomplete. Christ himself was the first "whole rational being, both body, and reason, and soul" (*Apol.* 2.10). Although Justin focuses primarily on the defense of Christianity to the Romans, he also refutes the teachings of Marcion, whom he says is being driven by demons to proclaim that God the Father of Jesus Christ is not the creator of the world. In another work, the *Dialog with Trypho*, Justin criticizes both the Marcionites and the followers of various Gnostic teachers for leading people astray. The fact that they are not true Christians, Justin says, is demonstrated by the fact that all these movements are named after their founders, whereas Christianity (i.e. his proto-orthodox understanding of Christianity) is named after Christ.

About 30 years after Justin, another Christian with a background in Greek philosophy wrote to the emperor Marcus Aurelius to urge him to stop treating Christians as enemies of the state. Athenagoras of Athens starts his letter by noting that Rome allows people all over the empire to worship whatever gods they want, so Christians should not be unjustly persecuted just for bearing the name of Christ. Some charges leveled against Christians are patently false, he says. For example, Christians are sometimes accused of atheism, but in fact they acknowledge one true God, whom they worship as Father, Son, and Holy Spirit. He notes that Greek philosophers themselves deny the literal existence of the Greek gods, and they often allegorize stories about the gods, equating Zeus with fire and Hera with the earth, for example. Some philosophers even say that those now acknowledged as gods were originally mortal humans. Another charge sometimes leveled against Christians is that they are cannibals, consuming human flesh (a charge probably based on the Eucharistic meal, in which the bread and wine are called the body and blood of Christ). How could Christians be cannibals, Athenagoras asks, when they not only forbid killing, but they also avoid gladiatorial contests, where killing occurs, and they condemn abortion and infanticide? A third charge leveled against Christians is that they engage in incest. This charge, based on the Christian practice of calling one another brother and sister, is ludicrous, Athenagoras says, because Christ taught that for a man even to look upon a woman with lust was as serious as adultery. Christians are people of high moral character, as any careful investigation will demonstrate, he tells the emperor.

Tertullian's objections to Greek philosophy and his eventual decision to follow the Montanist form of Christianity have already been noted, but Tertullian is also one of the most important apologists of the early church. Like the other apologists already mentioned, Tertullian urges Roman rulers to observe the moral lifestyle of Christians and realize that they are no threat to the empire. In his *Apology*, he argues that Christians are rounded up and punished simply for bearing the name of Christ, not for any actual misdeeds. It is true that some people allege that Christians commit atrocities, such as devouring children and engaging in incestuous relationships, but these charges are baseless, as any fair investigation would demonstrate, Tertullian says. In fact, a careful review of the lives of many who call themselves Christians will show that they became much better people after their conversion. Tertullian reviews many of the Greek and Roman myths, as well as aspects of Greco-Roman history, in order to demonstrate the innumerable examples of murder, rape, incest, dishonesty, and immorality that prevail in these accounts. It is unjust, he says, for those whose ancestors have committed such things to presume to judge Christians, of whom such acts are merely (and falsely) alleged. Christians are ideal Roman citizens, who are loyal to and pray for the emperor.

In addition to his *Apology* to the Romans, Tertullian also defends the proto-orthodox understanding of the faith against those with different understandings of Christianity. One of the primary reasons that Tertullian is so adamantly opposed to Greek philosophy is that many of the heresies that he opposes draw strength from the philosophical systems of the Stoics or Platonists. For example, he traces Valentinian Gnosticism to the teachings of Plato and Marcionism to the teachings of the Stoics. In contrast, Tertullian roots the Christian faith firmly in the soil of the Jewish scriptures, with Christ as the fulfillment of numerous messianic prophecies. Tertullian unleashes a torrid critique of Marcion, against whom he wrote five books. He focuses much of his attention on Marcion's "unknown god," who, contrary to what Marcion says, is not a better god at all, according to Tertullian. Marcion's god does not punish sin and allows injustice to prevail and so is a weak, feeble god. In contrast, Tertullian says, the God of the Old Testament created the universe. Far from hiding from his creation, as Marcion's god did, the true God has always been actively involved in the lives of the chosen people.

One of the primary arguments that Tertullian uses against the heretics, one used also by other apologists, is the argument concerning *apostolic succession*. Apostolic succession is the idea that the church in a given city could trace its heritage back through successive generations of bishops, or pastors, to one of the original apostles (including Paul, James the brother of Jesus, and other early Christian leaders). Tertullian says that none of the heretics can trace their lineage back to the apostles, whereas the churches in several locales, including Rome, Smyrna, Ephesus, Philippi, Corinth, and Thessalonica, can do so. He buttresses his argument from apostolic succession by noting that the churches that can trace their heritage back to an apostle share a common understanding of the faith. Since it is highly unlikely that all of these churches would have erred in the same direction independently, he argues, their interpretation of Christianity must be accurate. Apostolic succession became such an important argument for the apologists that it may be considered a third primary tool for ensuring orthodoxy, alongside the creed and the canon. While the creed focused on doctrine, and the canon was a mixture of doctrine and historical tradition, apostolic succession was a purely historical argument for the radical authenticity of particular churches.

Perhaps the greatest of the apologists was Irenaeus, bishop of Lyons in Gaul (modern France). Born in Asia Minor, he was a student of Polycarp and possibly also Justin Martyr. At some point he moved to Lyons. As a young man he escaped the martyrdom that claimed the lives of many in his congregation because he was away on church business, and when he returned he was chosen to replace the recently deceased bishop. Irenaeus was just as opposed to heresy as his contemporary Tertullian, but his approach was somewhat less combative, as his name implied (irenic = *peaceful*). In his greatest work, *Against Heresies*, which includes five separate books, Irenaeus describes the teachings of many of those whom he considers false teachers, including Marcion, but he spends the greatest amount of time refuting the teachings of various types of Gnostics.

Gnosticism, as noted in Chapter 1, was centered on the idea that salvation could only be attained through knowledge, usually secret knowledge of some kind. Gnostic teachers merged elements of more traditional Christianity with teachings prevalent in the Greco-Roman world in various ways to produce Christian Gnosticism. Although these Christian Gnostics held a wide variety of different beliefs, some doctrines were common to many different versions of Gnosticism. The belief in the efficacy of knowledge gave Gnostics their name, and the fact that many Gnostics spoke of a being called Sophia (wisdom) supports the importance of the role of knowledge. Gnostics believed that God was perfect and pure, living in a realm of light, separated from matter. God produced a pair of beings called *aeons*, from whom emanated more pairs of aeons, until there were a fairly large number of these beings. The lowest pair of aeons produced the *demiurge*, who created matter and formed the universe. In the process, bits of divinity were trapped inside the material universe. Christ was an aeon who inhabited the human Jesus in order to teach human beings to recognize and liberate the divine spark within them. Like more traditional Christian groups, Gnostics followed a wide variety of practices, ranging from extreme asceticism, to full acceptance of marriage and child-bearing, to libertinism, at least according to their critics. Most Gnostics probably tended toward asceticism, however, since the act of bringing children into the world trapped more divine sparks inside human bodies.

Gnostic teaching included a dualistic view of the world as divided between good and evil, light and dark, the divine and the material. An extreme form of dualism was practiced by a group called the Manicheans, whose belief system was influenced as well by Zoroastrianism, the religion of Persia. The Gnostics associated the original, uncreated God with the aeons to form a composite called the *pleroma*, or "fullness." In many forms of Gnosticism, it was this pleroma that sent the Christ into the material world to rescue humanity. Some of the concepts of Gnosticism can be found in the writings of Plato, who also speaks of a demiurge in the *Republic* and the *Timaeus*. It is not surprising, then, that a copy of Plato's *Republic* was discovered in the Gnostic Nag Hammadi "library" in Egypt.

Irenaeus lists several Gnostic teachers by name, describes their belief systems, and points out what he believes to be their errors. Some of the more important Gnostic teachers were Valentinus, Basilides, Saturninus, and Cerinthus. Irenaeus was not content simply to attack the views of the Gnostics; he also laid down his understanding of the Christian message in a great deal of detail. Among other aspects of his message were these:

- the God who created the world was also the father of Jesus Christ;
- the Old Testament scripture teaches that the universe was created out of nothing, not from pre-existent matter;
- the scriptures prophesied in advance many aspects of Jesus' life, death, and resurrection;
- Jesus was fathered by God and born of a virgin in the days of Pontius Pilate;
- Jesus was both divine and human;
- Jesus rose from the dead with a physical body;
- the four gospels of Matthew, Mark, Luke, and John are the only authoritative gospels;
- the faith of Christians is the same as the faith of Abraham and other righteous people in the Old Testament;
- Christ's death on the cross mediates salvation, which is transmitted to people through the Eucharist;
- faithful Christians will be raised from the dead and given new, physical bodies.

Many of these teachings were polar opposites from the doctrines that the Gnostics taught, particularly those that emphasize the identity of God as creator and the physical nature of Christ's body. Irenaeus's teachings were taken up and amplified by Hippolytus and many other Christian apologists, and within two centuries the teachings of Irenaeus and the other apologists were recognized as orthodoxy throughout most of the Christian world.

Justin, Athenagoras, Tertullian, and Irenaeus were all important apologists, but all were from the West. In the East, the greatest Christian apologist in the first three Christian centuries was Origen. Many of Origen's positions mirror those of his counterparts in the West. He opposed Marcion, the Gnostics, and other versions of Christianity that he deemed heretical. However, he also found some common ground with his opponents. For example, his description of the Son (Christ) as eternally begotten by the Father, as rays of light emanate from the sun, was similar to Gnostic descriptions of the aeons, though Origen understood something quite different. Origen also agreed with Marcion that the Old Testament, if taken literally, contained material that was either absurd or offensive, for example, in its description of God as a farmer planting a garden in Gen 2. Where he differed from Marcion was in his resolution of the problem. Whereas Marcion read the Old Testament literally and rejected it, Origen, influenced by Philo and Clement, his predecessors in Alexandria, advocated reading the Bible allegorically. In this way, Origen said, those aspects of the Old Testament that seem to show God in a bad light when read literally can be understood in a "spiritual" sense. An allegorical reading of the Hebrew Bible both protected its authority as Christian scripture and secured the integrity of God, according to Origen.

Origen was perhaps the most original thinker in the second and third Christian centuries, and his formulations of Christian doctrine were both influential and controversial. His description of the Trinity as the Father sending forth the Son, who in turn sends forth the Holy Spirit, was based on Platonic philosophy at least as much as it was on scripture, but it formed an integral part of the orthodox explanation of the Godhead. Some Christians, particularly in the East, opposed Origen's description of the Trinity, touting instead an understanding of the relationship between Father, Son, and Holy Spirit called *monarchianism*. Monarchianism was an attempt to preserve the unity and uniqueness of God, and monarchists opposed Origen and others as "ditheists." Two main forms of monarchianism existed. The first, *modalism*, stated that the Trinity was a reality, but that the three persons of the Trinity were simply three different aspects of God. The Sabellians, for example, taught that God acted as Father in creation, as Son in redemption, and as Spirit in prophecy and sanctification, thus preserving the unity of God but eliminating any real distinction among the different persons of the Trinity. The second form of monarchianism was *adoptionism*. Adoptionists believed that Jesus was fully human, though sinless, and God "adopted" him at some point in his life, either at his baptism or his resurrection, by means of the Holy Spirit. Paul of Samosata, for example, taught that Jesus was born fully human, but at his baptism the *logos* entered him and guided him in his public ministry. Origen opposed the modalists because he believed that modalism destroyed the distinction between the Father and the Son that was clearly taught in scripture. He opposed the adoptionists because they denied the full divinity of Christ. Although both modalism and adoptionism survived Origen, they were not to prosper for long, for the critiques of Origen and others of a similar mindset were incorporated into the still developing Christological doctrines of the orthodox church.

If Origen's ideas concerning the Trinity and the divine and human in Christ were appreciated by the proto-orthodox church, his ideas about the origin and destiny of souls were not as widely accepted. Origen believed that God created all souls at some point before the creation of the universe, and in fact before the creation of time itself. All souls fell except for the soul of Christ, which always remained firmly grounded in the divine. Origen accepted the idea of souls suffering for their sins, but he believed that that suffering would not be eternal. In the end, Christ would reconcile all souls to the Father, and even the devil himself would be saved. Salvation, for Origen, consisted in a grand reunion of souls with their creator, a view that approaches that of the Hindu concept of the soul's immersion in the divine, though without the consequent loss of individuality. Some later Christian writers, particularly in the West, condemned Origen, saying that he treated the Son as a created being, though Origen no doubt would have denied that interpretation. Others suggested that Origen's view that all souls would one day be reunited with God was contrary to scripture, which, they said, taught a doctrine of eternal punishment for the wicked. Although Origen was highly regarded during his lifetime, and his teachings influenced the development of orthodoxy, he was sometimes reviled by later Christians, who found aspects of his belief system objectionable, even heretical. Nevertheless, in his day, Origen's role as a champion of the developing orthodox position and his erudition on matters of biblical interpretation and theological formulation were widely recognized and appreciated.

External struggles

Early persecutions

> But to pass from the examples of ancient times, let us come to those champions who lived nearest to our time. Let us set before us the noble examples which belong to our own generation. Because of jealousy and envy the greatest and most righteous pillars were persecuted, and fought to the death. Let us set before our eyes the good Apostles. There was Peter, who, because of unrighteous jealousy, endured not one nor two but many trials, and thus having given his testimony went to his appointed place of glory. Because of jealousy and strife Paul by his example pointed out the way to the prize for patient endurance. After he had been seven times in chains, had been driven into exile, had been stoned, and had preached in the East and in the West, he won the genuine glory for his faith, having taught righteousness to the whole world and having reached the farthest limits of the West. Finally, when he had given his testimony before the rulers, he thus departed from the world and went to the holy place, having become an outstanding example of patient endurance.
>
> (*1 Clem 5*)

While many churches throughout the Roman empire and beyond were struggling to determine the nature of their faith during the first three Christian centuries, others were struggling simply for survival. The book of Acts speaks of occasional, sporadic instances of persecution of Christians by either Jewish or Roman leaders, and Paul describes himself as a former persecutor of Christians (1 Cor 15:9; Gal 1:13, 23). The first major outbreak of violence perpetrated against Christians, however, occurred during the reign of the Roman emperor Nero. In the summer of 64, a great fire broke out in Rome and destroyed much of the city. To deflect rumors that he had ordered the conflagration himself, Nero laid the blame on the Christians in the city, and he ordered the arrest and immediate execution of hundreds of them. Some were crucified, others were torn apart by wild animals in the Colosseum, and still others were covered with tar and set on fire as human torches to illuminate the night. Both Peter and Paul met their deaths during the Neronian persecution. Nero's cruel treatment of Christians was localized, and his policies toward Christians did not survive his death in 68. Nevertheless, occasional outbreaks of persecution arose throughout the Roman empire, particularly in those areas where Christianity was growing the fastest, in Asia Minor, Egypt, and Rome. Christian martyrs were revered by their coreligionists and held up as examples of the faith (e.g. Rev 2:10, 13; *1 Clem 5*).

By the time Trajan became emperor in 98, Christians were present in growing numbers throughout the empire. It was during his reign that the most notable martyrdom since the time of Nero occurred, the execution of Ignatius, bishop of Antioch. Ignatius was arrested in Antioch and transported to Rome for execution in the arena, where he was devoured by lions. While he was on his journey to Rome, he wrote letters to six churches and one to his fellow bishop Polycarp of Smyrna, extolling the Christian faith and urging Christians to be faithful. In 112 Pliny the Younger, who was an imperial legate in Bithynia in Asia Minor, wrote to Trajan asking for his guidance regarding the treatment of Christians who had been arrested. Pliny indicates in his letter that he willingly executed Christians who were brought before him, even if they had committed no crime, but only after giving them several chances to renounce their faith. He notes that Christianity was spreading in Asia Minor not only in the cities but also in smaller towns and villages, and its numbers included people of all classes and ages. So powerful is the Christian movement, Pliny says, that pagan temples in many areas are all but deserted. Nevertheless, he is sure that his treatment of Christians will eliminate the most rabidly devoted and cause most others to renounce the religion. Trajan's letter in response to Pliny endorses his actions, but he cautions that Christians should not be sought out, and those who are accused should be given every opportunity to prove their innocence by recanting their faith and worshiping the Roman gods.

Hadrian, who succeeded Trajan as emperor in 117, reversed Trajan's policy of persecuting Christians merely for the sake of their religious identity, and in fact he ordered those who falsely accused Christians of crime to be punished themselves. In the aftermath of the Second Jewish War, Hadrian punished the Jews in Judea by banishing them from Aelia Capitolina (Jerusalem), but because he recognized Christians as a separate religious group, they were not included in his edict. Throughout the second and early third centuries sporadic outbreaks of persecution occurred, usually as a result of the animosity of ordinary people against their Christian neighbors rather than because of official policy. During the reign of Antoninus Pius (138–161), Polycarp, bishop of Smyrna in Asia Minor, was burned at the stake in a public arena in Smyrna after the crowd that had gathered earlier to witness the execution of other Christians cried out for him to be found and killed. An outbreak of mob violence against Christians in the cities of Lyons and Vienne in Gaul during the reign of Marcus Aurelius (161–180) resulted in the beating, arrest, torture, and execution of many Christians. Several incidents of violence toward Christians occurred in Carthage, Alexandria, Rome, Antioch, Cappadocia, and elsewhere during this period, though without imperial sanction. In fact, the mother of the emperor Septimius Severus (193–211) invited Origen, whose own father had been martyred several years earlier, to the court for a discussion of religion, philosophy, and science. Despite the numerous examples of persecution during this period, Christians on the whole experienced relatively good relations with Rome for more than 100 years after the death of Trajan.

Figure 6.1 The most widespread and devastating persecution of Christians authorized by Rome occurred during the reign of the emperor Diocletian.

The first widespread, imperial persecutions

The ascent to the throne of Maximinus Thrax in 235 marked a decisive change in imperial policy toward Christians. Pliny's prediction that Christianity would soon die out proved to be incorrect, for since the time of Trajan, Christianity had grown enormously throughout the empire. Christian martyrdoms did not scare potential converts away. On the contrary, for every martyr numerous new converts stepped forward to take his or her place. Maximinus viewed Christians as enemies of Rome, and he instituted a new wave of persecution in various places throughout the empire. In Cappadocia churches were burned to the ground. The Roman bishop Pontian was exiled from Rome and sentenced to labor in the mines in Sardinia, where he died. The persecution of Maximinus ended with his death in 238. The reign of Maximinus marked a dire turning point in the history of Roman-Christian relations, not because of the large numbers of Christians killed – the numbers were not large – but because of the change in the official attitude toward Christians that it represented. Barbarian (i.e. non-Roman) tribes who originally lived north and east of the Rhine and Danube rivers had been encroaching on Roman territory from the earliest days of the empire, but between 235 and 284, a period known to historians as the Crisis of the Third Century, barbarian invasions were constant. Twenty-five different emperors reigned during this half century, and all but two were either murdered or killed in battle. Having grown accustomed to the *Pax Romana* that had existed from the time of Augustus, the first Roman emperor, the people, and often the emperors, looked for someone to fault for the empire's problems, and increasingly, blame was placed squarely on the shoulders of the Church.

Later Roman emperors important for their impact on Christianity

Marcus Aurelius (161–180)

Septimius Severus (193–211)

Antoninus (Caracalla) (211–217)

Maximinus Thrax (235–238)

Decius (249–251)

Valerian (253–260)

Diocletian (284–305)

Galerius (293–311)

Constantine I (306–337)

One advantage for the Church during the Crisis of the Third Century was that emperors were so busy fighting barbarians and rivals for the imperial throne that they often had little time to persecute Christians. The reign of Decius was different. Decius seized the throne in 249 after defeating his predecessor Philip the Arabian in battle. An extremely conservative man, Decius blamed the problems of Rome on the failure of its citizens to show proper respect to the gods. Christians, whose numbers were growing rapidly, were especially responsible in Decius's eyes. He had visions of restoring the military greatness of Rome, and he was convinced that worship of the Roman gods was a vitally important step along the path. Decius ordered all Roman citizens to sacrifice to the gods, and each person who did so was issued a *libellus*, or certificate proving that he had indeed offered a sacrifice. Those who refused to sacrifice were faced with harsh punishments, and many were summarily executed. The Decian persecution was the first empire-wide persecution of Christians, and though brief, its impact was severe. Fabian, the bishop of Rome, was arrested and died in prison, probably as a result of harsh treatment. Origen was arrested in Caesarea and imprisoned there. Although he survived the ordeal, his death within three years of his release may be attributed to the punishment he experienced in prison. Christian bishops from Antioch, Jerusalem, Carthage, and Pontus were also imprisoned or executed. The long period of relative peace with Rome had produced a church not accustomed to martyrdom. Many bishops and priests who were ordered on pain of death to sacrifice to the gods did so, and large numbers of ordinary Christians followed their examples. When the persecution ended in 251 with the death of Decius, who was killed in battle with the Goths (a Germanic tribe), many Christians had died, but many, many more had sacrificed to the Roman gods in order to save their lives. The result was a church in disarray, reeling from both the martyrdoms and the renunciations of the faith.

When the persecution in Rome subsided in 251, the Roman clergy elected a new bishop named Cornelius. One of his rivals, a priest named Novatian, angrily denounced the new bishop and had himself elected bishop of Rome by his supporters. At issue was the disposition of those Christians who had lapsed from the faith during the Decian persecution (this was the first of the "lapse controversies"). Novatian, supported by many in Rome and North Africa, and by the bishop of Antioch, argued that those who had sacrificed to the Roman gods could no longer be considered Christians and should not be readmitted to the church. Cornelius and a majority of the Roman clergy, however, believed it was in the best interest of the church to readmit their lapsed brothers and sisters, after a suitable period of penitence. Novatian's refusal to acknowledge the Roman clergy's choice of Cornelius resulted in his excommunication from the church of Rome, but it did not end the controversy. Novatian and his followers established rival churches throughout the Roman Empire, and though Novatian himself perished during the Valerian persecution in 258, Novatianist churches continued for several centuries. Christians who wanted to join a Novatianist church after having been baptized in a Catholic church (i.e. one allied with the main church in Rome) were only admitted after being rebaptized. The strict attitude of the Novatianists toward those who had denied the faith found a sympathetic ear in some Montanist Christians, and the two joined forced in some areas. Other Novatianists were readmitted to the Catholic church after renouncing their allegiance to the schismatic church. Cyprian, bishop of Carthage in North Africa, was strongly opposed to admitting the validity of Novatianist baptism, and he had wide support from many Christian leaders throughout the empire. Bishop Stephen of Rome (254–257), however, held the position that the efficacy of baptism was inherent in the rite itself and was not based on the relationship of the person performing the baptism to the Catholic church. Furthermore, since the Novatianists were orthodox in their views and merely *schismatics*, rather than heretics, their entry into the Catholic church should not be made too difficult. Stephen's more moderate position also had the support of Christian leaders throughout the empire, and it was his position that ultimately prevailed in this and the Donatist lapse controversy of the following century. The moderates believed that the church would suffer irreparable harm if it did not readmit those who had fallen away during times of persecution, not only because of the loss of large numbers of Christians, but also because denying readmittance to the church was in fact denying the willingness of God to forgive those who had sinned.

After Decius's death, Trebonianus Gallus reigned for two years. Although he sent Cornelius of Rome into exile, where he died, he does not seem to have restarted a broad persecution of Christians. The church had a respite, then, for a few years, during which time it wrestled with the issues of lapsed Christians and the Novatianist schism. Persecution became official Roman policy again in the reign of Valerian. Although Valerian put on the purple in 253, his attacks on Christians did not begin immediately, and at first he seems to have been somewhat favorably disposed toward them. For some reason in 257 he began a harsh, though sporadic, persecution of Christians, ordering them to participate in religious ceremonies dedicated to the Roman gods and forbidding them from gathering in cemeteries, which they considered holy ground, because they held the bones of martyrs. He ordered the execution of bishops, priests, and deacons, and he also prescribed other kinds of punishment for laypeople. On 6 August 258, Valerian's troops rushed into the catacomb, an underground burial chamber, where

Xystus, bishop of Rome, was presiding over a service and beheaded him on the spot, along with several deacons. Cyprian, bishop of Carthage, was exiled in 257 and then beheaded a year later. Bishop Dionysius of Alexandria was sent into exile but survived Valerian's rampage against Christians. In addition to his punishment of many individual Christians, Valerian also confiscated quite a bit of church property. In 260 the emperor was captured in a battle with the Persians, and he died in captivity. His son and successor Gallienus reversed his father's harsh treatment of Christians, allowing exiled leaders to return home and restoring property that had been taken.

The 43 years from the deposal of Valerian to the start of the next persecution under Diocletian were years of unprecedented success and prosperity for the church. Gallienus's 15-year reign provided a welcome respite from the short imperial tenures that plagued much of the third century, a relief that was good for the Roman Empire and good for the Church. Christianity in Asia Minor grew to such an extent that it became the majority religion in many provinces. In 301 Tiridates III, the king of Armenia, became a convert, and he declared Christianity the official religion of his kingdom, making Armenia the first Christian nation. The church also grew in North Africa, Western Europe, and Syria. A monastic movement had been developing in Egypt since the middle of the third century, and its most famous advocate was Anthony, an anchorite (solitary) monk who entered the desert at the age of 34 and remained there for more than seventy years. Many of his contemporaries followed his example, and Christianity grew in Egypt as a result of the testimony of the "desert saints." Growing numbers of people were converted to Christianity as a philosophy, much as Justin Martyr had earlier advocated. The last four decades of the third century were a time of tremendous growth for the Church in both East and West.

The great persecution

Christianity's era of peace with the Roman Empire came to an abrupt end in February of 303, when the emperor Diocletian issued his first edict against Christians. Diocletian had already been emperor for almost two decades, and he had shown little inclination to persecute Christians prior to issuing his edict. In fact, both his wife and his daughter, who was married to Galerius (see below), were Christians, as were many in his household. In order to ease his administrative burden, Diocletian had appointed an augustus (co-emperor), Maximian, and two caesars (vice emperors), Galerius in the East and Constantius in the West. It is likely that Galerius, a convinced pagan, was responsible for influencing Diocletian to begin his persecution of Christians, and in fact sporadic minor persecutions began before 303, concentrated in the East. Diocletian's persecution was well planned, and he hoped thereby to bring all Roman citizens back to the traditional worship of the Roman gods, as a means of strengthening the empire. He was aware of previous persecutions, and he had little desire to make martyrs, for he understood that making martyrs inevitably led to making more converts. Instead, he started by focusing on the church's infrastructure: its buildings and its scriptures. Diocletian's first edict ordered that church buildings throughout the empire be destroyed and that all copies of scripture be collected and burned. It also removed all Christians from public office and stripped Christians who were members of the upper classes of their privileges. The edict was carried out with glee by many pagan magistrates throughout the empire, who harbored resentment against Christians because of their remarkable growth over the past few decades, as well as for their rejection of ancient Roman traditions. The edict was quite successful on the surface. Buildings were destroyed, the wealth of many churches was confiscated, and, perhaps most devastatingly, a significant percentage of the extant copies of scripture was burned. A few Christians resisted and paid with their lives, but most cooperated with the authorities. In many cases, local authorities were sympathetic to the Christians under their charge, and they accepted as "scripture" bound for the flames a wide variety of writings, ranging from heretical writings to medical texts.

In the summer of 303, Diocletian turned up the heat on the Church. He issued a second edict ordering the arrest of all bishops and other Christian leaders, who would be forced to participate in the imperial cult, which involved offering a sacrifice of incense to the genius (protective spirit) of the emperor. Most who were arrested refused to participate in emperor worship, and soon the jails became overcrowded. A short time later Diocletian issued his third edict, commanding that all imprisoned clergy be forced to offer sacrifices and then released. In many places the edict was obeyed by physically forcing Christian leaders to sacrifice. In one instance, recorded by Eusebius, a man was physically carried to the altar, where his hands were pried open so that the incense he was forced to hold would fall into the fire. A few bishops offered sacrifices to the gods in the face of threats, but most had to be forced, and many went into hiding to avoid arrest in the first place. At this point, few Christians had yet been killed, and the church in many places was deprived of its leaders, either through martyrdom, imprisonment, voluntary exile, or dishonor. Christian influence throughout the empire was lessened, and Diocletian's plan seemed to be working, at least to some extent.

Sometime in 304 Diocletian fell seriously ill and contemplated abdicating the throne. He was still in office, however, when a fourth edict was issued in the spring of 304, one much harsher than the previous three, probably at the instigation of Galerius. This edict ordered that all Roman citizens – and by implication all Christians, not only clergy – offer sacrifice to the gods or forfeit their lives. The edict was largely ignored in the westernmost provinces, where Constantius was caesar, and it was implemented with limited enthusiasm throughout the areas over which Maximian and Diocletian himself presided, though many were in fact killed in those provinces. It was in the easternmost provinces, those ruled over by Galerius, that the edict was enforced most harshly. The exact number of Christian martyrs is unknown, but those killed in the East numbered at least in the hundreds, perhaps in the thousands. One reason that so many more Christians were killed in the Great Persecution of Diocletian than in the Decian persecution is that most Christians who were arrested under Diocletian refused to sacrifice to the gods. The persecution raged throughout 304 and early 305, particularly in the East, but on 1 May 305 the emperor Diocletian suddenly announced his retirement and stepped down from the throne, as did his co-emperor, Maximian. Diocletian's retirement did not yet signal an end to the persecution of Christians, however.

Upon the resignations of the two co-emperors, Galerius assumed the title augustus in the East, as did Constantius in the West, and Galerius appointed two new caesars as well, overlooking Constantius's son Constantine, whom many expected to be elevated to that rank. Galerius and his caesars continued their assault on Christians, and many more died or were sentenced to hard labor in the mines. When Constantius died in 306, his troops declared his son Constantine augustus in the West, and soon various claimants to the titles augustus and caesar were fighting one another. When the dust settled – temporarily – in 308, Galerius, Licinius, Constantine, and Maximinus Daia formed a new tetrarchy of rulers. Three years later Galerius, who was dying, and Licinius issued an Edict of Toleration, formally ending the persecution of Christians in their territories (although Maximinus Daia continued to attack Christians). The following year Constantine converted to Christianity, after winning the Battle of the Milvian Bridge against Maxentius, the son of the Diocletian's former co-emperor Maximian. Before the battle, which occurred near an important bridge crossing the Tiber north of Rome, Constantine had his troops paint the Christian symbol chi-rho (the first two Greek letters in the word Christ), on their shields, reportedly in response to a dream in which he saw the symbol and heard a voice saying "By this sign you will conquer." A later version of the story says that both Constantine and his troops saw a cross of light in the sky, accompanied by a voice proclaiming the aforementioned words. A year later, in 313, Constantine and Licinius, who were now co-emperors, issued the Edict of

Edict of Toleration (311)

Among the important cares which have occupied our mind for the utility and preservation of the empire, it was our intention to correct and re-establish all things according to the ancient laws and public discipline of the Romans. We were particularly desirous of reclaiming into the way of reason and nature the deluded Christians who had renounced the religion and ceremonies instituted by their fathers, and, presumptuously despising the practice of antiquity, had invented extravagant laws and opinions according to the dictates of their fancy, and had collected a various society from the different provinces of our empire. The edicts which we have published to enforce the worship of the gods having exposed many of the Christians to danger and distress, many having suffered death, and many more, who still persist in their impious folly, being left destitute of any public exercise of religion, we are disposed to extend to those unhappy men the effects of our wonted clemency. We permit them, therefore, freely to profess their private opinions, and to assemble in their conventicles without fear or molestation, provided always that they preserve a due respect to the established laws and government. By another rescript we shall signify our intentions to the judges and magistrates, and we hope that our indulgence will engage the Christians to offer up their prayers to the Deity whom they adore for our safety and prosperity, for their own, and for that of the republic.

Milan, officially recognizing Christianity as a legal religion within the Roman Empire. Land that had been confiscated from Christians was restored, and money for rebuilding churches was allocated. Unlike Constantine, Licinius was not a Christian, and despite the Edict of Milan, he still sought to subvert Christianity by denying its followers the right to hold civil office, denying bishops the right to hold synods, and other acts of discrimination. In 324 Constantine and Licinius, who had been at different times allies or rivals over the years, fought one another for control of the empire, and Constantine emerged victorious as sole emperor of the Roman Empire.

The Church had entered the second century with perhaps a few thousand adherents, scattered around the eastern Mediterranean world. Internal conflicts over the relationship between Christianity on the one hand and Judaism and philosophy on the other gave way to intense debates between rival visions of Christianity. As the second century gave way to the third, the Great Church began to emerge as the likely victor in the struggle to define Christian orthodoxy. Sporadic Roman persecution of Christians for two centuries was replaced with an empire-wide attack on Christians during the reigns of Decius and Valerian, followed by a much more far-reaching persecution under Diocletian and Galerius. Despite the devastating loss of life and property during the Great Persecution, the church emerged stronger than ever, and its reach extended all the way to the imperial purple. When the retired emperor Diocletian died, probably in the year 316, the man who had been ultimately responsible for the greatest persecution against Christians in history had lived to see the day when not only was Christianity a legal religion within the empire, but a Christian emperor was sitting on the throne.

Key points you need to know

- The earliest dominant forms of Christianity in some areas reflected beliefs and practices that would later be deemed heretical.
- One way in which the issue of orthodoxy was settled was with the creation of a canon of the New Testament. Christians who accepted books at variance with this canon were considered outside the Great Church.
- The size, prestige, and effective leadership of the church at Rome made it an ideal champion, and definer, of orthodoxy.
- The church at Rome, supported by likeminded leaders from other locations known as the Apologists – including Justin Martyr, Athenagoras, Tertullian, Irenaeus, and Origen – were able to establish their version of orthodoxy, in part through the use of tools such as the creed, the canon, and the idea of apostolic succession.
- Despite early, localized persecutions under emperors such as Nero and Trajan, Christianity flourished in many parts of the Roman Empire and beyond during the first two centuries of its existence.
- The first widespread, imperial persecution of Christians came in the middle of the third century under the emperor Decius, who blamed Christians for the failure of Roman

> citizens to show proper respect for the gods, and the subsequent problems the empire had with the barbarian tribes. This persecution was fierce but short-lived.
>
> - Valerian's persecution of Christians, beginning a few years after Decius's death, targeted church leaders, and was again fierce but relatively brief.
> - The Great Persecution of Christians was ordered by the emperor Diocletian in 303 and was continued in the east after his abdication by Galerius. This persecution resulted in the deaths of hundreds, perhaps thousands of Christians. It continued until Galerius and others signed the Edict of Toleration in 311, formally ending the persecution of Christians in most parts of the Roman Empire. Two years later Christianity was declared a legal religion.

Discussion questions

1. How closely did the orthodoxy proclaimed by the church at Rome and the Apologists match the understanding of the church in the first few decades of its existence?
2. In what ways were the creed, the canon, and apostolic succession effective tools for spreading and enforcing orthodoxy?
3. Which alternate form of Christianity posed the greatest threat to orthodoxy?
4. How effective were the various Roman persecutions at limiting the spread and influence of Christianity?
5. How did the Great Persecution affect the Church, both negatively and positively?

Further reading

Athenagoras, *A Plea for the Christians*.

Bauer, Walter 1971. *Orthodoxy and Heresy in Earliest Christianity*. Translated by Robert A. Kraft *et al*. Edited by Robert A. Kraft and Gerhard Krodel. Philadelphia, PA: Fortress.

Eusebius, *Church History*.

Irenaeus, *Against Heresies*.

Justin Martyr, *Apology*.

Justin Martyr, *Dialog with Trypho*.

Martyrdom of Polycarp.

Origen, *Against Celsus*.

Origen, *On First Principles*.

Plato, *Republic*.

Plato, *Timaeus*.

Quasten, Johannes and Angelo Di Berardino 1950–1986. *Patrology*. 4 vols. Vol. 4 translated by Placid Solari. Allen, TX: Christian Classics.

Robinson, James M. 1996. *The Nag Hammadi Library in English*. 4th edn, Leiden: Brill.

Tertullian, *Against Marcion*.

Tertullian, *Apology*.

7 The triumph of Christianity

According to the apostolic teaching and the doctrine of the Gospel, let us believe in the one deity of the Father, Son, and Holy Spirit, in equal majesty and in a holy Trinity. We authorize the followers of this law to assume the title Catholic Christians; but as for the others, since in our judgment they are foolish madmen, we decree that they shall be branded with the ignominious name of heretics, and shall not presume to give their conventicles the name of churches. They will suffer in the first place the chastisement of divine condemnation, and in the second the punishment which our authority, in accordance with the will of Heaven, shall decide to inflict.

(Theodosius I, *Code of Theodosius* 16.1.2)

In this chapter

With Constantine ruling as the first Christian emperor of the Roman Empire, Christianity spread more rapidly than ever, especially, but not exclusively, within the boundaries of the empire. Christian leaders from all around the Mediterranean world gathered in great councils – first at Nicaea, then at Constantinople, Ephesus, and Chalcedon – to define the boundaries of orthodox Christianity. Constantine, meanwhile, moved his capital from Rome to Constantinople, and the empire itself was divided into an eastern and a western half, to make it more manageable. Finally, under the emperor Theodosius I, Christianity became the official religion of the Roman Empire. While most Christians were thrilled with this turn of events, some Christians believed that Christianity was becoming too worldly, so they left their settled lives and fled to the deserts to live solitary lives of piety in search of God.

Main topics covered

- Overview of the reigns of the emperors Constantine, Julian the Apostate, and Theodosius I, especially their decisions regarding Christianity
- The Council of Nicaea, the Arian controversy, and the Nicene creed
- Semi-Arianism, the Council of Constantinople, and the revision of the Nicene creed
- The Great Cappadocians and John Chrysostom in the East

- Ambrose, Augustine, and Jerome in the West
- The rise of the monastic movement
- The relation of the divine and human in Christ, and the Councils of Ephesus and Chalcedon

Three early emperors

Thus, like a faithful and good servant, did [Constantine] act and testify, openly declaring and confessing himself the obedient minister of the supreme King. And God forthwith rewarded him, by making him ruler and sovereign, and victorious to such a degree that he alone of all rulers pursued a continual course of conquest, unsubdued and invincible, and through his trophies a greater ruler than tradition records ever to have been before. So dear was he to God, and so blessed; so pious and so fortunate in all that he undertook, that with the greatest facility he obtained the authority over more nations than any who had preceded him, and yet retained his power, undisturbed, to the very close of his life.

(Eusebius, *Life of Constantine* 6)

Constantine's defeat of Maxentius at the Milvian Bridge and his conversion to Christianity guaranteed that serious persecutions against Christians would cease. His

Figure 7.1   Though not yet a Christian at the time, the emperor Constantine attributed his victory at the Battle of the Milvian Bridge to Christ's intervention on his behalf. Soon thereafter he legalized Christianity. This medallion depicts "The undefeated Constantine."

defeat of Licinius 12 years later assured Christians a favored status within the empire. Constantine's level of personal commitment to Christianity is a matter of debate. His mother Helena was a devout Christian (famous for her later discovery of the "true cross"), but his father Constantius, though favorably disposed toward Christians, was a pagan. In his early days as a soldier, general, and emperor, Constantine worshiped Sol Invictus, "the undefeated Sun(-god)." Even after the traditional date of his conversion in 312, Roman coins bearing Constantine's name continued to carry a legend honoring Sol Invictus. It was only in 325, the year that the Council of Nicaea met, that Constantine had the Roman mint stop including the legend on official coinage. Furthermore, Constantine retained his title of Pontifex Maximus, or high priest of the Roman pantheon of gods, until his death in 337, and traditional pagan festivals and customs continued to be observed under the oversight of the emperor. Finally, Constantine was not baptized until shortly before his death, though it was a fairly common practice at the time to postpone baptism, in order to assure that the maximum number of sins would be washed away by the sacrament. At the same time, Constantine was a great benefactor of the church, donating large amounts of money and land. In particular, he donated the land on which the current Lateran Palace and Basilica of St. John Lateran stand, and he built a great church in honor of St. Peter, on the site of the current Basilica of St. Peter in the Vatican. He was also intimately involved in some of the most important decisions in the life of the fourth century Church, summoning bishops to discuss disputes involving the Donatist and Arian controversies.

The church historian Eusebius of Caesarea wrote the *Life of Constantine* shortly after Constantine's death. He considered the emperor to be a great Christian, a man blessed by God for his faithfulness and virtuous life. In fact, Eusebius said, God appointed Constantine to be emperor because he was a friend of God, an opponent of idolatry, a man of prayer, and a promoter of the Christian faith. Modern historians consider many of Eusebius's comments about Constantine to be fanciful exaggerations, and some doubt the emperor's personal commitment to the faith. They point to his execution of his son and wife, among others, as evidence of Constantine's failure to embrace the teachings of Christ. It is likely, they say, that Constantine saw Christianity as a tool by which he could cement his empire together, taking the place of the now obsolete pagan religious practices. Christianity would only serve the purpose of unifying his empire, however, if its doctrines and practices were standardized, so he attempted to settle disputed matters by decree. When that failed, he summoned the bishops together and charged them to settle their differences for the good of the church and the empire. The most important of these gatherings was the Council of Nicaea, which met in 325 to decide the Arian controversy, among other matters (see below). The question of Constantine's sincerity is impossible to answer with any certainty, but it seems likely that Constantine was indeed a convinced Christian, albeit one whose level of conviction grew over time and whose understanding of the fine points of Christian doctrine was limited at best. His commitment to the prosperity of the Roman Empire was at least as important to him as the prosperity of the Church. In fact, it is likely that he saw the two as intertwined. Constantine saw no contradiction between building the kingdom of Rome and building the kingdom of God, and many Christian leaders of his day agreed with him.

One of Constantine's most important acts as emperor was moving his capital from Rome in the West to Byzantium in the East. He commissioned a new city on the site of Byzantium, and he christened it Constantinople, the city of Constantine. Constantine saw the long-term danger of leaving the capital of the empire in Rome, because of the encroachment of the barbarian tribes that were growing ever stronger and more numerous. Constantine dreamed of a New Rome, whose wealth and prosperity would be the envy of every other city in the world. He not only moved his court to Constantinople, but he strongly urged many of the leading families of Rome, including the families of senators, to do the same. Within 100 years, Constantinople was indeed a great city, rivaling and eventually surpassing Rome in wealth and power. At the same time as he moved his capital, he divided the empire into two halves: the Eastern and Western Roman Empires, ruled over by augusti (co-emperors) and caesars, with the most powerful augustus usually reigning from Constantinople. Constantine's transfer of the capital to Constantinople allowed a portion of the Roman Empire to survive the fall of the city of Rome, along with the Western Roman Empire, more than a century later. The emperor's presence in Constantinople raised the importance of the city in ecclesiastical terms as well, and the rivalry between Rome and Constantinople during the days of the empire foreshadowed the rivalry that would develop between the eastern and western branches of the church.

Constantine was followed to the throne by his sons Constantine II, Constans, and Constantius, who divided the empire among themselves. The first two considered themselves Nicene Christians, that is, Christians who fully supported the positions favored by a majority of bishops at the Council of Nicaea concerning the relationship between God the Father and God the Son. Constantius, who ruled in the East, favored a slightly different understanding of the divine interrelationship, one supported by many Eastern bishops and based in large part on Origen's earlier formulation. It is hard to tell how seriously they held to these religious niceties, but they, and many emperors who followed them, used the religious differences to their advantage in gaining support against their adversaries from the bishops, the army, and the common people. Before long the three sons of Constantine were at war with one another, primarily over territory, though their religious differences played some role as well. Constantius accused members of his father's court, which included many family members, of plotting to overthrow his father, and he had many of them killed, sparing only young children, one of whom was his six-year-old cousin Julian.

Although Julian was raised as a Christian, he was interested in Greek philosophy and became a follower of Neo-Platonism sometime before his twentieth birthday. The fact that almost his whole family had been slaughtered by a self-proclaimed Christian emperor may have played a role in Julian's rejection of Christianity. Nevertheless, though he harbored animosity toward Constantius and other family members because of their role in the massacre of his own family, his attitude toward Christianity was not wholly negative. A few years after his adoption of Neo-Platonism, in 355, Julian was appointed caesar in the West, where he had a great deal of success in subduing the Germanic tribes. When the emperor Constantius died in 361, Julian became the new augustus and openly declared his adherence to paganism.

One of Julian's first acts was to remove the privileges that Christians had enjoyed in civil society, and he prohibited them from teaching rhetoric, grammar, and other classical disciplines, since they did not hold to the religious underpinnings of the courses they taught (i.e. paganism). He also ordered that exiled Christians be allowed to return home, probably to focus the church's attention on old, internal feuds rather than his own actions. Next, Julian organized the traditional pagan religion into a hierarchical structure modeled on the Christian churches, and he ordered all the priests and other cultic functionaries to live honorable lives, like the Christians. He further demanded that they show compassion for the poor and care for the dead as their Christian neighbors did, in part so that Christians could no longer win converts by pointing to their own holy lifestyles. Third, Julian, a skilled rhetorician, wrote treatises seeking to discredit Christianity as a recent, aberrant form of Judaism, a religion that was inferior to paganism but that at least had an ancient pedigree.

Julian had no interest in killing Christians simply for their faith, but he believed that paganism, if properly reformed and organized, would defeat Christianity in the realm of ideas. Julian's plan was well-conceived in many ways, but its chances of success were minimal from the outset. Christianity had been the favored religion within the empire for almost 50 years when Julian became emperor, and it was by now also the dominant religion in the empire. The fact that Julian sought to mimic its social concern and ecclesiastical organization shows that it was unlikely to be defeated by an old, obsolete religion that had lost its power to inspire its followers, regardless of the facelift that Julian sought to give it. The question of the viability of Julian's plan became moot, however, when Julian led his army east into Persian territory. After a number of initial victories, his forces met stiff resistance outside the city of Ctesiphon in Mesopotamia, and Julian was killed in battle, only two years after he assumed the throne. It is ironic that Julian was the last direct descendant of Constantine, the first Christian emperor, to wear the purple, and he did so as the last pagan emperor. Christian historians who wrote his history saw in his defeat God's hand of judgment, and they gave Julian a new name after his death: Julian the Apostate.

After Julian's death, the empire reverted to Christian rule. Various Germanic tribes – the Alamanni, Burgundians, Franks, Saxons, and Goths, among others – continued to harass the empire in the West, as did a new, non-Germanic tribe, the Huns. Roman emperors fought the barbarians, and they also warred with themselves over issues of land, power, and religion. In 378 a Spaniard, Theodosius I, was appointed emperor in Constantinople. His defeats of the barbarian tribes in battle brought stability to the empire, but he is perhaps most famous for being the emperor who declared Christianity to be the official religion of the Roman Empire in 391. Paganism was outlawed, as was Manichaeism. Non-orthodox or schismatic Christians, such as Arians and Donatists, were forced to convert to Catholic Christianity, and Jews were persecuted as well. The orthodox inhabitants of many locales took advantage of the new laws to loot and burn pagan temples or confiscate them for use as churches. In Athens the Parthenon was converted to a church. In Alexandria the Serapeum, the temple dedicated to Serapis, was destroyed by a combination of Roman soldiers and monks from the desert. It is possible that much of the Alexandrian library was destroyed at the same time.

The other important event associated with Theodosius that relates directly to the development of Christianity is the Council of Constantinople, which he summoned in 381 to address doctrinal matters that persisted or had developed since Nicaea (this council will be discussed in the next section). Near the end of his life, Theodosius divided his empire between his two sons, naming Arcadius his successor in the East and Honorius emperor in the West. When he died in 395, Theodosius was the last emperor of the whole Roman Empire.

The three emperors discussed in this section were the most important of the fourth century in terms of the development of Christianity and its relation with the Roman Empire. When Constantine began his rule in 306, Christianity was still an illicit religion, although sanctions against Christians were rarely enforced in the westernmost part of the empire, where Constantine began his rule. During his long reign – the longest reign of any emperor since Augustus – Christianity went from being illegal, to officially tolerated, to legal, to favored. The church grew enormously in wealth, influence, and popularity, as many people abandoned paganism to embrace Christianity. Julian's brief reign marked the last official resistance to Christianity from a Roman emperor, and though Julian failed in his effort to bring paganism back to a place of honor in the empire, the inability of a highly intelligent, well organized, powerful opponent of Christianity to make a significant dent in its hold on the people illustrates the heights to which Christianity had risen by the middle of the fourth century. In Theodosius, the pendulum which had briefly swung toward paganism during the reign of Julian swung back toward Christianity, this time for good. Theodosius carried the empire's attitude toward Christianity to its apparently logical conclusion, and the dream of Constantine that the empire would adopt a single religion that could bind its people together was realized. Christianity would continue to be the official religion of the Roman Empire in the East until its fall in 1453, and it would quickly regain its official status in the West after the fall of the Western Roman Empire and its reconstitution in various Germanic kingdoms.

The Councils of Nicaea and Constantinople

[Jesus Christ] is the image of the invisible God, the firstborn of all creation; for in him all things in heaven and on earth were created, things visible and invisible, whether thrones or dominions or rulers or powers – all things have been created through him and for him. He himself is before all things, and in him all things hold together. He is the head of the body, the church; he is the beginning, the firstborn from the dead, so that he might come to have first place in everything. For in him all the fullness of God was pleased to dwell, and through him God was pleased to reconcile to himself all things, whether on earth or in heaven, by making peace through the blood of his cross.

(Col 1:15–20)

Constantine saw Christianity as a potentially stabilizing force in the empire, but only if it was unified. Unfortunately, Constantine ruled over an empire in which Christians did not always agree with one another on doctrinal or practical issues. One example was the Donatists, a group of North African Christians who refused to readmit to the church other Christians who had recanted their faith, offered sacrifices to the pagan gods, or surrendered scripture to Roman officials during the Great Persecution of Diocletian. Like the Novatianists before them, the Donatists were not really heretics, for they accepted standard orthodox doctrine, but they were schismatics, who refused to accept the authority of the church at large. The Donatists also claimed that the sacraments administered by lapsed priests and bishops were invalid, and they rebaptized those who joined their churches after being baptized in Catholic churches. Many Donatists were sharply critical of wealthy bishops and churches, and they advocated a redistribution of wealth. One group of Donatists, the Circumcellions, sought the overthrow of the existing social order and were especially opposed to wealthy landowners who owned slaves. Constantine called a regional council at Arles in Gaul to deal with the Donatists, and the bishops decided against them, but the Donatists refused to accept the decree of the bishops. In response, Constantine sent imperial troops into Carthage to destroy Donatist churches and arrest, banish, and even execute Donatist Christians. Constantine succeeded in wreaking havoc among the Donatists, but the movement continued to grow in many areas, so his efforts to bring unity by the sword were unsuccessful.

Constantine tried another approach to deal with the Arian controversy. Arius, a priest from Alexandria, was a strong proponent of Origen's teachings regarding the distinction between the Father and the Son, which Origen had promulgated in opposition to monarchianism. Arius, however, went further than Origen had gone, stating that since the Son was begotten, "there was a time when he was not," and he also spoke of the Son as created. He was opposed by his own bishop Alexander, who, though he was also an Origenist, was uncomfortable with the language Arius used. He was also opposed by the entire Western (Latin-speaking) church, and by the monks from the Egyptian desert, whose theology tended toward modalism. Arius argued forcefully from scripture that his view was correct, and he had several influential supporters, most notably Eusebius of Nicomedia (not to be confused with the historian, Eusebius of Caesarea), who would become Constantine's personal chaplain and instructor in the faith. The opposition to Arius was led by another Alexandrian, the deacon Athanasius, who would soon become bishop of Alexandria. Before the Council of Nicaea met, Constantine tried to persuade Alexander and Arius to settle their differences and focus on their common faith, but they were unable or unwilling to do so. Constantine was determined to force unity, so he summoned bishops from all over the empire to Nicaea in 325. Most of the 250 or so bishops who attended were from the East, though an influential Western bishop, Hosius of Córdoba, Spain, presided. Sylvester I, bishop of Rome, declined to attend because of his advanced age, but he sent two priests to represent him.

Because Arius himself was unable to speak at the council, since he was not a bishop, his views were represented by proxy. The issue boiled down to a description of the relationship between the Father and the Son. Constantine proposed that the Greek term *homoousios*, "of the same substance," be used to describe the common faith, and the churches of the West immediately accepted the proposal, for they had long used Tertullian's Latin formulation "three persons in one substance." The term was less popular with the bishops from the East, in part because the same term was used by the adoptionist bishop of Antioch Paul of Samosata, a contemporary and opponent of Origen, but because the emperor insisted on using the term, all but two eventually accepted it. Some Eastern bishops, such as Eusebius of Caesarea, did not understand the term in exactly the same way as the Western bishops, an issue that would lead to future divisions within the church. In the end, the council produced a statement of faith, the Nicene Creed (see Box), which declared, among other things, its faith in "one Lord Jesus Christ, the Son of God, begotten from the Father, only-begotten, that is, from the substance of the Father, God from God, light from light, true God from true God, begotten not made, *of one substance with the Father.*" Arius's views – that "there was a time when [Christ] was not," that "before being born he was not," and that "he was of a different substance [*heteroousios*] from the Father" – were explicitly condemned. The term *homoiousios*, "of a similar substance to the Father," was favored by many Eastern bishops, who used it in place of *homoousios*. Other Eastern bishops wanted to avoid the troublesome *ousios*, "substance," altogether, preferring to say that the Son was "like" the Father, without any further specificity. (Those who preferred the terms *homoiousios* or *homoios* are often labeled semi-Arian, and in lieu of a better term, it will be used here, with the caveat that it is not particularly accurate.) Even the Spanish bishop Hosius agreed to this last formulation, which many believed could bring peace to the Church. In reality, further debate in the wake of the council's decision angered those who strongly supported the term *homoousios*, and arguments, banishments, and even wars were waged over the next half century over the inclusion or exclusion of the letter *i*. Bishop Athanasius of Alexandria, a strong proponent of the Nicene *homoousios* doctrine, was sent into exile and recalled no less than five times over his long tenure. The *homoousios/homoiousios* issue would not be finally resolved until the Council of Constantinople in 381.

In addition to the Arian question, the Council of Nicaea also dealt with other, less problematic issues. Some of the more important decisions were these:

- The bishops of Rome, Antioch, and Alexandria were recognized as having regional authority over other bishops.
- The bishop of Jerusalem was to be honored for the historic importance of the city but was not considered equivalent in status to the three bishops just mentioned.

Ecumenical creeds

The Nicene Creed (original 325 version)

We believe in one God, the Father, almighty, maker of all things visible and invisible;

And in one Lord Jesus Christ, the Son of God, begotten from the Father, only-begotten, that is, from the substance of the Father, God from God, light from light, true God from true God, begotten not made, of one substance with the Father, through whom all things came into being, things in heaven and things on earth, who because of us men, and because of our salvation came down and became incarnate, becoming man, suffered and rose again on the third day, ascended to the heavens, will come to judge the living and the dead;

And in the Holy Spirit.

(Kelly 1972: 215–16)

The Nicene Creed (as modified at Constantinople in 381)

We believe in one God, the Father, almighty, maker of heaven and earth, of all things visible and invisible;

And in one Lord Jesus Christ, the only begotten Son of God, begotten from the Father before all ages, light from light, true God from true God, begotten not made, of one substance with the Father, through whom all things came into existence, who because of us men and because of our salvation came down from heaven, and was incarnate from the Holy Spirit and the Virgin Mary and became man, and was crucified for us under Pontius Pilate, and suffered and was buried, and rose again on the third day according to the scriptures and ascended to heaven, and sits on the right hand of the Father, and will come again with glory to judge living and dead, of whose kingdom there will be no end;

And in the Holy Spirit, the Lord and life-giver, who proceeds from the Father (and the Son)*, who with the Father and the Son is together worshiped and together glorified, who spoke through the prophets;

In one holy catholic and apostolic Church; we confess one baptism to the remission of sins; we look forward to the resurrection of the dead and the life of the world to come. Amen.

(Kelly 1972: 297–8)

Latin: filioque. This phrase was added by the Western Church; see below, Chapter 10.

- Bishops could not move from see to see (a *see* was a region ruled over by a bishop).
- Easter was to be celebrated on Sunday, on a day to be determined by a consensus of the churches, rather than by reference to the Jewish calendar.

The Council of Nicaea is recognized today as the first of many ecumenical councils – the Roman Catholic Church reckons the number at 21, but only three since the

Protestant Reformation – that is, a council whose findings are considered binding on all Christians. Other councils have often been held, sometimes small regional councils and sometimes large councils with broad representation, but those councils deemed ecumenical have had the greatest influence on the development of Christian faith and practice.

The debate over Arianism, or, more accurately, "semi-Arianism," embroiled the church in a great debate from the moment the Council of Nicaea was closed. Under the influence of the two Eusebiuses, and despite the determination of the Council of Nicaea, Constantine adopted a semi-Arian understanding of the relationship between Father and Son. In the following century the great scholar Jerome said of that moment that the world awoke with a groan to find itself Arian! As already noted, true Arianism was rejected by most influential Christians, so Jerome's comment refers to the so-called semi-Arian position. Constantine's semi-Arianism was also held by his son Constantius and other emperors. Constantine's two other sons, in contrast, were Nicene Christians. Christians called regional councils and local synods to promote one position and condemn the other, and the battle raged in many areas for 50 years. Finally, in 381, the emperor Theodosius decided to summon bishops to Constantinople to deal with the matter once and for all.

The first order of business for the Council of Constantinople was to declare that no authoritative council had been held since Nicaea in 325 and that contrary decisions at earlier councils held in Sirmium, Ancyra, Constantinople, Antioch, and elsewhere were to be discarded. The council reaffirmed the use of the term *homoousios* and the Nicene Creed, but it made several changes to the latter. While the Nicene Creed (N) had said that Christ was the "begotten from the Father," the Constantinopolitan Creed (C) said "begotten from the Father *before all ages*," a direct contradiction of Arius's claim that "there was a time when he was not." C added specific details to N's treatment of Christ's incarnation, saying that he was "incarnate *from the Holy Spirit and the Virgin Mary*." In place of N's "he suffered," C has "*he was crucified for us under Pontius Pilate*, and suffered *and was buried*." C also adds the details that Christ's resurrection was predicted by scripture and that "*of his kingdom there will be no end*." The largest addition by far comes at the end of the creed. Whereas N ends simply with "[We believe in] the Holy Spirit," C elaborates extensively on the nature of the Spirit and the Spirit's relationship with the Father and the Son, additions that reflect the development of Trinitarian doctrine in the interim since Nicaea and also serve as condemnation of *Macedonianism*, which denied the divinity of the Holy Spirit. C also adds a statement about "*one holy catholic and apostolic Church*," a clear condemnation of the Donatists and other schismatic groups.

In addition to the changes to the creed, the Council of Constantinople rejected the teaching of Apollinaris, priest of Laodicea, who said that Christ had a human body but a divine mind. Apollinaris had based his belief in a divine mind on the assumption that if Jesus had had a human mind, he would have been subject to the possibility of sin, but the council rejected his logic because it diminished the humanity of Christ. The council also declared that the bishop of Constantinople should join the ranks of Rome, Antioch, and Alexandria as one of the principal rulers of the church, second in authority only to Rome. Ecumenical councils like Nicaea and Constantinople were very important in shaping the doctrine of the church, but any formulation put together by a committee was likely to be somewhat stodgy, less communicative, less innovative, and ultimately less influential than the theological reflections of brilliant theologians.

Theological reflection, East and West

In the fourth century, in the province of Cappadocia in eastern Asia Minor, a remarkable family lived. Two brothers, Basil and Gregory, lived with their older sister, Macrina, and the rest of their family. The family had deep Christian roots – their relatives had suffered during the Decian persecution, and one was a bishop – and they were both financially well off and educated. Macrina had been promised to a young man by her parents, but when he suddenly died, she declared her intention to live a solitary life devoted to God. She tried to convince her brother Basil to do the same, but Basil, who had studied in Athens with his friend Gregory (who would become bishop of Nazianzus) and the future emperor Julian the Apostate, had no time for such things. However, when his brother Naucratius died unexpectedly, Basil was devastated, and he decided to take Macrina's advice. Meanwhile, Macrina retired to some family land, along with her mother and several other women, and led a life of devotion. Her knowledge was so vast and her didactic skills so keen that she became known simply as the Teacher. She remained in retirement for the rest of her life, touching the lives of many women directly, and the lives of many men indirectly through the influence she had on her brothers.

Macrina's brother Basil, shaken by Naucratius's death, went to Egypt and other outlying areas of the Roman Empire to learn the monastic life from the desert saints. He returned and set up a monastery for men with his friend Gregory of Nazianzus, near the location of Macrina's retreat for women. After spending about six years as a monk, he was ordained a priest in Caesarea in 362, and he became bishop there in 370. Although he was an admirer of Origen, he came to believe strongly that the word *homoousios* was the term that was necessary for all orthodox Christians to accept in order to fight full-blown (*heteroousios* or *anomoios*, "not similar") Arianism, but he understood *homoousios* in a way similar to many who preferred *homoiousios*, that is, as a term that did not blur the distinction between Father and Son. Basil also believed in the full divinity of the Holy Spirit, writing an important book on the subject. He combined his understanding of the relationship between Father and Son with his emphasis on the full divinity of the Spirit to arrive at a formulation concerning the Trinity: one substance (*ousia*) but three persons, or identifying qualities (*hypostases*). Basil's Greek explanation of the Trinity was roughly equivalent to Tertullian's earlier Latin formulation of one substance (*substantia*) in three persons (*personae*). However, whereas Tertullian came at the problem of the Trinity by beginning with unity of substance, Basil began with an emphasis on the distinction of persons. Basil explained the difference between substance and person as the same as the difference between the general and the particular. For example, the human race represents the general, whereas the individual person represents the particular. Moreover, the *hypostases* were distinct in their relationship to one another: the Father begets, the Son is begotten, and the Spirit proceeds (from the Father).

Despite his numerous books and letters devoted to theological topics, Basil was a monk at heart, and he felt himself dragged into the theological debates of his day against his will, though he accepted his role as bishop and theologian as part of his service to God. Basil used his interest and experience in the monastic life to draw up a set of guidelines for monastic communities to follow. The guidelines he create served as the "rule" for monks in the region, and Basil became known as the father of eastern monasticism. Basil regularly suffered from bad health, as a child and as an adult, and he died sometime before reaching his fiftieth birthday, in 379. His accomplishments as bishop, theologian, and monastic organizer were such that he was honored in his own time for his erudition and commitment to fighting for orthodoxy, and he became known after his death as Basil the Great.

Macrina and Basil had a younger brother named Gregory, known as Gregory of Nyssa to distinguish him from Basil's friend Gregory of Nazianzus. Gregory, although devout, was not interested in the monastic life when he was young, so he married and may have fathered children. After his wife died, however, the pain of her loss drove him to a life of contemplation like his siblings. His abilities did not allow him to remain in the monastic life, however, and in about 371 his brother Basil recruited him as bishop of the town of Nyssa, near Caesarea. He worked closely with both Basil and Gregory of Nazianzus on developing the doctrine of the Trinity from an orthodox perspective. He was an ardent admirer of Origen, but he had no qualms about modifying Origen's teaching if he felt it needed to be updated. For example, like Origen, Gregory believed that evil, which is the absence of good, is not eternal, and when God eventually encompasses all in all (1 Cor 15:28), evil will no longer exist. Thus, by implication, people who had lived evil lives would be cleansed of their evil and could be reunited with God. Gregory also accepted Origen's "ransom theory of the atonement," which states that God gave Jesus to Satan as a ransom for the human race. Whereas Origen had said that God deceived Satan by raising Christ from the dead, Gregory argued that God was not being deceitful at all. Christ contained the fullness of divinity within him, and Satan was simply unable to hold him.

Gregory was not a very good administrator, and he longed to return to the life of a monk. Nevertheless, like Basil, he accepted his role as a defender of orthodoxy, and after Basil's death, he attended the second ecumenical council in Constantinople to represent the orthodox position. He remained a bishop for several years after the council, writing many books and letters on both theological and spiritual themes. An example of the latter is his commentary on the Song of Songs, which he interpreted allegorically. After some time, when he was convinced that orthodoxy was firmly established, he retired to pursue a life of contemplation and passed from the public stage.

Gregory of Nazianzus was the son of the bishop of Nazianzus, and like Basil and Gregory of Nyssa, he felt drawn to the solitary life. Nevertheless, Basil appointed him bishop of Sasima, a small town in Cappadocia. Although he did not remain long in the post, fleeing back to the monastic life, he accepted the position of bishop of the most important see in the East, Constantinople, in 379, where he was the first orthodox Nicene bishop in 40 years. Although he only remained there for two years, he was present when the new Nicene emperor Theodosius I first entered the city, and he was present at the opening of the Council of Constantinople in 381. During Gregory' brief tenure in Constantinople, he secured the return of all church property to the Nicene party. Famous for his rhetoric, his fiery sermons on the divinity of the *logos* gained immediate notoriety. After bishops from Egypt and Macedonia objected to his appointment as bishop of Constantinople, he resigned and returned to Nazianzus, where he worked for a few years. He spent his last few years engaged in literary pursuits and monastic duties.

Gregory of Nazianzus

Of the Great Cappadocians, Gregory of Nazianzus was the most skilled orator and the only poet. He composed some 30,000 verses of poetry and songs, about a third of which survive. Gregory's songs and poems were lyrical and theological at the same time, as this morning hymn demonstrates:

'Tis dawn: to God I lift my hand,
To regulate my way;
My passions rule, and unmoved stand,
And give to Thee the day:
Not one dark word or deed of sin,
Nor one base thought allow;
But watch all avenues within,
And wholly keep my vow.
Shamed were my age, should I decline;
Shamed were Thy table too,
At which I stand: – the will is mine:
Give grace, my Christ, to do.

Because Gregory worked closely with his friends Basil and Gregory of Nyssa, his views on the Trinity and the nature of Christ were identical, as his five Theological Orations (sermons) show. For example, in his Third Theological Oration, he says,

When did these come into being? They are above all "When." But, if I am to speak with something more of boldness, – when the Father did. And when did the Father come into being? There never was a time when He was not. And the same thing is true of the Son and the Holy Ghost. Ask me again, and again I will answer you,

When was the Son begotten? When the Father was not begotten. And when did the Holy Ghost proceed? When the Son was, not proceeding but, begotten – beyond the sphere of time, and above the grasp of reason; although we cannot set forth that which is above time, if we avoid as we desire any expression which conveys the idea of time.

Gregory's beautiful rhetoric and theological acumen earned him the title Gregory the Theologian in the Eastern church.

If Gregory of Nazianzus was the most skilled orator of the Great Cappadocians, the most skilled orator of the entire history of the Eastern church, and some would argue the greatest preacher in the history of the church, East or West, was their younger contemporary, John Chrysostom, whose name means "golden mouth," an appellation he earned for the sermons he preached while bishop of Constantinople. Born in Antioch about 347, he was raised in a wealthy Christian family, so he had both a theological and a classical education. After completing his education, he spent a few years leading a monastic life, after which he returned to Antioch to serve as a deacon, then a priest for several years. He answered the call to become bishop of Constantinople somewhat reluctantly, but after his installation as bishop in 398, he threw himself into the job. His somewhat choleric temperament, combined with his skill with words, made him a popular preacher to the masses of people, but the emperor and others in power, including many in the clergy, grew to dislike his moralistic outbursts. The emperor Arcadius, and especially the empress Eudoxia, took great offense when Chrysostom railed against the rich, calling on them to use their wealth for the benefit of the poor. He also made an enemy of Theophilus, bishop of Alexandria. After several antagonistic encounters with members of the court and clergy, and after several sermons in which Chrysostom criticized the empress directly, he was forbidden access to the church facilities and expelled from the city, and he died in exile.

Chrysostom did not possess the sharp intellect of Basil or the lyrical talents of Gregory of Nazianzus, but he had a tremendous oratorical gift, which he used to full advantage. He also had a deep compassion for the common people, and they loved him for it. In fact, his tenure as bishop of Constantinople would undoubtedly have ended sooner except for the intervention of the masses. Chrysostom was also a prolific writer, and his sermons, letters, and other writings take up 18 volumes in the standard scholarly collection of the writings of the Greek "fathers," far more than any other author represented in the 161 volume work. The three Great Cappadocians, Macrina, and John Chrysostom are honored by both the Eastern and Western churches as saints. Basil, Gregory of Nazianzus, and Chrysostom are also recognized by the Roman Catholic Church as doctors (that is, teachers) of the church, and they are referred to as the Three Hierarchs, or premier teachers and fathers, of the Eastern Orthodox Church.

If the East was blessed with many important bishops and theologians during the fourth and fifth centuries, the West was hardly bereft of them. Like their counterparts in the East, the western theologians that are today considered the most important were strong champions of Nicene orthodoxy. Unlike those in the East, they often wielded a surprising degree of political as well as ecclesiastical power, due to the fragile state of the Western Roman Empire and the relative weakness of the Western emperors, in comparison with their Byzantine colleagues.

The first important theologian in the West after the time of Constantine was Ambrose, bishop of Milan. When the previous bishop died in 373, Ambrose was an unbaptized layman and governor of Milan, which served for a time in the late fourth century as capital of the Western Roman Empire. A strong advocate for the Nicene position even as a *catechumen* (student of the faith), he was baptized, then ordained as deacon, priest, and bishop within one week, when he was only 34 years old. His governmental experience made him comfortable dealing with other political leaders, including emperors. He influenced the young emperor Gratian to stamp out all remnant of Arianism and semi-Arianism in his realm, and he was not afraid to appoint Nicene bishops even in territories controlled by the semi-Arian emperor Valentinian II and his mother Justina. On one occasion he intervened with the general (later emperor) Magnus Maximus of behalf of Valentinian II to keep the former from invading Italy. On another occasion he refused Justina's order to surrender the basilica of Milan to semi-Arian bishops and prevailed. On yet another occasion he harshly reprimanded the emperor Theodosius I for slaughtering 7,000 inhabitants of Thessalonica after one of his officers had been killed in the city, excommunicating him from the church and forcing him to do public penance for eight months before Ambrose readmitted him to communion. Ambrose believed in the superiority of the church to the state, stating that "bishops ought to judge Christian emperors, and not emperors bishops" (Ambrose, *To Valentinian* 21.4).

Before Ambrose came to power, the Western church considered the ascetic, or monastic, lifestyle, so frequently practiced in the East, to be an excessive and fanatical way of living the Christian life. Ambrose was also instrumental in validating asceticism as acceptable to those living in the West, and asceticism became increasingly more popular in the West, though it never had the following that it had in the East. Ambrose was a strong and forceful individual, unafraid to wield the power of his office, and undaunted by imperial power. His greatest contribution to Christianity, however, came about through his influence on a young teacher of rhetoric who settled in Milan, Augustine.

Augustine was born in Latin-speaking North Africa to an orthodox mother and a pagan father in 354. He went to Carthage when he was 17 to study, and he became interested in philosophy, especially the writings of Cicero. He read the Bible, but he failed to find value in the crude anthropomorphisms of the Old Testament. While in Carthage he took a mistress, who bore him a son. Augustine was a deeply spiritual and introspective man, in search of truth from an early age. He turned to Manichaeism, which taught a strict dualism of light and darkness, soul and body, good and evil. It also stressed Christ as savior, especially as revealed through the Apostle Paul. Augustine spent nine years as a Manichaean "hearer," never seeking full-fledged acceptance among "the perfect." He became a vegetarian, as Manichaeism taught, but he retained his mistress, thus violating one of the principal teachings of Manichaeism, celibacy (childbirth brought about a new mixture of light and darkness, which the Manichaeans sought to separate). After some time he became dissatisfied with some Manichaean teachings, and when the great Manichaean teacher Faustus was unable to answer some of his questions, he left the sect. He moved to Rome in 382 to teach rhetoric and soon became a Neo-Platonist.

Neo-Platonism was a spiritual form of Platonism based on the system of Plotinus. Augustine was drawn to it because it claimed to offer personal salvation, which Augustine deeply believed he needed. Plotinus described "the One" as that which exists in and of itself through its own thought processes. When the One begins to consider itself as "other," it becomes divided, and Being is created. These aspects of Neo-Platonic thought were fascinating to Augustine, and they were formative in the development of his thinking about the Trinity later in his life.

In 384 Augustine moved to Milan, and in order to appear respectable, he enrolled as a catechumen under the tutelage of Bishop Ambrose. As a rhetorician, he was also interested in evaluating Ambrose's rhetorical style. Augustine was amazed that Ambrose was able to harmonize the Bible with much Platonic thought through allegory, making it more palatable to him. He sent his mistress and son back to Carthage to await a proper marriage, but Augustine became more and more drawn to Christianity. He was especially impressed when he heard that a famous Neo-Platonist philosopher had been converted to Christianity through reading Athanasius's *Life of Anthony*, a biography of the desert saint. In 386, while he was in a garden struggling with a decision concerning Christianity, he heard a child playing a game, saying "take and read, take and read." He opened a Bible to Rom 13:13–14, and read, "Not in reveling and drunkenness, not in debauchery and licentiousness, not in quarreling and jealousy, but put on the Lord Jesus Christ, and make no provision for the flesh, to gratify its desires." His seeking at an end, he was baptized by Ambrose on Easter 387.

After returning to North Africa, Augustine sent his mistress away. Shortly thereafter both his mother and his son died, leaving him heartbroken. In 391 Valerius, bishop of Hippo, a nearby city, ordained him as a priest. He quickly became famous for his intellect, and he delighted in challenging Manichaeans who lived in the area to public debates, where he regularly got the better of them. He played a leading role in the regional Council of Hippo in 393, and in 395 he was elected co-bishop of Hippo. He became sole bishop after Valerius died, and he served in that capacity for the remainder of his life. During his tenure, he became the most influential theologian of the Western church, influencing both Roman Catholic and Protestant theology centuries after his death.

Augustine was a determined opponent of the Donatists, who were present in great numbers in North Africa. He considered them schismatics who were outside the church, and he supported the imperial edict which the emperor Honorius issued in 412 suppressing the Donatists. In a letter to a Roman general who was trying to persuade a Donatist bishop to give up his church, he said it was better that the bishop and his associates perish in the flames than that all Donatists should burn in hell. Augustine's willingness to use the power of the state to enforce religious conformity shows a clear dependence on the example of Ambrose.

Augustine's most famous theological argument was with a British monk named Pelagius, who was forced to flee his residence in Rome when Alaric the Goth sacked the city in 410. Pelagius taught that the whole gospel should be obeyed, including Jesus' saying, "Be perfect, as your heavenly Father is perfect." Pelagius saw sins as individuals failings, not as indicative of a fallen nature inherited from Adam. Since sin was the result of habit, not nature, Pelagius said, the individual believer should be able to overcome it. Augustine himself had struggled with sin and been *unable* to overcome it for years prior to his conversion to Christianity, so he believed in the doctrine of "original sin," which states that a sin nature is passed on through birth and can be traced back to Adam. He read Rom 5:12 as saying that all people sinned in Adam; that is, as a direct result of Adam's disobedience, all are guilty of Adam's sin. He emphasized the necessity of God's grace in the conversion experience, because the human will is not free to choose to follow God in and of itself. On the other hand, Augustine said, God's grace is irresistible and is directed toward those predestined for salvation. Pelagius had a particular problem with Augustine's statement (from *The Confessions*), "O God, give what you command and command what you will," because he thought it was ridiculous that God would command something that humans were unable to follow, then condemn them for not following it. Augustine countered that in his own experience, he was unable even to believe in God, which is the foundation of Christianity, but his mother's prayers caused God's grace to shine on him. Pelagius settled in the East, where people were more open to his point of view. "God is [the will's] helper whenever it chooses good; while man is himself in fault when he sins, as being under the influence of a free will," Pelagius said (Augustine, *On the Proceedings of Pelagius* 8). Pelagius was condemned at the Council of Carthage in 416. Although it declared Augustine's position orthodox, the later church actually taught a compromise between the strict Augustinian view and the teaching of Pelagius, a view sometimes called semi-Pelagianism. Because of Augustine's teaching on original sin, which was universally accepted in the West, infant baptism, which was seen as washing away original sin, became increasingly popular.

Unlike the Cappadocians, whose discussions of the Trinity began with the notion of the distinctions among Father, Son, and Holy Spirit and moved toward unity of substance, Augustine began with the concept of the unity of God, influenced by his Neo-Platonic background, and then developed the idea of three separate persons sharing the same essence. He agreed with the Cappadocians that the three persons of the Trinity are defined by their relationships with one another, not by any difference in essence: the Father begets, the Son is begotten, and the Spirit proceeds from the Father and the Son. The Trinity is an internal relationship within God, he said, independent of God's revelation to humanity or of salvation through Christ. The Trinity exists before creation and is independent of it.

Augustine is best known for two works, *The Confessions* and *The City of God*. In *The Confessions*, Augustine wrote a spiritual autobiography that was unique in the ancient world and remains a classic today. In it he traces his spiritual formation, his dalliances with sin, and his interest in various philosophies and religions. The form of the book is a confession to God, in which Augustine highlights his own foolish behavior and sin, and also that of all those who reject Christianity. He offers a particularly scathing critique of Manichaeism, to which he was formerly attracted. The book is a confession in two senses. First, it is an actual confession of sins (lust, pride, etc.). Second, it is a confession, or statement, of faith.

After the sack of Rome by the Goths, and with the Vandals and other Germanic tribes destroying the last vestiges of the Roman Empire all around him, Augustine wrote a book that expressed his political and theological theory of government. He proposed the idea of two cities, the City of God, built on love of God, and the Earthly City, built on love of self. Though the two cities are mingled with one another throughout history, they are in constant struggle, and in the end only the City of God will remain. All earthly cities, like Rome, will eventually fall. God preserved Rome to spread the gospel, Augustine said, but now that that has been accomplished, God allowed the city to fall. Christians, as citizens of the City of God, must remember that heaven is the Christian's true home, so excessive loyalty to any earthly city should be avoided. The purpose of the book was not primarily philosophical or political but pastoral. Christians throughout the West did not understand why God would let Rome fall, but Augustine counsels them to have hope for the future, thus showing the importance of interpreting current events in the light of theology.

If Augustine was the most important theologian in the West, the leading biblical scholar was his contemporary Hieronymus, usually known in English as Jerome. Jerome was drawn to asceticism in the West at a time when ascetics were not yet fully accepted by western society. He was highly educated, but he saw little value in pagan literature, with which he was very familiar. He saw a sharp distinction between Christianity and all aspects of pagan culture, and he was highly critical of those with whom he disagreed. He traveled widely in the East, where he failed to win many friends because of his harsh judgments. He was criticized in the West for excessive asceticism, which he observed and urged others to follow as well. Jerome was vigorously opposed to sex, believing that a holy life required perpetual virginity. He said that Adam and Eve did not engage in sexual activity before the Fall (i.e. the first sin), and marriage was inferior to perpetual virginity.

In 382 Jerome was appointed secretary to Damasus, bishop of Rome, who commissioned him to create a new translation of the Bible into Latin. Many Latin translations were already in existence (the Old Latin versions), but they were often quite different from one another, a situation that led to theological confusion in the Latin-speaking world. The Old Testament in the Old Latin versions was translated from the LXX rather than the Hebrew text, so Jerome decided to learn Hebrew so that he could translate his Latin version directly from the original language. After mastering the language, he became the only Western scholar of his day to know Hebrew. In fact, Jerome had an argument by correspondence with Augustine over the importance of resorting to Hebrew when translating the Old Testament. Jerome believed it was very important, while Augustine argued that since the LXX itself was inspired, going back to the Hebrew was unnecessary. Jerome began his task by revising existing Latin versions of the New Testament and Psalms, but he eventually translated the entire Old Testament from Hebrew into Latin. Jerome's translation, the Latin Vulgate, became the standard Bible of the Latin-speaking church for more than 1,500 years.

The monastic reaction

Many people flocked to the church in the wake of Constantine's conversion and declaration that Christianity was a legal religion. Some saw the Christian message as validated by Constantine's victories in battle. Others saw Christianity as a valuable new philosophy worthy of pursuit. Still others saw Christianity as the newest, preferred religion of the Roman Empire. Christianity was suddenly popular in comparison with other religion in the empire. Elaborate churches were built, and many people sought to become bishops of prestigious sees, such as Rome or Constantinople. In the wake of these changes in the church, many Christians began decrying the increasing worldliness of the church. A large number of them, particularly in the East, fled to the desert in search of a quiet, contemplative life. Although monasticism traces its origins to earlier times, it was after the Decian persecution that it began to grow in popularity. After Athanasius wrote his famous biography of Anthony, many more Christians decided to flee the cities for the solitude of the deserts of Egypt, Syria, and Palestine.

Figure 7.2   St Catherine's Monastery is situated on Jebel Musa, one of the mountains in the Sinai Peninsula identified as the mountain on which Moses received the Ten Commandments. Both male and female monastics fled the ease and temptations of civilized society to seek God in the desert.

The earliest Christian monks were *anchorites*, that is, solitary monks. These monks followed the *eremitic* lifestyle (i.e. the life of a hermit) because they wanted to find solitude in the desert to pray and meditate. Many monks were renowned for their piety and orthodoxy, so they were often sought out by Christians who still lived in society for their opinions and counsel. They made their living by begging or by weaving mats from reeds. They sometimes had small gardens, but they avoided meat, oil, and wine. Both men and women became monks, and they were sometimes known as Christian "athletes," because of the discipline required to live the life of a monk.

After a while, many monks began to live near one another in order to worship with one another one or two days a week. These monks were no longer strictly eremitic but had become *semi-eremitic*. Other monks began to gather together in communities, organized around a spiritual leader (abbot). This type of monasticism is called *cenobitic*, from a Greek word meaning "living together." The first organizer of cenobitic communities, at least the first whose name was preserved, was Pachomius, a fourth century monk. Pachomius insisted on complete obedience to one's superiors within the community, and he emphasized mutual service. His sister Mary formed a similar community for women as well.

The influence of monks on other Christians was great. Examples of leading secular Christians (i.e. those remaining in the world) who were heavily influenced by the monastic life include Athanasius, Jerome, Basil the Great, and Augustine. One of the most unusual developments in the history of the monastic movement was the emergence of *stylites*, or pillar saints, who climbed tall pillars and lived on them for years at a time. The first and most influential stylite was Simeon Stylites, who ascended his pillar in the Syrian desert in 423 and remained there until his death in 459, 36 years later. Simeon was known for his wisdom and revered for his saintliness, and people traveled from far and wide to see him. Over the years, Simeon was forced to increase the height of his pillar in order to maintain some measure of isolation. Simeon corresponded with emperors and bishops; his influence was felt in the court of Theodosius II and at the Council of Chalcedon.

Not all monks lived in the desert. In the second half of the fifth century, Patrick established Christian monasteries in Ireland. Irish monks became known for their rigorous asceticism, their customs that differed from the rest of the Western church, and their semi-eremitic communities. In the sixth century, another monk, Columba, took Christianity from Ireland to the Picts in Scotland, establishing monasteries as he worked. Back in Italy, a fifth century monk named Benedict established several monasteries and decided to write a rule for those living in his monasteries. He decreed eight times of prayer per day, one or two meals, and labor in the fields for his monks. The *Rule* of St. Benedict was copied and used in monasteries throughout Europe over the next several centuries, much as Basil's rule had been used in the East, and Benedict is known today as the father of western monasticism.

The Councils of Ephesus and Chalcedon

Two important ecumenical councils were held in the fourth century, both of which dealt further with the central issue arising out of the Councils of Nicaea and Constantinople: the relation of the divine and the human in Christ. Nestorius, the bishop of Constantinople from 428 to 431, was raised in Antioch, one of the important centers of Christian scholarship. He accepted without question the Nicene doctrine that Christ was fully divine and fully human, and, in keeping with the emphasis of many in the East, particularly in Antioch, he also held that it was vital to avoid mixing the divine and human natures so that they lost their particular characteristics in the person of Christ. Nestorius first drew attention to himself shortly after being appointed bishop of Constantinople. It was common in those days for people to speak of Mary as the *theotokos*, or "mother of God." Nestorius said that the word was inaccurate, for Mary should be called *christotokos*, "mother of Christ" instead, since it was impossible for God to have a mother. Cyril, bishop of Alexandria, was incensed by Nestorius's claim, because he believed that Nestorius was trying to separate the divine from the human nature in Christ, perhaps in the manner of the adoptionists, although Nestorius explicitly denied that interpretation of his words. Theological differences were not all that divided Nestorius and Cyril, for the latter, like other bishops of Alexandria, believed that Alexandria should be considered the preeminent see in the East, just as Rome was in the West. Constantinople may have been the new imperial city, but the Christian pedigree of Alexandria was much older. The Alexandrians had a natural ally in the church of Rome, for Rome was concerned that Constantinople would usurp the rightful place of leadership that Roman bishops believed belonged inherently to them. The bishop of the other major see, Antioch, sided with Nestorius, primarily for theological reasons – for of course, Nestorius was originally from Antioch, and his theology was thoroughly Antiochian.

The core of Nestorius's argument was that the divine and human natures in Christ remained distinct from one another, retaining their individual properties, even though they were inextricably bound together. Nestorius believed that unless the distinctiveness of the two natures was maintained, the result would be a third, combined nature that was neither completely divine nor completely human, but something altogether different. An analogy might be that when sodium and chlorine are combined, the result (salt) is something entirely new, having the properties of neither original element, whereas when salt and water are combined, the two mix together and cannot be separated, but the properties of both the salt and the water remain in the solution. Cyril argued that the two natures were indeed both present in Christ, but they were bound together in a "hypostatic union" that precluded dissolution. Thus, it was impossible for Mary to bear Christ without at the same time bearing God.

The emperor Theodosius II called an ecumenical council, which was to meet in Ephesus in 431 to decide the matter. Cyril and his allies arrived first and promptly declared Nestorius a heretic and deposed him from his position as bishop. When Nestorius and

The divine and the human in Christ

Early Christians struggled to explain in what sense Jesus was the Son of God, what human characteristics he had, and what divine characteristics he had. Some emphasized Jesus' humanity rather than his divinity, and some did the opposite. The following diagram illustrates some of these positions, and the final, orthodox position determined at the Council of Chalcedon, by using the vertical shaft of a cross to indicate Jesus' divinity and the horizontal shaft to indicate his humanity, in the minds of different individuals and groups.

Century/Year	Group/Person	Divinity	Humanity	Symbol
First	Docetists	Affirmed	Denied	
First	Ebionites	Denied	Affirmed	
Fourth	Arians	Reduced	Reduced, but emphasized	
Fourth	Apollinaris	Reduced, but emphasized	Reduced	
Fifth	Nestorius	Affirmed, but separate	Affirmed, but separate	
Fifth	Eutychians	Affirmed	Reduced	
451	Chalcedon	Affirmed	Affirmed	
			without confusion	
			without mutability	
			without division	
			without separation	

his allies arrived, they held their own meeting and deposed Cyril. Delegates from Rome then arrived and joined Cyril's council, because Cyril had agreed that the council would condemn Pelagianism, the primary concern of Rome, as well as Nestorianism. The emperor was not happy with the council's proceedings, and he imprisoned Nestorius and Cyril, as well as John of Antioch, Nestorius's chief supporter. Cyril soon convinced the emperor to release him and exile Nestorius, so the end result was that Nestorius was removed from his position as bishop of Constantinople, his theological position was condemned as heresy, and he was exiled.

Not surprisingly, the results of the third ecumenical council were not universally accepted, and debate over the relationship between the divine and the human in Christ continued. Many Christians considered Cyril's formulation heretical, for it seemed to subsume the human nature of Jesus under the more powerful divine nature, thus making him somewhat less than fully human. This was an important theological point, for Cyril's opponents argued that if Christ were not fully human, he would be unable to effect salvation for humanity, for he would no longer be a representative of the human race. Some time later Eutyches, a monk in Constantinople, proposed the idea that the flesh of Christ was from some heavenly source rather than derived from Mary. His proposal was intended to safeguard the sinlessness of Jesus by preserving him from any hint of corruption or original sin. He was supported by Dioscorus, Cyril's successor in Alexandria, but much of the church was adamantly opposed to Eutyches' proposal, seeing it as the logical conclusion of Cyril's questionable theological position. Not only was the bishop of Constantinople, Flavian, opposed to Eutyches, but so was Leo, the bishop of Rome. The emperor called another council to meet in Ephesus in 449, run by Dioscorus. Leo, who did not attend, sent a strongly worded letter condemning Eutyches' position, but the council was stacked with supporters of Eutyches, and Leo's letter (the *Tome* of Leo) was never read. Furthermore Flavian, who did attend, was physically beaten so severely that he died a few days later. Not surprisingly, Leo and many others refused to recognize the findings of the council, calling it the "Robber Synod."

After the death of Theodosius in 450, his wife Pulcheria called a new council at Chalcedon in 451. This time the whole Eastern church was represented, and Leo's *Tome* was read and approved by the council. The council decided that Christ did indeed have two natures, and these natures were combined "without confusion, without mutability, without division, and without separation." Still in exile, Nestorius heard the decision of the council and proclaimed himself vindicated. Nevertheless, the council did not lift the condemnation of Nestorius issued by the Council of Ephesus, nor did it condemn the view of the now-deceased Cyril of Alexandria, so the first went down in tradition as a heretic and the second as a saint. The council did condemn the view of Eutyches, and it elevated the role of Leo, the bishop of Rome. In fact, many scholars refer to Leo as the first Roman bishop worthy of the title "pope," or "father," for he asserted his authority to speak for the whole church, and many in the church listened. The power of the Roman bishop had been growing for some time, for while three patriarchs existed in the East, only one existed in the West. When conflicts arose among the Eastern bishops, they often appealed to Rome for support, thus elevating the perceived authority of the bishop of Rome. For example, Athanasius had appealed to Rome against the semi-Arians, the Great Cappadocians had joined Rome against Apollinaris, Cyril had appealed to Rome against Nestorius, and a majority of the East had agreed with Leo against Dioscorus and Eutyches. In all of these conflicts – as in most previous theological struggles – the Roman position had emerged victorious. Leo's assertion of the authority of the papacy and his success in dealing with issues such as Pelagianism, Nestorianism, and Eutychianism, led others to give him the title Leo "the Great," one of only two popes to be so honored.

The findings of the Council of Chalcedon were rejected by a sizeable minority in the East, centered around Egypt and Syria. The monophysites, whose name means "one nature," were convinced that Chalcedon's commitment to two natures in Christ was just another form of Nestorianism. Many Copts (Egyptian-speaking Christians) and Syrians separated themselves from the Chalcedonian definition of the faith, eventually forming what are now called Oriental Orthodox Churches in Egypt, Syria, Armenia, Ethiopia, and elsewhere. All attempts to heal the rift between Chalcedonians and monophysites were unsuccessful. The next two ecumenical councils, both held in Constantinople, continued to deal with related issues. Constantinople II (553) condemned Origen and his spiritual heirs Theodore of Mopsuestia, Theodoret of Cyrrhus, and Ibas of Edessa, whom many believed overemphasized the separate natures in Christ, as Nestorius had (all those condemned were already dead). On the other hand, Constantinople III (680–681) condemned monothelitism (belief that Christ had only one will) and monenergism (belief that Christ had only one "energy," or activity), which were both attempts to bridge the gap between the Chalcedonians and the monophysites. It is interesting to note that the monothelite compromise was supported in advance of the latter council by Pope Honorius I of Rome, by Patriarch Sergius of Constantinople, and by Byzantine Emperor Heraclius!

Key points you need to know

- Though he only became a Christian later in life, Constantine favored Christianity from the beginning of his reign as emperor and made it a legal religion for the first time.
- The last pagan Roman emperor, Julian the Apostate, tried to subvert Christianity not through persecution but by taking away Christians' privileges and by organizing the pagan religion after the Christian model.
- Christianity became the official religion of the Roman Empire under Theodosius I, and Jews, heterodox Christians, and pagans were all denied the same rights as orthodox Christians.
- The Council of Nicaea, the first ecumenical council, was called to address the Arian controversy, among other items. It produced the Nicene Creed, which defined orthodoxy for most Christians.
- After continuing controversy concerning the semi-Arian position, the Council of Constantinople was called to strengthen the orthodox, Nicene position, and the Nicene Creed was modified accordingly.
- Great scholars in both the East and the West during the fourth and fifth centuries helped to define standard Christian doctrines such as the Trinity and the relationship between the divine and the human in Christ.
- Jerome translated the Bible into Latin, and his Latin Vulgate became the official Bible of the Western Church for centuries.

- Many Christians fled to the deserts of Egypt, Syria, and Palestine in order to live secluded lives of contemplation.
- Ongoing controversies over the exact relationship between the divine and the human in Christ led to the Councils of Ephesus and Chalcedon. The former's decisions led to a split with the Nestorians, and the latter's led to a split with the Monophysites. As a result of these splits, the Oriental Orthodox Churches remain separated from the rest of the Christian Church to this day.

Discussion questions

1. Did Constantine choose Christianity as the preferred religion of his empire because he was convinced of its truth or because he believed it would cement his empire together under a common system of thought?
2. Why did the orthodox (Nicene) party within Christianity feel the need to modify the original Nicene Creed at the Council of Constantinople?
3. What are the different implications of the terms *homoousios, heteroousios, homoiousios,* and *homoios* in reference to Christ?
4. How did the formulations concerning the Trinity defined by Augustine differ from that defined by the Great Cappadocians? How does the doctrine of the Trinity accord with the teaching of the New Testament?
5. What factors led so many people to seek God in the desert during the third through fifth centuries?
6. Was Nestorius's position on the two natures of Christ vindicated by the Council of Chalcedon, as he claimed, or not, as his opponents claimed?

Further reading

Athanasius, *Life of Anthony.*
Augustine, *City of God.*
Augustine, *On the Proceedings of Pelagius.*
Augustine, *On the Trinity.*
Eusebius, *Life of Constantine.*
Frend, W. H. C. 1984. *The Rise of Christianity.* Philadelphia, PA: Fortress.
González, Justo 1984–1985. *The Story of Christianity.* 2 vols. New York: HarperSanFrancisco.
González, Justo 1987. *A History of Christian Thought.* Revised edn, 3 vols. Nashville, TN: Abingdon.
Latourette, Kenneth Scott 1975. *A History of Christianity.* Revised edn, 2 vols. New York: Harper & Row.
Pelikan, Jaroslav 1971–1989. *The Christian Tradition: A History of the Development of Doctrine.* 5 vols. Chicago, IL: University of Chicago Press.

Quasten, Johannes and Angelo Di Berardino 1950–1986. *Patrology*. 4 vols. Vol. 4 translated by Placid Solari. Allen, TX: Christian Classics.

Tillich, Paul 1968. *A History of Christian Thought*. Edited by Carl E. Braaten. New York: Simon and Schuster.

8   *Power shift*

In the age of Roman virtue the provinces were subject to the arms, and the citizens to the laws, of the republic, till those laws were subverted by civil discord, and both the city and the provinces became the servile property of a tyrant . ... During the same period, the barbarians had emerged from obscurity and contempt, and the warriors of Germany and Scythia were introduced into the provinces, as the servants, the allies, and at length the masters, of the Romans.

(Edward Gibbon, *The Decline and Fall of the Roman Empire*, Chapter 36)

In this chapter

Only 150 years after Christianity became the favored religion of the Roman Empire, the western half of that empire fell to the "barbarians," the predominantly Germanic tribes that had been encroaching on the empire's territory for centuries. The absence of strong, centralized leadership in the West increased the power of the pope, the bishop of Rome, both politically and spiritually. Meanwhile, the Eastern Roman Empire, now commonly called the Byzantine Empire, flourished in the East. The emergence of Islam in the seventh century, however, threatened the power of the Byzantine Empire, and in the Levant, Egypt, North Africa, and the Iberian peninsula Muslims conquered Christian nations and spread Islam. Within a few decades of the fall of the Western Roman Empire, the majority of the Germanic tribes on the European continent south of Scandinavia had converted to Christianity, and they would be followed by the tribes of Britain within a century.

Main topics covered

- The fall of the Western Roman Empire
- The rise of the Eastern Roman (Byzantine) Empire
- The emergence and spread of Islam
- The spread of Christianity in Europe and beyond

The fall of the Western Roman Empire

As the happiness of a *future* life is the great object of religion, we may hear, without surprise or scandal, that the introduction, or at least the abuse, of Christianity had some influence on the decline and fall of the Roman empire. The clergy successfully preached the doctrines of patience and pusillanimity; the active virtues of society were discouraged; and the last remains of the military spirit were buried in the cloister; a large portion of public and private wealth was consecrated to the specious demands of charity and devotion; and the soldiers' pay was lavished on the useless multitudes of both sexes, who could only plead the merits of abstinence and chastity. Faith, zeal, curiosity, and the more earthly passions of malice and ambition kindled the flame of theological discord; the church, and even the state, were distracted by religious factions, whose conflicts were sometimes bloody, and always implacable; the attention of the emperors was diverted from camps to synods; the Roman world was oppressed by a new species of tyranny; and the persecuted sects became the secret enemies of their country.

(Gibbon, *Decline and Fall of the Roman Empire*, Chapter 38)

Some of the important political changes that occurred in the Mediterranean world have already been mentioned, but it is worthwhile to include a brief, coherent narrative of the political developments that took place between the fall of Rome in 410 and the accession of Charlemagne to the throne of the new Western Roman Empire (later called the Holy Roman Empire) in 800. The increasingly untenable position of the city of Rome in the face of the barbarian invasions had been one factor in Constantine's decision to move the capital of the empire to Constantinople in 330. After the emperor Theodosius I permanently divided the empire into Eastern and Western segments in 395, the Western Roman Empire declined rapidly in power. Alaric the Goth sacked Rome in 410. The Vandals sacked Hippo in North Africa in 430, just days after Augustine's death. The Vandals also sacked Rome in 455. Attila the Hun wreaked havoc throughout Europe for two decades, invading the Balkans, laying siege to Constantinople, and driving the Western emperor from his capital of Ravenna. Finally, in 476, the Germanic chieftain Odoacer drove the last Western Roman emperor, Romulus Augustulus, from his throne and declared himself king of Italy. Historians often date the beginning of the Middle Ages to either the sack of Rome in 410 or the fall of the Western Roman Empire in 476.

Numerous tribes of people, called "barbarians" by the Romans, began encroaching on Roman territory as early as the first century c.e., one of the great migrations of people in the history of the world. Most of these tribes were of Germanic origin, but a few, like the Huns, originated further east. The most important of these tribes from the standpoint of European history, and thus the history of the Western Church, were the Angles, Saxons, and Jutes, who originated in northern Europe and settled in Britain; the Franks, who began in modern Germany and settled in Gaul (France); the Ostrogoths (Eastern Goths), who began in northeast Europe and settled in Italy and the Balkans;

> Since, then, the supreme good of the city of God is perfect and eternal peace, not such as mortals pass into and out of by birth and death, but the peace of freedom from all evil, in which the immortals ever abide, who can deny that that future life is most blessed, or that, in comparison with it, this life which now we live is most wretched, be it filled with all blessing of body and soul and external things? ... But, on the other hand, they who do not belong to this city of God shall inherit eternal misery, which is also called the second death, because the soul shall then be separated from God its life, and therefore cannot be said to live, and the body shall be subjected to eternal pains.
>
> (Augustine, *City of God* 19.20, 28)

the Visigoths (Western Goths), who likewise began in northeast Europe and settled in Spain and southern Gaul; and the Vandals, who began in northeast Europe and settled in North Africa. Other Germanic tribes, such as the Lombards, Burgundians, and Alamanni, played important though lesser roles in this historical period. The Huns were a special case. Although the Hun Empire, which occupied much of eastern Europe and western Asia did not survive Attila's death, the impact that the Huns made on Europeans is indicated by the incorporation of stories about Attila into Norse sagas and European legends.

The Germanic tribes were pagan when their invasions of Europe and Africa began, but over time they all converted to Christianity. In 339 Bishop Eusebius of Nicomedia ordained a Goth, Ulfilas, and commissioned him to bring Christianity to his people. Ulfilas translated the Bible into Gothic – the first translation into a Germanic language – and began preaching to the Goths. The Apostle to the Goths, as he was known, had phenomenal success, and the gospel spread from the Visigoths, to the Ostrogoths, to the Vandals and Burgundians. Because Eusebius of Nicomedia was a committed semi-Arian, the form of Christianity to which the Germanic tribes were first converted was also semi-Arian. Their theological differences with the majority of Christians in the West made their blending into European society even more difficult than it otherwise would have been. One important tribe, the Franks, was not immediately converted, but when it was, it accepted a Catholic (Nicene) form of Christianity. As the Franks grew in influence, and as the members of other Germanic tribes became more accustomed to life in their new homes, Catholic Christianity gradually eclipsed semi-Arian Christianity forever.

Another group of tribes that did not convert to Christianity, in part because they were so far from the centers of Christian population, was the group that invaded Britain: the Angles, Saxons, and Jutes. Britain had seen its first Christians centuries earlier, when the Romans still controlled the southern part of the island, but the Germanic tribes drove the Romans, and ecclesiastical Christianity, from Britain. Many monasteries remained in the British Isles, however, especially in Ireland, and a distinctive form of Christianity, Celtic Christianity, persisted and even grew though the efforts of Patrick, Columba, and others. In 597 Pope Gregory I sent a monk named Augustine to Britain, at the request of Ethelbert, king of Kent in southeast England. Ethelbert's wife was a Christian, and

Augustine worked with her to build the church among the Anglo-Saxons. Augustine settled in Canterbury, was ordained as bishop, and soon won numerous converts, including Ethelbert himself. The Anglo-Saxon church, which was directly affiliated with Rome, had some conflicts with the Celtic Church, which considered itself to represent the original, and correct, form of Christianity in the British Isles. In 664, at the Synod of Whitby, Celtic Christians met with their Anglo-Saxon counterparts and agreed to follow the practices of the larger Roman church.

Clovis became king of a group of Franks in 481, at the age of 15, and he was king of all the Franks by 491. He became a Catholic (as opposed to semi-Arian) Christian in 499, after making a vow to God prior to a battle with another tribe, the Alamanni. After he won the battle, he had all his troops baptized *en masse*, the first mass baptism of Germans into Catholic Christianity. Clovis conquered other Germanic tribes in the area, such as the Visigoths and the Burgundians, and at the time of his death in 511, Frankish Gaul was the strongest power west of the Alps. After Clovis's death, his descendants (the Merovingians) were unable to rule effectively, and power passed into the hands of Charles Martel, the "Mayor of the Palace," and *de facto* ruler of the Kingdom of the Franks. Charles led Frankish and Burgundian troops to victory at the Battle of Tours in 732, stopping the advance of Islam into Western Europe, and cementing his claim to leadership over the Franks. He was the founder of the Carolingian line, the grandfather of Charlemagne.

The Visigoths settled in the Iberian Peninsula (Spain and Portugal) after defeating other tribes in the region. Although originally semi-Arians, they converted to Catholic Christianity in 587. They remained in control of the peninsula until they were defeated by the Saracens, a Muslim tribe, in 711.

In North Africa, the Vandals ruled over the region from 430 to 534. This semi-Arian tribe was famous for destroying churches and burning cities occupied by Catholic Christians, thus giving rise to the modern English word *vandal*. Christian-on-Christian tension had been a way of life in North Africa since the days of the Donatists, and the Vandals continued that tradition by persecuting Catholic Christians, sometimes violently. The Vandals were defeated by the Byzantine emperor Justinian in 534.

Italy was ruled for several decades by the Ostrogoths, but it was conquered by Justinian in 540. After three decades of rule over the entire peninsula, Italy was split into three parts, controlled by the Byzantines in the south, the Lombards in the north and center, and the popes in the area right around Rome. The Lombards began to be converted from semi-Arian to Catholic Christianity around the end of the sixth century. The Lombard Kingdom fell to Charlemagne in 774.

The rise of the Eastern Roman Empire

Justice is the set and constant purpose which gives to every man his due. Jurisprudence is the knowledge of things divine and human, the science of the just and the unjust.

(*Code of Justinian* 1.1)

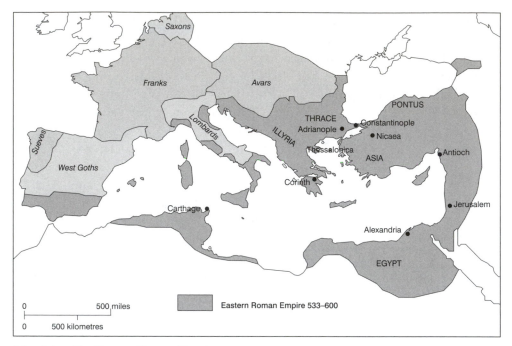

Map 8.1 The Eastern Roman Empire.

The political situation in the East was nowhere near as chaotic as that in the West, and Byzantine emperors enjoyed great power and wealth throughout the period. Theodosius II (408–450) had a long, relatively stable reign, and he was seen by his subjects as a perfect example of what a Christian ruler should be, but by far the most important ruler in the first five centuries of the Byzantine Empire was the emperor Justinian I (527–565). Justinian had risen to the purple from less than noble beginnings, and his wife, the Empress Theodora, was a commoner who had been an actress, a profession considered quite ignoble at the time. Perhaps in an effort to compensate for his humble background, Justinian became a tireless worker, and was sometimes known as "the emperor who never sleeps." He undertook great building programs in Constantinople and beyond, the greatest example of which was the construction of the Hagia Sophia, or Church of Holy Wisdom.

Justinian had a dream of restoring the former glory of the Roman Empire, and part of his efforts to accomplish this goal required him to organize and update the old Roman laws into a single code, the Code of Justinian. Gathering all the old Roman laws into one law code was an enormous undertaking, because the laws, imperial decrees, and judicial decisions of Rome had never been collected in a single place. In addition, because the laws were in Latin, while the language of most inhabitants of Byzantium was Greek, the laws had to be translated as well. Some of the laws that Justinian promulgated dealt with followers of non-Christian religions. The laws were particularly harsh toward pagans, forbidding them to practice their religion. It was during the reign of Justinian that the Academy in Athens, originally established by Plato, was closed permanently.

Figure 8.1 Empress Theodora, represented in this mosaic from Ravenna, was born a member of the lower classes and worked as an actress, an ignoble profession in the early Byzantine period. She later became a convinced adherent of monophysite Christianity and married Justinian I, the future emperor of the Byzantine Empire.

Laws against Samaritans, who were still fairly numerous in Palestine, were also quite restrictive, as were the laws against the Jews. Judaism was still considered a legal religion in Rome, but Jews were subject to numerous legal disparities, including prohibition from holding public office, prohibition from testifying in court against Christians, and prohibition of the use of Hebrew in worship. Justinian's law code served as the basis for legal decisions in the Byzantine Empire for the next 900 years.

If Justinian wanted to restore the glory of the Roman Empire, he would have to conquer an enormous amount of territory that had fallen to the Germanic tribes, and he set out to do just that. Although he began his drive for territory with campaigns against the Persians to the east, he soon concluded that he could not make serious inroads into Persia and made peace instead. He then turned his attention to the west, particularly to the Italian peninsula. His army marched west from his holdings in Egypt and conquered the Vandals in North Africa. From there his general launched the conquest of Sicily and Italy, and he captured both Rome and Ravenna, former capitals of the Western Empire, defeating the Ostrogoths. Finally, his troops moved into Spain, where he took territory from the Visigoths. Despite his victories in battle, the idea of a reunited Roman Empire was a dream that neither he nor any other emperor would be able to realize. War with the Persians heated up again, and he was unable to hold all the territory he had conquered in the West. Despite their temporary setbacks, the Germanic tribes could not be driven from the territories in which they had settled, and a new, much more powerful, military threat would soon face both the Byzantine Empire and the various Germanic kingdoms of the West: the Muslims.

Byzantine emperors came to see themselves as unquestioned rulers of the people and guardians of the church. In the Byzantine Empire, the church and the state were increasingly integrated, but it was clear who had the upper hand in any dispute: the emperor. Justinian had a special interest in healing the rift between Chalcedonian and monophysite Christians, since the Empress Theodora was herself a monophysite. The fact that he did not succeed shows how intractable the problem was. His condemnation of the "Three Chapters" (i.e. the writings of Theodore of Mopsuestia, Theodoret of Cyrrhus, and Ibas of Edessa) was an attempt to show the monophysites that the Chalcedonian position was opposed to Nestorianism, but the monophysites did not accept the gesture. Because he was in control of Rome for several years, Justinian was able to influence the election of popes, supporting those who agreed with his attempts to bridge the gap between the two sides in the Christological controversy. Meanwhile, the monophysite church was organizing and winning converts, often with the tacit support of Justinian and the overt support of Theodora. At the end of Justinian's reign, far from healing the rift, the monophysite church was larger and much better organized than it had been at the start of his reign.

Justinian was an enormously powerful and successful emperor, but his successors were unable to hold onto his territorial gains, and the Byzantine Empire began a slow, relatively steady decline – albeit with some notable reversals – in the face of the Muslim invasions of the following century. Never again would a Byzantine emperor hold the city of Rome, and in fact during the Crusades it was Roman troops who occupied Constantinople for many years. The Hagia Sophia was the zenith of Byzantine architecture, and Justinian's law code held sway for the remainder of the Middle Ages. Justinian was the greatest emperor in the thousand year history of the Byzantine Empire, the model to whom subsequent emperors looked for inspiration.

The emergence of Islam

One of the most significant events in Christian history was the rise of Islam. Muhammad was born in the Arabian city of Mecca in 570, and about 610, according to Muslim tradition, he began receiving revelations from the angel Gabriel. The religion that the Arabs were practicing, the angel said, was corrupt, and it was Muhammad's task to restore the original Abrahamic religion. Although Jews and Christians were heirs to the faith, both groups had strayed from the religion of Abraham. Abraham, Moses, and many other heroes from the Hebrew Bible were prophets, Muhammad said, as was Jesus, but God had appointed him as a prophet as well to turn his people back to the proper way. In 622, because he encountered resistance to his ideas in Mecca, he and his fairly numerous followers moved to the city of Medina, a journey known as the Hijra (or Hegira), "the migration." Shortly thereafter he engaged in battle with troops from Mecca, and after eight years of fighting, he defeated them. His troops entered Mecca triumphantly and removed all remnants of idolatry from the holy temple called the Kaaba. The majority of the city converted to Islam, and a short time later, in 632,

Muhammad died. He is revered today by Muslims as the last and most important of the prophets.

Islam grew rapidly in the period immediately following Muhammad's death, and within a few years Muslim forces had moved out of Arabia and defeated the Persian Empire, which included Persia, Syria, and Mesopotamia. Over the next few decades, the Muslims also captured Palestine, Egypt, and North Africa from the Byzantine Empire, as well as Spain from the Visigoths. Islam was thus encroaching on territory occupied by Christians, just as the Germanic tribes had encroached on the Roman Empire in earlier centuries. Charles Martel's victory at the Battle of Tours stopped their advances in the West, but Muslims had already taken much of the Byzantine Empire's land in the south, and they began to threaten Constantinople from the east as well. Much of the history of Christianity from the seventh century through at least the seventeenth century revolves around the interaction between Christianity and Islam, and especially between Christian and Muslim nations and empires.

Christianity reascendant

The term *Christendom* can be used to refer to all Christians collectively or to the Christian world (i.e. that part of the world under predominantly Christian influence). It can also be used with a more restrictive meaning, to refer to the amalgamation of Christian society with the political power of the state. In this latter sense, Christendom reached its pinnacle in the East during the reign of the emperor Justinian, suffered some retraction in the immediate aftermath of his death as the Germanic tribes reasserted themselves, suffered severe losses in the initial Muslim invasions of the seventh century, then slowly diminished over the following centuries under pressure from the Muslim East, and occasionally from the Christian West as well. In contrast, Christendom in the West had yet to reach its greatest extent. During the barbarian invasions of the fifth century, many Christians, including Augustine of Hippo, probably assumed that the church was in for a long period of repression at the hands of a new group of pagans, but the missionary efforts of Ulfilas, Patrick, Augustine of Canterbury, and others were wildly successful in converting the Germanic tribes *en masse* to Christianity. With the simultaneous conversion of the Franks to Catholic Christianity and their emergence as the dominant power in Western Europe, the Church, which had for some time been divided between Catholic (Nicene) and semi-Arian, was well on its way to becoming fully Catholic. When Charlemagne took the throne in 800 as emperor of the Holy Roman Empire (see the following chapter), most of Europe, with the exception of Muslims in Spain and remnants of paganism in Scandinavia and the Slavic areas, was Christian. In fact, there were now more Christians in Europe, both numerically and as a percentage of the population, than at any time in history, including during the late days of the Roman Empire.

Europe and western Asia were certainly the center of Christianity at the end of the period under discussion, but Christianity was alive and well in many other places as

Early Christian missions

Despite the troubles facing the Western Roman Empire, Christianity continued to spread beyond the borders of both the Western and the Eastern Empires. These are some of the early missionaries, individuals or groups, and the nations to which they bore witness. Usually, however, the individual who first brought Christianity to a new nation has long been forgotten.

Ulfilas (fourth century): Goths
Patrick (fifth century): Irish
Augustine of Canterbury (sixth–seventh century): Anglo-Saxons
Nestorians (eighth century): Chinese
Cyril and Methodius (ninth century): Slavs

well. The Muslim invasions had succeeded in converting many people to Islam, but Christianity remained strong in Egypt, where both Greek and Coptic Christians abounded, and where the monastic movement was still strong. Christians were also numerous to the south, in Nubia and Ethiopia. Smaller numbers continued to live in Palestine, Syria, and Mesopotamia. Christianity had also spread to India centuries before, and to Sogdia in Central Asia, from which point it would eventually reach China at the hands of Nestorian missionaries. It is interesting to note that many of the Christians who lived outside the traditional borders of the Roman Empire were those who did not subscribe to the orthodoxy of the majority, rejecting the findings of either the third ecumenical council (the Nestorians in Syria and beyond) or the fourth (the monophysites in Ethiopia, Mesopotamia, and Syria, as well as in Egypt). The tendency of Christian rulers to seek unanimity of doctrine was a common practice in the early Middle Ages, just as it was in the late Middle Ages and in the early centuries of the modern period. In fact, it harkens back to the time of Constantine, who wanted a religion which could help him hold his empire together. For most Christians in the Middle Ages, East or West, Christianity was ideally suited for the purpose of creating a united society.

Key points you need to know

- The collapse of the Western Roman Empire at the hands of the Germanic tribes was the end result of migrations and infiltrations into the empire that had been occurring since the earliest days of the empire.
- The Germanic tribes in the closest proximity to Rome converted to Christianity first, eventually followed by most of the other tribes over a period of about 150 years, with the exception of the Norse. The Slavs, a non-Germanic group, also failed to convert to Christianity during this time period.
- The Byzantine Empire reached its greatest extent during the reign of the emperor Justinian, who had a dream of restoring the former glory of the Roman Empire. However, his conquests in the West were short-lived.
- While the pope was gaining power in the West, in large part due to the lack of centralized political leadership, no single Christian leader in the East had equivalent power. Instead, the Byzantine emperor asserted control over both the state and the Church.
- Islam began threatening both the Byzantine Empire and the Germanic tribes in North Africa and the Iberian Peninsula in the seventh century, capturing much territory in Asia, Africa, and Europe. The Muslim advance was halted in the West by Charles Martel, but Muslims continued to threaten the East for centuries.
- In addition to the Germanic tribes that converted to Christianity, Christianity also spread east to many other parts of Asia. Christianity also maintained a presence in Egypt, Ethiopia, Palestine, and other places under Muslim control.

Discussion questions

1. What were the primary factors that led to the fall of the Western Roman Empire?
2. In the long term, was the fall of the Western Roman Empire a benefit or a detriment to Christianity in Western Europe?
3. How did the different fates of the two halves of the Roman Empire affect the development of Christianity in the East and the West?
4. What were the long-term consequences of the rise of Islam on Christianity?

Further reading

Frend, W. H. C. 1984. *The Rise of Christianity*. Philadelphia, PA: Fortress.

González, Justo 1984–1985. *The Story of Christianity*. 2 vols. New York: HarperSanFrancisco.

Hourani, Albert 1991. *A History of the Arab Peoples*. Cambridge, MA: Belknap (Harvard University Press).

Latourette, Kenneth Scott 1975. *A History of Christianity*. Revised edn, 2 vols. New York: Harper & Row.

Pelikan, Jaroslav 1971–1989. *The Christian Tradition: A History of the Development of Doctrine*. 5 vols. Chicago, IL: University of Chicago Press.

Roberts, J. M. 1993. *History of the World*. New York: Oxford University Press.

9 *Christendom at its height*

We knew not whether we were in heaven or earth, for on earth there is no such vision nor beauty, and we do not know how to describe it; we know only that there God dwells among men.

(Envoys of Prince Vladimir of Kiev, upon seeing Constantinople for the first time)

In this chapter

With the conversion of the Norse and the Slavs, most of Europe and Western Asia was Christian a millennium after the founding of Christianity. Despite its reduced size in the wake of the rise of Islam, the Byzantine Empire, and especially its capital Constantinople, was a center of wealth and culture unrivaled by any city or state in the West. Nevertheless, the intellectual and cultural achievements of Western Christendom began to grow during the time of Charlemagne, as did the West's political organization. The papacy became the most powerful institution in the West, and the power of popes often surpassed that of temporal rulers. When the Byzantine Empire was threatened by Muslim armies, popes launched a series of wars known collectively as the Crusades, whose repercussions are still felt today.

Main topics covered

- History of the Byzantine Empire from the eighth century until the fall of Constantinople
- History of the Holy Roman Empire and Christian Europe
- The increasing power of the papacy
- The Crusades

The Byzantine Empire

In the early centuries after the fall of Rome and the Western Roman Empire, the Germanic kings and rulers of the West continued to acknowledge the natural authority,

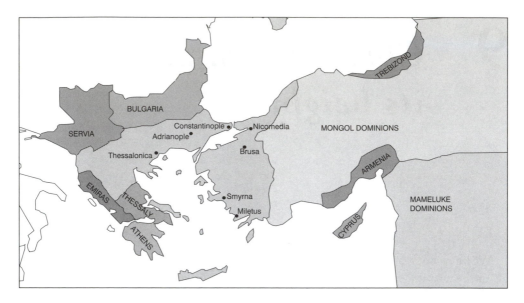

Map 9.1   The Byzantine Empire in 1265

even the natural superiority, of the emperor in Constantinople. And for several centuries, the Byzantine Empire, and especially the city of Constantinople itself, was far more advanced in terms of wealth, culture, and intellect, than any city or kingdom in the West. The East was more urbanized, and the great cities of Alexandria, Antioch, and Athens offered glories that visitors from the West could only dream about after returning to their homes. Even after the Arab conquests in the seventh century, Constantinople remained the shining city of Christianity, the center of Christian thought and culture. In fact, if anything the fall of Egypt and Syria to the Muslims made Constantinople that much greater, for it was now without dispute the greatest Christian city in the East, many would say the greatest city in the world. When a group of Russians visited the city in the late tenth century, they exclaimed, "We knew not whether we were in heaven or earth, for on earth there is no such vision nor beauty, and we do not know how to describe it; we know only that there God dwells among men" (Roberts 1993: 292).

The word *byzantine* is defined as "characterized by a devious and usually surreptitious manner of operation … : intricately involved" (Merriam-Webster, *loc. cit.*). The word conjures up in many people's minds the sort of arcane bureaucracies that Franz Kafka describes in his novels. There is some truth to these associations with the word. The Roman emperor, as the rulers of the Byzantine Empire consistently referred to themselves, was an autocratic leader without peer in the empire. He was supported by an impressive bureaucracy, which included informers who worked for the secret police. Life in the empire was well ordered, and the ultimate authority was always clear. While the patriarch of Constantinople crowned the new emperor, there was never any question of whose authority was greater. The emperor was both the ruler of the empire and the guarantor of the Christian faith. He could appoint and depose the patriarch of Constantinople or any other bishop on a whim, and there was nothing the church could do. More than that, there was nothing the church *wanted* to do, for Christians living in the empire saw the integration of Christianity with the Roman Empire (that is what they called their state) as part of God's divine will for the world.

Byzantium, and especially Constantinople, was the gateway between Europe, Africa, and Asia. Although it maintained relationships with the West after the empire was unable to hold onto most of its European territories outside the Balkans following Justinian's death, it had strong ties to the East as well. The Silk Road brought the wares of China and the Far East to the empire, and despite periodic wars, the empire also traded and exchanged ideas with the Muslim world as well. The model of the autocratic ruler may well have been modeled on the style of leadership in many Asian lands.

In 717 a new emperor, Leo III, ascended the throne of the Byzantine Empire, and he was immediately faced with the military might of the Arabs, who had invaded Asia Minor and were knocking on the door of Constantinople itself. He managed to repel the invaders, and the Arabs were pushed back from the city. When the dust settled after the initial wave of Arab conquests, the empire was greatly reduced in size, consisting only of the bulk of the peninsula of Asia Minor, Thrace (the region immediately across the Bosporus Strait from Asia), and a smattering of territories in mainland and insular Europe at the beginning of Leo's reign. Leo was a military commander who overthrew the previous emperor and established a new line of emperors, the Isaurian dynasty. The Isaurian emperors, especially Leo and his son Constantine V, were effective in pushing the Arab threat out of Asia Minor. They also expanded beyond Thrace into

Figure 9.1   Hagia Sophia, or Holy Wisdom, was the most impressive Byzantine church in the city of Constantinople (now Istanbul)

the greater part of the Balkan peninsula. Leo is infamous for the role he played in the early iconoclastic controversies that embroiled the East, and, to a lesser extent, the West (see below). In 797 Irene, mother of the emperor Constantine VI, had her son arrested and blinded, and she had herself crowned emperor (not empress!). A period of unrest followed, during which time Charlemagne, who had been ruling the Franks for many years, was crowned first emperor of the Holy Roman Empire, a move that caused some consternation in the Byzantine Empire, which still called itself the Roman Empire. Efforts to reunite the two empires by marriage never materialized, and the two empires, separated by language, culture, and eventually theology, drifted apart.

A series of weak rulers in the ninth century led to the founding of the Macedonian dynasty, the zenith of Byzantine success in the post-Justinian period. The greatest of the Macedonian emperors was Basil II, whose reign spanned almost 50 years, from 976 to 1025. Basil presided over the greatest expansion of the Byzantine empire in more that 400 years. His conquest of the Bulgars, a group of people originally from Central Asia who had settled north and west of the Black Sea, earned him the title Bulgar-slayer. He also expanded the empire into parts of Armenia and Georgia, more of the Balkan peninsula, and southern Italy. After Basil's death, a series of weak rulers gave up much of the land he had acquired for the empire. Near the end of the Macedonian dynasty, in 1054, the Eastern and Western churches split from one another permanently.

In 1071 the Byzantine army suffered a devastating loss to the Seljuk Turks, a group originally from Central Asia that was in the process of setting up a great empire of their own to the east of Byzantium. The initial Byzantine loss was exacerbated by further military losses to the Seljuks, and by 1081, almost all that was left of the Byzantine Empire was a sliver of land in far western Asia Minor and the land around Thrace and the Balkan peninsula. It was in that year that the emperor Alexius I Comnenus petitioned the Western church for help in defeating the Muslims and defending the Byzantine Empire. Fourteen years later the Crusades, a series of military campaigns – or more accurately, holy wars – began. Ostensibly launched to free the Holy Land from the Muslim "infidels," they achieved few of their goals over almost two centuries. On the contrary, they brought untold pain and misery to many people, Christians, Muslims, and Jews alike. The low point of the Crusades from the standpoint of the Byzantine Empire was the Fourth Crusade (1201–1204), when Western troops sacked the city of Constantinople. For three days in 1204, Western soldiers marauded through the streets of the city, stealing and destroying everything of value that they saw. They then set up the Latin Empire, a Roman Catholic state that claimed Constantinople as its capital. The Byzantine emperors were driven from the city, and they fled to the city of Nicaea to the east, where they ruled over a small portion of the former empire. The Latin Empire fell in 1261, when Byzantine Emperor Michael VIII Palaeologus recaptured Constantinople.

Despite regaining control of their capital, the emperors of the Palaeologus dynasty were unable to resist the advances of the Turks. The empire eventually lost all its territory in Asia Minor and all but a handful of cities in Thrace and Greece, including Constantinople and Thessalonica. Finally the empire fell to the Ottoman Turks on 29

May 1453, bringing an end to a state that could trace its heritage in an unbroken line of succession back to the beginning of the Roman Republic around the year 500 B.C.E. The fall of Constantinople sent shock waves through Europe as well as the East, and it also caused many Greek Christians to flee to the West. God's kingdom on earth, as many Eastern Christians had seen the empire, had fallen.

The Holy Roman Empire and Christian Europe

Charles had the gift of ready and fluent speech, and could express whatever he had to say with the utmost clearness. He was not satisfied with command of his native language merely, but gave attention to the study of foreign ones, and in particular was such a master of Latin that he could speak it as well as his native tongue; but he could understand Greek better than he could speak it. He was so eloquent, indeed, that he might have passed for a teacher of eloquence. He most zealously cultivated the liberal arts, held those who taught them in great esteem, and conferred great honors upon them.

(Einhard, *Life of Charlemagne* 25)

Charlemagne (Charles the Great) became king of the Franks in 768, ruling jointly with his brother Carloman until the latter's death in 771. He quickly moved against the Lombards in Italy, under the guise of protecting the pope and papal holdings around

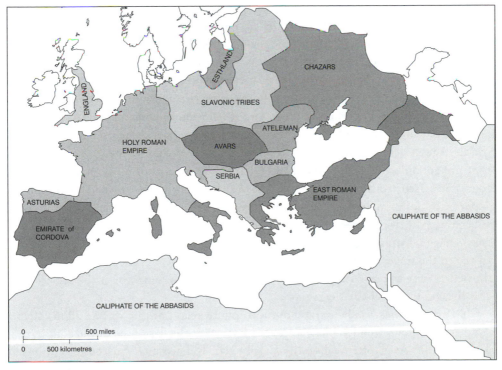

Map 9.2 The Holy Roman Empire at the death of Charlemagne (814)

Rome. Charlemagne defeated the Lombards in 774 and proclaimed himself king of the Lombards. After a series of wars against the Saxons lasting more than three decades, he also conquered them and forcibly converted them to Christianity. Over the course of his long reign (768–814), he also fought battles against the Frisians, Avars, Slavs, Saracens, Moors, Basques, Danes, and others. He suffered his most notable defeat at the hands of the Basques at Roncesvalles, while his army was returning home from an expedition in Spain. Although the loss was relatively minor, it achieved notoriety when a fanciful version of the story was composed and transmitted during the later Middle Ages as the *Song of Roland*. On Christmas Day in the year 800 – perhaps in response to events in the Byzantine Empire, perhaps to secure the position of the pope, or perhaps for a combination of reasons – Pope Leo III crowned Charlemagne Emperor of the Holy Roman Empire, the first emperor in the West since the fall of the Western Roman Empire in 476. By the end of his reign, the Holy Roman Empire consisted of most of Central and Western Europe west of the Elbe, south of Scandinavia and the British Isles, and north and east of the Pyrenees on the one hand and Rome on the other. The Holy Roman Empire never rivaled the original Roman Empire, or even the Western Roman Empire, in extent, but it immediately surpassed in size and military might, if not in wealth and grandeur, the Byzantine Empire.

Charlemagne was committed to the advancement of Christianity, and he saw himself as the protector of the papacy as well. His wars against pagan tribes, such as the Saxons and Frisians, often resulted not only in conquest but also in forced conversions. For reasons of political expediency, Charlemagne had married the daughter of Desiderius, king of the Lombards, but when the latter tried to assert control over Pope Stephen III, Charlemagne divorced his Lombard wife and marched to Italy to confront, and eventually defeat, Desiderius. The pope died shortly thereafter, and Charlemagne negotiated with the new pope, Hadrian I, the boundaries of the Papal States, that is, those lands around Rome that were under the direct administrative supervision of the pope. When Hadrian's successor, Pope Leo III, was forced from office and imprisoned in 799 by members of the Roman aristocracy – a circumstance not particularly uncommon in the Middle Ages – Charlemagne again stood on the side of the papacy. Leo had escaped from prison and came to his court, and Charlemagne, refusing to accept his removal from office, escorted him back to Rome. A year later the pope crowned Charlemagne emperor. In doing so, he asserted his independence from the Byzantine emperor, who still claimed the title Emperor of Rome. Furthermore, although he pledged obedience to Charlemagne, by placing the crown on his head, he also asserted the supremacy of the papacy to the imperial court (compare Napoleon's coronation centuries later in 1804). The debate over who had the greater power in the West, the emperor or the pope, began with the coronation of Charlemagne.

Charlemagne was barely literate, not learning to read until he was an adult, but he had a great appreciation for knowledge. He instigated the first great cultural flowering of the Middle Ages, often called the Carolingian Renaissance. Surrounding himself with literary men, Charlemagne set about to transform his ever-expanding kingdom into a state characterized by Christian piety, justice, and an educated citizenry. Alcuin of York, a renowned scholar and teacher, was representative of the Christian humanism that flourished in eighth century England, associated with such figures as the Venerable Bede and Alcuin himself. Alcuin had taught at a cathedral school in York famous for its humanistic leanings, and he brought that philosophy of education with him to Charlemagne's court in Aachen. His school taught the basics of a classical education: grammar, logic, rhetoric, mathematics, geometry, music, and astronomy. It taught these subjects in Latin, no longer a spoken language, but now the language of scholarship in Europe. Alcuin, a devout man, believed that a study of the liberal arts led to a better understanding of Christian doctrine. Some years after establishing his school, he was appointed abbot of the Abbey of St. Martin of Tours, where he supervised the work of monks copying biblical manuscripts, writings of leading Christian figures, and documents dating back to the Roman Empire. Other monasteries throughout the Frankish kingdom were also busy copying manuscripts of various sorts, and they were centers of education as well. Many of these manuscripts were gathered into a great library in Aachen and made accessible to those who studied there.

When he inherited his throne, the Frankish kingdom was not terribly well organized, but Charlemagne set out to remedy the problem. He divided his kingdom (later empire) into counties, each of which was administered by a count. He regularly sent pairs of men – one a cleric, the other a lay member of the court – throughout the kingdom to confer with the counts on the state of the kingdom, to ensure that justice was being administered properly, and to promulgate royal decrees. He also reformed the legal system and trained legal experts to help administer justice. He banned judges from taking bribes, and he revised existing law codes to fit the times.

Charlemagne's commitment to promoting classical education, Christian piety, and justice in his kingdom; his championing of manuscript copying and preservation; his commitment to protect the papacy; and even his forcible "conversion" of conquered subjects all point to a man with a simple but deep faith. He loved learning for its own sake, achieving some level of proficiency in both Latin and Greek, and studying other subjects as well. Most of all, though, he saw himself as a defender of the Christian faith. He built a great cathedral in Aachen to worship God, and, according to his biographer Einhard, he provided for the poor, both in his own kingdom and outside it. Many legends developed around Charlemagne in the Middle Ages concerning his piety, wisdom, strength, and bravery. While many of the stories are no doubt exaggerations or pure inventions, it is impossible to deny his impact on European history in the Middle Ages.

About 30 years after his death, Charlemagne's empire was divided among three of his grandsons, becoming three separate kingdoms, with the ruler of the so-called Middle Frankish Kingdom retaining the title "emperor." The Kingdom of the West Franks evolved into France, and the Kingdom of the East Franks was ruled initially by Louis the German. After the Carolingian line died out, Otto I became king of the Eastern kingdom in 936 and proclaimed himself heir to Charlemagne's imperial title. For the remainder of the Middle Ages, the Holy Roman Empire and France were the two most powerful states in Western Europe, but after a time French power waxed while the power of the Empire waned. This situation was caused in large part by the power that individual regions within the Empire had throughout its existence, and the correspondingly weak authority of the emperor under such a federal system. Meanwhile, the Normans, a group of people of mixed French and Norse heritage from the north of France, invaded and conquered England in 1066, establishing themselves on the English throne. After several generations, the Norman kings considered themselves English – and in fact they had English as well as French ancestry – but they also had territorial claims in France. Rivalry between the monarchs of France and England led to the Hundred Years' War, a period that saw several periods of extended warfare between France and England punctuated by periods of peace, and ending the same year as the fall of Constantinople, 1453. The three centuries immediately prior to the Hundred Years' War saw Christian Europe launch several Crusades against the Muslims in the East (see below).

By the end of Charlemagne's reign, only three large groups of people in Europe remained pagan: the Slavs, the Magyars, and the Norse. In the early ninth century, the Slavs occupied much of the Balkan peninsula and the region north of the Black Sea. Their territorial advances in recent decades had come at the expense of the Byzantine Empire, to whose capital a group of them had laid siege in the sixth century, so when in 862 an emissary from the Slavic king of Moravia asked Byzantine Emperor Michael III and Patriarch Photius of Constantinople to send them someone to teach them about Christianity, they readily complied. Photius recommended two brothers, Cyril and Methodius of Thessalonica, for the task. Since they were from the Balkan region, they already knew something of the language, which as yet had not been committed to writing. They devised an alphabet to record the language and proceeded to translate the Bible into the Old Bulgarian language, also known as Old Church Slavonic. Scholars are divided over whether the brothers created the Glagolitic alphabet, the related Cyrillic alphabet, or both. The most likely answer is that they created Glagolitic, and one of Cyril's students later created the Cyrillic alphabet and named it in his honor. At any rate, the Cyrillic alphabet, which was largely based on Greek letters, soon replaced Glagolitic in most places. Both Moravia and Bulgaria converted to Christianity, and the newly established churches used the translation of the Bible and the liturgy developed by Cyril and Methodius in Old Church Slavonic.

A large group of Slavs lived to the north of the Black Sea and had not yet converted to Christianity. The Russians were not yet an organized state in the ninth century, but their numbers had grown, and they were concentrated around the cities of Kiev and Novgorod. Native Slavs in this region were ruled over by a group of Norsemen who had invaded the region decades earlier in search of slaves and other goods to trade. The Norse rulers intermarried with the Slavs, and by the middle of the tenth century they were thoroughly Slavic themselves, adopting Slavic names and the Slavic culture. In 957 Olga, the widow of a prince of Kiev, visited Constantinople and was publicly baptized as a Christian in Hagia Sophia Church. About 20 years later the Russian prince Vladimir became a convert to Orthodox Christianity, and so did his subjects. Some of the Slavs, such as the Poles and the Croats, eventually accepted Roman Catholic forms of Christianity, but the majority of Slavs retained their ties to Orthodoxy. Russia eventually became the most powerful Slavic nation, and the Russian Orthodox Church flourished. However, the invasion of Slavic territory by Muslims in the south and Mongols in the north greatly diminished the territory controlled by the Christian Slavs from the eleventh through the fifteenth centuries. In the late fifteenth century a new Russia emerged, centered on Moscow, stronger militarily than before, and – with the recent fall of Constantinople – heir apparent to the title of Protector of Orthodoxy.

In the late ninth century the Magyars, a group of fierce warriors originally from the Ural Mountains, settled in present day Hungary. They engaged in repeated expeditions throughout Europe and were known for burning churches and killing priests. In 955 Holy Roman Emperor Otto I defeated the Magyars and stopped their advances, and soon some of them began converting to Christianity. In the year 1001 Stephen I, king of Hungary, converted to Christianity – along with his people – and asked Pope Sylvester II for a crown to symbolize his right to rule. The pope complied, and he also sent bishops to help organize the church. After a period of resistance to Christianity after Stephen's death, Christianity gained the upper hand by the end of the century.

The Norsemen were a group of warriors and raiders who originated in Scandinavia but whose exploits took them all over Europe and beyond. Starting in the eighth century, Norsemen began leaving Scandinavia, sometimes on raiding parties (the Vikings) and sometimes to settle in places like Russia, France, England, Iceland, Greenland, and even Newfoundland and Labrador (Vinland) in North America. They often gave their names to the places they settled (e.g. Normandy in France, Danelaw in England), and they were feared by the Christian inhabitants of the lands they raided. The Norsemen who settled outside Scandinavia, in Russia and Normandy, were the first to convert to Christianity, but in Scandinavia the first Christian king was Harald Bluetooth of Denmark, about the year 950. It was not until the reign of Canute, who ruled both Denmark and England, about 1020 that Christianity was firmly established in Denmark, the southernmost of the Scandinavian countries. Although Christian missionaries from the Holy Roman Empire did some work in Scandinavia, it was missionaries from England who succeeded in convincing the Danes to convert, perhaps because the English were less of a political threat at the time.

The conversion of Norway begins with the story of Olaf Tryggvason, a man who led an eventful life before becoming king. As a young boy he was captured by pirates and sold into slavery. After being rescued, he became a Viking and raided England, before converting to Christianity and being baptized by a monk. Upon his return to Norway in 995, he was made king, and he immediately began the process of converting the inhabitants of his land. The process was not completed in his lifetime but in the lifetime of another Olaf, Olaf Haraldsson, who became king in 1015.

Christians had lived in Sweden since the ninth century, and there were bishops in the country by the tenth century. However, neither the king nor the population as a whole had accepted the new religion. Christian missionaries from England had success in converting Swedes from the south of Sweden in the eleventh century, but it was only in the early twelfth century that Christianity reached the north of Sweden in large numbers.

Iceland was colonized by Norwegians beginning in the late ninth century, and many settlers were converted to Christianity during the reign of Olaf Tryggvason in Norway. Many pagans remained on the island, however, and to avoid war, both groups agreed that Christianity was the official religion, but anyone who was caught sacrificing to the traditional gods would not be severely punished. A few years later, however, paganism was abolished once and for all. Greenland was colonized by Eric the Red, a pagan from Iceland. His son, Leif Ericsson, was converted in Norway during the reign of Olaf Tryggvason, and he introduced priests, and Christianity, to Greenland.

In addition to the Slavs, Magyars, and Norse, two other areas of Europe lay outside the influence of the church in the middle of the ninth century, both controlled by Muslims: Sicily, ruled by the Saracens, and the Iberian peninsula, ruled by the Moors. The island of Sicily, just off the "toe" of the Italian peninsula, changed hands several times in the centuries after the fall of the Roman Empire. At the beginning of the ninth century, the island was under Byzantine rule, but over a period of several decades Saracen (Arab) armies from North Africa gradually conquered Sicily, holding it for almost 200 years. In the late eleventh century, over a period of 30 years, Norman soldiers who had emigrated to southern Italy began invading Sicily, conquering it in 1091 and bringing the island once again under Christian rule.

In 711 the first army of Moors crossed the Strait of Gibraltar from Morocco into Spain, ironically at the invitation of a Visigothic lord who was at odds with another Visigothic lord. The Moors won several decisive victories over the Christian Goths, and by 714 they had moved north and captured most of the Iberian peninsula. The northward march was stopped by Charles Martel in 732 at the Battle of Tours, and the Moors retreated to Iberia, where they set up an emirate that they called by the Arabic name Al-Andalus. Only in the extreme north, in Asturias and Navarre, did Christians retain control over the land. The *Reconquista*, or reconquest of Spain, began almost as soon as the Moors stopped their advances, though for the first few centuries the idea of reclaiming the entire peninsula for Christianity does not seem to have occurred to anyone. By the end of the eighth century Christians controlled a thin slice of territory in northern and northeastern Spain, including the Basque Country and Catalonia, the latter of which was controlled by the Franks. In 844, Christians won a great victory at the battle of Clavijo, where, according to legend, James the son of Zebedee, one of Jesus' disciples, appeared to the Christian troops and fought for them against the Moors, thus earning the name Saint James Matamoros, or "Moor-slayer." James was eventually recognized as the patron saint of Spain. Internal struggles within the Muslim leadership of Al-Andalus in the ninth through eleventh centuries resulted in the creation of many small independent Muslim states, which expended much energy waging war on one another, allowing the Christians in the north to organize politically and to repopulate areas that the Muslims had abandoned. The Almoravids, reinforcements from Africa, slowed down the Christian advance to the south, but in 1085 Alfonso the Brave of Castile conquered the city of Toledo, the former Visigothic capital, thus achieving a great symbolic victory. In the twelfth century, popes who called for Crusades against the Muslims in the East also proclaimed the fight against Muslim control of Spain a spiritual battle of equal importance, and many foreigners joined the fight. By the early thirteenth century, Christian kingdoms of Portugal, Leon, Castile, Navarre, and Aragon controlled more than half of the peninsula, and by the middle of the same century the Moorish kingdom of Granada was the only Muslim realm remaining in Spain, and it was in fact a vassal of Castile. In 1479, when her husband Ferdinand ascended to the throne of Aragon, Isabella of Castile and Ferdinand of Aragon became joint rulers of the two largest Christian states in the Iberian peninsula, forming a unified Christian Spain. In 1492 the Muslim king of Granada surrendered to the Spanish monarchs, and the *Reconquista* was complete. Later the same year, most Jews and Muslims living in Spain and Portugal were ordered to convert to Christianity or leave the country. A third significant event associated with Spain that occurred in 1492, Columbus's "discovery" of the New World, was destined to have an enormous impact on the history of Christianity.

The rise of the papacy

> Every Christian king, when he comes to die, seeks as a pitiful suppliant the aid of a priest, that he may escape hell's prison, may pass from the darkness into the light, and at the judgment of God may appear absolved from the bondage of his sins. Who, in his last hour (what layman, not to speak of priests), has ever implored the aid of an earthly king for the salvation of his soul? And what king or emperor is able, by reason of the office he holds, to rescue a Christian from the power of the devil through holy baptism, to number him among the sons of God, and to fortify him with the divine unction? Who of them can by his own words make the body and blood of our Lord – the greatest act in the Christian religion? Or who of them possesses the power of binding and loosing in heaven and on earth? From all of these considerations it is clear how greatly the priestly office excels in power.
>
> (Pope Gregory VII, *Letter to the Bishop of Metz*)

Even before the fall of the last Roman emperor in 476, Leo I, bishop of Rome (440–461) and considered by many to be the first who deserves the title "pope," insisted that the bishop of Rome held primacy over the entire church, both East and West. When he had his *Tome* supporting the orthodox position on Christology read at the Council of Chalcedon in 451, it is clear that he expected it to be followed by everyone because of his authority as pope. Many in the East disagreed with the proposition that the bishop of Rome should have such authority. On the contrary, they saw the bishops of Alexandria, Antioch, and Constantinople – whose leaders came to be called patriarchs – as having the same dignity and power as the bishop of Rome. At most, they said, the bishop of Rome is "first among equals."

Some important early and medieval popes

Although the church of Rome dates to at least the middle of the first century, its early bishops made little effort to exert anything other than moral authority over Christians beyond their immediate region. Beginning with Leo I, however, the first bishop of Rome who might legitimately be called a pope in the modern sense, popes began to assert their authority farther and farther afield. The refusal of the patriarch of Constantinople to accept the authority of the pope was an important factor that led to the Great Schism between the Orthodox and Catholic Churches in 1054. A list of important pre-Reformation popes follows.

Stephen I (254–257)
Sylvester I (314–335)
Damasus I (366–384)
Leo I "the Great" (440–461)
Gelasius I (492–496)
Gregory I "the Great" (590–604)
Gregory II (715–731)
Stephen II (752–757)
Hadrian I (772–795)
Nicholas I (858–867)
Leo IX (1049–1054)
Gregory VII (1073–1085)
Innocent III (1198–1216)
Gregory IX (1227–1241)
Boniface VIII (1294–1303)
Gregory XI (1370–1378)

After the emperors abandoned the city and moved the capital of the Western Empire to Milan and then Ravenna, the bishop of Rome was left with both religious and political power, and before long popes were vying for political authority outside the narrow confines of the city. Pope Gelasius I (492–496) asserted that the authority of the church, and particularly of the pope, was superior to that of the state. He is often credited with creating the theory of the two swords – which asserts that temporal authority (the first sword) rests with the state and spiritual authority (the second sword) with the church, but of the two, the spiritual authority is greater – in a letter to the Byzantine emperor. He was the first to use the term "vicar of Christ" (i.e. official representative of Christ) as a title for the pope, an assertion of ecclesiastical primacy over other bishops. As the *de facto* ruler of Rome, he dealt with the Ostrogoth king Theodoric, convincing him to donate food to the poor in the city.

After the Germanic tribes conquered the Roman Empire, they appointed rulers over Rome, but the pope still had immense influence over political affairs. Pope Gregory I "the Great" (590–604) had been the prefect, or mayor, of Rome prior to his ordination – although he had left political life to live in a monastery – so when he became pope he was uniquely qualified to organize the defense of the city against the Lombards and to negotiate with the Germanic tribes on various occasions on behalf of the citizens of Rome. He focused his attention on the affairs of the West rather than on the Roman church's ties with the Byzantine Empire. In particular, he used the resources and organization of the church to feed the poor. In addition to his political successes, he also organized the successful mission to Christianize the Anglo-Saxons in England, and he instituted major reforms in the worship of the church (Gregorian chants are named for him). Although he acknowledged his subservience to the emperor in Constantinople, he bristled at the patriarch of Constantinople's use of the title "ecumenical patriarch," which seemed to suggest an authority that reached beyond the East. Gregory insisted that there was no universal patriarch, even including, by implication, the pope! Although his words may have been intended mainly as a limitation on the power being asserted by the patriarch of Constantinople, few subsequent popes would utter words that could be used as arguments for limiting the power of the bishop of Rome.

Sometime in the eighth or ninth century popes began using a forged document, the *Donation of Constantine*, to bolster their claims to political and ecclesiastical power. The document, supposedly addressed by the emperor Constantine to Sylvester I, bishop of Rome, claimed that Constantine had granted the bishops of Rome authority over the three major sees of the East, over the city of Rome, and over the entire Western Roman Empire, while Constantine retained political authority in the East. The authenticity of the document was accepted without challenge in the West for centuries, and it had a tremendous impact on the claims for the authority of the papacy. Since everyone in the West agreed that the pope had authority over all the churches in the West, popes and their supporters used the *Donation* primarily to bolster their claim to political power in the face of challenges from the emperors of the Holy Roman Empire and others. With the revival of classical learning during the Renaissance, scholars demonstrated from anachronisms and linguistic style that the *Donation* was a fake, but by that time the die had already been cast in favor of the authority of the papacy.

Pope Nicholas I (858–867) clashed with Emperor Louis II, insisting on papal rights and the authority of the pope over secular rulers, and he asserted his authority over councils of bishops as well. Toward the end of the ninth and into the tenth century a serious decline in papal authority occurred, as some popes bought the office (a practice called simony) and others took mistresses and fathered children. Clerical celibacy was not yet an official rule, but it had become the accepted norm, especially for bishops (including the pope), so the moral lapses of the popes during this period brought discredit to the papacy. Between 896 and 955 18 different men served as pope, many of whom were deposed, imprisoned, or murdered before they could serve out a natural term of office. It was also during this time that one of the major fiascos of the medieval papacy occurred, when the body of a former pope (Formosus) was dug up and put on trial by the sitting pope (Stephen VI), an incident referred to as the Cadaver Synod.

In light of many scandals and irregularities involving the popes in this period, many in the church called for a reform of the papacy. Pope Leo IX (1049–1054) was appointed to the papacy by Emperor Henry III, but he insisted that the people and clergy of Rome approve his election, thus asserting that the church was not subservient to the state. He denounced simony, insisted on clerical celibacy (from bishops down to subdeacons), and instituted a number of other reforms. Even though the reforms instituted during this period are known today as the Gregorian reform, in honor of one of his collaborators and successors as pope, the movement to restore honor and order to the papacy began with Leo IX. During the last year of his reign envoys acting in Leo's name, while on a visit to Constantinople, pronounced the excommunication of the patriarch of Constantinople, who soon thereafter followed suit, excommunicating Leo IX. The Great Schism between the Eastern (Orthodox) and Western (Catholic) churches, which remains to this day, was the result.

The pope who gave his name to the reforms of the papacy that took place in the eleventh century was Gregory VII (1073–1085). Gregory was immensely powerful and influential, and he was controversial as well. His reforms sought to enforce clerical (including papal) morality, as a prelude to strengthening the authority of the pope to heights never before seen. He affirmed Leo IX's insistence on clerical celibacy and opposition to simony, opposed lay investiture (the appointment of bishops and abbots by temporal rulers rather than by the church), and he gave teeth to his decrees by threatening disobedient bishops with excommunication. Gregory was intent on elevating the authority of the pope in both the ecclesiastical and secular spheres. He was the first pope to claim authority over the entirety of the church, including not only clergy and religious, but also individual citizens and even rulers. In 1075 he issued a document claiming 27 different papal rights, including the exclusive right of the pope to claim universal sovereignty over the church; the authority not only of the pope but also of papal representatives over bishops; the exclusive authority of the pope to use the imperial insignia; the power to transfer bishops to different sees; the right to depose and reinstate bishops; and even the right to depose emperors. He further stated that the Roman church had never erred, and would never err, for all eternity. These were bold claims, for they claimed for the pope authority that he had never before had. Not surprisingly, his decree was not universally accepted. Many bishops opposed the pope making himself superior to a council of bishops, and the Holy Roman Emperor Henry IV asserted his own authority to name bishops and abbots in regions under his control. Technically, Henry was only king of the Eastern Frankish Empire, since he had not been officially crowned emperor by the pope, and his adversarial relationship with Gregory guaranteed that the latter would not do so. In January 1076 Henry convoked a synod of German bishops that deposed Gregory; in response, Gregory excommunicated Henry and released his subjects from their allegiance to him. To get Gregory to retract his order of excommunication, Henry was forced to kneel in the snow outside the Castle of

Canossa in northern Italy for three days, wearing the clothes of a penitent. Thereupon Gregory did lift the decree of excommunication, but the struggle between the two men continued. Finally, after several other incidents, Henry captured the city of Rome after a two-year siege, and with the pope safely inside the Castel Sant'Angelo, a rival pope (antipope) crowned Henry emperor. Gregory's intransigence in his dealings with Henry, among other matters, eventually turned the citizenry of Rome against Gregory, and they drove him from the city, where he died in exile shortly thereafter. Despite the inglorious end to his papacy, Gregory stands as one of the most important popes in the history of the church, and with him papal authority expanded immensely.

The height of papal power, at least in the temporal sphere, is identified with the reign of Pope Innocent III (1198–1216). Innocent not only claimed authority over both church and state, as Gregory had, he repeatedly exercised it as well. During his investiture as pope, he recited the words of Jer 1:10: "See, today I appoint you over nations." The state has authority over the body, Innocent said, but the church has authority over the soul. Just as the soul is superior to the body, so also is the authority of the church superior to that of the state. He intervened, or interfered, in political matters in many different parts of Europe, and he increased the wealth of the church in the process. When two rivals vied for the throne of the Holy Roman Empire, Innocent chose the one who both swore loyalty to him and also promised to increase the territory of the Papal States, the region in central Italy ruled directly by the pope, though he later deposed him and appointed his rival as emperor. He temporarily excommunicated King John of England over the appointment of the archbishop of Canterbury, but after the king submitted to papal authority and granted him some land as a papal fief (i.e. land from which he would draw income), the pope agreed to condemn the *Magna Carta*, a document expressing the rights of English citizens that King John had been forced to sign. Innocent meddled in the political affairs of numerous other nations as well, including France, Aragon, and Poland in the West and Bulgaria, Cyprus, and Armenia in the East. He presided over the Fourth Crusade, which resulted in the seizure of Constantinople by Catholic troops and the establishment of a Latin kingdom there, and he prepared for the Fifth Crusade, which started the year following his death. Innocent III was a powerful pope, but his interference in matters of state ruffled the feathers of many rulers, who resented the papacy's claim to sovereignty over temporal as well as spiritual affairs.

The struggle between popes and princes over temporal authority came to a head in the papacy of Pope Boniface VIII (1294–1303). Obsessed with accumulating power and wealth not only for the papacy but also for himself and his family, he sometimes appeared in public wearing imperial regalia, implying that he was caesar as well as pope. His attempts to intervene in matters of state were often unsuccessful, as rulers sometimes ignored his decisions. His most troublesome rival was King Philip IV of France. When Boniface issued a papal bull to stop Philip from taxing the clergy to finance his war with England, Philip issued decrees that hurt the pope financially, so he was forced to rescind his bull and canonize Philip's grandfather. After a later conflict with Philip, he issued the bull *Unam sanctam* (One Holy Church), a document famous for its audacious claims to papal authority. Among other things, the bull claimed that outside the Roman Catholic Church there is no salvation and furthermore that it is necessary for salvation for every person to be subject to the pope. *Unam sanctam* is most famous, though, for its claim that the pope had the authority to wield the two swords of authority, both the temporal and the spiritual. Boniface issued haughty words, but he overreached. Philip was not impressed with Boniface's claims to temporal authority, and he retaliated by calling for a council to depose the pope. A short time later the pope was arrested by allies of Philip, and though he was later rescued, the impotence of the papacy in the temporal realm was evident. Popes still commanded great respect by virtue of their position as ruler of the church, but never again would kings tremble at the thought of excommunication. The papacy had already seen the zenith of its temporal power, and a sharp drop in papal prestige and authority was poised to begin.

After the brief reign of Boniface's successor, Pope Clement V of France was elected by a pro-French faction of cardinals in 1305. He never set foot in Rome, but remained in France, eventually establishing his residence in the city of Avignon in the south of France. Thus began what historians call the Avignon Papacy, and what opponents often derided as the Babylonian Captivity of the popes. The reasons for the move to Avignon were complex. Many in the church believed that the papacy was becoming increasingly controlled by powerful families in Rome whose family members often occupied the chair of Peter. The king of France, on the other hand, wanted to assert his own influence over the papacy. The next several popes were effectively puppets of the kings of France, so Pope Gregory XI (1370–1378) decided to move the papal court back to Rome in 1377, encouraged by Catherine of Siena, who claimed to have received visions from God directing the popes to return to Rome. Gregory's return did not end the controversies surrounding the control of the papacy by powerful temporal leaders, as subsequent events demonstrate.

After the death of Gregory XI, cardinals did not want the new pope to return to Avignon, so they elected an Italian, Urban VI (1378–1389). Urban was interested in reforming the church, but he was so undiplomatic in his efforts – threatening his opponents with excommunication – that some of the cardinals who had elected Urban declared him deposed and elected Clement VI in his place. Clement promptly moved the papal residence back to Avignon, so the church now had two men claiming to be popes, an event known as the Great Western Schism. France and Scotland supported the pope at Avignon, while England, Scandinavia, Flanders, Hungary, and Poland supported the pope at Rome. Other European powers wavered back and forth over the next several papacies. Clement and Urban went to war with each other, but neither side was able to score a decisive victory on the battlefield. Though subsequent Roman and Avignon popes gave lip service to healing the schism, none was willing to take the first step and renounce the papal throne. Finally in 1409, tired of the now 30-year-old schism, cardinals representing both sets of popes called a church council in Pisa to decide the rightful heir to the see of Peter. The Council of Pisa declared both popes deposed and installed a new pope, Alexander V, with the result that now three different men claimed to be pope at the same time. In 1415 the Council of Constance, which had previously deposed Alexander's successor in Pisa, accepted the resignation of Gregory XII of Rome, ignored the claims of Benedict XIII of Avignon, and declared the papacy vacant. In 1417 the Council appointed Martin V as the new pope, in Rome, finally ending the schism. Although the Roman Catholic Church today considers all the men in Avignon during the Great Western Schism who claimed the title of pope to be in fact antipopes, it was certainly not clear for more than 30 years which of the two was the legitimate successor to Peter. The rift in the Western church healed, the next several popes were able to deal with other matters, particularly the question of reform. That issue came to a head in 1517, in the conflict with a young monk named Martin Luther.

Holy war

> The Christian who slays the unbeliever in the Holy War is sure of his reward, the more sure if he himself is slain. The Christian glories in the death of the pagan, because Christ is glorified.
>
> (Bernard of Clairvaux, *Letter to the Knights Templar*)

"I, or rather the Lord, beseech you as Christ's heralds to publish this everywhere and to persuade all people of whatever rank, foot-soldiers and knights, poor and rich, to carry aid promptly to those Christians and to destroy that vile race from the lands of our friends. I say this to those who are present, it is meant also for those who are absent. Moreover, Christ commands it." With these words Pope Urban II in 1095 launched the First Crusade, summoning the Christian West to go to Jerusalem and wrest it from the hands of its Muslim overlords. "That vile race" was the Seljuk Turks, who had taken control of Jerusalem in 1077, but the city had been in Muslim hands since the Arabs took it from the Byzantine Empire in 638. Clearly the presence of Muslims in the city was nothing new, so why did Byzantine Emperor Alexius I Comnenus appeal to the pope to send his army at that time? Apparently Alexius's original aim was the rescue not of Jerusalem but of Constantinople itself. Byzantine armies had lost a large amount of territory to the Turks in Anatolia, so that the Turkish army was alarmingly close to the capital of the empire. Two factors sent the crusaders to Jerusalem instead of Constantinople. First, Jerusalem, the city where Jesus had been crucified and where the early church had begun, had an exotic and devotional appeal to Christians in the West in a way that Constantinople never did. Second, Urban had heard stories of atrocities committed against Christians in the city, including torture, murder, and the burning of churches. Some of the stories were true, but they reported events that had occurred more than 80 years earlier, during the reign of a single Arab ruler, Al-Hakim bi-Amr Allah, who was noted for his bizarre and provocative behavior. He had indeed killed both Jews and Christians and burned the Church of the Holy Sepulcher to the ground, but after his death his successor, with help from the Byzantine Empire, rebuilt the church. The fact of the matter is that both Jews and Christians had generally fared fairly well in the lands ruled by Muslims. That Urban refers to the Eastern Christians as "our friends" is notable, because the Great Schism between the two major branches of Christianity had begun only 40 years earlier, but some thawing of relationships had begun. It is likely that recent Christian advances in Spain associated with the *Reconquista* encouraged other European Christians to believe in the justice of their cause. Finally, the troubles that Christian pilgrims from the West sometimes had when visiting the East may also have attracted the attention of the pope. For all these reasons, Urban called Christians to war.

The attitude of Christians toward war has been ambivalent throughout history. Jesus told his disciples to love their enemies (Matt 5:44) and to "turn the other cheek" (Matt 5:39). During the first three centuries, Christians were rarely part of the power structure of the Roman Empire, and few were in the Roman legions, so the question of making war was a theoretical one that few asked. With the advent of Constantine, however, the attitude of many in the church changed. God had apparently granted Constantine a great victory at the Battle of the Milvian Bridge, specifically telling him to fight with Christian symbols emblazoned on his soldiers' shields. Christians as far back as Paul had acknowledged the right of governments to use force in order to keep the peace and punish evildoers (Rom 13:1–5), so many Christians in Constantine's day argued that service in the government or military was a perfectly legitimate undertaking for Christians.

The most important contribution in the early period to the discussion about the proper Christian attitude toward war and the use of violence was made by Augustine of Hippo in the fifth century. Augustine, who had seen Rome sacked by the barbarians and observed what he considered to be harmful heresies and schisms rock the church, developed a formulation for thinking about the use of force that has come to be called the Just War theory. In his various writings, Augustine's thoughts concerning the Just War – that is, a war in which a Christian ruler and nation may justly participate – may be summarized in five points:

1. The war must have a just cause, primarily self-defense, but also the failure of another state to act justly toward its inhabitants.
2. The war must be motivated by the cause of justice rather than a desire to inflict harm, gain power, and so forth.
3. The war must be waged by a legitimate authority (i.e. a state).
4. War must be a last resort.
5. The war must be conducted justly.

Augustine's idea of a Just War continued to be developed by other Christians through the Middle Ages, but it was accepted as a given in the eleventh century that fighting to regain former Christian territory from non-Christians was a valid justification for war. In fact, about 20 years earlier Pope Gregory VII had come close to launching the First Crusade himself.

The First Crusade actually began in 1096, the year after Urban II's summons, and over the next two centuries nine official crusades sponsored by the church were fought, in addition to other campaigns sometimes referred to as crusades but not officially sanctioned by a pope. They involved mass movements of people from West to East, and they brought many western Christians into contact with the East for the first time. Soldiers were often recruited with the promise of a plenary indulgence, that is, the forgiveness of all one's sins, if a soldier died in battle. Some were attracted by the adventure of traveling to foreign lands, and others went because of a burning religious zeal, while still others hoped to win fame or fortune along the way. The Christians who went to the East saw themselves as fighting a Holy War, sanctioned by God, and many wore the sign of the cross on their helmets or breastplates, or painted it on their shields. The were the army of God, fighting against the forces of darkness. There was no way they could lose.

During the Crusades several Christian "military orders" were founded to support the Crusades in one way or another. The most famous of these orders were the Templars, the Hospitallers, and the Teutonic Knights, though there were many others. Members of these orders, like members of the mendicant orders (see below), were required to take vows and follow strict rules of discipline, but the focus was on military service rather than prayer, poverty, or preaching. These orders were also involved in ministering to the sick and wounded, raising money to ransom captives, and providing Christian pilgrims with transportation and safe passage on their visits to the Holy Land. The medieval idea of the chivalric knight is based to a large extent on the members of these groups.

The First Crusade (1096–1099) was by far the most successful crusade in terms of meeting its stated goals. The crusaders, led by several European knights and nobles, managed to capture Edessa and Antioch in 1098 and Jerusalem in 1099, but they did not restore any of them to Byzantine hands. Instead, they established the first Crusader States – the County of Edessa, the Principality of Antioch, and the Latin Kingdom of Jerusalem – all of whose rulers were loyal to the pope. Jerusalem remained in Christian hands for almost 90 years before falling to Saladin, sultan of Egypt, in 1187. The Latin Kingdom of Jerusalem continued to exist for another 100 years, though without its eponymous capital city. By capturing Jerusalem, the First Crusade set the bar high for future crusades, too high, in fact, for any of them to reach. This crusade also set a standard for the behavior of Christian warriors, a low standard that unfortunately was met by soldiers involved in future crusades. When the crusaders finally captured Jerusalem after a siege lasting almost six weeks, they began the systematic slaughter of almost every inhabitant, young or old, male or female, Muslim, Jew, or Eastern Christian (they had done the same when they captured Antioch a year earlier). In addition to the Jews killed in the East, many died in the West as well, in violent pogroms perpetrated by certain Christian leaders, in a series of incidents known as the German Crusade. While many Christians used the crusade to justify their attacks on the Jews, others abhorred the violence and offered the Jews shelter from their enemies. The assault on European Jews would become a trademark of every subsequent crusade as well. The First Crusade ended with Jerusalem in Christian hands, the city populated almost exclusively by Christians, thousands of Western Christians dead, and many more inhabitants of the East dead.

For more than 40 years following the end of the First Crusade, Christians and Muslims in the Middle East lived next to one another in relative peace, but the fall of the County of Edessa to the Muslims in 1144 spurred Pope Eugene III to call the Second Crusade (1145–1149). This crusade was led by the kings of the two Frankish states, Louis VII of France and Conrad III of Germany (i.e. the Holy Roman Empire), and it was strongly supported by Bernard of Clairvaux, an abbot and eloquent preacher. Bernard traveled through France and Germany urging men to join the crusade, and at the same time cautioning the overzealous against killing European Jews, as some were already advocating. The crusader armies did not achieve their objectives. They were defeated on their journey by armies of Turks, and when they arrived in Jerusalem, they took stock of their situation. Although they had already suffered serious losses from battle and disease, the majority agreed to besiege Damascus. The siege was unsuccessful, and the crusaders were forced to return to Jerusalem. Bernard was devastated by the failure of the crusade, whose success he had confidently predicted, but he blamed the failure on the behavior of the crusaders. As was typical of all the crusades, many of the individual armies, who traveled to the East by different means and along different routes, had looted cities along the way, including cities belonging to the Byzantine Empire. The crusaders' behavior in the previous crusade, as well as reports from incidents in Greece and elsewhere in the present crusade, gave the Byzantine Emperor Manuel I Comnenus reason to be concerned about the crusader armies passing near Constantinople on their pilgrimage to Jerusalem. The Second Crusade ended in failure, and the kings and their armies returned home.

Saladin's capture of Jerusalem in 1187 precipitated the Third Crusade (1189–1192). This crusade was a fiasco almost from the beginning. Of the three original kings who began the crusade – Frederick Barbarossa of the Holy Roman Empire, Richard the Lionheart of England, and Philip II Augustus of France – Frederick drowned after being thrown from his horse while crossing a river before he ever arrived in the Holy Land, Philip got into a dispute with Richard and left before the crusaders had accomplished their goal of recapturing Jerusalem, and Richard was captured by his enemies and held for ransom in Germany while on his journey back to England. Although the crusaders did manage to win some victories, they could not capture Jerusalem, and eventually only Richard and his army were left on the field of battle, along with soldiers from the Kingdom of Jerusalem. Richard negotiated a treaty with Saladin, whereby unarmed Christian pilgrims could enter Jerusalem, and then he left the Holy Land, ending the Third Crusade. It is interesting to note that Richard and other Christians who dealt with Saladin had great respect for him, so much so that popular legends about his exploits circulated in Europe, and Dante included him among the virtuous pagans in *The Inferno*.

The Fourth Crusade (1201–1204) was perhaps the low point of the officially sanctioned holy wars. Shortly after the Third Crusade failed to recapture Jerusalem from

Saladin, Pope Innocent III called the Fourth Crusade to try again. However, instead of going to Jerusalem, the crusaders, who found themselves short on both soldiers and money, were convinced by the son of a recently deposed Byzantine emperor to travel to Constantinople instead and put him on the throne, in exchange for a large sum of money. The crusaders sacked the city and captured it in 1204, slaughtering many of its inhabitants and pillaging many of its treasures. They divided the Byzantine Empire into several Crusader states, one of which, the Latin Empire, was based in Constantinople. They were unable to control all the former territory of the Byzantine Empire, however, so territories still calling themselves the Roman Empire (they never called themselves the Byzantine Empire) continued to exist. This division of the empire led to the somewhat confusing situation in which three different political entities claimed the right to call themselves the Roman Empire: the Latin Empire of the Catholics, the rump Byzantine Empire of the Orthodox, and the Holy Roman Empire in Germany. To make matters more confusing, the Turks in the territory immediately adjacent to the Byzantine states in Anatolia called their land the Sultanate of Rum (i.e. Rome). The Latin Empire existed until 1261, when it was recaptured by the Byzantine army. Pope Innocent III, who had called the crusade, decried the outcome, railing against the crusaders for fighting their fellow Christians and preferring earthly riches to heavenly riches.

The remaining crusades can be summarized briefly. The Fifth Crusade (1217–1221) saw crusading armies capture some cities in Egypt, but they were prevented by the flooding Nile from capturing Cairo and forced to surrender. The leader of the Sixth Crusade (1228–1229), Holy Roman Emperor Frederick II, managed to obtain through negotiation what other crusaders were unable to obtain through force of arms: Christian control of Jerusalem, Nazareth, and Bethlehem; however, Christians only held these cities for ten years. The Seventh Crusade (1248–1254) was led by King Louis VIII of France against Cyprus, Egypt, and Syria, but Louis was taken prisoner in Egypt and held for ransom. After the ransom was paid and Louis was released, Louis led the Eighth Crusade (1270), but after being diverted from his original target of Egypt, he arrived in Tunis, where he died of a stomach ailment. The Ninth Crusade (1271–1272) also failed to capture any Muslim strongholds in the Middle East, and in fact the Arabs and Turks managed to conquer all of the Crusader States in the Levant and Anatolia either before or shortly after this crusade. No other crusades to the Holy Land were mounted after the ninth, for both religious and political leaders realized the futility of undertaking such costly expeditions.

In the whole sorry history of the Crusades, no event was more tragic than the aborted attempt to recruit young people as warriors for God, the so-called Children's Crusade. Legends about the Children's Crusade sprang up quickly in the Middle Ages, and it is difficult to separate fact from fiction. There may have been more than one movement associated with children, but one occurred in 1212, when Nicholas, a young shepherd from Germany, convinced other children to follow him on a journey to Jerusalem. Some of the children died on the journey, others were captured and sold into slavery, and others simply went back home, but none of them reached the Holy Land. The same year Stephen, a young man from Cloyes-sur-le-Loir, led children across France to Marseilles, where they were taken by unscrupulous ship captains to slavery or death. The number of children who were lost in these events is uncertain, but it is likely to have numbered in the thousands. It is possible that the medieval legend of the Pied Piper of Hamelin, who lured more than a hundred children out of their village and into a cave, never to be seen again, was influenced by stories about the Children's Crusade, or a similar event.

Overall, the crusades were an abysmal failure in the short term, and in the long term the consequences were even worse. The primary, overarching goal of the Crusades, to help preserve the Byzantine Empire from conquest by the Turks and restore the Holy

The Crusades

Nine Crusades to liberate the Holy Land were officially called by popes. The following list gives the dates, the pope who called the Crusade, and the immediate results.

First Crusade (1096–1099): called by Pope Urban II; captured Edessa, Antioch, and Jerusalem, establishing Crusader States.

Second Crusade (1145–1149): called by Pope Eugene III after the fall of the County of Edessa, one of the Crusader States; unsuccessfully attempted to besiege Damascus.

Third Crusade (1189–1192): called by Pope Clement III after the fall of Jerusalem to Saladin; failed to capture Jerusalem, but Richard the Lionheart of England negotiated with Saladin to allow unarmed Christian pilgrims to enter Jerusalem.

Fourth Crusade (1201–1204): called by Pope Innocent III; instead of trying to recapture Jerusalem as planned, crusaders sacked Constantinople and carved several Crusader States out of parts of the Byzantine Empire, including the Latin Empire of Constantinople.

Fifth Crusade (1217–1221): called by Pope Honorius III; captured some cities in Egypt, but forced to retreat before reaching the Holy Land.

Sixth Crusade (1228–1229): called by Pope Gregory IX; negotiated for control of Jerusalem, Nazareth, and Bethlehem for ten years, while the Egyptian sultan was busy with other battles.

Seventh Crusade (1248–1254): called by Pope Innocent IV; some successes in Egypt, but ultimately unable to capture any important territory in Egypt or the Holy Land.

Eighth Crusade (1270): called by no pope, but rather by King Louis VIII of France, during a papal vacancy; Louis died only two months after reaching Tunis, so the Crusade ended.

Ninth Crusade (1271–1272): called by no pope, but rather by Prince Edward of England and King Louis IX of France, during a papal vacancy; failed to capture any important territory, and Muslim forces defeated all the remaining Crusader States about this time, ending the Crusades.

Land to Christian control, was partially successful, since Jerusalem and some other territories were captured and incorporated into the Crusader States, which lasted for a few decades or perhaps a century or more. However, these "successes" are greatly overshadowed by the wanton destruction and slaughter experienced by the inhabitants of the East, by Jews in Europe, and even by the crusaders themselves. The Byzantine Empire, with help from the West, managed to hold off the Turks for another 350 years, though it also experienced the humiliating conquest of Constantinople by the very crusaders who were supposed to be their saviors. For the church as a whole the Crusades were a disaster, resulting in centuries of continuing animosity with Muslims, worsening relations between the Western and Eastern branches of the church, and the slaughter of hundreds of thousands of people, including many noncombatants. On a more positive note, many who traveled to the East were able to observe the great achievements of both the Byzantines and the Muslims in scholarship and the arts. This new reconnection with the East opened new doors to trade and allowed access to the knowledge of the East. Trade in turn led to the increasing wealth of the merchant class, and the concomitant rise of the middle classes in European society. Trade also led to the great bubonic plague epidemic called the Black Death in 1348. Contact with Eastern scholarship and art led directly to the Renaissance, the flowering of learning and culture that spread across Europe during the late Middle Ages. In particular, contact with scholars in the East allowed Western scholars to rediscover their classical heritage, especially the philosopher whose works had the greatest influence on Renaissance scholars: Aristotle.

Key points you need to know

- Though the Byzantine Empire gradually lost much of its territory to the Muslims from the seventh century on, the city of Constantinople remained a center of wealth and culture until its fall.
- Constantinople, and with it the Byzantine Empire, fell to the Turks in 1453.
- After Charlemagne, king of the Franks, consolidated his power, he had himself crowned emperor of the Holy Roman Empire by the pope in the year 800, the first emperor in the West since the fall of the Western Roman Empire.
- Charlemagne's promotion of learning led to the Carolingian Renaissance, the first great cultural flowering of the Middle Ages.
- With the conversion to Christianity of the Slavs, the Magyars, and the Norse, the only parts of Europe outside the control of a Christian state were Sicily and parts of the Iberian peninsula, both controled by Muslims, and both reconquered by Christians by the end of the Middle Ages.
- The reconquest of the Iberian Peninsula led the Christian rulers of Spain to expel Muslims and Jews from their country.
- Columbus's "discovery" of the New World in 1492 set the stage for the spread of Christianity, as well as European dominion, in the Western Hemisphere.

- Disputes between leaders of the Eastern and Western branches of the Church resulted in a permanent split between the two largest branches of Christianity in 1054, the Great Schism. The resulting Churches are the Roman Catholic Church in the West and the Eastern Orthodox Church in the East.
- Papal power increased throughout the Middle Ages, with popes serving as political leaders of the Papal States as well as rulers of the Roman Catholic Church.
- In response to an initial request for help by the Byzantine emperor, Pope Urban II called for the First Crusade in 1095, and it was launched the following year.
- A total of nine official Crusades were called by the popes over about two centuries. Despite limited success in retaking land from the Muslims during the First Crusade, the wars as a whole failed to achieve the goal of permanently driving the Muslims from the Holy Land or of protecting the Byzantine Empire.

Discussion questions

1. What factors led to the fall of the Byzantine Empire?
2. Why were popes able to achieve such high levels of power in the West, despite the presence of powerful leaders such as the Holy Roman Emperor?
3. What short-term effects did the Crusades have on Western Europe? on Eastern Europe and Western Asia?
4. What long-term effects did the Crusades have on the relations between Christianity and Islam? on the relations between the Roman Catholic and the Eastern Orthodox Churches?

Further reading

Bax, Douglas S. 1987. "From Constantine to Calvin: The Doctrine of the Just War." In *Theology and Violence: The South African Debate*, 147–71. Edited by Charles Villa-Vicencio. Johannesburg: Skotaville.

Carroll, James 2001. *Constantine's Sword: The Church and the Jews*. Boston, MA: Houghton Mifflin.

González, Justo 1984–1985. *The Story of Christianity*. 2 vols. New York: HarperSanFrancisco.

Latourette, Kenneth Scott 1975. *A History of Christianity*. Revised edn, 2 vols. New York: Harper & Row.

McBrien, Richard P. 1997. *Lives of the Popes*. New York: HarperSanFrancisco.

Papal Encyclicals Online. http://www.papalencyclicals.net.

Pelikan, Jaroslav 1971–1989. *The Christian Tradition: A History of the Development of Doctrine*. 5 vols. Chicago, IL: University of Chicago Press.

Roberts, J. M. 1993. *History of the World*. New York: Oxford University Press.

10 *Winds of change*

Tell me, poor men, if you really are poor what is gold doing in the sanctuary?

(Bernard of Clairvaux, *Apology*)

In this chapter

The final centuries of the Middle Ages saw developments in many areas of Christian theology, including debates over the veneration of icons, the continued division between the Roman Catholic and Orthodox branches of the Church, the increasingly popular veneration of Mary, and the scholastic movement. The Renaissance began in Florence and spread throughout Europe, as scholars moved away from their reliance on tradition in all areas of life, beginning with art and literature but eventually including matters of faith and practice as well, a movement known as Christian humanism. Abuse of power in the Roman Catholic Church led to calls for reform, but the hierarchy of the Church, while willing to reign in corruption, resisted all calls for major change, yet the calls for change persisted on many fronts. Priests accompanied or followed Spanish and Portuguese conquistadors to the New World, and after a slow start, Christianity spread rapidly throughout Ibero-America in the wake of the appearance of the Virgin Mary to Juan Diego, a Mexican Indian peasant.

Main topics covered

- Theological developments in the East and West
- The Renaissance and Christian humanism
- Efforts to reform the Church prior to the Protestant Reformation
- Christianity beyond the Mediterranean world

Theological developments

While no single theological issue dominated the middle to late medieval period like the Christological controversies did in the previous centuries, several important developments in and debates over Christian doctrine mark the period. The first important issue to arise was the debate over the use of *icons*, two-dimensional representations of sacred people, symbols, or scenes that were widely used as aids to worship. Christians in both East and West had been using painted images since the earliest days of the church, but by the eighth century some in the church were convinced that images had become the objects of idolatry and should be banned or destroyed. It is possible that the Muslim prohibition of images, coupled with numerous Muslim victories over Christians in battle during the previous several decades, fueled the antipathy toward images by the *iconoclasts* (those who wanted to remove or destroy the images). The central figure in the early iconoclastic controversy was the Byzantine emperor Leo III. Sometime shortly before 730 Leo issued a series of orders banning the use of images in worship. He was supported in his efforts by several Eastern bishops, but he was opposed by even more bishops, by many irate citizens, by all the Eastern monks, and by almost the entire Western church. Angry words and orders of excommunication flew back and forth between East and West. The patriarch of Constantinople, an *iconodule* (supporter of the use of images), resigned and was replaced by an iconoclast. Hastily called local synods condemned either the iconoclasts or the iconodules, depending on who called the meeting. Leo's son Emperor Constantine V, a convinced iconoclast, continued his father's policies. John of Damascus, a Syrian monk and priest whose family served as officials under the Umayyads, the Muslim rulers of Damascus, was the most ardent supporter of the iconodule position, writing several treatises against the emperors and in favor of the use of images. Constantine's son Leo IV was married to Irene, an iconodule who encouraged the appointment of fellow iconodules privately while Leo was still alive and publicly after his death, when she ruled as coregent with her son Constantine VI and for a time as sole emperor after her son's death. She called a council to discuss the matter of icons, and the Second Council of Nicaea in 787, recognized by both the Eastern and Western churches as the seventh ecumenical council, repudiated iconoclasm. The council did make an important distinction, however, between the *worship* of icons, which was still prohibited, and the *veneration* of images, which was permitted, a distinction that was perhaps a nod in the direction of the iconoclasts. Nevertheless, the council was a clear victory for the iconodule position, and the veneration of images became an especially important part of both the devotional life and public worship of Eastern Christians. A second period of iconoclasm was instituted in the early ninth century by Emperor Leo V and his two immediate successors. After the emperor Theophilos died in 842, however, his widow Theodora, who held power as her young son's regent, promoted once again the iconodule position, and icons were officially restored to their position of honor on the first Sunday of Lent, celebrated by the Orthodox church today as the Feast of Orthodoxy.

One residual effect of the Christological controversies of the previous centuries began to make itself felt about the time of Charlemagne, and its power was such that it contributed to schism between the Eastern and Western churches. It was called the *filioque* controversy. The original text of the Nicene Creed, as modified by the Council of Constantinople, said, "We believe in the Holy Spirit, the Lord, the giver of life, who proceeds from the Father." At some point, apparently in Spain, the Western church added the Latin word *filioque*, "and the Son," to indicate that the Holy Spirit proceeds from both the Father and the Son (cf. John 15:26). This addition to the creed was an attempt to bolster the equality of the Son with the Father in the days of the Christological controversies, and it became the traditional way that the creed was recited in the West. Although of more recent vintage, it could claim support in the writings of the great theologian Augustine, whose definition of the Trinity was normative in the West. In the time of Charlemagne it came to the attention of certain Eastern Christians that the West had inserted the *filioque* clause into the text, and they were aghast. Not only did the West's insertion of *filioque* change the text agreed upon by an ecumenical council, but it also asserted the pope's authority to establish orthodoxy, for although a pope had not actually added the word to the creed, several popes, including Pope Nicholas I, asserted their authority over the Eastern as well as the Western church. It was Nicholas who, for various reasons, excommunicated Photius, the popular and influential patriarch of Constantinople (whom the pope had previously supported), in 863. In turn, Photius excommunicated the pope, citing, among other matters, the insertion of *filioque* into the creed. The so-called Schism of Photius, which divided the Eastern and Western church until Photius's death around 895, was a precursor of the Great Schism that permanently divided the church a century and a half later.

The Great Schism was precipitated by the rash actions of papal legate Cardinal Humbert, who, while on a visit to Constantinople in 1054 to try to resolve various differences between the East and West, walked into the Hagia Sophia cathedral and placed on the altar a decree of excommunication against Patriarch Michael Cerularius of Constantinople. The patriarch responded in kind, and the church was officially divided into two halves. Schisms between East and West had occurred before, associated with Emperor Zeno and Patriarch Acacius, the Three Chapters controversy, and Patriarch Photius, so it is likely that Christians on both sides of the schism thought that this new schism would be healed in time, once cooler heads prevailed. However, the churches in the East and West by this time had drifted too far apart from one another for reconciliation to be effected. The issues that divided them were many. The West continued to insist that *filioque* was an essential part of the creed, while the East rejected it as an unwelcome innovation. The East used leavened bread in the Eucharist, while the West used unleavened bread. The East allowed priests to be married, while the West did not (after the time of Pope Leo IX, who, ironically, was the pope who sent Cardinal Humbert to Constantinople). The West asserted the authority of the church over the state, especially in matters such as the appointment of bishops, while the Byzantine emperor had the power to depose even the patriarch of Constantinople. The most important single factor that made this schism permanent was the authority that popes from at least the time of Gregory VII claimed for themselves in relation to the rest of the church. The patriarch of Constantinople – indeed, no Eastern Christian in communion with Constantinople – could admit that the bishop of Rome had authority over Christians in the East, even over the patriarch of Constantinople himself. Although relations between East and West improved somewhat following the dual excommunications in 1054, the Crusades, which might have been an opportunity for Eastern and Western Christians to work together to achieve a common goal, actually made the relationship between the two sides much worse, particularly after the occupation of Constantinople during and after the Fourth Crusade.

One of the issues just mentioned, clerical celibacy, was a matter of some contention in the West for centuries. Although many early Christian leaders, including Peter, were married, others, such as Paul, were not. Some Christians in the first few centuries saw marriage as an honorable state that was fully compatible with a vocation to the clergy, and many priests, bishops, and even popes were married. Another group of Christians saw marriage either as incompatible with full devotion to God or at least as a distraction to those who were supposed to be the leaders of the church. The tradition practiced by some prelates (Christian leaders with authority to govern others, such as bishops or abbots) of appointing their sons as successors in ecclesiastical offices was also pointed to by proponents of clergy celibacy as a problem associated with married clergy. Pope Leo IX was an avid supported of clerical celibacy, and Gregory VII endorsed Leo's policies and enforced them rigorously. From that time clerical celibacy has been the official position of the Roman Catholic Church.

The doctrine of *transubstantiation* stated that the bread and wine used in the Eucharist are transformed into the literal body and blood of Jesus, from the moment the priest consecrates it. Thus, Jesus' words, "This is my body," which he spoke during his last meal with his disciples, were interpreted in a literal fashion by those who accepted this doctrine. The elements of the Eucharistic meal had long been considered to be more than just ordinary bread and wine. Ignatius of Antioch in the early second century called the Eucharist "the medicine of immortality." Ambrose of Milan said that bread that is ordinary bread before being consecrated becomes the flesh of Christ afterwards. On the other hand, Augustine and other patristic authors did not hesitate to use terms such as *sign* and *symbol* when discussing the relationship between the Eucharist and the body of Christ. The term transubstantiation itself did not arise before the eleventh century, though the sentiment was present much earlier. The Fourth Lateran Council, held by the Roman Catholic Church in 1215, made transubstantiation the official doctrine of the Catholic Church, and this view was upheld by the Council of Trent (1545–1563), in reaction to the denial of the doctrine by Protestants. The Orthodox Church never used the Latin term transubstantiation, and in general they avoided speculation about the specific mechanics of the transformation of the elements into the body and blood of Christ, preferring to refer to the process as a *mystery*. They did, however, agree with the essential idea behind the doctrine.

As noted above, Christians both East and West made a point of distinguishing between worship or adoration, which is owed only to God, and veneration, a lesser form of honor bestowed upon sacred objects such as icons and relics, and upon departed saints as well. Of all the saints venerated by the church, the highest degree of veneration was given to Mary, the mother of Jesus. Historically, Marian veneration can be connected with the controversies over the use of the term *theotokos*, rejected by Nestorius but accepted by most Christians of the day. The veneration of Mary was especially popular among the common people and the monks, particularly in the East, but it got a fresh impetus in the West from the preaching and writing of Bernard of Clairvaux in the twelfth century. Bernard rejected the rationalism of the scholastic movement (see below) and favored a more immediate, even mystical approach to Christianity. For Bernard, this more intimate form of Christianity was mediated by the Blessed Virgin, who interceded in heaven for believers. Veneration of Mary grew immensely in late medieval Christianity, as evidenced by the numerous books of Christian devotion that focused on the Christian's relationship with Mary (e.g. Thomas à Kempis's *On the Imitation of Mary* and Hildegard of Bingen's numerous hymns to Mary). The practice of directing prayers to Mary, such as the traditional "Ave Maria" ("Hail Mary"), also dates from this time. Many medieval churches and cathedrals were dedicated to Mary, who was sometimes called the Queen of Heaven (e.g. the Notre Dame cathedral in Paris). The reported appearance of the Virgin Mary to the Mexican Indian Juan Diego in 1531 (the Virgin of Guadalupe) may be tied to this late medieval emphasis on Marian devotion.

At the opposite end of the spectrum from Marian veneration was a movement known as *scholasticism*. The rediscovery by the West of the works of Aristotle, which had been preserved by Muslim scholars in Spain and in the East, led to a revolution in the theology of the Western church, whose primary philosophical basis up to that point had been Platonism. Whereas Plato saw ultimate reality in eternal Forms, Aristotle believed that ultimate reality was in physical objects, which could be known from experience. Every object, according to Aristotle, had both essence (its ultimate identity, comparable to Plato's Form) and accidence (its observable characteristics). Although the idea of transubstantiation predates scholasticism, the Aristotelian understanding of reality opened the door to a way of buttressing transubstantiation theologically, by proposing that the *essence* of the host (bread) is transformed into the body of Christ at the point of consecration, while the *accidence* of the bread (i.e. its taste and texture) remains.

Anselm of Canterbury, a forerunner of the scholastic movement, applied reason to questions of Christian doctrine, not as a substitute for faith but as a tool of inquiry. He developed the *ontological argument* for the existence of God, which argues that because the greatest possible being imaginable would have to include the property of existence, therefore God must exist. He also used reason to develop the substitutionary (or objective) theory of the atonement, which states that the holiness of God demands a perfect sacrifice to pay for the sins of humanity, and that sacrifice occurred in the death of Jesus on the cross, who was a substitute for the rest of humanity. Another forerunner of scholasticism was Abelard, who wrote a work entitled *Sic et Non* (Yes and No), in which he developed the method of quoting authorities on all sides of a theological question and examining all the arguments before finally settling on a preferred solution. Abelard's method provided the model for many scholastic inquiries.

The scholastic movement grew out of cathedral schools but developed especially in the newly established universities. The influence of the philosophy of Aristotle is unmistakable in the works of the scholastics. The greatest of the scholastic teachers was Thomas Aquinas, who took Abelard's method of quoting authorities on all sides of a theological question, then added his own resolutions which tended to support particular authorities while arriving at definite conclusions. The work most clearly associated with the work of the scholastics was Aquinas's work *Summa Theologica*, a summary of Christian doctrine.

Scholasticism, with its emphasis on combining faith and reason, continued to develop beyond the writings of Thomas Aquinas. John Duns Scotus (1266–1308) was famous for intricate scholastic arguments, but he also questioned whether divinely revealed doctrines like the immortality of the soul could be proved by means of reason alone. Going a step further, William of Occam (1280–1349) concluded that reason alone can prove nothing about God. Furthermore, God's actions cannot be interpreted, much less predicted, by means of reason. God does not do what is good, for whatever God does is the definition of good. Earlier theologians had claimed that the Incarnation was necessary because God *must* become human in order to redeem humanity, but Occam said that God could act in whatever way God wanted to act, and God could have redeemed humanity without becoming human. He said that both councils and popes could err, so the only ultimate source of authority was the Bible. Occam is perhaps best known for his statement known as Occam's Razor: "one should make no more assumptions than necessary"; in other words, the least complicated explanation is the best.

Though scholasticism was quite influential, it was not universally accepted. Detractors came in two varieties. Some, like Bernard of Clairvaux, saw scholasticism as a dangerous attempt to build the Christian faith on the rules of logic and rhetoric rather than on direct experience with God. Others, such as the humanists, whose approach to learning came out of the Renaissance, saw scholasticism as too rigid and formalistic. The conclusions of the scholastics on doctrinal matters were often challenged by the Protestants in the next period of Christian history, but the Protestants eventually developed scholastic methods of their own and wrote voluminous summaries of Christian theology.

The Renaissance and Christian humanism

Encounters with the Byzantine Empire and Muslims introduced Western Europe to great classical thinkers, orators, and writers like Aristotle and Cicero, as well as Greco-Roman art. As a result, scholars in the West began to move away from a reliance on tradition. The rallying cry of the Renaissance was *Ad fontes!* ("back to the sources!"). The sources in question were the Greek and Roman classics in literature and art that had long been forgotten in the West. The name Renaissance, or rebirth, implies a sharp break from the previous period, the Middle Ages, which interrupted the flow of culture from Greco-Roman antiquity to the present. Although most modern historians see the Renaissance as the end of the Middle Ages rather than as a completely separate

Figure 10.1 Renaissance art discarded the stylized forms of the earlier medieval period and focused on realistic renditions of objects, especially human figures. Michelangelo's David captures the youthful exuberance and vigor of the young biblical hero as he contemplates battle with the giant Goliath.

age, the terminology of rebirth persists. In truth, scholars in the Renaissance drew on both medieval and classical forms of art, literature, music, and thought. Renaissance artists put a new emphasis on perspective and realism in their work, and they focused on ordinary human subjects rather than exclusively on religious subjects. They studied human anatomy in order to paint or sculpt authentic human bodies. Renaissance writers tried to imitate the literary style of classical authors. The term *humanism* came to be applied to those influenced by the spirit of the Renaissance, who valued the study of the humanities, or liberal arts, including art, literature, music, history, philosophy, and religion.

The Renaissance began in fourteenth-century Florence – a center of trade and finance, and so in regular contact with the East – but it quickly spread throughout the rest of Europe. The Renaissance signaled the beginning of the end for the Middle Ages. The final end was brought about by the invention of the printing press in 1450, the fall of Constantinople in 1453, and the discovery of the New World in 1492. The fall of Constantinople in particular resulted in a new influx of refugees from the East, many of whom were familiar with classical thought, either directly from Greek and Latin sources or indirectly through Arabic translations. The Renaissance marked the rebirth of critical thinking and disciplines such as textual criticism (establishing the original text of a work by analyzing existing copies) and textual analysis (evaluating traditional claims regarding the date, authorship, and unity of literary works). For example, the papal secretary Lorenzo Valla, using these techniques, was able to demonstrate that the *Donation of Constantine* was a forgery, and he also noted that the Apostles' Creed did not date back to the first century, as tradition said. The humanism that arose during the Renaissance put a new emphasis on humans as actors in their own dramas and subjects in their own lives, not merely objects of divine whim. Ordinary people once more began to think for themselves.

Efforts to reform the Church

Mendicant monasticism

> The rule and life of the lesser brothers is this: To observe the holy gospel of our Lord Jesus Christ, living in obedience without anything of our own, and in chastity.
>
> (*Rule of the Franciscan Order*)

One of the earliest moves in the direction of ecclesiastical reform began in the monasteries as early as the tenth century, when a series of abbots at a monastery in Cluny, France, set about to follow the *Rule* of Benedict with greater fidelity than was usually observed in contemporary monasteries. The success of the reform in Cluny led monks to leave there and travel to other monasteries, instituting the same reforms in hundreds of them and starting new monasteries as well. The successes of the Cluniac reform led to two monks involved in the reform becoming reform-minded popes: Leo IX and Gregory VII. Eventually the Cluniac reform buckled under the weight of its own success, as monasteries accrued great wealth and monks gradually slipped into more relaxed lifestyles. A new reform movement in the monasteries was called the Cistercian reform, and its most famous advocate was Bernard of Clairvaux. Again the monasteries prospered, but the common people outside the walls of the monasteries saw little change in the church.

All that changed with the rise of the mendicant orders – that is, religious orders whose members do not live in a cloistered community – in the early thirteenth century, the most famous of which were the Franciscans and the Dominicans. Francis of Assisi was the son of a wealthy merchant, who abandoned riches for a life of poverty. He saw wealth as the greatest temptation in the Christian life, and he mistrusted education, which could lead to arrogance. Over time he gathered many disciples, who petitioned the pope to allow them to form a new religious community, the Order of Friars (Brothers) Minor. The order demanded complete poverty of both individuals and the community. Most importantly, Franciscan monks did not live in a walled monastery but in the real world. The order sent its brothers out to preach the gospel, and they worked with lepers and the other neediest people in society. They tried to follow the life of the earthly Jesus literally. Francis had enjoyed the songs of French troubadours in his youth, so he used his knowledge of this musical tradition to write prayers and songs for his community.

He preached to Christians, non-Christians, and even animals, He encouraged his friend Clara Sciffi to found a similar community for women, the Order of Poor Ladies, or, as it is more commonly known, the Poor Clares. Francis eventually gave up his leadership of the order and retired to the country to spend time in prayer and contemplation.

By the time of his death, the Franciscan order was a phenomenal success, and Francis himself was widely recognized as a saint. The *Little Flowers of Saint Francis* is a collection of legends that began circulating about him during his own lifetime. The most famous of these legends says that while Francis was fasting during Lent, the five wounds of Christ, or *stigmata*, appeared on his body (e.g. scars on his hands and feet from the nails used during the crucifixion). In fact, Francis's devotion and lifestyle led many to call him the "Second Christ." His order sought to live out the gospel through service to others, especially the weak, and their impact on the church was notable.

About the time that Francis was starting to organize his order, a priest and scholar named Dominic was growing increasingly concerned about the success of a group of unorthodox Christians living in southern France, the Albigensians, also known as the Cathars, whose beliefs included elements of earlier Gnosticism and a belief in reincarnation rather than literal resurrection of the dead. Dominic was impressed with their strict lifestyles (the word Cathar means "pure"), and he believed that force would be ineffective in refuting their errors. Instead, he formed a new mendicant order devoted to poverty, scholarship, and preaching. The Order of Preachers required poverty of its members, though the community could own property in the furtherance of its goals. The primary goal of the order was the conversion of heretics, Jews, and Muslims, but one side effect of the founding of the Dominican order was a new emphasis on scholarship and the creation of cathedral schools and universities. Two of the leading Dominican theologians of the period were Albert the Great and Thomas Aquinas.

Mystics

> The divine erotic force also produces ecstasy, compelling those who love to belong not to themselves but to those whom they love. This is shown by superior beings through their care of inferiors, by those of equal dignity through their mutual union, and by lower beings through their divine conversion towards those that are highest in rank. It was in consequence of this that St. Paul, possessed as he was by this divine erotic force and partaking of its ecstatic power, was inspired to say: "I no longer live, but Christ lives in me" (Gal 2:20). He uttered these words as a true lover and, as he himself says, as one who has gone out from himself to God (cf. 2 Cor 5:13), not living his own life but that of the beloved, because of his fervent love for Him.
>
> (Maximus the Confessor, in the *Philokalia*)

In contrast to the mendicant orders, which sought to effect change through active engagement in the world, Christian mystics hoped to change themselves through direct contact with the divine. Hildegard of Bingen (1098–1179) began seeing visions when

Figure 10.2 Catherine of Siena, a medieval mystic who had the ear of more than one pope, influenced Pope Gregory XI to return the papacy to Rome from Avignon, France, where popes had been living for about 70 years. Renaissance artist Agostino Carracci depicts Catherine fainting into the arms of angels after experiencing a vision of Christ. In 1970 Pope Paul VI declared Catherine a Doctor of the Church, one of only three women so recognized.

she was only five years old. Over time she learned to keep her visions to herself, but when she was about 48 years old, she saw a vision commanding her to write down what she saw for the sake of posterity. She did, and she eventually produced three books of her visions, which she viewed as "God's mysteries," along with her interpretation of the visions. In addition to writing down her visions, she wrote many songs and other works. She was the director of a convent, and she was recognized in her own day as an accomplished scholar. She communicated with popes and emperors, and she was widely revered for both her accomplishments and her piety.

Meister Eckhart (*c.* 1260–1327) was a Dominican monk from Germany. An accomplished scholar, he became famous for the unusual descriptions of God in his sermons. Influenced by both Aristotelianism and Neo-Platonism, as well as his own mystical experiences, he discussed theological matters in novel and, some of his contemporaries thought, alarming ways. He believed that each human soul contained a divine spark that was somehow identified with God. He valued his mystical experiences of God, but his encounters with God were peaceful and quiet rather than full of emotion. Although he was accused of heresy at the end of his life by his enemies, he denied the accusations, but he died before his case was decided. His writings were popular throughout Germany, particularly, in his own day and in subsequent centuries.

Unlike the two previous mystics, Catherine of Siena (1347–1380) had no formal education. She joined a convent when she was 18, and she began receiving visions within a couple of years, often after rounds of severe, self-imposed fasting. She described her early mystical experiences as a "mystical marriage" with Christ. Eventually she left the cloistered life and began writing letters to popes and rulers, urging the latter to make peace with one another and the former to return the papacy to Rome from Avignon. She was successful in convincing Pope Gregory XI to return the papal court to Rome, and she spent her last years in Rome as a guest of Pope Urban VI and his successors.

Joan of Arc (1412–1431) combined mysticism and direct action in a unique way during the Hundred Years' War. Joan began receiving visions as a young girl, and they directed her to help the French recover land lost to the English during the war. She convinced the dauphin Charles, the heir to the throne of France, to let her ride with the soldiers to lift the siege of Orleans, which she said God would deliver into French hands. When she succeeded in rallying the troops to defeat the English in only nine days, many hailed her as a saint sent from heaven. She participated in several other victorious campaigns, but she was eventually captured, tried for witchcraft by the English, and executed at the age of 19. Nevertheless, the new vigor she had infused into the French troops survived her death, and the emboldened French eventually pushed the English army out of French territory. She was immediately regarded by the common people as a national heroine.

Because the patriarchs of the Eastern Orthodox Church never had the kind of political power that the popes in Rome had, the history of Eastern Orthodoxy followed a different path from that of the Roman Catholic Church. Instead of focusing on the relative authority of church and state, the Eastern church accepted the idea that patriarchs and bishops had authority over spiritual matters, while the emperor had authority over temporal matters. The Islamic conquests from the seventh century onward also affected Orthodox Christians, most of whom lived in lands either already controlled by Muslim leaders or in danger of falling under Muslim hegemony. In response, the Orthodox church turned its eyes inward, stressing the development of the soul in relationship to God. Symeon the New Theologian lived in the late tenth and early eleventh centuries, and he taught his followers that the purest form of Christianity was the mystical contemplation of God through prayer and worship. He composed many songs (*Hymns of Divine Love*) to help Christians focus their attention on God and thus develop their inner, spiritual lives. Although Symeon believed that monks were especially well suited to seeking the face of God through prayer and worship, he acknowledged that laypeople too were able to become "partakers of the divine nature." Eastern Orthodox Christians saw the Eucharist as a particularly important means of strengthening the inner life, not because of any magical power innate in the bread and wine, but because the Spirit worked through the elements to impart life. Many of the works of Orthodox Christians on spirituality, including some by Symeon, are contained in a multivolume work called the *Philokalia*.

The Conciliar Movement

The moral excesses of many medieval popes, the control that outside forces often had over the papacy, the failure of reforming popes to effect substantive change from within, and especially the Babylonian Captivity of the papacy and the subsequent Great Western Schism, all led many bishops to believe that for meaningful reform to occur, it would have to be led by councils of bishops. Along with the frustrations that many in the church felt about the poor state of the papacy, many bishops had also grown tired of the increasingly grandiose claims to authority that popes were making. Although they supported the authority of the pope, many in the Conciliar Movement believed that a duly called ecumenical church council had greater authority than any single pope, a sentiment with which the Eastern Orthodox Church would certainly agree. Many bishops believed that the solution to the problem of having simultaneous popes in Rome and Avignon was to call a council to decide the matter. Unfortunately for them, the existing popes simply ignored the Council of Pisa's (1409) declaration that they were deposed, so the situation resulted in the creation of a third pope. The Council of Constance (1414–1418) was called to remedy the situation, which it succeeded in doing, and early in the proceedings it pronounced the supremacy of the decisions of ecumenical councils over even papal decrees. However, that statement was later declared invalid, since the representatives of Pope Gregory XII, the Roman pope, had not yet arrived.

One of the decisions that was later invalidated required the pope to call periodic ecumenical councils to discuss matters of importance to the church. Pope Martin V complied with this decision, and the Council of Florence (also called the Council of Basel, after the first city in which it met, 1431–1445) was summoned. Future popes did not follow through on Martin's commitment, and when Pope Julius II (1503–1513) failed to call a council, other bishops called one at Pisa in 1511. Julius hastened to call his own council, the Fifth Lateran Council (1512–1517), which promptly invalidated the Council of Pisa and declared the Conciliar Movement invalid. With a single vote in an ecumenical council, the hopes of reforming the church through councils of bishops died.

Forerunners of the Protestant Reformation

Preaching on the streets of Lyon beginning in 1173, Peter Waldo called on his fellow Christians to reform themselves and reform the church. Waldo stressed that Christians should live simple lives of poverty, and he advocated his beliefs through public preaching. Unlike most Christians in his day, he read the Bible literally rather than allegorically. Because of his emphasis on the authority of scripture, as read in a literal fashion, he opposed oaths, the doctrine of purgatory, and the veneration of relics and icons. Many of his critiques of the church were similar to those of the Franciscans, but he also foreshadowed themes that would reappear in both the Protestant and the Radical Reformations. Although his views were declared heretical by the Catholic Church, he continued preaching, and his followers persisted in France and northern Italy until the

Early reformers

Christians had been calling for a variety of different types of reform for centuries before the Protestant Reformation broke out in 1517. Some of the more important figures who either called for or implemented some type of reform are listed below.

Cluniac monks (tenth century)
Pope Leo IX (eleventh century)
Pope Gregory VII (eleventh century)
Bernard of Clairvaux (twelfth century)
Peter Waldo (twelfth century)
Francis of Assisi (thirteenth century)
Catherine of Siena (fourteenth century)
John Wycliffe (fourteenth century)
Jan Hus (15th century)
Conciliar Movement (fourteenth–fifteenth centuries)
Girolamo Savonarola (fifteenth century)

Protestant Reformation, sometimes suffering intense persecution at the hands of the institutional church.

John Wycliffe, a fourteenth-century Oxford scholar, believed that both temporal and ecclesiastical authorities should follow the example of Christ, who came to serve, not profit himself. He opposed excesses of both types of authorities as illegitimate. The true church, he said, is embodied not in the pope, nor in the bishops, but in the invisible body of believers who are predestined for salvation. He opposed the Catholic doctrine of transubstantiation, saying the while Christ is mystically present in the bread and wine, the bread and wine are still really present as well. His most influential teaching involved his belief that the Bible should be in the hands of the people, in language they could understanding. Consequently, he translated the Bible into Middle English, and copies circulated widely among his followers, called the Lollards. The Lollards had great support from the lower classes, and they eventually joined and strengthened the Protestant movement in England. Although Wycliffe died 30 years before the Council of Constance, the council condemned him as a heretic anyway and ordered that his body be dug up, burned, and dumped in the River Swift.

Perhaps the most famous of the pre-reformers was Jan Hus, who became rector of the University of Prague in Bohemia in 1402. He sought the reformation of the church, though he was primarily concerned at first with the behavior of the clergy rather than doctrinal reform. He came under the influence of Wycliffe's writings, and he came to accept many of Wycliffe's teachings (though he continued to support transubstantiation). The Czechs, including Hus, supported the Pisan popes (i.e. those popes selected by the Council of Pisa), so the archbishop of Prague prohibited Hus from preaching. When

Hus refused to stop, he was excommunicated. Hus came to believe that unworthy popes should not be obeyed and that the Bible is the final authority for all Christians, including the pope. He opposed the sale of indulgences, on the grounds that only God can forgive sins and that Christian nations should not go to war against one another merely to satisfy a pope's political ambitions. Hus was summoned to the Council of Constance in 1414, under a promise of safe passage. However, he was arrested upon his arrival, and when he refused to submit to the assembly's authority by recanting his beliefs, he was burned at the stake. His supporters in Bohemia were outraged at the council's violation of safe passage and rebelled against the authority of the pope. After several attempts to suppress the rebellion by force failed, the Roman Catholic Church offered some doctrinal compromises, such as the right to take the Eucharist "in both kinds" (i.e. to receive both bread and wine), enforcement of clerical poverty, rejection of simony, and freedom to preach the Bible. Some Hussites separated from the main group and evolved into the group known as the Moravian Brethren.

A reformer of a different sort was Girolamo Savonarola, a Dominican friar from Ferrara who came to Florence in 1490 and began an intense preaching campaign. Savonarola ferociously attacked the evils of the time, including excessive wealth and power, offending both clergy and secular authorities, including his former supporter Lorenzo de Medici. Nevertheless, Savonarola continued his preaching, and his church was packed with people. In 1494 King Charles VIII of France invaded Florence and overthrew the ruling Medici family, and Savonarola became the ruler of the city. He instituted numerous reforms, including making homosexuality a capital offense. He called for a "Bonfire of the Vanities," where citizens of Florence would bring items associated with a loose moral life, vanity, or other sin to the middle of the city and throw them on an immense bonfire. Mirrors, jewelry, books, and priceless works of art were destroyed in the bonfire, in which the citizens of Florence apparently participated of their own free will. They eventually grew tired of his constant railing against sin, and in 1497 people began to rebel against him. Pope Alexander VI, a pope from the Borgia family and a great supporter of the arts, condemned Savonarola and two associates as heretics, and he had them burned at the stake on the same spot where Savonarola's bonfire had earlier stood.

Christianity beyond the Mediterranean world

> Wherever we find that we may offer a first sample of ourselves, by words and works, let it be peace. And let it be no different with the Indians, Gentiles, Greeks, or barbarians: for there is one Lord of all, who died for all without distinction.
>
> (Bartolomé de las Casas, *History of the Indies* 1.17)

On 12 October 1492, Christopher Columbus, in search of a western route to the Indies, sighted a small island, which he named San Salvador (the exact location is disputed), and he also explored the islands of Cuba and Hispaniola in the Caribbean Sea. He established a fort on Hispaniola during his first voyage, but when he returned to the island with missionaries and settlers the following year, natives of the island had destroyed the fort and killed its inhabitants, apparently in response to atrocities committed against them by the Spaniards. Columbus's response was to "pacify" the island by force. The early policies of the church and state toward the native inhabitants of the Caribbean islands may be described as varying from cultural destruction, to forced subjugation, to slavery, and even to genocide. The state wanted slaves, the church wanted converts, and the Indians of Hispaniola and the other Caribbean islands wanted to be neither. These desires for slaves and converts were combined in institutions known as *encomiendas*, or "trusts." The managers, or *encomenderos*, of these *encomiendos* "civilized" the Indians and taught them about Christianity, and the Indians, in return, were to serve them.

Reaction against the abuse of Indians began with the Dominican monk Antonio Montesinos in 1511, but it was the work of a priest named Bartolomé de las Casas that garnered the most attention, both positive and negative. Las Casas, who was an *encomendero*, heard Montesinos preach and was converted to his way of thinking about the relationship between the Spanish and the Indians. At first he advocated importing slaves from Africa to relieve the burden on the Indians, but he soon came to believe that any form of slavery was wrong, and he opposed both Indian and African slavery. He traveled several times to Spain and wrote many books in opposition to the exploitation of the Indians. He joined the Dominican order and eventually became bishop of Chiapas in Mexico. He won many supporters, but he had even more adversaries, both among the rich and among the church hierarchy, who considered the Europeans to be morally, intellectually, and spiritually superior to the natives of the Americas. His books were banned in Peru during his lifetime, and they were added to the Inquisition's list of banned books during the following century. As a result of the protests of Montesinos, Las Casas, and others, King Charles V, grandson of Ferdinand and Isabella, passed "New Laws of the Indies" in 1542 limiting the power of Spanish settlers over the Indians. However, the laws were rarely enforced, so they had little impact.

In the early sixteenth century the Franciscans had some success in converting the Indians of Mexico to Christianity, largely because they practiced a lifestyle of poverty and lived among the common people. Many early converts were baptized according to a simplified ritual, which the church hierarchy opposed. Secular bishops (i.e. bishops not members of a religious order) were generally opposed to educating the Indians, believing them to be incapable of learning, or else fearing that they would rise up against their masters. The Dominicans did not allow any Indians to become members of the clergy, while the Franciscans allowed them only to occupy the lowest levels of the clergy (e.g. lectors and acolytes). Neither group allowed Indians to become even lay brothers in their monasteries. The situation changed dramatically beginning in 1531, when, according to legend, a Mexican Indian, Juan Diego, saw a vision of the Virgin Mary, who told him to climb a certain hill to pick flowers, even though it was December and flowers should not be blooming, to prove to the bishop that she had appeared to him. A chapel was later built on the hill, and Juan Diego's cloak, where he carried the flowers, was imprinted with the image of the Virgin of Guadalupe (that is, the Virgin Mary), who appeared as a pregnant Indian woman. This event signified to many that Christ

Figure 10.3 Christianity had made little headway in the New World until the Mexican Indian
Juan Diego reported seeing the Virgin Mary on a hill near the present-day Mexico
City. The image of the Virgin of Guadalupe depicted Mary as an Indian woman
pregnant with her son Jesus.

was "born again" among the peoples in the New World. As the story of Juan Diego's
encounter spread, Indians flocked to the church in droves, and the Virgin of Guadalupe
became the symbol not only of the Catholic Church in the Americas but also a symbol
of Mexican nationalism.

While many Spanish conquistadors looked for gold or the fountain of youth, the
Franciscans established missions throughout Mexico and Central America, including
areas that are now in California, Arizona, New Mexico, and Texas. The outreach by the
Franciscans, combined with the miracle of Guadalupe and the intermarriage of Spaniards
and Indians, resulted in rapid growth for the church. By the end of the sixteenth century,
most inhabitants of Mexico and Central America considered themselves Christians.
Christianity spread rapidly in South America as well, through the work of Dominicans,
Jesuits, Franciscans, and secular priests and bishops. Advocates for the Indians and
other poor in Latin America, generally the religious orders and the priests, often ran
into opposition from the authorities of both the church and state, setting the stage for
the independence movements that would flourish in the nineteenth century.

Before the Spanish unification under Ferdinand and Isabella, Portugal was the dominant Christian nation in the Iberian peninsula, having expelled the Moors in the thirteenth century. Early Portuguese explorers concentrated on finding a sea route around Africa to the Far East in order to avoid going through Muslim lands, and in 1487 Vasco da Gama succeeded in sailing around the Cape of Good Hope and across the Indian Ocean to the Indies. The Portuguese established several settlements along both the west and east coasts of Africa (Congo, São Tomé, Angola, and Mozambique), primarily to support Portuguese traders on their way to and from the Far East. Soon Portuguese missionaries came to the settlements and began working among the Africans who lived nearby, though with limited success.

The Portuguese also established a base of operations in Goa, India, and from there they expanded their colonial settlements to Ceylon, Japan, and China (Macau). Francis Xavier, a Jesuit missionary who was one of the founders of the order, arrived in Goa in 1542, and after early work in India, he sailed for Japan, where he won many converts to Christianity. Shortly after his death Christianity was banned in Japan, but an underground church survived, resurfacing only in the nineteenth century. Xavier had hoped to enter China to do mission work there as well, but he was never able to, because the Chinese rulers were suspicious of establishing relationships with foreigners. One factor that led to Chinese suspicion of foreigners was that most missionaries at the time equated European customs and even names with Christianity, and the Chinese were not interested in becoming more European. In order to build relationships with the Chinese, some missionaries began adopting Chinese styles of dress and submerging themselves in Chinese culture and philosophy, and as a result, churches began to be established in China as well.

In 1500 a Portuguese squadron sailing for the Far East was steering a wide course around Africa and sighted land in South America. Soon Portuguese traders and settlers came to the land, Brazil, and began enslaving Indians to work on sugar plantations. When many Indians proved to be recalcitrant, the Portuguese began importing slaves from Africa. While many in the church hierarchy cared little about the treatment of Indians by the Portuguese, the Jesuits in Brazil did their best to protect them. After various plagues and other disasters, the Indians and black slaves in Brazil began to combine Christianity with traditional religious practices to create *santidade* and other syncretistic systems of belief. These new religions offered Indians and blacks dignity that traditional Christianity denied them, so they grew in popularity in many areas.

Key points you need to know

- Christian doctrine continued to develop throughout the Middle Ages. Issues such as the veneration of icons, the *filioque* controversy, transubstantiation, the veneration of Mary, and scholasticism were important during the last few centuries of the medieval period.
- Renaissance scholars called for the rejection of tradition and a return to the ancient sources, especially in art and literature. This call to return to the sources led some Christians to advocate a return to the authority of the Bible and a rejection of the traditions of the Church that had accumulated over the centuries, a call that would reach its zenith with the Protestant Reformation.
- Many Christians, both within the ecclesiastical power structure and without, called for reform. Those calling for reform included the mendicant religious orders, Christian mystics, supporters of the Conciliar Movement, and individual forerunners of the Protestant Reformation, including Waldo, Wycliffe, Hus, and, in a different way, Savonarola.
- Roman Catholic Christianity spread to the New World, Africa, India, and East Asia, following the path blazed by explorers and traders.
- The harsh treatment that many European Christians showed to the native inhabitants of the lands they explored led some to resist, some to acquiesce to the new religion, and others to combine elements of Christianity with traditional religious practices.
- The introduction of African slaves to the New World brought additional new religious traditions to the region, which were sometimes combined with Christian traditions.
- A few Europeans, such as Antonio Montesinos and Bartolomé de las Casas protested the treatment of Native Americans but had little effect on the practices of either the Church or the state.

Discussion questions

1. Which theological developments had the greatest long-term significance for the Church?
2. How did the traditional Renaissance cry, "To the sources!" affect Christian theology?
3. In what ways were the calls to reform by mendicant monasticism, Christian mystics, and the Conciliar Movement similar? In what ways were they different?
4. Which group or individual calling for reform ultimately had the greatest impact on the Church?
5. Why did the Roman Catholic hierarchy initially decline to act on the reports of abuse of the native population by Spanish and Portuguese soldiers, for example by threatening to excommunicate either the soldiers involved or the monarchs who sent them?

Further reading

Abelard. *Sic et Non.*

Anselm. *Proslogion.*

Aquinas, Thomas. *Summa Theologica.*

González, Justo 1984–1985. *The Story of Christianity.* 2 vols. New York: HarperSanFrancisco.

González, Justo 1987. *A History of Christian Thought.* Revised edn, 3 vols. Nashville, TN: Abingdon.

Gutiérrez, Gustavo 1993. *Las Casas: In Search of the Poor of Jesus Christ.* Translated by Robert R. Barr. Maryknoll, NY: Orbis.

Kempis, Thomas à. *On the Imitation of Mary.*

Latourette, Kenneth Scott 1975. *A History of Christianity.* Revised edn, 2 vols. New York: Harper & Row.

McBrien, Richard P. 1997. *Lives of the Popes.* New York: HarperSanFrancisco.

Palmer, G. E. H., Philip Sherrard, and Kallistos Ware, trans. and ed. 1979–1995. *The Philokalia.* 4 vols. London: Faber and Faber.

Pelikan, Jaroslav 1971–1989. *The Christian Tradition: A History of the Development of Doctrine.* 5 vols. Chicago, IL: University of Chicago Press.

Roberts, J. M. 1993. *History of the World.* New York: Oxford University Press.

Symeon the New Theologian. *Hymns of Divine Love.*

The Little Flowers of Saint Francis.

Tillich, Paul 1968. *A History of Christian Thought.* Edited by Carl E. Braaten. New York: Simon and Schuster.

11 Upheaval in the Church

Unless I am convicted by scripture and plain reason – I do not accept the authority of popes and councils for they have contradicted each other – my conscience is captive to the Word of God. I cannot and I will not recant anything, for to go against conscience is neither right nor safe. Here I stand, I cannot do otherwise, God help me. Amen.
(Martin Luther, *Address to the Diet of Worms*)

In this chapter

The end of the Middle Ages brought several changes in perspective to Christians living in the Mediterranean world. The fall of the Byzantine Empire signaled a shift in power within Christendom from East to West, and the discovery of the New World opened the door to many different opportunities. The invention of the printing press allowed Martin Luther and other Reformers to spread their ideas throughout Europe and beyond, and Protestantism took root in many parts of Northern Europe, including Britain. The Roman Catholic Church responded belatedly to calls for reform by implementing several measures to purify the Church, though without admitting the need for doctrinal change. In the West Protestants fought Catholics, and sometimes one another, until the Peace of Westphalia brought an end to the religious wars between nations and established the principle of the sovereign nation-state. Fighting continued inside the borders of European countries, however, with Catholics prevailing in France and Protestant Puritans prevailing in England.

Main topics covered

- Causes and effects of the end of the Middle Ages
- Luther and the Protestant Reformation in Germany
- Zwingli and the Protestant Reformation in Switzerland
- Anabaptists and the Radical Reformation
- Calvin and the Reformed tradition
- The Reformation in England, Scotland, and Scandinavia
- The Catholic Reformation

- The Thirty Years' War and the Peace of Westphalia
- The Persecution of the French Huguenots
- The Puritan Revolution in England

The end of the Middle Ages

As the sixteenth century dawned, the church found itself in a new world. Three major events of the past half-century had changed life as medieval Christians had known it, and the world would never be able to return to what it had been before. First, in 1453 the Turks captured the Christian city of Constantinople, bringing an end to the Byzantine Roman Empire that had ruled the East since the fall of Rome a thousand years earlier. Of the five major metropolitan areas that had dominated Christian life and thought during the first few centuries, only Rome remained in Christian hands; Jerusalem, Alexandria, Antioch, and Constantinople now lay under the power of the Muslims. Second, in 1492 Christopher Columbus discovered the Western Hemisphere. Of course, it wasn't really lost, since Native Americans had lived there for thousands of years, but from a European perspective, the voyages of Columbus were nothing short of revolutionary, for they offered new opportunities for commerce, provided a new stage on which rivalries among European powers could play out, and spurred a new missionary emphasis in the church. The third major event of the fifteenth century was perhaps the most dramatic of all. About 1450 Johannes Gutenberg invented the printing press, a device that allowed people to produce multiple copies of books and other works in a short period of time and relatively inexpensively. The printing press was the most effective tool ever invented for disseminating information to large numbers of people, and it spurred the growth of literacy, higher education, the middle class, and reform within the church. Although the Latin Bible was probably the first major work printed on the new presses, and Hebrew Bibles had similarly been printed as early as 1488, it was the publication of the first Greek New Testament in 1516 that really set the stage for the Protestant Reformation that would begin the following year.

The Protestant Reformation

Luther and the Reformation in Germany

In addition to the three major changes just mentioned, the church itself was undergoing calls for change from various quarters. The excesses of the papacy in the late Middle Ages led to renewal movements and calls for reform. One such movement was the Conciliar Movement, an attempt to wrest absolute authority in the Roman Catholic Church from the pope and distribute it among other bishops. Sometimes reformers within the church were successful in electing one of their supporters as pope, so the papacy instituted a few reforms from within. Christian humanists, such as Erasmus of Rotterdam, looked to advances in science and the arts as inspiration for reform within the church. A number of other reformers arose among the priests and the common people and addressed problems that they saw with the church. This group included John Wycliffe in England, Girolamo Savonarola in Florence, Jan Hus in Bohemia, and Peter Waldo in France. Although none of these people had the widespread or lasting impact of Luther, each addressed concerns that large numbers of people had with the church, and they laid the foundation for the success of the Protestant Reformation.

Martin Luther, a Roman Catholic priest and Augustinian monk, began questioning some of the tenets of the church as he taught classes in the University of Wittenberg. He questioned whether certain church teachings such as the doctrine of purgatory were biblical. He also questioned the need for works in salvation, believing instead that faith alone was sufficient. These questions might have gone largely unnoticed had he not also questioned the efficacy of indulgences that were being sold to raise money to build St. Peter's Basilica in Rome. Luther said that if the pope really had the authority to forgive sins and release souls from purgatory, he ought to release everyone at once for the sake of mercy. Luther's disputes with the church hierarchy led to his excommunication, and a price was put on his head. Nevertheless, Luther had powerful protectors among European rulers, and the pope was unable to touch him. For Luther, the Protestant Reformation was about the proper understanding of Christian theology, but for many others, European politics played at least as important a role as did theology.

Lutheran theology is sometimes described as consisting of three principles: *sola scriptura* (only scripture), *sola fide* (only faith), and *sola gratia* (only grace). Two other

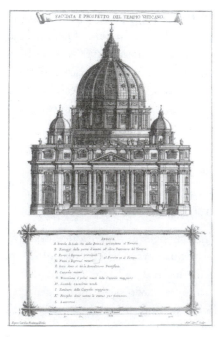

Figure 11.1 St. Peter's Basilica in Rome was financed in part through the sale of indulgences, certificates of remission of sin. Martin Luther and other Protestant reformers railed against the sale of indulgences.

principles are sometimes added: *solus Christus* (only Christ), and *soli Deo gloria* (only for the glory of God). These descriptions are oversimplifications, but they do describe emphases that the Reformers incorporated into their preaching and teaching.

First, Luther came to believe that the Bible was the ultimate source of authority for the church. Moreover, he recommended major changes to the canons of the Old and New Testaments. Most Protestants accepted his proposal to eliminate from the Old Testament those books not found in the Hebrew Bible (i.e. the Apocrypha, or Deuterocanonical books), but they rejected his proposal to eliminate books such as James, Jude, and Revelation from the New Testament. Luther still valued the books of the Apocrypha, as well as the teachings of earlier church leaders such as Augustine and Aquinas, but he believed that the testimony of sacred scripture should be the final arbiter of doctrine.

Second, Luther understood salvation to be rooted in faith in Christ alone, not in works. He took Paul's words in Romans 1:16 to heart: "[The gospel] is the power of God for salvation to everyone who believes." Good works were important to Luther as proof of genuine faith, but faith alone was necessary to enter into a relationship with God. Because of Luther's love of Paul's formulation of the relationship between faith and salvation, he found James's emphasis on the necessity of both faith and works difficult to accept, and he even went so far as to call the book of James "an epistle of straw."

Third, Luther believed that divine grace was the ultimate cause of reconciliation between humanity and God. Though faith was the necessary human response to God, humans could not muster faith on their own, apart from God's grace. God, then, supplied grace in sending Christ to die for people's sins, and then God gave humans the grace to respond in faith to the divine initiative.

The final two *"solas"* describe Luther's emphasis on Christ's mediation alone (and the corresponding reduced emphasis on Mary and the saints) and the desire that all that Christians do be done for the glory of God. Johann Sebastian Bach, a Lutheran musician of the Baroque era, often wrote the words *soli Deo gloria* on his manuscripts.

Another of Luther's emphases was the distinction between Law and Gospel. Luther himself struggled for years with his awareness of his own sinfulness, and it was for this reason that his discovery of salvation by faith alone was so important. Nevertheless, he believed that the Law continues to have an impact on the lives of believers, because it reminds them that they are sinners. God's justification does not remove the reality of the sin, only its punishment. Therefore, because of humans' sinful natures, the state, the enforcer of the Law, remains essential for human society.

Closely related to the question of Law and Gospel was Luther's belief in the two kingdoms, one under the Law and one under the Gospel, the State and the Church. Drawing on Augustine's *City of God* and medieval developments of Augustine's thought, Luther taught that the two kingdoms were both important but that they had separate responsibilities. In particular, the State should not enforce doctrinal purity on behalf of the Church. In practice, Luther's commitment to this distinction often broke down, as when he advocated state suppression of Anabaptists, Jews, and others.

Unlike many of his fellow reformers, Luther was deeply suspicious of the trustworthiness of human reason to aid in the pursuit of either salvation or truth. In response to Erasmus's book *On Free Will*, in which the leading Christian humanist of the day argued that God creates humans with the ability to choose either to follow or to reject God, Luther wrote *On the Bondage of the Will*, in which he proclaimed the human will hopelessly corrupted by sin. Only by the grace of God, Luther said, can the will be restored to its pristine state, overcoming the effects of sin and the Fall, and become capable of responding positively to God's call.

One of the major areas of reform to come out of the Protestant Reformation concerned the Christian understanding of sacraments. Since the very beginning the church had observed Communion and Baptism as sacred rites of great importance. Over the centuries, other rites had joined these two as means by which God communicated grace directly to individual Christians: Confirmation, Marriage, Confession, Holy Orders, and Holy Anointing (Last Rites). Luther rejected most of these later rites as of lesser importance than the first two. Furthermore, he rejected the idea that the communion host literally became the body of Christ, and was thus sacrificed anew, during Communion, the doctrine of transubstantiation. However, he continued to believe that Christ's presence was more than just symbolic in the bread, so the Lutheran doctrine is sometimes called consubstantiation.

Luther's views so outraged the leaders of the Roman Catholic Church that they sought to silence him, permanently if necessary. Luther was summoned to the Diet of Worms to defend his beliefs, and the same diet (assembly of German princes) condemned Luther and his views. While Luther's supporters argued with his opponents over his fate, Luther was spirited away to the castle at Wartburg, where he remained in hiding for more than a year. During that time, he translated the New Testament from Greek into German, an undertaking that was important both for the spread of Protestantism and for the development and standardization of the German language.

While Luther was in hiding at Wartburg, his colleagues in Wittenberg, Andreas Karlstadt and Philipp Melanchthon, instituted a number of reforms. They urged priests and nuns to marry, they began offering wine as well as bread to people during communion, and services were held in German rather than Latin. Soon, questions arose concerning exactly how far the reforms should carry, and when political realities forced Luther's opponents to relent concerning his punishment, he returned to Wittenberg. Despite the fact that his name is the one most closely associated with the Protestant Reformation, Luther often served as a moderating influence, reigning in some of the more radical changes proposed by his colleagues and by others who were influenced by his teachings. When a large number of peasants revolted against the German princes in 1524, although Luther agreed with many of the peasants' complaints against their rulers, he sided with the state when the revolts turned violent. His alliance with the state caused many peasants to abandon Protestantism and return to the Catholic fold, while others sought more radical forms of Christianity among the Anabaptists.

Protestant princes joined in an alliance called the League of Schmalkald to defend themselves from the Catholic princes, but political expediency again intervened, and

Figure 11.2 Unlike earlier would-be reformers, Luther was successful in starting a mass movement of Christians willing to stand against the authority of the Roman Catholic Church.

Protestants and Catholics signed a peace treaty in 1532. One stipulation of the treaty was that Protestants would not try to spread their views among Catholics in other provinces, but their views did spread fairly quickly, in large part because of printed pamphlets advocating Protestant viewpoints.

Zwingli and the Swiss Reformation

Ulrich Zwingli was a Roman Catholic priest who, like Luther, saw a great need for reform within the church. Unlike Luther, who was driven by an inner sense of his own sin and need for justification, Zwingli came to his theology primarily through the study of the Bible and the application of Christian humanist principles. Because of this background, Zwingli had a much more positive view of reason than Luther did. Nevertheless, the two agreed on many points, and in 1529 Luther, Zwingli, and other Protestant leaders came together in Marburg to try to reach consensus on various issues. Although they achieved accord on many issues, the idea of the presence of Christ in the communion bread proved to be an insurmountable sticking point. Whereas Luther held out for the real presence of Christ in the bread, Zwingli believed Christ's presence to be purely symbolic. Years later, leaders of the German and Swiss branches of Protestantism were able to reach accord even on this issue.

Zwingli was opposed to the practice of Swiss cantons (provinces) raising mercenary troops to send into battle for other sovereigns, such as the king of France. He urged the government of Zürich, where he lived, to resist the call to arms, not because he was opposed to war but because he believed that the mercenary life led to a breakdown in morals, among other evils. Eventually the government of Zürich threw its weight behind

Zwingli, and other cantons followed as well. When the Catholic cantons joined forces to fight against Zürich in 1531, Zwingli went out to battle with the troops, where he was killed. Just a month later, the Protestant and Catholic canons came to an agreement that averted further war. The Swiss Reformation, bereft of its leader, was eventually subsumed under the banner of Lutheranism, though other Swiss reformers continued to work and think for themselves.

Zwingli's theology was similar to Luther's in many ways. Two major differences were evident, however. The first was the disagreement over whether the bread in communion was in some sense really Christ's body (Luther) or merely a symbol of Christ's body (Zwingli). The second was that Luther taught that whatever the Bible did not disallow was implicitly allowed, while Zwingli taught that whatever the Bible did not explicitly allow was disallowed. Thus, while Lutheran worship continued to use artwork and music to enhance the experience of the faithful, Zwinglian worship was much more austere. Zwingli removed organs from his churches and disallowed the use of other musical instruments, since they were not mentioned in the New Testament, and he also removed statues and other forms of art from places of worship. Other leaders in the Swiss Reformation reversed these measures after his death.

Anabaptists and the Radical Reformation

Luther, Zwingli, Calvin, and their allies led a movement sometimes called the Magisterial Reformation, because of the support they received from the magistrates, or political leaders of their day. Another reform movement, parallel to this one but lacking the support of important political leaders, is sometimes called the Radical Reformation, and sometimes the Anabaptist Reformation. Neither term is perfect. Though most of the participants in the movement were radical in the sense of discarding church tradition and going back to Christianity's biblical roots for guidance (*radical* comes from the Latin word for *root*), some were also radical in the sense of being political revolutionaries, while many others were complete pacifists. Again, while most could be called Anabaptists ("to baptize again") because they advocated adult, believer's baptism, there were exceptions. The movement was fragmented and lacked a common spokesperson, in large measure because leaders of the movement were often rounded up and imprisoned or even executed by Catholics and Protestants alike. After some early, spectacular failures, such as Thomas Müntzer, a leader of the Peasants Revolt, and the Münster rebellion of 1533–1534, most Anabaptists rejected violence as a legitimate tool of social change. Many believed that Christ would return soon, but they trusted God to provide the force necessary to overwhelm their enemies.

Two of the most influential early Anabaptist leaders were George Blaurock and Conrad Grebel, both of whom were early disciples of Zwingli in Zürich. Blaurock and Grebel, after failing to convince Zwingli to support more radical changes in Christian practice, formed their own congregation and began baptizing converts. They held that only believer's baptism is valid, since babies are incapable of making a conscious choice of faith in Christ. They advocated pacifism, rejected oaths, and taught that the church was made up only of those who truly believed: no one was born into the church. They believed in a sharp distinction between the role of the church and the role of the state. Because of their refusal to take oaths or swear loyalty to the state, political authorities, supported by Zwingli, turned on the Anabaptists and began persecuting them. Many were executed for their beliefs. Apparently the first to suffer this fate was Felix Manz, an associate of Blaurock and Grebel, who was drowned in Lake Zürich in 1527 after refusing to recant his beliefs.

A somewhat later Anabaptist leader was Menno Simons of Friesland (a region in the Netherlands), a former priest who became an Anabaptist in 1536. Because of his effective preaching and long ministry, his followers began to be called Mennonites. Despite persecutions, the Mennonites grew, and their quiet lifestyles and advocacy of peace eventually won them favor with both their neighbors and the authorities.

Calvin and the Reformed tradition

By predestination we mean the eternal decree of God, by which he determined with himself whatever he wished to happen with regard to every man. All are not created on equal terms, but some are preordained to eternal life, others to eternal damnation; and, accordingly, as each has been created for one or other of these ends, we say that he has been predestinated to life or to death.

(John Calvin, *Institutes of the Christian Religion* 3.21.5)

Although Luther is legitimately called the founder of the Protestant Reformation, John Calvin was its first great systematizer. Because he was born almost 30 years later than Luther, Calvin avoided many of the greatest early conflicts between Catholics and Protestants. As a result, his set his mind to develop a presentation of the entirety of Protestant thought, not focusing on the primary issues of conflict of earlier decades, such as the sale of indulgences. Calvin's most important work, *Institutes of the Christian Religion*, began as a relatively short work of six chapters in 1536. He continued expanding it over the years, and by the time of his death in 1564, the *Institutes* had grown to four books, containing 80 chapters. This work was by far the most thorough and most influential theological work that any Protestant had produced. In fact, its importance as a systematic theology was rivaled in the entire history of Christianity to that point only by Thomas Aquinas's *Summa Theologica*, written in the thirteenth century. It continued to be an authoritative statement of Protestantism for two centuries, up to the Enlightenment in the eighteenth century.

Luther thought highly of Calvin's *Institutes*, and although the two reformers differed on certain points, they respected each other greatly. The main point of contention between the two seems to have been the question of the presence of Christ in the Eucharist. Though he denied the Catholic doctrine of transubstantiation, Luther believed Christ's presence to be real in the Eucharist. Calvin preferred to speak of Christ's presence as spiritual in the Eucharist, but he denied that the Eucharist was merely a symbol, as

Zwingli and the Anabaptists held. Martin Bucer, a reformer from Alsace, worked over the years to forge a compromise between Luther and the Swiss successors to Zwingli on the one hand, and between the Lutherans and the Reformed (i.e. Calvinists) on the other, with a great deal of success. After the deaths of the principal actors, however, differences between Lutheran and Reformed points of view calcified, with the result that they came to be considered two distinct Protestant groups.

Calvin was born in Noyon, France; was educated in Paris, Orleans, and Bourges; and spent several years in Strasbourg (then a free city in the Holy Roman Empire), but his greatest work, and his notoriety, stemmed from the years he spent in Geneva, Switzerland. When he arrived in Geneva, he originally intended to spend only a short time there, but he was persuaded to invest himself in the life of the city, and he did so with gusto. In addition to writing the *Institutes* and various exegetical and other works there, he also became highly influential in the city government. Like other magisterial

Reformers of the Church

Luther and Calvin were the most famous reformers during the sixteenth century, but they were by no means the only important figures leading the reform movement. Some of the more important early reformers are listed below, along with an indication of their faith tradition (although some are difficult to classify in a single faith tradition).

Martin Luther (Lutheran)

Philipp Melanchthon (Lutheran)

Andreas Karlstadt (Lutheran)

Ulrich Zwingli (Lutheran)

Martin Bucer (Lutheran)

Johannes Oecolampadius (Lutheran)

Heinrich Bullinger (Lutheran)

John Calvin (Reformed)

Theodore Beza (Reformed)

John Knox (Reformed)

Jan Laski (Reformed)

Thomas Cranmer (Anglican)

William Tyndale (Anglican)

Hugh Latimer (Anglican)

Nicholas Ridley (Anglican)

Balthasar Hübmaier (Anabaptist)

Menno Simons (Anabaptist)

Felix Manz (Anabaptist)

Conrad Grebel (Anabaptist)

Faustus Socinus (Unitarian)

reformers, he equated the population of a given region with the membership of the church. Under that theory of the relationship between church and state, he taught that the local government had the right to enforce strict religious rules among its citizens and to punish lax moral behavior and heresy.

The most infamous example of Calvin's mingling of church and state occurred when the Spanish physician Michael Servetus was apprehended while passing through Geneva in 1553. Servetus was a fugitive from the Catholic Inquisition, and he fled east hoping to find more tolerant views among the Protestants. Servetus denied the doctrine of the Trinity, and he criticized the practice of infant baptism. Interestingly, Servetus had corresponded with Calvin in previous years, and the two had carried on heated exchanges concerning Servetus's theological ideas. Servetus actually stopped in Geneva to hear Calvin preach, hoping to pass unrecognized, but he was recognized by someone in the crowd and arrested. Calvin and the government of Geneva condemned Servetus to be burned at the stake, and the other Protestant cantons concurred in his punishment. Servetus is sometimes loosely associated with the Radical Reformation because of his rejection of infant baptism, but he seems to have arrived at his views primarily on his own, apart from a community of fellow believers. His views were indeed similar to the Socinians, a group of anti-Trinitarians who were to thrive in Zürich, the Netherlands, Transylvania, and Poland over the next several decades.

The Reformation in England

Henry VIII ascended the throne of England shortly before the Protestant Reformation began on the Continent. Early in his reign he wrote against the Protestants, and he was rewarded by being named Defender of the Faith by the pope. Henry's break from the Roman Catholic Church had more to do with politics than with religious beliefs. For political reasons, he had married Catherine of Aragon, daughter of Ferdinand and Isabella of Spain. After several years, however, Catherine had not produced a male heir, only a daughter, Mary Tudor. Henry desperately wanted a male heir, so he decided that he needed a divorce from Catherine. When the pope refused to grant it (for political rather than religious reasons; Spain was a strong supporter of the papacy), Henry pulled the English church away from the Roman church by declaring that English churches owed their loyalty to the English crown rather than the pope. As head of the Church of England, Henry granted himself a divorce. He ultimately married five other women, only one of whom produced a male heir, Edward VI, but Henry's quest for a son led directly to the Church of England's break with Rome.

Of course, many English clergy and laity, including Thomas Cranmer, archbishop of Canterbury, had theological reasons for wanting reform. Those with the most influence wanted a more gradual, less radical reform than had taken place in the Holy Roman Empire and Switzerland, and since Henry wasn't really an advocate of reform at all, the moderate view prevailed. Henry was not moderate, however, when it came to loyalty to the crown. Thomas More, a former Lord Chancellor and a friend of Henry's, refused to swear loyalty to the king as head of the church, because he regarded the pope as the only legitimate ruler of the church. Despite intense efforts by his friends and family to get him to recant, he refused to do so, and he was executed.

After Henry's death, Edward VI was only nine years old, and he reigned for only six years. His regents, the Dukes of Somerset and Northumberland, were strong advocates for Protestant reform, and they instituted a number of changes to the church, including worship in English, married clergy, and serving wine as well as bread to the people during communion. The most important innovation was the *Book of Common Prayer*, the first liturgy in the English language. It served to unite the churches in worship.

Upon Edward's death, the throne passed to his half-sister, Mary Tudor, a Catholic. A staunch believer, Mary removed Protestants from their religious posts and restored Catholicism to its former status as the official religion of the kingdom. She ordered the execution of many Protestants, including the Archbishop of Canterbury, Thomas Cranmer. So many Protestants were killed during her brief five-year reign that her enemies referred to her as "Bloody Mary."

After Mary died, her half-sister Elizabeth, a Protestant, ascended to the throne. Like her father, she was not an advocate of radical reform, but she did restore Protestants to power, and she also imprisoned and executed many Catholics, on the grounds that they were plotting against her (as some certainly were). Through a number of intrigues, Elizabeth ruled with strength for forty-five years, and Protestantism, albeit of a fairly conservative variety, was firmly entrenched in England upon her death.

The Reformation in Scotland

Bot or he haid done with his sermont he was sa active and vigorus, that he was lyk to ding that pulpit in blads and flie out of it. [But before he had done with his sermon, he was so active and vigorous that he was likely to break the pulpit into pieces and fly out of it.]

(*Diary of Mr. James Melville*, on John Knox)

The political intrigues that engulfed England during this period affected Scotland as well. The two countries were independent of one another, though their dynasties were related by blood, and often by marriage as well. Scotland had traditionally been allied with France, which supported it in its conflicts with England, so for this reason the Scottish king, James V, opposed the Protestants, who were natural allies with the English. His successor, Mary Stuart (Mary, Queen of Scots), for a time favored the Protestant camp, though she remained a Catholic herself. She coveted the throne of England, however, and her political missteps cost her first her throne and eventually her life. She was executed by her cousin Elizabeth for plotting to overthrow her.

The leader of the Protestant cause in Scotland, at least from the religious side, was John Knox. Knox, a former Catholic priest, had traveled on the Continent and had studied and worked with both Calvin and Heinrich Bullinger, Zwingli's successor in Zürich. He was a strong advocate of the Reformed type of Protestantism, and when he returned to Scotland after his travels he helped organize the Church of Scotland, with a Reformed theology and a presbyterian structure. He opposed Mary Stuart when she turned against the Protestants late in her reign, and he ultimately saw the Church of Scotland gain ascendancy after Mary was deposed.

Protestantism in Scandinavia

Scandinavia was undergoing many of the same conflicts that the rest of Europe was seeing: conflicts over religious ideas, conflicts between kings and the nobility, conflicts between ecclesiastical authorities and secular leaders. In the midst of a variety of crises, a Lutheran form of Protestantism came to Scandinavia, and despite political difficulties and conflicts, Protestantism was almost universal by about the middle of the sixteenth century.

The spread of Protestantism

The spread of Protestantism in Europe in the sixteenth and early seventeenth centuries is inextricably bound to the course of European history during that time. As Europe emerged from the Middle Ages, the power of the pope was on the wane, though his influence remained great throughout this period. However, the pope's authority was challenged by absolute or near-absolute monarchs, such as the kings of England, France, Spain, and the Holy Roman Empire. Because the American and French Revolutions two centuries later were democratic reactions against entrenched monarchies, it is sometimes hard to see the development of strong monarchies during the sixteenth century as a step forward in the lives of the common people, but in fact the fate of peasants under various monarchies was often better than under the feudal system that prevailed during the medieval period. In addition to the growing influence of hereditary dynasties around Europe, the middle class was also becoming a power to be reckoned with for the first time in history. Although the bourgeoisie (another name for the middle class) eventually turned against the monarchy in favor of democratic institutions, in the early Reformation period, it often sided with the monarchs. At other times the bourgeoisie sided with the nobility against the kings.

The Holy Roman Empire was a special case. Voltaire said of the Holy Roman Empire that it was not holy, was not Roman, and was not an empire. In fact, by the sixteenth century the Holy Roman Empire was basically the German-speaking parts of Europe, plus a few surrounding lands. The empire was divided into many quasi-independent states (at one point more than 200), some very small, whose leaders chose the emperor. The emperor was a powerful figure, but he needed the support of the larger German states in his confederation in order to enforce his decisions. For this reason, states were constantly jockeying for political position, allying themselves with other states for or against the emperor, for or against the pope, for or against the surrounding nations. The Reformation allowed states to remain Christian, while at the same time opposing the papacy. Rulers within the Holy Roman Empire who converted to Protestantism sometimes did so out of religious conviction, sometimes for the sake of political expediency, and sometimes for both reasons. The common people more often converted to Protestantism for reasons of religious conviction, but mixed motives might have influenced members of the middle class from time to time.

The Low Countries (modern day Netherlands, Belgium, and Luxembourg) during this period were first part of the Holy Roman Empire, then Spain, and the Reformation swept into the region early in the sixteenth century. (The Radical Reformation took root in the Low Countries as well.) Protestants were particularly strong in the north, in the area that is now the Netherlands. Wars over religion and nationalism were fought in the region for several decades, with Philip II of Spain on the side of the Catholics, and the Empire and William the Silent (or William of Orange) on the side of the Protestants. The conflicts were numerous and bloody, and the final resolution of 1607 did not appear until several years after the deaths of the two main protagonists. When the dust settled, the area that now makes up the Netherlands was Protestant, while the area that now comprises Belgium and Luxembourg was Catholic.

Protestantism did not spread into France as rapidly as it did into other parts of Western and Central Europe – the first Protestant church wasn't established until 1555 – but once it took root, it flourished. The French kings, who were Catholic, sometimes persecuted French Protestants (Huguenots) and sometimes allowed them a measure of freedom, depending on the political circumstances. Soon, some of the highest French nobility were Protestants. The highest ranking Protestant figure was Henry Bourbon, king of Navarre (a neighboring kingdom in the Iberian peninsula), and also in the French royal lineage. In 1571, on the day of the wedding between Henry Bourbon and the French king's sister, Margaret of Valois, Henry of Guise, a fierce opponent of the Protestants and a rival of Henry Bourbon, had someone try to assassinate the leader of the Huguenots, Admiral Coligny. Although Coligny escaped the attempt on his life, a year later, on August 24, 1572, Guise planned and executed the massacre of about 2,000 Protestants in Paris, the St. Bartholomew's Day Massacre. One of the victims was Admiral Coligny, and Henry Bourbon was imprisoned and forced to renounce Protestantism. In the aftermath of this slaughter, persecutions against Huguenots sprang up all over France, and tens of thousands were killed.

In 1576 Henry Bourbon escaped from prison and returned to Navarre. Shortly thereafter, after a series of untimely deaths to other members of the royal family, Henry found himself in line to inherit the throne of France, after the current king, Henry III, who had no heirs, died. Henry of Guise, unable to tolerate the idea of a Protestant king and lusting for the throne himself, declared himself the legitimate heir, on the basis of a forged document. This dispute escalated into a conflict known as the War of the Three Henrys, which lasted several years. Even after the deaths of two of the Henrys at the hands of assassins, the war continued. However, Henry Bourbon, who adopted the title Henry IV of France, was a strong ruler, and after proclaiming his conversion to Catholicism (the fifth "conversion" of his life), he was accepted by the majority of France as the legitimate king. Despite the lip-service he gave to Catholicism, he showed favor to the Huguenots who had long been his most ardent supporters. In 1598, he issued the Edict of Nantes, an important statement that gave Protestants the right to worship throughout France, with the exception of Paris.

The Catholic Reformation

Let everyone understand that real love of God does not consist in tear-shedding, nor in that sweetness and tenderness for which we usually long, just because they console us, but in serving God in justice, fortitude of soul, and humility.

(Teresa of Ávila)

Although it has often been called the Counter-Reformation by Protestants, in fact the Catholic Reformation began before the time of Martin Luther. As noted earlier, Christians such as Wycliffe, Hus, Savonarola, Waldo, the Conciliar Movement, and the humanists had been calling for reform within the Roman Catholic Church for at least two centuries. Items called into question by these advocates of reform included corruption, nepotism, absenteeism, pluralism, the sale of indulgences, lax morality, the decline of monasteries, and doctrine. One of the first successful attempts at reform occurred in Spain and was led by Queen Isabella of Castille and Cardinal Cisneros. The main targets of their reform were religious laxity and the decline of the monasteries. They personally visited many of the most important monasteries, insisting that their leaders reform their practices and return to the more austere ways of their predecessors. Isabella also took steps to ensure that men who held ecclesiastical posts did so because of their faithfulness and competence, not because of their political or family connections. It was not enough that church leaders observe a stricter form of Catholicism; Isabella wanted her subjects to as well. Therefore, she and her husband Ferdinand, king of Aragon, instigated the Spanish Inquisition, led by the Dominican friar Tomás de Torquemada, whose goal was to enforce doctrinal purity and suppress heresy. They forced all the Jews of Spain to convert to Christianity or leave the country. About 200,000 did leave, but many stayed in Spain and supposedly converted. Many of these "converts," though outwardly Catholic, secretly continued to practice their faith and became known as crypto-Jews or Marrano Jews (the word *marrano*, which means "pig" in Spanish, comes from an Arabic word meaning "ritually unclean"). Isabella and Ferdinand also forced many Muslims into either exile or conversion, despite earlier promising them that they would be allowed to practice their faith freely.

Clearly the reform that Isabella and Cisneros instituted in Spain (similar events transpired in Portugal) was quite different from the Reformation that took place on the Continent under Luther, Zwingli, and Calvin. One important difference was that the Protestant Reformation included sweeping doctrinal reforms, while the Catholic Reformation in Spain did not. Another important difference was that Luther and the other Protestants renounced all loyalty to the pope and the Roman Church, while the

Catholic Reformation renounced those who *rejected* the papacy and the Church. One way in which the two forms of reformation did not differ, except perhaps in degree, was the desire for uniformity of doctrine and practice, and the measures church leaders were willing to take in order to ensure that uniformity. While the Spanish Inquisition was claiming the lives of thousands of suspected heretics on the Iberian Peninsula, Protestants to the east were burning heretics at the stake or, particularly when the victims were Anabaptists, drowning them in rivers and lakes.

In addition to the efforts of Isabella and Cisneros to reform the monasteries of Spain, two other Spanish religious made major contributions in this area during the sixteenth century. Teresa of Ávila, while a nun in a Carmelite convent, began receiving visions encouraging her to lead a more devout, disciplined life. She founded another convent, which eventually led to the creation of a new monastic order, the Discalced Carmelites (although Discalced means "barefoot," they actually wore sandals rather than regular shoes). This order observed a rigor that other Carmelite monasteries did not follow, and Teresa founded many other convents of this type around Spain. She was joined in her efforts by John of the Cross, a monk who helped start monasteries for men that followed Teresa's example. Both Teresa and John wrote books that became Christian spiritual classics, such as Teresa's *The Life of Teresa of Jesus* (her autobiography) and John's *The Dark Night of the Soul*. Both were also named Doctors of the Church, a select list of 33 important Christians, by different popes. Teresa was only the second woman so named (the first was Catherine of Siena, named Doctor of the Church earlier in the same year, 1970, by Pope Paul VI; Pope John Paul II named a third woman, Thérèse of Lisieux, a Doctor of the Church in 1997).

The second monastic reformer in the sixteenth century was Ignatius Loyola, the founder of the Society of Jesus, more commonly known as the Jesuits. Thwarted in his attempts to pursue a military life by a wound he received in battle, he retreated into a private, monastic life. After experiencing the grace of God – the exact circumstances are unclear – Loyola pursued a formal education. A few years later Loyola and some of his followers took vows of poverty, chastity, and obedience to the pope and founded the new order. Unlike the Discalced Carmelites, whose focus was inner spiritual development, the Jesuits were focused on service to others, both in the mission field and in the arena of scholarship. Jesuit missionaries worked in areas as far-flung as South America and East Asia (the movie *The Mission* and the book *Silence*, by the Japanese Christian Shusaku Endo, are both based on the work of Jesuit missionaries). Those who concentrated on scholarship were often formidable intellectual adversaries of the Protestants, and they were true heirs of the traditions of Christian humanism. The most influential Jesuit opponent of Protestantism in the sixteenth and early seventeenth centuries was Robert Bellarmine, who was a professor of theology in Rome for 12 years and who wrote the most important anti-Protestant polemic in the history of the Catholic Church, *On the Controversies of the Christian Faith*.

One thing that almost all reformers agreed upon was the need to reform the papacy, which during the Middle Ages had become an office often occupied by corrupt, morally lax men who were more interested in the acquisition of power than in the care of souls.

The situation began to change in the sixteenth century, when a few reform-minded popes held office. The most important of these were Paul III, who called the Council of Trent, and Paul IV, who had been appointed to a commission on reformation by Paul III. Paul IV succeeded in reforming the Roman curia (the leaders of the Roman Catholic Church) and in heading off a movement designed to shift the authority of the popes to councils of bishops, and from this point reformers had less to complain about in regard to the papacy. However, the terrors of the Inquisition in the Catholic kingdoms increased under his leadership, and the *Index of Forbidden Books* swelled with the works not only of Protestants but also of devoted Catholics.

The most important event in the early years of the Catholic Reformation was the Council of Trent. In his early years, Luther had called for an ecumenical council to debate the points he had raised, but the Council of Trent, which met on and off from 1545 to 1563, was decades too late for Luther. The council, which was primarily a response to Protestant challenges, addressed a number of issues raised by Luther and others. In every case the council came down on the side of traditional Roman Catholic teaching, though it clarified several points that had previously been ambiguous. Among the more important decisions of the council were these:

- The books rejected as Apocrypha by most Protestants were officially recognized as canonical by the council.
- The Latin Vulgate was made the standard for Catholic scriptural exegesis, having an authority that superseded even the Hebrew and Greek originals.
- The number of sacraments was set at seven.
- Church tradition was declared of equal authority with scripture.
- Both faith and good works were declared to be essential for salvation.
- Indulgences, the veneration of relics, and prayer to the saints were affirmed.
- Protestants and others considered to be heretics were declared to be outside the church.

The Council of Trent did address some of the most egregious abuses in the sale of indulgences, the moral laxity of monasteries and convents, pluralism, and absenteeism, among other issues, but it was not willing to budge on matters of doctrine. The Council of Trent set the stage for the development of the modern Roman Catholic Church, and it remained the most important modern council until Vatican II, which met from 1962–1965 and profoundly reformed the Church.

Protestantism settles in

The Thirty Years' War

Europe underwent extensive, important changes in the centuries following the start of the Protestant Reformation. Nationalism, the confrontation of nobles and kings, the rise of the middle class, and religious differences played key roles in the first century and a half of this period. (Democracy, imperialism, and workers' rights provided the basis for conflict in subsequent centuries.) The Treaty of Augsburg (also known as the Peace of Augsburg, signed in 1555) had established the principle that individual German rulers within the Holy Roman Empire had the right to determine the form of Christianity that their territory would follow, either Lutheran or Catholic. The treaty was followed more in the breach than in the observance over the next decades, however. The rise of Calvinism established a third major branch of Christianity within Europe, and since Augsburg did not contemplate further Christian groups, it was found to be inadequate. Just as important as the religious motivations behind the wars that followed were the political rivalries among the various European dynasties, particularly the Habsburgs in Spain, Austria, and the Holy Roman Empire; the Bourbon dynasty in France; and the kingdoms of England and Sweden. That the wars were not exclusively over religious differences is demonstrated by the fact that Catholic France sided with the Protestants against the Catholic Habsburgs.

The Thirty Years' War started in 1618 and was disastrous in its impact, particularly on citizens of the Empire. The immediate cause of the war was a revolt of Protestants against the Catholic monarch Ferdinand II in Bohemia (modern Czech Republic), but war had been brewing for quite a while. Protestants banded together in the Evangelical Union, a group that included Protestants in states throughout the empire. Other states joined themselves together in the Catholic League to oppose the Protestants. The war went against the Protestants in the first several years, and Protestants in Bohemia were forced to flee in huge numbers or face execution. The Protestant cause was strengthened when England, the Netherlands, and Denmark sided with them in 1625 and sent troops into Germany. The greatest boost to the Protestant cause, however, was the entry of Sweden into the war in 1630. Led by their king Gustavus Adolphus, the Swedes, who were Lutheran, defeated the army of the Catholic League in several important battles. After this point the tide of fortune turned to the Protestants. Even though Gustavus Adolphus was killed in battle in 1632, the Protestants continued to prevail, and many Catholics, including their general Albert of Wallenstein, tired of war. Peace talks began, and after several years, the Peace of Westphalia was signed in 1648.

The Peace of Westphalia marked the end of the religious wars in Europe and, according to many scholars, the beginning of the modern era in Europe. The Peace of Westphalia was important for several reasons. First, it established the sovereignty of European nation-states. No longer would the ruler with the largest army be able to intervene in affairs of neighboring states at will. Second, it established the principle of legal equality among states. Smaller, poorer states had the same legal status as larger, richer states. Third, it established the principle of binding treaties between states. Agreements were no longer between individual rulers or families but between sovereign nations. The Peace of Westphalia left intact the Holy Roman Empire, but it weakened the power of the emperor by strengthening the hand of the rulers of the numerous autonomous regions within the Empire. This provision of the treaty delayed German unification for about two centuries. Italy also remained a collection of small states, and it would remain so until the mid-nineteenth century. The treaty gave Calvinists legal recognition for the first time (on a continent-wide basis – as we will see, persecution of French Protestants broke out again some decades later). Persecution of smaller Christian groups, including the Anabaptists, continued in many areas after this time, however. Finally, the treaty established the independence of the new states (which had been functionally independent prior to this time) of Switzerland and the (Protestant) Netherlands.

Persecution of the French Huguenots

During the Thirty Years' War, Cardinal Richelieu was the power behind the throne in France, advising the ineffectual king Louis XIII for two decades. Although a cardinal in the Roman Catholic Church, Richelieu's chief concern was to increase the power and wealth of the French crown, and thus his own power and wealth. Because he believed the Habsburg dynasty in Spain, Austria, and the Holy Roman Empire to be France's chief rival in Europe, he clandestinely supported the Protestant side in the Thirty Years' War. At the end of the war, the Habsburgs had lost some of their power, and France had gained territory and prestige. While Richelieu supported the Protestants in the Empire during the war, he suppressed Protestant rebellions at home in France. After finally breaking their political power in 1629, because he did not want to see France dragged into a civil war over religion, as was happening in the Empire, he issued an edict of toleration for the Huguenots. Although Richelieu died a few years before the end of the Thirty Years' War, his successor, Cardinal Mazarin, who led France during the minority of Louis XIV, continued his policies, including toleration of the Huguenots.

The situation took a dramatic turn after Mazarin's death. Louis XIV was now 23 years old and ready to reign on his own. He angered the Vatican by refusing to appoint a successor to Mazarin, thus asserting France's independence from the control of the Catholic Church. Nevertheless, he was a staunch Catholic, and he disagreed with the policy of Richelieu and Mazarin regarding French Protestants. Louis thought that allowing Protestants to remain in France would weaken the country, so he attempted various tactics to get them to convert, including threats and bribery. In 1685 he issued the Edict of Fontainebleau, which reversed the policy of the Edict of Nantes that his ancestor, Henry IV, had promulgated, which had given Protestants civil rights and political protection in France. As a result of Louis's edict, huge numbers of Huguenots – somewhere between 200,000 and 500,000 – left France for more tolerant countries, such as England, the Netherlands, Switzerland, the Holy Roman Empire, and British America. Some Huguenots even made it as far as the Cape of Good Hope in South Africa, where they settled by the hundreds. The Huguenot exodus had a significant, negative impact on the French economy, as many skilled and educated people left France for other lands. Some Huguenots remained in France and practiced their faith in secret, calling themselves the Christians of the Desert. Although Louis XIV was perhaps the

Figure 11.3 French Protestants, or Huguenots, fled persecution under Kings Louis XIV, Louis XV, and Louis XVI and scattered around the world. The Huguenot Memorial in Franschhoek, South Africa, marks one site where the Huguenots settled.

greatest king of France in terms of the battles he won and the wealth he brought to the nation, his policy toward the Huguenots resulted in internal strife and resentment whose effects lingered for 100 years, culminating in the French Revolution.

Louis XIV died in 1715, after a reign of 72 years (he had ascended the throne at the age of five), and he was succeeded by his great-grandson, Louis XV, after four older male heirs died within a three year period from either smallpox or measles. Louis XV's regent, Philippe, the Duke of Orleans, continued to persecute the Huguenots, but the latter began to organize and grow throughout France. Protestant pastors trained in Lausanne, Switzerland, and returned to France to minister to their flocks. Persecutions continued through the 59-year reign of Louis XV and into the reign of his successor, Louis XVI. Finally in 1787, Louis XVI reinstated the principle of religious tolerance. In 1789 an angry mob stormed the Bastille, spelling the beginning of the end for the French monarchy. In January 1793 Louis XVI and his wife, Marie Antoinette, were executed. The French Revolution had begun.

The Puritan revolution

The Protestant Reformation had come to England not through the mediation of a dynamic reformer like Luther or Calvin but largely as a statement of political independence from Rome by King Henry VIII. Although the reforms of the English church were genuine, under Henry and his immediate successors they were not particularly far-reaching. In particular, they preserved the episcopalian system of church governance (i.e. rule by bishops), and the official theology might be described as mildly Calvinistic (Reformed). Under the strongest of Henry's successors, Elizabeth, both Catholics (except those suspected of collusion with Mary Stuart) and Protestants of a more radical bent were often tolerated, even though the only legal church was the Anglican state church. However, when James I ascended the throne of England (he was already King James VI of Scotland), the situation changed. A group of Protestants advocating more radical reforms to the churches of England and Scotland emerged, and these people were called the Puritans. They were actually a fairly diverse group, including those who wanted to institute a presbyterian form of church governance (i.e. rule by elders rather than bishops) and independents, who believed each church should govern itself. The Puritans were generally strong supporters of the British Parliament, in part because they distrusted the king, whose mother, Mary, Queen of Scots, had been a staunch Catholic. James, in contrast, wanted to establish the British king as an absolute monarch, as in France. To this end, he increased the power of the bishops in the Church of England, who were among his strongest supporters. In 1604 the archbishop of Canterbury, the leader of the Church of England (after the king, who was the titular head), declared that bishops ruled the church by divine right, just as kings ruled their subjects by divine right. Not surprisingly, members of the House of Commons, which included many Puritans, rejected this claim.

Enmity between James and Parliament continued to grow, and James called Parliament into session as infrequently as possible. However, since only Parliament was authorized to institute new taxes, he was forced to reconvene Parliament in order to address England's serious economic crisis. New Parliamentary elections resulted in a House of Commons that favored Puritans even more heavily, so James dissolved that Parliament and relied on money he raised from bishops and nobles, who in turn got their money from the common people, especially the poor. Although James supported the Protestant cause in the Thirty Years' War, he was unable or unwilling to offer them financial support, and this failure caused many Puritans in England to be suspicious of the king's true religious allegiance. In addition to the struggle between the Crown and Parliament, two other significant events occurred during James's reign. The first was the Gunpowder Plot in 1605, in which Catholic opponents of the king planned to blow up the Parliament building while the king was addressing the assembly, killing both the king and a large number of Puritan leaders. The plot was foiled, however, and many of the conspirators, including Guy Fawkes, a demolition expert, and several leading British Catholics, were captured and executed. The second important event was the publication of the King James Bible in 1611. Several other English Bibles had been published in recent years, including the Great Bible, the Bishop's Bible, and the Geneva Bible (the Bible Shakespeare used in his plays), but the King James Version, put together by the leading biblical scholars and linguists of England, was so successful that it was the overwhelming favorite of English-speaking Protestants for more than 300 years.

Between 1625 and 1640, the Puritans grew stronger, as did the royal opposition to them. Charles I convened Parliament sporadically during his early years on the throne, then tried to rule without Parliament for eleven years, but the need for funds eventually led him to convene the assembly again in 1640. The new assembly, called the Long Parliament, passed a law preventing the king from dissolving the body without its own approval. Economic woes led to unrest among the poor and the middle class, where the Puritans' support was strongest. Rebellions in Scotland and Ireland fueled the chaos, and when Charles tried to arrest the leaders of the House of Commons, the royalists and the Puritans had reached a breaking point. Parliament began assembling its own militia, which Charles correctly saw as a threat to his position as king, and soon civil war broke out. Parliament abolished episcopacy and instituted a presbyterian form of church government favored by many, but by no means all, Puritans. Independents, who believed each church should govern itself, initially backed the presbyterian reform, because they preferred it to the rule by bishops. Oliver Cromwell, a wealthy Puritan who was a member of Parliament, raised a small cavalry and led Parliament's militia in battle, winning several victories. The Scots, allies of Parliament, captured the king, and the civil war ended. Shortly thereafter Cromwell, sensing that chaos was inevitable in England, seized power as Lord Protector, ruling with the support of a Rump Parliament (i.e. one that had been purged of all but Puritans). He ordered the execution of King Charles I in January 1649. With the power of government on their side, Cromwell and the Parliament instituted a number of laws that enforced Puritan beliefs, such as enforced observance of the Lord's Day (Sunday) and outlawing or restricting certain "frivolities," such as sports or theater. Puritans also banned the observance of Christmas, swearing, and immodest dress.

Upon Cromwell's death in 1658, the country had had enough of Puritan extremes, and the Parliament invited Charles's son Charles II to retake the English throne (he had already ruled for some time in Scotland). He did so, but his Catholic leanings did not make either the English or the Scots happy, and his deathbed conversion to Catholicism was proof to his opponents that new blood was needed on the throne. His son James II's attempts to make Catholicism once again the official religion led to another rebellion, called the Glorious Revolution, on largely religious grounds. Parliament invited William of Orange and his wife Mary, the daughter of James II, to take the thrones of England and Scotland, which they did in 1688. Staunch Protestants, they organized the Church of Scotland along presbyterian lines, and they granted tolerance to all who would swear to follow the Thirty-Nine Articles (defining Anglican belief) and obey the English sovereigns. Those whose religious beliefs prevented taking oaths (e.g. the Anabaptists) were also allowed to practice their religious beliefs, as long as they did not participate in revolts against the crown.

Key points you need to know

- The three key events that signaled the end of the Middle Ages were the invention of the printing press, the fall of Constantinople, and the "discovery" of the New World.

- Martin Luther, a Roman Catholic monk and priest in the Holy Roman Empire (Germany), called for a debate on various points of doctrine within the Roman Catholic Church. When his request for debate over doctrinal matters was denied, he led the movement to reform the Church, the Protestant Reformation.

- Ulrich Zwingli led a similar reform movement in Switzerland, where he was killed in battle.

- Many Christians called for more radical reforms to Christianity, including adult baptism, pacifism, and a distinct separation of church and state. These Christians were called Anabaptists, and their reform movement was called the Radical Reformation.

- John Calvin was the first great systematizer of Protestantism, and he developed a form of Protestantism called Reformed Christianity, or Calvinism.

- The Reformation in England was occasioned by King Henry VIII's personal difficulties with the Roman Catholic Church, and the reforms implemented by the Church of England were initially fairly mild, in comparison to way in which the Reformation was progressing on the Continent.

- Outside England, Protestant nations or regions in Europe declared themselves either Lutheran or Reformed. Anabaptists were often persecuted by Catholic and Protestant alike.

- Queen Isabella of Spain and Cardinal Cisneros instituted reforms of the Roman Catholic monasteries in her country before the Protestant Reformation began.

- The Catholic Reformation was codified by the decisions of the Council of Trent, which rejected all calls for doctrinal reform and officially adopted a version of the Old Testament that differed from that of most Protestants.

- The Thirty Years' War was fought between Catholics and Protestants, and it ended with both sides signing the Peace of Westphalia, which allowed each nation-state to select which form of Christianity (Catholic, Lutheran, or Reformed) it would observe.

- The French crown's persecution of Protestant Huguenots drove many of them from France, setting the stage for the French Revolution in the following century.

- The Puritan Revolution in England resulted in the temporary overthrow of the British monarchy, but the excesses of Puritan rule led most of the British to welcome the return of the monarchy, as well as a milder form of Anglicanism.

Discussion questions

1. Why do you think Martin Luther's efforts at reform succeeded, while earlier efforts did not?
2. How did the "discovery" of the Americas affect the direction of the development of the church?
3. How did the support (or lack of support) of political leaders help or hinder the Magisterial Reform and the Anabaptist Reform?
4. Was the English Reformation more of a religious movement or a political movement?
5. How did religion affect politics, and vice versa, in England during that period?
6. How did economic and political developments such as the rise of the middle class, the emergence of powerful monarchs, and the rise of nationalism affect the spread of Protestantism during the sixteenth century?
7. Where did Protestantism plant its strongest roots during the sixteenth century? Why was it more successful in these areas than in other places?
8. What positive steps did the Catholic church take toward reform in the wake of the Protestant Reformation? What steps were negative?
9. How did the persecution of the Huguenots ultimately result in the destruction of the French monarchy?

Further reading

Bainton, Roland H. 1950. *Here I Stand: A Life of Martin Luther.* New York: Penguin.

Calvin, John 1986. *Institutes of the Christian Religion.* Translated by Ford Lewis Battles. Grand Rapids, MI: Eerdmans.

Erasmus, Desiderius 1989. *Discourse on Free Will.* Translated and edited by Ernst F. Winter. New York: Continuum.

González, Justo 1984–1985. *The Story of Christianity.* 2 vols. New York: HarperSanFrancisco.

González, Justo 1987. *A History of Christian Thought.* Revised edn, 3 vols. Nashville, TN: Abingdon.

Latourette, Kenneth Scott 1975. *A History of Christianity.* Revised ed. 2 vols. New York: Harper & Row.

Luther, Martin 1957. *Martin Luther on the Bondage of the Will.* Translated by J. I. Packer and O. R. Johnston. Westwood, NJ: Revell.

Pelikan, Jaroslav 1971–1989. *The Christian Tradition: A History of the Development of Doctrine.* 5 vols. Chicago: University of Chicago Press.

Roberts, J. M. 1993. *History of the World.* New York: Oxford University Press.

Tillich, Paul 1968. *A History of Christian Thought.* Edited by Carl E. Braaten. New York: Simon and Schuster.

Williams, George Huntston 1992. *The Radical Reformation,* 3rd edn. Kirksville, MO: Sixteenth Century Journal Publishers.

12 *Orthodoxy*

The whole counsel of God, concerning all things necessary for his own glory, man's salvation, faith, and life, is either expressly set down in Scripture, or by good and necessary consequence may be deduced from Scripture: unto which nothing at any time is to be added, whether by new revelations of the Spirit, or traditions of men.

(Westminster Confession of Faith, 6)

In this chapter

After the European wars of religion came to a halt following the Peace of Westphalia, Christians of all faith traditions had the opportunity to rethink and standardize their beliefs. All three major branches of Christianity in the West – Roman Catholic, Lutheran, and Reformed – produced great systematic works that encapsulated orthodoxy as they saw it. The Eastern Orthodox Church, whose center of creative thought shifted from Constantinople to Russia, also began systematizing its beliefs. Reactions to these new definitions of orthodoxy took many forms, as scholars and ordinary Christians responded to the religious landscape with mindsets shaped by rationalism, spiritualism, and pietism.

Main topics covered

- Catholic orthodoxy
- Lutheran orthodoxy
- Reformed orthodoxy
- Eastern orthodoxy
- Rationalism
- Spiritualism
- Pietism

Different types of orthodoxy

Catholic orthodoxy

The term "orthodoxy" means the belief in correct doctrine, but it also carries with it the idea of adhering to an official, defined standard. In the early church, the question of what was orthodox and what was heretical was a matter of debate during the centuries prior to the victory of the Emperor Constantine and the legalization of Christianity. When that early form of orthodoxy was established, the power of the sword was sometimes as influential as the power of persuasion in determining its parameters. The various forms of orthodoxy that arose during the seventeenth and eighteenth centuries among Catholics, Lutherans, and Calvinists were based on documents and decisions made in the sixteenth century, but they clarified and systematized certain aspects of the various faiths, and they often used the political power at their disposal to attempt to enforce official church doctrine. The form of orthodoxy that developed in the Eastern Orthodox Church was based on decisions made at councils in the sixteenth and seventeenth centuries, but because of the different political climate in the East, doctrine was not enforced there with the sword.

For Catholics, the official statements of faith on which most orthodoxy was based were those promulgated by the Council of Trent, which met from 1545 to 1563. It was the last ecumenical council recognized by the Roman Catholic Church until the two Vatican councils of the nineteenth and twentieth centuries, respectively, and therefore it set the standard for official Catholic thought for the entire early modern period, up to the Enlightenment, the French Revolution, and its aftermath. Because the Council of Trent was called in reaction to Martin Luther and the Protestant Reformation, its attitude toward Protestants and their beliefs was harsh. Protestants were condemned as heretics, and their right to call themselves Christians was denied. This declaration alone was enough to stifle serious dialog for centuries. In addition, the Tridentine ("of or pertaining to Trent") declaration of the limits of the Old Testament canon, which included those books that Protestants called Apocrypha, established another barrier to dialog, much less reconciliation, even though the Catholics clearly had the weight of tradition on their side in this particular dispute. Another teaching of the Council of Trent dealt with the question of grace and human activity in justification. In an explicit denial of the prevailing Protestant doctrine that God's grace alone was sufficient for human salvation (by stimulating the response of faith), Trent said that while God's grace was the primary cause of salvation, humans were responsible for responding in faith, supplemented by works that demonstrated the validity of their faith. Although the debate was more complicated than this, one essential point of difference between Catholics and Protestants was the debate over whether humans were free to choose to accept God's grace (free will, the Catholic position) or whether humans were overwhelmed by God's irresistible grace (enslaved will, the Protestant position). As it turned out, both Catholics and Protestants debated their faith's predominant position on this matter, as on others.

Many Catholics believed that the position on grace that the Council of Trent had adopted rejected the teachings of Augustine and tended toward Pelagianism. One such group were the Jansenists, named after Cornelius Jansenius, whose book *Augustine* was published in 1640, though a similar evaluation of Trent had circulated in Catholic circles for several decades prior to this. The Jansenists were particularly opposed to the Jesuits, who held strongly to the teachings of the Council of Trent. Probably the most famous Jansenist was the French mathematician and scientist Blaise Pascal, who wrote a series of "Provincial Letters" ridiculing the positions of the Jesuits and supporting Jansenism. The popes during this period mostly opposed Jansenism, though their reaction to it and its proponents varied. King Louis XIV, whose brutal policies against the Huguenots drove hundreds of thousands from France, showed no more toleration for the Jansenists, believing them to be a threat to the unity of the church and, more importantly, the unity of France under an absolute monarch. Finally, in 1713, Pope Clement XI condemned Jansenism in the papal bull *Unigenitus* (Only Begotten Son of God). This condemnation did not stamp out Jansenism, however, which had by now morphed into a reform movement within Catholicism, opposing papal authority, ecclesiastical corruption, and enforced dogmatism.

One of the currents into which Jansenism merged was Gallicanism, a movement that opposed the Tridentine centralization of power in the papacy. Many Catholics believed that ultimate power in the church should reside in the bishops as a group, a position shared with Eastern Orthodoxy and Anglicanism. The name Gallicanism comes from the ancient Roman name for France, Gaul, and it stressed the independence of the French clergy from Roman control. That the movement was named Gallicanism is ironic in light of the control that France exerted over the papacy during the so-called Babylonian Captivity of the Church, when popes ruled from Avignon, France, during most of the fourteenth century. Alongside Gallicanism in France, Febronianism and Josephism in other parts of Europe also challenged papal authority, on political, ecclesiastical, and intellectual grounds. One direct result of these various movements was that the Jesuit order, which constituted one of the strongest supporters of the papacy, was banned from Portugal, France, Spain, and Naples, as monarchs exerted their independence from Rome. Finally, bowing to pressure from the Catholic kings, in 1773 Pope Clement XIV dissolved the Jesuit order, and they disbanded everywhere except in Russia, where Catherine the Great prevented the papal decree from being published. They were reconstituted in 1814. Gallicanism and its related movements, as well as the suppression of the Jesuits, resulted in a papacy that was considerably weakened from the height of its power in the thirteenth century, and even from the power that it had had in the sixteenth century.

In 1675 the Spaniard Miguel de Molinos published a book called *Spiritual Guide*, which advocated a form of devotion to Christ based on total passivity before God. Gone were the spiritual exercises taught by the religious orders and read by the pious, and the good works which many ordinary Catholics believed were required of them were also set aside as ultimately unimportant. When Molinos was brought to trial before the Spanish

Inquisition, he refused to defend himself but recanted his beliefs without the slightest hesitation, thus demonstrating to all that he practiced what he preached. In France, Madame Guyon wrote a book entitled *A Short and Simple Means of Prayer* (sometimes published today under the title *Experiencing the Depths of Jesus Christ*). Guyon was a mystic who saw Quietism as a means of growing closer to God. Like every other non-standard form of Christianity, Quietism was opposed by Louis XIV, but no pope was willing to condemn it, though they did warn that it might tend to lead some people into error.

Lutheran orthodoxy

The primary document on which Lutheran orthodoxy of the seventeenth and eighteenth centuries was based was the Augsburg Confession of 1530. While Martin Luther was still alive, he remained the primary interpreter of Lutheranism, but he had amicable disagreements over points of doctrine with other teachers. After his death, Philipp Melanchthon took over as primary spokesperson for the Lutheran position. Melanchthon had always disagreed with Luther on certain points of doctrine, as well as in style. Melanchthon was strongly influenced by humanism and remained friends with Erasmus and others after Luther broke with them. Thus, he had a more positive view of the role of reason in Christian theology than Luther did. Because of his ties with humanism, Melanchthon held on to the hope of reconciliation between Lutherans and Catholics for longer than did many other Lutherans. Eventually he acknowledged that reconciliation was not to be, but he still refused to condemn those who disagreed with Lutheranism on matters that he considered to be of secondary importance. For example, he disagreed with Luther's idea that humans had an enslaved will that was incapable of responding to God's gracious call. He also took a view of Christ's presence in the Eucharist that was less literal than Luther's, and thus closer to the views of Zwingli or Calvin. In contrast to Melanchthon, strict Lutherans like Matthias Flacius stressed the need for absolute conformity with Luther's teachings on the enslaved will and the literal presence of Christ in the Eucharist. They further insisted on the need to uphold even so-called "secondary" positions of the faith. A mediating position between strict Lutheranism and Philippism, as Melanchthon's positions came to be called, was developed in the Formula of Concord of 1577. Although more moderate than strict Lutheranism, it insisted on the literal presence of Christ in the Eucharist, a position that came to be known as consubstantiation.

Beginning in the seventeenth century, Lutheran theologians began working on large, multi-volume works of systematic theology, similar to the great scholastic works of late medieval Catholic scholars like Thomas Aquinas and Nicholas of Lyra. The idea was to develop comprehensive, quasi-official expressions of orthodox Lutheran belief that would state the Lutheran position unequivocally. Like their Catholic predecessors, the developers of Lutheran scholasticism often relied on methodologies derived from Aristotle, especially his logic and metaphysics. This use of Aristotle directly contradicted Luther's own approach to theology, which emphasized divine revelation and was wary of entanglements with Greek philosophy (part of his aversion to humanism). These orthodox Lutheran scholastic theologies were the work of university scholars and were taught in the schools, rather than originating with pastors and being taught in the parishes, as previous generations of Lutheranism had been. Although the Lutheran scholastics made use of Aristotelian methods, they agreed with Luther's emphasis on divine revelation in scripture, going farther than Luther himself in their understanding of inspiration. Luther had always taught that scripture was important not in and of itself but because it pointed to divine revelation, but the scholastics came to regard the biblical text itself as inspired in a way that approached a theory of dictation. Whereas Luther felt free to criticize those parts of scripture which he believed to be less inspired than others (e.g. the book of James), the scholastics taught a strict form of inspiration that would not allow such latitude of thought. An interesting corollary of their position was that they concluded that the medieval Jewish scribes who added vowel points to the Hebrew Bible had been inspired by God to do so, a theory at odds with their usual, somewhat negative attitude toward the Jews.

While the scholastics were erecting a superstructure of impregnable orthodoxy around Luther's teachings, some Lutherans advocated a more moderate position. Georg Calixtus was a strong proponent of Lutheranism, but he found it ridiculous to suppose, as many rigidly orthodox Lutherans did, that disagreement on nonessential aspects of Christianity precluded one from being a faithful Christian. In particular, he held that both Catholics and Calvinists were legitimate Christians, even though they were in error on certain points of doctrine. Calixtus proposed that any doctrine that had not been decided by the fifth century could not be used to deny a person's valid Christianity. In this sentiment, he recalled the statement of Vincent of Lerins, who advocated as doctrines "what has been believed always, everywhere, and by all." According to Calixtus's definition, primary doctrines of faith included such items as the Trinity and the Virgin Birth, while secondary doctrines included justification by faith and the literal presence of Christ in the Eucharist, which arose later than the fifth century. Although Calixtus won some supporters, he did not sway the majority of orthodox Lutheran teachers, many of whom insisted on unswerving loyalty to even minor theological points. Like Catholic orthodoxy, Lutheran orthodoxy was becoming more entrenched in its positions.

Reformed orthodoxy

> Man's chief end is to glorify God, and to enjoy him forever.
> (*Shorter Catechism* of the Westminster Assembly, 1643)

Like the Catholics and the Lutherans, Reformed Christianity in the seventeenth and early eighteenth centuries struggled with self-definition, and one result was a "circle the wagons" approach to theology. Reformed theology was based primarily on Calvin's *Institutes*, but Calvinists specified and refined their beliefs further at the Synod of Dort and in the Westminster Confession, both of which reflected the controversy surrounding Arminianism. Jacobus Arminius was a Dutch pastor who had been raised in the Reformed tradition, studying at Geneva with Theodore Beza, Calvin's successor.

After studying the doctrine of predestination in the Bible and in the church fathers, he became convinced that it was based on God's foreknowledge of those who would come to believe in Jesus Christ. Although he believed that this understanding was consistent with Calvin's views, his opponents, the strict Calvinists, contended that Calvin taught that predestination meant that God chose those who would be saved prior to the creation of the world. The debate soon expanded to other aspects of Calvin's work, and Arminius and his successors (he died in 1609) held out for a less stringent form of Calvinism, while the strict Calvinists insisted on a stronger form.

The followers of Arminius, or Remonstrants, issued a document that outlined five basic points that were under debate and described their position on the issues. First, they defined predestination loosely, so that it could either mean God's foreknowledge of those specific people who would be saved or God's open decree that whoever believed would be saved. Second, they stated their belief that Jesus' death was potentially efficacious for all people, though only the saved actually benefited. Third, they denied accusations of Pelagianism (the belief that humans could do good without the benefit of God's grace), stating that the grace of God is necessary for humans to engage in good works. Fourth, they denied Augustine's contention that grace was irresistible. Fifth, they admitted indecision on the matter of whether believers could lose their salvation and "fall from grace." In a direct response to these published positions, the Synod of Dort (1618–1619) stated the positions that came to be identified with orthodox Calvinism. First, predestination meant that God chose certain people for salvation and not others, as a result of God's sovereign will. Second, Jesus' death was efficacious only for the elect. Third, human beings in their fallen state are completely unable to do good works of any value. Fourth, God's grace is indeed irresistible. Fifth, those who have received God's grace through faith will never fall from that state of grace and lose their salvation. Those who refused to accept these strict definitions of Calvinism were driven from their preaching and teaching posts, fined, imprisoned, and even killed in the Netherlands for several years after the Synod of Dort, before persecutions were relaxed, and tolerance was eventually granted in 1631.

In England, the Westminster Confession of 1646 was produced by the theologians called to Westminster to advise Parliament on theological matters during the English Civil War. It followed the lines of Reformed orthodoxy already promulgated by the Synod of Dort three decades earlier, but it was much more expansive in its coverage. It emphasized God's absolute sovereignty, including God's predestination from all eternity of all events that will eventually transpire. Included in this section was a statement that some people have been predestined for salvation and others for condemnation, a doctrine known as double predestination. It upheld the traditional five points of strict Calvinism, and it became the basis for orthodox Reformed theology for the next two centuries. One group of English Baptists, the Particular Baptists (so-called because of their view in particular, or limited, atonement) used the Westminster Confession as the basis for their own confession of faith, the Second London Confession, published and officially approved in 1689, though it was written in 1677 during less tolerant times.

TULIP

If these five points of orthodox Calvinism are rearranged, they may be described by the acronym TULIP:

1 Total depravity
2 Unconditional election
3 Limited atonement
4 Irresistible grace
5 Perseverance of the saints.

The various forms of Western orthodoxy – Catholic, Lutheran, and Reformed – have certain commonalities. First, they all came about after various internal struggles over doctrinal issues. In particular, the roles of divine grace and human free will played a part in theological discussions within each group: Jansenists vs. Jesuits, strict Lutherans vs. Philippists, strict Calvinists vs. Arminians, Particular Baptists vs. General Baptists. A second characteristic that the various forms of Western orthodoxy had in common was a strong tendency toward rigorous definitions of the faith and religious exclusivism. The Reformed orthodox were certain that not only Catholics and Lutherans were going to hell, but so were less strict Calvinists; the same held for orthodox Catholics and Lutherans as well. The great freedom of thought that the Protestant Reformation had promised to individual Christians had taken a detour for many who held orthodox positions among Lutherans and Calvinists. Strict orthodoxy would hold sway over most Protestant Christians until the Enlightenment and the French Revolution began to swing opinions in different directions. For Catholics, true reformation awaited Vatican II in the 1960s.

Eastern orthodoxy

Whereas theologians in the West, from Thomas Aquinas to Martin Luther to John Calvin to Robert Bellarmine, sought to explain in increasingly great detail the nature of God, Christ, and the church, Eastern theologians accepted God as a divine mystery. It is not that they made no effort to learn about or explain God, but their approach was radically different. Whereas Western Christians used rational arguments to explore God and God's work in the world, Eastern Christians saw prayer and contemplation as the preferred means of exploring the realm of the divine. Direct knowledge of God was impossible, said the fourteenth-century theologian Palamas, not only because of the finite limitations of sinful humans, but also because of the divine transcendence of God. Silence (i.e. contemplation) rather than reason was the true path to knowledge about God for the Eastern Orthodox.

After the Protestant Reformation began, Luther appealed to the existence of the Orthodox church as proof that Christian communities could exist quite happily apart from the rule of the pope, as the Eastern church had for centuries. Melanchthon translated the Augsburg Confession into Greek, producing a translation that was not merely literal but one that was sensitive to Eastern sensibilities (e.g. the rendering of the word "justification" by "sanctification," in recognition of the Eastern emphasis on this doctrine). However, this early attempt at ecumenism was rebuffed, for though Jeremiah, the patriarch of Constantinople, was sympathetic to certain Protestant teachings, he rejected the notion of faith alone as sufficient for salvation, for "the catholic church demands a living faith, one that gives witness of itself through good works." The Orthodox church also rejected the continued Protestant use of the *filioque* clause in the creed (the idea that the Holy Spirit proceeds from the Father *and the Son*). The Old Testament canon that the Orthodox promulgated at the Council of Jerusalem in 1672 included several books that the Protestants had relegated to the Apocrypha, such as Sirach and the books of Maccabees, thus approximating the canon of the Roman Catholic Church. On the other hand, the Orthodox rejected the Catholic doctrine of purgatory, believing that it was based on excessive speculation on a subject of which Christians had no definite knowledge. Perhaps Orthodoxy's biggest argument with Protestantism was the latter's rejection of the teachings of the church fathers and their understanding of scripture. The Protestants argued that it was necessary to go back to the sources, the biblical books themselves, to find the true meaning of scripture, but the Orthodox maintained that the Holy Spirit had spoken through the patristic writers, so their teachings could not simply be set aside or ignored. In their ongoing conversations with the Catholics and the Protestants, the Orthodox often borrowed from Protestant teachings to refute aspects of Catholicism and from Catholic teachings to refute aspects of Protestantism. For the first time in their history, the Orthodox church in the sixteenth and seventeenth centuries set down in a more or less systematic fashion its most important beliefs and practices, and it also clarified the ways in which Orthodox Christians differed from both Catholics and Protestants. After the fall of Constantinople to the Turks in 1453, Orthodoxy continued to be practiced and to develop in the former Byzantine Empire, but the center of developing Orthodox thought and doctrine shifted to the Slavic lands, especially Russia.

Reactions to orthodoxy

Rationalism

> I think, therefore I am.
> (René Descartes)

Orthodoxy in the West – whether of the Catholic, Lutheran, or Reformed variety – erected great edifices of doctrine that attempted to specify the most minute matters of Christian faith. Despite differences in detail, they were alike in one important way: they purported to provide Christian believers with answers to almost any imaginable question about the Christian religion. All three forms of orthodoxy used the data of divine revelation (i.e. the Bible for the Protestants, the Bible and church tradition for the Catholics) as the primary content for their system, and they used Aristotelian philosophy as the structural glue to hold the system together.

Almost as soon as the most spectacular of the various orthodox theologies were developed, however, reaction against them set in from several different quarters. One angle of attack came from the rationalists, people who thought that reason rather than revelation should provide the primary data for both the Christian religion and for modern thought in general. The founder of the rationalist movement was René Descartes, a Frenchman who lived at the beginning of the seventeenth century. Descartes was a brilliant mathematician, and he saw in the logical processes of mathematical thought a new way to approach the quest for knowledge that would be purely rational. He started by doubting all that he could doubt, then found that he could not doubt his own existence, uttering the famous words, "I think, therefore I am." After proving (to his own satisfaction) his own existence, he proceeded to prove the existence of God, the world, and other things. It is important to note that Descartes, who was particularly attracted to the geometrical proofs based on Euclid's 18 postulates (Euclidean geometry), had made limited use of postulates in his philosophical musings, basing almost everything on the axiom of self-existence, which he considered self-evident. The philosophy of Descartes, or Cartesianism, was enormously popular in Descartes' own day. It led to the overthrow of the orthodox systems of theology, and it laid the groundwork for the Enlightenment, which encompassed the seventeenth and eighteenth centuries.

One of the questions that Descartes wrestled with was the issue of the relationship between the soul (the rational) and the body (the physical) in human beings. If soul and body are distinct entities, as Descartes maintained, how does one communicate with the other? Three main theories were offered to answer the question. First, the idea of occasionalism (associated with Arnold Geulincx and Nicolas Malebranche) suggested that God is the intermediary between soul and body, communicating the soul's ideas to the body so that it can react, and conversely communicating the body's sensory stimuli to the soul so that it can process the data. Second, Baruch de Spinoza offered a solution that is called monism, which postulated that soul and body are really a single substance. Similarly, God and the universe must be merely different attributes of a single substance. Third, Gottfried Wilhelm Leibniz proposed the idea of monads (not to be confused with monism, which is completely the opposite). Leibniz contended that God created an infinite number of monads, or substances, which are completely separate from one another and do not communicate with other monads. The fact that the universe appears organized is the result of God's wise plan, although in fact the organization is a matter of appearance rather than fact. None of these three attempts to solve the problem of the soul and the body was particularly successful, so rationalists began to look for different solutions to these and other problems.

Whereas Descartes based his philosophical system on pure reason (internal), the Empiricists Locke, Berkeley, and Hume believed that true knowledge comes only from human experience (both internal and external, with a greater emphasis on the external). John Locke, the founder of the movement, believed that the human mind is a *tabula rasa*, or empty slate, at birth, and it is filled with knowledge through its experiences in life. Locke believed that all human knowledge was based on three types of experience: (1) humans' experience of themselves; (2) humans' experience of the world through their senses; and (3) humans' experience of God, whose existence is proven through human self-experience (similar to Descartes' idea). All certain knowledge comes from one of these three modes of experience. However, in addition to certain knowledge, Locke proposed that humans can also gain knowledge based on probability rather than certainty. That is, humans can conclude that a certain postulate is true because their rational judgment tells them that the probability of that postulate being true is great. Of course, such "knowledge" is not absolutely certain, for it remains at least somewhat uncertain. Faith is based on revelation, which is knowledge that, though probable, is not certain. For this reason Locke urged religious toleration, since absolute certainty in matters of religion (e.g. that certainty implied in the orthodox systems) was impossible. One of Locke's conclusions was that, although Christianity was the most reasonable of all religions, any divine revelation that might be associated with it added little or nothing to what believers could have derived from reason alone.

George Berkeley, an Anglican bishop from Ireland, developed Locke's empiricist ideas further. Whereas Locke believed that human knowledge can come through the senses, Berkeley argued that there is no way to demonstrate that what the senses perceive has independent existence. On the contrary, Berkeley said, "to be is to be perceived." Berkeley distinguished thoughts that the mind generated on the basis of memory or imagination from the perception of external objects by the senses such as sight, smell, and taste. If perception determines existence, does it follow that objects that are not perceived cease to exist until they are perceived again? No, said Berkeley, for even when humans or animals do not perceive an object, its existence is guaranteed by the fact that God perceives it. In fact, God's perception is just another name for God's creation. The fact that sense perception is so much stronger in the mind than pure, self-generated thought was proof to Berkeley of the existence of a greater mind that produced objects that forced themselves upon the senses, the mind of God.

David Hume was a Scottish philosopher who both carried empiricism to its logical conclusion and drew attention to the limitations of empiricism. Empiricists claimed that knowledge was based on the experience of the senses, but Hume pointed out that many of the ideas we assume to be true are merely patterns of thought rather than actual observations. For example, the Latin expression *post hoc ergo propter hoc* ("after this, therefore because of this") was a statement regarding the "law" of cause and effect. It was a law that people observed in everyday life, and it was integral to the developing scientific knowledge put forward by scientists such as Isaac Newton, whose Third Law of Motion declared that for every action there was an equal and opposite reaction, an application of cause and effect to the material world. Hume denied that the notion of cause and effect was rational. All we can observe, Hume said, was that one event follows another.

Limericks inspired by Berkeley

Berkeley's unique brand of empiricism was described in two witty limericks by a twentieth-century cleric, Ronald Knox:

There once was a man who said, "God
Must think it exceedingly odd
If he finds that this tree
Continues to be
When there's no one about in the Quad."

"Dear Sir
Your astonishment's odd:
I am always about in the Quad
And that's why the tree
Will continue to be,
Since observed by.
Yours faithfully,
God."

Since we don't actually observe causation, we cannot claim that it is rational knowledge. Rather, it is a construct of the mind. Similarly, the idea that a substance external to ourselves consists of certain properties such as color, taste, and weight is another mental construct, since although we can observe certain properties with our senses, we have no way of proving that the substance itself is real. All we have perceived are the properties. David Hume did not deny the reality of ideas like cause and effect. He simply pointed out that such ideas could not be proven rationally, so the amount of knowledge that we can gather through our senses is limited indeed.

While the empiricists Locke and Berkeley saw their philosophical speculations as supportive of Christianity, the Enlightenment also produced many people who used rationalism to justify their rejection of traditional Christian ways of thinking about God. The Deists were a group of people whose beliefs about God were determined primarily by reason. They rejected the bickering of various Christian sects, and even the arguments between Christianity and other religions. Deists were strongly influenced by Newtonian mechanics, which stated that the universe ran on the basis of a set of universal laws that determined motion, interactions of bodies, and so forth. The Deists saw God as a deity who set the universe in motion, then retired to watch it play out according to purely naturalistic principles. Anything contrary to reason, such as the belief in miracles or the divinity of Christ, was foreign to the Deist conception of God and the universe. Deism was enormously influential, first in England, and then in France and the American colonies. It began to decline in popularity in England by the middle of the eighteenth century and had lost most of its influence in Europe by 1800, though it continued to have celebrated adherents in the U.S. through the first two or three decades of the nineteenth century. Famous Deists include Lord Herbert of Cherbury (considered the founder of the movement), Voltaire, Rousseau, Thomas Paine, Thomas Jefferson, George Washington, and Benjamin Franklin. The philosophical writings of David Hume and Immanuel Kant questioned the validity of the Deists' idea of God as the First Cause, and the excesses of the French Revolution, which had the support of many prominent Deists on both sides of the Atlantic, led to a decline in the influence of Deism. Deism ceased to exist as an influential school of thought, but many of its followers made the transition to other movements, including Unitarianism, the Ethical Culture Movement, and various strains of nineteenth-century liberal Christianity.

In France, rationalists such as Voltaire, Montesquieu, and Rousseau used reason to criticize both traditional religion and current forms of government. Voltaire criticized both Christians and many Deists for claiming to know more than he believed it was

Figure 12.1 The ideas of Jean-Jacques Rousseau, French philosopher and political theorist, were influential in the days leading up to the French Revolution. He used reason to criticize both Christianity and the government.

possible to know about God and the ways of God in the world. Jean-Jacques Rousseau advocated a return to "natural religion," which he defined as belief in God, the immortality of the soul, and moral living. Voltaire and Rousseau were also critical of the institution of the monarchy. They believed that rulers had their positions in order to provide freedom and justice for their subjects, so in effect, rulers should be seen as servants of the people. Montesquieu expanded on these ideas and concluded that a republic, in which the people elect their own representatives in government, was the ideal form of government. He also argued for a separation of powers into three branches of government: the executive, legislative, and judicial branches. The French rationalists wanted to throw off the tyranny of tradition in all its forms, whether religious or political.

Enlightenment thinking reached its zenith, and also met its end, or rather its transformation into (political) liberalism and modernism, in the writings of Immanuel Kant. Kant was a rationalist in his younger days, but after reading David Hume's critique of aspects of rationalism, Kant became convinced that rationalism as currently being pursued was a dead end. He accepted Hume's reasoning that empirical knowledge was limited. In fact, Kant said, purely objective knowledge was nonexistent. In his *Critique of Pure Reason*, he argued that, contrary to the contention of Locke and the other empiricists, people are not born with a mind that is a *tabula rasa*. Instead, the human mind comes equipped from birth with certain predetermined categories that help us to organize the input we get from our senses. Some of the categories that Kant hypothesized include time, space, causality, existence, and substance. Kant's writings demonstrated that simplistic rationalism, and religious expressions based on rationalism, were no longer tenable. Kant did not thereby deny the truth of religion or religious beliefs, including the belief in God, but he claimed that religious knowledge is of a different sort than rational knowledge. He dealt with religion, which he based in morality, in his book *Critique of Practical Reason*. Kant expressed both the direction and the optimism of the Enlightenment in his essay entitled "What Is Enlightenment?" He said that the motto of the Enlightenment was "Have courage to use your own understanding."

Spiritualism

Whereas the rationalists reacted against the dogmatic orthodoxy of their day by appealing to reason, the spiritualists rejected both dogmatic orthodoxy and rationalism, relying instead on God's revelation through the Spirit to individuals within the movement. Those classified as spiritualists shared a common belief that the Spirit was speaking directly to them, or at least to their leaders, but they disagreed on many other matters, and it is thus more accurate to speak about spiritualist *movements* rather than a single spiritualist *movement*.

The first noted leader of spiritualism was Jakob Böhme, a German cobbler who became disillusioned at an early age with the Lutheran orthodoxy in which he was raised. As he wandered the region as a traveling cobbler, he encountered a wide variety of different religious opinions that were in conflict with his own ideas, which be believed to be confirmed by visions and other spiritual experiences. Although he was not a preacher, he did write down many of his ideas, and his writings caused him to be persecuted in more than one locale. In his later writings he made use of ambiguous statements and phrases, so that even the most educated Lutheran theologians of Saxony were unable to determine their precise meaning. Böhme believed that "the letter kills, but the Spirit gives life" (2 Cor 3:6), and he believed that the Holy Spirit's message to him was more relevant for his life than the scripture written by inspired writers of an earlier period.

By far the most influential of the spiritualists was George Fox, the founder of the Quaker movement. Like Böhme, he began his working life as a cobbler's apprentice, but he soon abandoned the profession in a search for illumination. After visiting the services of many different groups, he came to the conclusion that all were wrong, in large measure because their worship practices inhibited the work of the Holy Spirit. Church buildings, sermons, sacraments, creeds, and hymns all "tied the hands" of the Spirit, and Fox advocated a form of worship that was entirely free-form and Spirit-based. Having come to his own understanding of the Spirit's leadership in his life through visions and other experiences, Fox began interrupting services of various churches to proclaim what he said the Spirit was teaching. Although he was expelled from many churches and was frequently arrested, he soon gained a large following. The Friends, as they called themselves, or Quakers, as others called them, observed completely unstructured services, but they also emphasized the importance of community and love. They were pacifists and lacked any formal clergy, and they believed in the contributions of Spirit-filled women as well as men. Fox traveled throughout the British Isles, parts of continental Europe, the Caribbean, and North America, spreading the message of the Spirit. One of Fox's most influential followers was William Penn, the founder and first governor of the Pennsylvania colony in British North America. Pennsylvania, along with Rhode Island, offered its settlers complete religious freedom. Furthermore, unlike other colonial governors, Penn made friends with the local Indian tribes, buying their land rather than simply taking it. Many Quakers found a home in Pennsylvania, and from there they spread throughout the rest of the U.S. after the new nation adopted the principle of religious freedom.

Unlike Böhme and Fox, Emanuel Swedenborg was from an aristocratic family and was well educated. Born and educated in Sweden, he spent several years traveling through Europe in search of knowledge. He became a respected scientist, particularly famous for his discoveries in human anatomy. His interest in science led to his pursuit of religious knowledge as well, but it was not until he was 56 years old that he had his first vision of the last judgment and the second coming of Christ and began formulating his own, distinct system of beliefs. He spent the last decades of his life studying and writing. Many of his beliefs were common to most Christians of his day, but he rejected the doctrine of the Trinity as illogical, believing Father, Son, and Holy Spirit to be three different aspects of the one God (modalism). He also differed from Luther on the centrality of faith for Christianity; Swedenborg believed that love was more important. Swedenborg had a small but devoted following during his lifetime, and the Swedenborgian Society was founded shortly after his death in 1772 to publish and distribute his writings. The Swedenborgian Church, also called the New Church, was founded by Swedenborgians after his death.

Pietism

Despite the numerous followers of George Fox, the spiritualist movements had little immediate impact on either Christianity or society as a whole. The largest impact on Orthodoxy, particularly Protestant Orthodoxy, came from the Pietist movement, which also offered an alternative to rationalism. The founder of Pietism was Philipp Jakob Spener, who was born in Alsace, near the border of France and the Holy Roman Empire. A Lutheran pastor who accepted orthodox doctrine, Spener was nevertheless convinced that doctrinal purity was not enough for the Christian. He believed that laity as well as clergy should be thoroughly conversant with and obedient to the scripture. Furthermore, Christians who had been justified by faith should seek to be sanctified by God. Because the emphasis on sanctification was more characteristic of Calvinism than Lutheranism, Spener found himself in trouble with some supporters of Lutheran orthodoxy. However, his influence soon extended beyond the boundaries of the Lutheran church, and he found followers among the German Reformed Christians as well. His follower August Hermann Francke emphasized the joy that he experienced from following Christ, and pietism was characterized by an emotionalism that more traditional Protestants found worrying. Its influence was great, however, for it was embraced by many lay Christians and by an increasing number of the clergy as well. Pietism also led to the sending out of the first Protestant missionaries to India, Lapland, and Greenland.

Count von Zinzendorf was the godson of Spener, and he was raised in a pietist family. After studying at the University of Halle under Francke, Zinzendorf studied in and traveled to various places in Europe. In Dresden he met a group of about 200 Hussites (followers of Jan Hus) who had fled from Moravia to escape religious persecution. Zinzendorf offered them sanctuary on his estates, and he was soon influenced to join their group. He had always been interested in missions, and when he met a group of Eskimos who had been converted by a Lutheran missionary, he encouraged his own community to send out missionaries. Within a few years the Moravians had sent out missionaries to Africa, India, North America, and South America. The Moravians had ongoing difficulties with the Lutheran church in their area, both because they were not of German origin and because of their pietist beliefs and practices. Although the Moravian church was never very large, their greatest historical impact came through an encounter that a young Anglican priest named John Wesley had with a group of Moravian missionaries bound for the English colony of Georgia.

John Wesley was the son and grandson of Anglican priests, and he took his commitment to God very seriously. During his days at Oxford University, he and his brother Charles were members of a group of students known to their detractors as the "holy club" or the "methodists" because of the time they spent in study of scripture and their commitment to a rigorous life of Christian service. Nevertheless, when a storm at sea forced John Wesley to compare his faith to that of his Moravian shipmates, he found himself wanting. He sought the advice of Moravians both during his pastorate in Savannah, Georgia, and after his return to England. He eventually came to the conclusion that he lacked saving faith, but his advisor counseled him to continue preaching until he got it, then to continue preaching after that *because* he had it. Wesley attended a service in 1738, during which he felt his heart "strangely warmed." Now having assurance of his own salvation, he preached with renewed vigor. He joined forces with another former member of the Holy Club, George Whitefield, who had had a conversion experience similar to Wesley's a few years earlier. Although they were men of different temperaments and had theological differences as well, they worked well together in Bristol for several years.

When Whitefield returned to Georgia, where he had a second church, Wesley took over the Bristol congregation. At first he was Whitefield's assistant, but over time Wesley became the leader of the movement. Although both Wesley and Whitefield considered themselves Calvinists, Wesley held Arminian positions in regard to predestination and free will, whereas Whitefield held to a stricter form of Calvinism. Although they remained friends, they ultimately agreed to follow their own paths. Whitefield founded the Calvinist Methodist Church, based in Wales, while Wesley remained within the Anglican church. Wesley organized his growing number of followers into Methodist "societies," including women's societies led by women. Wesley's concern for the poor and members of the working class was evident in the number of people from these groups who joined the movement. A shortage of ordained Anglican priests led Wesley to use lay preachers, and as the movement grew, he further organized groups of societies into a "circuit" led by a superintendent.

Wesley differed from Whitefield and his followers in regard to Calvinist-Arminian positions, and he differed from the Moravians in regard to the latter group's understanding of the role of the Spirit in the Christian life. His biggest conflicts, however, were with other Anglicans, many of whom were suspicious of, or outright opposed to, the Methodist movement. While many of his followers advocated a clean break from the Anglican church, Wesley refused to allow it, but by the end of his life it was clear that such a break was inevitable. Wesley's evangelistic concern pushed him to allow preaching without regard to parish boundaries (including open-air preaching), even in opposition to official Anglican practice. Wesley also allowed Methodist preachers to register their church buildings, as English law required, even though the Anglican Church didn't recognize them as legitimate churches. Finally, Wesley became convinced from his study of the New Testament that the offices of bishop, presbyter (priest), and elder were one and the same. This understanding led him to permit priests, such as himself, to ordain other priests, a privilege reserved for bishops in the Anglican (and Catholic) Church. In response to a shortage of ordained clergy in the U.S. following the American Revolution, Wesley sent two lay preachers, whom he ordained as priests, to America, with instructions to ordain priests as necessary.

In England, Methodism found the greatest number of its early adherents in the cities that attracted increasing numbers of people to work in the factories created as part of the Industrial Revolution. In America, it was the rapid westward shift of the population that led to the need for more Methodist pastors, which in turn resulted in more converts to Methodism. American Methodists broke with English Methodists over loyalties during the American Revolution, and at the same time the American Methodists broke with the Anglican church. Another difference in the two branches of the Methodist church was that the American church continued to recognize bishops as a separate level of clergy, even after the English Methodists had eliminated the position. In America, the new Methodist church was called the Methodist Episcopal Church. After Wesley's death, Methodists in England also broke from the Anglican church and formed a new denomination.

Key points you need to know

- Roman Catholic orthodoxy from the sixteenth through the twentieth century was based largely on the decisions rendered at the Council of Trent.
- Lutheran orthodoxy was based on the Augsburg Confession, but both moderate and strict schools of thought existed among Lutherans. Large systematic theologies encapsulating Lutheran thought, a kind of Lutheran scholasticism, were produced in the seventeenth and eighteenth centuries.
- Reformed orthodoxy was based on Calvin's *Institutes*, as interpreted by the Synod of Dort and the Westminster Confession. Followers of a milder form of Calvinism were known as Arminians.
- All three Western forms of orthodoxy share certain characteristics: they arose out of debates over divine grace and free will, they had a strong tendency toward rigorous definitions of the faith and religious exclusivism, and they discouraged freedom of thought outside certain narrow parameters.
- Eastern Orthodox theologians were never as concerned with producing systematic analyses of the faith as their Western counterparts, preferring to leave room for mystery in their theology. However, at the Council of Jerusalem, Orthodox leaders came together to define many of their doctrines.
- Rationalists valued reason over divine revelation, some advocating the superiority of reason over revelation and others denying the very reality of divine revelation.

- Some rationalists believed that reason supported the basic tenets of Christianity, while others believed that it called into question many of the traditional doctrines of the faith.
- Spiritualists believed that God communicated with believers directly through the Holy Spirit, if they were attuned to the voice of the Spirit. The most influential of the spiritualists was George Fox, the founder of the Quakers.
- Pietists rejected rationalism, and while they were often theologically orthodox, they thought that living a sanctified life was more important than having correct doctrine. Although pietists could be found in many Protestant denominations, their greatest impact came through the ministry of John Wesley, the founder of the Methodist Church.

Discussion questions

1. Which issues in the following debates are similar, and which are different: the Jesuits vs. Jansenism, strict Lutherans vs. the Philippists, strict Calvinism vs. Arminianism?
2. How do these debates compare with the debates between Athanasius and Arias, and between Augustine and Pelagius?
3. How did Philipp Melanchthon's ties with humanism influence his theological views in comparison with Martin Luther?
4. What aspects of Protestant Orthodoxy were of the greatest concern to rationalists? to spiritualists? to pietists?
5. How does Kant's proposal that humans have built-in constructs for analyzing sense data (e.g. time, place, causality) relate to the modern understanding of the human genome?
6. Did Wesley's Arminianism cause him to be more successful in reaching people than Whitefield's stricter form of Calvinism, or were other factors involved?

Further reading

González, Justo 1984–1985. *The Story of Christianity*. 2 vols. New York: HarperSanFrancisco.

González, Justo 1987. *A History of Christian Thought*. Revised edn, 3 vols. Nashville, TN: Abingdon.

Guyon, Jeanne 1975. *Experiencing the Depths of Jesus Christ*. Auburn, ME: Christian Books.

Kant, Immanuel 1990. *The Critique of Pure Reason, The Critique of Practical Reason, and Other Ethical Treatises*. Translated by J. M. D. Meiklejohn *et al*. Chicago, IL: Encyclopaedia Britannica.

Latourette, Kenneth Scott 1975. *A History of Christianity*. Revised edn, 2 vols. New York: Harper & Row.

Pelikan, Jaroslav 1971–1989. *The Christian Tradition: A History of the Development of Doctrine.* 5 vols. Chicago, IL: University of Chicago Press.

Roberts, J. M. 1993. *History of the World.* New York: Oxford University Press.

Tillich, Paul 1968. *A History of Christian Thought.* Edited by Carl E. Braaten. New York: Simon and Schuster.

13 *Old world and new world*

Thus the world is divided into two great political parties; the difference between them is, that one party choose Satan as the god of this world, yield obedience to his laws, and are devoted to his interest. Selfishness is the law of Satan's empire, and all impenitent sinners yield it a willing obedience. The other party choose Jehovah for their governor, and consecrate themselves, with all their interests, to his service and glory.

(Charles G. Finney, "Sinners Bound to Change Their Own Hearts")

In this chapter

Christianity came to North America in old clothing, but it quickly acquired new apparel. In the colonial period the dominant forms of Christianity were Anglicanism (often in Puritan garb), Lutheranism, Calvinism (often in Congregational form), and Roman Catholicism. After the American Revolution, the ranks of Baptists and Methodists exploded, especially on the frontier, and new forms of Christianity, such as Unitarianism, Seventh-day Adventism, the Stone-Campbell Restoration movement, Pentecostalism, Mormonism, Jehovah's Witnesses, and Christian Science arose, fueled in part by two Great Awakenings. In Europe, the French Revolution led to abortive attempts to suppress Christianity, Napoleon's rise to power restored some of the privileges of the Roman Catholic Church, and conflict between France and the Papacy – and later between Italian nationalists and the Papacy – led to the pope's political power being curtailed. Catholicism reigned supreme throughout much of Latin America and the Caribbean, but the Church's close ties with the colonial powers, and later with the powerful elite in this region, led many people to see the Church, and especially the bishops and the Vatican, as their enemy in the struggle for freedom.

Main topics covered

- The Church in the United States during the colonial period
- The Great Awakening
- Christianity in the United States after the American Revolution

- The U.S. Civil War and its aftermath
- The Church in Post-Reconstruction America
- The Church and its relations with the new nations of Europe
- The Church of Latin America and the Caribbean

The Church in the United States

The colonial period

Although the Spanish and Portuguese had established colonies in Central and South America and the Caribbean as early as the late fifteenth century, the British were not able to colonize the New World until the beginning of the seventeenth century. By that time, the regions with the greatest mineral wealth were already in the hands of the Spanish and Portuguese, so only the east coast of North America remained to be colonized (as well as the interior of the continent). Like the Spanish and Portuguese, the British saw the New World as having tremendous economic potential, but that potential would have to be realized from agriculture rather than precious metals. The earliest British colony was Virginia, where the Jamestown settlement was established in 1607. After a difficult beginning for the settlers, which included several encounters with the local Algonquian Indians, both peaceful and bellicose, the settlement was restocked with provisions and people from Britain, peace with the Algonquians was concluded (in part through the marriage of Pocahontas to John Rolfe), and other settlements began to be established throughout Virginia.

The Jamestown colony was established primarily as an economic venture, and in 1619 the colony began importing African slaves to work the tobacco plantations. The Anglican form of Christianity was the official religion of colony, and many Puritans were included among the inhabitants. However, the rancorous relationship between the Puritans and other Anglicans in Britain – including the Civil War and the execution of the king – had little impact on Virginians. In fact, the zeal to establish a Christian community in the New World waned significantly as the years went by, and the church excited little enthusiasm among most inhabitants. Ancient prohibitions against Christians owning other Christians as slaves were observed for a while, with the result that little effort was made to evangelize the African slaves. After a law was passed in 1667 that overturned the ancient prohibition, an effort was made in some quarters to establish Christianity among the slave population, but most slave owners preferred to keep their slaves ignorant and submissive.

The southern colonies of North Carolina, South Carolina, and Georgia were also based on agriculture, and they also made use of slaves purchased from Africa. In addition to its agriculture-based economy, Georgia was also founded to halt the northern advance of Spain from its colony in Florida, and it served as a dumping ground for people released from debtors prisons in Britain. Religious observance was minimal in the early days of the southern colonies, but the preaching of George Whitefield during the eighteenth century won a number of converts to a more committed form of Christianity. Although

Whitefield advocated a Calvinist form of Anglicanism, many of his converts became Methodists and especially Baptists. Whitefield is reported to have remarked, "My chickens have turned to ducks!"

In 1620 a group of Puritan separatists from England, who had lived for a while in the Netherlands, landed their ship *Mayflower* on the shore of territory north of the Virginia colony, founding the Plymouth settlement. Unlike their compatriots to the south, this group of settlers had come to the New World primarily for religious reasons. They wanted to establish a colony where they could practice their religion according to their understanding of the biblical text. The Pilgrims, as they are often called, suffered through a harsh winter, but with help from local Indians, about half were able to survive. As more settlers arrived to reinforce the population, and as they were able to harvest both food and animal pelts, they began to prosper. About ten years later the Massachusetts Bay Company received a grant from King Charles I to establish a colony which included Plymouth and much more territory. The Company was founded by English Puritans who, though not Separatists like the Mayflower Pilgrims, wanted to establish a colony run on Puritan principles. During the persecutions that Archbishop Laud instituted in England prior to the English Civil War, as many as 10,000 Puritans fled to Massachusetts Bay and the new colonies of Connecticut and New Haven (later absorbed into Connecticut).

The Puritans of New England believed in the importance of a conversion experience in order to be truly a part of the church. Most of them also believed in the importance of infant baptism as a seal of the covenant that God had made with each individual in the colonies. Although the Baptists among them urged them to abandon infant baptism, the majority of Puritans, who were intent on establishing a Christian society, opted for a different solution, the "half-way Covenant." Under this arrangement, those who had been baptized but had had no conversion experience were considered members of the community, but not full members with the right to participate in decision making.

The Salem witch trials

The most notorious event of this era to take place in New England was the Salem witch trials. In 1692 several young girls accused an Indian slave woman named Tituba of being a witch, and Tituba in turn "confessed" (in order to save her life) and accused several other people. A five-judge panel, led by chief justice William Stoughton, presided over the trials. Eventually 14 women and six men were executed for being witches, and two dogs were executed as accomplices. At least four other women accused of witchcraft died in prison, and more than 100 other people were arrested. Governor Phips intervened to put a stop to the proceedings, perhaps because his wife was one of many who had been accused. Although many participants in the trial later apologized, Stoughton was unrepentant, and in fact he criticized Phips for interfering in the work of God. Stoughton became the next governor of Massachusetts.

Questions of church government led most Puritans to adopt a congregational form of church polity, though they insisted that all churches adopt a Confession of Faith based on the Westminster Confession.

The principle of religious freedom, so important in American history, was first put into practice by Roger Williams, a pastor who, after living in and being expelled from various places in New England, founded the colony of Providence in 1636, which later merged with surrounding territories to become the Colony of Rhode Island and Providence Plantations in 1642. Williams published a tract called *The Bloudy Tenent of Persecution for the Cause of Conscience Discussed*, in which he argued that freedom of religion was required for the true worship of God. Williams also believed that the land on which British colonists had settled actually belonged to the Indians, so he insisted on paying for lands that the king or Parliament had granted him. Anne Hutchinson, after being banished from Massachusetts for insisting that people could communicate directly with God, without the need for a minister as an intermediary, established the settlement of Portsmouth on Aquidneck Island, later renamed Rhode Island. In 1652 Rhode Island became the first colony in North America to outlaw slavery. Williams's church in Providence became the first Baptist church established in North America, but Williams left the church after a short time to continue his religious journey as a Seeker. He nevertheless remained on friendly terms with the Baptists, and he also remained involved in the politics of the colony, always fighting to maintain its strong principles of religious liberty. Baptists, Quakers, Jews, and many other people seeking the freedom to worship as they saw fit migrated to Rhode Island in the years after it was founded.

Although the first Baptist church founded in what is now the U.S. was Roger Williams's church in Providence, Rhode Island, Baptist congregations in other colonies sprang up soon afterward. At that time, Baptists in both the colonies and in Britain were divided into two groups, General and Particular. The General Baptists accepted an Arminian theology that taught that Christ died for all people. The Particular Baptists were strict Calvinists who believed that Christ died only for those predestined for salvation. In the early decades of the Baptist presence in the colonies, the General Baptists were the larger group, but the Great Awakening, with its emphasis on Reformed theology, led to a surge in the number of Particular Baptists. Baptists were persecuted in many colonies, but as religious tolerance became the rule rather than the exception, Baptist churches were founded throughout the thirteen colonies.

In 1632 King Charles I granted Lord Baltimore the right to establish the colony of Maryland in British America, carving the colony out of land previously granted to Virginia. The first settlers arrived in 1634, and from the beginning Maryland was different from most other British colonies, in that the majority of its leading citizens were Catholic. Sporadic religious persecution in Virginia to the south caused some settlers to migrate to Maryland, where religious tolerance (for Christians) was practiced. In 1649 the Maryland Toleration Act was passed, which declared that all Christians of any persuasion were free to practice their faith in Maryland. After this act was passed, a large number of more observant Puritans moved from Virginia to Maryland, after finding

Virginia's laws mandating Anglican observance objectionable. The fact that a majority of the population was Protestant, however, led to constant struggles for political power between Catholics and Protestants, and after the Glorious Revolution of 1688, when the Protestant monarchs William and Mary assumed the British throne, Anglicanism became the official religion of the colony.

Religion in the Mid-Atlantic colonies of New York, New Jersey, Pennsylvania, and Delaware was predominantly Protestant, with Anglicans, Puritans, Quakers, and others mixing with one another. The official tolerance of religion practiced in Pennsylvania was not mirrored in the other colonies, but because these colonies were not founded by people seeking religious freedom, most of the time people in these colonies were fairly tolerant of those with different beliefs. Over time, all of the colonies became increasingly tolerant of religious diversity, following the examples of Rhode Island and Pennsylvania, where tolerance was the law.

The Great Awakening

In 1734 Jonathan Edwards, the pastor of a Congregational church in Northampton, Massachusetts, noticed that people began to respond to his sermons in surprising, emotional ways. Edwards was a strict Calvinist, but he had always emphasized the need for a personal encounter with God that included the conviction of sin and the experience of divine forgiveness. His preaching style was not particularly emotional, so he attributed the results he was seeing to an outpouring of the Holy Spirit. Pastors in other churches in the area began noticing similar experiences among their congregants, and the movement spread into Connecticut as well. However, after a fairly short time, the phenomenon ceased. Three years later, the Anglican preacher George Whitefield came to New England, and Edwards invited him to address his congregation. Soon a wave of emotional conversions spread, and Whitefield and other dynamic preachers were in great demand throughout the region. This outbreak of repentance and conversion was not limited to a single denomination but embraced them all.

The Great Awakening should probably be seen as part of a larger phenomenon that was related to pietism in Germany and the evangelism of slaves in the British colonies. Unlike subsequent awakenings, the Great Awakening primarily affected people who were already members of local churches, imbuing them with a new sense of the immediate presence of Christ in their lives. Congregationalist, Presbyterian, and other denominations with strong Calvinist theologies were greatly affected, as were newer, smaller denominations like the Methodists and Baptists. In particular, the emphasis on a personal conversion experience pushed many people into the Baptist camp, after they began to question the validity of infant baptism. Many Christians influenced by the Great Awakening, especially Baptists and Methodists, moved to the western frontiers of the colonies, organizing churches and becoming the predominant denominations on the frontier. The Great Awakening also made many inhabitants of the colonies begin to appreciate the commonalities they shared with those in other colonies, and many people began thinking of themselves as Americans rather than English for the first time.

The new nation

A growing nationalism in the American colonies was exacerbated by the lack of political power that many felt. Many felt that the British government did not treat them fairly, as exemplified by the quartering of a large number of British troops in America and the lack of representation in the British Parliament. Disputes over the perceived right of Americans to expand their settlements to the west also raised tensions. Finally, in April 1775, a rebellion began on the fields of Lexington and Concord, Massachusetts. The war expanded, and independence was declared on July 4, 1776. The Declaration of Independence invoked both the "Law of Nature" and "Nature's God" to defend the Americans' right to revolt, also referring to the "Supreme Judge of the world" and "Divine Providence." The language of the Declaration makes clear that belief in God was common among the signers, but it also demonstrates that the nature of that belief for many of them tended toward Deism and other forms of rationalism.

Shortly after American independence was won in 1783, with the assistance of Spain and especially France, who were rivals to Britain in Europe and abroad, Christianity in the United States began to grow in new and surprising ways. Unitarians, who rejected the concept of the Trinity primarily on rational grounds, began establishing churches in Boston and elsewhere in New England, peeling off members from Anglican and Congregationalist churches. At about the same time, Universalists, who rejected the concept of eternal punishment, arose primarily from the ranks of Methodists who believed that God's love precluded the idea of hell. These movements eventually coalesced into a single denomination, the Unitarian-Universalists. Another religious movement influenced by rationalism was Transcendentalism, which turned the rationalist eye inward and promoted self-knowledge and self-understanding. Leading Transcendentalists included Ralph Waldo Emerson, Henry David Thoreau, and Bronson Alcott.

Churches with historical ties to England – especially Anglicans and Methodists – moved to distinguish themselves from their British counterparts. Anglicans in America became the Protestant Episcopal church, and American Methodists also asserted their independence under the leadership of Francis Asbury. Baptists also had English roots, but because of their congregational church polity, the ties were not institutional, so American Baptists had little difficulty asserting their independence. The rise of so many distinct Christian groups in America gave rise to the idea of denominations, that is, groups of (Protestant) Christians that were organizationally separate, yet shared a number of common beliefs and practices. In response to growing denominationalism, Barton Stone, together with Thomas and Alexander Campbell, founded the Disciples of Christ, also known as the Christian Church, whose goal was to create a church based on the New Testament that would unify all Protestant Christians (now called the Stone-Campbell Restoration Movement). The result, however, was the formation of another denomination, and yet another when the Church of Christ split from the Disciples in 1906.

In the wake of the American Revolution, large numbers of immigrants came to the United States. Whereas the majority of people living in the thirteen colonies had been British, soon their numbers were equaled and even surpassed in some areas by immigrants from France, Germany, Ireland, Italy, Poland, and elsewhere in Europe. At the same time, southern landowners were importing large numbers of African slaves to work the cotton and tobacco fields. The number of Roman Catholic immigrants from Europe swelled the ranks of the American Catholic church, and the number of Catholics exploded after the Louisiana Purchase of 1803, the annexation of Texas in 1845, and the Mexican War of 1846–1848. The sudden influx of non-Anglo, non-English speaking Catholics caused tension within the hierarchy of the Catholic Church in America, but eventually the Catholic Church was able to overcome these difficulties to become one of the most integrated and linguistically diverse denominations in the U.S.

An anti-Catholic, anti-immigrant backlash arose in certain areas, particularly, but not exclusively, in the South. This unrest found its most visible representation in the Knights of the Ku Klux Klan, a racist, xenophobic organization that arose from the ashes of the Southern defeat in the Civil War and waged a terror campaign against African Americans, Jews, Catholics, and others deemed unacceptable to white, "Christian" values.

Like the First Great Awakening, the Second Great Awakening started in New England in the first two decades of the nineteenth century, but it quickly spread from there to the American frontier. One of the leaders of the Second Great Awakening was Charles Finney, a former lawyer who became a preacher in New York. He conducted revival meetings in Utica, Rochester, and many other locales, preaching a Calvinist theology tempered by an emphasis on humans as free moral agents, capable of obtaining salvation by answering God's call. On the frontier, camp meetings were a popular way of spreading the gospel, and they also served an important social function in unifying the community in places where the population was dispersed. A number of Christian social agencies and movements were founded during this time, including the American Board of Commissioners for Foreign Missions, the American Bible Society, the American Society for the Promotion of Temperance, and the Women's Christian Temperance Union. In addition to promoting temperance, the latter group became a champion of women's rights. Other social movements that came to prominence under the influence of the Second Great Awakening were groups organized for the abolition of slavery, the end of dueling, and support for public education. The number of registered church members grew considerably during this period, particularly among the Baptists and Methodists in frontier areas.

The Texas Revolution of 1836 separated a huge chunk of territory from Mexico, and Texas's annexation by the U.S. in 1845 was seen by many Anglo-Americans as an example of the "manifest destiny" of the U.S. to extend its western border all the way to the Pacific Ocean. Accordingly, the Mexican War of 1846–1848 further extended U.S. territory to the west, in the processing taking in enormous swaths of land formerly claimed by Mexico and inhabited almost exclusively by Native Americans and *Mestizos* (people of mixed Indian and European descent). In addition to the many former Mexican citizens who were added to the population of the U.S., most of them Catholic, the U.S.

conquest of the American Southwest brought with it the specter of slavery. Slavery, which had been abolished in Mexico in 1829, was one of the reasons behind the Texas Revolution, and questions of slavery in the new territories caused grave concern in the rest of the U.S., where the balance of power between slaveholding states and free states was in question. Former president John Quincy Adams and other anti-slavery advocates strongly opposed the U.S. appropriation of Mexican territory, so both Texas annexation and the Mexican War were precursors of the Civil War that was soon to begin.

The American Civil War and its aftermath

> With malice toward none, with charity for all, with firmness in the right as God gives us to see the right, let us strive on to finish the work we are in, to bind up the nation's wounds, to care for him who shall have borne the battle and for his widow and his orphan, to do all which may achieve and cherish a just and lasting peace among ourselves and with all nations.
>
> (Abraham Lincoln, *Second Inaugural Address*)

The U.S. Constitution implicitly allowed slavery, stipulating that all those who were not "free Persons" be counted as three-fifths of a person for census purposes. Some states outlawed slavery, while others permitted it. The disagreement between elected leaders of free states and elected leaders of slave states grew in the aftermath of the Mexican War, and it grew into open conflict after the passage of the Fugitive Slave Act (1850) and the Supreme Court's *Dred Scott* decision (1856). The abolitionist movement in Britain had been championed by William Wilberforce, a British Member of Parliament, beginning in 1789. Slave trade was ended in the British Empire in 1807, and all slaves were freed in the Empire in 1833. Abolitionists in the U.S., such as Frederick Douglass, Harriet Beecher Stowe, Ralph Waldo Emerson, and Harriet Tubman, carried the fight to end slavery to the U.S., and many argued that slavery was contrary to the teachings of the Bible, and particularly to the teachings of Jesus. Other Christians pointed to passages that they said supported slavery, and denominations such as the Baptists and Methodists split over the issue. The 1831 slave revolt led by Nat Turner, who claimed to have received messages from God, and the 1859 attack on Harpers Ferry, led by John Brown, were violent attempts to overthrow slavery that accompanied the generally peaceful abolitionist movement. Finally, in 1861, after the election of Abraham Lincoln, the southern states seceded from the Union, and the first shots of the Civil War were fired at Fort Sumter in Charleston, South Carolina.

The American Civil War was relatively short, lasting four years, but extremely costly in terms of human lives. Issues such as states' rights and economic policies played a role, but the central issue behind the Civil War was slavery. Lincoln opposed slavery but initially advocated a "go-slow" approach. After the war started, however, Lincoln decided it was time to issue his Emancipation Proclamation, which declared all slaves who lived in areas that were rebelling against the Union free (but not those slaves in states that

Figure 13.1 President Abraham Lincoln, shown in this photograph standing between intelligence
director Allan Pinkerton and General John A. McClernand, hoped to preserve the
Union without war. When several southern states seceded from the Union and
attacked the Union armies, Lincoln presided over a bloody Civil War. In 1863 he
issued the Emancipation Proclamation, freeing the slaves who lived in territories
controlled by the Confederacy.

did not secede or in regions that were under Union control, such as New Orleans). The
North had much more money than the South, and in the end, the South was unable to
overcome the financial deficit, and Lee surrendered to Grant. In his Second Inaugural
Address, delivered shortly before the end of the war, Lincoln noted that both sides in the
conflict prayed to the same God, and neither side had had all their prayers granted.

Lincoln was assassinated just after the war ended, and the Reconstruction of the
South proceeded along lines that were undoubtedly harsher than Lincoln would have
liked. Many northerners took advantage of the economic collapse of the South to
make wild profits, thus earning the wrath of many southerners. On the other hand,
during Reconstruction many African-American men were able to assume positions of
authority in city governments, state legislatures, and even the U.S. House and Senate.
Black participation in government did not last long, however, as political and economic
forces in the North and South, combined with White racism, put an end to meaningful
Black integration into the political process in the South for the next century. While
segregation ruled supreme in the South, it also continued in the churches, and it was not
until the modern Civil Rights Movement that many denominations would reunite.

Post-reconstruction America

After the Civil War, Americans from the east moved west in droves, building new cities, founding new states, and bringing to its culmination the Native American holocaust. Already driven from their original homelands in the east, many Indians were again uprooted and herded onto reservations in the west, such as the Indian Territory (Oklahoma), New Mexico, and Arizona. After years of only sporadic violent resistance, many Indians decided to band together to fight the expansion of Americans into the West. Despite some successes along the way, the Indians were outnumbered and outgunned, and most who wanted to hang onto their heritage reluctantly accepted life on the reservation (the first reservations were set up by President Ulysses S. Grant). Christian agencies were established to evangelize the Indians, but the approach these groups took usually resulted in the destruction of Indian culture as well as belief.

The attitude of many Christians toward Native Americans – the belief that Americans of European descent were inherently superior both intellectually and spiritually – was evident in the attitudes that many Christians took toward other groups in Post-Reconstruction America, including African-Americans, Latinos, and Chinese immigrants. Even Europeans from certain areas – such as Italy, Ireland, or Poland – were often treated as inferiors by other Americans, who identified themselves as Christians. Other Christians, however, particularly in urban settings, believed that the gospel demanded that they love all their neighbors, regardless of their race or national origin. Revivalists such as D. L. Moody reached out to the urban masses, regardless of ethnic background. Other organizations such as the YMCA, YWCA, and Salvation Army combined social services with the gospel message. Walter Rauschenbusch, a Baptist preacher and scholar from New York, provided a theological foundation for those Christians who believed that commitment to Christ demanded a commitment to the social betterment of all God's children. This idea was designated the "social gospel."

A number of new Christian groups or movements emerged or became prominent after the Civil War. The holiness movement, associated with churches such as the Church of the Nazarene, grew out of Methodism but emphasized Wesley's teachings on sanctification in the Christian life. The Pentecostal movement traces its roots to the Azusa Street revival of 1906, where believers experienced the "baptism of the Holy Spirit" that resulted in their speaking in tongues. The Seventh-day Adventist church grew after a failed predication that Christ would return in 1843 led some former followers of William Miller to follow Ellen G. White, who reinterpreted some of Miller's teachings and moved the group toward sabbatarianism and an interest in missions. Protestant liberalism flourished as well, fed by the development in Europe of critical tools for studying the Bible and influenced as well by advancements in science, such as Darwin's theory of evolution. In reaction to this trend, many Christians rallied around an inerrant view of the Bible and a set of fundamental principles that they identified as essential for salvation; this movement identified itself as fundamentalism. An interpretation of the end times known as dispensationalism, developed by John Nelson Darby in England

New denominations

Several new Christian denominations arose in the United States during the nineteenth and early twentieth centuries, many of which spread well beyond the borders of the U.S. The theology of some of these new denominations was quite orthodox, while other groups held decidedly unorthodox positions on certain matters. Some of the denominations that arose during this period include:

Church of the Nazarene
Wesleyan Church
Seventh-day Adventist Church
Church of Jesus Christ of Latter-day Saints (Mormons)
Jehovah's Witnesses
Christian Science Church
Disciples of Christ
Church of Christ
Assemblies of God

and popularized by C. I. Scofield through his edition of the King James Bible, grew out of the fundamentalist movement. Joseph Smith founded the Church of Jesus Christ of Latter-day Saints, commonly known as the Mormons, in New York, and he moved the group as far west as Missouri, where he was killed. Subsequently, Brigham Young took the group to Utah, where they established a community patterned after their own beliefs, which included, at that time, polygamy (they officially abandoned the practice in 1890). Charles T. Russell founded the Jehovah's Witnesses, a group that rejected the divinity of Christ and predicted the end of the world in 1914. When the end did not occur, Judge Rutherford reorganized the movement and reinterpreted those scriptures that Russell had used to predict the 1914 date. Finally, the Christian Science church grew out of a mixture of Christianity, spiritualism, and other religious philosophies, under the leadership of Mary Baker Eddy. This group believed that illness was a "mental error," and spiritual "science" could be used to cure oneself from disease.

The Church in Europe

> Liberty consists in the freedom to do everything which injures no one else; hence the exercise of the natural rights of each man has no limits except those which assure to the other members of the society the enjoyment of the same rights. These limits can only be determined by law.
>
> (Declaration of the Rights of Man and of the Citizen, France, 1789)

The history of Europe from the beginning of the Protestant Reformation in 1517 was characterized by numerous wars and internal struggles between Catholics and

Protestants. The Peace of Westphalia in 1648 ended the overt international conflicts over religion within Europe, but religious affiliation continued to drive internal politics in many countries, most notably the English Civil War and the persecution of the French Huguenots. The continuing influence of religious belief in European unrest led many to embrace forms of religion that de-emphasized dogmatic formulations (rationalism and Deism) or emphasized the spiritual aspects of religion (spiritualism and pietism). The same conditions led others to reject religion altogether as a negative force in world history, in conflict with modern scientific understanding and contrary to the wellbeing of humanity (atheism). The relationship between religion and the state took a drastic, irreversible turn at the end of the eighteenth century.

Although the American Revolution began in 1775, more than ten years prior to the French Revolution, it was the latter that had the most profound effect on European history. One reason, of course, was distance. America was a British colony separated from Europe by several thousand miles of ocean. Another reason was the relatively moderate nature of the American Revolution, and of American revolutionaries. The British colonies in America had seen religious liberty work in both Rhode Island and Pennsylvania, and despite isolated outbreaks of religious intolerance (the Salem witch trials were an aberration, related to superstition rather than religious differences), most Americans had not suffered greatly from religious persecution, especially in the decades leading up to the American Revolution. A third reason that the American Revolution did not have an immediate, profound impact on European history was that when the revolution ended in 1783 with the signing of the Treaty of Paris, King George III was still on the British throne.

In France the situation was different. First, King Louis XVI's edict of toleration for Protestants in 1787 did little to assuage the bitterness of more than 100 years of persecution. Second, the French kings' persecution of the Huguenots had driven tens of thousands of them into other countries, thus weakening France economically. Thus, France faced dire economic circumstances during the reign of Louis XVI. Third, a sizeable number of French revolutionary leaders were atheists, who despised both the monarchy and the papacy, because they believed that the one supported the other to the detriment of ordinary French citizens. Fourth, the extravagant living of Louis XVI and his court was constantly before the eyes of the people of France, leading the masses to seek the destruction of the monarchy. Fifth, abuses of power among high-ranking Roman Catholic clergy led many of the French, Catholic and Protestant alike, to oppose them. One connection between the American and French revolutions was important, however. During the American Revolution, France, which had been in a more or less constant state of antagonism with Britain for several centuries, was a strong supporter of the American revolutionaries, despite their avowed aim to rid themselves of the authority of the British king. Unlike Cardinal Richelieu, who was able to support anti-papal forces abroad while stifling anti-papal sentiment at home, Louis XVI was unable to keep the germ of revolution from spreading among the French people while supporting revolution in America. In 1789, after several unsuccessful attempts to involve the French populace in the governing of France, Paris erupted in riots, culminating in the storming of the

Bastille prison on July 14. The National Constituent Assembly, which represented the people, issued the "Declaration of the Rights of Man and of the Citizen," a document that expressed the essence of the battle cry of the French Revolution: Liberty, Equality, and Fraternity. When Louis XVI refused to sign the declaration and other documents issued by the assembly, he and his family were placed under virtual house arrest. Although he later agreed to the 1791 constitution, in 1793 he and his wife, Marie Antoinette, were executed for treason.

The French Assembly allowed freedom of religion, but it also assumed responsibility for reforming certain aspects of the dominant Roman Catholic Church. Drawing on a long tradition of relative independence from the papacy in matters of clerical appointments (Gallicanism), the Assembly ordered several reforms of the church within the borders of France, including dissolution of clergy as a distinct political entity (estate), the nationalization of all ecclesiastical land, and equalization of clergy salaries. These reforms did not sit well with all Catholics, and they were almost universally rejected by the bishops, who had enjoyed both wealth and political influence under the monarchy. Those bishops and others who refused to swear an oath to obey the Civil Constitution of France were suspected of opposing the French Revolution, and many were imprisoned and executed over the next few years.

Meanwhile, war broke out between France and many of its neighbors on the continent, beginning with the Holy Roman Empire, whose emperor was the brother of Marie Antoinette. Monarchs in neighboring states were concerned that republican sentiment would spread into their territories, while the leaders of the new French Republic were anxious to reduce the power of their neighbors to counteract their revolution. In the wake of the French Revolution, France fought many of its neighbors, including Great Britain, Austria, Prussia, and Spain. Despite early losses, France eventually gained supremacy over most of its neighbors, in large measure as a result of forced mass conscriptions.

While the armies were fighting, anti-religious sentiment at home was growing among the leaders of the revolution. Although the Civil Constitution called for religious liberty, which was extended to Jews as well as Christians, many revolutionaries pushed for the establishment of a new state religion, either the Cult of Reason (atheists) or the Cult of the Supreme Being (Deists). Changes to the calendar eliminated references to Christian holidays, and even the ancient seven-day week, and a list of officially recognized saints included such famous thinkers as Socrates, Jesus, Marcus Aurelius, and Jean-Jacques Rousseau. A period of political persecution, often with religious overtones, broke out, known as the Reign of Terror. Thousands of people were executed by the guillotine, including many of the original leaders of the French Revolution. The terror lessened as the army took more control of the situation in France, and in 1799 one of the revolution's leading generals, Napoleon Bonaparte, became ruler of France, with the title of First Consul.

Napoleon recognized that the anarchy of the Reign of Terror was detrimental to both the revolution and the wellbeing of France, so he acted to curb the worst abuses. In particular, he negotiated an understanding with Pope Pius VII, whose predecessor

Pius VI had been captured by French troops during an invasion of the Papal States and who had died in French captivity. Napoleon adopted the title French Emperor in 1804, in a ceremony attended by the pope. As emperor, Napoleon granted full religious freedom to French Protestants, but he also allowed a greater measure of authority over French Catholic clergy to the Pope, in an effort to secure the pope's continued support. Napoleon fell out of the pope's good graces, however, both because of his divorce from Josephine and because of his wars with his neighbors, which ended in 1815.

In the aftermath of the Napoleonic Wars, the political situation in Europe had changed substantially. The Holy Roman Empire, which had been losing power for more than a century, had been finally dissolved, and two powerful states emerged from its rubble, Austria and Prussia. Hereditary monarchs sitting on the thrones of several of France's neighbors had been overthrown or deposed, and those who were restored to power generally found themselves with less authority than they had previously enjoyed. Over the next century, several states (e.g. Germany, Portugal, Finland, and France itself, which restored the Bourbon line to the throne for a time) became constitutional monarchies, and others became republics in the wake of the two world wars of the twentieth century.

The industrial revolution, which had begun in Britain in the late eighteenth century, spread to Europe early in the nineteenth century, accompanied by the theory of economic liberalism, or free enterprise. People flocked to the cities to find work in the new factories that were springing up everywhere, and some members of the middle class began accumulating enormous amounts of wealth in the form of capital. The idea behind economic liberalism was that the growth of capital and the creation of wealth would benefit the entire society. When such promises failed to materialize by the middle of the nineteenth century, alternative views of economics, such as socialism and communism, became popular among the masses, championed above all by Karl Marx, whose book *Capital* enumerated the abuses of the capitalist system on the lower classes.

1848 is sometimes called the Year of Revolution because of the many revolutions that erupted in Europe that year as a result of economic and social unrest. Beginning in Sicily, the revolutions among the lower and middle classes spread to France, Austria, Prussia, and Poland, among other areas. Although most of the revolutions were suppressed, they led to changes in the political landscape, including a new constitution in Switzerland and the establishment of the Second Republic in France. The long-term consequences of the social unrest were profound. In 1851 Napoleon III declared himself French emperor, and Count von Metternich, the long-time chancellor of Austria, was forced into exile. Over the next few decades, both Germany and Italy finally achieved the unification that many Germans and Italians had sought for years. The final piece to fall into place in Italy was the Papal States, which the pope finally agreed to cede to a united Italy in 1929, though the region had been controlled by Italy since 1870.

The separation of church and state that followed the French Revolution throughout much of Europe resulted in the growth of "free churches," that is, churches supported by the voluntary contributions of members, rather than by contributions from the state.

The pietist movement, both within the state churches and the free churches, encouraged the growth of both missionary societies and ministries to the poor, especially the urban poor whose numbers had multiplied so greatly under the influence of the Industrial Revolution. Some of the greatest work in this area occurred in Great Britain, where Wesley and Whitefield a century earlier had emphasized the church's responsibility to minister to the poor. Organizations such as the Young Men's Christian Association (YMCA), the Young Women's Christian Association (YWCA), and the Salvation Army, which became a distinct Christian denomination, worked largely with the poor in the cities. Other groups worked to form labor unions, institute prison reform, and outlaw child labor. The Sunday Schools were initially intended to educate poor children who had no other educational opportunities. The most important societal change that grew out of the reform movements within the Anglican church was the abolition of the slave trade, first, then of slavery itself within the British Empire. Led by William Wilberforce, a British Member of Parliament, slavery was once and for all outlawed in 1833, and Britain began seeking slavery's abolition in other countries as well.

The Church in Latin America and the Caribbean

> Among individuals, as among nations, respect for the rights of others is peace.
> (Benito Juárez, President of Mexico)

From the time of the Spanish *conquistadores* until the early nineteenth century, South America and the southern and western portions of North America had been under the political control of Spain and, in Brazil, Portugal. The Caribbean islands were divided among the European powers of Spain, Portugal, France, the Netherlands, and Great Britain. Great cities had been built all over Latin America, and generations of people of European descent had lived alongside Native Americans and African slaves, often intermarrying with them, for three centuries. Nevertheless, the European powers tended to view their colonies primarily as resources for enriching themselves, and they neglected to take advantage of the native-born leadership that was proliferating in every area of the New World. By 1800, unrest was growing in Latin America and the Caribbean, for three reasons. First, the tendency of Spain and Portugal to appoint European-born rulers and bishops instead of using native-born people of European descent (creoles) had begun to cause a tremendous amount of antipathy toward the European powers. Second, many wealthy creoles who traveled back and forth from the New World to Europe had caught the republican fever that swept the continent in the wake of the French Revolution. Third, the American Revolution also inspired many to consider declaring independence from their European overlords.

Haiti was the first Caribbean nation to declare its independence in 1804, after the vicissitudes of the French Revolution drained resources away from the French colonists in the country. The vast majority of the country consisted of slaves, who rose up against their masters in the first successful slave revolt in history.

Figure 13.2 Simón Bolívar led successful revolutions against Spain that resulted in the creation of several new South American countries, including Venezuela, Colombia, Ecuador, Peru, and Bolivia.

Mexico, the northernmost Spanish colony, was the first country in Latin America to declare its independence in 1810. Unlike the situation in most of the rest of Latin America, the rebellion in Mexico was supported by the lower-class Indians and *mestizos*, in addition to the creoles. Revolutionary fervor spread south, as one country after another declared itself free from European rule. In northern South America, Simón Bolívar led independence movements that resulted in establishing the new countries of Colombia, Venezuela, Ecuador, Peru, and Bolivia. Further south, Argentina, Paraguay, Uruguay, and Chile all gained their independence from Spain as well. In 1821, Central America declared its independence from Spain, and in 1822 Brazil declared its independence from Portugal.

The result of all these independence movements was to decrease the influence of the major European colonial powers and to increase the wealth of a small minority of people in Latin America, mostly those of European descent. With the exception of Mexico, the common people had little or no voice in the government, regardless of whether the rulers were more conservative (favoring close ties with Spain and a controlled economy) or liberal (favoring ties to more liberal European regimes and a capitalist economy). In many cases, military dictators took control of countries and stifled moves toward either political freedom or a more even distribution of wealth.

The Roman Catholic Church found itself in a difficult situation with regard to the revolutionary movements of the nineteenth century. On the one hand, most inhabitants of the new countries were Catholics. On the other hand, recognition of the new states threatened to harm relations with powerful nations such as Spain and Portugal. After trying to please both sides for a couple of decades and pleasing neither, Pope Gregory XVI finally acknowledged the new republics and appointed bishops for them. This acquiescence on the part of the pope did not resolve all of the difficulties that the Roman Catholic Church faced in the New World, however. The bishops who were appointed were primarily European rather than native-born, and their sympathies usually lay with the wealthy. Parish priests, in contrast, usually supported the revolutionary movements and the people of the lower classes. Tensions with Rome continued to grow, with the result that although most Latin Americans still considered themselves Catholics, few attended services, and many became strongly anti-clerical in outlook. Latin American states became increasingly secular, as many of their leaders believed that the church was aligned with the European powers against the interests of the new nations.

The animosity between the Catholic Church and the new states led many of them to proclaim religious liberty for their citizens. One result of this trend was that many Protestants from other parts of the world came to Latin America to settle, and in the absence of a strongly supported Catholic Church, Protestantism flourished in many areas.

Discussion questions

1.   What were the religious factors that led to the Salem witch trials? Did these events happen as a result of the prevailing Puritanism of the region, or might they have happened just as easily in settings in which the prevailing form of Christianity was different?
2.   Why was the religious liberty that Roger Williams preached so hard for many to accept? How different might the U.S. have been without the principle of religious liberty enshrined in the Bill of Rights?

Key points you need to know

- Many English colonists came to the New World to escape religious persecution or to be able to practice their religion freely. Many others came for purely economic reasons.
- The Great Awakening in the early eighteenth century brought many people back to the Church, and it also caused many colonists to begin thinking of themselves as Americans rather than British for the first time.
- In part because of the separation of church and state enshrined in the U.S. Constitution, many new Christian denominations sprang up after the American Revolution, and the denominations that experienced the most rapid growth were not the traditional Protestant denominations that enjoyed state support in Europe.
- The Louisiana Purchase, as well as the conquest of the American Southwest as a result of the Texas Revolution and the Mexican-American War brought large numbers of Roman Catholics of mixed Spanish and Indian descent into the United States. This demographic shift challenged both the Roman Catholic Church and Protestant Churches.

- The Pentecostal movement, which would change the face of global Christianity, was born in California during the 1906 Azusa Street Revival.
- The Roman Catholic Church lost its political power in Europe as a result of the French Revolution, which showed the military impotence of the papacy, and the unification of Italy, which annexed the Papal States to the new nation of Italy.
- Christian social activism led to many changes in society, including a renewed concern for the poor, the formation of labor unions, prison reform, outlawing child labor, and the abolition of first the slave trade and then of slavery itself.
- Almost all of Latin America and the Caribbean declared its independence from European colonial powers during the first two decades of the nineteenth century. The Roman Catholic Church struggled to maintain its ties with both the European powers and the new nations.

3. Why did the French Revolution take a much bloodier turn than the American Revolution? Why did the fighting continue for so long (including the Napoleonic Wars)?
4. How did the French Revolution affect the history of Europe throughout the nineteenth century?
5. What were the most positive movements within Christianity during the nineteenth century? What were the most negative?
6. How did independence in Latin America affect the average citizen?

Further reading

Edwards, Jonathan 1741. *Sinners in the Hands of an Angry God*. Christian Classics Ethereal Library. http://www.ccel.org/e/edwards/sermons/sinners.html.

González, Justo 1984–1985. *The Story of Christianity*. 2 vols. New York: HarperSanFrancisco.

Hudson, Winthrop S. 1981. *Religion in America*, 3rd edn. New York: Scribner.

Latourette, Kenneth Scott 1975. *A History of Christianity*. Revised edn, 2 vols. New York: Harper & Row.

Pelikan, Jaroslav 1971–1989. *The Christian Tradition: A History of the Development of Doctrine*. 5 vols. Chicago, IL: University of Chicago Press.

Rauschenbusch, Walter 1997. *A Theology for the Social Gospel*. Louisville, KY: Westminster John Knox.

Williams, Roger 2001. *The Bloudy Tenent of Persecution for Cause of Conscience*. Macon, GA: Mercer University Press.

14 *Diversification and expansion*

Expect great things from God. Attempt great things for God.

(William Carey)

In this chapter

In the aftermath of the Napoleonic Wars, Europe underwent huge changes, with traditional monarchies replaced throughout the continent by representative democracies. Many Protestant scholars set aside traditional models of theology as well, developing approaches to Christianity that put an emphasis on reason, feeling, or ethical behavior. The quest for the historical Jesus followed the rules of scientific historical investigation, and scholars applied critical tools to the study of the Bible. Catholics, meanwhile, held much more closely to traditional dogmatic theology, and as the papacy was losing its temporal power, its spiritual authority increased enormously when the pope declared himself to be infallible in matters of dogma. Toward the end of the nineteenth century, the Catholic Church took some tentative steps toward acknowledging both the value of modern critical tools of study and the staying power of representative democracies. Both Protestants and Catholics launched great global mission efforts in the nineteenth century, often in conjunction with the neocolonial exploits of the world's most powerful nations. As a result, Christianity reached areas of Asia and Africa where it was previously unknown, and Christianity showed the first signs of becoming a truly global religion.

Major topics covered

- Developments in Protestant theology
- Emergence of the critical study of Christian history and the Bible
- Developments in Roman Catholic theology
- Growth in the papacy's spiritual authority in the wake of the First Vatican Council
- The Modern Missions Movement

Developing theology

Protestant theology

> I do not lack the courage to think a thought whole.
>
> (Søren Kierkegaard, *Fear and Trembling*)

Although it began decades earlier, after the end of the Napoleonic Wars in Europe in 1815 the Industrial Revolution proceeded at full strength throughout Europe and, shortly thereafter, in North America as well. The Industrial Revolution brought with it huge changes in society. People moved from rural to urban areas in search of work. Factories were built on farmland. Extended families were replaced in function by nuclear families. Even ways of looking at life in general changed. The focus of most educated people in the nineteenth century shifted from the past to the future. Rather than seeing the past as an era of greatness to be emulated, people began to believe in the idea of progress. Advances in science and philosophy led to changes in theology as well. While the Catholic Church resisted these movements of progress, many in the Protestant churches embraced them, so the leading theological thinkers of this era were predominantly Protestants.

Friedrich Schleiermacher was raised in the home of a Reformed pastor, but he was strongly influenced by the pietism of the Moravians and by the romantic movement that challenged the stark rationalism of the day. Unlike the orthodox, who tried to base religion on logical reason, or Kant, who tried to base religion on moral reason, Schleiermacher drew on the romantic critique of rationalism by recognizing that human beings are more than just rational, moral beings. They are also beings that can feel; specifically, they can feel a sense of profound dependence which can only be filled by the divine. For Schleiermacher, the purpose of theology is not to propound dogmatic truths but rather to explore the feeling of dependence that all Christians feel in relation to themselves, their communities, and God. The factuality of biblical stories was unimportant to Schleiermacher, because disputes about creation, the historicity of certain accounts, or the supernatural did not touch directly on the central question of dependence. Thus, Schleiermacher saw no conflict between the findings of modern science or history and authentic Christianity.

In contrast to Schleiermacher, G. W. F. Hegel put a great deal of emphasis on reason. In fact, for Hegel, reality and reason were one and the same. History was the working out of ideas in the real world, and the progress of history demonstrates the progress of human thought. Hegel proposed a process that explains the nature of progress within

> Religion is the sigh of the oppressed creature, the heart of a heartless world, just as it is the spirit of a spiritless situation. It is the opium of the people.
>
> (Karl Marx, "Introduction to a Contribution to a Critique of Hegel's Philosophy of Right")

human reason and history. First, an idea is put forward and examined in its entirety. Second, a competing idea is similarly examined. Third, the best parts of the two ideas are combined into a new, better idea – thesis, antithesis, synthesis. Hegel saw history as the unfolding of the divine idea, as grasped incompletely by humans. He saw Christianity and Christian doctrines such as the Incarnation and Trinity as the culmination of divine (or Spiritual) thought, but he saw value in other religions and schools of thought as well. Hegel's followers saw Hegel's system of dialectical idealism as a means by which the whole of reality might be understood.

Søren Kierkegaard, a Danish Lutheran philosopher, was not convinced by the immense claims of the Hegelian system of thought. He rejected the romanticism of Schleiermacher and the rationalism of Hegel, opting instead for the alternative of faith. Christianity, for Kierkegaard, was not based on either reason or a sense of absolute dependence, but on faith in God who has chosen to be revealed in scripture and in Jesus Christ. However, the faith that Kierkegaard proposed was not escapism from the realities of the world. On the contrary, faith required great risk, and it was not easy. The great enemy of Christianity, Kierkegaard proclaimed, was not Judaism or Islam, but rather Christendom itself, the amalgamation of church and state that allows someone born in a particular place and time to consider himself a Christian without any other effort. Christianity required sacrifice in one's personal life, and as such Kierkegaard proposed a profoundly individualistic vision of the faith. Each person struggles with his or her own existence, Kierkegaard taught, dealing with pain, doubt, and despair. Existence cannot be reduced to a single system, like Hegelianism, for it is constantly changing, and it is different for each individual. The challenge of Christian existence, Kierkegaard said, is to live a life characterized by faith, taking risks for God.

In the nineteenth century, many people found a new appreciation for and understanding of history. Old formulations were rejected, and scholars looked again at historical questions. Traditional understandings of biblical authorship and dating were rejected by the Tübingen school of F. C. Baur and others. Adolf von Harnack proposed that Christian history showed the development of doctrine from the very earliest time, so that the classical expressions of dogma were far from the original teaching of Jesus. The quest for the historical Jesus led scholars like H. S. Reimarus, Ernest Renan, and Albert Schweitzer to attempt to write historical biographies of Jesus. The theologian Albrecht Ritschl proposed that Christianity was neither about reason nor about a feeling of absolute dependence but about practical living. Karl Marx modified Hegel's dialectical idealism into dialectical materialism and proposed that human history is moving forward by means of clashes between social classes that would eventually lead to the dictatorship of the proletariat, and ultimately to a classless society. Charles Darwin applied the idea of progress to biology, proposing a theory of evolution of living beings by means of natural selection. Everywhere scholars were seeing the progressive development of human institutions and thought, even of the whole world, and the overall outlook of most people was generally positive. Surely human progress would soon bring about a better world! This optimistic feeling was dashed soon after the advent of the twentieth century, in the fields of Verdun, the peninsula of Gallipoli, and the trenches of the Western front.

Catholic theology

While many, but by no means all, Protestants in the eighteenth and nineteenth centuries were characterized by an attitude of liberalism – that is, a willingness to question traditional doctrine and explore new ways of expressing the Christian faith – the Roman Catholic Church was staunchly conservative. The reason for this difference in outlook can be traced to the Protestant Reformation and the Catholic response. While many Catholics in the early sixteenth century were calling for reforms in clergy behavior, the monasteries, and the papacy, the Protestants went a step further by calling for major changes in doctrinal positions as well. After failing to subdue Martin Luther after the Diet of Worms, the Roman Catholic Church faced losing millions of adherents to a new form of Christianity. Their reaction, as codified by the Council of Trent, was to correct some glaring problems in how the church was run, while refusing to consider changes to traditional Catholic doctrine. This conservative attitude set the stage for the next 400 years within the Roman Catholic Church, an approach that would not be radically challenged until the Second Vatican Council in 1962–1965.

Ecclesiastical conservatism within the Catholic Church was by no means limited to matters of doctrine. Popes Pius VI and Pius VII both opposed the French Revolution on the grounds that monarchy was the proper form of temporal government, while the republican democracy was a dangerous innovation. Pius VI became pope in 1775 and ruled for 24 years, thus becoming the longest-reigning pope to that time. He began his pontificate by issuing a papal encyclical entitled *Inscrutabile*, in which he harshly criticized those who advocated radical changes in the structure of government: "They keep proclaiming that man is born free and subject to no one, that society accordingly is a crowd of foolish men who stupidly yield to priests who deceive them and to kings who oppress them, so that the harmony of priest and ruler is only a monstrous conspiracy against the innate liberty of man" (sec. 7). He tried to dissuade Holy Roman Emperor Joseph II from granting toleration to Protestants and limiting the pope's power within the empire to spiritual matters. When the French Revolution began in 1789, he opposed it vociferously as contrary to the divinely established social order. When he continued to oppose the new French government and its foundational proclamations (e.g. the Declaration of the Rights of Man and the Civil Constitution), French troops seized papal properties in France, and in 1796 Napoleon Bonaparte conquered the Papal States in Italy, making the pope a virtual prisoner of the French. The French moved the pope from place to place for security reasons, and he died in Valence in 1799. Many thought that the papacy itself had come to an end with his death, but he had left secret plans for the election of the next pope in a conclave held outside Rome, which was still held by the French.

The next pope took the name Pius VII, and he opposed the results of the French Revolution just like his predecessor. Nevertheless, after Napoleon became First Consul in 1799, relations between France and the papacy began to thaw, and Napoleon granted the pope more control over the church in France. Significantly, under the settlement agreed to by both Napoleon and Pius VII, the pope for the first time in history gained the power to remove a sitting bishop from office, a move that further separated the Bishop of Rome from all other bishops in the church and gave the pope near monarchical powers within the church. When Napoleon declared himself emperor in 1804, Pius traveled to Paris to participate in the coronation. The next year Napoleon's troops again invaded the Papal States, and in 1808 they captured Rome and took Pius prisoner. He remained a prisoner for the remainder of Napoleon's reign, but he emerged from captivity to continue reigning as pope until 1823. In 1814 Pius VII reinstated the Jesuit order, which had been banned about 40 years earlier by Pope Clement XIV, standing up to the Catholic monarchs of Europe to do so.

The three successors to Pope Pius VII – Leo XII, Pius VIII, and Gregory XVI – continued the policies of their immediate predecessors, opposing the political pluralism and philosophical liberalism associated with the French Revolution, as well as religious toleration and the increased use of the laity in the administration of the Papal States, a trend that had been gaining ground in recent years. Leo XII added new titles to the Index of Forbidden Books, strengthened the Holy Office of Inquisition, and carefully scrutinized the orthodoxy of professors at Catholic universities. Gregory XVI, the last monk to be elected pope, opposed Italian nationalism, calling on Austrian troops on two occasions to quell unrest in the Papal States. He also prohibited the use of railroads in the Papal States and banned street lights, because he was worried that people would plot at night against the authorities. He sharply opposed the French priest Félicité Robert de Lamennais, who supported religious liberty and separation of church and state, taking the extraordinary step of condemning him personally in one of his encyclicals. Gregory was a strong supporter of Christian missions, appointing almost 200 missionary bishops and establishing about 70 new dioceses and vicariates apostolic (mission areas).

Without doubt the most important pope of the nineteenth century was Gregory's successor, Pope Pius IX, often called by his Italian title Pio Nono, even in the English-speaking world. His pontificate stretched from 1846 to 1878, the longest in history, and he was in office during the Year of Revolution (1848), the unifications of Germany and Italy, and the loss of the Papal States to the new Kingdom of Italy. Conservative, like the popes who preceded him in the nineteenth century, he may nevertheless be considered the first modern pope, since from 1870 he had only spiritual authority over the Roman Catholic Church, having lost all claims to temporal authority when Rome was annexed into Italy.

The impact of the Year of Revolution was felt in Rome, where the Republic of Rome was declared in 1849, driving Pius from the city. Restored with the help of French troops, he failed to acknowledge the trend toward democracy and political liberalism in Europe, ruling as an absolute monarch within the Papal States and expanding the powers of the

Figure 14.1 Pope Pius IX presided over the First Vatican Council, which declared the doctrine of Papal Infallibility. His immense power over the Roman Catholic Church was balanced by his loss of political power to the new Kingdom of Italy, which claimed Rome.

papacy within the church itself. Although he was unable to hold onto political power, he was successful in increasing his own authority in the spiritual realm. When he proclaimed the doctrine of the Immaculate Conception of Mary in 1854, he was the first pope ever to define a dogma on his own, without the support of a church council. The doctrine itself had long been accepted by most Catholics, so it was the unilateral action of the pope rather than the teaching itself that was significant. In 1864 he published his *Syllabus of Errors*, a list of 80 propositions that all Catholics must accept.

The outcome of the battle was not yet evident, however, at least in the spiritual realm. Pius called the First Vatican Council, which met from 1869 to 1870, to deal with the problems of modernism. The Council ratified his response to the errors he cited in his *Syllabus* and supported his overall resistance to the trends of modernity. Most importantly, the Council stated the doctrine of papal infallibility, which stated that the pope cannot be in error when speaking *ex cathedra*, that is, from the papal chair. This doctrine was revolutionary in the power it asserted for the pope, and it was widely ridiculed by Protestants, as well as by some Catholics. The danger of this doctrine was immediately evident to historians of the church, who could point to numerous instances of popes proclaiming doctrines that were later officially considered to be in error. Popes since Vatican I have been extremely wary of playing the infallibility card, and in fact it has only been used once, in 1950, when Pope Pius XII proclaimed the doctrine of the Bodily Assumption of Mary. Ironically, just after the First Vatican Council closed its meetings, with the papacy at the height of its powers with regard to religious matters,

Pope Pius IX's *Syllabus of Errors*

Included in Pius IX's list of erroneous statements are the following:

5   Divine revelation is imperfect, and therefore subject to a continual and indefinite progress, corresponding with the advancement of human reason.

11   The church not only ought never to pass judgment on philosophy, but ought to tolerate the errors of philosophy, leaving it to correct itself.

13   The method and principles by which the old scholastic doctors cultivated theology are no longer suitable to the demands of our times and to the progress of the sciences.

15   Every man is free to embrace and profess that religion which, guided by the light of reason, he shall consider true.

18   Protestantism is nothing more than another form of the same true Christian religion, in which form it is given to please God equally as in the Catholic Church.

20   The ecclesiastical power ought not to exercise its authority without the permission and assent of the civil government.

24   The Church has not the power of using force, nor has she any temporal power, direct or indirect.

26   The Church has no innate and legitimate right of acquiring and possessing property.

38   The Roman pontiffs have, by their too arbitrary conduct, contributed to the division of the Church into Eastern and Western.

42   In the case of conflicting laws enacted by the two powers, the civil law prevails.

45   The entire government of public schools in which the youth of a Christian state is educated ... may and ought to appertain to the civil power, and belong to it so far that no other authority whatsoever shall be recognized as having any right to interfere in the discipline of the schools, the arrangement of the studies, the conferring of degrees, in the choice or approval of the teachers.

55   The Church ought to be separated from the state, and the state from the Church.

63   It is lawful to refuse obedience to legitimate princes, and even to rebel against them.

67   By the law of nature, the marriage tie is not indissoluble, and in many cases divorce properly so called may be decreed by the civil authority.

77   In the present day it is no longer expedient that the Catholic religion should be held as the only religion of the State, to the exclusion of all other forms of worship.

78   Hence it has been wisely decided by law, in some Catholic countries, that persons coming to reside therein shall enjoy the public exercise of their own peculiar worship.

80   The Roman Pontiff can, and ought to, reconcile himself, and come to terms with progress, liberalism and modern civilization.

This selection of "erroneous statements" conveys a sense of the extent to which Pius IX opposed the changes that had taken place since the time of the Protestant Reformation, and particularly since the French Revolution. Statement 80 sums up the rest, signifying the pope's opposition to progress, liberalism, and modern civilization, a battle he was destined to lose.

List of ecumenical councils

Vatican I was the twentieth ecumenical council recognized by the Roman Catholic Church. Despite the name "ecumenical," Christians outside the Roman Catholic Church do not accept any of the most recent councils as authoritative. A complete list of Ecumenical Councils, together with an indication of which Churches accept these Councils, follows. In this context, "Accepted by all" indicates the acceptance of all those Christians who accept *any* council as ecumenical.

1   First Council of Nicaea (325): accepted by all; condemned Arius; said the Son was of the same substance (*homoousios*) as the Father; produced the Nicene Creed.

2   First Council of Constantinople (381): accepted by all; clarified and expanded Nicene Creed; proclaimed the divinity of the Holy Spirit, condemned Apollinaris.

3   Council of Ephesus (431): accepted by all except Nestorians (i.e. the Assyrian Church of the East); condemned Nestorius; called Mary the "God-bearer" (*theotokos*).

4   Council of Chalcedon (451): accepted by all except Nestorians and Monophysites (i.e. the Oriental Orthodox Churches); condemned Eutyches and monophysitism (one nature in Christ); proclaimed two natures, divine and human, in Christ, "without confusion, without mutability, without division, without separation."

5   Second Council of Constantinople (553): accepted by Catholics, Orthodox, and some Protestants; condemned the "Three Chapters" (Theodore of Mopsuestia, Theodoret of Cyrrhus, Ibas of Edessa).

6   Third Council of Constantinople (680–681): accepted by Catholics, Orthodox, and some Protestants; condemned Pope Honorius I and monotheletism (one will in Christ).

7   Second Council of Nicaea (787): accepted by Catholics, Orthodox, and some Protestants; condemned iconoclasts; promoted veneration, but not worship, of icons.

8   Fourth Council of Constantinople (869–870): Accepted by Catholics; deposed Patriarch Photius of Constantinople.

9   First Lateran Council (1123): accepted by Catholics; confirmed the Concordat of Worms, which specified that only the Church could appoint bishops and invest them with spiritual authority.

10   Second Lateran Council (1139): accepted by Catholics; compelled clerical celibacy.

11   Third Lateran Council (1179): accepted by Catholics; clarified that only cardinals were eligible to vote for pope, who required a two-thirds vote for election; set thirty as the minimum age for bishops.

12   Fourth Lateran Council (1215): accepted by Catholics; declared doctrine of transubstantiation; condemned various people as heretics; proclaimed the primacy of the pope over other patriarchs of ancient sees; demanded confession and communion at least once per year; put restrictions on Jews and Muslims.

13   First Council of Lyons (1245): accepted by Catholics; excommunicated and deposed Emperor Frederick II of the Holy Roman Empire.

14   Second Council of Lyons (1274): accepted by Catholics; attempted to end Great Schism; declared that when a vacancy in the papacy occurred, cardinals who assembled to vote

could not leave until they decided on a new pope (thus the word "conclave," which means they were locked in with a key); clarified that there were seven sacraments.

15 Council of Vienne (1311–1312): accepted by Catholics; suppressed the Knights Templar.

16 Council of Constance (1414–1418): accepted by Catholics; ended Great Western Schism; condemned Jan Hus.

17 Council of Florence (1431–1445): accepted by Catholics; attempted to end Great Schism.

18 Fifth Lateran Council (1512–1517): accepted by Catholics; condemned Council of Pisa as schismatic.

19 Council of Trent (1545–1563): accepted by Catholics; condemned Protestants; proclaimed authority of both scripture and tradition; defined the extent of the canon, including the apocryphal/deutercanonical books in the Old Testament; took measures to reform the Roman Catholic Church.

20 First Vatican Council (1870): accepted by Catholics; proclaimed papal infallibility.

21 Second Vatican Council (1962–1965): accepted by Catholics; allowed use of vernacular languages in worship; accepted non-Catholics as Christians; showed respect for other religions; declared support for religious liberty.

Some Eastern Orthodox churches substitute different councils for numbers 9 and 10 on this list, namely the Fourth Council of Constantinople (879–880), which restored Patriarch Photius to his see and condemned changes to the Niceno-Constantinopolitan Creed (i.e. the *filioque* clause); and the Fifth Council of Constantinople (1341–1351), which affirmed the hesychastic tradition of prayer practiced by many in the East, and described in the *Philokalia.*

the city of Rome surrendered to the army of King Victor Emmanuel of Italy, removing forever the power of the pope in matters of state.

Pius IX's successor was Pope Leo XIII, who also reigned as pope for more than two decades. Although he continued to deny the right of the unified Italian state to exist, since Italy had annexed the Papal States, he made peace with both the newly unified German Republic and the French Third Republic. In so doing, he recognized the inevitable march of history away from dynastic monarchies and toward democratic states, and he also sought to counteract some of the anticlerical measures taken in those countries. Leo's greatest legacy was his involvement in the thorny problem of labor relations. Although he rejected Marxist teachings regarding the inevitability of class struggle, the scandal of private property, and of course the rejection of God, he acknowledged the Marxist critique of capitalism, which often concentrated wealth in the hands of a few, while the workers who produced the wealth were very poorly rewarded for their work. Leo advocated the creation of Catholic labor unions, recognizing the value of organizing and collective bargaining, while at the same time worrying about labor unions that had no religious underpinnings. His papal bull *Rerum novarum* sometimes offered somewhat simplistic solutions, such as encouraging the rich to care for the poor and urging the poor not to hate the rich, but it nevertheless showed a commitment of the modern papacy to deal with matters of social concern, even when they do not directly treat issues with which popes had traditionally concerned themselves. Leo also issued the bull called *Providentissimus Deus*, which cautiously admitted the value of the critical study of the Bible, as well as of historical and theological issues, studies that had been going on in Protestant circles for decades.

Pope Pius X, who ruled the Catholic Church from the death of Leo XIII until the beginning of World War I, returned to the more conservative policies of his namesake, Pius IX. He opposed the critical study of the Bible and of modernism in general. His efforts caused many scholars to leave the church, along with some laypeople. Furthermore, his extreme conservatism strengthened the rift between Catholicism and Protestantism, a rift that had begun to be bridged during the previous pontificate. The Catholic Church, then, entered the modern era as an extremely conservative institution on the surface, but all the papal bulls and encyclicals in the world could not keep modern trends from influencing Catholics, whether in the pew, the pulpit, or the university study.

Global missions

While the nineteenth century saw the expansion of Roman Catholic missions under the leadership of popes like Gregory XVI, it was the Protestants who made the nineteenth century the age of missionary expansion that gave birth to the Modern Missions Movement. Mission activities, however, were preceded – and sometimes accompanied – by neocolonialism. The Napoleonic Wars proved the naval superiority of the British, for though they were held in check in Europe by Napoleon's army, the British navy ruled the seas all over the world. So powerful was their navy, in fact, that by the end of the war in 1815, the British controlled several former French and Dutch territories. European nations began scrambling around the world to look for new markets for their goods and new sources of raw materials for their industries. The United States similarly sought to expand its sphere of economic influence, beginning in the Caribbean and Latin America and eventually expanding to the islands of the Pacific Ocean. Neocolonialism manifested itself in two different ways: outright conquest and political rule over foreign lands, and enforced economic influence. Africa was largely divided among Great Britain, France, Germany, Belgium, Portugal, Italy, and the Netherlands in an effort to control the vast mineral wealth of the continent. In Asia, some areas were ruled directly, like India, and others were merely subjected to economic oversight, as in China and Japan. The colonial powers often had the cooperation of wealthy landowners in the countries they dealt with. For example, the creoles of Latin America saw an opportunity to increase their holdings by dealing with American and European trading partners, so they opened the doors to economic exploitation of their fellow citizens.

Some Christians in Europe and America protested the treatment of native peoples in the new colonies, but others pointed to the benefits that the industrialized West was bringing to the poor, "backward" people of the southern and eastern lands, including mechanization, medicine, agricultural improvements, and western law. Another benefit that the West offered was Christianity. Many in the West believed it was the "white man's burden" to bring civilization to the rest of the world, even though civilized societies had existed in some of those regions long before the advent of modern cities in many parts of Europe. Not surprisingly, many of the people who were offered the "benefits" of Western civilization were less than grateful, and a powerful backlash against neocolonialism erupted in the middle of the twentieth century.

In 1792, William Carey, the father of modern missions, founded the Particular Baptist Society for Propagating the Gospel among the Heathen, which supported his missionary efforts in India. Soon other Protestant groups – such as the Methodists, Presbyterians, Congregationalists, and Anglicans – were sending out missionaries as well. The British and Foreign Bible Society, founded in 1804, saw as its mission the translation of the Bible into foreign languages and the publication and distribution of those Bibles. Missionary societies sprang up all over Europe and North America, and eventually thousands of missionaries were sent out, primarily in places where Western neocolonialism was also occurring. Because neither countries nor denominations played a major role in raising funds for the missions enterprise, at least at first, the missionary societies were supported primarily by interested individuals and churches. Women were particularly important in raising both money and awareness. At first most missionaries were men, but by the middle of nineteenth century numerous women were on the mission field as well, some working alongside their husbands, but others working on their own as nurses, teachers, and even preachers, something very uncommon in their home countries. The leadership roles that women filled on the mission field often led to the demand that they be allowed to exercise the same authority at home in their own churches, and thus the missions movement was one of the bases for the expansion of the role of women within many Protestant denominations.

The first mission field in Asia to see a large number of Western missionaries was the Indian subcontinent: modern India, Pakistan, Bangladesh, and Sri Lanka. William Carey, a Baptist teacher and cobbler, became convinced that Christians needed to take the gospel to the lands of the East that had recently come to the attention of the West through the travels of Captain Cook and others. After arriving in India in 1793, he worked tirelessly for years, learning several native languages, winning converts, establishing churches, and translating the Bible into 35 different languages. His successes inspired other Christians to come join him, and by the time of Carey's death in 1834, the Protestant church in India was firmly established. In addition to preaching the gospel, many missionaries in India sought to enact social changes. Carey himself worked to abolish the practice of widows being burned to death on their husbands' funeral pyres. Other missionaries proclaimed the injustice of the caste system, which kept the vast majority of poor Indians in a state of abject poverty from generation to generation. Opposition to the caste system in particular led to the conversion of masses of the poor, and when India gained its independence from Great Britain in 1947, many of its new leaders were either Christians or had been strongly influenced by Christianity. Mahatma Gandhi, the father of modern India, fell into this latter category.

Both Catholic and Protestant missionaries worked in Southeast Asia. In French Indochina, Catholic missionaries won converts and organized entire villages of Catholics, alongside more traditional Buddhist villages. In Burma, controlled by the British, Protestant missionaries such as Adoniram Judson translated the Bible into Burmese, Thai, and other languages. As a result of their efforts, many in the Karen tribe converted to Christianity. In Siam, which retained its independence, both Catholics and Protestants worked.

Christianity first reached China during the Middle Ages in the form of Nestorian missionaries who traveled from Central Asia with the gospel. However, this original form of Christianity had almost entirely vanished when Catholic (Jesuit) and Protestant missionaries began arriving in the early nineteenth century. After several years with few results, Scottish missionary Robert Morrison succeeded in translating the Bible into Chinese, and converts began to multiply slowly. Missionary efforts in China were complicated by the military and political struggles between the Chinese government and Western powers, especially Britain. The Opium War (1839–1842) and the Boxer Rebellion (1899–1901) were expressions of opposition to Western influence in China and resulted in thousands of deaths. Nevertheless, Christianity continued to spread, under the influence of missionaries such as Lottie Moon and the organizational efforts of people like Hudson Taylor.

The Christian church which had been planted in Japan by the Jesuit missionary Francis Xavier in the sixteenth century had been furiously suppressed for about 300 years, yet when Western missionaries were again allowed in the country following a showing of Western military might in the middle of the nineteenth century, about 100,000 Christians had survived in and around the city of Nagasaki. The Japanese government adopted Western weapons and attitudes regarding expansion, and soon they were knocking on the doors of Korea and China, demanding access to their natural resources. Japan's intervention in Korea also opened the door for missionary expansion into Korea, and within a few decades Korea had the highest percentage of Christians in their country of any country in Asia, with the exception of the Philippines.

The British colonization of Australia and New Zealand resulted in an extermination of the native population in proportions similar to the devastation of Native Americans in the United States. Military conquest and disease decimated the population of Aborigines in Australia and the Maori in New Zealand. The church accompanied European settlers in those lands, and soon both Australia and New Zealand were predominantly Christian. By the end of the century, only a few remote islands and the interior of New Guinea had not yet heard the gospel of Jesus Christ.

By the end of the nineteenth century, it was evident that the Ottoman Empire, which controlled much of the Middle East and North Africa, was fading in influence, and European powers began stripping away parts of the empire, beginning in North Africa. Western missionaries soon began working in the area, sometimes attempting to draw the ancient Christian communions into their fold (the Catholic approach) and at other times trying to work alongside Eastern Christians (the Protestant approach).

Missionaries also sought to convert Muslims, without great success, although they did win some converts in Egypt, Syria, and Lebanon.

David Livingstone, a British missionary and government representative, began exploring sub-Saharan Africa in the middle of the nineteenth century, reporting on the natural beauty of the region as well as the devastation caused by the slave trade. After diamonds were discovered in South Africa in 1867, European powers rushed into Africa and began dividing up the land. At the beginning of World War I, only Ethiopia and Liberia remained independent countries, with the rest of the continent divided among Britain, France, Germany, Portugal, Spain, Italy, and Belgium. Missionaries followed the neocolonial governments, with Catholic missionaries predominating in regions controlled by Catholic countries and Protestant missionaries in regions controlled by Protestant countries.

The Roman Catholic Church was firmly entrenched in Latin America and in much of the Caribbean, but following the independence movements in the early nineteenth century, the newly independent nations began inviting immigrants from Europe, the United States, and elsewhere to live in their countries and bring their talents and skills. They also brought their religious beliefs, and as a result, Protestant forms of Christianity took root in Latin America and began to spread throughout the century. The spread of Protestantism in Latin America sometimes led to harsh confrontations with the Catholic hierarchy. While many Protestant groups were careful to focus their work among various Indian tribes, others worked for converts among the Catholics, leading each side to charge that the other was not truly Christian. Despite the growth of Protestantism throughout the century, Protestants were still a small minority throughout the region, and many Protestants banded together for comfort and fellowship, overcoming denominational barriers that they had brought with them from their countries of origin.

This spirit of cooperation was beginning to be felt in other parts of the world as well, as Christians of different Protestant denominations began to feel that they had more in common with one another than they had differences. This new mood led to the birth of the Ecumenical Movement, the effort on the part of Christians to form a universal church, with representatives from every part of the globe. William Carey had foreseen the need for cooperation among Christians of different denominations, having proposed an international missions conference in Cape Town, South Africa, in 1810. It was not until 100 years later that his vision was fulfilled. In 1910 the World Missionary Conference first met in Edinburgh. At this meeting, proselytism from one form of Christianity to another was explicitly rejected as a subject for conversation, so delegates who met talked only about the conversion of non-Christians to Christianity. This meeting, though small, paved the way for future meetings of the same nature. Eventually this meeting led to the establishment in 1948 of the World Council of Churches.

Key points you need to know

- The Industrial Revolution of the nineteenth century caused great changes to society, beginning in Europe but spreading first to North America and then elsewhere. The view that history was progressing affected Christian thinking in many ways.
- Many Protestant thinkers were affected by contemporary movements such as romanticism (Schleiermacher) and rationalism (Hegel).
- Other Protestants, such as Kierkegaard, rejected both romanticism and rationalism, opting instead for a focus on individualistic faith. Kierkegaard's emphasis on the actions of the individual gave rise to existentialism.
- Many Protestants adopted a scientific approach to studying both history and the Bible. One result of this emphasis was the so-called quest for the historical Jesus, an attempt to write a scholarly, historically accurate account of Jesus, stripped of the accretions of post-Easter faith.
- Roman Catholic scholars tended to be much more conservative in their approach to the new critical tools, adopting them only slowly. Many were committed to retaining as many of the traditional teachings of the Church as possible.
- Popes from the time of the French Revolution were extremely conservative in outlook, opposing the new democratic governments of Europe and demanding that their temporal rule over the Papal States be respected, refusing to recognize Italian sovereignty over Rome for decades after the unification of Italy.
- Pope Pius IX claimed great spiritual authority for the papacy, and the First Vatican Council proclaimed the infallibility of the pope on doctrinal matters.
- The Modern Missions Movement began with the work of William Carey in India, but it soon became a global movement, spreading Christianity into many parts of Asia and Africa. Both Protestants and Catholics sent out missionaries.
- Protestant missionaries who represented many different denominations in their home countries realized once they met on the mission field that their common faith was more important that their theological differences, and they began cooperating with one another in unprecedented ways. This spirit of cooperation laid the groundwork for the modern ecumenical movement.

Discussion questions

1. How do you evaluate the ideas that Christianity should be based on a sense of absolute dependence (Schleiermacher), reason (Hegel), or faith (Kierkegaard)?
2. Why was the Roman Catholic Church so resistant to doctrinal and political change during the period from the French Revolution to World War I? Why did the popes see changes from monarchies to representative democracies as a threat?
3. Why has papal infallibility been used so sparingly (i.e. only once) since it was declared an official Catholic doctrine in the nineteenth century?

4. How did neocolonialism affect the modern missions movement? Would the spread of Christianity have been as dramatic in the nineteenth century apart from neocolonial activities on the parts of European and American governments?

Further reading

González, Justo 1984–1985. *The Story of Christianity*. 2 vols. New York: HarperSanFrancisco.

González, Justo 1987. *A History of Christian Thought*. Revised edn, 3 vols. Nashville, TN: Abingdon.

Kierkegaard, Søren 1954. *Fear and Trembling and Sickness unto Death*. Translated by Walter Lowrie. Princeton, NJ: Princeton University Press.

Latourette, Kenneth Scott 1975. *A History of Christianity*. Revised edn, 2 vols. New York: Harper & Row.

Papal Encyclicals Online. http://www.papalencyclicals.net.

Pelikan, Jaroslav 1971–1989. *The Christian Tradition: A History of the Development of Doctrine*. 5 vols. Chicago, IL: University of Chicago Press.

Roberts, J. M. 1993. *History of the World*. New York: Oxford University Press.

Schleiermacher, Friedrich 1958. *On Religion: Speeches to Its Cultured Despisers*. Translated by John Oman. New York: Harper & Row.

Schweitzer, Albert 1968. *The Quest of the Historical Jesus*. Translated by W. Montgomery, with an Introduction by James M. Robinson. New York: Macmillan.

Tillich, Paul 1968. *A History of Christian Thought*. Edited by Carl E. Braaten. New York: Simon and Schuster.

15 The Church and the modern world

The joys and the hopes, the griefs and the anxieties of the men of this age, especially those who are poor or in any way afflicted, these are the joys and hopes, the griefs and anxieties of the followers of Christ. Indeed, nothing genuinely human fails to raise an echo in their hearts. For theirs is a community composed of men. United in Christ, they are led by the Holy Spirit in their journey to the Kingdom of their Father and they have welcomed the news of salvation which is meant for every man. That is why this community realizes that it is truly linked with mankind and its history by the deepest of bonds.

(Vatican II Document: *On the Church in the Modern World*)

In this chapter

The twentieth century began with a great World War, a harbinger of the globalization that increasingly affects the modern world. The spirit of unbridled optimism that characterized many thinkers in the early twentieth century was derailed by World War I and completely crushed by World War II. The failure of Christianity to prevent the wars caused great angst among many Christians, causing them to rethink their approach to theology. The dominant movement among Protestants in the first half of the twentieth century was neo-orthodoxy, but Protestant fundamentalism flourished as well in many places, especially the United States. Later in the century Christian realism, Christian existentialism, liberation theology, Black theology, feminist theology, and other new approaches arose. Despite World War II, the greatest conflict of the twentieth century was not between representative democracies and fascism but between capitalist democracies and communist autocratic states. The fall of Soviet communism in the late 1980s revealed a vital Eastern Orthodox Church that many in the West had forgotten about or had assumed was moribund. The most profound development in the Roman Catholic Church in centuries came courtesy of the Second Vatican Council, which authorized worship in vernacular languages, acknowledged Protestants as Christian brothers and sisters, and brought the Catholic Church fully into the modern world. The devastation of World War II and the birth of the atomic age gave new impetus to

Christian emphases on both peace and justice, on the one hand, and the ecumenical movement, on the other. Christians played active roles in combating racial and sexual discrimination, opposing wars, and standing for workers' rights.

Main topics covered

- Globalization and its effect on war, economy, technology, and Christianity
- Eastern Christianity
- Roman Catholicism
- Neo-orthodoxy, Christian realism, and Christian existentialism
- The Rise of Protestant fundamentalism
- World War II and its aftermath
- The ecumenical movement

Globalization: war, economy, technology, Christianity

> I have a dream that one day every valley shall be exalted, every hill and mountain shall be made low, the rough places will be made plain, and the crooked places will be made straight, and the glory of the Lord shall be revealed, and all flesh shall see it together.
>
> (Martin Luther King, Jr.)

The nineteenth century and early twentieth century in Europe and the United States were characterized by a sense of almost unbridled optimism. The Napoleonic Wars ended in the defeat of a tyrant, and liberal democracies spread throughout Europe. Italy and Germany were united nations for the first time in centuries. The Industrial Revolution brought wealth and prosperity in measures hitherto unseen in human history. The United States survived a bloody civil war and joined the rest of the industrialized world in abolishing slavery. And Christian missions were flourishing throughout the world, particularly in China and other areas of Asia. The growth in prosperity, the extended period of relative peace in the Western world, and enthusiastic reporsts from the mission field led many to believe that the millennial kingdom of God was just around the corner. It is true that the optimism and prosperity were concentrated primarily in the wealthiest nations and among the rich and middle class citizens of those nations, but since these people made up the intelligentsia, who wrote the books and newspapers and taught in the universities and seminaries – and who read the books and newspapers and studied in the universities and seminaries – those who were relatively or extremely well off had much about which to be optimistic.

Looking back, historians today can see what many in that era were unable to see: the underlying weakness of many of the assumptions on which such optimism was based. Despite the birth of liberal democracies throughout Europe, longstanding rivalries and deep-seated suspicion and prejudice still underlay the relationships among European countries. The unifications of Italy and of Germany led citizens of these nations to develop strong nationalistic tendencies, tendencies that would eventually feed the fascism of the 1920s and beyond. The Industrial Revolution, which brought wealth to the upper and middle classes, created a new class of urban poor, and the number of poor in the cities grew dramatically throughout the period. The abolition of slavery in the United States was followed by a brief period of relative equality for Black Americans, but then the end of Reconstruction signaled the birth of a new period of oppression for the former slaves and their descendants. Finally, while it is true that Christianity reached many new converts throughout the world, many natives of the countries who received Christian missionaries considered Christianity an ally of the neocolonial enterprise that was robbing their countries of their wealth, independence, and culture, and they were right in many respects. Many Western Christians of the period viewed colonialism as a positive development for the unfortunate inhabitants of less developed lands, improving their lives by bringing them the "three C's": Christianity, commerce, and civilization. Thus, all of the trends that leaders in the West saw as positive developments had their darker side as well.

One of the most important aspects of the Industrial Revolution was technological innovation. Technology promised to make life easier, and often it did, but the mechanization of factories also resulted in the need for fewer workers to run the machines, and hence fewer jobs, at least in the short term. The growth of national wealth allowed many countries to develop new and better weapon systems: tanks, dirigibles, airplanes, submarines, battleships, machine guns, hand grenades, land mines, chemical weapons, and vastly more powerful bombs. The concept of "total war," the complete eradication of the enemy's ability to respond militarily, was a new development in the late nineteenth century, and its adoption as the universal philosophy of war by the European powers built the bomb that lay just under the surface of the deceptive peace that covered Europe. The growth of international alliances, both within Europe and among the various colonies (political or economic) of Europe and the United States, which committed nations to come to the aid of other nations if they were attacked, laid the fuse of inevitable conflict among European nations in the early twentieth century. The chaotic situation in the Balkans, recently freed from the control of the Ottoman Empire, lit the match that would set off the bomb. On June 28, 1914, the fuse was lit when a Serbian nationalist assassinated Archduke Franz Ferdinand in Sarajevo. The resulting explosion was World War I, the largest, most deadly war the world had ever seen.

The Great War, or the War to End All Wars, as it was also called, resulted in the deaths of between 8 and 10 million soldiers, plus millions of civilians as well. When it ended in 1918, Europe was devastated, and the victorious Allied Powers imposed harsh strictures on the defeated Central Powers. The Allies saw the destructive results of the war and vowed never to wage such a war again. They formed the League of Nations, an organization whose primary intent was to prevent the recurrence of a major war. Although the European countries joined the League, the United States took an isolationist stance and refused to join, despite the fact that the League of Nations had been to a large extent the brainchild of President Woodrow Wilson. The combination of the refusal of the U.S. to join the League, the harsh penalties exacted from the nations that lost the war, and the worldwide economic depression that started in 1929 led to the failure of the League of Nations and the start of World War II.

A decade of economic prosperity that immediately followed the war was succeeded by a decade of economic difficulty. Nowhere was the economic situation more dire than in Germany. Humiliated by their defeat in the war and the conditions imposed on them as a member of the Central Powers, Germany did not prosper in the 1920s as most of the Western world did. Instead, the country suffered from astronomic rates of inflation, loss of territory to neighboring countries, and the humiliation of not being allowed to redevelop their military. Preaching a gospel of German patriotism, Adolf Hitler was appointed chancellor in 1933, after his Nazi Party became the largest single party in the Reichstag. After consolidating all the political power of Germany in his new role as Führer and Reich Chancellor in 1934, Hitler led a remarkable rebuilding of the German economy, military, and nationalism over the next five years. After incorporating both Czechoslovakia and Austria into an enlarged German Reich (empire) without firing a shot, Hitler's invasion of Poland on September 1, 1939, triggered a response. Since the total war principle and web of international alliances still held in Europe, Great Britain, France, and other countries declared war on Germany, and Italy and Japan, allies of Germany (the Axis Powers), were soon included as well. Germany's most natural ideological enemy was the Soviet Union, a communist state formed in the wake of the overthrow of the czarist system in the 1917 Bolshevik Revolution. However, Hitler and Joseph Stalin, the leaders of Germany and the Soviet Union, respectively, had secretly signed a nonaggression pact, so Hitler was free to encroach upon its neighbors' territory, while Stalin took advantage of the pact to annex the Baltic states. Both leaders knew that conflict was inevitable, and it was Hitler who broke the pact by invading the U.S.S.R. in June 1941. The Japanese attack on Pearl Harbor pulled the U.S. into the war on December 7, 1941, and war engulfed the globe.

The Allied victory over General Rommel in North Africa, the Allied toehold in Italy, and especially the Normandy invasion on June 6, 1944, signaled the beginning of the end for Germany and its allies. Italy fell to the Allies on September 8, 1943, Germany surrendered on May 7, 1945, and Japan surrendered on August 14, 1945, ending the war. More than 60 million people died in the war, including between 6 and 12 million Jews, Roma (gypsies), homosexuals, Jehovah's Witnesses, and others who were killed in the Holocaust. The war ended with two awesome displays of military destruction, the atomic bombs that American planes dropped on Hiroshima and Nagasaki. Having learned valuable lessons from the aftermath of World War I, the Allied victors took a different approach to the defeated Axis countries in the aftermath of World War II. The Marshall Plan used American money to rebuild Europe, including Germany, Italy, and other Axis partners. Germany and its allies were permitted to rebuild their militaries, with the proviso that they be used only for defensive purposes.

The end of the shooting war (or hot war) in 1945 almost immediately led to a Cold War between the Soviet Union and the major Western powers: the U.S., Britain, and France. The Soviets enveloped most of Eastern Europe into their sphere of influence, leading former Prime Minister Winston Churchill to remark in a 1946 speech,

> A shadow has fallen upon the scenes so lately lighted by the Allied victory … From Stettin in the Baltic to Trieste in the Adriatic an iron curtain has descended across the Continent. Behind that line lie all the capitals of the ancient states of Central and Eastern Europe. Warsaw, Berlin, Prague, Vienna, Budapest, Belgrade, Bucharest and Sofia, all these famous cities and the populations around them lie in what I must call the Soviet sphere, and all are subject in one form or another, not only to Soviet influence but to a very high and, in some cases, increasing measure of control from Moscow.

The conflict between the Western-style democracies (First World) and the Communist countries (Second World) dominated international politics for most of the second half of the twentieth century. Soviet development of nuclear weapons in the late 1940s precluded a direct attack on the U.S.S.R. by the U.S., and a fragile peace between the world's two "superpowers" was maintained by a principle aptly abbreviated MAD: mutually assured destruction. Instead of attacking one another directly, the U.S. and the U.S.S.R. fought many battles by proxy, supporting opposing sides in wars in Korea (China was a Russian ally at the time), Vietnam, Angola, Nicaragua, and elsewhere. While the First World and Second World countries were engaged in ideological struggles, nonaligned nations struggled with more mundane issues such as economic development, overpopulation, and poverty. These Third World countries (also called the Two-Thirds World, because of their overall population) saw themselves as allies of neither the democratic capitalists or the communists, though both sides tried to court them.

In the fall of 1989, nations in Eastern Europe one after another declared themselves free of Soviet domination and communist control. The first nation to declare its independence from Soviet influence was Poland, followed quickly by Hungary. Within a matter of weeks Czechoslovakia, Bulgaria, and every other communist state in Eastern Europe declared itself free of Soviet control, almost exclusively in the absence of bloodshed. The lone exception was Romania, where the brutal dictator Nicolae Ceaușescu was overthrown and killed in a coup. On November 9, the Berlin Wall was opened to allow inhabitants of East Berlin to travel freely to West Berlin, and over the next several weeks citizens from both sides of the wall, and in fact from all over the world, painted the wall with graffiti and eventually broke it down with sledge hammers, so that today only short sections of the Wall remain as a historical reminder. In 1991 the Soviet Union itself collapsed, with each "soviet" declaring itself an independent state, the largest and most populous of which was Russia. The same year saw the dissolution of Yugoslavia, when Croatia and Slovenia declared their independence. Several years of war followed in the former Yugoslavia, and eventually Macedonia, Bosnia-Herzegovina, Serbia, and Montenegro became independent states as well. Many other communist regimes across the globe renounced communism in the wake of the collapse of Soviet communism in Europe, with the notable exceptions of China and Cuba. China, however, gradually adopted many principles of capitalism and opened its markets to trade with the rest of the world.

Another major trend that began after World War II was the movement among women and oppressed minorities (and occasionally oppressed majorities) to struggle for their equal treatment in society. After serving with distinction in World War II, many American women and African Americans returned home to a society in which they were treated as inferior to white men. Although women had won the right to vote in the U.S. in 1920 by the adoption of the 19th Amendment to the Constitution, both social custom and the men who largely ran both businesses and government expected women to limit themselves to being housewives, raising children, or filling certain stereotypical women's jobs, such as teachers or nurses. Women's groups like the National Organization of Women rallied women to demand equality in the job market and in the home, and they pushed an Equal Rights Amendment to the Constitution. Although the Amendment failed to be ratified, women did achieve large measures of success, with the result that women were much better represented in executive offices, boardrooms, and government office in the early twenty-first century than at any time in history.

Black Americans returning from the war found themselves discriminated against in housing, education, and even voting, especially in the South. Furthermore, the criminal justice system was anything but just for them, and extrajudicial murders (lynchings) were an all too common occurrence in parts of the Deep South. Sporadic protests occurred for many years, but when Rosa Parks refused to give up her seat and move to the back of the bus on December 1, 1955, the Civil Rights Movement was born. The Montgomery Bus Boycott introduced the spokesman for the new movement, Dr. Martin Luther King, Jr. King and his supporters spoke fervently in favor of desegregation and equal treatment, participated in marches, and even went to jail for their beliefs. King won the Nobel Peace Prize in 1964 for his work, and two pieces of landmark legislation were signed into law by President Johnson: the Civil Rights Act of 1964 and the Voting Rights Act of 1965. Although King was assassinated in 1968, the movement for equal treatment of African Americans and others of minority origin continued. César Chávez, leader of the United Farm Workers, for example, led a movement to reform the treatment of migrant farm workers, the vast majority of whom were Hispanics. Outside the U.S., the white minority government in South Africa fell in 1990, the system of legal discrimination known as apartheid ended, and Nelson Mandela was elected the first black president of South Africa in 1994.

Another trend that flowed from the experiences of World War II was the effective end of political colonialism. In 1950 Ethiopia and Liberia were the only independent countries in Africa, that is, the only countries not governed by European colonial powers. The first African country to achieve independence was Libya in 1951, followed by Egypt

(1953), Sudan, Tunisia, and Morocco (1956), and Ghana (1957). Seventeen African countries became independent in 1960, and by 1980 only four countries remained under the domination of foreign nations – three of them within Africa itself – or ethnic minorities of European ancestry. Namibia gained its independence from South Africa in 1990, Eritrea from Ethiopia in 1993, and in 1994 South Africa renounced minority white rule. Only Western Sahara lacks total independence today. In conjunction with political independence, many African Christians, beginning in the early twentieth century, declared their independence from European and American Christian denominations, forming a large number of independent churches and denominations that are collectively called African Independent Churches.

Scientific advances and technological developments changed life dramatically in the second half of the twentieth century and the beginning of the twenty-first. The decoding of the DNA molecule by Watson and Crick started an avalanche of research on chromosomes and genes, culminating in the publication of the (essentially) complete human genome in 2003. Scientists developed techniques to measure cosmic distances and observe infinitesimal objects, and they came to new understandings of the structure of the atom. Perhaps the most influential technological innovation was the development of the computer. In 1951 Univac, the first commercial computer, went on sale. Initially selling for $159,000, it weighed about 13 metric tons and covered 33 square meters of floor space. The development of the microprocessor in the 1970s brought computers into the home, and the construction of the Internet, beginning in 1969, provided the infrastructure of what would become the Information Superhighway. The Internet became a tool for individual use with the invention of the World Wide Web by Tim Berners-Lee. Although the Web was invented in 1991, it came to the public's attention only in 1993, when the White House went online with its own Web pages. The Web has revolutionized the dissemination of information in much the same way that Gutenberg's printing press did in the 1450s, so that today billions of Web pages, including innumerable personal Web logs, or blogs, exist on the Web.

All of these developments, and more, signal a century of radical change. One common thread unites these disparate movements, the move toward globalization. The two world wars demonstrated the diplomatic and military ties among countries, and the Great Depression proved the interconnectedness of world economies. The global availability of information, first in print form and later electronically via the Web, spurred similar freedom movements around the world. As a result of missionary efforts in the nineteenth century and renewed efforts in the twentieth and twenty-first centuries, Christianity is a global religion as well. Encompassing about one-third of the world population, Christianity is both the largest religion in the world and the most widely distributed, claiming adherents in every country on the globe. Christianity is the majority religion in about 120 countries. The developments in the past century have all affected Christianity, in a variety of ways.

Eastern Christianity

The Eastern Orthodox Church survived and often flourished in the modern period, despite the frequently hostile political context in which it found itself. Although the traditional leadership of the church remained with the Patriarch of Constantinople, now under Ottoman rule, the center of influence and growth shifted to Moscow and the Russian Orthodox Church. When Ivan IV took the title czar (i.e. caesar) for the first time in 1547, he was asserting that Russia was the natural successor to the empires of Rome and Byzantium. Czar Peter the Great (1689–1725) opened the doors of Russia to the West, encouraging his subjects to wear clothes and think thoughts that reflected the fashion of the West. Many in the Russian Orthodox Church did just that, adopting the arguments of Catholics or Protestants in theological discussions. Others, however, thought that Eastern Orthodox traditions were superior to those traditions that some were trying to import from the West, and they strove to develop a form of Orthodoxy that was true to their own traditions but at the same time cognizant of Western developments in philosophy and science.

In addition to the pursuit of philosophical and theological questions based on Western thinkers like Descartes, Hegel, and the romanticists, Orthodox Christians also shared with Western Christians an emphasis on missions. One of the prime examples of Orthodox missions was the Russian Orthodox mission to Alaska. After the Aleutian Islands and the Alaska mainland were mapped by Russian explorers early

Figure 15.1 Ecumenical Patriarch Bartholomew I is the titular head of the Eastern Orthodox Churches, but he exercises no direct authority over Orthodox Christians outside the Ecumenical Patriarchate of Constantinople.

in the eighteenth century, a fur rush began, drawing thousands of Russians to the East in search of fortunes to be made by trapping sea otters. In 1794 a group of ten Orthodox monks, led by Father Joasaph, landed on Kodiak Island and began the work of spreading the gospel among the inhabitants of Alaska. The Orthodox had great success, recording thousands of baptisms and founding many churches, but opposition from both the native Alaskans and the Russian fur traders and their descendants resulted in the martyrdom of many of the monks. The last surviving member of the original party was a monk named Father Herman, who came to be known as St. Herman of Alaska. The Orthodox sent more missionaries to the area and established churches throughout Alaska, especially along the coast and in the Aleutian Islands. When political authority over Alaska shifted to the United States in 1867, most ethnic Russians returned to Russia, but about 12,000 native Orthodox Christians remained behind, comprising nine parishes, and the Orthodox Church in Alaska continued to grow under indigenous leadership. In addition to the Alaska mission, the Orthodox Church also undertook successful missions to Lapland, Finland, Korea, Japan, and China.

Not all Orthodox Christians embraced the Russian Orthodox Church as the natural successor to Constantinople. Orthodox Christians in Greece were unwilling to accept Russian hegemony over their church and asserted their independence. As the Ottoman Empire disintegrated during the late nineteenth and early twentieth centuries, Orthodox communions in Serbia, Bulgaria, and Romania similarly claimed independence from direct oversight of either Constantinople or Moscow. The debate over Russian oversight was brought to a sudden close by the Bolshevik Revolution in 1917. The new communist constitution of Russia decreed separation of church and state, guaranteeing the rights of both religious worship and "anti-religious propaganda." Other Orthodox Christians in Eastern Europe, with the exception of Greece, also found themselves under communist governments that no longer supported their mission, and in some cases actively opposed it. In Russia, all the seminaries were closed from 1925 to 1943, when they were allowed to reopen. Despite decades of opposition to Christianity in the Soviet Union and elsewhere in Eastern Europe, the Orthodox Church survived, largely through emphasis on liturgical worship and personal devotion. Outside the communist world Orthodoxy grew throughout the twentieth century, generally as a result of the Orthodox diaspora in Western Europe, North America, and elsewhere.

When communist regimes in Europe began falling in 1989, the world discovered that Orthodoxy had done more than merely survive communist opposition, it had maintained much of its vitality. In Russia, the Orthodox Church sought to claim preferential treatment among the various religious groups that existed in the country, drawing opposition from Catholics, Protestants, and members of other religions. In most countries, however, the Orthodox Church was content to continue its traditional activities in the light of day, without having to worry about opposition from the government. After some initial skepticism, many Orthodox churches joined the World Council of Churches, an ecumenical umbrella organization whose goal was to foster dialog and reconciliation among the numerous Christian groups around the world.

The Orthodox Church also took some steps to repair the breach between itself and the Roman Catholic Church, which dates to 1054. Ecumenical Patriarch Bartholomew I of Constantinople welcomed visits by Pope Benedict XVI in 2006, the third such papal visit to Constantinople at the invitation of the patriarch (the first two were by Pope Paul VI in 1967 and Pope John Paul II in 1979).

In addition to those churches in the Eastern Orthodox communion, a number of other ancient Eastern churches continue to exist, both in their original geographical settings and in areas of the West. Included in this group are the Assyrian Orthodox Church, the Coptic Orthodox Church, the Ethiopic Orthodox Church, the Armenian Orthodox Church, and the Syrian Monophysite (Jacobite) Church. Opposition between Turkey and Armenian Christians living within the boundaries of the Ottoman Empire led to the massacre of up to a million Armenians around the turn of the twentieth century, the so-called Armenian Holocaust. Turkey's refusal to acknowledge its role in the massacre, despite being prodded to do so by the Turkish 2006 Nobel Literature Prize laureate Orhan Pamuk, has interfered with Turkey's attempts to join the European Union. At the beginning of the twenty-first century, the Web site Adherents.com reported approximately 240 million Eastern Christians in the world, from both the Orthodox and the smaller Eastern communions.

Roman Catholicism

The three popes who served from World War I until the late 1950s were cut from the same conservative mold as their immediate predecessors, yet they also laid the groundwork for the great changes of Vatican II. Pope Benedict XV became pope in the early days of World War I. Like his predecessors, he refused to accept Italy's annexation of the Papal States, despite the papacy's functional loss of control almost fifty years earlier. He was a man committed to peace, and although his efforts to halt the violence of war were unsuccessful, he made more progress in quelling the internecine conflict within the Catholic Church which his immediate predecessor Pius X had launched in his harsh attacks on modernism. Within two months of being installed as pope, he issued an encyclical entitled *Ad beatissimi Apostolorum* (At the Threshold of the Most Blessed Apostles), calling for an end to infighting among Catholics. After the war he strove for reconciliation among formerly warring states, and he supported the formation of the League of Nations. His canonization of Joan of Arc in 1920 was part of an effort to make peace between the papacy and France. His efforts to bring peace with Turkey and the East included his proclamation of St. Ephraem Syrus as a Doctor of the Church, and his work was recognized by the Turks, who erected a statue of him in Istanbul.

Pius XI was pope in the days leading up to World War II, from 1922 to 1939. He spoke out passionately against communism because of its promotion of atheism, but he did not oppose fascism with equal fervor. In fact, he supported Benito Mussolini in the early days of his reign, and it was Pius XI who finally signed an agreement with the Italian government recognizing Italy's legitimate control of the former Papal States, at the same time restoring a modicum of temporal power by establishing Vatican City as a self-governing state within Rome. He appreciated the authoritarian style and conservative leanings of fascism, even though he eventually turned against the excesses of both Italian and German fascism, including its racist policies concerning Jews. He continued to support the Spanish fascism of Francisco Franco. In 1937 he issued encyclicals against both Nazism, which he saw as a form of neo-paganism, and communism. Pius pursued dialog with the Orthodox Church, with no success, and he gave increased support to the Eastern-rite Catholic churches, for example, by issuing an encyclical called *Rerum Orientalium* (Concerning the Eastern Churches), which called for a greater understanding of the Eastern churches. He did not soften the traditional anti-Protestant stance of the Church, however, forbidding Catholics from participating in ecumenical conferences with Protestants. He also condemned the use of artificial birth control as immoral. A scholar and former Vatican librarian, Pius XI promoted the study of the sciences such as archaeology and astronomy.

Some important modern popes

Although popes in the era after the Protestant Reformation did not hold sway over political leaders as they had done during the Middle Ages, they continued to be powerful influences in both the church and the world. After Pope Pius IX lost control of the Papal States, and thus the last vestiges of temporal power, the authority of the pope over spiritual matters only increased, particularly when the doctrine of papal infallibility was declared by the First Vatican Council. Here is a list of some of the most important popes in the period after the Reformation.

Paul III (1534–1549)
Pius IV (1559–1565)
Gregory XIII (1572–1585)
Innocent XI (1611–1689)
Innocent XII (1691–1700)
Benedict XIV (1740–1758)
Pius VII (1800–1823)
Pius IX (1846–1878)
Leo XIII (1878–1903)
Benedict XV (1914–1922)
Pius XI (1922–1939)
Pius XII (1939–1958)
John XXIII (1958–1963)
Paul VI (1963–1978)
John Paul II (1978–2005)

The pope who reigned during World War II was Pius XII, an opponent of Hitler who nevertheless declined to speak out against Nazi atrocities against the Jews, of which the pope was aware, while at the same time condemning vociferously the persecution of Catholics in Poland. Although he condemned Nazism, he was at least as fearful of communism, and after the war he did all he could to halt its spread. In 1950 Pius XII became the only pope to invoke the principle of papal infallibility by proclaiming the doctrine of the Bodily Assumption of Mary, a pronouncement that further complicated his desire for reconciliation with the Eastern church. He was suspicious of theological innovation and suppressed many theologians, including the priest-paleontologist Pierre Teilhard de Chardin, whose works, such as *The Future of Man* and *The Divine Milieu*, were banned from publication until after Teilhard's death in 1955; Karl Rahner, one of the most influential Catholic theologians of the twentieth century; and Yves Congar and Henri de Lubac, both of whom later became cardinals. Ironically, his encyclical *Divino afflante Spiritu* (Inspired by the Divine Spirit) encouraged modern methods of biblical study, methods which Protestants had already been using for almost 100 years. He called for greater participation of the laity in the life of the church, and he supported the participation of non-European, and especially non-Italian, bishops in the church hierarchy. He also supported the formation of regional bodies of bishops such as CELAM (the Conference of Latin American Bishops) to discuss matters of interest to the church in specific geographical areas.

The most influential, and one of the most-loved, popes of the twentieth century was Pope John XXIII. Despite his short reign (1958–1963), his vision for "updating" the church culminated in the most important ecumenical council since the Council of Trent, Vatican II. John opened the Council on October 11, 1962, encouraging the delegates to interact with the modern world rather than condemning it. The Council was unique in including many non-Catholic observers, and the makeup of the Council was quite diverse, with 42 percent of the delegates hailing from Latin America, Asia, and sub-Saharan Africa. Far from affirming traditional Catholic doctrine and practice and condemning its opponents, as Trent had done, Vatican II produced documents that proposed significant changes in the life and teaching of the Church. When John XXIII died in 1963, his successor Pope Paul VI continued the work of the Council, despite his own more conservative tendencies. Some of the innovations of Vatican II include the following:

- The liturgy of the church was revised, and the Latin mass was replaced with mass carried out in local vernacular languages.
- Protestants and other non-Catholic Christians were recognized as genuine Christians.
- The Church recognized that God speaks to and through non-Christian religions.
- Antisemitism, based on the theory that the Jews were responsible for the death of Christ, was condemned.
- Infant baptism was de-emphasized, and the instruction and induction into the Church of new believers was emphasized.

- The Church took a generally positive stance toward many aspects of modernity, including science and technology, economic and social issues, and politics.
- The study of scripture in the original languages, or in translations made from the original languages, was encouraged.
- The role of bishops as colleagues, with the pope as their leader, was promoted.

The Catholic Church that emerged after Vatican II was a much different church from the pre-Vatican II church, and not surprisingly, many traditionalists within the church opposed some or all of the Vatican II innovations. Nevertheless, the official position of the Church is that the reforms instituted in Vatican II are to be observed by all Catholics, and even the more conservative popes who have followed John XXIII have upheld the validity of the Council's decisions.

Pope Paul VI, despite presiding over the majority of the Vatican II Council, was conservative in many ways, as evidenced by his strong stance against all methods of artificial birth control. During Paul's reign, many bishops around the world used their newly found authority to speak out against issues such as the nuclear arms race and the exploitation of the poor. In 1975 Paul released perhaps the most important document of his papacy, apart from the Vatican II documents, an apostolic exhortation entitled *Evangelii nuntiandi* (On Evangelism in the Modern World). He defined the word "evangelism" broadly in a way that emphasized its root meaning of "proclaiming the good news." He proposed three questions, which he said those concerned with evangelism must keep in mind:

- In our day, what has happened to that hidden energy of the Good News, which is able to have a powerful effect on man's conscience?
- To what extent and in what way is that evangelical force capable of really transforming the people of this century?
- What methods should be followed in order that the power of the Gospel may have its effect?

For Pope Paul VI, evangelism included not only the conversion of non-Christians to the Christian faith but also the announcement to all people, Christian or not, that God loves them and cares about every aspect of their lives.

One of the most creative theological movements to emerge from the Roman Catholic Church in modern times was liberation theology, a type of contextual theology in which theologians, whether clerics or laypeople, begin their theological inquiry by analyzing their own social situation. Only after they have come to an understanding of who they are as members of a particular social class do they turn to scripture and theological tradition to try to make sense of God and God's work in the world. Liberation theology arose in Latin America among priests and the poor people with whom they worked. Laypeople and priests came together in Ecclesial Base Communities to discuss their situation of poverty and oppression, then they turned to scripture and tradition for answers. Not only did they seek answers, however; they also sought practical solutions to their problems and took action (praxis) to bring about radical change. Liberation theologians often speak of "orthopraxy," or right practice, as the forerunner to orthodoxy, or right belief. The first book to bring liberation theology to the attention of the general public was Gustavo Gutiérrez's *Teología de la liberación*, first published in 1972, and translated into English as *A Theology of Liberation* in 1973. Over the next 30 years numerous books on liberation theology – at first concentrating on the situation in Latin America and then focusing on the situation in South Africa, Asia, Israel/Palestine, and elsewhere – were published, despite the Catholic Church's, and particularly Pope John Paul II's, deep skepticism about the movement. Liberation theology spread beyond Catholicism and became popular among Protestants, and even Jews, as well. It also influenced, and was influenced by, other contextual theological movements, such as feminist theology and Black theology in the U.S.

After the untimely death of Pope John Paul I, following a one-month reign, Pope John Paul II became the first non-Italian pope in 450 years. The former archbishop of Krakow, Poland, was a strong opponent of communism and supporter of Polish labor movements even before becoming pope. The second-longest reigning pope in history, John Paul was a tireless ambassador for the church, traveling the world more than any other pope had ever done. His conservative beliefs led him to oppose many liberation theologians in Latin America, suspecting them of being overly influenced by Marxist teachings. Nevertheless, he was a strong advocate for the poor throughout the world, and he condemned the excesses of capitalism alongside the atheistic doctrine of communism. His first encyclical, *Redemptor hominis* (Redeemer of Humanity) emphasized the dignity and worth of all people, condemned the wanton destruction of the environment, opposed consumerism, and condemned the arms race. John Paul was critical of the amount of money that both capitalist and communist nations spent preparing for war, which he believed would be better spent alleviating poverty, disease, and other forms of human suffering. He was a vigorous opponent of war, capital punishment, abortion, artificial birth control, and human rights abuses.

John Paul's reign started off on a controversial note. He revoked world-renowned theologian Hans Küng's status as an official church theologian, subjected Dutch theologian Edward Schillebeeckx to severe scrutiny, prohibited Brazilian liberation theologian Leonardo Boff from writing or teaching for a year, forced the expulsion of American Catholic theologian Charles Curran from the theological faculty of the Catholic University of America, and excommunicated Sri Lankan theologian Tissa Balasuriya for his questioning of both excesses in Marian devotion and the issue of the ordination of women. He appointed vast numbers of conservative bishops to vacant sees around the world, so that when he died, of the 117 cardinals eligible to vote for his successor, John Paul II had appointed all but three of them.

Despite his conservative theological stance and his opposition to communism, John Paul II was progressive in regard to the church's relationship with modern science. In an address to the Pontifical Academy of Sciences on October 22, 1996, the pope said,

In order to delineate the field of their own study, the exegete and the theologian must keep informed about the results achieved by the natural sciences ... Today, almost half a century after the publication of the encyclical [*Humani Generis*], new knowledge has led to the recognition of the theory of evolution as more than a hypothesis. It is indeed remarkable that this theory has been progressively accepted by researchers, following a series of discoveries in various fields of knowledge. The convergence, neither sought nor fabricated, of the results of work that was conducted independently is in itself a significant argument in favor of this theory.

This willingness to embrace the theory of evolution led to some controversy within the Catholic Church, although most Catholic leaders who spoke out on the subject supported the pope. One who gave a somewhat less positive response was John Paul's advisor and Prefect of the Congregation for the Doctrine of the Faith, Cardinal Joseph Ratzinger.

Perhaps the worst blight on John Paul II's papacy was the clergy sex scandal, which broke in January 2002. Although sexual impropriety among clergy has a long history among both Protestants and Catholics, the magnitude of this scandal, coupled with both accusations that the Catholic Church tried to cover it up and enormous payments to victims of the scandal, made it worse than earlier scandals in the minds of many. The scandal began in Boston, with accusations that a local priest had molested young boys for years, while the local archdiocese merely reassigned the priest when people in the parish complained. Soon the scandal spread throughout the U.S., as dozens of people came forward to allege that priests had abused them as children. The Vatican harshly condemned the priests involved, but many laypeople involved in support groups for the victims charged that the Vatican had done too little to stop a problem that had been around for decades.

After Pope John Paul II's death on April 2, 2005, the college of cardinals elected Cardinal Joseph Ratzinger pope, and he took the name Pope Benedict XVI. Although he was not as charismatic a figure as John Paul II, he undertook a busy travel schedule almost immediately. He did not shy away from his roots as a scholar, and comments concerning the relationship between Islam and violence led to controversy in 2006, particularly in largely Muslim countries. The pope's subsequent visit to a Turkish mosque and his words of reconciliation mollified some of his harshest critics, but his reputation as an outspoken leader, as well as his well-known conservative bent, have caused many Vatican observers to expect more fireworks during his term in office.

Neo-orthodoxy, Christian realism, and Christian existentialism

When Christ calls a man, he bids him come and die.
(Dietrich Bonhoeffer, *The Cost of Discipleship*)

Whereas the Roman Catholic Church in the early twentieth century reacted to modernism by attempting to stem its tide, many Protestants, particularly in Europe, but also many in North America, were much more welcoming. They developed the theology of Protestant liberalism, which was optimistic about human progress and about what God was doing in the world. Many Protestants saw the world getting ever better as advances in technology solved problems related to poverty, health, and work. Some believed that the promised kingdom of God was just around the corner and would soon be ushered in by Christians committed to spreading "Christian civilization" to the rest of the world.

World War I put a serious damper on the optimism of the previous period. Never before had a war so deadly and involving so many nations been fought. What was more, the war was centered in Europe, the heartland of Protestant Christianity. It became evident to many that classical Protestant liberalism held a naïve and fundamentally unsound view of humanity. Whereas liberalism focused on the good that lay within all people, it did not take sufficiently into account the evil that was also present. In a word, Protestant liberalism ignored the problem of sin. European theologians, and American theologians intimately involved with their European colleagues, sought a different approach to theology.

The most influential movement to grow out of the tremendous disillusion of the Great War was known by many names: crisis theology, dialectical theology, and neo-orthodoxy. The primary exponent of neo-orthodoxy was Karl Barth, a Swiss theologian who taught at universities in Göttingen, Münster, Bonn, and Basel. Barth rejected the philosophical basis of liberal theology and sought to base his theology on the Word of God found in scripture. He did not equate the Bible with the Word of God, but believed that the Bible pointed to the revelation of God, most profoundly expressed in Jesus Christ. In putting a renewed emphasis on the Bible, Barth and other neo-orthodox theologians harkened back to the emphases of Luther and Calvin on hearing the voice of God through the exposition of scripture. They did not, however, elevate the Bible to a position of excessive authority, for they accepted the Bible as a product of inspired human effort, susceptible to illumination through the scholarly use of critical tools developed in the nineteenth and twentieth centuries. The movement is sometimes called crisis theology because, as Emil Brunner says in *A Theology of Crisis*, it calls for a complete change in the very essence of faith, one that rejects rationalists' claim that all knowledge can be gained by reason alone and that rejects the traditional orthodox claim that fails to grasp the true nature of the Bible. "He who would know what constitutes the word of God in the Bible, *must* devote himself to Biblical criticism," Brunner says, for otherwise one might "mistake ancient cosmology and Israelitish chronology for the word of God" (Brunner 1931: 20).

The initial presentation of neo-orthodox thinking was Barth's 1918 commentary *Epistle to the Romans*, a work that he revised thoroughly in 1922 and again more modestly in subsequent years. Barth argues in his commentary that God cannot be allied with any specific human culture, even one that sees itself as based on the teachings of Christ, because God must always stand outside culture as "wholly other." The definitive work on neo-orthodox theology is Barth's *Church Dogmatics*, a 13-part work that Barth worked on from 1932 until his death in 1968. Among other things, Barth argued in *Church Dogmatics* that since Christianity is God's attempt to reach humankind, whereas other religions are humankind's attempt to reach God, Christianity is not really a religion at all.

Soon after the publication of Barth's initial volume of *Church Dogmatics* in 1932, the church in Germany was faced with a crisis for which Protestant liberalism had ill prepared it. Adolf Hitler had risen to power in Germany on a tide of strong nationalism and a feeling of racial and cultural superiority. Many classical liberal theologians went along with Hitler's efforts to unify the German Protestant church as a bastion of German nationalism, but Barth and other theologians influenced by neo-orthodoxy refused to go along. In 1934 many theologians signed the Barmen Declaration, which opposed the movement of "German Christians," an amalgamation of the church with the Nazi party. Those who opposed Hitler and his attempts to control the church comprised the "Confessing Church," and its members were harassed by the German government throughout the period of Nazi rule.

The most famous victim of the assault on the Confessing Church was Dietrich Bonhoeffer, a German pastor and theologian who, while pastoring in London, was invited by the Confessing Church to return to Germany and start a clandestine seminary, after the government had shut down previously existing seminaries. Bonhoeffer agreed, and when his seminary was closed by the Nazis two years later, he continued meeting with theological students informally. During a brief stay in America, Bonhoeffer became convinced that God had called him to stand alongside his German brothers and sisters in opposition to Hitler. He returned to Germany, got involved in a plot to assassinate Hitler, and was arrested in 1943. He was executed in 1945, just days before the Allied liberation of Berlin. Bonhoeffer's books include *The Cost of Discipleship*, an exposition of the Sermon on the Mount, and *Letters and Papers from Prison*, assembled after his death. Although Bonhoeffer agreed with much of Barth's theology, he criticized Barth for putting too much confidence in the human ability to understand God's revelation. He mused about the possibility of a "religionless Christianity," in which traditional ways of thinking about God were no longer important. The senseless death of so many people in World War II, particularly in the Holocaust, profoundly influenced discussions about God in the remainder of the twentieth century,

One American scholar who influenced Bonhoeffer during his brief stay in America was Reinhold Niebuhr, professor of practical theology at Union Theological Seminary in New York. Although strongly influenced by Barth's neo-orthodoxy, Niebuhr saw himself as a realist rather than an idealist, advocating action, even violence, when necessary to stop a tyrant. As the founder of the Christian Realism movement, Niebuhr rejected the pacifism of his youth and supported the war against Hitler. He was also a strong advocate for social justice, and he supported those approaches to the ills of society that he believed were most likely to result in steps forward. His book *Moral Man and Immoral Society* examined the problem of morality as applied to individuals and to nations, and he was the founding editor of the magazine *Christianity and Crisis*, which addressed social issues from a Christian perspective. His work was quite influential in post-War America, including the fledgling civil rights movement led by Martin Luther King, Jr.

Another important theologian in the early and middle twentieth century who was critical of Protestant liberalism was Paul Tillich, a German theologian who moved to the U.S. to teach with Niebuhr at Union Theological Seminary. His theology was based on the philosophical existentialism of Martin Heidegger, and he reevaluated traditional Christian themes such as the kingdom of God and the Trinity from an existentialist perspective. He focused particularly on the question of "ultimate concern" and described God as the "ground of being," rather than "a being" itself, even a divine being.

The rise of Protestant fundamentalism

Many Protestants in the U.S. took an entirely different approach to the issue of modernism, rejecting it and all its trappings. Between 1910 and 1915, a group of American and British Protestants wrote a series of pamphlets entitled *The Fundamentals: A Testimony to the Truth*. The writers railed against biblical criticism, Darwinian evolution, and modern philosophy, and they promoted biblical inerrancy. This series of books gave its name to a movement that was particularly strong in America: fundamentalism. Although the word is often used pejoratively now, in the early twentieth century many conservatives applied it to themselves. For example, in 1919 Minneapolis Baptist pastor William Riley founded the World Christian Fundamentals Association. Fundamentalists opposed modernism as a threat to traditional Christianity, much as Roman Catholics of the same period had done.

Of particular fascination to many outside the debate, both in the U.S. and throughout the world, was the fundamentalist opposition to evolution. By the 1920s, most scientists and educated people in the U.S. and Europe had accepted Darwin's theory of evolution – descent with modification through natural selection – as a proven fact of science, so it was with amusement and disbelief that they watched the so-called Scopes Monkey Trial unfold in Dayton, Tennessee, in 1925. Although teacher John Scopes was found guilty of teaching evolution, contrary to Tennessee law, and fined $100, the verdict was eventually overturned on a technicality. Fundamentalist forces lost the battle of public relations following *Scopes*, but the battle over evolution was not yet over. In the 1960s Henry Morris and others started a new movement called creation science (or creationism), which purported to use science both to refute evolution and to uphold the traditional interpretation of the first chapter of Genesis that the world was less than 10,000 years old. Creationism was opposed by both scientists and many mainstream Christians, but it was quite popular in conservative Protestant circles. In the late 1990s and early 2000s a new anti-evolution approach known as intelligent design supplanted creationism as the leading movement opposed to evolution. Although its proponents generally tried to avoid religious language, a U.S. federal court in Dover, Delaware, expelled it from the public schools in 2006, ruling that it was a form of religion, not science. Few believe that the debate between supporters and opponents of evolution is over.

Some Christian fundamentalists in the South combined conservative theology with racism and anti-Semitism, resulting in the birth or rebirth of white supremacist hate groups such as the Ku Klux Klan. Klan members opposed the "mixing of the races," Jews, the Roman Catholic Church, and communism. Other fundamentalists rejected the extreme racism of the Klan, but their opposition to communism and socialism in all its forms often led them to support the fascist governments in Europe. Most Christian supporters of fascism in the U.S. turned against Germany and Italy after the Japanese bombing of Pearl Harbor in 1941 catapulted the U.S. into World War II, but the fierce anti-communist sentiment arose again in the 1950s, as exemplified in the Senate hearings aimed to root communist sympathizers out of government, led by Senator Joseph McCarthy.

World War II and its aftermath

> We must love one another or die.
> (W. H. Auden, "September 1, 1939")

World War II was profoundly devastating for most Europeans, and it had a strong negative impact on Christianity as well. How could countries whose citizens held themselves up as Christians have engaged in such wholesale destruction? The postwar revelations concerning the Jewish Holocaust added more fuel to the fire. If Christianity could stand idly by while millions of Jews and others were slaughtered, what good was it? In the decades following the war many Europeans turned from the church, convinced that it was increasingly irrelevant at best, or dangerous at worst. Some Christians, however, believed that only a proper understanding of Christianity could save Europe from a third world war. Elton Trueblood, a Quaker theologian, wrote a book in 1946 entitled *Foundations for Reconstruction*. Trueblood examined the Ten Commandments and found in a proper understanding of these ancient laws hope for rebuilding the world. German theologian Jürgen Moltmann argued in his book *Theology of Hope* that God lives in the future and calls Christians to the future, a future in which the struggles of this world, such as poverty and war, have finally been overcome.

While neo-orthodoxy provided answers that many Christians found compelling in the years following the war, other looked for a more radical reform of Christianity. Rudolph Bultmann was originally an advocate of neo-orthodoxy, and a signatory of the Barmen Declaration, but he became convinced that the traditional approach to the Bible and

Figure 15.2 The advent of the nuclear age in 1945 led many Christians to wonder whether humanity's pursuit of science had led it to ignore its obligation to make wise, ethical choices for the future.

theology that Barth offered could not meet the needs of modern Christians. Bultmann, a New Testament scholar, advocated a way of reading the Bible called "demythologizing." The New Testament, Bultmann said, is written in mythological language, and modern Christians will miss the truth of the New Testament if they confuse its call to faith with a call to accept its mythological language as literal.

Other theologians went even further from the neo-orthodox emphasis on the revelation of God through the Bible, questioning not the existence of God, but the existence of the traditional God of theism. John A. T. Robinson, Bishop of Woolwich, wrote a short book in 1963 called *Honest to God*, in which he documented his own questions about the traditional view of God. Three years later Thomas Altizer and William Hamilton issued *Radical Theology and the Death of God*, which documented the growth of theology away from traditional ways of expressing faith in God to more radical forms of God-talk. The "Death of God" school had borrowed a phrase from Nietzsche to express modern society's discontent with the traditional view of God and the structures of society. Episcopal Bishop of Newark Shelby Spong articulated this belief from a faith perspective in his popular book *Why Christianity Must Change or Die*. Yet another approach to understanding God that arose in the mid-twentieth century was process theology, which saw the history of the universe as the result of the decisions of innumerable agents of free will. God was not omnipotent (or chose not to act in an omnipotent, coercive manner), but influenced the development of the universe through divine persuasion. Furthermore, God contains the universe, but is not part of it (a view known as *panentheism*).

By no means did all Protestants accept such nontraditional notions about God or question the continued relevance of the church. Harvey Cox's 1965 book *The Secular*

City is subtitled *A Celebration of Its Liberties and an Invitation to Its Discipline*. Cox, following an approach influenced by neo-orthodoxy, says that Christianity cannot stop the increasing secularization of the modern world, but neither should it try. Instead, it should embrace the changes that arise and use the genius of Christianity to transform society. In the late twentieth and early twenty-first centuries, increasing secularization in society combined with a movement called postmodernism, which questioned the rationality of the Enlightenment and the entire modern period, as well as the validity of authoritative systems of meaning and value. Some, particularly in Europe, referred to this period as the post-Christian era, because of the decreasing influence of the church on public life, but Christians around the world continued to struggle to find ways to make Christianity relevant to a changing world.

Both mainline Protestants and Catholics in the postwar era continued to investigate the Bible and the history of the church using critical tools developed, to some extent, in other fields of study. Remarkable archaeological finds, such as the Oxyrhynchus Papyri and the Dead Sea Scrolls, added new data for scholars to study. Biblical textual critics took the new information and created new texts of the Bible in Hebrew and Greek for scholars to translate into modern languages. The Revised Standard Version, published in 1952, was the first English translation since the King James Version of 1611 to achieve widespread acceptance by the general public, and by the end of the century, dozens of new translations of the Bible into English were in print. One of the most visible attempts to use modern critical tools of scholarship to investigate the Bible was associated with a group known as the Jesus Seminar. This group of scholars investigated the question of how much of the material in the gospels was historically accurate, famously "voting" on whether Jesus said this or that statement attributed to him. Not surprisingly, both the results of the Jesus Seminar's work and its method of reaching conclusions generated much controversy among Christians, and the Seminar had both strident opponents and ardent supporters.

Evangelicalism and Pentecostalism grew rapidly in the years following World War II. These movements, while differing in some important respects, such as the role of women in ministry and speaking in tongues, shared a similar approach to modernism: cautious acceptance of certain aspects of it; outright rejection of other aspects. Revivalism was key to the growth of both movements, beginning in the 1950s with mass rallies by people like Billy Graham (Evangelical) and Oral Roberts (Pentecostal), and continuing in the 1960s and beyond with an active presence on radio and television (e.g. Jim and Tammy Faye Bakker and Pat Robertson). Both groups decried the increasing secularization of society, including the removal of teacher-led prayer and Bible courses from the public schools in the U.S. After some initial resistance, particularly on the part of southern Evangelicals, to racial integration, both groups sought closer ties with African American Christians, and eventually with Christians from other ethnic backgrounds as well. The formation of the Moral Majority in 1979 gave Evangelicals and Pentecostals political clout in the U.S., and though the organization was dissolved in 1989, other organizations such as the Christian Coalition continued to offer considerable political support to social conservatives opposed to abortion, homosexuality, embryonic stem cell research, and other issues against which Evangelicals and Pentecostals – frequently joined by many Catholics – spoke out.

While most Evangelicals and Pentecostals in the U.S. identified themselves with the American political right in the late twentieth and early twenty-first centuries, others argued for a more balanced approach to social issues. Ron Sider, who wrote *Rich Christians in an Age of Hunger*, formed a group called Evangelicals for Social Action in 1973. Other Evangelicals such as Anthony Campolo and Jim Wallis warned Evangelicals to beware of excessive entanglements with one political movement in American politics, and they called all Christians to take seriously the biblical call for justice. In 2006 Joel Hunter was tapped to become the new president of the Christian Coalition, but his stated intention to move the organization in the direction of becoming involved with social justice and environmental issues – in addition to its traditional opposition to abortion and homosexuality – led to his resignation before his term in office began.

The American Civil Rights movement, which began with the Montgomery bus boycott in 1955, was strongly influenced by a traditional form of Protestant Christianity. Martin Luther King, Jr., received his seminary training at Boston University, and he was influenced by the neo-orthodox emphasis on the power of scripture in preaching, as well as by his own roots in African American culture, and by the passive resistance approach advocated by Gandhi. Many in the movement, including Ralph David Abernathy, John Lewis, and Jesse Jackson, were Protestant pastors and theologians whose reading of scripture moved them to call for social justice. James Cone, professor of systematic theology at Union Theological Seminary, influenced by King and others in the Civil Rights Movement, wrote *Black Theology and Black Power* in 1969 and *A Black Theology of Liberation* in 1970. These books drew on the civil rights movement and movements such as liberation theology in Latin America, as well as on theologians such as Barth and Tillich, to urge Black Americans to unite in opposition to institutionalized oppression.

Like liberation theology and black theology, another example of contextual theology that arose in the mid to late twentieth century was feminist theology. Women had made great strides in society over the previous century, winning the right to vote in democracies around the world between 1860 and 1930; the United States passed the Nineteenth Amendment to the Constitution in 1920, guaranteeing women the right to vote. Along with the right to vote, women could now stand for election to public office, and many began to do so, and win. After a few decades there were women heads of government, such as Golda Meir in Israel, Margaret Thatcher in the U.K., and Indira Gandhi in India. Despite their gains in the secular world, however, women were still largely shut out of leadership positions in many churches. One important exception was the Pentecostal movement, which allowed women to serve in a variety of leadership roles, including senior pastors, from the beginning of the movement in 1906. As the twentieth century wore on, more Protestant denominations welcomed women into ministry, so that by the early twenty-first century, most mainline Protestant denominations, most Pentecostal denominations, and many Evangelical denominations allowed women to serve in many or all leadership positions. Women were still denied access to the priesthood in Orthodox and Catholic churches, however. Feminist theology (sometimes called womanist theology by African American women) was responsible in part for the growing prominence of women in the modern church, but its proponents focused on many other issues as well, including the exploitation of women by men, interpreting scripture with an awareness of its patriarchal background, and feminine images of God.

The ecumenical movement

One of the most momentous changes to the church in the middle and late twentieth century was the emergence of the ecumenical movement. After centuries of fighting with both weapons and words, Protestant Christians in the early twentieth century decided to try dialog instead. The World Missionary Conference of 1910 was the first large, international meeting of Protestant Christians who sought ways of working together to spread the gospel. Subsequent meetings increased Protestant awareness of other groups within the Protestant fold, as well as their willingness to work with one another, despite theological differences.

Other groups of Protestants met to discuss Faith and Order, on the one hand, and Life and Work, on the other. After several conferences, these two groups formed the World Council of Churches in 1948. Speakers at the inaugural meeting included Karl Barth, Reinhold Niebuhr, and Martin Niemöller, a Berlin pastor who was imprisoned by

Figure 15.3 The World Council of Churches offers Christians from a variety of backgrounds the opportunity to converse, study, worship, and work together.

Hitler for his opposition to the Nazis. In 1961 the World Missionary Conference joined the WCC. The stated goal of the World Council of Churches is Christian unity, and the total church membership of the WCC exceeds half a billion Christians, including most Orthodox communions. The Roman Catholic Church has declined to join the WCC, but it holds regular dialogs with the Council and sends observers to its meetings. Altogether, the number of Christians that belong to either member denominations of the WCC or denominations that regularly dialog with the WCC exceeds 1.6 billion, leaving less than half a billion Christians uninvolved in the worldwide ecumenical movement. National and regional councils of churches have also been created in many countries since the early twentieth century. After centuries of fighting among themselves, many Christians in the twenty-first century have found that the faith they share is more important than the individual beliefs and practices that divide them.

Key points you need to know

- Wide-ranging international military alliances, an increasingly intertwined global economy, and the unprecedented growth in technology which began in the late nineteenth and early twentieth centuries set the stage for modern globalization. Christianity reacted to these changes in a variety of ways, including embracing the modern world, rejecting modernity in its entirety, and participating in the world while at the same time critiquing in.

- In response to developments in the modern world, many new movements within Christianity arose in the twentieth century, including fundamentalism, Evangelicalism, Pentecostalism, Neo-orthodoxy, liberation theology, feminist theology, and Black theology.

- Although concentrated in lands controlled by either Muslims or communists throughout much of the twentieth century, the Eastern Orthodox Church survived, and even thrived, emerging from the fall of the Iron Curtain as a vital community of faith.

- After centuries of political and theological conservatism, the Roman Catholic Church saw sweeping changes take place as a result of the Second Vatican Council. As a result of the Council, Catholics worshiped in their vernacular languages; engaged in fellowship with Orthodox and Protestant Christians; dialogued respectfully with Jews, Muslims, and people from other faith traditions; and fully engaged the modern world.

- Neo-orthodoxy, Christian realism, and Christian existentialism were three Christian reactions to the changes in the modern world that took seriously scientific and technological advances, while at the same time facing the challenges of the Church in a world characterized by the threat of annihilation.

- Protestant fundamentalism rejected both many of the claims of modern science and the approaches to Christianity that took those claims seriously.

- After World War II, some Christians advocated radical new approaches to theology, such as the "Death of God" school, while others sought to reinvigorate traditional theology to make it relevant for the modern age.
- Many Christians spoke out strongly in favor of social justice around the world, from the American Civil Rights Movement, to criticism of the South African apartheid regime, to advocating equal rights for women.
- A desire for Christian unity led many denominations to launch the ecumenical movement, which culminated in the creation of the World Council of Churches. Counting both member Churches and the Roman Catholic Church, which regularly engages in dialog with the World Council of Churches, about three-fourths of the world's two billion Christians are part of the ecumenical movement.

Discussion questions

1. On what was the pervasive optimism of the late nineteenth and early twentieth centuries based?
2. Why was the optimists' analysis of the world so mistaken, or was it?
3. How has technology changed the way people "do church"? What are the larger implications of the pervasiveness of technology for the future of the church?
4. How has Vatican II affected the way in which Catholics view the Bible, other Christians, and people of other faiths? How has it affected the way in which other people view Catholics?
5. What was the rationale behind Barth's contention that Christianity is not really a religion? What does Bonhoeffer mean by "religionless Christianity"?
6. Why did so many nontraditional approaches to theology arise in the twentieth century? In what ways is Protestant fundamentalism a reaction to the modern world?
7. What are the pros and the cons of the ecumenical movement? What are the advantages of having diverse groups of Christians involved in ongoing conversation with one another?

Further reading

Adherents.com. http://www.adherents.com.

Altizer, Thomas J. J. and William Hamilton 1966. *Radical Theology and the Death of God*. Indianapolis, IN: Bobbs-Merrill.

Barth, Karl 1968. *The Epistle to the Romans*. Translated from the sixth German edition by Edwyn C. Hoskyns. London: Oxford University Press.

Bonhoeffer, Dietrich 1959. *The Cost of Discipleship*. 2nd edn. New York: Collier.

Bonhoeffer, Dietrich 1967. *Letters and Papers from Prison*. Revised edn. Edited by Eberhard Bethge. Translated by Reginald Fuller. New York: Macmillan.

Brunner, H. Emil 1931. *A Theology of Crisis*. New York: Scribner.

Cone, James 1969. *Black Theology and Black Power*. New York: Seabury.

Cone, James 1970. *A Black Theology of Liberation*. Philadelphia, PA: Lippincott.

Cox, Harvey 1965. *The Secular City*. New York: Macmillan.

FitzGerald, Thomas E. 2004. *The Ecumenical Movement: An Introductory History*. Westport, CT: Praeger.

Flannery, Austin, ed. 1996. *Vatican Council II*. Vol. 1: *The Conciliar and Post Conciliar Documents*. New revised edn. Northport, NY: Costello.

González, Justo 1984–1985. *The Story of Christianity*. 2 vols. New York: HarperSanFrancisco.

González, Justo 1987. *A History of Christian Thought*. Revised edn, 3 vols. Nashville: Abingdon.

Gutiérrez, Gustavo 1973. *A Theology of Liberation*. Translated and edited by Caridad Inda and John Eagleson. Maryknoll, NY: Orbis.

Latourette, Kenneth Scott 1975. *A History of Christianity*. Revised edn, 2 vols. New York: Harper & Row.

Lewis, John and Michael D'Orso 1998. *Walking with the Wind: A Memoir of the Movement*. San Diego, CA: Harcourt Brace & Company.

Moltmann, Jürgen 1967. *Theology of Hope*. London: SCM.

Niebuhr, H. Richard 1951. *Christ and Culture*. New York: Harper & Row.

Niebuhr, Reinhold 1932. *Moral Man and Immoral Society*. New York: Scribner.

Oleksa, Michael 1992. *Orthodox Alaska: A Theology of Mission*. Crestwood, NY: St. Vladimir's Seminary Press.

Papal Encyclicals Online. http://www.papalencyclicals.net.

Pelikan, Jaroslav 1971–1989. *The Christian Tradition: A History of the Development of Doctrine*. 5 vols. Chicago, IL: University of Chicago Press.

Roberts, J. M. 1993. *History of the World*. New York: Oxford University Press.

Robinson, John A. T. 1963. *Honest to God*. Philadelphia, IL: Westminster.

Sider, Ronald J. 1977. *Rich Christians in an Age of Hunger*. Downer's Grove, IL: Inter-Varsity Press.

Spong, John Shelby 1998. *Why Christianity Must Change or Die*. New York: HarperSanFrancisco.

The Fundamentals: A Testimony 1910. 12 vols. Chicago, IL: Testimony Publishing Co.

Tillich, Paul, 1951–1963. *Systematic Theology*. 3 vols. Chicago, IL: University of Chicago Press.

Tillich, Paul 1952. *The Courage to Be*. New Haven, CT: Yale University Press.

Tillich, Paul 1968. *A History of Christian Thought*. Edited by Carl E. Braaten. New York: Simon and Schuster.

Trueblood, Elton 1946. *Foundations for Reconstruction*. New York: Harper & Brothers.

Part III

The varieties of Christianity

16 *A denominational/ traditional perspective*

Over 9,000 Christian Denominations are represented in the World Christian Database.

(World Christian Database)

In this chapter

Christianity has grown from a handful of followers of Jesus to 2 billion adherents. Along the way, disagreements over matters of doctrine and practice – as well as the boundaries of nationality, ethnicity, and language – have led to the formation of thousands of distinct denominations. Nevertheless, Christians can be grouped into large faith traditions, most containing many different denominations, which share a common heritage, system of beliefs, and organizational structure. This chapter divides Christians into six large faith traditions and examines their similarities and differences.

Main topics covered

- Varieties of church polity
- Catholic Churches
- Eastern and Oriental Orthodox Churches
- Anglican and Episcopal Churches
- Churches of the Magisterial Reform
- Free Churches
- Pentecostal and Neocharismatic Churches
- Another way to look at denominations

From the very earliest days of the church, Christians have held differences of opinion on religious issues, and they have organized themselves into groups that maintained active relationships with other Christians like themselves and that declined to interact with Christians who were significantly different in some way. In the second century the Great Church, Marcionites, Montanists, and various types of Gnostics formed fairly distinct groups. After the Council of Nicaea in the early fourth century, Nicene Christians, Donatists, Arians, and Semi-Arians could be distinguished from one another. After the Council of Chalcedon in 451, Catholic/Orthodox Christians, Nestorians, and Monophysites could be distinguished. After the Great Schism in 1054, Catholics and Orthodox were divided (and the other groups persisted as well). The Magisterial and Radical Reformations led to several new groups, as Protestants (in a broad sense) split into ever more numerous groups as their numbers increased. Only in the past century or so have individual groups joined forces with one another to form united denominations in fairly large numbers, though further divisions continue to occur as well.

The word *denomination* refers to a group of Christians whose common beliefs and practices have led them to associate with one another to experience worship, train ministers and laity, engage in mission, and celebrate life together. Denominations usually have regional or national offices, often have some sort of hierarchical structure, and generally adhere to a defined set of beliefs and practices. Denominations often cooperate with other denominations to accomplish common goals, and they sometimes engage in dialog with one another to identify similarities or differences, to explore avenues of cooperation, or even to consider joining forces formally. Denominations also sometimes fight with one another, with arms in the past, with words now.

One way in which denominations show their disapproval of other groups that identify themselves as Christian is by calling themselves a *church* and referring to others by a different, ostensibly less worthy name, such as denomination or sect. Alternatively, denominations might refer to another Christian group as a sect or, worse, a cult, words that imply inferior Christian status or even a position outside the Christian family entirely. The terminology adopted in this book uses the words church, denomination, and Christian group interchangeably, though in context the word *church* might refer to an individual congregation, or even a building. In a narrow sense, *church* refers to people, not the buildings in which they meet, but in a broader sense the word can refer to an individual congregation, a building in which Christians meet, a denomination, the worldwide body of Christian believers, or even the totality of all Christian believers living or dead. The specific way in which the term is used below should be clear from the context of the discussion, though it will often be capitalized to clarify that reference is being made to one or more denominations.

Above the level of individual denominations is the *faith tradition*. Other than the Roman Catholic Church, most denominations are limited to a set geographical area, perhaps a single country or a group of countries in geographical proximity to one another. Thus, numerous independent Orthodox denominations exist, as well as numerous Anglican/Episcopalian denominations, Baptist denominations, and more. The discussion below treats groups of denominations that share a common faith tradition, usually one rooted in the histories of the various denominations, even though in many ways a denomination may be more similar to a denomination that is part of a different historical faith tradition. Thus, for example, Presbyterians, some Baptists, and Anglicans/Episcopalians are often grouped together as *mainline churches*, but since they belong to three different faith traditions, they will be considered in three different categories. Later sections, such as that entitled "A Doctrinal Perspective," will group the denominations together differently.

The presentation below focuses on those Christian groups whose stated beliefs include adherence to the definition of Christianity determined to be orthodox by the ecumenical Council of Nicaea, or churches that developed historically from the Nicene tradition. Groups that either no longer identify themselves as Christian in this sense (e.g. Unitarians/Universalists) or groups of recent vintage whose beliefs differ substantially from traditional Nicene Christianity, even though they may self-identify as Christians (e.g. Mormons, Jehovah's Witnesses, and Christian Scientists) will be discussed more briefly. Groups that have adopted names taken from ancient Christian history (e.g. Gnostics) or whose path diverged from Christianity in the distant past, and was even then tenuous at best (e.g. Manicheans, Mandaeans) will not be considered here.

Varieties of church polity

Before individual denominations are discussed, it is useful to look at four different models of church polity that different denominations share. *Polity* refers to the form of government an organization has, in this case of a religious organization. Polity deals with issues such as authority, organization, and the succession of leaders. The first polity model is the episcopal model. This model is so named not because it is associated with the Episcopal Church (though the Episcopal Church does use the episcopal model), but because of the root meaning of the word. *Episcopal* comes from a Greek word that means overseer or supervisor, but in a religious context it is usually translated *bishop*. In the simplest form of the episcopal model, the church is ruled by a bishop. In this model, the bishop makes decisions concerning doctrine and practice. The bishop may get input from other individuals or groups, but he or she is under no obligation to follow the will of the majority of advisors. A common assumption behind the episcopal model is that the bishop is especially in tune with God, either because God reveals Godself in a direct way to the bishop, or because the bishop is considered to be especially sensitive to God's voice. One variation on the episcopal model introduces a hierarchy of rulers, for example, priests, bishops, archbishops, and the pope in the Roman Catholic Church; the hierarchical variation is often necessary in large denominations. Another variation places a group of people, or council, at the top of the hierarchy, rather than a single individual. In the United Methodist Church (in the U.S.), for example, ultimate authority rests not in a single individual bishop but in the General Conference that is held every four years. Another characteristic of the episcopal model is that when a vacancy occurs in an episcopate, it is other bishops who choose the new bishop. For this reason, many churches with an episcopal polity claim to be able to trace their bishops back through an unbroken line of succession to one of the apostles. Churches that follow some sort of episcopal model include the Roman Catholic Church, the Eastern Orthodox churches, the various smaller Oriental Orthodox churches, the Anglican and Episcopal churches, and the Church of Jesus Christ of Latter-day Saints (i.e. the Mormon Church). Many

Methodist and Lutheran denominations also have an episcopal polity. More than 70 percent of the world's Christians belong to churches that subscribe to some form of episcopal polity.

A second model of church polity is the presbyterian model. The word *presbyterian* is based on a Greek word meaning elder, though the word is often translated *priest* or simply transliterated as *presbyter*. Churches that follow this model have no clergy of higher rank than presbyter; in other words, they have no bishops. Although they recognize that the term bishop (*episcopos*) occurs in the New Testament, they consider it to be a synonym for elder (*presbyteros*). Groups of presbyters govern individual churches, and they elect a representative to stand for them in the Presbytery, the next higher level of organization. Presbyteries elect people to represent their geographical region in a Synod, which represents a still larger area, and finally Synods elect representatives for the General Assembly, which has authority over the whole denomination. (Not every denomination that uses the presbyterian model has this many levels of governing bodies.) These various assemblies of presbyters are also called church courts. Unlike the episcopal model, members of one church court do not fill replacements that arise on their own. Instead, the replacement is elected from the court immediately below. The presbyterian system, then, is a system of hierarchical representative governments. The presbyterian model is followed by most churches within the Reformed tradition, such as the various denominations that include the word Presbyterian in their name, the Church of Scotland, and many denominations with the word Reformed in their name. The Seventh-day Adventist Church has a polity that is largely presbyterian, except that local churches do not elect their own pastors, which are appointed by the local conference.

A third model of church polity is the congregational model. Denominations that follow this model do not have any authoritative structures above the level of the local church. These churches elect their leaders (variously called pastors, elders, ministers, or bishops), and their leaders serve at the pleasure of the congregation. In a church that follows the congregational polity, an individual pastor may serve the congregation alone, or a group of pastors may guide the church, perhaps led by a senior pastor. In other churches, a church board or board of deacons may assist the pastor, or the pastor may be under the authority of the board. Churches with a congregational polity often organize themselves into committees, associations, or conventions in order to work together on common projects (e.g. missions, feeding the hungry, higher education, or political advocacy) or to worship and fellowship together. Other churches of this sort avoid forming any kind of denominational structure. Even those congregational churches that do join other churches to form associations do not recognize the authority of those associations over individual churches. Churches may join whichever associations they want (provided the association votes to receive them), and they may leave whenever they want. A congregational church may be a member of different regional organizations (e.g. city, state, and national in the U.S.), but even the regional organizations do not form hierarchies of any sort, since the national organization cannot dictate to the state organizations, for example. Congregational polity is the second most popular form of church polity, after episcopal polity. Churches that have a congregational polity include Baptists, Mennonites, Amish, Disciples of Christ, Church of Christ, United Church of Christ, Pentecostals, Congregationalists, many African Independent Churches, many Evangelical churches, and some Reformed churches.

The fourth kind of church polity, the society form of government, has no hierarchical structure either outside or inside the individual church. Like congregational churches, the local church is subject to the authority of no other association or individual. Unlike congregational churches, those that follow the society model also recognize no authority structure within the local church itself. These churches have no clergy, and their services are sometimes completely unstructured, as they wait for the Spirit of God to move individuals to address the congregation. Individual churches often cooperate with one another in associations, or *meetings*, as the Quakers call them, and they also typically support educational institutions, social service organizations, and other similar entities. The Society of Friends, or Quakers, is the Christian group most often identified with the societal form of church polity.

Before moving to an examination of some of the beliefs and practices of individual denominations or groups of denominations, it is important to recognize that in any denomination with many members, differences of opinion will exist, sometimes quite profound differences. In addition, official church dogma or practices often change over time, so the views of the church in the sixteenth century, for example, will frequently be different from those of the descendants of those churches in the twenty-first century. The characterizations given below represent the official position of the church today, or the position of the majority of members if no official position exists. Divergent views will be discussed to some extent, especially when a sizeable minority within the church advocates change, but the primary purpose of this overview is to provide readers with an accurate, though necessarily limited, thumbnail sketch of the largest denominations or groups of denominations in Christianity today.

Catholic Churches

The Roman Catholic Church is by far the single largest denomination in Christendom, with a membership of slightly more than one billion, a little more than half of all believers worldwide. The leader of the Roman Catholic Church is the pope, who resides in Vatican City, an independent city-state completely surrounded by the city of Rome and under the full control of the Church. Other titles used by the pope, and the different roles they represent, include:

- Bishop of Rome: overseer of the Christians who live in Rome and its environs
- Vicar of Christ: representative of Christ on earth
- Supreme Pontiff (in Latin, Pontifex Maximus): high priest of the Christian church (borrowing a title used by Roman emperors to indicate their role as head of the state religion)

- Prince of the Apostles: a title that originally referred to Peter, and now is held by his successors in Rome

As noted above, the Roman Catholic Church has an episcopal form of government, with a single individual leading the church: the pope. Beneath the pope in honor and power are the cardinals, a collection of bishops who serve in a variety of capacities around the world or in the Vatican. There are currently almost 200 cardinals, all appointed by the pope, and divided into three categories: cardinal bishops, cardinal priests, and cardinal deacons. Cardinal bishops are the leaders of the Roman Curia, the central government of the Roman Catholic Church, based in the Vatican (e.g. the Secretary of State for Vatican City or the Prefect of the Congregation for the Oriental Churches). Cardinal priests serve primarily as archbishops of geographical regions around the world, usually centered around one or more large metropolitan areas (e.g. the Archbishop of Los Angeles or the Archbishop of Bangkok). Cardinal deacons, like cardinal bishops, serve in various posts in the Curia (e.g. Archivist and Librarian of the Holy See and Prefect of the Congregation for the Doctrine of the Faith). At one time all the cardinal bishops led churches in the immediate vicinity of Rome, and all cardinal priests and deacons worked in specific churches in Rome, but today the office of cardinal is purely titular, that is, they serve in a variety of capacities and, as noted, live around the world. There is no distinction in authority among cardinal bishops, priests, and deacons. Together they make up the Sacred College of Cardinals, and, in addition to their other duties, they periodically come to Rome (if not already based there) and advise the pope on matters of importance. Perhaps the most important duty of cardinals is to select a new pope when the previous one dies, usually from their own number. No man who was not already a cardinal has been chosen pope in over 600 years.

Most of the cardinal priests serve as archbishops of regions known as archdioceses, a juridical region within the Roman Catholic Church that often has oversight of other, usually less populous dioceses. An archdiocese is led by an archbishop, and a diocese is led by a bishop, and sometimes other bishops are assigned to assist in the diocese or archdiocese. Despite the gradation of titles in bishop, archbishop, and cardinal, all are in fact considered bishops in the Roman Catholic Church so are in the highest level of clergy. (Arch)bishops supervise a number of individual parishes, each of which is led by a priest, the intermediate level of ordained clergy. Each parish is centered in a particular Catholic church. Priests in turn are assisted by deacons and possibly other lay people, such as acolytes (those who serve at the altar) and lectors (readers). Bishops, priests, and deacons are installed in their offices through a ceremony called *ordination*, while acolytes and lectors, who are not ordained, are installed in their offices through a ceremony called *institution*. Bishops and priests are unmarried, while deacons, acolytes, and lectors may be married. All must be male; there are no female members of clergy in the Roman Catholic Church.

To this point we have been discussing the *secular* organization of the Roman Catholic Church, that is, that part of the church whose primary ministry is to the world. A second organization, or rather collection of organizations, exists in the Roman Catholic Church that deals with communities of religious, both *brothers* and *sisters*. Numerous religious orders exist within the Church, some focused on life within a monastery (for men) or convent (for women), and others focused on specific types of ministry to the world. *Cloistered* brothers (i.e. those who live in a monastery) are called *monks*, and cloistered sisters are called *nuns*. Those who are members of a religious order take vows of obedience when entering the order, and they live according to the Rule, or set of guidelines, adopted by the order. Individual monasteries are led by an abbot, and convents are led by an abbess, or mother superior. Abbots and abbesses report to superiors in a hierarchical structure, which is headed by the leader of the order, the superior general. A similar structure exists for the mendicant orders, which are not cloistered. Individual abbots or monks may be priests or bishops, but they need not be, and members of most orders of brothers are laity, and all sisters in the Roman Catholic Church are laity. The Catholic Church also has religious orders (usually called congregations) that are exclusively for lay people or which lay people may join without taking the vows required of religious. Some familiar Catholic religious orders are the Jesuits (mendicant men), Franciscans (mendicant men), Dominicans (mendicant men), Trappists (cloistered men), Carmelites (several cloistered orders for women and men), and Missionaries of Charity (mendicant women).

The term *Roman* Catholic Church implies the primacy of the bishop of Rome, but it also suggests the Latin heritage that most Catholics share. Although since the Vatican II Council (1962–1965) Catholics worship in their vernacular language – English, Spanish, Chinese, Xhosa, and so forth – most Catholics are members of *Latin Rite* churches, that is, churches which trace their ancestry to churches originally founded in Europe or North Africa, where Latin was the predominant language at one time. Many Catholic churches, however, trace their ancestry to the East, where the traditional language of worship was Greek, Syriac, Armenian, or other languages. The *Eastern Rite* churches have their own hierarchy, usually headed by an archbishop or patriarch, and their order of worship may vary slightly or significantly from the Latin Rite used in most Catholic churches, but they are in communion with Rome, recognize the pope as their spiritual leader, and are full-fledged members of the Roman Catholic Church. There are also *Anglican Rite* churches, congregations of Anglican or Episcopal churches that have converted to Roman Catholicism but still use a form of worship based on the traditional Anglican liturgy, as well as a small number of Roman Catholic churches that follow other rites.

Roman Catholics accept the teachings of 21 ecumenical councils, from Nicaea in 325 to Vatican II in 1962–1965. In many ways, they are the very definition of orthodoxy, at least in the West, although Protestants, who split from the Catholics after 1517, differ from them on a number of points. Catholics believe in the full humanity and divinity of Christ and in the doctrine of the Trinity. They have three sources of authority: the Bible, traditions of the Church, and the pope, but all three may be viewed as different facets of the single authority of the Church, especially as represented by its bishops. They accept both the Nicene and Apostles' Creeds. Believers in apostolic succession, they claim the ability to trace an unbroken chain of succession from every modern bishop back to the apostles in the first century. They count seven sacraments: Baptism, Confirmation, Eucharist, Penance (Confession), Marriage, Holy Orders, and the Anointing of the Sick. When Catholics celebrate communion by partaking of the Eucharist, they believe that the bread and wine are transformed into the literal body and blood of Christ, a doctrine called *transubstantiation*. Catholics believe that the ultimate destination for all people in the afterlife is either Heaven or Hell, but they also believe that souls not yet ready for heaven go first to Purgatory, where they are "cleansed" (the root meaning behind the word *Purgatory*) through punishment. For this reason, prayer for the dead is important in the Roman Catholic Church, because they consider prayer efficacious in reducing the time a soul may have to spend in Purgatory. Catholics view Christians of other denominations as mistaken in certain beliefs and practices but brothers and sisters in Christ nonetheless. Without conceding their own firmly-held beliefs, Catholics view adherents of other religions with respect, for they see them engaged in a common struggle to understand life's deepest mysteries. Catholics have a deep respect for human life, and they oppose artificial birth control, abortion, euthanasia, and capital punishment. Although they are in the Just War rather than the Pacifist tradition, the modern Roman Catholic Church has developed a profound suspicion of war and is generally loath to advocate the use of force. Their respect for life also leads the Catholic Church to be involved in a wide variety of social ministries to the poor, sick, and outcast. One typically becomes a member of the Roman Catholic Church by being born into a Catholic family and baptized as a baby, although baptism may be administered to converts of any age.

In response to the decision of the First Vatican Council in 1870 to proclaim the doctrine of papal infallibility, many Catholic churches in Europe split from the Roman Catholic Church and formed a new denomination, the Old Catholic Church. This church continues to hold many of the beliefs and follow many of the liturgical practices of the Roman Catholic Church, but it differs from the latter in allowing priests to marry, permitting women to be ordained as deacons and priests and in accepting artificial contraception as fully compatible with Christian values.

Eastern and Oriental Orthodox Churches

> So then, brothers and sisters, stand firm and hold fast to the traditions that you were taught by us, either by word of mouth or by our letter.
>
> (2 Thess 2:15)

It is technically more accurate to speak of Eastern Orthodox Churches rather than *the* Eastern Orthodox Church, because several different administratively independent denominations consider themselves part of the Orthodox communion and related to the traditional leader of the Church, the patriarch of Constantinople (Istanbul). Most of these groups are based in particular countries, such as the Greek Orthodox Church, Russian Orthodox Church, or Albanian Orthodox Church. However, since the Church has spread over time as the Orthodox immigrated to other countries, one can find Orthodox churches of different ancestries in the same city, particularly in the Western

Hemisphere. Eastern Orthodox Churches worldwide number between 215 and 250 million members, making them the second largest Christian communion, after Roman Catholics.

The pedigree of Eastern Orthodox Churches is just as ancient as that of the Roman Catholic Church, since three of their major patriarchal sees – Alexandria, Antioch, and Jerusalem – were all founded in the first century, as the New Testament itself attests. Constantinople became a patriarchal church after Constantine moved his capital there in the early fourth century, but the Orthodox trace the founding of the church in Byzantium, the former name of Constantinople, to the apostle Andrew in the first century as well. The Orthodox Church has an episcopal structure, but the patriarch of Constantinople, its titular head, has no authority comparable to that of the pope in the Roman Catholic Church. Instead, the patriarch of Constantinople is considered "first among equals," and major decisions affecting the entire Orthodox communion are only made in consultation with other bishops of the Church. The Orthodox have a threefold hierarchy of clergy: bishops, priests, and deacons. Priests and deacons are allowed to marry, if they do so before their ordination, but bishops must remain celibate. All members of the clergy in the Orthodox Church are male. The church is organized into dioceses and parishes, with a bishop leading the former and a priest the latter.

Monasticism has a long and important tradition within Orthodoxy, for it was in the East that the monastic movement began, in the deserts of Egypt, Syria, and Palestine. Although the Eastern Orthodox Church lacks formal religious orders, it has many monks and nuns, who may be referred to collectively as monastics. Monastics may live in communities following a common Rule (cenobitic monasticism), they may live in isolation (eremitic monasticism, whose practitioners are called *hermits*), or they may live in partial isolation, coming together periodically with other monastics to share in worship (semi-eremitic monasticism). Some monks live outside cloistered communities in order to serve those in the world, for example, in a parish church. The highest concentration of monks in the world live on Mt. Athos in Greece. The peninsula on which Mt. Athos is found hosts 20 different Orthodox monasteries, plus many *sketes* (collections of monks who practice a semi-eremitic lifestyle) and hermitages, housing over 2,000 monks.

Most Eastern Orthodox Christians accept only seven ecumenical councils, from the First Council of Nicaea to the Second Council of Nicaea, though some accept two others as well. Thus, they accept the Nicene and Chalcedonian definitions of Christ as both divine and human and the doctrine of the Trinity. The recite the Nicene Creed, as modified by the First Council of Constantinople, but reject both the addition of the *filioque* to the Nicene Creed and the Apostles' Creed, because neither was approved by an ecumenical council. The 1672 Synod of Jerusalem, though not officially considered an ecumenical council, has continuing importance for all Orthodox today, because it defined who the Orthodox were in comparison to Roman Catholics on the one hand and Protestants on the other. Authority in the Orthodox Church has three sources: scripture, tradition, and the ecumenical councils. However, the Orthodox see these three sources as essentially one: sacred tradition, as given by Jesus to his disciples and transmitted faithfully through apostolic succession to the Orthodox Church today.

The orthodox have no official statement on the number of mysteries (sacraments) that they accept, but most recognize Baptism, Eucharist, Chrismation (anointing with oil, a form of confirmation), Fasting, Almsgiving, Repentance, Marriage, Monasticism, and Holy Orders. In fact, any act that brings one in contact with God may be regarded as a mystery in this sense. Although the Orthodox believe that the bread and wine are transformed into the actual body and blood of Christ in the Eucharist, they do not have an official position on the precise mechanism involved, so they cannot be said to endorse the Catholic view of transubstantiation, strictly speaking. The Orthodox reject the Catholic doctrine of Purgatory as a recent innovation, outside the transmission of tradition within the Church. Many Orthodox Churches are involved in the ecumenical movement, and they are also in frequent dialog with the Roman Catholic Church. Because of their distinctive history in the Byzantine Empire and under Muslim rule, the Orthodox have traditionally focused on development of the inner person through prayer and contemplation. An example of this is the practice of praying the Jesus Prayer ("Lord Jesus Christ, Son of God, have mercy on me, a sinner") repeatedly as a form of devotion. People join an Orthodox church by baptism, either as a child dedicated by his or her parents, or as an adult believer who accepts the Orthodox faith.

The Assyrian Church of the East, sometimes called the Assyrian Orthodox Church, is a church that was once based in the western part of the Persian Empire, with its first churches probably located in northern Mesopotamia (ancient Assyria). It is in communion with neither the Roman Catholic Church, the Eastern Orthodox Churches, nor the Oriental Orthodox Churches. The Assyrian Orthodox Church split from the Catholic/Orthodox Church over disputes revolving around Nestorius, patriarch of Constantinople, who was condemned by the Council of Ephesus in 431 (the third ecumenical council) for supposedly teaching that the divine and the human in Jesus were separate entities, a charge Nestorius himself denied. Although Nestorius claimed to be vindicated by the formulation concerning the divine and human in Christ decreed by the Council of Chalcedon in 451 (the fourth ecumenical council), the churches that followed his teachings never rejoined the Chalcedonian churches. Today the Assyrian Church of the East has a few hundred thousand members, concentrated in Iraq, Iran, Syria, and Turkey, but with fairly large populations in the U.S., Australia, and elsewhere around the world as well.

The Oriental Orthodox Churches are not in communion with either the Eastern Orthodox Churches or the Roman Catholic Church, though they are in communion with each other. The Oriental Orthodox Churches separated from the Catholic/Orthodox Church over disagreements concerning the decisions of the Council of Chalcedon, over 600 years prior to the final split between the Roman Catholic and Eastern Orthodox Churches. The Oriental Orthodox Churches believed that the definition of the faith promulgated by the Council of Chalcedon was Nestorian in nature, dividing Christ into two distinct parts, divine and human. These churches preferred a view that is typically called Monophysite, emphasizing the single nature of Christ, which was both divine and human. The Coptic Orthodox, Armenian Orthodox, Syriac Orthodox, Ethiopian Orthodox, Eritrean Orthodox, and Indian Orthodox Churches comprise the Oriental Orthodox family, with more than 40 million adherents worldwide, the greatest number of whom concentrated in an arc stretching from Ethiopia to India. Although their historical split with the larger church has prevented reunification of the Oriental Orthodox with Eastern Orthodox or Roman Catholic Churches for more than 1,500 years, the doctrines and practices of these churches are quite similar in many ways, and recent dialogs have soothed ancient tensions among these groups. The Ethiopian Orthodox Church has two distinctives that make it unique among Christian denominations. First, its canon of scripture contains several books not found in the canon of any other Christian tradition, in both the Old and the New Testaments. Second, its Church of Our Lady Mary of Zion, the oldest church in Ethiopia, located in Axum, claims to house the original Ark of the Covenant mentioned in the Hebrew Bible.

Anglican and Episcopal Churches

Anglicans comprise the third largest communion of Christians worldwide, numbering perhaps 80 million followers. They may safely be considered larger than other Protestant groups that represent particular faith traditions because none of the other groups has a structure that is as cohesive on a worldwide scale as the Anglicans (thus the reference to Anglicans as the third largest *communion*, not third largest *faith tradition*). The Anglican Church split from the Roman Catholic Church in the sixteenth century during the reign of Henry VIII, but as a church that values apostolic tradition, it traces its pedigree from modern Anglican and Episcopalian churches back to the first Anglican archbishop of Canterbury, Thomas Cranmer, through the previous archbishops of Canterbury back to Augustine of Canterbury, and from Augustine back to the church of Rome. Anglicans may properly be considered Protestants, because of their historical break from the Roman Catholic Church, but in practice many Anglicans consider themselves Anglo-Catholics, that is, Anglicans who value the continuity of tradition that exists between Anglicans and the Roman Catholic Church. On the other hand, other Anglicans are proud of their Protestant roots and have no desire to be reabsorbed into the Roman Catholic Church. The Archbishop of Canterbury is the symbolic head of the Anglican Communion, but the Archbishop has no authority over the various independent Anglican denominations that make up the worldwide Anglican Church, which sometimes go by the name Episcopalian rather than Anglican.

Like Catholics and Orthodox, Anglicans have a three-tiered clergy, with bishops, priests, and deacons, within the typical episcopal structure of diocese and parish. In most Anglican Churches, all three levels of clergy can be married. Women can be ordained as deacons or priests in most Anglican Churches and as bishops in many. Many different religious orders and Christian communities exist within the Anglican Church, many of them open to both laity and clergy. A major difference between religious orders and Christian communities is that religious orders require celibacy and communal sharing of property, while Christian communities do not.

Anglicans generally accept the teachings of the first seven ecumenical councils, though they do not ascribe the same level of authority to them as either Catholics or Orthodox. The reason for this is rooted in the Protestant basis for the Anglican Church and its

Figure 16.1 After the Great Fire of London, which destroyed much of the city in 1666, Christopher Wren was commissioned to rebuild St. Paul's Cathedral, an Anglican church, on the site of the previous church, which was destroyed in the fire.

emphasis on *sola scriptura*, the principle that the ultimate authority for the church is the Bible. Thus, they accept the traditional orthodox teachings concerning the divinity and humanity of Christ and the Trinity, not necessarily because they were defined by ecumenical councils, but because the ecumenical councils correctly interpreted the scripture when dealing with these issues. Anglicans accept both the Nicene and the Apostles' Creeds. Other than scripture, the most important writing for Anglicans is the *Book of Common Prayer*, which includes the creeds, the lectionary (daily scripture readings), many prayers, the Psalms, and liturgies for many occasions. In fact, in many ways it is the *Book of Common Prayer* that unites Anglicans when other issues threaten to divide them. Like other Protestants, Anglicans accept only two sacraments, Baptism and the Eucharist, as fully normative for the Church, but they often attribute greater or lesser degrees of importance to the other five sacraments recognized by the Roman Catholic Church. Anglicans generally reject the Catholic doctrine of transubstantiation, though they do believe in the "Real Presence" of Christ in the elements of the Eucharist.

Churches of the Magisterial Reform

Those Protestant denominations that stem from the work of the early Magisterial Reformers Luther, Zwingli, Calvin, and their colleagues may be conveniently grouped together since they share similar polity and systems of belief. The largest of these groups of faith traditions are the Lutherans and the Reformed/Presbyterian churches (including the Church of Scotland). These Protestant churches generally have a commitment to the traditional emphases of the Protestant Reformation, such as the sole authority of scripture and the priesthood of the believer. They may generally be classified as orthodox, in the sense that they adhere to the teachings of the Councils of Nicaea through Chalcedon, and perhaps other ecumenical councils as well, but there is rarely much of an emphasis on the councils in these denominations. Their polity is generally either episcopal, presbyterian, or some combination of the two, perhaps with elements of congregationalism thrown in. These churches may have three levels of clergy – bishop, priest/elder, and deacon – or they may only have the latter two. Both men and women may serve as clergy in most of these denominations, and there is no injunction against married clergy. As traditional Protestants, their primary – often sole – source of authority is the Bible. They often use the Apostles' or Nicene creeds in their services. With a few exceptions, even the churches in this group that have bishops do not claim to have true apostolic succession back to the earliest days of the church.

Most Magisterial churches adhere to a fairly strict idea of predestination, particularly the Reformed churches. They accept only two sacraments: Baptist and the Eucharist. They reject transubstantiation, but Lutherans still speak of the true body and blood of Christ "in, with, and under" the bread and wine, an idea sometimes called *consubstantiation*. Others in this group see Christ's presence in the elements as either spiritual or even as purely symbolic. Christians who belong to these churches, like other Protestants, reject the idea of Purgatory as unbiblical, particularly since they also reject the apocryphal or deuterocanonical books as (fully) authoritative. Denominations within this group sometimes consider themselves in communion with others outside their immediate faith tradition. For example, certain Lutheran and Anglican/Episcopalian denominations explicitly consider themselves in communion with one another, so that an Episcopal priest can serve in a Lutheran church that is unable to find a suitable priest. People typically become members of these churches by being baptized into the church as infants and later confirmed.

Free Churches

> For freedom Christ has set us free. Stand firm, therefore, and do not submit again to a yoke of slavery.
>
> (Gal 5:1)

Perhaps it is inevitable in any attempt to group Christian churches into a small number of categories that at least one category will contain a fairly disparate collection of denominations. In the scheme given in this chapter, it is the Free Churches which contain the most heterogeneous mix of denominations. All of the faith traditions we have discussed to this point either are now or have at some point been granted some sort of official status as a state church. For example, the Roman Catholic Church is the official religion in several Latin American and European countries, including, of course Vatican City; an Eastern Orthodox Church is the state church in Greece and Cyprus, and the Russian Orthodox Church was the official church of Russia prior to

Some denominations, or groups of denominations, in the Free Church tradition

African Independent Churches (some)

Amish

Baptist

Bible Churches

Christian Church

Christian Scientist

Church of Christ

Church of Jesus Christ of Latter-day Saints (Mormons)

Church of the Nazarene

Congregational

Disciples of Christ

Evangelical Free Church

Jehovah's Witnesses

Mennonite

Methodist

Moravian Brethren

Nondenominational Churches (some)

Seventh-day Adventist

Society of Friends (Quakers)

Unitarian Universalist

United Church of Christ

Waldensian

Wesleyan

the Bolshevik Revolution; the Church of England (Anglican) is the official religion of England; the Church of Scotland (Presbyterian) is the national church of Scotland; and a Lutheran denomination is the official church in Denmark, Norway, and Iceland. In the past, many more countries recognized representatives of these denominations as official or state churches. The Free Churches represent faith traditions that have historically rejected any official affiliation with the state, and their combined memberships make them the largest category of Protestant Christians, although they do not form what might be called a single communion, like the Anglicans do. In fact, their combined membership is larger than that of the Eastern Orthodox Church as well, numbering more than 250 million adherents.

Churches that fall into the category of Free Churches frequently have a congregational church polity, but episcopal, presbyterian, and societal polities are also represented among the Free Churches. Denominations that may be called Free Churches include Methodists and other churches in the Wesleyan tradition, including the Holiness

Churches; Baptists of many different varieties; members of the Stone-Campbell Restoration Movement (Disciples of Christ, Christian Churches, Church of Christ); various denominations that identify themselves as Evangelicals, including those that call themselves Bible Churches and Non-denominational Churches; Anabaptists and other Historic Peace Churches (e.g. Quakers, Moravian Brethren, Mennonites, Amish); the United Church of Christ and other Congregational Churches; Seventh-day Adventists; Unitarian Universalists; Jehovah's Witnesses; Christian Scientists; and the Church of Jesus Christ of Latter-day Saints (Mormons) and other groups that split from the larger Mormon denomination.

The historical origins of these churches vary. The oldest denominations among the Free Churches, the Waldensian Church and the Moravian Brethren, have roots that predate the Protestant Reformation in 1517. Some of the Anabaptist Churches are nearly as old, dating to the Radical Reformation, which was more or less contemporaneous with the Magisterial (Protestant) Reformation. All these churches broke off directly from the Roman Catholic Church. Other Free Churches split off from other Protestant faith traditions. The Wesleyan churches arose historically as an offshoot of the Anglican Church, and in fact John Wesley remained an Anglican priest until the time of his death. Baptists originated among the Separatists and Puritans in England in the seventeenth century, and they had some limited contact with early Anabaptists as well. Congregationalist Churches and the United Church of Christ were born out of churches in the Reformed tradition. The Society of Friends (Quakers) was founded by George Fox, an English dissenter from the Anglican Church, in the seventeenth century. The Unitarian Universalists arose in New England among Congregationalist and other Protestant churches, though they had many indirect historical antecedents. The founders of the Stone-Campbell Restoration Movement were both Presbyterians, though they drew their followers from different traditions. Joseph Smith, the founder of the Mormon Church, grew up under the influence of evangelical forms of Protestantism and was strongly influenced by the revivalist movements associated with the Second Great Awakening in the U.S. William Miller, the founder of the Seventh-day Adventist Church, was originally a Baptist. Charles Taze Russell, founder of the Jehovah's Witnesses, had roots in both Congregational and Adventist churches. Mary Baker Eddy, founder of the Christian Science Church, grew up in a Congregational church.

The beliefs and practices of the Free Churches vary widely. Most, but not all, adhere to Nicene and Chalcedonian orthodoxy. Of those that do not, the Jehovah's Witnesses see Christ in a more or less Arian fashion, as God's first creation, and thus also reject the doctrine of the Trinity. While accepting some traditional tenets of orthodoxy such as the Virgin Birth and the Resurrection of Jesus, Christian Scientists view Jesus in a manner similar to the Adoptionists, distinguishing the man Jesus from the divine Christ, and their view of the world is sharply dualistic, similar to the Gnostics. The group whose beliefs stray furthest from traditional Christian orthodoxy is the Church of Jesus Christ of Latter-day Saints, whose members are commonly called Mormons. Although much of their terminology is similar to that of traditional Christianity, their meaning is quite different. For example, they talk about faith in the Father, Son, and

Holy Spirit, but they view the three persons of the "Trinity" as three distinct individuals, with Jesus as the literal son of God and his wife. Furthermore, faithful Mormons, they believe, will one day be exalted and become gods themselves, and husbands and wives will populate new planets. One last denomination grouped with the Free Churches is the Unitarian Universalist Church, which, as the name implies, rejects the doctrine of the Trinity and also rejects the concept of Hell as a place of eternal punishment. Although both the Unitarians and the Universalists began as explicitly Christian denominations, albeit unorthodox ones, many members of Unitarian Universalist churches today (the two denominations merged in 1961) would not identify themselves as Christians at all, preferring to identify themselves simply as religious people, people of faith, or spiritual people. Because of the divergence of the denominations listed in this paragraph from traditional Christian orthodoxy, the paragraphs that follow will deal only with those Free Churches that either explicitly accept or more closely approximate traditional orthodox positions.

Even among the orthodox Free Churches, wide diversity of opinion and practice exists. Most Free Church denominations recognize two levels of clergy – pastors/elders and deacons – but some, such as many Methodists, add bishops as well. The Quakers have no official clergy at all. All clergy in the Free Churches are allowed to marry. While some of these churches allow women to become clergy, others do not. Most Free churches associate with other like-minded churches in an organized, denominational structure, while others eschew any formal organization above the level of the individual church. For this reason, some groups in the Free Church category dismiss the label "denomination" as an accurate description of their churches (though the label is retained in this discussion for the sake of consistency). Most orthodox Free Churches hold that the Bible alone is their source of authority, and – aside from the Methodists – they make no use of either the Nicene or the Apostles' Creed, even though most of them would concur with the statements contained in these creeds. On the other hand, several of the denominations do have historically important *confessions* of faith, such as the Schleitheim Confession, favored by many Anabaptists, such as the Mennonites, and the various editions of the Baptist Faith and Message, favored by different Baptist denominations in the U.S.

Free Churches disagree on many doctrinal matters as well. Although some Baptists, for example, are strict Calvinists in regard to doctrines like predestination and limited atonement (e.g. Primitive Baptists and some Southern Baptists), most in the Free Church tradition are either moderate Calvinists or Arminians (e.g. Methodists, Church of Christ). Although many Free Churches have either a very conservative (fundamentalist) or fairly conservative theological profile in relation to traditional orthodoxy, a large number can fairly be described theologically as either moderate or liberal. Free Churches typically observe the Eucharist (which many call the Lord's Supper or Communion) and Baptism, but Seventh-day Adventists and Primitive Baptists also practice foot-washing on a regular basis. Although many Methodists speak of the Real Presence of Christ in the Eucharist, most Free Churches see the bread and wine (or grape juice, in some denominations) as symbols of Christ's death. Thus, they often refer to the sacraments as *ordinances*, that is, religious activities ordained by Christ but possessing no special ability to impart grace.

Quakers observe no sacraments at all, because they believe that people can experience God directly, without the mediation of sacraments. Those denominations that use the term "ordinances" would likely agree in sentiment with the Quakers on this last point. Although some Free Churches, such as some Methodists, practice Infant Baptism (*Pedobaptism*), almost all other Free Church denominations practice Believer's Baptism (*Credobaptism*). That is, they insist that Baptism is a rite than can only follow an informed decision to follow Christ, so it should be limited to adults and older children and adolescents. In fact, two of the largest groups of Free Church faith traditions, Baptists and Anabaptists, were so named (by their opponents) because of their insistence on Believer's Baptism. Most Free Churches that practice Believer's Baptism see it as an essential step in becoming a member of the church. Seventh-day Adventists, as their name implies, worship on the Sabbath (Saturday), rather than on Sunday, as most other Christians do; they are joined in this practice by the Seventh Day Baptists.

One of the largest subsets of the Free Churches consists of those churches that consider themselves Evangelicals. The name *Evangelical* comes from the Greek word that means "gospel," or "good news." Evangelical denominations focus much effort on evangelism – that is, preaching or otherwise sharing the good news of Jesus Christ – and missions, usually thought of as evangelism in areas with little or no previous Christian witness. What constitutes a "Christian witness" is a matter of some debate among Evangelicals. Some see their own denomination, or perhaps a fairly small set of denominations like theirs, as the only true Christians. Others are willing to acknowledge that anyone who has had a true *conversion experience* – that is, a moment in which they had a profound encounter with God through Jesus Christ – is a Christian. Still others take a broader view. There is deep suspicion among some Evangelicals, and some others in the Free Church tradition, about whether members of other denominations are "saved," that is, whether they are truly Christians bound for heaven. Other Evangelicals are more welcoming of other types of Christians, while clinging firmly to their own understanding of the nature of salvation. The vast majority of Evangelicals would consider groups like the Mormons, Jehovah's Witnesses, and Christian Scientists, because of their departure from traditional orthodoxy, as outside the bounds of Christianity. Some would put the Catholics and the Orthodox outside the camp as well. Like other Free Churches, new members can join Evangelical churches by being baptized (usually immersed in water), but only after praying some version of the *Sinner's Prayer* (not a specific set of words, but the sentiment expressed), indicating that the person has repented of sin and wants to "accept Jesus Christ into his/her heart." Because of their focus on sharing the good news with other people, Evangelical denominations are some of the fastest growing in the world.

The Anabaptists form an interesting subset of Free Churches. Consisting of groups like the Mennonites, Hutterites, and Amish, Anabaptists typically strive to live simple lives, sometimes in communities of like-minded believers. The Amish and some Mennonites refuse to take advantage of modern technology, preferring to live like their ancestors did in earlier centuries. They separate themselves from the rest of society (to a greater or lesser extent), do not take oaths, and are pacifists. They are joined by the Quakers, Moravian Brethren, and others in making pacifism a central tenet of their faith.

Pentecostal and Neocharismatic Churches

> When the day of Pentecost had come, they were all together in one place. And suddenly from heaven there came a sound like the rush of a violent wind, and it filled the entire house where they were sitting. Divided tongues, as of fire, appeared among them, and a tongue rested on each of them. All of them were filled with the Holy Spirit and began to speak in other languages, as the Spirit gave them ability.
>
> (Acts 2:1–4)

Because of the distinctive origins of the Pentecostal and Neocharismatic churches, as well as their emphasis on the manifestations of the Holy Spirit, they will be treated in a separate section, despite their similarities in structure and theology to many of the Free Churches, and especially to the Evangelicals.

Though it had earlier roots in Holiness churches (many in the Wesleyan tradition), the Welsh Revival (1904–1905), and elsewhere, the birth of the Pentecostal movement is often dated to the start of the Azusa Street Revival in Los Angeles, California. William J. Seymour, an African American preacher, and some other Christians with him, experienced what he described as the Baptism of the Holy Spirit for the first time on 14 April 1906. Evidence that Seymour and the others had received spirit baptism was the fact that they began *speaking in tongues* (a phenomenon also called *glossolalia*), which they tied to experiences described as occurring on the Day of Pentecost in Acts 2:1–4. They soon ran out of room in the church in which they were meeting, so they moved to a building on Azusa Street, and the movement spread dramatically from there. Many Christians who had experienced spirit baptism left their denominations and joined with others to form new, Pentecostal denominations, like the Assemblies of God and the Church of God in Christ. Others stayed in their original denominations but continued to have experiences of the Holy Spirit that were manifested as glossolalia, prophecy, healing, and miracles. The Charismatic movement gained great momentum in the 1960s, associated in part with the Latter Rain Movement, and its practitioners considered the increase in practicing Charismatic Christians to be a Second Wave of the Holy Spirit. These Second Wave Charismatics either stayed in their original denominations or joined Pentecostal churches; for the most part they did not start new denominations. A Third Wave of the Holy Spirit began in the 1980s, when new manifestations of the Spirit were associated with such events as the Toronto Blessing and the Vineyard Movement. In the Third Wave, many Christians formed new, *Neocharismatic*, denominations such as the Association of Vineyard Churches and the House Church movement in China. Though many Third Wave Christians practice glossolalia, they tend to de-emphasize it, in comparison with classical Pentecostals, and stress the other manifestations of the Spirit.

Within 100 years of the Azusa Street Revival, various Pentecostal denominations (i.e. First Wave Pentecostals) claimed between 100 and 150 million members worldwide. If the Neocharismatic denominations are included, the total soars to almost 400 million members, by some estimates. Other Christians who had been baptized by the Holy

Some denominations, or groups of denominations, in the Pentecostal/Neocharismatic tradition

African Independent Churches (some)
Apostolic Church
Apostolic Faith Mission
Assemblies of God
Christ Apostolic Church
Christian Congregation of Brazil
Church of God
Church of God in Christ
Church of Jesus Christ of Prophecy
Igreja Pentecostal e Apostólica Missão Jesus
International Church of the Foursquare Gospel
Kimbanguist Church
Nondenominational Churches (some)
Pentecostal Mission
United Christian Church
United Pentecostal Church
Vineyard Churches
Zion Christian Church

Spirit stayed in their original denominations but shared their experiences with others, beginning *Charismatic movements* within a large number of denominations. This section will consider only separate Pentecostal and Neocharismatic denominations.

The largest Pentecostal denomination is the Assemblies of God, based in the U.S. but with more than 50 million members around the world. Other Pentecostal or Neocharismatic denominations include the Kimbanguist Church, based in the Democratic Republic of Congo; the Apostolic Church, based in Wales; the Christian Congregation of Brazil; and the Christ Apostolic Church, based in Nigeria. Although Pentecostalism began in the U.S., it boasts more members in both Africa and South America than in North America, making it a major factor in the growth of Christianity in the Southern Hemisphere. The largest individual Pentecostal church – in fact, the largest Christian church of any sort – is in Seoul, South Korea, and has about 800,000 members. Most Pentecostal/Neocharismatic churches are organized into denominational structures that provide support, but not oversight, for churches (i.e. congregational polity). In many cases the denominational structure is very informal, or even nonexistent. These churches typically recognize two levels of clergy, pastors/elders and deacons, allowing both married and women clergy. Their ultimate authority is the Bible, although in some smaller denominations the interpretation of a specific prophet (such as the denomination's founder) is particularly revered. They practice Baptism and the Lord's Supper (Eucharist), seeing the latter primarily as a symbol of Christ's death. Some groups and individual churches also practice foot washing.

Most Pentecostals and Neocharismatics believe in the standard Nicene and Chalcedonian orthodoxy concerning the Trinity, but a minority of Pentecostals, called Oneness Pentecostals, reject the orthodox view of the Trinity and hold a belief that has traditionally been called Modalism, in which God is manifested as Father, Son, and Holy Spirit, but the three are not distinct persons. (This view differs from Unitarianism, in which God is identified with the Father, but Jesus is simply human, and the Holy Spirit is the power or extension of the Father.) The largest group of Oneness Pentecostals is the United Pentecostal Church, which has about 3 million members worldwide. Oneness Pentecostals baptize in the name of Jesus alone, whereas most Pentecostals and Neocharismatics, like the vast majority of Christians generally, baptize in the name of the Father, Son, and Holy Spirit. Most Neocharismatics subscribe to traditional orthodoxy, but many of the African Independent Churches that are charismatic in nature, while holding to Nicene and Chalcedonian orthodoxy, differ in certain beliefs from most other Christians by virtue of the fact that they combine aspects of traditional African beliefs, such as a belief in the reality of ancestral spirits, with otherwise orthodox Christianity (for more on African Independent Churches, see below, "A Geographical Perspective"). Most Pentecostal and Neocharismatic churches accept members who have prayed the Sinner's Prayer and seek to be admitted to the church through baptism, as in Evangelical churches. They also typically expect that manifestations of the Holy Spirit – glossolalia, prophecy, or perhaps being *slain in the Spirit* (falling to the floor in a trance-like state) – will accompany the baptism of the Spirit, either at the point of conversion or at some later time, and repeatedly thereafter.

Another way to look at denominations

In 2001 David R. Barrett, Todd M. Johnson, and George T. Kurian published a book entitled *World Christian Encyclopedia: A Comparative Survey of Churches and Religions in the Modern World*, in two volumes (second edition; the first edition appeared in 1982). The first two authors also published a third volume, *World Christian Trends: AD 30 to AD 2200*, which interprets the data from the *Encyclopedia* and projects trends two centuries into the future. These books contain enormous amounts of demographic data and statistics on the current state of Christianity, as well as a historical overview of the growth of the church and projections of future trends. They group Christians into six *megablocs*. The first four are the traditional faith traditions identified as Catholic, Orthodox, Anglican, and Protestant. The fifth megabloc, Independents, includes those Christians who do not consider themselves to be affiliated with one of the traditional four megablocs. Included in this category are members of the African Independent Churches, members of various groups who think of themselves as "postdenominationalists" (those who think of denominational structures themselves as outmoded), as many Neocharismatics see themselves, and many, many others. In

The ecumenical movement

Despite the many differences that separate Christians from one another, most Christians in the twenty-first century have come to the conclusion that what unites Christians into one faith is more important than what divides them. They take as their starting point the Pauline exhortation in Eph 4:1–6:

> I therefore, the prisoner in the Lord, beg you to lead a life worthy of the calling to which you have been called, with all humility and gentleness, with patience, bearing with one another in love, making every effort to maintain the unity of the Spirit in the bond of peace. There is one body and one Spirit, just as you were called to the one hope of your calling, one Lord, one faith, one baptism, one God and Father of all, who is above all and through all and in all.

Although fracturing of the Christian family into separate groups had occurred earlier in church history – most notably after the Councils of Ephesus and Chalcedon, and after the Great Schism of 1054 – it was the Protestant Reformation in 1517 that led to the massive proliferation of Christian denominations claiming full or partial independence from one another. At the same time, some Protestant churches did sometimes try to heal rifts, such as with the Lutherans and the Reformed, and sometimes they succeeded, as when the German and Swiss branches of the Lutherans resolved the differences that their original leaders Luther and Zwingli had been unable to; both these events occurred in the sixteenth century. Despite occasional successes, however, fragmentation rather than unification of Protestant groups was the norm during the period following the Reformation.

The nineteenth century Stone-Campbell Restoration movement was an attempt in the U.S. to find common ground on which Protestants could unite, but it resulted in the formation of more denominations, not fewer. Only in the twentieth century did large numbers of Protestant denominations start to merge with one another. In the U.S., several larger denominations were formed from the merger of smaller denominations within the same faith-tradition. For example, in 1987 the Evangelical Lutheran Church in America formed from a merger of smaller groups, many of whom in turn had been formed by mergers earlier in the century. Around the world, denominations from the same faith tradition began coalescing into larger groups. In 1905 the Baptist World Alliance was formed as an umbrella organization for Baptist denominations, and today it has more than two hundred member conventions and unions, although it does not function as a single denomination. In 1968 a new denomination, the United Methodist Church, based in the U.S. but with members around the world, was formed with member churches that were previously members of various Methodist churches, the Church of the United Brethren, and the Evangelical Association.

In addition to denominations that have merged or otherwise affiliated with one another within a single faith tradition, or among closely related faith traditions, some denominations in the twentieth century started seeking alliances further afield. These new denominations, referred to as United and Uniting Churches, formed from the merger of somewhat more disparate denominations. Sometimes the mergers were small, as when the Waldensian Evangelical Church, which traces its roots to Peter Waldo in the twelfth century, merged with the Italian Methodist Church to form the Union of Waldensian and Methodist Churches. Sometimes they were larger. For example, in 1957 the United Church of Christ was formed from the merger of the Evangelical and Reformed Church and the Congregational Christian Churches, both of which were also the results of earlier mergers of U.S. churches; and in 1977 the Uniting Church in Australia formed from the merger of Congregationalist, Methodist, and Presbyterian Churches. The movement toward merger across the lines of faith tradition is especially strong outside Europe and North America, particularly in places where Protestant Christians are in the minority. For example, the Church of North India was founded in 1970 from a merger of Anglican, Baptist, Methodist, Disciples of Christ, Presbyterian, Congregational, and Brethren Churches; and the Organization of African Instituted Churches was formed in 1978 to represent many of the AICs.

Interdenominational dialog, that is, formal discussion between member churches representing different major faith traditions within the Christian church, abounded in the twentieth century and continues today. One of the most notable examples of progress being made as the result of this type of dialog was the Joint Declaration on the Doctrine of Justification, produced as a result of discussions between Roman Catholic and Lutheran Christians. Numerous associations of Christian churches within single countries – national councils of churches – were formed in the twentieth century, but the organization that most clearly exemplifies the ecumenical movement is the World Council of Churches, formed in 1948. The WCC currently represents 348 distinct denominations in more than 120 countries. If the membership of the Roman Catholic Church, a regular dialog partner with the WCC, is added to the membership of the constituent churches of the WCC, approximately 1.6 billion Christians and their denominations are participating in the ecumenical movement, representing about three-fourths of all Christians worldwide.

fact, according to the statistics cited in *Encyclopedia*, which is updated in the *World Christian Database*, the number of Independents (386 million) surpasses the number of Protestants (342 million), excluding Anglicans. The sixth megabloc, Marginal Christians, are those denominations that hold unorthodox views concerning the nature of Christ or the Trinity, including Mormons, Jehovah's Witnesses, Christian Scientists, and Unitarian Universalists. Not included in this category is the United Pentecostal Church, which is listed among the Protestants, but, like other Oneness Pentecostals, holds a view of the Trinity that is outside the historical orthodox tradition.

The classification scheme used by the *World Christian Encyclopedia* has the advantage of focusing attention on a major trend in twentieth and twenty-first century Christianity, the tendency for Christians to define themselves in ways that are not bound by tradition (in the case of the Independents, not the so-called Marginal Christians). One disadvantage is that it allows self-identification to supersede other important factors in classification, so that groups of Christians that share a common heritage and are quite similar in terms of doctrine and practice may find themselves on opposite sides of the Protestant-Independent fence. For example, the Southern Baptist Convention, the largest Baptist denomination in the U.S., is listed among the Protestants, but the next three largest Baptist denominations in the U.S. – the National Baptist Convention, USA; the National Baptist Convention of America; and the Progressive National Baptist Convention – are all listed among the Independents. The reason for listing the various National Baptist groups with the Independents is that they are historically Black churches, and denominations that are identified primarily with a particular racial or ethnic group are placed in the Independent category. The same distribution between the two megablocs also occurs among U.S. Methodists, with the United Methodist Church placed in the Protestant category and the African Methodist Episcopal Church numbered among the Independents. Similarly, the Pentecostals are primarily placed in the Protestant camp, but the Neocharismatics are placed in the Independent camp.

Although self-identification is important to consider when classifying Christian groups, the rise of huge numbers of Christians since the early twentieth century who belong to denominations that think of themselves as Independents, separated from older denominations, suggests that Christian independence movements are to a large extent part of the continuing backlash against colonialist and repressive policies that characterized so much of European and North American Christianity since the late fifteenth century. Furthermore, lack of formal ties between denominations that share similar beliefs and practices does not keep them from associating with one another in a variety of settings, such as work on social issues of common concern. With one of the tendencies of modern Protestant Christianity being a trend for denominations with much in common to merge into larger denominations, it is likely that many of those groups that now self-identify as Independents will eventually join with other denominations, whether Independents or Protestants, to enhance their own ability to carry out their mission. There is no doubt that many of the groups listed among the Independents have beliefs or practices that are divergent enough to preclude them from joining forces with more traditional denominations any time in the near future, and it is also evident that the tendency toward postdenominationalism will continue to grow in the near future. Nevertheless, it is not clear that many, perhaps most, of the Christian groups that the *Encyclopedia* classifies as Independent are significantly different from Christian denominations listed among the Protestants. For these reasons, the use of the "Independent" category has not been adopted in this chapter. Instead, Free Churches and Pentecostals/Neocharismatics have been classified separately from other Protestants, and those groups included in the *Encyclopedia* as Marginal Christians have been placed among the Free Churches, as indicated above. Both classifications schemes have their advantages and disadvantages, and the six megablocs of Barrett and his colleagues will undoubtedly continue to be both influential and helpful to those studying modern Christianity.

Key points you need to know

- A denomination is a group of Christian churches that have common beliefs and practices and that are associated with one another in some organized fashion.
- A faith tradition is a group of Christian denominations that share a common historical ancestry, as well as certain beliefs and practices that distinguish them from other faith traditions.
- Four main types of church polity, or organizational structure, are episcopal, presbyterian, congregational, and societal.
- The Roman Catholic Church is by far the largest individual Christian denomination, and the Catholic faith tradition, which also includes the Old Catholic Church, is the largest of the Christian faith traditions. The Roman Catholic Church is led by the pope, the bishop of Rome, and follows an episcopal form of church government.
- The Eastern Orthodox Churches are made up of several autonomous Churches, led by the ecumenical patriarch of Constantinople. The ecumenical patriarch, however, has no actual authority over Orthodox Christians outside his own Orthodox Church of Constantinople. The Eastern Orthodox Churches follow an episcopal form of church government.
- The Oriental Orthodox Churches, which diverged from the Great Church in the fifth century, while not in communion with the Eastern Orthodox Churches, share many traditions and practices with them.
- Anglican and Episcopal Churches are made up of several different regional bodies, which share a common episcopal structure. The nominal leader of the Anglican communion is the Archbishop of Canterbury.
- Churches of the Magisterial Reform are those denominations that arose directly as a result of the work of the early Protestant Reformers, such as Luther, Zwingli, and Calvin. Lutherans and Reformed/Presbyterians are the two largest subgroups within this faith tradition. Their polity is generally either episcopal, presbyterian, or some combination of the two, although some Churches in this tradition practice congregationalism.
- Free Churches are all those denominations, with the exception of Pentecostal and Neocharismatic denominations, that may be classified as Protestant but have never been an official state church and thus have historically rejected any official affiliation with the state. Although most Churches in this category follow a congregational church polity, the other three types of polity are represented as well in some denominations within this faith tradition.
- Pentecostal and Neocharismatic denominations, while sharing many characteristics with the Free Churches, are unique in the special importance they attribute to the work of the Holy Spirit in the lives of individual Christians. Christians in these denominations often speak in tongues or exhibit other manifestations attributed to the work of the Spirit.

Discussion questions

1. What are the historical and pragmatic reasons behind the development of each of the forms of church polity?
2. What accounts for the success of the Roman Catholic Church in terms of the number of adherents?
3. How do Eastern Orthodox beliefs and practice compare with those of Roman Catholics? of Protestants?
4. How do Anglican/Episcopalian beliefs and practice compare with those of Roman Catholics? of other Protestants?
5. Has the support of the state helped or hindered the work of Lutheran and Reformed Churches in those areas where they are still the official state church? How have these denominations fared in areas where they were not the official state church?
6. In what ways does the notion of congregational polity contribute to the large amount of diversity found among Free Churches? How does the Free Church understanding of the concept of authority compare with that of other Christian faith traditions?
7. How are Christians identified with the First, Second, and Third Waves of the Holy Spirit similar and different in their views of the Spirit and in their understanding of their relationship with other Christians?

Further reading

Adherents.com. http://www.adherents.com.

Barrett, David R. and Todd M. Johnson 2001. *World Christian Trends*. Pasadena, CA: William Carey Library.

Barrett, David R. *et al.* 2001. *World Christian Encyclopedia: A Comparative Survey of Churches and Religions in the Modern World*. 2nd edn. New York: Oxford University Press.

Day, Peter 2003. *A Dictionary of Christian Denominations*. London: Continuum.

McBrien, Richard R. 1994. *Catholicism*. 2nd edn. New York: HarperSanFrancisco.

Ware, Timothy 1997. *The Orthodox Church*. 2nd edn. New York: Penguin.

World Christian Database. Online database. http://worldchristiandatabase.org/wcd/.

17 A geographical perspective

You will be my witnesses in Jerusalem, in all Judea and Samaria, and to the ends of the earth.

(Acts 1:8)

In this chapter

Christian churches can be found in every region of the world. Christianity is the dominant religion in Europe, the Americas, and Australia/Oceania, but while Christianity is slowly losing ground to other religions and secularism in Europe, it is growing rapidly in sub-Saharan Africa and parts of Asia, places where the world's population is also growing rapidly. Denominational affiliations are shifting in many places, with Protestantism, particularly of a Pentecostal or Neocharismatic variety, encroaching on traditional Roman Catholic and Eastern Orthodox lands. African Independent Churches, which are independent of European or North American denominations, are also growing rapidly.

Main topics covered

- The Church in Europe
- The Church in Asia
- The Church in North America
- The Church in Latin America and the Caribbean
- The Church in Africa
- The Church in Australia and Oceania

The church was born in a small, eastern province of the Roman Empire, near the eastern frontier of the empire. The church spread rapidly within the boundaries of the Roman Empire, as well as in neighboring regions just beyond the borders, so that when the emperor Constantine declared Christianity a legal religion in the empire, the map of the Christian world was not much larger than the map of the Roman Empire, with the exception of a Christian presence in and around Armenia, just east of the empire. Small outposts of Christianity existed as well in parts of the Persian Empire, south of Egypt in Nubia and Ethiopia, and in India. Over the centuries, Christianity spread throughout the Mediterranean world and north into the rest of Europe, but its growth to the east was hindered, though not completely stopped, by the rise of Islam. In fact, places where Christians were formerly highly concentrated, such as Egypt, North Africa, Syria, Spain, and especially Anatolia, became predominantly Muslim. During the Middle Ages, Christianity was concentrated in the ever shrinking Byzantine Empire, centered on Constantinople, and in Europe. With the arrival of the modern period, Christianity experienced new and rapid growth, at first in the Western Hemisphere, then later in Australia, Oceania, sub-Saharan Africa, and parts of Asia. Christianity often accompanied colonialism in these new areas, but in recent decades the church in many areas once under the rule or influence of Europe has changed markedly, often taking on a flavor that is influenced by regional interests and customs. The statistics listed in this section are derived primarily from the *World Christian Database*, an updated version of the statistics from the *World Christian Encyclopedia*.

The Church in Europe

Despite its birth in western Asia, the spiritual, if not necessarily the statistical, center of Christianity over the past 1,500 years has traditionally been Europe. Rome was the heart of the Church in the West, and Constantinople of the Church in the East. The fall of Constantinople to the Muslims in 1453 greatly reduced its influence over European Christians, and the Protestant Reformation in 1517 began a process that gradually reduced the influence of the Church in Rome, as Northern and Western Europe became increasingly Protestant. It was the *secularism* that grew out of the Enlightenment and the Industrial Revolution, however, that has shaped modern Europe, turning it into a region in which Christianity, while still the dominant religious tradition in most areas, is waning in influence and membership, as a percentage of the population. The decline in European Christianity should not be exaggerated – it still claims about 75 percent of the population – but this figure is down from the figure of 95 percent or more that Europe claimed at the beginning of the twentieth century (statistics for Europe in this section include the Asian part of Russia). The Christian presence in Europe would be in even more decline if not for the influx of immigrants from Africa and Asia, many of whom bring their commitment to Christianity with them when they enter Europe in search of jobs and to escape war and poverty (many also bring commitments to other religions). Another factor in the decreasing impact of Europe on the Christian church is the fact that, according to demographers, the population of Europe will remain more or less stable over the next half century, while many countries in Africa, Asia, and Latin America will experience remarkable growth. Corresponding to the growth in general population will be growth in the Christian population, especially in Africa and Latin America, so that European Christians will comprise a smaller and smaller percentage of the worldwide Christian population as the twenty-first century progresses.

Christianity in Europe has traditionally been divided between the Catholic south, the Orthodox east, and the Protestant north, and those patterns of distribution remain largely true today. However, secularism has made headway in many parts of Europe, so that today almost 20 percent of Europeans claim to be either atheists or nonreligious. A large majority of Christians in Europe still belong to one of the large faith traditions: Catholic, Orthodox, Anglican, or Magisterial Protestant, though the number of those in other traditions is increasing, often at the expense of the current and former state churches. Despite declines over the past century, Europe continues to claim the most Christians of any region, 553 million, or 26 percent of the worldwide Christian population.

The Church in Asia

> And Jesus came and said to them, "All authority in heaven and on earth has been given to me. Go therefore and make disciples of all nations, baptizing them in the name of the Father and of the Son and of the Holy Spirit, and teaching them to obey everything that I have commanded you. And remember, I am with you always, to the end of the age."
>
> (Matt 28:18–20)

Christianity began in western Asia, and it saw some of its greatest early growth in Palestine, Syria, Armenia, and Anatolia. Christianity also gained a toehold in India and the Persian Empire prior to the rise of Islam. Even after the advent of Islam severely reduced its numbers, some regions in Western Asia continued to have relatively high concentrations of Christians, even outside the borders of the Byzantine Empire. In 1900, Christians and Jews together made up perhaps 30 percent of the population of the Ottoman Empire (which included Egypt). Over the next century or so the population of Christians in Western Asia plummeted precipitously, under the influence of events such as the massacres of Armenians and other Christians by the Turks, the fall of the Ottoman Empire, the end of the British and French mandates in the Middle East, the founding of the state of Israel, the civil war in Lebanon, the Iranian Revolution, the Palestinian *intifadas*, and the two Iraq wars led by the U.S. As late as 1950 about half the population of Lebanon and some 15 percent of Arabs in Palestine were Christians, and sizeable minorities of Christians existed in Iraq and Syria. The numbers today are quite different. Christians still make up between 35 percent and 40 percent of the population of Lebanon, but in Syria (5 percent), Jordan (3 percent), Palestine (2 percent), Iraq (3 percent), Israel (3 percent), and Turkey (less than 1 percent), the percentage of Christians is much lower than at any point in the past 1,800 years. Only in the traditionally Christian nations of Armenia and Georgia has Christianity remained dominant, with about 83 percent of Armenians and 64 percent of Georgians describing themselves as Christians. Christianity also makes up close to 10 percent of the population in the United Arab Emirates, Kuwait, and Bahrain. Orthodoxy, especially Oriental Orthodoxy, is the affiliation of about 60 percent of the Christians in Western Asia.

In some other parts of Asia, the church is growing rapidly, along with the rest of the population. Christianity makes up less than 10 percent of the populations of China and India, but the total number of Christians in those countries, 111 million and 68 million, respectively, make them the countries with the third and seventh largest populations of Christians in the world. In China, 64 percent of Christians belong to Neocharismatic groups, and in India 47 percent belong to either Pentecostal or Neocharismatic denominations. South Korea is the country in East and South Asia, on the continent itself, with the largest percentage of Christians, 42 percent, with Pentecostals/Neocharismatics outnumbering both Catholics and Protestants. By far the most Christian nation in Asia east of Armenia is the Philippines, which is 89 percent Christian, mostly Catholic. The picture of Christianity in Asia is one of decline in many parts of the West but growth in the East and South, with the most rapid growth among Neocharismatic denominations. About 350 million Christians live in Asia, or 16 percent of Christians worldwide. (The Asian part of Russia is predominantly Russian Orthodox, but statistics for Russia as a whole were grouped with the statistics for Europe, above.)

The Church in North America

Christianity in the U.S. and Canada came with European settlers, beginning in the early seventeenth century. Protestantism dominated the earliest period of settlement on the East coast of North America, while at about the same time Spaniards were pushing north with the gospel into what is now Florida and the U.S. Southwest, making these regions predominantly Catholic. Today Protestants of all types outnumber Catholics about 2 to 1 in North America. A sizeable population of Mormons is concentrated in the Western states, particularly Utah, where its adherents constitute the majority of the population. The Roman Catholic Church is the largest denomination in the U.S., followed by the Southern Baptist Convention, the National Baptist Convention, USA, and the United Methodist Church. Almost 75 percent of all Protestants are either Neocharismatics, Evangelicals, or Pentecostals. The low birth rate and high saturation rate (83 percent) of Christianity in North America suggests that future developments in Christianity will primarily involve movements from one Christian denomination to another rather than a large increase in the percentage or a significant increase in the total number of Christians. The 277 million Christians in North America comprise about 13 percent of the global population of Christians.

The Church in Latin America and the Caribbean

The region that includes Mexico, Central America, South America, and the Caribbean is the most thoroughly Christian region on earth. Five hundred and seventeen million Christians live in the area, and they make up about 93 percent of the total population. The Roman Catholic Church has about 93 percent of Christians in its records as members, but more than 20 percent of the people claim to be Protestants or other non-Catholic Christians. The reason for the discrepancy in the figures is that many people who are baptized into the Catholic Church as babies have joined other churches as adults, but since their baptism makes them Catholics for life, unless they explicitly ask to be removed from the rolls, they are counted by both Catholics and Protestants. The true numbers are probably closer to 80 percent Catholic and 20 percent Protestant throughout the region, with Protestant churches gaining ground on the Roman Catholic Church. Jamaica, Trinidad and Tobago, and Guyana – all former British colonies – are the only majority Protestant countries in the region with more than half a million inhabitants. Brazil, the most populous country in Latin America, also has the highest concentration of Protestants, more than 30 percent of the Christian population, and more than 80 percent of Protestants in Brazil are Pentecostals and Neocharismatics. More than 30 percent of the population of Chile is also Protestant, the vast majority of whom are Neocharismatic. Other Latin American and Caribbean countries (with populations greater than 500,000) with sizeable percentages of Protestants include Guatemala (27 percent), Haiti (27 percent), El Salvador (25 percent), and Nicaragua (21 percent). Although the Latin American and Caribbean region is the most thoroughly Christian on the planet, so that it is doubtful that the percentage of Christians there will rise in the foreseeable future, the high growth rate of the overall population (projected at almost 60 percent over the next half century) almost guarantees that the number of Christians in the region will increase dramatically, with the greatest growth coming among Protestants, and particularly among Neocharismatics. The Christian population of Latin America and the Caribbean is now approximately 517 million, which constitutes 24 percent of the worldwide Christian population.

The Church in Africa

Of all the major regions in the world, over the past century the church has grown the most rapidly in Africa. Christianity arrived in Africa in the first century, as the gospel reached Egypt and North Africa and those regions soon became predominantly Christian. The gospel also spread south along the Nile to Nubia (northern Sudan and southern Egypt) and Ethiopia. The rise of Islam all but destroyed Christianity in North Africa, but the Christian church held on tenaciously in Egypt, particularly in the form of the Coptic Orthodox Church, and today Christians make up about 15 percent of the population. Historically, Ethiopia has remained a predominantly Christian nation, and it remains so today, with about 55 percent of its population professing Christianity. The highest rate of growth for Christianity in recent times, however, has been south of the Sahara. There Nigeria, the most populous country, is also the most populous Christian country on the continent, with 61 million Christians, about 47 percent of the total population. The Democratic Republic of Congo has the second largest Christian population, 53 million, representing 95 percent of the population. Throughout the sub-Saharan region the story is much the same. Christianity is the majority religion in most of Africa's 60 countries, all of them south of the Sahara. In fact, the continent of Africa

African Independent Churches

In addition to Africa's ancient churches, such as the Coptic and Ethiopian Orthodox churches, and to African churches closely allied with faith traditions or denominations that originated in Europe, Western Asia, or North America, Africa has many denominations that have no organizational ties with Churches outside the continent. Most of these churches, called AICs (which may stand for African Independent Churches, African Indigenous Churches, African Initiated Churches, or African Instituted Churches) are distributed among the Free Church and Pentecostal/Neocharismatic faith traditions, but some share beliefs, traditions, and practices with Roman Catholic, Orthodox, Anglican, and Magisterial Reform Churches. A list of some of AICs follows:

African Congregational Church
Apostles of Johane Maranke
Celestial Church of Christ
Christ Apostolic Church
Church of the Lord (Aladura)
Kimbanguist Church
Nazareth Baptist Church
Zion Christian Church
Zulu Congregational Church

is almost evenly divided between Muslims in the north and Christians in the south, with practitioners of traditional African religions concentrated south of the Sahara as well.

Oriental Orthodox Christians make up the vast majorities of the Christian population in Egypt (Coptic Orthodox) and in Ethiopia and Eritrea (Ethiopian Orthodox). Otherwise, Protestants of all sorts outnumber Catholics by about 7 to 4 throughout the rest of Africa. One of the most interesting developments in Christianity over the past 100 years is the rise of the African Independent Churches, also called African Initiated Churches, African Indigenous Churches, or African Instituted Churches (AICs). These churches are made up of Christians who left traditional, colonial Christian denominations and started new churches or denominations that often have a strong African flavor. Although Christianity in sub-Saharan Africa was sparked in many areas by European and North American missionaries, the growth of the church was too rapid in many places for missionaries to handle effectively. In addition, African resistance to colonial political powers had its counterpart in the church, and new denominations, often different in significant ways from the colonial churches, sprang up. A few examples will illustrate the nature of the African Independent Churches.

The Kikuyu people are Kenya's largest tribe, and they began their conversion to Christianity with the arrival of the first white missionaries in the first decade of the twentieth century. Soon Kikuyu Christians ran into conflicts with the missionaries. In the late 1920s, the missionaries tried to put a stop to the custom of female circumcision, which the Kikuyu had been practicing since time immemorial. This conflict led many Kikuyu to leave the mission churches and start their own, independent churches. Others started churches that were focused on influencing the Kenyan government, then under British administration. Still others formed "praying" churches that abhorred any involvement in politics. One emphasis that most of these movements shared was a commitment to reading and interpreting the Bible for themselves. When they found no laws condemning female circumcision, but they did find many stories describing the polygamy practiced by Old Testament men of faith, they argued with the missionaries over their strictures on traditional Kikuyu practices. Over the ensuing decades, the variety of forms of Christianity multiplied among the Kikuyu. Today, some Kikuyu Christians claim that the salvation spoken of in the Bible has no connection with issues of social justice. Others say that only the Second Coming of Christ will bring justice to the world. At the same time, other Kikuyu Christians argue that the state is responsible before God for making sure that justice reigns. The Kikuyu today are predominantly Christian, spread among a wide variety of independent and traditional (colonial) forms of Christianity.

In 1921 Simon Kimbangu, a Christian convert in the Belgian Congo (the modern Democratic Republic of Congo), started his own church, putting an emphasis on healing and biblical teaching. Although imprisoned by the colonial authorities, his movement grew, and today it numbers between 1 and 3 million followers. Church teachings are quite similar to what Kimbangu learned from the Baptist missionaries who instructed him in his youth. The Kimbanguist Church condemns polygamy, which was widely practiced in that region of Africa, and it forbids the production or consumption of traditional palm wine. Members of the church suffered widespread, albeit intermittent, persecution under the Belgian authorities, before finally achieving recognition as an official church near the end of the colonial period. In 1970 the Kimbanguist Church joined the World Council of Churches. A small minority of Kimbanguist churches today revere Simon Kimbangu as a prophet.

Among the Yoruba people of Nigeria, the Aladura Churches were started in 1930 by Josiah Olunowo Ositelu and several associates. Most of the founders came out of the Anglican tradition, but the church grew to emphasize the power of the Holy Spirit (i.e. Pentecostal/Charismatic emphases) and a distinctive method of reading the Bible, which takes into account the cultural background of the Yoruba people. Because the missionaries who first converted the Yoruba to Christianity required them to stop using traditional incantations, medicines, or charms to protect themselves from the evil spirits unleashed by their enemies, they turned to the scripture for help. They found in certain Psalms words that proved themselves to be powerful deterrents of evil. In Psalm 55, for example, they found an effective means of protecting themselves, because the psalm, when recited repeatedly, causes evildoers to die (cf. Ps 55:15, 23). Certain psalms were also written down and kept as amulets to ward off evil. For Yoruba Christians, the spirit world is a powerful reality that did not disappear with the advent of Christianity, and their distinctive interpretation of the Bible helps them come to terms with both their new religion and their traditional culture.

The precise number of Christians who belong to AICs is disputed, with figures ranging from a low of 35 million to more than 100 million. The actual number is perhaps as high as 90 million, depending primarily on how one classifies specific African denominations. Those AICs that incorporate elements of traditional African culture and systems of belief perhaps deserve to be considered independently of traditional forms of Christianity whose roots lie in Europe or North America. On the other hand, the similarities between AICs and other churches are numerous, so maybe it is best to take a two-pronged approach, recognizing the indigenous origins of AICs while at the same time looking for points of commonality between them and other churches around the world.

Christianity surpassed Islam as the dominant religion in Africa within the past decade, and it currently has about 411 million adherents, compared with 358 million Muslims and 107 million practitioners of traditional religions. Because it still comprises only 46 percent of the total population of Africa, its potential for growth over the next few decades is large, though it faces a formidable challenge from Islam, particularly in the north. Projected population growth rates, along with trends that indicate continued growth in the number of Christians, suggest that Africa will become the continent with the largest number of Christians sometime in the next 50 years.

The Church in Australia and Oceania

Christianity arrived in Australia and the Pacific islands with missionaries and traders, and eventually with colonists starting in the late eighteenth century, after the voyages of Captain Cook. In Australia and New Zealand the number of British settlers, both voluntary and involuntary (Australia was founded as a penal colony), soon surpassed the population of displaced Aborigines and Maoris native to those lands, and they brought their Christian religion with them. European powers and the U.S. eventually took control of almost every island in the Pacific, and those islands, too, soon became predominantly Christian. Roman Catholics make up the largest number of Christians in the region (9 million), followed closely by non-Anglican Protestants (8 million), then Anglicans (5 million). Unlike in other regions, the number of Pentecostals and Neocharismatics is relatively small, comprising less than 10 percent of the total number of Christians. Approximately 26 million Christians live in Australia and Oceania today, comprising about 80 percent of the total population. The Christian population of this region is only about 1 percent of the total world Christian population. Projected growth rates for the overall population are small, and the saturation level of Christianity in the region probably precludes large increases in the percentage of the population that is Christian, so the next few decades will probably see only a modest growth in the total number of Christians in the area.

Patterns of Christian growth over the past century have significantly redefined both the location and the nature of the center of Christendom. In 1900, 82 percent of all Christians lived either in Europe or in North America. They were divided among Catholics, Orthodox, Anglicans, Mainline Protestants, and Free Churches; the Asuza Street Revival, which gave birth to the Pentecostal/Charismatic movement, had not yet occurred. Today, a little more than 100 years later, the picture is very different. Less than 40 percent of all Christians live in Europe or North America, and more than 40 percent live in Africa or Latin America. Another 19 percent live in Asia. This shift to the south and, to a lesser extent, to the east, will define Christianity for the next several decades, particularly as the overall populations of Africa, Latin America, and Asia grow dramatically and the populations of Europe and North America more or less stabilize. In addition to the shifting demographics of Christianity, the growth of Independent denominations, particularly those associated with the Charismatic movement in one way or another, will create a form of Christianity that is less committed to old denominational structures, and that is also less committed to old ideas, or at least to old formulations of traditional Christian doctrine. The Christianity of 50 years from now will likely be concentrated in the south, with more than half of all Christians living in Africa or Latin America, and another 20 percent or so in Asia. Europeans and North Americans will still have important contributions to make to the development of Christian ideas and practices, but they will no longer be in the driver's seat.

Key points you need to know

- Christianity is still the dominant religion in Europe, but the presence of Islam and the growth of secularism are cutting into the overall population of Christians in Europe.
- Although the Church was born in Western Asia, Christianity has largely been replaced by Islam in that region, although large numbers of Christians remain in a few countries, such as Lebanon, Armenia, and Georgia.
- Christianity is growing rapidly in parts of South and East Asia, though Christians remain in the minority there (except in the Philippines).
- Christianity is the religious affiliation of most people living in the United States and Canada, with Protestants outnumbering Catholics 2 to 1. Roman Catholics are the predominant denomination, however, in many parts of the Southwest U.S., which has a large Hispanic population, and Mormons are the majority denomination in Utah.
- The Church in Latin America and the Caribbean is overwhelmingly Catholic, but Protestants – particularly Pentecostals and Neocharismatics – are growing rapidly in countries like Brazil and Chile.
- Christianity has grown more rapidly in Africa over the past century than in any other region. Christians have been present in Egypt and Ethiopia for well over 1,000 years, but

Christianity is now growing the fastest in sub-Saharan Africa. Other than Egypt, Eritrea, and Ethiopia, whose Christians are predominantly Oriental Orthodox, Protestants, including those in African Independent Churches, make up the majority of African Christians.

- Christians constitute the majority of people in Australia and Oceania, divided among Catholics, Anglicans, and non-Anglican Protestants.

Discussion questions

1. Why has secularism grown faster in Europe than in other regions?
2. How will the diminishing influence of European Christians over the next several decades affect Christianity, and especially those Churches whose home bases are in Europe, such as Roman Catholics, Eastern Orthodox, and Anglicans?
3. Why has Christianity grown more rapidly in places like India and China and less rapidly in Western Asia?
4. What demographic, political, and social trends are likely to affect the face of North American Christianity over the next 50 years?
5. Why is the Roman Catholic Church losing ground to certain Protestant denominations in many parts of Latin America and the Caribbean?
6. What is the significance of the growth of African Independent Churches?

Further reading

Barrett, David R. and Todd M. Johnson 2001. *World Christian Trends*. Pasadena, CA: William Carey Library.

Barrett, David R. *et al.* 2001. *World Christian Encyclopedia: A Comparative Survey of Churches and Religions in the Modern World*. 2nd edn. New York: Oxford University Press.

Jenkins, Philip 2002. *The Next Christendom: The Coming of Global Christianity*. Oxford: Oxford University Press.

Maxwell, David 1998. *Christianity and the African Imagination*. Leiden: Brill.

West, Gerald O. and Musa W. Duba, eds 2001. *The Bible in Africa*. Boston, MA: Brill.

World Christian Database. Online database. http://worldchristiandatabase.org/wcd/.

18 *A doctrinal perspective*

One Lord, one faith, one baptism.

(Eph 4:5)

In this chapter

From the very beginning, Christians have understood the person and work of Jesus Christ in different ways, and they have also had diverse opinions on other doctrinal matters as well. Shared beliefs and perspectives do not always follow strict denominational lines, often cutting across the boundaries of denominations and even faith traditions. This chapter will examine several doctrinal issues on which Christians disagree.

Main topics covered

- The Trinity
- The Holy Spirit
- Justification by Faith
- Church and State
- Eschatology
- Traditional and progressive churches

Recently a group of Baptist theologians, representing different Baptist denominations from around the world, and a group of Roman Catholic theologians held a meeting to discuss issues of importance to both Baptists and Catholics and to draw up position papers on these issues. They soon discovered, however, that the differences of opinion among Baptists from different parts of the world were often greater than the differences of opinion between many of the Baptists present and the Catholics. This story illustrates the point that denominational affiliation, while an important indicator of a particular Christian's beliefs and practices, in no way completely defines them. Christians regularly ally themselves across denominational lines to support or oppose certain causes, or to take a stand for a certain set of beliefs. They frequently find themselves in opposition to other Christians from their same faith tradition, or even from their same denomination. Another way to examine the varieties of Christianity, then, is to look at specific theological issues on which Christians, often within the same denomination or faith tradition, disagree.

The Trinity

One of the defining issues for Christians throughout the history of the church has been the question of the Trinity. The first ecumenical council, held at Nicaea in 325, dealt with an issue – the relation of the divine and human in Christ – that was key to the still developing doctrine of the Trinity. Augustine and the Great Cappadocians, relying on earlier work by Tertullian, Origen, and others, formulated what came to be considered the normative, orthodox view of the Trinity. The Trinity, they said, consisted of one God in three Persons, distinct from one another and yet united in substance. The term "Tri-unity" might better describe the orthodox position than the more traditional "Trinity." Debate over the nature, or even the existence, of the Trinity did not stop, of course, just because respected theologians offered their understanding of the nature of God. The idea that Jesus was not fully divine, or at least not completely the Father's equal in the Godhead, was voiced by the Ebionites, the Arians, and the Adoptionists prior to the Council of Nicaea, and the idea continued to resurface from time to time, for example, in Michael Servetus, the Socinians, and the Deists.

Similarly unorthodox views are advocated today by Unitarians, Jehovah's Witnesses, and the Church of Jesus Christ of Latter-day Saints. The Unitarians' position on the Trinity is simple. Like the Socinians and the Deists, they view Jesus as a great teacher, but he was not divine, and thus there is no Trinity at all, only a single, sovereign God. The Jehovah's Witness position on the Trinity is closer to that of Arius than to the Deists. They believe that Jesus was the first created being, God's only Son, and God used him to create everything else in the universe. The view of the Mormons regarding the Trinity is quite idiosyncratic, and it is based as much on the *Book of Mormon* and other sectarian Mormon documents as on the Bible. The Mormons speak of the reality of the Trinity, but they view God as the literal father of Jesus Christ, born to him by his wife through natural processes. After living an exemplary life, Jesus was elevated to the status of the divine, as God and his wife had been in the distant past.

A second deviation from traditional orthodoxy regarding the Trinity moves in the opposite direction from the Ebionites and their followers. Instead of viewing Jesus as less than fully equal to God, groups like the Docetists, the Sabellians, and the Modalists held that to divide the Godhead at all into separate Persons was to deny Jesus full divinity. Those who held Modalist positions saw the three "Persons" of the Trinity as three different expressions of God, not as distinct at all. God was Father in creation and in relationship to the Son, Son in redemption and relationship to the Father and the Spirit, and Spirit in regeneration of believers and in relationship to the Father and Son, yet the three were completely indistinct. This type of view is expressed today in the official position of Oneness Pentecostals such as the United Pentecostal Church and by followers of Emanuel Swedenborg. These Christians do not deny the full humanity of Jesus, but they believe that the doctrine of the Trinity is unbiblical, separating God and destroying God's unity.

The Modalist position, though the official view of only a small number of Christian denominations, expresses a view of the Father, Son, and Holy Spirit that many ordinary Christians would voice if asked what the doctrine of the Trinity means to them. This way of thinking communicates their understanding of Jesus as fully divine, in contrast to the view held by Unitarians and others that Jesus is not divine at all, except in the sense that all humans are created in God's image and (may) contain a divine spark within. It might be more accurate, then, to view the Modalist position as a variant of the orthodox position, and contrast it with those views that see Jesus as less than fully divine.

The Holy Spirit

> For all who are led by the Spirit of God are children of God. For you did not receive a spirit of slavery to fall back into fear, but you have received a spirit of adoption. When we cry, "Abba! Father!" it is that very Spirit bearing witness with our spirit that we are children of God, and if children, then heirs, heirs of God and joint heirs with Christ – if, in fact, we suffer with him so that we may also be glorified with him.
>
> (Rom 8:14–17)

The original version of the Nicene Creed, before it was elaborated upon by the Council of Constantinople, had somewhat developed sections on what Christians were to believe about God the Father and especially the Son. Concerning the third Person of the Trinity, however, the creed simply says, "We believe ... in the Holy Spirit." What exactly did the early church believe about the Holy Spirit? Some New Testament writers present the Holy Spirit, or Spirit of God, as a manifestation of divine power, sent to people to "inspire" them to speak the words of God. Paul describes the Spirit in more personal terms, as something that lives within individual believers and interacts with their own spirit, sometimes communicating with God when the normal human spirit was unable to express its needs effectively (Rom 8:26–27). John goes even further, calling the Holy Spirit the Comforter, whom God will send to believers after Jesus' departure to teach them and help them remember everything that Jesus said (John 14:26). After the classical doctrine of the Trinity was formulated, Christians saw the Holy Spirit as an equal part of the Trinity. The Spirit was active in regeneration, that is, in removing the sin of believers and helping them live righteous lives. The Spirit was especially important in the lives of many mystics, and in Orthodox Christians as well, who put a special emphasis on the Spirit's role in *sanctification* (making believers holy). It is fair to say, however, that the Holy Spirit was in many ways the most neglected Person of the Trinity, especially in Western Christianity, both Catholic and Protestant.

This neglect of the Holy Spirit in the West began to change in the nineteenth century with the development of the Holiness Churches of the Wesleyan tradition. Christians in these churches, which were influenced by the Pietist movement as well as the teachings of John Wesley, emphasized the sanctifying power of the Holy Spirit in their lives, and today's Holiness denominations, such as the Church of the Nazarene, believe that the goal of all Christians should be perfection (or "entire sanctification"), which is a work of grace that can only be accomplished by the Christian's submission to the Holy Spirit. Christian perfection does not imply a final state of sinlessness, as though the temptations of sin had been completely overcome, much less a perfection of wisdom, but rather a perfection of love.

The Azusa Street Revival of 1906 grew out of the Holiness movement and launched a new movement that put increased emphasis on the relationship between Christians and the Holy Spirit, the Charismatic movement (from the Greek word *charisma*, "gift" or "grace"). Christians involved with the movement spoke of their experience as the Baptism of the Holy Spirit, a second, post-salvation encounter with God that manifested itself in a number of ways, including glossolalia, miracles, healing, prophecy, and even casting out demons (*exorcism*). The early practitioners of Pentecostalism, as it was also called, put special emphasis on speaking in tongues as God's special sign that they had encountered the Spirit. They viewed Spirit baptism not as a single, isolated event in the believer's life but as an ongoing reality. True, Spirit-filled believers would continue to experience manifestations of the Holy Spirit in their daily lives and in their worship experiences as a community of faith. One group of Pentecostals in the rural Appalachia region of the U.S., influenced by their reading of Mark 16:15–18, adopted the practice of handling poisonous snakes during worship services as a sign of their faith in God and of their sanctification by the Spirit. Such extremes, however, were condemned by the vast majority of Pentecostals, who quickly became one of the fastest growing segments of Christianity.

A second wave of Pentecostalism broke out in the 1950s and 1960s, this time among Christians whose experiences with the Holy Spirit led them to speak in tongues and experience miracles and other signs of the Spirit's presence, but did not lead them to leave their own denominations, for the most part. The Charismatic movement of the mid-twentieth century attracted Christians from all faith traditions to seek Spirit baptism and the signs of sanctification. A third wave of Christian encounter with the Holy Spirit began in the 1980s, chiefly among Protestants in the Free Church tradition. Christians involved in the Neocharismatic movement, as it is sometimes called, stressed the importance of having personal encounters with the Holy Spirit, but they consciously sought to avoid what they considered the excesses of the earlier Charismatic movements. Specifically, they put more emphasis on healing and miracles (answered prayer) than on speaking in tongues, and in fact they generally do not consider glossolalia to be an essential sign of an encounter with the Holy Spirit. Instead, they see glossolalia as a gift of the Spirit that is allotted to some Christians and not to others, according to the sovereign decree of God.

The Christian Renewal movement, as the three waves of the Holy Spirit are sometimes called, has had a tremendous impact on Christianity, involving perhaps as many as a quarter of all Christians, a third of whom have remained in their original denominations. Those Christians who do not consider themselves part of the movement have had a variety of reactions to these developments. One common critique of the Charismatic movement is that it puts too much emphasis on emotion, potentially distracting the attention of Christians from their other obligations, such as involvement in ministry of one sort or another. A similar critique comes from anthropologists, who note that glossolalia and the other "manifestations of the spirit" are practiced by adherents of other religions as well, such as practitioners of Haitian Vodou. A few attack glossolalia from a theological perspective, claiming that although it was present in the early church as a sign of God's Spirit working among unbelievers, at some point early in church history it ceased to be a valid gift of the Spirit. Although this last point is rejected by all involved in the Renewal movement, many in the movement acknowledge the excesses that they themselves perceive as being practiced by others in the movement. Many Christians who do not count themselves part of the movement and may disagree with some of its emphases nevertheless credit the movement with breathing new life into Christianity, and they recognize its importance in those parts of the world where Christianity is adding the greatest number of new believers: Africa, Latin America, and Asia.

Justification by faith

> For by grace you have been saved through faith, and this is not your own doing; it is the gift of God – not the result of works, so that no one may boast. For we are what he has made us, created in Christ Jesus for good works, which God prepared beforehand to be our way of life.
>
> (Eph 2:8–10)

One of Martin Luther's strongest arguments with the Roman Catholic Church revolved around the issue of *justification*, or gaining a right standing before God. Luther, based on his reading of Rom 1:16–17, proclaimed the doctrine of *sola fide*, or justification by faith alone. In response to what they perceived as Luther's deviation from the traditional faith, the Roman Catholic Church at the Council of Trent (1545–1563) codified its understanding of the doctrine of justification, which the Council said was predicated upon both faith *and* good works. They explicitly rejected the idea that grace was received by people in a totally passive manner, purely on the basis of faith. Instead, they said that some human effort was involved in the process of justification. The rift between Protestants and Catholics over this issue caused many Catholics to accuse Protestants of preaching an antinomian (lawless) gospel that minimized the importance of following Jesus' life and teaching in their daily lives. In return, many Protestants accused Catholics of preaching a doctrine of justification by works, as though one could work one's way to heaven without the necessity of God's grace. Both these accusations were caricatures of the positions actually held by either side.

On October 31, 1999, the anniversary of the start of the Protestant Reformation, Lutherans and Roman Catholics came together to sign a "Joint Declaration on the

Doctrine of Justification," a document that was the result of years of dialog and debate worldwide between the two parties. The document laid out a common understanding of the doctrine of justification. Although it did not resolve every difference between Catholic and Lutheran expressions of the doctrine, it acknowledged that the differences that remained were minor and that Catholics' and Lutherans' mutual condemnations of one another, dating to the sixteenth century, were rescinded. The summary of their joint understanding was this: "By grace alone, in faith in Christ's saving work and not because of any merit on our part, we are accepted by God and receive the Holy Spirit, who renews our hearts while equipping and calling us to good works" ("Joint Declaration" 15). This important document demonstrated to many Christians that doctrinal differences, even differences that were once considered to be fundamental to the faith of the respective parties, can often be overcome through dialog, or if not completely overcome, then at least the two sides can better understand the position of their opponent and respond to actual beliefs, not exaggerated misstatements about those beliefs, as has too often been done throughout church history.

Church and state

> We must obey God rather than any human authority.
>
> (Acts 5:29)

Since the time of Constantine, Christianity has often held a favored position in relation to the state. The emperor Theodosius declared Christianity the official religion of the Roman Empire in 391, and Christianity retained its status as official state religion until the fall of Constantinople in 1453. In the meantime, while Eastern Orthodoxy was the favored form of Christianity in the East, Roman Catholicism became the official religion of many of the barbarian kingdoms and their descendants in the West, including the Holy Roman Empire, France, and the newly united Spain of Isabella and Ferdinand. After the Protestant Reformation, Protestantism became the official religion of several provinces within the Holy Roman Empire and several Swiss cantons. When John Calvin established the Reformed version of Christianity in Geneva and the surrounding areas as the state religion, two forms of Protestantism functioned as state churches on the Continent, and a third became the Church of England. Meanwhile, Anabaptists, Separatists, and others formed churches that operated outside the official, state-sponsored churches. Many of these groups developed the idea that state sponsorship of any religion, even their own, was a bad idea. Roger Williams established the first American colony that took religious liberty (opposition to state churches) as a founding principle. As Protestant denominations flourished, many of them agreed with the principle of religious liberty, which Thomas Jefferson called the separation of church and state. Other denominations, including the Roman Catholic Church and the Russian Orthodox Church, among many others, continued to insist on the value of state sponsorship of Christianity. In many cases denominations even insisted that their particular version of Christianity was somehow more worthy of state sponsorship than other forms of Christianity, not to mention other religions in general. Over time, more and more nations declared an official policy of secularism. The rise of Soviet communism disenfranchised all the state churches in the Soviet bloc. After communism fell, some in the Russian Orthodox Church argued for their church to be enshrined once again as the official state church.

Many Christians today in countries with state churches resent the idea of having their taxes used to support a denomination of which they are not a member. They also resist the favoritism of the state churches that they see played out on the national scene. Even in countries where no state church exists, Christians are often at odds with one another over whether the government should favor one religion or denomination over another, or whether specific state policies constitute favoritism. In the U.S., for example, while most Christian denominations agree officially that government favoritism of one religion over another is wrong, many people claim that the U.S. is a Christian nation, so there is no problem with favoring Christianity, or, as some would phrase it, favoring "the Judeo-Christian ethic." The issue of what constitutes government support or opposition to religion is problematic. Does doing away with state-sponsored prayer in the schools, as the U.S. Supreme Court did in 1963, constitute appropriate governmental restraint from sponsorship a particular religion (Protestant Christianity), or does it constitute opposition to the free expression of religion? Does mandating the teaching of evolution in schools and the banning of creation science and intelligent design from the classroom constitute the advocacy of the religion of secular humanism, as some claim, or is it a legitimate attempt to oppose the teaching of one specific form of religion (conservative Christianity)? Is a law outlawing the use of peyote, a hallucinogenic cactus, a legitimate restriction on a traditional Native American religious practice that is necessary for the public welfare, or is it an unnecessary burden placed on an unfavored, minority religion? Is a French law banning the wearing of headscarves by Muslim schoolgirls an infringement of their right to practice their religion, or is it a legitimate attempt to remove potential causes of conflict in the state school classroom? On these and many other issues Christians are divided, sometimes finding themselves on opposite sides of an issue from Christians in other denominations, and sometimes from Christians within their own denomination.

Christian denominations sometimes join forces with other likeminded Christians, or even with likeminded people of other faiths or no faith, to form permanent organizations or temporary alliances to deal with church-state issues. In the U.S., the Baptist Joint Committee on Religious Liberty is an organization that represents 14 different Baptist denominations and organizations on religious liberty matters. It often works with organizations such as the National Council of Churches, the American Jewish Congress, the American Civil Liberties Union, and Americans United for the Separation of Church and State on issues of concern. On the other hand, a founding member and formerly the largest denominational sponsor of the Committee, the Southern Baptist Convention, withdrew from the organization in 1993 over concerns that the Committee was no longer representing points of view with which it agreed.

Now the Baptist Joint Committee often – but not always! – finds itself on opposite sides of an issue with a former supporter. On the other hand, in the Second Vatican Council, the Roman Catholic Church issued a *Declaration on Religious Freedom* that proclaimed that religious freedom was a basic human right and cannot be coerced by the state. These tales illustrate the fact that Christians' views on church and state, like their views on other topics, can change over time, because of changes in society, changes in understanding, or changes in leadership.

Eschatology

One of the most fascinating areas of disagreement among Christians revolves around the question of how the world will end. The New Testament often speaks of Christ's future return to earth to judge humankind and establish his kingdom. The Apostles' Creed states Christians' belief that "he will come again to judge the living and the dead" (the Nicene Creed is similar). The New Testament book of Revelation is an *apocalypse*, a document that purports to reveal a secret truth concerning the divine plan for the future. Using graphic and sometimes mystifying imagery, it describes a situation in which Christians are suffering at the hands of an evil state. God intervenes by having angels pour out different types of divine retribution on the earth. An evil beast rules over the state that is persecuting the faithful, but in the end a savior on a white horse comes from heaven to earth, slaughters the beast and his armies, and establishes a kingdom that will last for 1,000 years. After the millennial reign, Satan is released from prison, foments more trouble, and is cast forever into a lake of fire, where he suffers eternal torment, along with his followers. The book of Revelation is different from every other New Testament book, so different, in fact, that many in the early church argued for keeping it out of the developing canon. It was eventually accepted; however, readings from the book were not included in the standard ancient lectionary cycles of the church. Today, the book of Revelation is included in the lectionaries of the Roman Catholic and Protestant churches that use lectionaries, but it is still omitted from Orthodox lectionaries.

Christians in the first few centuries agreed on the idea that Christ would one day return to earth and establish his reign, but they disagreed as to the details of Christ's return. During the days of Roman persecution of the church, many believed that the persecutions would grow steadily worse until Christ suddenly intervened, brought judgment on the wicked empire, and established his kingdom. This position is called *premillennial* (i.e. Christ returns *before* the millennial rule). After Christianity was legalized, attitudes shifted, and Augustine was one of the first people to see Christ's millennial rule as his symbolic rule over the church in the present age. This view is called *amillennial* (there is no literal millennial rule), and it was the dominant view of the church for many centuries and was adopted by the Protestants after the Protestant Reformation. In the eighteenth and nineteenth centuries several new ways of understanding Christian eschatology arose. First, many who were influenced by the Enlightenment, as well as its application in Christian biblical and theological studies through a historical-critical reading of the text of scripture, advocated reading the book of Revelation as a message to a suffering, late first-century church that needed to be reassured that their suffering was not in vain and that Christ would come to deliver the church from its oppressor, the Roman Empire. The difference between the critical reading of Revelation and the early premillennial views was that the early Christians were looking for a literal fulfillment of many of the events described in the book, whereas the critical scholars saw the book as containing symbols designed to communicate comfort but not to predict the future. This approach to the book may be called the critical approach, or one version of the *idealist* approach.

A second new position on eschatology held that many of the events described in Revelation were fulfilled throughout history, and only a few remain to be fulfilled. This approach, championed by the founders of both the Seventh-day Adventist Church and the Jehovah's Witnesses, expected Christ to return to earth sometime in the nineteenth century. When the Second Coming did not materialize, these Christian groups were forced to reevaluate their positions, but although they both modified their understandings somewhat, they did not abandon their overall approach, which might be called the *historicist* approach. A similar approach, the *preterist* approach, believes most or all of the events described in Revelation were fulfilled in the first century.

Another new approach to eschatology that arose in the nineteenth century grew out of a positive world view that saw progress everywhere and believed that the world, under the guidance of the church, would continue to improve until the kingdom of God was established on earth, after which Christ would return. This view, the *postmillennial* view (because Christ returns *after* the millennium), was largely abandoned after the disasters of two world wars in the early twentieth century, but it has since gained some new proponents. The three views called premillennial, amillennial, and postmillennial are often referred to collectively as *futurist* approaches.

One of the most elaborate and interesting approaches to eschatology was developed in the nineteenth century by a man named John Nelson Darby and popularized by C. I. Scofield in his notes to the King James Version of the Bible, which sold innumerable copies. This view, the premillennial *dispensationalist* approach, divides the history of the world into seven different ages, or dispensations. The current age, the Church Age (or Age of Grace) will end with a sudden event known as the Rapture, in which all true Christians will disappear from the planet. The world will descend into chaos, and the Antichrist will arise to control much of the world. Newly converted Christians (including many Jews) will suffer tremendously during this period, known as the Great Tribulation. Finally, after seven years, as armies gather to attack the state of Israel, Christ will return to stop the suffering of his people, punish the wicked, and establish his kingdom. This general overview of the dispensationalist position does not take into account the numerous variations proposed by different people regarding the timing of the Rapture, among other things.

The dispensationalist view has been popularized in recent years by the publication of books such as Hal Lindsey's *The Late Great Planet Earth* in 1970, the *Ryrie Study Bible*

Dispensational premillennialism

The seven dispensations into which dispensationalists divide the history of the world are:

1   Dispensation of Innocence (from creation to the Fall of Adam)

2   Dispensation of Conscience (from the Fall of Adam to Noah's flood)

3   Dispensation of Government (from Noah's flood to Abraham's journey to the Promised Land)

4   Dispensation of Patriarchal Rule (from Abraham's journey to the Promised Land to Moses' reception of the Law on Mt. Sinai)

5   Dispensation of the Mosaic Law (from Moses' reception of the Law on Mt. Sinai to the Day of Pentecost, after Jesus' resurrection)

6   Dispensation of Grace (from the Day of Pentecost to Jesus' Second Coming)

7   The Millennial Kingdom (1,000-year reign of Christ after his Second Coming

The Dispensation of Grace, also called the Church Age, is the present period, which will end with a series of events called the Rapture, the Great Tribulation, and the Second Coming Christ. Dispensationalism is rooted in the teachings of John Nelson Darby, a nineteenth-century Anglican priest in Ireland who later joined the Plymouth Brethren.

and other dispensationalist study Bibles (i.e. Bibles with notes interpreting the text from a dispensationalist standpoint), and especially the *Left Behind* books by Tim LaHaye and Jerry Jenkins, a series of novels based on dispensationalist theology. This point of view is particularly influential among Evangelical and Pentecostal/Neocharismatic Christians. In fact, some denominations require their clergy to subscribe to the dispensationalist position as an article of faith. The Roman Catholic and Orthodox churches, as well as many Protestant churches, reject dispensationalism and continue to advocate the amillennial position, which is compatible with the critical position as well. Controversy over the different approaches to eschatology becomes most inflamed when one side accuses people on the other side of not being real Christians because they believe in the wrong eschatological position. Non-dispensationalists sometimes accuse dispensationalists of trying to influence international politics in an effort to set events in motion that will ultimately result in Christ's Second Coming, such as policies designed (their critics say) to inflame Israeli-Arab dissention. Of all the issues over which Christians disagree with one another, it is eschatology that often seems to generate the most passion and that has the potential to have the greatest impact on the world as a whole.

Figure 18.1 The Rev. Martin Luther King, Jr. greets President Lyndon Johnson after the latter signed the Voting Rights Act in 1965.

Traditional and progressive churches

Traditional and progressive, conservative and liberal, fundamentalist and mainstream – these are all labels that Christians apply to themselves and to one another to describe their positions on a variety of issues in a single word. The various nuances of these terms, and the complete set of doctrines that they imply, is beyond the scope of this book to explore. However, since the terms are often used in public discourse, a general understanding is in order. One may group the terms traditional, conservative, and fundamentalist together as implying, in different degrees, a commitment to a traditional understanding of both the Bible (and perhaps other sources of authority) and Christian theology. For many, this commitment includes an understanding of the Bible as *inerrant* (correct in every detail), as well as an overall belief in the literal reading of the Bible. On the other side are the terms progressive, liberal, and mainstream, words that imply, again in different degrees, a commitment to a critical reading of the Bible (i.e. one informed by widely accepted scholarly approaches), an open approach to theology, and a rejection of both inerrancy and extremely literal readings of the Bible. It is important to note that these terms are used in the present context only to describe a general approach to the Bible and theology, not politics, where the same words are often used. Someone who is conservative theologically may be moderate or liberal politically, and someone who is liberal theologically may be quite conservative politically. The correlation between liberal positions on theology and politics is not strong, and the same can be said for conservative positions. It should also be noted that some Christians consider the word *fundamentalist* to be pejorative and would not use it to describe themselves, even if they think of themselves as quite conservative. Similarly, some Christians do not like the word *liberal* and prefer to call themselves either progressive or mainstream, or even moderate.

Traditionalists and progressives can both be found in many denominations of all faith traditions. With more than 1 billion members, it should not be surprising that the Roman Catholic Church contains large numbers of both traditionalists and progressives with regard to their views on the Bible and theology. The same is true, though perhaps to a lesser extent, among the Orthodox, who have a tendency to put more emphasis on the importance of continuity with their tradition than do many Catholics, so, on average, the Orthodox, especially the Oriental Orthodox, might be somewhat more conservative theologically than the Catholics. Anglicans, on the other hand, probably lean a little more to the progressive end of the spectrum theologically. This is especially true of North American and European Anglicans; their African, Latin American, and Asia counterparts tend to be more conservative in some ways.

Protestants are in some ways easier to categorize, though again it must be emphasized that these observations are generalizations, for which many specific exceptions exist. Magisterial Protestants – Lutherans and those in the Reformed tradition – trend more progressive than many other Protestants, the Lutherans perhaps more so than the Reformed. However, there are definite exceptions, such as the Missouri Synod Lutherans in the U.S., which are conservative theologically. Among those in the Wesleyan tradition, those who call themselves Methodists tend to be more progressive than the Holiness churches of the Wesleyan tradition. Evangelicals, Pentecostals, Neocharismatics, and Anabaptists all have a reputation for being quite conservative, but there are several progressive Baptist denominations in the U.S., though as a general rule, U.S. Baptists tend to be more conservative theologically than their international counterparts. Among the Stone-Campbell Restorationists, the Disciples of Christ tend more toward the progressive side of the scale, while the Church of Christ occupies the traditionalist side. Quakers are often, though not always, progressive theologically, and the United Church of Christ is definitely progressive.

It is important not to overgeneralize when using terms like traditionalist and progressive or conservative and liberal, since individuals or groups within any given faith tradition or denomination can hold views that go against the grain. Nevertheless, the characterizations given here are probably fairly accurate in describing the overall positions of the faith traditions and subtraditions mentioned above in regard to their approach to the biblical text and to theology.

Key points you need to know

- The debate over relationship between the divine and the human in Christ played a major part in the first four ecumenical councils: Nicaea I, Constantinople I, Ephesus, and Chalcedon. Resolution of this matter, in turn, led to the development of the doctrine of the Trinity, a belief that God is one but at the same time consists of three Persons: Father, Son, and Holy Spirit. The doctrine of the Trinity is accepted by most Christians, though a minority reject it.

- The New Testament portrays the Holy Spirit in various ways: as equivalent to the power of God, as an indwelling presence in believers that helps them commune with God, and as the Comforter sent by God to the faithful after Jesus' departure, among others. In addition to being considered the third Person of the Trinity by orthodox Christians, the Holy Spirit came to be considered particularly important in the process of sanctification by the Holiness Churches. In the twentieth century, three "Waves of the Spirit" are associated with the birth of Pentecostalism, the Charismatic movement, and the Neocharismatic movement.

- One of the issues that divided Catholics and Protestants during the early days of the Protestant Reformation was the question of justification by faith. Luther and other Protestants believed that faith alone was sufficient for attaining right standing with God, whereas the Roman Catholic Church at the Council of Trent declared that faith, unless accompanied by good works as evidence of the genuineness of faith, was insufficient for justification. Catholics and Lutherans in the 1990s issued a "Joint Declaration on the Doctrine of Justification," in which both Churches agreed that faith alone was sufficient for justification, but that such faith would inevitably result in good works.

- From the time of Constantine, the Church was often the favored or official religion of nations in the Mediterranean world, and later in the Americas and elsewhere. Anabaptists, Separatists, and other Protestant groups outside the tradition of the churches of Magisterial Reform argued that religious belief or practice could not be coerced by the state, since religion was a matter of conscience. Although Christianity, or some specific Christian denomination, remains the official religion in some countries, freedom of religion is accepted by most Christians as a basic human right. However, specific implications of religious liberty are a matter of ongoing debate among Christians.

- Although the doctrine of the Second Coming of Christ is accepted by most Christians, questions about the nature of the end times, the days just prior to Christ's return, evoke great debate and disagreement. The traditional amillennial position, accepted by most Catholics and Orthodox, as well as by many Protestants, is challenged by several other points of view. The most visible, and probably the most widespread, challenger to the traditional position is called dispensational premillennialism, or simply dispensationalism, which expects a rapture of faithful Christians into heaven, a seven-year period of increasingly severe conflict known as the Great Tribulation, and finally the physical return of Christ to rule the earth.

- Traditional churches and individuals (sometimes called conservative or fundamentalist) have a traditional understanding of both the Bible (and perhaps other sources of authority) and Christian theology. Some traditionalists believe that the Bible is inerrant and should be read literally in most cases. Progressive churches and individuals (sometimes called liberal or mainstream) accept a critical reading of the Bible, an open approach to theology, and a rejection of both inerrancy and extremely literal readings of the Bible. Both traditionalists and progressives can be found in every faith tradition, as well as in many individual denominations.

Discussion questions

1. Most of the early attempts to define both the nature of Christ and the relationship among the different Persons in the Trinity were based on particular Greek philosophical traditions which no longer hold sway, such as Neo-Platonism. How do different approaches to philosophy today affect traditional theological beliefs?
2. How does the view of the Holy Spirit among Pentecostals and Charismatics differ from that among other Christians?
3. Since Catholics and Lutherans now claim a common understanding of the doctrine of justification, did the theological understanding of one or both groups change, or was the difference in the two groups' positions exaggerated in the sixteenth century?
4. What are the advantages and disadvantages to Christianity of a favored relationship with the state?
5. How may a Christian's approach to global politics be affected by his or her view of eschatology?

Further reading

Catechism of the Catholic Church 1997. 2nd edn. Vatican City: Libreria Editrice Vaticana.

Cobb, John B., ed. 2003. *Progressive Christians Speak.* Louisville, KY: Westminster John Knox.

González, Justo 1987. *A History of Christian Thought.* Revised edn, 3 vols. Nashville, TN: Abingdon.

Lindsey, Hal and C. C. Carlson 1970. *The Late Great Planet Earth.* Grand Rapids, MI: Zondervan.

Lutheran World Federation and Roman Catholic Church 1999. "Joint Declaration on the Doctrine of Justification." http://www.vatican.va/roman_curia/pontifical_

councils/chrstuni/documents/rc_pc_chrstuni_doc_31101999_cath-luth-joint-declaration_en.html.

Papal Encyclicals Online. http://www.papalencyclicals.net.

Scofield, C. I. 1917. *The Scofield Reference Bible.* 2nd edn. New York: Oxford University Press.

Tillich, Paul 1968. *A History of Christian Thought.* Edited by Carl E. Braaten. New York: Simon and Schuster.

19 *A liturgical perspective*

Church unity is vital to the health of the church and to the future of the human family … Christ – the life of the world – unites heaven and earth, God and world, spiritual and secular. His body and blood, given to us in the elements of bread and wine, integrate liturgy and diaconate, proclamation and acts of healing … Our eucharistic vision thus encompasses the whole reality of Christian worship, life and witness.

(World Council of Churches, Vancouver Assembly, 1983)

In this chapter

Worship has been at the center of Christian life from the earliest days, when Jesus and his followers worshiped in the synagogues of Galilee, to Jesus' instructions on prayer and his institution of the sacrament of communion at the Last Supper. Early Christian worship mimicked many aspects of Jewish worship in the synagogues, with the addition of distinctive Christian elements. Christian worship began to vary considerably after the Reformation, and a wide variety of worship styles are practiced today. Three common styles of worship may be called liturgical (high-church), traditional (low-church), and contemplative.

Main topics covered

- Early Christian worship
- Liturgical (high-church) worship
- Traditional (low-church) worship
- Contemplative worship
- Clergy attire

Worship is at the center of the Christian life. When Christians come together to worship, they gather themselves as a community of faith, leaving aside the cares of the world and differences of opinion to sing, pray, read, confess, and proclaim the word of

God. Although the most common time for Christians to gather for worship is Sunday morning, some Christians regularly worship on Saturday morning instead, and some worship regularly at other times during the week as well, such as Sunday, Wednesday, Thursday, or Saturday evening. Christians also worship together on special occasions: holy days, like Christmas and Good Friday; joyful celebrations, like weddings and graduation ceremonies; times of sorrow, like funerals and memorials for the dead; special days of consecration, like Ash Wednesday or Maundy Thursday.

Christian worship takes many forms. Worship can occur when one person or a small group seek to commune with God, and it can occur when hundreds or thousands meet in one place to celebrate their common faith. Worship can occur when clergy are present and when clergy are absent. Worship can occur in a Baroque cathedral, a modern church made of glass and steel, a modest brick building, a small wooden hut with a thatched roof, a store-front mission, or out of doors alongside a stream. Worship can occur on consecrated ground, on an ocean liner, in a prison, or in a spacecraft hurtling through space. Worship can occur any time, anywhere, under a wide variety of circumstances. The focus of this section will be on worship traditions that occur at regularly scheduled intervals, typically on Sunday mornings.

The word *liturgy* comes from a Greek word meaning *service*, that is, service that is rendered to God. In a formal sense, the word "liturgy" can mean a Christian's service to God through worship, and the meaning of the word can even extend to other types of service that do not involve worship. In typical use, however, "liturgy" refers to the form of worship, or even the content of a service. Worship styles are typically divided into two main types: liturgical and non-liturgical, but within each category is a wealth of variety. For example, within the liturgical traditions there are many levels of gradation between what is sometimes called *high-church* liturgy (i.e. a very formal and traditional service) and *low-church* liturgy (i.e. a less formal service). Many Christians, especially in the Free Church and Pentecostal traditions, do not use the term "liturgy" at all to describe their services – hence the rubric "non-liturgical" – but they often follow traditional patterns of worship just the same, which may therefore be designated as liturgies. Thus, the word "non-liturgical" is actually a misnomer in many cases, for unless a service is completely unstructured and unplanned, as in some Quaker services for example, there is some sort of liturgy involved, even if it is applied very loosely.

Rather than describe in great detail the immense variety of worship practices observed by contemporary Christians, a brief sketch of several typical services from different liturgical traditions will be offered, with limited comments. First, however, a short overview of worship in the early church will be offered as a backdrop for subsequent discussion.

Early Christian worship

Early Christian worship was evidently modeled on the synagogue service. Christian worship involved the singing of hymns or Psalms, readings from the scripture (i.e. the LXX) and from whatever Christian writings might be available (Justin Martyr, a second-century Christian, mentions the "memoirs of the apostles," possibly the gospels), prayer, and exhortation. In contrast to the Jews, who worshiped on Saturday, Christians worshiped on Sunday, in commemoration of Jesus' resurrection on the first day of the week. The Roman historian Pliny the Younger, writing about 112, describes a Christian service as follows:

> On an appointed day they had been accustomed to meet before daybreak, and to recite a hymn antiphonally to Christ, as to a god, and to bind themselves by an oath, not for the commission of any crime but to abstain from theft, robbery, adultery, and breach of faith, and not to deny a deposit when it was claimed. After the conclusion of this ceremony it was their custom to depart and meet again to take food.

The *Didache*, a Christian treatise dating from the late first or early second century, is an early Christian instruction manual that covers aspects of organizing and running a church, including instructions on matters of importance for worship. Here are some of the instructions found in the *Didache*:

> Now concerning baptism, baptize as follows: after you have reviewed all these things, baptize "in the name of the Father and of the Son and of the Holy Spirit" in running water. But if you have no running water, then baptize in some other water; and if you are not able to baptize in cold water, then do so in warm. But if you have neither, then pour water on the head three times "in the name of Father and Son and Holy Spirit."

> "Pray like this," just as the Lord commanded in his Gospel: "Our Father in heaven, hallowed be your name, your kingdom come, your will be done on earth as it is in heaven. Give us today our daily bread, and forgive us our debt, as we also forgive our debtors; and do not lead us into temptation, but deliver us from the evil one; for yours is the power and the glory forever." Pray like this three times a day.

> Now concerning the Eucharist, give thanks as follows. First, concerning the cup: We give you thanks, our Father, for the holy vine of David your servant, which you have made known to us through Jesus, your servant; to you be the glory forever. And concerning the broken bread: We give you thanks, our Father, for the life and knowledge which you have made known to us through Jesus, your servant; to you be the glory forever. Just as this broken bread was scattered upon the mountains and then was gathered together and become one, so may your church be gathered together from the ends of the earth into your kingdom; for yours is the glory and the power through Jesus Christ forever.

The Lord's Prayer

The Lord's Prayer is found in Matt 6:9–13. It is used in most Christian traditions and is the most widespread of the traditional prayers.

A modern version
Our Father in heaven,
  hallowed be your name.
Your kingdom come.
Your will be done,
  on earth as it is in heaven.
Give us this day our daily bread.
And forgive us our debts,
  as we also have forgiven our debtors.
And do not bring us to the time of trial,
  but rescue us from the evil one.
(New Revised Standard Version)

An older, traditional version, used by Protestants
Our Father which art in heaven, hallowed be thy name.
Thy kingdom come, thy will be done in earth, as it is in heaven.
Give us this day our daily bread.
And forgive us our debts, as we forgive our debtors.
And lead us not into temptation, but deliver us from evil:
For thine is the kingdom, and the power, and the glory, for ever. Amen
(King James Version)

A traditional Roman Catholic version
Our Father, who art in heaven, hallowed be thy name.
Thy kingdom come, thy will be done, on earth, as it is in heaven.
Give us this day our daily bread.
And forgive us our trespasses as we forgive those who trespass against us.
And lead us not into temptation, but deliver us from evil. Amen.

After this, the *Didache* offers a sample prayer that the one presiding over the service may wish to offer, though it indicates that the prayer may be modified. After some other comments, this instruction is offered:

> On the Lord's own day gather together and break bread and give thanks, having first confessed your sins so that your sacrifice may be pure.

Already in the first or second century the pattern that would establish itself as dominant for Christian worship for the next 2,000 years appeared. Christian worship, the *Didache* advises, should occur at least once a week and should include the gathering together of the community, the observance of the Eucharist, and the confession of sins. Other parts of the *Didache* suggest that prayer, particularly the Lord's Prayer, was already a regular part of the normal Christian worship experience.

Liturgical (high-church) worship

> Let the word of Christ dwell in you richly; teach and admonish one another in all wisdom; and with gratitude in your hearts sing psalms, hymns, and spiritual songs to God.
>
> (Col 3:16)

Liturgical worship is highly structured and planned. The scriptures read and the prayers prayed are often taken from an official schedule published by the denomination or regional body so that all churches under its jurisdiction will have similar worship experiences on any given day of worship. Nevertheless, some degree of freedom is almost always present, for example, in the selection of music or in the *homily* or *sermon* (a meditation or proclamation based on a passage of scripture). In the Roman Catholic Church, for example, the typical service is divided into two main parts, the Liturgy of the Word and the Liturgy of the Eucharist, preceded by Introductory Rites and followed by Concluding Rites. A typical service might look like this:

Entrance: *The priest, deacon, and other ministers enter the sanctuary to the accompaniment of a chant or a reading.*

Greeting: *The priest and deacon bow before the altar, which is at the front of the sanctuary and elevated, then they turn and greet the congregants, making the sign of the cross. The priest says,* "In the name of the Father, and of the Son, and of the Holy Spirit," *and the people respond,* "Amen." *The priest says,* "The Lord be with you," *and the people respond,* "And also with you."

The Act of Penitence: *The priest leads the people to confess their sins, which they do as a litany (in antiphonal fashion).*

The Kyrie Eleison: *The priest leads a litany in which he says, and the people repeat, these phrases:* "Kyrie, eleison; Christe, eleison; Kyrie, eleison," *or, in English,* "Lord, have mercy; Christ, have mercy; Lord, have mercy."

The Gloria: *The congregation or the choir sing or recite a traditional hymn called the Gloria, which begins, "Glory to God in the highest, and peace to his people on earth."*

The Collect, or Opening Prayer: *The priest leads the people in prayer, and the people respond, "Amen."*

The Biblical Readings: *The Liturgy of the Word begins with a series of scripture readings from the Apostle portion of the New Testament (i.e. something other than the Gospels), usually followed by a Psalm and another reading, often from the Old Testament. A chant called the Alleluia is sung. The last reading is from one of the Gospels. After each reading, the lector says, "The Word of the Lord," to which the congregation responds, "Thanks be to God." After the Gospel reading, however, the deacon or priest says, "The Gospel of the Lord," and the congregation responds, "Praise to you, Lord Jesus Christ."*

The Homily: *The priest delivers the homily, a reflection on one of the scripture passages read previously.*

Profession of Faith: *The priest leads the congregation in saying either the Nicene or the Apostles' Creed.*

The Prayer of the Faithful: *The priest leads the congregation in a series of prayers, which the priest voices, for the needs of the church, for the world and its authorities, for those with special needs, and for the local community. After each brief petition, the congregation responds, "Lord, hear our prayer."*

Presentation of the Gifts: *The Liturgy of the Altar begins with the ministers bringing the bread and wine to the altar. The priest praises God for the bread and wine that will become the body and blood of Christ, and the people respond after each of these praises, "Blessed be God forever." The priest then invites the people to pray, and he leads the congregation in a brief prayer for the Lord to accept their sacrifice, to which the congregation responds with a similar prayer.*

Prayer over the Gifts: *The priest prays, and the people respond, "Amen."*

Eucharistic Prayer: *The priest leads the congregation in a prayer, which begins with this interchange: Priest: "The Lord be with you." Congregation: "And also with you." Priest: "Lift up your hearts." Congregation: "We lift them up to the Lord." Priest: "Let us give thanks to the Lord, our God." Congregation, "It is right to give him thanks and praise." The priest then leads in the recitation of the Sanctus, which begins, "Holy, holy, holy Lord, God of power and might," followed by the words, "Let us proclaim the mystery of faith." The people respond, "Christ has died, Christ is risen, Christ will come again." The prayer ends with a doxology, and the people respond, "Amen."*

Lord's Prayer: *The priest begins the Communion Rite by leading the congregation to recite the Lord's Prayer.*

Rite of Peace: *The priest reminds the people that Jesus promised to leave his peace with them, and the congregation exchanges the sign of peace (a handshake or embrace) with those near them in the sanctuary.*

The Fraction, or Breaking of the Bread: *While the choir or cantor is singing the Agnus Dei (Lamb of God), the priest breaks the bread at the altar and prepares to distribute it to the people.*

Communion: *The priest prays, then elevates the host (the bread) so that the congregation can see it. He prays a prayer, such as,* "This is the Lamb of God who takes away the sins of the world. Happy are those who are called to his supper," *and the congregation responds appropriately. The people then file to the front of the sanctuary to receive communion from the priest and other ministers. As the priest gives the communicant the bread dipped in wine, he says,* "The body of Christ," *and the communicant responds,* "Amen." *Finally, the priest receives communion himself.*

Communion Song, Period of Silence, and Prayer: *After communion is finished and the people have returned to their seats, the priest leads the congregation in these observances.*

Concluding Rites: *The service concludes with the greeting of the priest,* "The Lord be with you," *and the people answer,* "And also with you." *This is followed by a blessing in the name of the Father, Son, and Holy Spirit, and finally a dismissal,* "Go in the peace of Christ," *to which the people respond,* "Thanks be to God."

In contrast to the Roman Catholic Mass, which usually lasts about an hour, or perhaps less, the Eastern Orthodox service can last up to three hours. The reason for this is that the actual Divine Liturgy, the portion of the service that corresponds to the Roman Catholic mass, is preceded by a number of introductory services, such as the *Matins*, a morning service (*Vespers* is the evening service) that includes prayers, songs, chants, scripture readings, the burning of incense, and the veneration of icons, but no celebration of the Eucharist. Several short preparatory services come after Matins, followed by the Divine Liturgy, the highlight of the Orthodox service. The Divine Liturgy shares many characteristics, including the overall structure with the Roman Catholic liturgy of the Mass. However, it is typically longer, includes more hymns (sung by the cantor and choir) and prayers, and arranges certain items in a different order from the Catholic Mass. The Divine Liturgy is divided into three parts: the Liturgy of Preparation, the Liturgy of the Catechumens (so-called because in earlier times catechumens, who were not yet baptized, would have to leave the service after this liturgy was completed), and the Liturgy of the Faithful, which includes the Eucharist.

Some Anglican churches have services that closely mirror the Roman Catholic service, while others opt for a less formal service, generally based on the *Book of Common Prayer*. Most other Protestants observe a style of worship that might be called traditional.

Several short traditional prayers, used especially in liturgical worship or private meditation

The Jesus Prayer

Lord Jesus Christ, Son of God, have mercy on me, a sinner.

Although used in other traditions as well, the Jesus Prayer is especially associated with the Eastern Orthodox Church. It is often repeated continually as a means of "centering" the mind and preparing for a time of meditation.

Ave Maria (Hail Mary)

Hail Mary, full of grace, the Lord is with thee. Blessed art thou among women, and blessed is the fruit of thy womb, Jesus. Holy Mary, Mother of God, pray for us sinners, now, and at the hour of our death. Amen.

Gloria Patri (Glory to the Father)

Glory to the Father, and to the Son, and to the Holy Spirit: as it was in the beginning, is now, and will be for ever. Amen.

The Rosary

The Rosary, a traditional Roman Catholic prayer, consists of reciting the Lord's Prayer, ten iterations of the Hail Mary, and the Glory to the Father. A series of meditations on different subjects is often included when praying the Rosary.

Kyrie Eleison (Lord, Have Mercy)

As recited in Eastern Orthodox litanies
Kyrie eleison *(sometimes repeated three times).*
As recited in Roman Catholic litanies
Kyrie eleison, Christe eleison, Kyrie eleison
(i.e. Lord have mercy, Christ have mercy, Lord have mercy).

Sanctus

Holy, holy, holy Lord, God of power and might,
heaven and earth are full of your glory.
Hosanna in the highest.

Agnus Dei (Lamb of God)

Jesus, Lamb of God, have mercy on us.
Jesus, bearer of our sins, have mercy on us.
Jesus, redeemer of the world, grant us peace.

The last phrase of the third line, "grant us peace," is sometimes separated from the rest of this prayer and sung in Latin as "Dona nobis pacem."

Te Deum

We praise you, O God,

we acclaim you as Lord;

all creation worships you,

the Father everlasting.

To you all angels, all the powers of heaven,

the cherubim and seraphim, sing in endless praise:

Holy, holy, holy Lord, God of power and might, heaven and earth

     are full of your glory.

The glorious company of apostles praise you.

The noble fellowship of prophets praise you.

The white-robed army of martyrs praise you.

Throughout the world the holy Church acclaims you:

Father, of majesty unbounded,

your true and only Son, worthy of all praise,

the Holy Spirit, advocate and guide.

You, Christ, are the king of glory,

the eternal Son of the Father.

When you took our flesh to set us free

you humbly chose the Virgin's womb.

You overcame the sting of death

and opened the kingdom of heaven to all believers

You are seated at God's right hand in glory.

We believe that you will come to be our judge.

Come then, Lord, and help your people,

bought with the price of your own blood,

and bring us with your saints to glory everlasting.

Traditional (low-church) worship

> And let us consider how to provoke one another to love and good deeds, not neglecting to meet together, as is the habit of some, but encouraging one another, and all the more as you see the Day approaching.
>
> (Heb 10:24–25)

Lutherans, Presbyterians, and Methodists, among others, typically observe a form of worship that, while following both a set liturgical structure and a lectionary cycle that determines the scriptures to be read during the service, allows a great deal of flexibility in the details. A typical Presbyterian service looks something like this:

Figure 19.1 Argentine Evangelist Luis Palau preaches to a crowd at a revival meeting. Extemporaneous preaching is one characteristic of traditional, non-liturgical worship.

Prelude: *The church organist plays music while the congregation meditates silently to begin the service.*

Lighting of the Christ Candle: *A member of the congregation lights the candle that represents Christ.*

Introit: *The congregation, led by the minister of music, sings an opening hymn.*

Call to Worship: *A worship leader leads the congregation in a litany of praise.*

Prayer of Adoration: *The pastor offers a prayer of praise to God.*

Hymn of Adoration: *The minister of music leads the congregation in singing a hymn.*

Prayer of Confession: *The pastor offers a public prayer of confession, after which the members of the congregation silently pray and confess their sins.*

Assurance of Forgiveness: *Following a period of silent prayer, the pastor leads the congregation in a litany acknowledging God's forgiveness of their sins.*

Gloria Patri: *The congregation sings a traditional hymn of praise to God.*

Nicene Creed: *The pastor leads the congregation in the recitation of the creed.*

Sharing the Peace of God: *The worship leader says, "Peace be with you," and the congregation responds, "And also with you." Members of the congregation then exchange greetings of peace with those near them.*

Prayer for Illumination: *A designated member of the congregation asks God to open the minds and hearts of the congregants to receive God's instruction.*

Old Testament Reading

New Testament Reading: *After these two readings, the lector says, "This is the word of the Lord," and the congregation responds, "Thanks be to God."*

Anthem: *The choir sings an anthem.*

Sermon: *The pastor preaches a sermon, typically based on one of the daily scripture readings.*

Hymn of Response: *The minister of music leads the congregation in a hymn of response and dedication to God.*

Holy Communion: *The pastor and deacons bless the bread and wine, and the congregants come forward to receive communion, after the following exchange: Pastor: "Lift up your hearts." People: "We lift them up to the Lord." Pastor: "Let us give thanks to the Lord our God." People: "It is right to give him thanks and praise."*

Prayers: *The pastor leads the congregation in prayers for congregants who are ill and for other needs of the church, followed by the Lord's Prayer, which all recite together.*

Offertory: *While ushers pass through the congregation with baskets or metal plates, the members of the congregation give their monetary offerings. The organist or another musician plays during the offertory.*

The Doxology: *The congregation sings a traditional hymn of praise.*

Offertory Prayer: *An usher or deacon offers a prayer dedicating the offerings to God.*

Closing Hymn: *The minister of music leads the congregation in a closing hymn.*

Benediction: *The pastor offers a closing blessing, which is followed by a choral Amen.*

Postlude: *The organist plays a song while the pastor and other ministers exit the podium.*

Services like this are typical among so-called low-church Protestants, although important variations exist in certain traditions. Many churches in the Pentecostal, Neocharismatic, and Evangelical traditions, for example, do not follow any lectionary cycle of scripture readings, so their services may only have one scripture reading, which is the text on which the pastor will preach his or her sermon. These same denominations

A prayer commonly attributed to Francis of Assisi

Lord, make me an instrument of your peace.
Where there is hatred, let me sow love;
where there is injury, pardon;
where there is doubt, faith;
where there is despair, hope;
where there is darkness, light;
and where there is sadness, joy.

O Divine Master, grant that I may not so much seek
to be consoled as to console;
to be understood as to understand;
to be loved as to love.
For it is in giving that we receive;
it is in pardoning that we are pardoned;
and it is in dying that we are born to eternal life. Amen

The attribution of this prayer to Francis of Assisi is doubtful.

Sinner's prayer

Lord Jesus, I need You. Thank You for dying on the cross for my sins. I open the door of my life and receive You as my Savior and Lord. Thank You for forgiving my sins and giving me eternal life. Take control of the throne of my life. Make me the kind of person You want me to be.

There is no fixed form of the Sinner's Prayer, but some variant of it is often prayed by people who are committing themselves to follow Christ in Evangelical traditions. This form of the Sinner's Prayer is taken from the popular Evangelical tract called "The Four Spiritual Laws."

almost always include an *altar call* at the end of their services, inviting people to accept Jesus as their Savior by praying the Sinner's Prayer and receiving baptism. During the altar call, the pastor normally invites all those making public decisions to walk to the front of the church, and those that do are presented to the congregation prior to the Benediction. Although the service above includes a celebration of the Eucharist (communion), many in the Free Church and Pentecostal traditions, as well as some Magisterial Reform churches, do not celebrate the Eucharist every week, but rather on a monthly or even tri-monthly schedule. Again, although the service listed above refers to organ music, many Protestant services – and some Catholic services as well – feature musicians who play piano, violin, or other orchestral instruments, while others include the music of "praise bands," which typically include electric guitars, drums, and other instruments. Music is sometimes led by "praise groups" rather than a minister of music, but in some churches the congregation sings without anyone specifically directing them. Services that are informal, include praise bands, and use technological innovations like multimedia or PowerPoint presentations are often called *seeker sensitive* services, and they are most often associated with Evangelical or Neocharismatic churches. Most Christian churches allow instrumental music in their worship, but some, such as the Church of Christ, do not. Finally, Pentecostal services will often have a place reserved in the service for people to praise God extemporaneously, including by speaking in tongues. Sometimes this opportunity occurs several times within the service.

Contemplative worship

Be still, and know that I am God!

(Ps 46:10)

Another form of worship that is common to all faith traditions is the service that focuses on contemplation. These services generally do not include the Eucharist, and they are often much less structured than either high-church or low-church liturgies, or at least they contain fewer elements. One popular contemplative type of service is the

Taizé service, which originated in the Taizé community in France. This community was founded by Brother Roger in 1940 and includes both Catholic and Protestant brothers, that is, men who dedicate their lives to celibacy, sharing with one another spiritually, and a simple life. The community welcomes visitors, and the form of contemplative worship that it developed is now used around the world. A Taizé service focuses on vocalized meditative prayer, singing, and periods of silence for prayer and meditation. Icons or other inspirational religious art may be displayed at the front of the sanctuary during a Taizé service, and people are invited to let the art help them focus on their communion with God. An instrumental or vocal chorus may be part of the service as well, providing music during times of prayer and meditation to help worshipers focus their minds and spirits on God. Contemplative services have for centuries been part of the routine inside monasteries and convents, but many consider the value of such services to ordinary, secular Christians (i.e. Christians who live in the world) to be great.

Clergy attire

In many churches bishops, priests, pastors, and other ministers wear special clothing (vestments) while presiding over a service. The main garment is a robe, which is worn over the minister's ordinary clothes. It may be an academic robe, indicating by means of standard colors and designs on the sleeves and elsewhere the level of education that the minister has (e.g. a doctoral robe for a pastor who has a Ph.D. or other doctoral degree), it may be a plain black robe, or it may be a colorful ecclesiastical robe. The colors and patterns on ecclesiastical robes are often keyed to the season of the Christian year, for example, Advent or Eastertide. Ministers often wear a stole as well, a long sash that drapes around the neck and whose color often indicates the color associated with the current Christian season: dark blue or purple for Advent, white or gold for Christmas and Easter, red for Pentecost, and so forth. Some also wear a clerical collar, to indicate their status as clergy, and in some traditions bishops and priests wear special headgear, such as a miter or biretta, and a special ring. Clergy in denominations that are typified by high liturgical worship styles – Catholics, Orthodox, and Anglicans – almost always wear robes and other special attire when conducting services. Many clergy and ministers in other denominations do as well, but Evangelicals and other Free Church denominations, as well as Pentecostals and Neocharismatics typically do not wear robes in worship. One exception to this generalization is those denominations that are closely associated historically with African Americans. Ministers of African Methodist Episcopal and National Baptist churches often wear robes, even when their counterparts in predominantly Anglo congregations in the same faith traditions do not.

Key points you need to know

- Worship is an important part of Christian life. Although an individual Christian can worship God, worship is usually done in a group setting, often following a set order or outline, known as a liturgy.
- Early Christians often worshiped in houses, in catacombs or other cemeteries, or in some outdoor location. Their services were modeled on synagogue services and included the singing of psalms or hymns, readings from scripture or Christian writings, prayer, and an exhortation. The most common day for worship was Sunday, in commemoration of Jesus' resurrection.
- Characteristically Christian rites such as baptism and the Eucharist (communion) have been a part of Christian worship since the beginning of Christian history.
- Liturgical, or high-church, worship is highly structured and is often based on an official schedule of prayers and scripture readings, coordinated with the season on the Christian calendar. Roman Catholics, Orthodox, and some Anglicans regularly practice liturgical worship.
- Traditional, or low-church, worship often follows a set structure, sometimes based on an official schedule of prayers and/or scripture readings, but the details are much more flexible than liturgical worship. In many denominations, individual churches determine the prayers and scripture readings for a particular service, which may or may not be related to the season of the Christian year (which is not observed by all Christians).
- Contemplative worship often includes only prayer, singing, periods of silence, and possibly readings from scripture or other sources.
- Clergy in many Christian traditions wear vestments and other accoutrements that carry some particular, symbolic value (e.g. stoles that reflect the color associated with the season of the Christian year, a cross, a clerical collar, and special headgear).

Discussion questions

1. After Christianity became a predominantly Gentile religion, why did they continue to follow the pattern of synagogue worship developed by the Jews?
2. What are some of the advantages and disadvantages of liturgical worship, from the perspective of the individual worshiper's experience with the divine?
3. What are some of the advantages and disadvantages of traditional worship, from the perspective of the individual worshiper's experience with the divine?
4. Why is contemplative worship becoming increasingly popular in many areas?
5. In those churches whose clergy wear it, how does clergy attire such as different colored stoles, rings, and special headgear contribute to the worship experience?

Further reading

Church of England 1987. *The Book of Common Prayer*. Cambridge: Cambridge University Press.

The Didache.

Mathewes-Green, Frederica 1999. *At the Corner of East and Now: A Modern Life in Ancient Christian Orthodoxy*. New York: Tarcher/Putnam.

Norris, Herbert 1950. *Church Vestments*. New York: Dutton.

Smolarski, Dennis Chester 2003. *The General Instruction of the Roman Missal*. Collegeville, MN: Liturgical Press.

Part IV

Christianity's interaction with the world

20 *Christianity and science*

Some of the most creative work today involves collaboration between scientists and theologians in drawing from the ongoing experience of a religious community while taking seriously the discoveries of modern science.

(Ian G. Barbour, *When Science Meets Religion*, 14)

In this chapter

The relationship between Christianity and science has been rocky throughout much of the history of modern science. The Reformation's iconoclastic approach to ecclesiastical authority led scientists, both Catholic and Protestant, to think in new ways about the universe and the world around them. The heliocentric universe proposed by Copernicus and Galileo was a direct challenge to the official Roman Catholic understanding of the scripture. Lyell's proposals concerning geology and the age of the earth, late twentieth-century ideas about the origin of the universe, and especially Darwin's theory of evolution by means of natural selection presented challenges to many Protestants and well as Catholics. Gradually, however, many Christians were able to reconcile their theology and understanding of the Bible with the modern scientific viewpoint.

Main topics covered

- Cosmology I: the heliocentric universe
- Geology: uniformitarianism and the age of the earth
- Cosmology II: the Big Bang
- Biology: evolution

Cosmology I: the heliocentric universe

The birth of modern science has its roots in the work of Muslim scholars like Alhacen, the eleventh-century father of optics, and the thirteenth-century Franciscan monk Roger Bacon, who developed the method of scientific induction, which specified the repeated use of observation, hypothesis, experiment, and verification. These methods conflicted with the standard Aristotelian method prominent in the late Middle Ages and used by Christians for both theological and scientific inquiry. As a result, Roger Bacon ran into opposition from within the church for his methods and was forbidden to teach his ideas for about eight years.

The invention of the printing press gave birth to a renewed interest in the pursuit of science, as scientific discoveries could be shared more easily with other scholars and with the public at large. The Protestant Reformation's doctrine of the priesthood of the believer encouraged individual Christians to "think outside the box," and many began to reexamine their core beliefs, in the realms of philosophy, theology, and science. The inclination to rethink traditional positions on scientific issues, based in European Christianity, affected Catholics as well as Protestants. The first major figure whose scientific views conflicted with the official position of the church was Nicolaus Copernicus, who published an anonymous work claiming that the sun, not the earth, was the center of the solar system. The traditional, earth-centered view, associated with a second-century Egyptian natural philosopher named Ptolemy, had been the accepted teaching of the Church from the beginning, in part because it accorded well with both observation and a literal reading of scripture. Copernicus died in 1543, before his work was widely enough known, or widely enough associated with him, to cause him personal problems. However, his book *On the Revolution of the Celestial Spheres* was added to the Index of Forbidden Books maintained by the Roman Catholic Church, and Christians were forbidden to read it.

Galileo Galilei (1564–1642) built telescopes and began looking through them at the heavens. He was familiar with the work of Copernicus, and his own studies confirmed the heliocentric (sun-centered) view of the solar system. However, in 1616 he was forbidden from teaching the truth of the Copernican view, though he was allowed to teach it as a hypothesis. In 1632 Galileo published a book called *Dialogue on the Two Chief World Systems* (i.e. those of Ptolemy and Copernicus). Although the title of the book made it sound as though the two views would be treated as having equal validity, it is clear that Galileo favored the Copernican view. The Roman Catholic Church forced Galileo to recant his beliefs, and his *Dialogue* was added to the Index. Galileo himself remained under house arrest until his death eight years later, but he nevertheless maintained his views in private.

Although the works of both Copernicus and Galileo were condemned by the hierarchy of the Roman Catholic Church, they became quickly accepted by Protestants, and by many individual Catholics as well, who were impressed by the scientific methodology that the scientists used. In order to reconcile this new view of the universe with the Bible, which most Protestants considered to be sacrosanct, they reinterpreted passages that at one time were interpreted as proving that the earth was stationary (Ps 75:3) or that the sun revolved around the earth (i.e. that it literally rose and set; Ps 50:1), explaining the language of the Bible as figurative rather than literal. The problem, many Christians began to see, was not with science, nor with the Bible, but with improper interpretations of the Bible, for example, forcing it to be literal when it should have been taken figuratively or phenomenologically (i.e. describing events as they appear from a human perspective, like the "rising" of the sun).

Slowly but surely, the Christian acceptance of modern scientific cosmology attracted more and more adherents. Some scientists, like Isaac Newton and Blaise Pascal, dabbled in theology as well as science. Most others remained loyal to the church. In 1741, a century after Galileo's death, Pope Benedict XIV formally removed the censure against Galileo and authorized the publication of all his scientific works. By the mid-eighteenth century, the consensus of opinion of most Christians, including those in positions of authority within both Catholic and Protestant churches, was that science and the Bible were fully compatible. The Copernican model of the universe had won the day, but other battles lay in the future.

Figure 20.1 This painting by an unknown French artist of the late seventeenth century depicts Noah building his ark in anticipation of the great flood that covered the surface of the whole earth. Charles Lyell introduced the geological principle of uniformitarianism, which proposed that geological phenomena like strata and fossils were better explained by slow, constant processes that occurred over millions of years than by a universal flood, as suggested by a literal reading of the early chapters of Genesis.

Geology

> In the beginning when God created the heavens and the earth, the earth was a formless void and darkness covered the face of the deep, while a wind from God swept over the face of the waters. Then God said, "Let there be light"; and there was light.
>
> (Gen 1:1–3)

Prior to the rise of the modern sciences of astronomy and geology, most Christians believed that the earth was created about 4,000 years before the birth of Christ. For example, the Venerable Bede dated the creation of the world to 3952 B.C.E., Joseph Scaliger dated it to 3949 B.C.E., and Archbishop Ussher dated it to 4004 B.C.E. (or, to be more exact, at nightfall on the evening preceding 23 October 4004 B.C.E.). These dates were based on tracking genealogical material in the Bible. Other people, who relied on observations of the world around them, believed that the earth was much older. The eighteenth-century Russian naturalist Mikhail Lomonosov thought that the earth was several hundred thousand years old. A contemporary French scientist, the Comte du Buffon, estimated the age of the earth at 75,000 years, based on the rate of cooling that he had measured. British naturalists William Smith and John Phillips observed the deposition of fossils in regular strata throughout Britain and estimated the age of the earth at 96 million years.

Charles Lyell, the father of modern geology, published his *Principles of Geology* in three volumes between 1830 and 1833. By observing such geological phenomena as the stratification of rocks and the action of volcanoes, Lyell came up with an idea that explained the past history of the earth by observing the present. He called his idea the principle of uniformitarianism, which stated that the processes that are currently going on in the earth have been going on more or less unabated since the earth's creation. Uniformitarianism quickly supplanted the previously dominant model of the earth's history, catastrophism, which was based primarily on a literal reading of the biblical record, and particularly the story of Noah's flood. Uniformitarianism led to even older estimates of the earth's age than had previously been proposed, and many scientists in Lyell's day accepted an age of as much as 400 million years for the earth. In the first two decades of the twentieth century, several geologists proposed the idea of Continental Drift, which suggested that the continents had moved relative to one another over the ages. At first dismissed by many as ridiculous, the theory, now called Tectonic Plate Theory, or simply Plate Tectonics, gained wide acceptance in the 1960s, as a result of an accumulation of scientific evidence. Most Christians today accept the theory of uniformitarianism, as well as its implications for the age of the earth, which is now estimated to be approximately 4.5 billion years old. A vocal minority of Christians, however, who continue to read the Genesis creation accounts literally, cling to catastrophism and its 6,000 year old earth.

Cosmology II: the Big Bang

While geologists were looking down at the earth, astronomers were looking up at the heavens. Improvements in optics after the time of Galileo made possible stronger and stronger telescopes, and scientists began observing the universe more closely than was possible at an earlier time. Through careful observations and measurements, they were able to determine that the universe was expanding, and measurements of the red-shift

Dating the earth and the universe

Modern scientists make use of a number of techniques that suggest that the ages of both the earth and the universe are much older than the 6,000 or so years that are derived from a literal reading of the Bible. These techniques, and the implications that scientists draw from their use, include:

- Measuring the red-shift of light from distant galaxies: measurements suggests an age of the universe of between 13 and 15 billion years.
- Radioisotope dating: based on observed ratios between different isotopes of radioactive elements, this technique dates some rocks on earth as older than 4.4 billion years (examples of radioisotope methods used to date objects include carbon-14, uranium-thorium, and potassium-argon dating).
- Plate tectonics: the slow movement of plates of the earth's crust floating on the underlying magma require the age of the earth to be at least 1 billion years old;
- Optically stimulated luminescence: this method of dating materials based on stored ionizing radiation can date items more than 300,000 years old.
- Thermoluminescence: this method of dating materials based on stored nuclear energy can date items more than 80,000 years old.
- Archaeomagnetism: based on observations of reversals in the earth's magnetic field (evidenced in rocks containing iron), this technique is capable of precise age measurements up to 10,000 years, but geomagnetic reversals are observable in rocks dating back hundreds of millions of years.
- Electronic spin resonance: based on observations of unpaired electrons trapped in crystal lattices, this method can date items at least tens of thousands of years old.
- Pollen analysis: this technique tracks the existence of particular species of plant pollen, which can be preserved for up to 400 million years.
- Ice core dating: this technique samples the earth's atmosphere at dates of up to at least 650,000 years ago, and perhaps up to a million years ago, for Antarctic samples.
- Soil creation by earthworms: this method suggests an age for the earth of at least several tens of thousands of years for current soil levels, assuming no erosion;
- Erosion rates: the erosion rate of Colorado River into the Grand Canyon indicates an age of several million years.

in the visible spectrum of stars at the edge of the visible universe eventually led scientists to estimate the age of the universe as between 13 and 15 billion years. Subsequent measurements of other types, for example, based on observations of the relative frequency of radioactive elements with extremely long half-lives, generally support this date.

The current theory that holds sway with the vast majority of astronomers concerning the origin of the universe is called the Big Bang Theory, which posits the age of the universe at between 13 and 14 billion years. The theory is based on the observation of phenomena such as black holes and quasars, as well as the measurement of the size of the current universe, and the observation that the universe is expanding. Its theoretical basis goes back to Einstein's theory of general relativity, but its place as the leading theory to explain the scientific origin did not arrive until 1964, when measurements of the cosmic microwave background radiation of the universe supported the theory.

Although many Christians oppose any theory that proposes an age of the universe (or earth) that is more than just a few thousand years old, most Christians have accepted scientists' contention that the age of the universe must be measured in units of billions of years rather than thousands. Of particular interest to many Christians today is the fact that no scientific consensus has arisen concerning what occurred immediately before the Big Bang, which general relativity theory posits as a gravitational singularity. What produced the matter that makes up the universe in the first place, and what led to the great explosion behind the Big Bang, whose effects are still observable today? For many Christians whose interests in theology and science overlap, these are fruitful questions for future inquiry.

Biology

> Perhaps we will one day be able at least to admit of a God possessing sufficient majesty and expansiveness to transcend the limits of our own imaginations and experience. But meanwhile, … we might do well to look upon the inadequacy of our concepts of God as the truest mirror of those limitations that define our condition.
>
> (Ian Tattersall, *Becoming Human*)

The largest crisis between science and Christianity since the time of Galileo arose in the mid-nineteenth century, when Charles Darwin published his book *The Origin of Species*, which proposed the theory of biological evolution of species by means of natural selection. In his earlier life Darwin had studied for the Christian ministry, but he became engrossed in the idea of biological evolution after serving as the resident naturalist aboard the *Beagle* as it sailed around the world, stopping in such places as South America and the Galapagos Islands. On this voyage Darwin encountered evidence of great diversity between animals of the distant past and those of the present. For example, he saw fossilized bones of long-extinct animals, and on different Galapagos islands he observed differences among various species of birds that were obviously closely related, yet distinctly adapted to their environments. Darwin also read with interest the first volume of Lyell's *Principles of Geology*, which asserted that the earth was much older than the traditional 6,000 years calculated by Bishop Ussher and others, based on biblical genealogies and a literal reading of scripture.

Reaction to *The Origin of Species* was mixed. Most scientists, including devout Christians, had long been convinced from a study of the increasingly large fossil record that evolution was a fact, but they had been unable to explain it satisfactorily. Darwin's proposal of descent with modification as a result of natural selection seemed to fit the evidence better than any other previous theory. Many scientists agreed with the concept of evolution, but they doubted that natural selection was a sufficiently powerful factor to drive species to change over time. Such large-scale changes, they argued, were driven primarily by factors internal to living beings that led to advancement up the evolutionary ladder; natural selection worked only on the margins, leading primarily to evolutionary dead ends. Defenders of a competing evolutionary theory, proposed by Jean-Baptiste Lamarck earlier in the century, argued that evolution occurred

MR. BERGH TO THE RESCUE.

THE DEFRAUDED GORILLA. "That *Man* wants to claim my Pedigree. He says he is one of my Descendants."
Mr. BERGH. "Now, Mr. DARWIN, how could you insult him so?"

Figure 20.2 Darwin's theory of evolution proposed descent with modification by natural selection. His proposal that humans and apes were descended from a common ancestor was ridiculed by many people of his day, as evidenced by this cartoon. Though Darwin's theory is the fundamental principle of modern biology, it is still a contentious idea for many Christians today.

when organisms inherited acquired characteristics. Lamarck's theory gave Darwin's continued competition for decades, since it proposed an observable means of acquiring heritable characteristics, namely, by means of experiences that had changed an organism throughout its life (e.g. continued stretching produced a slightly longer neck, chewing tough grasses produced slightly more powerful jaw muscles), whereas the mechanism for modifying the characteristics inherited from one's parents, the genetic code, had not yet been discovered. Still other scientists opposed Darwin's theory because it seemed to conflict with two biblical principles: immutability of species and the relatively young age of the earth.

Advances in knowledge in many scientific fields over the next 150 years – genetics, paleontology, molecular biology, subatomic particle physics – have generally confirmed both the age of the earth and Darwin's theory, at least in the minds of the vast majority of scientists, as well as many Christians. Most Christians worldwide today see Darwin's theory of evolution by means of natural selection as compatible with both the fossil record and with Christianity. They have modified their interpretations of the Bible to accommodate the theory of evolution. For example, the Roman Catholic Church officially acknowledged in 1950 that the theory of evolution was not in conflict with Christian doctrine (Pope Pius XII, *Humani Generis*). In 1996 Pope John Paul II, in an address to the Pontifical Academy of Sciences, said,

> Today, almost half a century after the publication of the encyclical [*Humani Generis*], new knowledge has led to the recognition of the theory of evolution as more than a hypothesis. It is indeed remarkable that this theory has been progressively accepted by researchers, following a series of discoveries in various fields of knowledge. The convergence, neither sought nor fabricated, of the results of work that was conducted independently is in itself a significant argument in favor of this theory.

Most scientists who identify themselves as Protestants also accept Darwin's theory as foundational to the modern, scientific study of biology. Other Christians continue to oppose the theory itself, some of whom also reject the idea that the universe is billions of years old. Those who oppose evolution often substitute various versions of the idea known as Creation Science, which bases its proposals on the authority of the Bible, read literally, and rejects all scientific conclusions that do not agree with their reading of the Bible. A more recent proposal that is popular among many Christians, Intelligent Design (ID), accepts many of the findings of modern science, such as the ancient age of the earth, and it even concedes that evolution by natural selection probably occurs on a small scale (microevolution), but it continues to dispute the idea that macroevolution – evolution that results in the creation of new families, orders, classes, or phyla – is explained by natural selection. In particular, ID advocates zero in on the issue of alleged irreducible complexity, that is, the existence of interacting systems that are too complex to have arisen in stages (e.g. the biochemistry behind the clotting of blood, or the complex bacterial flagellum). ID proponents suggest that an intelligent designer (i.e.

God, although many books on ID omit any overt mention of God) must be posited to explain certain aspects of evolution. In return, many scientists have pushed back, proposing mechanisms that might give purely naturalistic explanations for supposedly irreducibly complex systems. In the U.S., the courts have fairly consistently ruled against the teaching of either Creation Science or Intelligent Design in public school classrooms, saying that they are religious rather than scientific points of view. The debate is not by any means limited to the U.S., however, as some leading Roman Catholic scholars from around the world have weighed in on both sides of the debate, and the issue has also divided Christian communities in places like Kenya, where some of the most ancient fossil hominids have been discovered.

The question of the evolution of human beings from ancestral species is a particularly thorny issue for many Christians today. If Genesis 1 is read theologically rather than literally, as many Christians suggest, numerous questions concerning both the age of the universe and the origin and development of life are resolved. One question that remains, however, involves the origin of humankind. Direct creation of a single man and woman, as a literal reading of Genesis 1 suggests, appears to be an easy solution, at least on the surface. Indeed, some Christians argue that God used natural processes to create the rest of the universe but created humans as an act of special creation at a certain point in the not-too-distant past. This solution, however, does not address many pertinent issues raised by science, such as the existence of an extensive fossil record that includes ancient hominids, the genetic similarity between humans and other organisms, the evidence of widespread and continuous human occupation of different parts of the world, and the

Evidence of human ancestors

Since the initial discoveries of ancient, human-like skeletons in the Neander Valley in Germany in the nineteenth century, paleoanthropologists have uncovered a vast quantity of remains that appear more or less human. Scientists today group the more primitive remains into genera called *Australopithecus*, (*Paranthropus*,) *Ardipithecus*, *Orrorin*, and *Sahelanthropus*. More advanced remains are called *Homo*. Even within *Homo* scientists find many distinct species, including *H. habilis*, *H. erectus*, *H. ergaster*, *H. rudolfensis*, *H. heidelbergensis*, *H. antecessor*, *H. neanderthalensis*, *H. sapiens* (modern humans), and the recently discovered *H. floresiensis*, a diminutive specimen that survived until as recently as 13,000 years ago on the island of Flores in Indonesia. Modern humans overlapped chronologically with both Flores and Neanderthal individuals. Were all of these species human? Were only some of them, and if so, which ones? An important question to answer first is, what makes us human? From a theological perspective, many Christians argue that it is the image of God that makes us human. If so, could the image of God have been present in any of the other species listed here? These are questions that Christians struggle to answer in the light of the scientific evidence.

molecular evidence that suggests that the most recent common female ancestor of all living humans (called "Mitochondrial Eve") lived about 100,000 years ago.

In 2003 the Human Genome Project completed its mapping of the complete human genome and published the results. In 2005 a similar mapping of the chimpanzee genome was released. Depending on how one calculates similarities and differences, the two genomes differed by only 1.2 percent to 2.7 percent. In other words, human and chimpanzee DNA are between 97.3 percent and 98.8 percent the same. Genetic similarity is used as a tool by molecular biologists to construct family trees of related species, a technique known as cladistics. Christians interested in the interplay between science and Christianity ask the question, what is the significance of the human-chimpanzee genome similarity from a theological perspective?

Most special creation proposals posit a creation sometime within the past 10,000 years, perhaps accompanied by a more recent worldwide flood. However, Christians who support the conclusions of scientists argue that archaeological evidence suggests that modern humans have inhabited the continent of Australia constantly for between 40,000 and 60,000 years, and the American continents for at least 13,000 years. Furthermore, linguistic diversity suggests that human languages separated from one another at least 10,000 years ago. Christians who disagree with the scientific consensus dispute both the techniques used and the interpretation of data, but more and more Christians are coming to terms with the findings of science. Some Christians, when confronted by scientific evidence, have abandoned their faith altogether, finding it incompatible with their modern, scientific worldview. However, other Christians find the questions raised by science to be stimulating challenges to deal with theologically, while remaining firmly rooted in their faith. It seems doubtful at this juncture that science will reverse itself on the major issues discussed in this section, and the trend among Christianity as a whole is to adjust its beliefs in order to accommodate the discoveries of scientists, much as it did with the earlier crisis concerning Galileo and his heliocentric universe. At the same time, mathematicians and scientists themselves over the past century have defined some of the limits that science has in its attempts to explain the universe, as Kurt Gödel's Incompleteness Theorem, Werner Heisenberg's Uncertainty Principle, and Chaos Theory demonstrate. It seems likely, then, that the way forward in the conversation between science and religion will require mutual respect, new ways of thinking about old problems, and a fair amount of humility.

Key points you need to know

- The Protestant Reformation, with its emphasis on individuality and its antipathy toward traditional ways of thinking, created an environment in which creative thinking about science was possible. The printing press, invented the previous century, helped spread modern scientific ideas.

- Galileo Galilei promoted and further developed the theory of Nicolaus Copernicus that the earth revolved around the sun, not vice versa. He was forbidden by the Roman Catholic Church from teaching his ideas. Many Protestants immediately accepted his work, as did the Roman Catholic Church a century later.

- Charles Lyell proposed the geological theory of uniformitarianism, and contemporary scientists used this theory to estimate the age of the earth at several hundred million years. The current scientifically accepted estimate is about 4.5 billion (10^9) years.

- Observations of the furthermost reaches of the universe, accompanied by careful measurements of the cosmic background radiation, have led scientists to suggest that the universe began with a gigantic explosion, the Big Bang, between 13 and 15 billion years ago.

- Charles Darwin proposed that all life evolves over time by the process of natural selection, and that therefore all living organisms are descended from common ancestors.

- Although many Christians believe that the modern scientific concepts of geological uniformitarianism, the Big Bang, and especially evolution by natural selection conflict with their understanding of the Bible and/or theology, many other Christians fully accept the findings of modern science, finding them fully compatible with their understanding of God, the Bible, and Christian theology.

Discussion questions

1. Why were Protestant leaders in general more ready to accept Galileo's ideas than Roman Catholic leaders?

2. How did Lyell's proposals concerning uniformitarianism and an earth that is at least millions of years old challenge the typical Christian's understanding of the Bible?

3. Is the Big Bang compatible with the traditional Christian idea of *creatio ex nihilo* (creation from nothing)?

4. Why do many Christians who accept an ancient earth and the Big Bang have difficulty with Darwin's ideas concerning evolution?

5. How does the theory of evolution, if accepted, affect theological concepts such as the creation of human beings in the image of God, the Fall (the origin of sin), and the idea of God as creator?

6. Does the idea of Intelligent Design help bridge the perceived gap between Christianity and science, or is it merely an updated form of Creation Science?

Further reading

Barbour, Ian G. 2000. *When Science Meets Religion*. New York: HarperSanFrancisco.

Collins, Francis S. 2006. *The Language of God*. New York: Free Press.

Darwin, Charles 2003. *The Origin of Species and the Voyage of the Beagle*. Everyman's Library. New York: Knopf.

Dembski, William A. 1999. *Intelligent Design: The Bridge between Science and Theology*. Downer's Grove, IL: InterVarsity Press.

Dowe, Phil 2005. *Galileo, Darwin, and Hawking: The Interplay of Science, Reason, and Religion*. Grand Rapids, MI: Eerdmans.

Gingerich, Owen 2006. *God's Universe*. Cambridge, MA: Belknap Press.

Johanson, Donald and Blake Edgar 2006. *From Lucy to Language*. Revised edn. New York: Simon and Schuster.

Lyell, Charles 1997. *Principles of Geology*. Edited with an Introduction by James A. Secord. London: Penguin.

Margenau, Henry and Roy Abraham Varghese 1992. *Cosmos, Bios, Theos: Scientists Reflect on Science, God, and the Origins of the Universe, Life, and* Homo sapiens. La Salle, IL: Open Court.

Miller, Kenneth R. 1999. *Finding Darwin's God*. New York: Cliff Street Books.

Olson, Steve 2003. *Mapping Human History*. Boston, MA: Houghton Mifflin.

Papal Encyclicals Online. http://www.papalencyclicals.net.

Tattersall, Ian 1998. *Becoming Human*. San Diego, CA: Harcourt Brace & Company.

21 Christianity and the arts

Beauty is truth, truth beauty, – that is all
Ye know on earth, and all ye need to know.
                    (John Keats, "Ode on a Grecian Urn")

In this chapter

Christians have been using art to represent their understanding of Jesus Christ, Christianity, and God's interaction with the world from the earliest days of the Church, when they painted images of Christ as the Good Shepherd on the walls of catacombs. Christians have used the visual arts, architecture, music, drama, and literature through the ages to express their faith. They have also used the arts to critique or question Christianity in general and contemporary expressions of Christianity in particular, or to document various ways in which Christianity affects people's lives.

Main topics covered

- Visual arts
- Architecture
- Music
- Drama
- Literature

Visual arts

The link between Christianity and the arts is an ancient one, and it has often been controversial as well, at times approaching a love-hate relationship. Many in the early church, influenced by both the Jewish prohibition of making images of God and the Roman use of images to promote the imperial cult (e.g. images of the emperors on coins and in statues), saw the visual arts as an inappropriate means for expressing the Christian faith. For example, Clement of Alexandria, in *Exhortation to the Heathen*, rails against those who use idols, images, and great temples to represent the pagan gods, because these images are motionless, insensate, and utterly powerless. In *Stromata* 2.18, he praises the wisdom of the Mosaic law for teaching the "abstinence from sensible images." On the other hand, the human desire to express its deepest feelings artistically, which can be traced back to Cro Magnon cave paintings in the Paleolithic period, was a strong draw, and Christian art from catacombs abounds from the earliest era of Christianity. Furthermore, the Bible itself speaks of human beings as created in the image of God (Gen 1:26–27) and of Christ himself being the idealized image of God (Col 1:15). Christian martyrs proved to be subjects of particular interest from the fourth century, the period of the great Roman persecutions of Christians. In his *Church History*, Eusebius of Caesarea, writing in the fourth century, reports seeing both painted images and statues of Jesus and the disciples, an indication that the visual arts were becoming popular means of expressing religious devotion, at least in some areas, even before the time of Constantine.

After Constantine declared Christianity a legal religion, many Christian leaders continued to condemn the use of images, especially to represent God or Christ, fearing that they would lead to idolatry. However, images were becoming important not only to many of the common people but to the monks as well. Augustine, in his treatise *On the Trinity* 12, describes Adam and Eve as carriers of the divine image and powerful pointers back to God. In *City of God* 8.6, he argues that beauty itself is evidence that God exists, implying the possibility of intrinsic value in art. The Great Cappadocians were more straightforward in their support of Christian art, advocating the decoration of churches with visual images. In about 600, Pope Gregory I the Great wrote to Serenus, bishop of Marseilles, criticizing him for destroying images, which serve as the "Bible of the poor."

By the Early Middle Ages, the use of icons by both monks and ordinary Christians was widespread, especially in the East, when the Iconoclastic Controversies broke out, beginning in the eighth century. The Byzantine emperors and theologians who opposed the use of icons in worship, on the grounds that they had become idols, did not succeed in removing the popular icons, but they did force those who supported the use of icons in worship, such as John of Damascus, to stipulate that images were to be venerated rather than adored (worshiped). Although some Western theologians were against the veneration as well as the adoration of images, by the time of the High Middle Ages veneration of images was generally accepted in the West as well. In about the twelfth century religious sculpture, as well as two-dimensional images, began to be used in the West, often in conjunction with the increased reverence of relics. Despite efforts by Bernard of Clairvaux and others to oppose the use of statues, they soon became commonplace in the West, though not in the East.

Prior to the Renaissance, Christian art had been mostly stylized rather than realistic. The rediscovery of perspective and realism in art caused a new wave of controversy in the West, though not in the East, where traditions of icon "writing" were well established. Despite opposition, however, realistic images and statues multiplied. Monks were allowed to have images in their cells. Churches were adorned with both images and statues,

Figure 21.1 Gianlorenzo Bernini's sculpture The Ecstasy of St. Teresa depicts in a graphic way Teresa of Ávila's encounter with the divine.

all realistically rendered. By the fourteenth century, Christians who viewed sacred art could be granted indulgences, a development that further spurred the production of Christian art. Artists sometimes painted contemporary figures, such as their patrons, into religious scenes depicting biblical times or other significant events in the history of the church, thus creating an explicit link for those individuals between the faith of the present and the past. Also during this period great monumental sculpture, often with a religious theme, was placed in public areas in European cities like Florence and Venice.

The early Reformers were often iconoclasts, removing visual representations of God, Christ, and the saints from the churches they took over, and frequently destroying them. Their primary concern was the elimination of what they saw as idolatry, and the association of art with indulgences was particularly troubling to many. On the other hand, the excesses of some early Reformers caused a backlash, and art slowly made its way back into the great churches of Protestantism. After the Great Fire of London destroyed St. Paul's Cathedral in 1666, Sir Christopher Wren was commissioned to build a new cathedral on the same spot. Wren left the interior of the cathedral largely undecorated (by paintings), but he planned to add images to the interior of the great dome. The images that were added, by James Thornhill, were rendered entirely in various shades of brown and black, suggesting that by the late seventeenth century, sacred art was starting to make a comeback, albeit a tentative one, in Protestant England. In contrast, subsequent additions to the cathedral, particularly in the Victorian period, exhibit a wide array of color, and even statuary art makes a reappearance.

The Roman Catholic Church, in contrast to the early Reformers, reveled in artistic expression during the Baroque period (roughly 1600–1750), and afterwards as well. A new type of art, easel painting, became the most popular type of visual art during this period, especially for private collections, in contrast to the murals and frescos of the earlier period. The inside of churches, particularly the altars, became more elaborate, and churches were filled with religious statuary.

Secular art – that is, art produced for its own sake – became popular in the Romantic period, and it came to predominate in the Modern period. The separation between Christianity and the visual arts was caused in part by the rationalist critiques of Christianity and the rise of republican governments following the French Revolution. It was also spurred by a new freedom that artists felt to express themselves as laws imposing sometimes onerous restrictions on the production of art were gradually lifted. In general, the increase in popularity of secular art can be seen more as a celebration of human freedom than as an overt critique of the Church. Although explicitly religious art continued to be produced, Christian theologians, aesthetes, and critics of culture began turning more and more to secular art for religious themes and imagery. Just to name a few examples, Christians analyzed works like Picasso's *Guernica*, Dalí's *The Temptation of St. Anthony*, Chagall's *White Crucifixion*, and Munch's *The Scream* for clues about the modern world's views on religion, meaning, and value.

Most of the discussion to this point has focused on the relationship between Christianity and art in the West, particularly in Europe. In the Eastern Church, the relationship between church and art was much more conservative, especially in those areas where Christians continued to live under Muslim rule. The Muslim prohibition of human figures in art led to the development within Islam of an amazingly rich approach to two-dimensional rendering based largely on geometric patterns. While Christians of the Eastern church did not emulate Muslim art, they were influenced by it, and it is likely that the Muslim prohibition of human images retarded the Eastern Church's adoption of realism in Christian art. On the other hand, the production of stylized icons continued unabated, and the Eastern church today produces icons of startling beauty, quite different from the realistic images that those in the West have come to expect in art.

Christian art in the nineteenth-century mission areas of Asia, Africa, and Latin America at first largely imitated Western artistic styles, and the art itself was often commissioned with an evangelistic intent. Quickly, however, native artists began to infuse their pieces with aspects of their own local artistic traditions. One early example of this phenomenon, long predating the colonial period, comes from China, where a Nestorian Christian carved a cross rising from a lotus blossom, the traditional symbol of Buddhism. In Africa, for example, images of a hermaphroditic Christ on the cross emphasize the local tradition that perfection is both male and female at the same time. Another example from Africa is a crucifix on which Christ is represented by a tribal mask. The painting *Stilling of the Tempest* by Chinese artist Monika Liu Ho-Peh depicts Jesus and his disciples rendered as Chinese men, against a backdrop of sea and mountains that is presented in the style of traditional Chinese paintings. Finally, Miriam-Rose

Ungunmerr, an Australian Aborigine, produced a series of painted Stations of the Cross which combine Aboriginal designs and techniques with a very traditional Christian setting.

Architecture

Early Christians met in homes, alongside river banks, and in cemeteries. By the second and third centuries, some churches were meeting in modest houses that were owned by the church itself, rather than by an individual member. Many of the buildings owned by churches, particularly in the East, were destroyed or confiscated during the Great Persecution under Diocletian, just before the time of Constantine. When Constantine became emperor, he gave orders for the church buildings to be given back to the churches, and he also donated great amounts of money to church building projects. Constantine's greatest building project of all was his new capital, Constantinople. Locating it on the site of the ancient city of Byzantium, Constantine extended the city walls so that the area encompassed by the walls doubled, and he undertook a massive building campaign, which included the construction of many churches. With the huge influx of people into the church during Constantine's reign, new church buildings were needed all over the empire. Every large city built many churches to accommodate the worshipers.

After the fall of the Western Roman Empire in 476, the construction of large, new church buildings almost completely stopped. The churches that were built in the West

Figure 21.2 St Basil's Cathedral in Moscow incorporates large, onion-shaped domes, typical of Russian architecture, into its design.

over the next six hundred years or so were modest in comparison to the great cathedrals and basilicas that existed in the East. Although a modest Renaissance in church architecture occurred during the reign of Charlemagne, with buildings modeled on old Rome, the next great period of architectural innovation, as far as church buildings were concerned, was the eleventh century, the Romanesque Period, so-called because many of the designs were conscious imitations of the architecture of ancient Rome. It was during the Gothic Period, however, that medieval architecture reached its greatest heights, literally. The Gothic Period extends from the twelfth to the fifteenth century, and its buildings are characterized by their reach toward the heavens. Gothic churches were designed to inspire and uplift the worshiper, capturing copious amounts of sky and light in a massive structure. Gothic domes and towers could be built higher that ever before and more windows could be constructed because of several architectural innovations, including the ribbed vault, pointed ceiling vaults, and flying buttresses, all of which reduced stress on the load bearing walls.

The following periods, the Renaissance and Baroque, saw the construction of great cathedrals whose dominant characteristics were not tall spires and high ceilings but massive domes and, particularly in the Baroque period, florid decoration. The two

Figure 21.3 The Crystal Cathedral in Garden Grove, California, led until 2006 by pastor Robert Schuller, is one of the most recognizable churches in the world. Formerly known as the Garden Grove Community Church, the congregation that meets in the Crystal Cathedral is part of the Free Church tradition.

greatest examples of Renaissance cathedrals come from the beginning and the end of the period, the cathedral (Il Duomo) of Florence and St. Peter's Basilica in Rome. Although many of the great architectural projects of Florence were funded by the ruling Medici family, St. Peter's Basilica in Rome required the sale of indulgences, a funding decision that helped spark the Protestant Reformation.

Protestant churches that were part of the Magisterial Reformation were able simply to take over existing Catholic buildings, at least at first, and they also had the support of the state to undertake new construction. The Free Churches, however, had no such luxury, and their buildings were often crude and artless in comparison. Over time, however, as their numbers grew, large wealthy congregations of Free Churches were also able to build impressive church buildings, although not on the same scale as the great cathedrals of Europe, or even of the Catholic cathedrals of the New World. Boston's Old North Church was built in 1723, and its design was inspired by the work of Christopher Wren, the architect of St. Paul's Cathedral in London. It was an impressive building in comparison to others in Boston in the early eighteenth century, but its size and architectural style were hardly on a par with the great publicly supported churches. Nevertheless, it, and other similar buildings that were owned by individual churches or denominations and paid for by parishioners, provided models by which subsequent Free Church buildings could be measured.

The rise of the Protestant *megachurch* in the twentieth century sparked the building of many new, impressive church buildings whose styles were quite different than the great cathedrals of the state churches. Some of these churches built huge structures whose architectural style differed little from typical brick or stone churches designed to house smaller congregations; they were just bigger. Other megachurches built large rectangular buildings whose interiors somewhat resembled great warehouses, designed to hold people rather than goods. Perhaps the most innovative church building associated with a twentieth century megachurch was the Crystal Cathedral of Orange County, California, built to house the congregation led by Pastor Robert Schuller. The building is an enormous glass and steel structure designed to connect worshipers with the world around them.

Christian attitudes towards monumental church architecture have been mixed over the years. While no one can deny the grandeur of a great cathedral or basilica, some Christians question whether the amount of money spent on such huge structures is an appropriate use of church funds that might better be spent, they argue, for social ministries, new church planting, or evangelism. On the other hand, other Christians argue that church architecture is a form of art, and beautiful architecture inspires just like great art and great music do. It is interesting to note that many of the new church buildings today that put the most emphasis on aesthetics in architectural design belong to churches whose worship practices are highly liturgical, while the buildings that are built with an eye primarily focused on utility, with relatively minimal attention paid to aesthetics, often belong to churches whose worship practices are less structured and more free form.

Music

Hallelujah!
For the Lord God omnipotent reigneth.
Hallelujah!

(George Frederick Handel, *Messiah*, "Hallelujah Chorus")

Services in the first century included the singing of "psalms, hymns, and spiritual songs," according to Col 3:16. Many scholars believe that the New Testament itself contains fragments of early Christian hymns (e.g. parts of John 1:1–18; Phil 2:5–11; Luke 2:14). Pliny the Younger's letter to the emperor Hadrian in the early second century indicates that the Christians in his area were in the habit of meeting together and, among other things, "singing a hymn antiphonally to Christ, as to a god." The exact content of many of these early Christian hymns is unknown, as is the music involved, though it can probably be assumed that they followed musical traditions that were common to Jews, in many cases, or perhaps to pagans (though the Jewish impact on Christian hymnody was probably greater).

Several well-known early Christian writers were composers of hymns, including Ephrem Syrus, Basil the Great, Gregory of Nazianzus, and John Chrysostom. Bar Daisan, the leader of a major branch of the church in Syria, and who was later declared to be unorthodox, was famous in his day for composing hymns to help teach his version of the Christian faith (many of Ephrem's hymns were written to counteract those of Bar Daisan). One of the most important figures in the early medieval period for the development of Christian music was Pope Gregory I the Great. He instituted changes to the Western liturgical tradition that caused the songs used in worship to vary according to the calendar of the Christian year. He was so interested in a form of chant called plainsong that his name came to be associated with a particular form of it two centuries later, the Gregorian chant. The Carolingian Renaissance in the ninth and tenth centuries popularized this particular form of the chant, and it largely replaced other forms of chant used in the West at that time, such as Celtic and Mozarabic chants. Meanwhile, in the East, a distinctive form of music called the Byzantine chant reigned supreme until the fall of Constantinople. Symeon the New Theologian's *Hymns of Divine Love* are one of many examples of Byzantine hymn writing.

The Protestant Reformation brought with it a series of innovations in church music. Through the Middle Ages, Christian music was almost entirely sung *a capella*, without instruments. Advances in the technology required to build modern instruments, including the violin, organ, and harpsichord, led to the composition of great musical works by Protestant and Catholic musicians alike. In the Baroque period the Protestant composers Bach and Handel wrote countless masses, oratorios, and other types of music to support the church. Two of the most famous were Handel's *Messiah* and Bach's *Mass in B Minor*. In Venice their Catholic contemporary, the "Red Priest" Antonio Vivaldi, was busy composing many choral works of his own, many written explicitly for use in the church, such as his renowned *Gloria*.

Composers in the subsequent Classical, Romantic, and Modern periods also composed music for the church, but their efforts were often focused on more secular forms, such as the symphony and the opera. In addition to the great works of classical music produced during this period, the sixteenth through the nineteenth centuries were also productive ones for the composition of hymns, especially by Protestants. Martin Luther himself was a well-known composer, having written the hymn "A Mighty Fortress Is Our God," among many others. Charles Wesley, John Wesley's brother, wrote many hymns adopted by Methodists and others. Perhaps the greatest English hymn writer of the period was Isaac Watts, the "Father of English Hymnody," who composed some 750 hymns, many of which are still used in churches today. Perhaps the most influential single hymn ever written was composed not by a professional musician but by a former slave trader turned preacher, John Newton. After abandoning the slave trading business, Newton became a fierce abolitionist, and his hymn "Amazing Grace" verbalizes his deep remorse over what he saw as his earlier life of sin, and God's willingness to forgive him. The hymn became a favorite of Protestant churches around the world and is still popular today. The music to "Amazing Grace" has appeared in innumerable movies and television shows, and the impact of the song on people around the U.S. was examined in a multi-part documentary by journalist Bill Moyers.

Music has frequently been a force that unites Christians in worship, but it can also be a factor that divides Christians from one another. Many congregations, particularly in Protestant churches, have argued vociferously over the type of music that is appropriate for church services. Traditionalists argue that the great hymns of the past, accompanied by new songs of a similar ilk, are the best way to preserve the reverence and dignity that a proper church service should convey. Advocates of more modern music contend that the older music does not connect with either younger members of the congregation or

Christian protest music

Many Christians have used music to express frustration with their current life and hope for a better future. Music has been a particularly powerful tool for projecting the suffering and aspirations of oppressed groups. Black slaves in the United States composed many songs that spoke of their deliverance from oppression in both the temporal and the eternal world. Works such as "Joshua Fit the Battle of Jericho" and "Nobody Knows the Trouble I've Seen" speak openly of hope in God's deliverance in the afterlife, but they also convey the singers' expectation that a God of justice will begin to work in the present time. The American Civil Rights Movement drew on such African American spirituals for strength, and participants frequently sang the protest song, "We Shall Overcome," which, while the lyrics are not explicitly Christian, drew on both Christian themes and the tune of an old spiritual. The official anthem of the South African anti-apartheid movement was entitled "Nkosi Sikelel' iAfrika," a song whose Xhosa/Zulu title means "God bless Africa."

unchurched *seekers* who might be visiting a church for the first time. Some churches have removed pianos and organs and replaced them with guitars, synthesizers, and drums. Others have staunchly resisted change. Still others, after removing the piano and organ, decided to bring them back again. One of great struggles of any Christian generation is how best to reach new people with the gospel while at the same time holding onto existing members of the congregation, and the use of music is at the forefront of many such discussions in the contemporary church.

Drama

> I call him Jesus, and he calls me Sonny.
> (*The Apostle*)

All Christian worship that includes the observance of the Eucharist is sacred drama. One of the main purposes of worship in many religious traditions, including Christianity, is to reenact important parts of the sacred story, and the breaking of bread and the drinking of wine either symbolizes Christ's death or offers his sacrifice again to God, depending on which view of the Eucharist one holds. Outside worship, the dramatic arts developed into an important medium for communicating the Christian message during the High Middle Ages, with the advent of mystery plays, morality plays, and passion plays. Mystery plays retold a specific Bible story, such as the story of Cain and Abel, with a great deal of creative license. The plays were performed by actor's guilds who made a living moving from town to town performing their plays. Morality plays were not based on specific biblical passages but were allegorical representations of different aspects of the lives of Christians. One of the most famous morality plays in the English language was called *Everyman*, a play in which a man destined for death is given the opportunity to take along a companion, but of the numerous companions he invites – Fellowship, Goods, and Kindred, to name a few – none is willing to go except Good Deeds, and she is unable to go unless Everyman strengthens her by visiting the priest, confessing his sins, and doing penance. A third type of play that originated in the medieval period is the passion play, which reenacts the New Testament accounts of Jesus' betrayal, arrest, trials, crucifixion, and resurrection. These plays, usually performed during Lent, proved to be enormously popular, and some of them, such as the Oberammergau Passion Play in Germany, are still performed today.

Dramatized reenactments of biblical stories have been performed on the stage in the modern period, and more recently in feature-length films. Many early Protestant pastors spoke out against the evils of the theater, and some more recent Christian leaders have said similar things about films, urging Christians to stay away from movie theaters. Many other Christians have taken a more positive stance toward both plays and movies, preferring to make judgments about whether to see individual films instead of rejecting all movies out of hand. Still other Christians have fully engaged the film industry, either making movies of their own or leading other Christians through analyses of a wide variety of films from a Christian perspective.

In 1979 a movie called *Jesus*, but commonly known as *The Jesus Film*, was released in theaters. Although it had only limited success at the box office, the Jesus Film Project was created as an organization designed to translate the film into numerous languages. The success of the film worldwide has been spectacular. Its proponents, and some neutral observers as well, claim that the film has been seen by more people than any other movie ever made. Its distributors claim that it has been translated into 971 languages and has been seen in 228 countries. Many other movies about Jesus have been created in recent years, some intentionally based on a literal reading of the biblical text, such as *Jesus of Nazareth*, *The Gospel According to St. Matthew*, and *The Passion of the Christ*. Other movies were loose adaptations of the gospel story, such as *Jesus Christ Superstar*, *Godspell*, *The Last Temptation of Christ*, and *Son of Man*.

A new discipline that has been introduced into the curriculum of many universities and seminaries, as well as into the education programs of many churches, is the analysis of films from a Christian point of view. Some of the movies that are popular to analyze have overt religious themes, such as *Jesus of Montreal*, *The Apostle*, *To End All Wars*, *Joyeux Noel*, and *Amazing Grace*. Others do not, such as *Sophie's Choice*, *Star Wars*, *The Matrix*, *The Lord of the Rings*, *Signs*, *Munich*, and *The Last Supper*. These analyses are usually self-consciously subjective, and they encourage each individual to interact with the film from his or her own perspective. That Christian perspectives on movies can vary widely is abundantly exemplified by the widely divergent reactions Christians had to Mel Gibson's movie *The Passion of the Christ*. The movie was hailed by some as the most important Christian film ever made, and it was vilified by others as anti-Semitic and gratuitously violent. Its violent imagery gained it an R rating (intended for adults only), but its intense publicity made it one of the top film attractions of 2004, even though the whole movie was filmed in Aramaic, ancient Greek, and Latin, without a word of English or any other modern language.

Literature

> This is what self-centered religion does to us: it allows us to use it to further our own ends.
>
> (John Irving, *A Prayer for Owen Meany*)

Whatever else it may be – sacred scripture, historical document, collection of religious treatises – the Bible is also literature. If literature is defined as "imaginative or creative writing, especially of recognized artistic value," the Bible certainly qualifies. It is literature as opposed to raw data, or annals, or technical writing, because it shows every sign of skilled human authorship throughout, and it also has artistic value in and of itself, apart from other considerations. In recent decades, many Christians have begun to read the Bible as literature and to compare it to other works of literature, in order to gain a better understanding of its message.

People who read the Bible as literature read it in light of other works of "literature" in a broad sense, including novels, short stories, poetry, plays, and even visual arts, music, and architecture. A literary reading of Genesis 1, for example, might compare the creation account with J. R. R. Tolkien's myth of the "Ainulindalë," found in *The Silmarillion*, which reworks the idea of the fall of the angels into a story involving divine music, harmony, and cacophony. The literary reader of the Bible will ask how Tolkien's creation myth sheds light on the themes of Genesis 1.

Authors frequently write stories that include characters that may be considered "Christ figures," so it is relevant to compare the manner in which Jesus is portrayed in the gospels with Christ figures in stories such as Hermann Melville's "Billy Budd," Tolkien's Gandalf in *The Lord of the Rings*, and Stephen Crane's Jim Conklin in *The Red Badge of Courage*. The literary reader asks how these characters are similar and how they are different from Jesus in the gospels, for example, in regard to self-sacrifice.

Readers of the conquest narrative in Joshua might compare the entry of the Israelites into the "Promised Land" with the reception the Joads received upon entry into the promised land of California in John Steinbeck's *The Grapes of Wrath*. They will also want to read the first half of the book of Judges for contrasting narratives within the Bible itself.

The visual arts as well as literature per se might profitably be used in reading the Bible from a literary perspective. For example, the battle scenes in Revelation, with their intricate symbolism, might be compared with Pablo Picasso's portrayal of the Spanish Civil War in his painting *Guernica*. The portrayal of the crucifixion in the four gospels might be compared with any of the innumerable paintings of the crucifixion that have been done over the years by artists such as Chagall, Dalí, or Dürer. Finally, the description of the temple in Ezekiel 40–48 might be compared with any of the great cathedrals of Europe or Latin America.

In addition to the Bible itself, Christians have used literature to express, challenge, and analyze their faith for centuries. Several examples have already been mentioned in previous chapters. Augustine's *Confessions* is an autobiographical account of his inner struggle to find a meaningful approach to life. Ephrem Syrus, Bar Daisan, and Gregory of Nazianzus expressed their faith through poetry. Hildegard of Bingen wrote numerous hymns to Mary, among other works of literary value. Dante Alighieri composed a poetic vision of the afterlife in his *Divine Comedy*. In the post-Reformation period, literary works by Christians with an overt Christian theme are too many to mention, but include such works as John Milton's *Paradise Lost*, the poems of John Donne and William Blake, John Bunyan's allegory *The Pilgrim's Progress*, Johann Wolfgang von Goethe's *Faust*, C. S. Lewis's *The Chronicles of Narnia*, Shusaku Endo's *Silence*, William Styron's *The Confessions of Nat Turner*, Nikos Kazantzakis's *The Last Temptation of Christ*, Umberto Eco's *The Name of the Rose*, Barbara Kingsolver's *The Poisonwood Bible*, Anne Rice's *Christ the Lord*, and many, many others.

In addition to works whose primary theme is religious, many authors – whether Christian or not – work themes related to Christianity into their works in significant ways. As with literature that deals with Christianity in a more overt way, works that contain significant Christian themes are innumerable, so a few examples, primarily of relatively recent works, will have to suffice. Leo Tolstoy, a Russian author, wrote many short stories that deal with issues such as community, poverty, and faith. William Faulkner set his novels in the fictitious Yoknapatawpha County in Mississippi, and Christianity frequently comes into play in books such as *As I Lay Dying* and *The Sound and the Fury*, often by highlighting hypocrisy or disillusionment with religion. Russian novelist Fyodor Dostoyevsky's *The Brothers Karamazov* presents four brothers who struggle with faith, doubt, and issues of morality in response to their father's death. In Chinua Achebe's *Things Fall Apart*, the traditional life of an African tribal leader is challenged and eventually destroyed by the changes wrought by modernity, including the introduction of Christianity into the region. Alice Walker's *The Color Purple* deals with themes such as love, hatred, and forgiveness in a novel set in the American South. Maya Angelou, in her autobiographical works and her poetry, portrays the African American experience, including the strong influence of the church in the Black community. John Irving's *A Prayer for Owen Meany* records the life of a fictional, iconoclastic boy whose encounters with religion are usually unsatisfying, yet who manages nevertheless to develop a deep faith in God's purpose for his life. Many of Sandra Cisneros's short stories, such as "Mericans" and "Little Miracles, Kept Promises" reflect the influence of Roman Catholicism on the lives of Mexican Americans. Finally, Margaret Atwood's *The Handmaid's Tale* offers a frightening glimpse of religious tradition and control in a post-apocalyptic world where few women are capable of giving birth. These are just a few examples of the ways in which Christianity and literature interact in meaningful, and sometimes surprising, ways.

Key points you need to know

- Despite the opposition of some Christian leaders during certain times and in certain places to the use of visual arts by Christians, most Christians, both historically and today, have found the arts a valuable tool for expressing – or critiquing, or questioning – their faith.
- Architecture, particularly the creation of church buildings great and small, is another way in which Christians express their faith, often through the symbolic use of space, such as vaulted ceilings and the cruciform floor plan of many churches.
- Christians have been composing hymns and other songs of faith from the first century, often borrowing from contemporary musical forms.
- Drama, including films, is a powerful way to express ideas, and many have used the medium to treat both overtly Christian issues (in a supportive or critical light) and themes that are of concern to Christians.
- Another common way in which Christian stories and themes are presented and analyzed is through literature. The Bible itself may be read as literature and compared and contrasted with other literary works. Supporters, critics, and observers of Christianity all use literature effectively to deal with issues of interest to Christians.

Discussion questions

1. Why were the iconoclasts of the medieval and Reformation periods opposed to the use of the visual arts to present Christian ideas?
2. How do local church buildings use symbols, including the use of sacred space, to represent Christian themes and concepts? How effectively do they do so? Are there some church buildings whose symbolism appears to conflict with the ideas the church strives to present?
3. What are the advantages and disadvantages of using popular music styles, or even specific tunes taken from secular music, to present the Christian message?
4. Which movies tend to be more effective at communicating the Christian message: movies that reproduce biblical stories, other movies that deal with overtly Christian themes, or movies that deal with themes of interest to Christians more subtly?
5. Is reading the Bible as literature a legitimate way of reading the Bible? Why or why not?
6. In addition to those listed in the chapter, what other modern literary works deal effectively with Christian themes in an overt way? What other modern literary works deal effectively, yet less overtly, with themes of interest to Christians? Are there works whose attempts to deal with such themes fail to be effective?

Further reading, listening, watching, or observing

Achebe, Chinua 1994. *Things Fall Apart*. New York: Anchor Books.

Atwood, Margaret 1998. *The Handmaid's Tale*. New York: Anchor Books.

The Benedictine Monks of Santo Domingo de Silos 1994. *Chant*. New York: Angel Records. (music)

Christianson, Eric S. *et al.* eds 2005. *Cinéma Divinité: Religion, Theology and the Bible in Film*. London: SCM.

Duval, Robert. *The Apostle*. (film)

Endo, Shusaku 1969. *Silence*. Translated by William Johnston. New York: Taplinger.

Ferguson, George 1966. *Signs and Symbol in Christian Art*. London: Oxford University Press.

Gibson, Mel. *The Passion of the Christ*. (film)

Handel, George Frederick. *Messiah*. (music)

Haydn, Franz Joseph. *The Creation*. (music)

Jewison, Norman. *Jesus Christ Superstar*. (film)

Johnston, Robert K. 2000. *Reel Spirituality: Theology and Film in Dialogue*. Grand Rapids, MI: Baker Academic.

Kingsolver, Barbara 1998. *The Poisonwood Bible*. New York: HarperPerennial.

Pelikan, Jaroslav 1997. *The Illustrated Jesus through the Centuries*. New Haven, CT: Yale University Press.

Religion Past and Present 2007. S.v. "Art and Religion." Leiden: Brill.

Taylor, Richard 2005. *How to Read a Church: A Guide to Symbols and Images in Churches and Cathedrals*. Mahwah, NJ: HiddenSpring.

Vivaldi, Antonio. *Gloria*. (music)

22 Christian ethics and politics

Throughout the Bible God appears as the liberator of the oppressed. He is not neutral. He does not attempt to reconcile Moses and Pharaoh, to reconcile the Hebrew slaves with their Egyptian oppressors or to reconcile the Jewish people with any of their late oppressors. Oppression is sin and it cannot be compromised with, it must be done away with. God takes sides with the oppressed.

(Kairos Document, 1985)

In this chapter

Christianity involves more than just a system of beliefs. It demands that its adherents live moral lives, bearing witness to the world by lived example and by prophetic proclamation. For most Christians, active involvement in society is a vital part of the Christian life. A wide diversity of opinion exists among Christians concerning the proper application of the gospel to issues such as sexual mores, issues of life and death, and wealth and poverty. Accordingly, Christians support many different political parties in the countries in which they live, determined in part by their interpretation of the implications of Christianity concerning ethical issues.

Main topics covered

- Christ and culture
- Sexual mores
- Life and death
- Wealth and poverty
- Christianity and politics

Christ and culture

Christians have always understood that their commitment to Christ includes a commitment to live moral lives, but they have not always agreed on the precise parameters of the morality required of Christians. Some early Christians believed it was necessary to obey certain aspects of the Jewish law, such as male circumcision and dietary restrictions, while others believed that Christ had set them free from such obligations. Some believed that abstaining from meat that had previously been offered to pagan gods was a vital part of their Christian witness, while others had no problem eating meat sacrificed to idols, since the pagan gods were not real. Some believed that it was important to observe certain days of the week or year as holy, and others believed that every day was a gift from God and thus equal to every other day. Of course, there are many issues on which all Christians would probably agree, in principle: commitment to both one's family and to fellow Christians, love for one's neighbor, forgiving those who have sinned against them. The Golden Rule summarizes for many the essence of Christian ethics, at least on a personal level: "Do unto others as you would have others do unto you" (Matt 7:12).

The question of whether Christian ethics can be transferred from the personal to the national level is debated by Christian ethicists today. In the past, the debate might never have occurred, because when the church and state were closely intertwined, as they were in many places throughout the history of Christianity, Christian rulers could have theoretically led their nations to follow such New Testament imperatives as loving their enemies, though few, if any, ever did so. In a world in which even official state churches hold little sway over modern governments, should the church expect the state to abide by Christian ethical principles? Reinhold Niebuhr, in his book *Moral Man and Immoral Society*, argues that nations can never be held to the same moral standards as individuals, in part because the use of coercive force, which all nations must wield to stay in power, by its very nature tends toward the principle that the end justifies the means, a notion that almost all Christian ethicists would reject if applied to individual Christians. While some Christians agree with Niebuhr's analysis, others assert that while no nation is Christian in the same sense as individuals are, Christian citizens within a nation can still insist that its policies approximate those that Christ demanded of individuals. Some of the ethical debates that exercise Christians today, such as war and peace or the issue of poverty, revolve around the issue of individual versus national ethical obligations.

H. Richard Niebuhr, brother of Reinhold, wrote an influential 1951 book entitled *Christ and Culture*, which examined the various ways in which Christians have historically related to society. The five paradigms he studied are all of interest to Christians today who struggle with the issue of how their faith and their own ethical commitments should be applied to Christian living in the world today, but three seem especially relevant in the modern world. In one option, which Niebuhr calls "Christ Against Culture," Christians see themselves as separate from the world, "in the world but not of it," so they do not even consider trying to change what they see as a hopelessly evil world. The Amish, an Anabaptist group that purposely limits its contacts with the rest of society and rejects most modern conveniences, are a good example of a modern group that follows this paradigm, as are many modern Christian religious who live cloistered lives in monasteries or convents. A second option, "The Christ of Culture," recognizes the importance of communicating the gospel to men and women of today, and it sees the Christian message as compatible with the dominant worldview. What some Christians might call unwarranted compromise with the world, "Christ of Culture" Christians call necessary accommodation of the gospel to the prevailing culture as a means of communicating the message effectively. A third option, "Christ the Transformer of Culture," acknowledges the inherent distance between Christianity and any culture, but it seeks to transform culture nevertheless, not so that it becomes Christian, but so that the highest ideals of Christianity are reflected in culture to as great an extent as possible. This approach to the question of the proper relationship between Christ and culture is probably the dominant one among Christians today, though many remain committed to the second, "Christ of Culture," option.

Christ and culture

The five approaches to the question of how the Church should relate to society, as identified by H. Richard Niebuhr, are:

1   Christ Against Culture: Christians are called to be "in the world but not of it," and thus separate themselves from the world as a witness.
2   The Christ of Culture: Christians should accommodate their practices as much as possible to the prevailing culture in order to communicate the gospel message to others from the perspective of one immersed in the culture.
3   Christ Above Culture: Christians live in God's good creation and must participate in it, yet without compromising the essential teachings and example of Christ; the goal is to find a synthesis of Christ with culture.
4   Christ and Culture in Paradox: All human acts and efforts are sinful, unless sanctified by God's grace, so culture itself, whether of a secular or a Christian nature, is opposed to God, and Christians must learn to accept themselves as redeemed sinners who are called to follow the voice of God in a sinful world.
5   Christ the Transformer of Culture: Christians must recognize that the world is corrupt, but through Christ they seek to transform it so that it approximates the highest ideals of Christianity, though it will never reach it.

Sexual mores

> If the God you believe in hates all the same people you do, then you know you've created God in your own image.

(Anne Lamott)

Almost all religions and cultures have rules and taboos that elucidate proper and improper expressions of sexuality in a culture, and Christianity is no exception. Early Christians adopted many of the Jewish customs regarding marriage and sexuality. For example, Paul rebukes a man in Corinth for cohabiting with his (presumably former) stepmother (1 Cor 5:1; cf. Lev 18:8). He also condemns various forms of "sexual immorality," such as engaging in sex with prostitutes. One way in which Christians differed from both the Jewish and Roman law was in their attitude towards divorce. Jewish law allowed men to divorce their wives, and Roman law also allowed women to divorce their husbands. However, Christians, pointing to Jesus' teaching, strongly discouraged divorce. Elders and deacons, according to 1 Tim 3:2 and 12, must be "husbands of one wife," which probably reflects a prohibition of divorce among church leaders, though some scholars believe it refers to polygamy instead. The question of divorce continues to face Christians today, especially in the West, where divorce, once a cultural taboo, has become widely accepted. Most churches have many members who are divorced, and churches generally do their best to minister to their needs, just as they do other members. However, churches differ over the question of whether divorced people are eligible to serve as deacons, pastors, or other ministers. Some allow divorced people to serve in any capacity, and others do not.

At some point in the first century or so of Christian history, the idea became current among many Christians that celibacy was the path to greater holiness and that remaining single was preferable to being married. In the second century and beyond, this belief was probably based more on the dualistic notion, derived from the surrounding Greek culture, that spirit was good and matter was evil, than on the earlier, first century idea that the Parousia was imminent, which seems to have been Paul's rationale for urging those who were single to remain single (1 Cor 7). Most later Christians rejected extreme dualism, though many returned to the Pauline idea that a life of celibacy was more consistent with a life of complete devotion to God. Symeon the New Theologian, a medieval Eastern Christian, saw the monastic life as ideally suited for the pursuit of the purest form of Christianity. The canon law enacted in the eleventh century that mandated clerical celibacy in the Western Church was formulated both because of the idea that complete commitment to God precluded the entangling commitment to a wife and because of the corruption inherent in the practice of appointing one's children to positions of power within the church. The Reformers explicitly rejected the idea of clerical celibacy, however, as a recent innovation. Today clerical celibacy is the rule for Catholic bishops and priests and for Orthodox bishops. Other Christian denominations do not have any restrictions against married clergy.

One of the most divisive sexual issues facing churches today is the question of the proper Christian approach to homosexuality. Homosexual activity has traditionally been considered a sin in the church, and many Christians point to selected passages from both the Old Testament and New Testament to support the traditional view (e.g. Lev 18:22; Rom 1:26–27). Other Christians believe that the modern understanding of human physiology and psychology, including evidence that supports a genetic component behind homosexuality, suggests that traditional Christian attitudes toward homosexuality need to be reconsidered. Many Christians make a distinction between homosexual tendencies and homosexual activity. Only a few Christian denominations currently allow practicing homosexuals to serve as clergy or to marry in the church, though the number is slowly increasing. The issue has caused heated debate in several individual Protestant denominations, and the worldwide Anglican communion has struggled to deal with the U.S. Episcopal Church's ordination of an openly gay bishop, as some autonomous Anglican bodies have advocated forcing the U.S. Church to rescind its practice of ordaining homosexuals or face expulsion from the Anglican family. Similarly divisive is the issue of whether Christians should support legalizing gay marriage (already legal in a few jurisdictions worldwide), oppose it, or stay out of the controversy entirely. The controversy over the proper roles that gays, lesbians, bisexuals, and transgender persons can play within the church has spawned at least one entirely new denomination, the Metropolitan Community Churches, which originated in 1968

Figure 22.1 Bishop Gene Robinson was the first openly gay bishop to be ordained in the Episcopal Church (USA). His ordination set off strong protests in many other Anglican bodies around the world.

as a church that openly welcomed GLBT persons into its fellowship. Strident voices exist on both sides of this issue, but many Christians have chosen to sit down with one another and try to achieve mutual understanding with those who have a different point of view. This issue is, at least in part, related to the larger issue of the relationship between the teaching of the Church and the discoveries of science, so future information that scientists discover either supporting or denying the link between genetics and homosexuality will undoubtedly be part of the ongoing discussion.

Life and death

> God's haiku on Iraq
> Some think I condone
> the bombing of my children.
> They must not know me.
> *(Progressive Theology)*

Issues dealing with life and death are some of the most important and difficult that Christians have to face. The main issues may be subdivided into two subsets of issues, those dealing with the beginning of life and those dealing with the end of life. Artificial birth control, artificial insemination, surrogate motherhood, abortion, cloning, and embryonic stem cell research all deal in one way or another with beginning of life issues. Some denominations, notably the Roman Catholic Church, are on record as officially opposing all these procedures or areas of investigation because, the official policy of the Church states, they kill a human being. Many ordinary Catholics apparently disagree, at least in part, since large numbers practice artificial birth control as a means of family planning. Many Evangelical and Pentecostal Churches would similarly disagree with many of the items listed above, with the exception of artificial birth control and perhaps artificial insemination and surrogacy. Again, however, a considerable gap often exists between the stated view of the denomination as a whole and the view of individual Christians who belong to a church affiliated with the denomination.

Proponents of artificial birth control say that opposition is based on the pre-scientific notion that conception occurs when the man "plants his seed" in the soil of the woman's womb, whereas modern biology shows that both the man and the woman contribute 50 percent of the genetic material that their child has. They also say that in a world with more than six billion humans on it, it is the Christian's responsibility not to contribute to overpopulation, which puts an undue burden on the poor, especially in the developing world. Opponents of birth control concede the point that women as well as men contribute genetic material to their offspring, but they counter that birth control takes out of God's hands the question of whether a child will be born from the act of sexual intercourse. They use a similar argument when opposing artificial insemination and surrogacy, except this time the point is that humans, through artificial means, are creating life that God may not have ordained.

Few issues are as controversial as abortion, and though advocates on both sides of the issue often claim that the path to the right decision on this matter is straightforward, many Christians do not believe that it is. First, proponents of abortion rights – that is, the right of a woman to terminate her pregnancy prematurely – must admit that, although it is not mentioned explicitly in the New Testament, early Christians apparently viewed abortion, along with infanticide, also common in the Roman Empire, as wrong. The *Didache* specifically says, "You shall not abort a child nor commit infanticide" (*Did.* 2.2), and other early Christian texts voice similar strictures. On the other hand, opponents of abortion rights must admit that most people in society, perhaps including most Christians, make a distinction between the use of a pill that will prevent a fertilized egg from being implanted in the uterus and ending the life of a six month old fetus. Does life begin at conception? Many Christians say yes, but others point out that many doctors define pregnancy as starting with implantation of the fertilized egg. Others would draw the line at the distinction between embryo and fetus (about eight weeks), or at the point of viability (currently about 24 weeks). Other Christians point out that although abortion is not ideal, in certain circumstances, such as rape, incest, or the immaturity or family situation of the mother, bringing a baby to full term might have dire consequences for the mother's wellbeing. Despite what some say, there is no single, "Christian" position on the topic. Recent attempts by abortion opponents to try to reach a political and/or theological compromise with abortion rights advocates prove that dialog on this issue is possible and perhaps even productive.

Opposition to embryonic stem cell research shares a similar theoretical basis with opposition to abortion. If life begins at conception, as many Christians argue, then a fertilized egg represents human life, even if it is in a Petrie dish. Other Christians argue that since the egg is never allowed to develop beyond the stage where it has eight cells, and since it had no chance of implantation in a uterus, it cannot be classified as human life. Furthermore, proponents of the research say, the potential benefits of stem-cell research are so great that the moral objections of a minority should not be allowed to decide the issue. Some scientists are currently working on ways to derive similar results from stem cells that were not originally derived from an eight-celled embryo, and a breakthrough in this area might turn some Christian opponents of the research into advocates.

Two types of human cloning are contemplated by researchers: reproductive cloning and therapeutic cloning. Almost all Christians agree at this point that reproductive cloning is ethically problematic, but opinion is divided over therapeutic cloning. Therapeutic cloning is an attempt to grow certain types of tissue, for example, a liver or pancreas, from a single cell. In addition to concerns involving the use of embryonic stem cells in therapeutic cloning, some Christians are concerned that developing the techniques necessary to produce a particular organ from a single cell will greatly increase the danger that similar techniques could be used to create an entire cloned human, and based on cloning successes with several mammal species over the past decade, they say, such concern is warranted. Christian proponents of therapeutic cloning reply that the practice represents an important step forward in medical research and treatment, one that is preferable to the practice whereby parents purposely conceive a child so that the new baby's tissues, a kidney, for example, can be used to help a gravely ill sibling (without, of course, killing the baby). Furthermore, they say, the "slippery slope" argument is invalid, and what is needed is strict prohibitions against using cloning techniques to produce a living human. Based on the rapidity with which cloning technology has advanced over the past decade or two, and despite worldwide restrictions on reproductive cloning, it seems likely that soon Christians will have the face the issue of how to deal with babies that were produced by the cloning process.

On end of life issues, such as euthanasia and capital punishment, Christians similarly have differences of opinion, and the opinions of individual Christians do not always match the official position of their denominations. Euthanasia, or mercy killing, as it is sometimes called, is decried by most Christians, and probably by all Christian denominations that have taken an explicit stand on the issue, but the question of when life ends is not an easy one. Many people today spend their last days in a hospital hooked up to machines that supply medicine and food, relieve pain, stabilize the heartbeat, filter the blood, and force air in and out of the lungs. Does turning off one or more of these machines constitute euthanasia, or does doing so simply let nature take its course? Does increasing medication to relieve pain, when doing so might result in a death that could otherwise have been postponed, constitute euthanasia, or is it simply compassionate pain management? These are issues that families, medical staff, and spiritual advisors often have to face, and most clergy who regularly work with families going through these sorts of difficult decisions have come to the conclusion that under such circumstances, no decision should be subject to second-guessing from outsiders who have no involvement with the family. The most difficult situations are those in which family members themselves disagree on the proper course of treatment, and it is the role of spiritual advisors, clergy, or chaplains in such a predicament not to take sides but rather to help the family work through the issues in a way that is faithful to their Christian beliefs and also shows concern for their sick family member.

Many denominations, including the Roman Catholic Church, Anglicans, Eastern Orthodox, Lutherans, Methodists, and others oppose capital punishment under any circumstances, citing Jesus' command to love one's enemies as a reason for their opposition. Other denominations, including many that fall under the Evangelical or Pentecostal banners, support the judicious use of capital punishment for perpetrators of certain serious crimes, pointing to the Old Testament *lex talionis*, calling for "an eye for an eye, and a tooth for a tooth." This issue is one that affects the U.S. Church more than any other, since few countries in the world that are either predominantly Christian or that are industrially developed employ the death penalty. Capital punishment is another example of an ethical issue in which the official positions of the Church do not always comport with the opinions of believers in the pews. Christian critics of capital punishment point to many of the same arguments that secular opponents use – the lack of a deterrent effect, the racially biased way in which it is implemented, the futility of using violence to combat violence – but they also add arguments from a specifically Christian perspective. For example, they argue that Jesus' command to love one's enemies is not consistent with executing someone. Some, particularly in the Evangelical community, argue that executing someone who has not yet accepted Jesus as Savior will condemn that person to hell. Still others argue that since it is inconceivable that Jesus himself would have taken part in the execution of another person, Christians should not do so, either. For their part, supporters of the death penalty say that Jesus' command to love one's enemies does not preclude the possibility of capital punishment, and at any rate the command was meant for the individual, not the state. Support for capital punishment among citizens in the U.S., as well as among Christians specifically, is greater than 50 percent, though the percentage has been slipping somewhat in recent years. Still, it is clear that for American Christians, in any case, the proper Christian position on the death penalty is debatable.

The Roman Catholic Church, Orthodox Churches, the Anglican Church, and most Protestant Churches have either officially or unofficially adopted the Just War theory as their approach to evaluating the validity of a nation going to war. Using the Augustinian model, they look at such issues as the justice of the cause, the imminence of the threat, and the likelihood of success. They may disagree with other Christians on the conclusions drawn from a Just War analysis of a particular situation, but they go through many of the same steps to make their determination as their opponents do. The Historic Peace Churches – including the Mennonites and other Anabaptists, the Moravian Brethren, and the Quakers – have a different attitude toward war. They are pacifists, opposing any war, no matter the circumstances. Some in the Just War camp criticize the pacifism of the Peace Churches as idealistic, unsuited to the realities of the modern world, where the use of lethal force in war is sometimes necessary. On the other hand, many denominations in the Just War camp have slid toward the pacifist stance in recent decades, as many Christians in those traditions point out that *every* war is a just war in the mind of the country going to war. For this reason, many Christians from a variety of denominations that support both the Just War tradition and Pacifism have proposed a third solution, Peacemaking. Unlike Pacifism, which critics charge is entirely passive, the Peacemaking approach advocates extensive efforts to avert wars that appear ready to start by working in troubled areas to teach people how to resolve conflicts peacefully. Some peacemakers also support sending unarmed Christian civilians into potential war zones to discourage nations from dropping bombs on the citizens, knowing that they would be killing Christian peacemakers as well. Efforts in the direction of Peacemaking are still relatively recent, and critics sometimes dismiss the approach as naïve. Whether it develops into a third major tradition, alongside Just War and Pacifist approaches, remains to be seen.

Wealth and poverty

Most of Jesus' followers during his public ministry were from the peasant class, and most early Christians were poor as well. Paul speaks of his concern for the poor in several of his letters, and he encourages his readers to contribute financially to the relief fund he is collecting for the poor in Jerusalem. Throughout most of Christian history, in fact, the poor have made up the bulk of the Christian Church. Those who were not poor were always encouraged by the Church to contribute to the needs of the poor as part of their Christian duty. At some point in the twentieth century a different attitude towards the issue of wealth and poverty arose in some quarters of the Church. Some preachers, including some well-known televangelists, began to teach that wealth and good health were blessings from God and that those who were faithful to God would be blessed both physically and financially. The implication of this prosperity, or "health and wealth," gospel was that those who were poor, both individuals and countries, were poor because they had been unfaithful to God. The health and wealth message was widely condemned by most denominations, but it tapped into deep-seated resentment that many Christians felt about spending their "hard-earned" money, either through taxes or through offerings to the church, on the needs of poor people. This attitude was found among wealthy and middle class Christians from a variety of different denominations, but it was especially identified – fairly or unfairly – with Evangelicals, Pentecostals, and other theologically conservative Protestants.

In 1977 Ronald J. Sider, an Evangelical Christian and the founder of Evangelicals for Social Action, published a book that became very influential, especially among other Evangelicals: *Rich Christians in an Age of Hunger*. Sider examined both the biblical text and statistics regarding poverty to present his case that rich Christians (including especially the middle class) should take action to serve the poor in a variety of ways, including giving directly to Christian relief organizations, as a matter of sacred duty. The Roman Catholic Church, which had sometimes been criticized in the past for seeming to side with the rich and powerful (e.g. in colonial Latin America), issued a number of papal encyclicals and other documents calling on Christians around the world to support the poor, beginning with Pope Leo XIII's 1891 encyclical *Rerum Novarum* (On Capital and Labor), and continuing with Pope John XXIII's *Pacem in Terris* (Peace on Earth, 1963), Pope Paul VI's *Populorum Progressio* (On the Development of Peoples, 1967), and Pope John Paul II's *Sollicitudo Rei Socialis* (The Social Concern of the Church, 1988). Roman Catholic bishops from Latin America also pushed the Church in the direction of paying more attention to ministry to the poor, particularly in their conferences at Medellín (1968) and Puebla (1979). Some Catholics have criticized portions of these documents for not going far enough in their condemnation of oppressive structures that adversely affect the poor (e.g. Leo XIII was criticized for condemning the potential evils of socialism without addressing the potential evils of capitalism), but taken as a whole, they do push Catholic Christians, and all Christians who read and agree with them, toward a concern for the poor that is in accord with consistently enunciated historic Christian values.

Christianity and politics

The issues revolving around the relationship between church and state have already been discussed, so this section will concentrate on the church's attitude toward specific political systems (monarchies vs. republics) and politico-economic theories (communism vs. capitalism).

Ever since the days of Constantine, the church had supported the Christian state and the Christian emperor, king, or ruler. When the barbarians destroyed the Western Roman Empire, Germanic Christian kings replaced Roman emperors, but the Church's support for Christian rulers continued. When Constantinople fell to the Turks, many in the Eastern Church had no new Christian emperor to support, although the Russian Orthodox Church transferred its loyalty to the czar. In the West, the idea of the "divine right of kings" developed, an idea that claimed that those who were on the throne were put there by God and were specially chosen, as were their families. The Roman Catholic Church supported the Christian kings, as did the leading Protestant Churches at first. However, the French Revolution and the rise to power of Napoleon divided the Protestant churches. On the one hand, many were aghast at the French Republic's attempt to reduce the influence of Christianity in society, not mention the excesses of the Reign of Terror. On the other hand, Napoleon presented himself at first as one who could bring order to the chaos and who was more favorably disposed to the church. Napoleon's expansionistic moves, however, cost him the support of both the Catholic Church (Napoleon captured the Papal States) and the Protestant churches outside France, in the countries that Napoleon's troops invaded. The Year of Revolution, 1848, led to the adoption of representative forms of government in many European nations, and the Protestant churches for the most part accepted them, even though the new republics no longer recognized any particular state church, or, if they did, the state church had little political influence. The Roman Catholic Church, on the other hand, remained adamantly opposed to the very idea of representative government, which was contrary to the organization of the Church and, the popes argued, contrary to the desire of God. Particularly galling to the Church was the capture of the Rome by King Victor Emmanuel II in 1870. Pope Pius IX refused to acknowledge the Church's loss of sovereignty over Rome, as did his successors, until in 1929 Pope Pius XI finally signed the Lateran Treaty that restored the pope's temporal powers by creating the Vatican City. The overthrow of the ruling families of Europe was finally more or less completed at the end of World War I, when the Habsburgs of Austria and the Hohenzollerns of Germany were removed from power. Those monarchs that remained in Europe reigned over constitutional monarchies in which their powers were greatly restricted.

The long association of the Roman Catholic Church with European monarchs helps explain, in part, their opposition to the politico-economic systems called socialism and communism. In the mid-nineteenth century, Karl Marx advocated a new form of government in which the means of production (capital) would be taken from the owners of the factories (capitalists) and given to the workers (the proletariat). The middle classes (the bourgeoisie), which tended to support the upper classes and the capitalists against the proletariat, would lose their influence as well. All these changes would require revolution, Marx said, but eventually a classless society would result. Marx, an avowed atheist, also advocated the removal of all religious institutions from positions of authority. Both the call for revolution, with its ensuing disorder, and the attack on Christianity, which was after all the dominant religious tradition in Europe, alarmed

Catholics, Orthodox, and Protestants alike. The Russian Revolution of 1917, which again destroyed a Christian empire affiliated with the Orthodox Church, was alarming to the Catholic Church and to most Protestants as well. However, some Protestants argued that Marx's critiques of the capitalist system were accurate, and even his attacks on Christianity had their merits, because the church had all too often sided with the rich against the poor. Some Protestants, then, became supporters of Christian socialism, which rejected both atheism and, in most cases, the need for revolution, but adopted many of Marx's concerns about capitalism. The Roman Catholic Church, still wary of the new republics in Europe, was strongly opposed to all aspects of communism. Pope Leo XIII, in his 1891 encyclical *Rerum Novarum* (On Capital and Labor), harshly criticized communist/socialist proposals as harmful to the poor, but did not direct a similarly harsh critique against capitalists who, their critics claimed, were making their fortunes on the backs of the poor. As World War II approached, Pope Pius XI was an early supporter of fascism in Italy, chiefly because of Mussolini's opposition to communism. He eventually turned against both Mussolini and Hitler, but he continued to support Franco's fascist regime in Spain, for the same reason that he had originally supported Mussolini: Franco's opposition to communism.

Pope John Paul II was a fierce opponent of communism, and many historians credit his papacy with being one of the important factors in the downfall of communism in Europe. Although he was deeply concerned for the poor, his innate anti-communist

Figure 22.2 Oscar Romero, the Roman Catholic archbishop of El Salvador, paid for his outspoken support of the poor with his life. He was assassinated in 1980 while celebrating mass.

tendencies led him to crack down hard on liberation theologians within his own church who used certain aspects of Marxist theory in their theological and historical analyses. Ironically, liberation theology received greater acceptance in many Protestant churches, which were not as ideologically opposed to all aspects of communism as many popes were. John Paul was also a harsh critic of unbridled capitalism as well as communism, however, so his attitude toward both communism and capitalism may be described as critical. In conservative Protestant churches, especially associated with the Evangelical and Pentecostal/Neocharismatic branches of the church, many church leaders spoke out strongly against "godless communism." They promoted capitalism, free trade, and democracy, believing them to be the key components of the politico-economic system that was ordained by God to bring people political freedom and personal wellbeing, and to allow the gospel to spread further throughout the world. Christian critics of this approach, Catholic and Protestant alike, pointed out that "godless capitalism" was just as big a problem as "godless communism," and in fact it was capitalist democracies in the industrialized West that were responsible for much of the suffering around the world. The debate over the relative merits of socialism and capitalism continues unabated today, as does the issue of whether democracy can or should be imposed on countries that now have other forms of government, such as dictatorships.

Key points you need to know

- Reinhold Niebuhr argued that nations cannot be held to the same moral standards as individual Christians, even if the nation is predominantly Christian. Though Niebuhr won some support, many Christian scholars and ethicists disagreed with his analysis.

- While most Christian groups believe that engaging culture is a duty demanded by their faith, a few advocate remaining outside the dominant culture. Some who engage culture generally see the Christian message as compatible with the dominant worldview, while others believe that the two are radically different but that it is their obligation to work to transform their culture.

- Christians disagree over the proper stance regarding such issues as divorce, clerical celibacy, and homosexuality. Debates over homosexuality in particular have divided, or are threatening to divide, some denominations.

- Although almost all Christians proclaim their belief in the sanctity of life, significant differences of opinion concerning issues such as artificial birth control, abortion, embryonic stem cell research, therapeutic cloning, capital punishment, and euthanasia exist. Most Christians are wary of, or reject outright, the idea of reproductive cloning of human beings.

- Although the Just War theory is widely accepted among most Christian groups, an increasing number of contemporary Christians are questioning either the validity or the practicality of that approach to war, advocating instead the alternative of Peacemaking. The Historic Peace Churches advocate a stance of pacifism.

- Christianity has traditionally advocated care for the poor in society, but during some historical periods the Church has been derelict in its duties to the poor. Although some Christians have understood the gospel message as promising prosperity to the faithful, most reject that analysis.
- Christians support many different political parties – left, right, and center – as their views of the needs of the world, the demands of the gospel, and the efficacy of the politicians varies.

Discussion questions

1. What are the relative merits and weaknesses of the "Christ Against Culture," "Christ Of Culture," and "Christ the Transformer of Culture" positions?
2. Why do debates among Christians over sexual mores often seem to drown out other issues?
3. How do opinions regarding beginning of life issues relate to opinions regarding end of life issues?
4. Has the Church been committed to care for the poor throughout its history, or was such concern merely lip service? How committed is the Church today to care for the poor?
5. Is socialism, capitalism, or some other option more consistent with the teaching and example of Jesus Christ?

Further reading

The Didache.

Kairos Theologians 1986. *The Kairos Document: Challenge to the Church.* 2nd edn. Braamfontein, South Africa: Skotaville.

King, Martin Luther, Jr. 1963. *Strength to Love.* Philadelphia, PA: Fortress.

Marx, Karl and Friedrich Engels 1990. *Capital* and *Manifesto of the Communist Party.* 2nd edn. Chicago, IL: Encyclopaedia Britannica.

Niebuhr, H. Richard 1951. *Christ and Culture.* New York: Harper & Row.

Niebuhr, Reinhold 1932. *Moral Man and Immoral Society.* New York: Scribner.

Papal Encyclicals Online. http://www.papalencyclicals.net.

Rauschenbusch, Walter 1997. *A Theology for the Social Gospel.* Louisville, KY: Westminster John Knox.

Sider, Ronald J. 1977. *Rich Christians in an Age of Hunger.* Downer's Grove, IL: Inter-Varsity Press.

Villa-Vicencio, Charles, ed. 1987. *Theology and Violence: The South African Debate.* Johannesburg: Skotaville.

23 Christianity and other religions

There will be no peace in the world until there is peace among religions.

(Hans Küng)

In this chapter

Christianity has a checkered past with regard to its relationship with other religions. In particular, its relations with Judaism and Islam throughout its history have often been characterized by conflict or animosity, though matters have improved in recent decades. Christians have been engaging proponents of some eastern religions in dialog for many years, and they are just starting to engage adherents of other eastern religions. Christianity shares a concern for spirituality with other world religions, but Christian attitudes toward these religions vary from concern for people on the wrong path to respect for fellow travelers in the quest for the divine. A new challenge to Christianity in many parts of the world is the growth in the number of atheists, agnostics, and nonreligious people, especially in regions where Christianity was once overwhelmingly dominant.

Main topics covered

- Christianity and spirituality
- Christian approaches to other religions
- Christianity and Judaism
- Christianity and Islam
- Christianity and the religions of South and East Asia
- Christianity and Secularism

Christianity and spirituality

In the 1944 novel *The Razor's Edge*, Somerset Maugham tells the story of Larry Darrell, a former fighter pilot in World War I who returns home from the war to find that his whole outlook on life has changed, and he spends the next several years seeking the meaning of life, an odyssey that eventually leads him to spend five years in India, before finally returning home, giving away all his worldly goods, and continuing his pursuit of wisdom and the spirit. Jack Kerouac wrote a somewhat autobiographical, somewhat fictionalized account of a series of trips he made with his friends to find adventure and something of value in life, a 1955 book called *On the Road*. Robert Pirsig's 1974 autobiographical book *Zen and the Art of Motorcycle Maintenance* tells the story of a road trip across America that the author took with his young son; the subtitle of the book is *An Inquiry into Values*. All three of these books use the metaphor of a journey, real or fictional, to describe the process of discovery that the characters undertake on their various roads to wisdom. Spirituality may similarly be described as the path one takes from the mundane world of ordinary human experience to the transcendent world of the divine.

The post-World War II era has seen a tremendous surge in the number of people in the industrialized West, in particular, who claim to be interested in spirituality, but not religion. In some cases, this stance corresponds with an interest in gleaning the wisdom of eastern religions, such as Buddhism and Hinduism, which are viewed by many as more spiritual than Christianity. The Beatles famously traveled to India in 1968 to study Transcendental Meditation with the Maharishi Mahesh Yogi. The Dalai Lama, who fled Tibet in 1959, is a popular speaker and proponent of Tibetan Buddhism, and he has achieved an almost rock-star-like fame. Sufism, a mystical branch of Islam, and mystical Jewish traditions of Kabbalah have also attracted the attention of many in the West in recent years. What many people do not seem to realize is that Christianity itself has an ancient tradition of spirituality that dates back almost 2,000 years.

The words *spirituality* and *mysticism* are often used more or less interchangeably, and there is indeed a great deal of overlap in their use. Both terms express direct encounters between the human and the divine. The difference between the two terms is one of degree rather than content. The mystical experience is more intense, more psychically overwhelming than the spiritual experience, though of course no sharp differentiation can be established between a *spiritual experience* and a *mystical experience*. The word *spiritual* is a broader term that implies divine-human communion of either a passing or an intense nature. *Mystical*, in contrast, is always intense, sometimes even *ecstatic* in the sense of being out of the body, at least apparently. Mystical encounters often involve visions, auditory revelations, or moments of immense spiritual clarity. Christians throughout history, as well as Christians living today, have reported experiences both spiritual and mystical.

Some people assert that the visions attributed to John, the author of the book of Revelation, are a New Testament example of a mystical experience. Others point to Paul's vision of the third heaven, recounted in 2 Cor 12:1–4, as a mystical journey. By at least the third century, Christians in Egypt, Syria, and Palestine were leaving their homes and all they had and journeying into the desert to find God. Many went and quickly returned, but some stayed for months, years, or decades. The words and experiences of those who stayed were recorded in various collections often called the *Sayings of the Desert Fathers*, but since the voices of women were also preserved, the name Sayings of the Desert Saints is preferable. The Desert Saints experienced the hardships of life, and their reactions were often what one would expect: anger, fatigue, pride, even despair. What make their saying and stories noteworthy, however, is that they often arrived at insights or had experiences that they, and many others since, believed came from God. One did not go to the desert because he or she already had the answers to life. One went to the desert to find the answers to life.

In the Middle Ages, many Christians had ongoing communion with God, sometimes punctuated by brief periods of intense mystical experience, that were recorded by themselves or others. Augustine wrote a spiritual autobiography called *The Confessions*. Stories about Francis of Assisi began to be collected even before his death in a small volume called *The Little Flowers of St. Francis*. Other books that provide records of Christian spirituality from this period include the diaries of Hildegard of Bingen, *The Imitation of Christ* and *The Imitation of Mary* by Thomas à Kempis, the letters of Catherine of Siena, the *Hymns of Divine Love* by Symeon the New Theologian, and the *Philokalia*, an Eastern collection of spiritual texts. In the modern period, works by Christian mystics include *The Dark Night of the Soul* by John of the Cross, *The Life of*

The Desert Saints

From at least the third century, some Christians abandoned civilization to pursue a life of quiet and contemplation, in which they could seek and hear God. Here are some examples of their wisdom and humility.

"What am I to do, Abba, since passions and demons beset me?" a young monk asked the holy Sisoes. "Do not say that you are bothered by demons, child," answered the elder, "because the greater part of us are beset by our own evil desires."

A brother who had sinned was turned out of the church by the priest; Abba Bessarion got up and went with him, saying, "I, too, am a sinner."

"There are three things especially pleasing to God," said Abba Joseph the Thebite. "Illnesses suffered with patience, works done without ostentation and for His love only, and submission to a spiritual elder with perfect self-denial. This last thing will gain the greatest crown."

Once some elders went to visit Abba Antonios. Along with them was Abba Joseph. The Great Father, to test them, chose a certain written maxim and asked each of them, one by one, to tell its meaning. So each one began to explain it according to his understanding. "You did not find its meaning," he answered each of them. Then came Abba Joseph's turn. "What do you have to say about this, Joseph?" Antonios the Great asked him. "I do not know of such things," he replied. "Abba Joseph gave the correct answer," the holy one then said, marveling at Abba Joseph's humility.

Teresa of Jesus by Teresa of Ávila, *The Practice of the Presence of God* by Brother Lawrence, *Experiencing the Depths of Jesus Christ* by Madame Guyon, *The Story of a Soul* by Thérèse de Lisieux, *The Spiritual Life* by Evelyn Underhill, *The Seven Storey Mountain* by Thomas Merton, and *Celebration of Discipline* by Richard Foster.

Although the interplay between Christianity and other religions will be explored in the following section, it may be noted here that some of the most fruitful interactions have occurred between mystics of different religious traditions, including Christianity. Christian, Muslim, Jewish, and Buddhist mystics (among others) often express their encounters with the divine in similar ways. The speak of a sense of unity that they feel with all of reality, an all-pervasive love for all humankind, and a profound sense of both joy and awe. Many books on Christian spirituality, both classics from the past and entirely new publications, have been published in the past four decades, and many who left the church in search of spiritual meaning and experience have returned to find it in the faith of their fathers and mothers.

Christian approaches to other religions

> God is love.
> (1 John 4:8)

In the conclusion to his book *When Religion Becomes Evil*, Charles Kimball defines three ways in which Christians can view other religions in regard to the questions of salvation and truth. The first option is *exclusivism*, an approach that stresses the uniqueness of God's revelation in Jesus Christ and says that salvation can only be found in the Church. A slightly softer form of exclusivism maintains that while Christianity is the only way to salvation, other religions might have some truth in them, and it is possible that God will choose to save some who have not become Christians, but if so, God will save them through the blood of Christ. A second option for Christians is *inclusivism*, which believes that God does indeed reveal truths to adherents of other religions and offers them salvation as well through their own religions, but that Jesus Christ is the "full, definitive revelation of God." The third option that Kimball mentions is *pluralism*, which asserts that Christianity is neither the only way to salvation, nor is it the fulfillment of other religious traditions, but it is a path to God whose way was first shown by Jesus Christ. The Christian pluralist defines Christianity not by its borders – that which separates it from other traditions – but by its roots in the historic testimony of those Christians who have gone before. Christians who have extensive contact with people in other religious traditions may hold any one of these three positions, or they many place themselves somewhere on the continuum between two of these options, or they may simply admit a level of agnosticism regarding the question.

While exclusivism has been the stance that the Church has most often taken officially with regard to other religions, there have been many fruitful, respectful interchanges between Christians and Jews dating to the first century, between Christians and Muslims dating to the seventh century, and between Christians and followers of other religious traditions since first contact was established between Christianity and the various faiths. In *Nostra Aetate* (Declaration on the Relation of the Church to Non-Christian Religions), the Second Vatican Council decreed that other major world religions give evidence of access to truth, which comes only from God. Therefore, the declaration says,

> The Catholic Church rejects nothing that is true and holy in these religions. She regards with sincere reverence those ways of conduct and of life, those precepts and teachings which, though differing in many aspects from the ones she holds and sets forth, nonetheless often reflect a ray of that Truth which enlightens all men ... The Church, therefore, exhorts her sons, that through dialogue and collaboration with the followers of other religions, carried out with prudence and love and in witness to the Christian faith and life, they recognize, preserve and promote the good things, spiritual and moral, as well as the socio-cultural values found among these men.

This declaration was a monumental step forward in the communication between the Roman Catholic Church and other religions, for although it still acknowledged its belief that God's truth was most fully revealed in Jesus Christ, it at the same time admitted that truth existed in other religious traditions (thus adopting an inclusivist view, as discussed above), and it called for dialog between Christians and people of other faiths. Many Protestant denominations, though by no means all, have also seen value in holding discussions, drafting documents, and even worshiping with people of other faiths. The following sections will briefly survey some of the important historical contacts between Christianity and other religions, and they will also comment on current interactions.

Christianity and Judaism

The story of Christianity's encounter with Judaism is an account that is both intimate and tragic, inspiring and horrifying. Christianity began as a reform movement within Judaism. Jesus was a Jew, as were all of his earliest followers. The greatest spokesperson for Christianity in the first century, Paul of Tarsus, was a Jew. The scriptures that the earliest Christians used were the scriptures of the Jews, and even after the New Testament was written, about 80 percent of the Christian Bible is still the Jewish scriptures – and most of the writers of the New Testament itself were Jews. It is true that some of the Jewish leaders in Jerusalem played a role in the arrest of Jesus, according to the gospel accounts. It is also true that Jews in the early days of the church sometimes persecuted Christians, as Paul himself admits to having done. It is furthermore true that toward the end of the first century Jews expelled the few remaining Christians from their synagogues, though most, perhaps all, Christian Jews had already left to worship on their own terms. The Christian acclamation of Jesus as messiah, the developing theology of Christianity, the Roman-Jewish wars, the growing number of Gentiles in the church, and the recognition by the Roman government that Christianity was a different religion from Judaism, all

> He hath disgraced me, and
> hindered me half a million; laughed at my losses,
> mocked at my gains, scorned my nation, thwarted my
> bargains, cooled my friends, heated mine
> enemies; and what's his reason? I am a Jew. Hath
> not a Jew eyes? hath not a Jew hands, organs,
> dimensions, senses, affections, passions? fed with
> the same food, hurt with the same weapons, subject
> to the same diseases, healed by the same means,
> warmed and cooled by the same winter and summer, as
> a Christian is? If you prick us, do we not bleed?
> if you tickle us, do we not laugh? if you poison
> us, do we not die? and if you wrong us, shall we not
> revenge? If we are like you in the rest, we will
> resemble you in that. If a Jew wrong a Christian,
> what is his humility? Revenge. If a Christian
> wrong a Jew, what should his sufferance be by
> Christian example? Why, revenge. The villany you
> teach me, I will execute, and it shall go hard but I
> will better the instruction.
>
> (Shylock, in William Shakespeare, *The Merchant of Venice* Act 3, Scene 1)

led to the permanent split between Judaism and Christianity. Despite all these factors, relations between Jews and Christians remained relatively cordial throughout the first three Christian centuries. When Marcion urged his followers to discard the Old Testament in its entirety and purge the Gospel of Luke of its references to the Jewish scriptures, he did so primarily because he had a problem with the God of the Hebrew Bible, not its people.

The situation began to change when Constantine became emperor. He made Christianity not only a legal religion, but also the favored religion, which he himself adopted. Constantine prohibited Jews from trying to convert Christians to their religion, and he placed other restrictions on them as well, just as he did to other religions besides Christianity. His son Constantius made it illegal for Jews to own a Christian slave, and he prohibited Jewish men from marrying Christian women. Theodosius I, who made Christianity the official religion of the empire, restricted Jews from holding public office, and he ordered any new synagogue that the Jews might build to be confiscated and handed over to the church. The emperor Justinian would not allow Jews to testify in court against an orthodox Christian, although they could testify against an unorthodox Christian (i.e. one who didn't accept the stance of the Council of Chalcedon). He also prohibited Jews from reading the Mishna in the synagogues. Not all imperial legislation concerning the Jews was a burden. For example, the emperor Arcadius promulgated a law

Figure 23.1 The Hakhurba (or Hurba) Synagogue in Jerusalem's Jewish Quarter was one of the most important synagogues in the city for centuries.

giving Jewish rabbis the same privileges under the law as Christian clergy. Theodosius II allowed Jews to observe their traditional holiday seasons without interference. Nevertheless the general trend in both the Roman and Byzantine law codes, and in the law codes of the new Germanic kingdoms in the West as well, was more restrictions for the Jews, not fewer.

If the legal restrictions placed on the Jews by Christian emperors and kings was onerous, the words of bishops and theologians were often worse, for they stirred up animosity between the Christian majority and the Jewish minority in many places. John Chrysostom, the great pulpiteer of Constantinople, preached a series of eight sermons entitled *Against the Jews*, whose harsh rhetoric stirred up Christians against their Jewish neighbors. There is some modern debate over whether Chrysostom's words were directed against Jews per se or against Judaizers within the Christian family who were urging other Christians to adopt many of the Jewish laws and customs. A careful reading of his sermons suggests that some of his words may have been directed against Christian Judaizers, but others were undoubtedly directed against Jews. The words of Chrysostom and other bishops, East and West, demonized the Jews and resulted in mistrust, hatred, and even violence toward them. Bernard of Clairvaux, following the lead of Augustine several centuries earlier, passionately urged Christians not to kill the Jews, as had recently happened in certain parts of Europe, but outbreaks of violence against Jews continued throughout the Middle Ages. Some Christians accused Jews of the crime of deicide ("murder of God"), calling them Christ-killers. At the same time, however, Jewish and Christian scholars sometimes enjoyed periods of intellectual cooperation, such as during the Jewish Renaissance that preceded, and some say sparked, the Florentine Renaissance of the fourteenth century. Hugh of St. Victor, a Christian scholar, was familiar with and made use of the work of the famous Jewish scholars known today as Rashi and Rashbam, and he and his associates may well have had personal interaction with the men as well as with their writings.

In the modern period, relationships between Jews and Christians were sometimes better, but often even worse than in the medieval period. In 1492 monarchs Ferdinand and Isabella expelled all the Jews from Spain. Martin Luther is known to have made several intemperate remarks concerning the Jews. Shakespeare, hardly a theologian but nevertheless a person who reflected the society around him, wrote a play, *The Merchant of Venice*, which portrays the Jewish merchant, Shylock, in a stereotypically negative way. In Eastern Europe, pogroms against the Jews were common. In the two decades surrounding the turn of the twentieth century, a famous anti-Semitic incident in France, which came to be called the Dreyfus Affair, resulted in the sentencing of an innocent Jew, Alfred Dreyfus, for the crime of treason, before eventually being recalled from imprisonment on Devil's Island and exonerated. Without question, however, the most devastating single event in the entire history of Jewish-Christian interaction was the Holocaust, carried out by Hitler and his Nazi regime between 1933 and 1945, with the knowledge and cooperation of many Christians. Six million Jews were brutally and mercilessly slaughtered in a land that often viewed itself as the epitome of Christian learning and culture.

Relations between Christians and Jews have improved greatly on the whole since the end of World War II, and various Christian groups have offered apologies to Jews for their past behavior. Nevertheless, the ancient rift between Jews and Christians that began in the first century continues to manifest itself today, anti-Semitic incidents still occur, and anti-Semitic rhetoric is still spouted by Christians. On a more positive note, interfaith dialogs between Jews and Christians are going on constantly around the world, and interfaith organizations have sprung up in many cities and countries. *Nostra Aetate*, the same Vatican II document quoted above regarding the attitude of the Roman Catholic Church toward other religions in general, has this to say concerning the proper Christian attitude toward the Jews: "In her rejection of every persecution against any man, the Church, mindful of the patrimony she shares with the Jews and moved not by political reasons but by the Gospel's spiritual love, decries hatred, persecutions, displays of anti-Semitism, directed against Jews at any time and by anyone."

An interesting relationship has developed between many Evangelical Christians and a particular set of Jews, namely, those living in the State of Israel, particularly those associated with the Israeli government. Although the Evangelical position regarding people of others faiths, including Jews, is generally exclusivist, many prominent Evangelicals, especially in the U.S., have held numerous meetings with Israeli Jewish leaders, often in conjunction with conferences on Bible prophecy. These Evangelical supporters of Israel, who hold a dispensationalist view of eschatology, believe that the modern state of Israel is the fulfillment of biblical prophecy. Furthermore, they believe the Jerusalem temple will soon be rebuilt, and the Rapture will jump-start the end times. The apparent anomaly of exclusivist Christians dealing so intimately with Jews without attempting to convert them to Christianity is explained by the fact that these Christian leaders believe that the Rapture is right around the corner, and Jews will convert in huge numbers as a result of their newfound understanding of scriptural prophecy concerning Jesus after the Rapture occurs. Many non-dispensationalist Christians, and some other Evangelicals and Jews as well, view the friendship that the Evangelical Christians are showing to the Israeli Jews as disingenuous, since it masks a hidden desire to see all Jews converted to Christianity, one way or another. Evangelical Christians, for their part, respond that their attitude toward Israeli Jews is the same as their attitude toward other Jews, and indeed toward people of any other faith. The fact that they work so closely with the Israelis, they say, is simply a reflection of their understanding of biblical prophecy.

Christianity and Islam

The relationship between Christianity and Islam is nearly as old and nearly as violent as that between Christianity and Judaism. Some would argue that it is even more violent. Islam arose in the Arabian peninsula in the seventh century, and it quickly spread through formerly Christian lands at the hands of conquering Arab tribes. Muslims entered Europe in Spain, and they advanced as far as the Pyrenees before being stopped by Charles Martel, ruler of the Franks. The on-again, off-again wars in the Iberian peninsula paled in comparison to the massive undertakings in the East known as the Crusades, starting in 1096. Armies of Christians and Muslims fought each other many times, and countless people were slaughtered. Eventually the Muslims prevailed in the East, though they were driven from Spain and Portugal in the West at about the same time as the Turks captured the city of Constantinople. Life for Christians under Muslim rule was generally tolerable. Although Christians typically did not have the same rights as Muslims, they were respected as one of the three "peoples of the book." Christians served in a number of key positions throughout Muslim governments, a circumstance that was not reciprocated in the West, although admittedly there were few Muslims there. Following the fall of Constantinople, warfare between Christians and Muslims continued in Eastern Europe, particularly in the Balkan peninsula, for centuries, and Muslim troops advanced as far as the gates of Vienna at one point. The Ottoman Empire, the last true Muslim empire, fell to the Allied Powers in World War I, and its territory was divided among the victors of the war, though the intention was that the newly created states – Iraq, Syria, Jordan, Lebanon – would soon become independent. Creation of the state of Israel in 1948 set off a series of wars between Israel and its neighbors, and the Muslim inhabitants of Palestine, along with many of their Muslim neighbors in surrounding countries, saw the Western support of Israel as indicative of the larger, historical Christian-Muslim conflict. The Iranian Revolution in 1979 further deepened the distrust between Christians and Muslims in many areas, particularly after Muslim students captured and held hostage many American hostages in the U.S., Embassy for 444 days. Terrorist bombings by Muslim extremists and the two wars in Iraq only exacerbated the problems between Muslims and Christians, and in many places today the level of trust and cooperation between the two groups is at an all time low.

Despite these circumstances, Christian-Muslim dialog, and often Jewish-Christian-Muslim dialog, is occurring in many places. The Quran, the Muslim scriptures, contains references both to many prominent figures from the Hebrew Bible and to Jesus himself, whom the Quran calls *Isa*. The Quran says that Isa was born of a virgin, lived a sinless life, and was a great prophet. It denies that he died on the cross or was raised from the dead, though it does say that he ascended to heaven after his message was rejected by the Jews. In addition to sharing many traditions about Jesus and his Jewish predecessors, Christianity and Islam also share many doctrines, such as heaven and hell, the final judgment, and the oneness of God. Muslims believe that the Christian doctrine of the Trinity is a repudiation of the oneness of God, a charge that Christians deny. Islam also teaches ethical principles that Christianity shares: care for the poor, obligations to family, and the value of prayer, for example. Muslim-Christian dialog has many common bases on which to build mutual understanding and respect for one another, but the prospects of success are tempered by the animosity that many Christians feel toward Muslims and many Muslims feel toward Christians. Nevertheless, talks are ongoing, and most Christians hope fervently that dialogs will produce better understanding between Christians and Muslims worldwide.

Christianity and the religions of South and East Asia

Interfaith dialog between Christianity and the major religions of South and East Asia, such as Hinduism, Buddhism, Sikhism, Jainism, Bahá'í, the traditional Chinese religions (Taoism and Confucianism), and Shinto, the traditional religion of Japan, has not been as frequent as dialogs with Judaism and Islam, nor has it received the same publicity, for a number of reasons. First, there is no single leader of any of these religious traditions. For example, the Dalai Lama, the official spokesperson for Tibetan Buddhism, represents less than 5 percent of Buddhists worldwide. Second, Christianity has not had the same long-term, historical contacts with these religions as it has had with Judaism and Israel. Third, the informal organizational structure of some of these religions make it difficult to identify potential dialog partners for Christians. Fourth, the common ground that Christianity shares with Judaism and Islam – worship of the same God, acceptance of similar scriptures and religious traditions, acceptance of many of the same values and doctrines – is not present in the same ways in the Religions of South and East Asia. The worldview of many people living in South and East Asia is quite different from the Christian worldview, and in particular, Asians in these religious traditions do not share the concept of a single God who rules over the entire universe. The numerous gods of the Hindus and the absence of God for the Buddhists are quite different from the religious assumptions found in the three great monotheistic religions.

Despite these important differences, and perhaps to some extent because of them, many people in the West have been fascinated with the religions of the East for the past several decades, perhaps longer. This fascination led in the 1960s and beyond to the introduction to the West of Eastern religious traditions, some traditional and others an adaptation of traditional beliefs and practices for a Western audience. Some of the Eastern and Eastern-inspired religious traditions that were introduced during this period include Hare Krishna, Transcendental Meditation, Tibetan Buddhism, and Zen Buddhism. Forms of exercise based on Eastern religious traditions, such as Yoga and Falun Gong; sex guides based on Hindu Tantric practices; and numerous books with words in their titles that come from Eastern religions, such as *The Tao of Pooh*, *The Te of Piglet*, *Zen and the Art of Motorcycle Maintenance*, and *Zen in the Art of Archery*, just to name a few, all attest to an interest in the religions of the East that is more than a passing phase.

Christians and adherents of various Eastern religions work together in interfaith organizations to instill an understanding and respect for practitioners of these religions among Christians. On a more theological level, of all the religions of East and South Asia, probably the most numerous and productive dialogs have occurred between Christians and Buddhists. The Dalai Lama has been invited to speak on many occasions to largely Christian audiences, and even at Christian universities and seminaries around the world. In 2007 he was appointed as a distinguished professor at Emory University in Atlanta,

Figure 23.2 Overlooking Rio de Janeiro, Brazil, the statue of Christ the Redeemer welcomes all who come to him. After two thousand years, Christianity is still a vital and vibrant religion.

Georgia. Emory, a university with historical ties to the Methodist Church, has made a commitment to promote an understanding of Buddhist teaching and Tibetan culture to students and the community, both of which are largely Christian. In 1996 a group of Catholic and Buddhist monastics met at the Abbey of Our Lady of Gethsemani in Kentucky, the former home of the Trappist monk Thomas Merton. Over the course of five days the participants in the Gethsemani Encounter, as it was called, discussed many issues of shared interest to Buddhists and Christians. Five of the seven fastest growing religions in the U.S. – Sikhism, Jainism, Hinduism, Buddhism, and Bahá'í – originated in South or East Asia. Buddhists, Hindus, and Bahá'ís rank second through fourth on the list of fastest growing religions in the U.K., behind only Zoroastrianism. The continued fascination with Eastern religions in the West, the influx of immigrants who practice these religions, and the importance of expanding the Christian dialog to include these religions that together claim roughly a quarter of the world's population suggest that dialog between Christianity and the religions of South and East Asia are just in their beginning stage and are poised to increase substantially in the coming years.

Christianity and secularism

> The Christian religion, as organized in its churches, has been and still is the principal enemy of moral progress in the world.
>
> (Bertrand Russell, "Why I Am Not a Christian")

The word *secular* means "of or relating to the world," and it has at least two connotations in a Christian context. First, it refers to priests and bishops in the Roman Catholic Church who are stationed in diocesan parishes or engaged in other areas of ministry rather than associated with religious orders. Second, it can mean the world outside the church. It is in this second sense that the term is used in this section. A world in which the Church no longer holds sway over governments may be said to be secular, and that is the kind of world that exists today. Many Christians balk at the secularism of the modern world, seeing it as a threat to Christianity. The phrase *secular humanism* is used by some Christians to refer to a supposed common, anti-Christian worldview that pervades today's world and, allegedly, is being promoted by a conspiracy of secular institutions. Most Christians reject the threat posed by secular humanism as exaggerated, but they are still concerned about the increasing secularization of the world around them. Atheism is currently the fasting growing "religion" in the U.S., and Atheists and those who identify themselves as nonreligious account for almost 15 percent of the global population. Despite any qualms that individual Christians might have, many believe that is in the Church's best interest to talk with secularists about the similarities and differences that they have with Christians.

Harvey Cox's 1965 book *The Secular City* takes a different approach to the increasing secularism of the modern world. Noting that Christians are just as much a part of the secular world as non-Christians, he challenges them to accept the fact that the Church will never again have the kind of authority over governments and citizens as it has had in the past, and to consider that that might be a good thing. The secular city, Cox says, is the place where Christians live their lives, the place where they work and play. Wishing the situation were different will not make it so, so it is better to learn how the secular city works and to engage it fully in the name of Christ. Many Christians since Cox's time have taken up his challenge to live without fear or regret in a secular world, without giving up their commitment to Christianity. "Dialogs" between Christians and atheists in the past have largely been diatribes rather than dialogs proper. A good example of the diatribe is the series of charges and countercharges made by evolutionary biologist Richard Dawkins, an atheist, and his detractors against one another, most recently concerning his book *The God Delusion*, an attempt to portray all religion as contrary to an honest appraisal of widely accepted, well-known scientific evidence. More productive was the attitude of another evolutionary biologist, also an atheist, Stephen Jay Gould. Gould argued that the realm of science and the realm of religion were separate from one another, so they could not in reality be in conflict, unless one or the other tried to overstep its bounds. Not all would agree with Gould's approach, whether scientists or theologians, but at least his approach points to a direction for possible dialog. The growth of secularism worldwide, both in the sense of the decreasing influence of religion on the state and in the sense of the increased numbers of Atheists and nonreligious worldwide, suggests that the time for dialog between Christians and secularists is now.

Key points you need to know

- The Western world in particular has seen a growing interest in spirituality, concern with encountering the divine, over the past several decades. Spirituality, and in its more intense form mysticism, have been important traditions within Christianity from its inception.
- Three possible Christian approaches to other religions are (1) exclusivism, which stresses the uniqueness of God's revelation in Jesus Christ and posits salvation only in the Church; (2) inclusivism, which sees Jesus Christ as the full, definitive revelation of God but accepts the premise that God also reveals truths to adherents of other religions; and (3) pluralism, which sees Christianity as the path to God first revealed by Jesus Christ, but accepts the notion that God is revealed in other religions as well.
- Although Christianity originated as a reform movement within Judaism and the earliest followers of Jesus were Jews, as was Jesus himself, animosity between Jews and Christians began in the first century and only increased as the Church became predominantly Gentile.
- Christianity's growth to become the dominant religion in the Western world was accompanied by repression, as well as sporadic persecution, of Jews by Christians. The horrors of the Jewish Holocaust at the hands of the Nazis during World War II forced

many Christians to acknowledge the history of the Church's animosity toward the Jews, opening dialogs and avenues of cooperation between Jews and Christians never before undertaken.

- Conflict between Christianity and Islam began with the emergence of Islam, when Muslims captured territory formerly controlled by Christians, continued through the Middle Ages with the *reconquista* in the Iberian peninsula and the Crusades, and extends to today's conflicts in the Middle East and with Muslim extremists in various parts of the world.
- Christian-Muslim dialog, and often Jewish-Christian-Muslim dialog, is widespread today, as Christians and Muslims explore common areas of faith and common interests, such as concern for the poor, obligations to family, and the value of prayer.
- Although the connection between Christianity and the religions of South and East Asia is not as direct either historically or doctrinally, important discussions between representatives of Christianity and Asian religions, such as Buddhism, have begun in recent years. Meanwhile, concepts that originated in the religions of the East – derived from Zen Buddhism, Taoism, or Hinduism, for example – are having an increasing impact on Western consciousness.
- The increasing presence of secularism in Western society has prompted many interesting and fruitful interactions between Christians and those who hold various secular viewpoints, for example, among scientists.

Discussion questions

1. What elements of traditional Christianity might make it of interest to people in search of spirituality? What elements of traditional Christianity might discourage such people? Historically, what has been the dominant Christian approach to other religions? What is the dominant approach today?
2. What steps can Jews and Christians take together to ensure that another Holocaust never occurs? How has the Holocaust affected Christian thinking about the Jews?
3. How does the political situation in the Middle East affect the Christian-Muslim dialog?
4. With which religions of South and East Asia does Christianity have the most in common? the least in common?
5. Are there particular characteristics of Christianity that account for the fact that the growth in secularism worldwide is most prevalent in areas that are, or have historically been, predominantly Christian? Is secularism likely to spread to areas now dominated by other religious traditions?

Further reading

Armstrong, Karen 1994. *A History of God: The 4000-Year Quest of Judaism, Christianity and Islam*. New York: Knopf.

Carroll, James 2001. *Constantine's Sword: The Church and the Jews*. Boston, MA: Houghton Mifflin.

Charlesworth, James H., ed. 1990. *Jews and Christians: Exploring the Past, Present, and Future*. New York: Crossroads.

Chrysostom, John. *Against the Jews*.

Cox, Harvey, 1965. *The Secular City*. New York: Macmillan.

Cox, Harvey 1984. *Religion in the Secular City: Toward a Postmodern Theology*. New York: Simon and Schuster.

The Dalai Lama 1999. *Ethics for a New Millennium*. New York: Riverhead Books.

Dawkins, Richard 2006. *The God Delusion*. Boston, MA: Houghton Mifflin.

Foster, Richard J. 1998. *Celebration of Discipline: The Path to Spiritual Growth*. New York: HarperSanFrancisco.

Kimball, Charles 2002. *When Religion Becomes Evil*. New York: HarperSanFrancisco.

Merton, Thomas 1948. *The Seven Storey Mountain*. New York: Harcourt, Brace and Company.

Papal Encyclicals Online. http://www.papalencyclicals.net.

Pirsig, Robert M. 1974. *Zen and the Art of Motorcycle Maintenance: An Inquiry into Values*. New York: Quill.

Ward, Benedicta, trans. 1975. *The Sayings of the Desert Fathers*. London: Mowbray.

24 *Conclusion*

Probably, the continuing vitality of Christianity will remain dependent upon how fully Christians engage the question of Jesus, and how radically they are willing to consider what devotion to him means for them.

(Larry Hurtado, *Lord Jesus Christ*, 653)

Have mercy upon us.
Have mercy upon our efforts,
That we before Thee,
In love and in faith,
Righteousness and humility,
May follow Thee,
With self-denial, steadfastness,
 and courage,
And meet Thee in the silence.

Give us a pure heart
That we may see Thee,
A humble heart
That we may hear Thee,
A heart of love
That we may serve Thee,
A heart of faith
That we may live Thee,

Thou
Whom I do not know
But Whose I am.
Thou
Whom I do not comprehend
But Who hast dedicated me
To my fate.
Thou –

Dag Hammarskjöld, *Markings*

Christianity is a large, diverse, and growing religion. Originating in a small province on the eastern edge of the Roman Empire, it has grown over the past 2,000 years into a religion that claims the allegiance of more than 2 billion people, about one-third of the world's population. It has adherents on every continent and in every country. Every week Christians around the world gather in cathedrals, megachurches, small country churches, store-front rooms, and out of doors to worship and to celebrate their common commitment to God through their faith in Jesus Christ. Christians hold a wide diversity of beliefs, they practice their faith in many different ways, and their worship styles vary immensely. Despite these differences, there are some core beliefs that Christians share. They believe that there is only one God. They believe Jesus Christ is God's Son in some unique way. They take the teachings of Jesus of Nazareth as a model for their own faith and practice. They believe that their communion with God through faith in Christ is one of the most meaningful experiences in life. Although the name *Christian* was probably originally applied to them as a term of derision, they proudly wear the name today as a reminder of Jesus Christ, the Pioneer and Perfecter of their faith (Heb 12:2).

Over 2,000 years of Christian history, many important events have shaped the life and future of the church. Of all that has transpired over that time, after the Christ-event itself, the following ten events, or clusters of events, have perhaps been the most important for creating the church as it is today. They are listed chronologically.

1. *Ministry and letters of the Apostle Paul.* According to Paul's own testimony in his letter to the churches of Galatia, he agreed with Peter and the other "pillars of the church" that they would concentrate on taking the gospel to the Jews, and he would take the gospel to the Gentiles. Whether that arrangement was really an equitable division of labor, Paul undertook the challenge with gusto. He founded churches on two continents and in several different Roman provinces, and his letters to those churches make up a significant amount of the New Testament. Moreover, his mission to the Gentiles, within the boundaries of the Roman Empire, defined the shape of the church for centuries to come.

2. *Second century.* After the first generation of Christians, those who had known Jesus and the apostles, died, and when the Parousia did not occur within the time frame that many expected, Christians in the second century were faced with the task of defining the parameters of Christianity. In the face of challenges from Marcion, Montanus, and the Gnostics, the early leaders of the Great Church – which was in many places great only in spirit rather than in numbers – began assembling the books that would become the sacred scripture of Christianity, alongside the sacred texts they had inherited from the Jews. Furthermore, they started to define their faith using philosophy and other tools at their disposal, so that the message of the gospel would speak to their generation and not wither on the vine.

3. *Emperor Constantine.* Constantine's conversion to Christianity and his edict making Christianity a legal religion changed the Church in profound ways. Hordes of new believers poured into the churches, and grand new structures for Christian worship

were built all over the empire. Constantine called the first ecumenical church council to deal with the problem of Arianism, establishing the principle that decisions made by ecumenical councils were binding. He moved his capital to Constantinople, and in so doing preserved the Roman Empire in the East for another 1,000 years.

4. *Fall of Rome/Rise of Islam.* The barbarian destruction of Rome in the West and the rise of Islam in the East set the stage for the next 1,000 years of church history. While the West struggled to recover, the Byzantine Empire flourished. When Muslim troops captured large portions of the Byzantine Empire, and even managed to capture the Iberian peninsula, the newly Christian Germanic kingdoms fought back. Christians in both the East and the West would spend centuries fighting their Muslim neighbors, and the greatest error in judgment in Christian history, the Crusades, were a delayed response to the encroachment of Islam onto formerly Christian territory.

5. *Great Schism.* After years of drifting apart and bickering over various issues, the Eastern and Western churches split apart permanently in 1054. The histories of the two halves of the church would follow different paths from this time on, as the Eastern Church was subject first to a powerful Christian emperor and then to a powerful Muslim caliph, while the Western Church, in the person of the pope, found itself able to wield more and more power, political as well as spiritual.

6. *Renaissance/Modern Age/Protestant Reformation.* The rediscovery of the wisdom of the ancient Greeks and Romans set the stage for an incredible burst of creative power, first in Florence, then in Rome, and then throughout Europe. New ways of thinking could be shared once the printing press, the most important invention since the wheel and the plow, began the mass production of knowledge and ideas. The Protestant Reformation, which was based on the inspiration of the Renaissance and the technology of the printing press, changed the face of the Church in ways that would ultimately make a greater impact than even the Great Schism.

7. *Peace of Westphalia/French Revolution/Enlightenment.* The Peace of Westphalia marked the end of international conflict in Europe based on religion, but as it turned out, it allowed states to redirect their efforts from fighting nations that were loyal to a different form of Christianity to rooting out different forms of Christianity within a single country. These persecutions, when they were carried out in France, led to the exodus of the Huguenots, the collapse of the French economy, and eventually the French Revolution. Contemporaneous with this period was the Enlightenment, which inspired the French and American Revolutions and also spurred the growth of science through the development of the scientific method. Advances in philosophy during the Enlightenment brought about the downfall of the great systems of Protestant orthodoxy that had been built in the previous century.

8. *Fall of Papal States.* The fall of the Papal States was not so much an important event in itself, though it led to the unification of Italy for the first time since the fall of the Western Roman Empire. The significance of the fall of the Papal States was that it forced the papacy to turn its attention away from political matters to focus exclusively on spiritual matters, a focus that had been sorely lacking in the previous

several centuries and that had forced the papacy into a series of compromises with power that were detrimental to both the institution of the Church and to individual Christians.

9. *Holocaust/Vatican II.* The horrors of World War II, and especially of the Holocaust, caused the Vatican to rethink its policies concerning the Jews, as well as in many other areas. Vatican II turned the Roman Catholic Church from an institution that was living in the past, afraid to confront the modernism that surround it, into a revived institution whose members could now worship in their own languages, that pledged to heal the rift with Protestants, and that charted a new course with regard to other religions as well.

10. *Missions/ecumenical movement.* The modern missions movement of the nineteenth century led directly to the ecumenical movement of the twentieth century. The World Council of Churches, combined with its regular dialog partner, the Roman Catholic Church, comprised an umbrella organization that represented three-fourths of the world's Christians. Furthermore, the Ecumenical movement charted a course that envisioned dialog and cooperation rather than verbal assaults and opposition, a decided improvement over the relations between the churches since at least the time of the Protestant Reformation.

As noted above, some culture commentators contend that we live today in a post-Christian age. If by that term they mean that the Church no longer wields authority over nations and empires as it did as recently as the nineteenth century, they are correct. If the Church wants to influence political decisions today, it must use its moral authority, since it no longer has armies at its beck and call. On the other hand, if by "post-Christian" age they mean that the church is lifeless, moribund, and increasingly irrelevant, they could not be more wrong. Christianity is growing rapidly in many areas, particularly in the global south: in Africa, Latin America, and parts of Asia. Furthermore, various renewal movements are keeping the church vital and in touch with the wellspring of the Spirit that gives it strength. The Ecumenical movement is strong and growing stronger, as Christians realize that they need one another's support and wisdom. Finally, interfaith dialog is building bridges between Christianity and other religions, and even between Christianity and the secular world, as the Church has come to understand that it shares the planet with more than 4 billion other people whose ideas, aspirations, and dreams are often not that different from its own. As the twenty-first century progresses, Christianity's place in the world of religion, the world of ideas, and even the world of politics is assured.

Appendix

Timeline of Christian history

World history	Christian history
63 B.C.E: Roman conquest of Judea	
27 B.C.E.–14 C.E.: Reign of Caesar Augustus, the first Roman emperor	
	c. 8–6 B.C.E.: Birth of Jesus
	c. 27–30 C.E.: Public ministry of Jesus
	c. 30: Crucifixion and resurrection of Jesus
	c. 36–64: Public ministry of Paul
	c. 49: Jerusalem Council, deciding the appropriate way of receiving Gentile converts into the Church
	c. 50–120: Composition of the New Testament
	64: Great Fire of Rome leads Nero to persecute Christians, executing Peter and Paul
70: Roman destruction of the Second Temple in Jerusalem	
	c. 100: Final split of Christianity from Judaism
	c. 107: Martyrdom of Ignatius, bishop of Antioch
117–138: Roman Empire reaches its greatest extent under Emperor Hadrian	

World history	Christian history
	c. 140–200: Great Church faces internal crises related to Marcion, Montanus, and the Gnostics, begins to establish canon of New Testament
	c. 175: Tatian composes the Diatessaron, a gospel harmony used for several centuries by Syriac Christians
235–284: Crisis of the Third Century sees barbarian tribes encroaching on Roman territory	249–260: Widespread Roman persecution of Christians under Decius and Valerian
284–305: Reign of Emperor Diocletian	303–311: Great Persecution begun by Diocletian, continued by Galerius in the East after Diocletian's retirement
306–327: Reign of Emperor Constantine I, first in the West, then over whole Roman Empire	311: Edict of Toleration stops imperial persecution of Christians
	313: Edict of Milan recognizes Christianity as a legal religion in the Roman Empire
	325: First Council of Nicaea (First Ecumenical Council)
330: Constantine renames Byzantium Constantinople and moves his capital there from Rome	
	c. 340–350: Ulfilas translates the New Testament into Gothic and uses it to convert the Goths to Christianity
361–363: Reign of Emperor Julian, known to later Christians as Julian the Apostate	
	367: Athanasius, bishop of Alexandria, is the first to list the 27 books of the New Testament as authoritative
378–395: Reign of Emperor Theodosius I	381: First Council of Constantinople (Second Ecumenical Council)
	382: Pope Damasus I commissions Jerome to create the Latin Vulgate, the official Latin translation of the Bible for the Western Church for more than 1,000 years

World history	Christian history
	391: Theodosius declares Christianity the official religion of the Roman Empire
395: Upon the death of Theodosius, the Roman Empire is permanently split into separate Eastern and Western empires	
410: Sack of Rome by Alaric the Goth	
	423–459: Syrian monk Simeon Stylites lives an ascetic life on a pillar in the Syrian desert
	c. 425: Augustine completes City of God, begun in the aftermath of the fall of Rome
	431: Council of Ephesus (Third Ecumenical Council), split of Nestorians from the Great Church
	440–461: Reign of Pope Leo I, considered by many to be the first bishop of Rome worthy of the title "Pope"
	451: Council of Chalcedon (Fourth Ecumenical Council), split of Monophysites from the Great Church
476: Fall of the Western Roman Empire	
	499: Clovis I, King of the Franks, converts to orthodox (Nicene) Christianity, as do his people
527–565: Reign of Byzantine Emperor Justinian I, during whose reign Byzantine Empire reaches its greatest extent	
	597: Pope Gregory I sends the monk Augustine to England to convert the Angles and Saxons
622: Hijra of Muhammad and his followers to Medina, an important event in the emergence of Islam	
	c. 640–700: Muslims conquer territory in Palestine and North Africa from Byzantine Empire

World history	Christian history
	664: At Synod of Whitby, Celtic Christians meet with Anglo–Saxon Christians and commit to follow the practices of the Roman Church
	710: Muslims begin their conquest of the Iberian peninsula, wresting it from Christian hands
	730–787: First Iconoclastic controversy
	732: Charles Martel stops the expansion of Muslim control in Western Europe at the Pyrenees in the Battle of Tours
	787: Second Council of Nicaea (Seventh Ecumenical Council) settles the first Iconoclastic controversy
768–814: Reign of Charlemagne as King of the Franks and Emperor of the Holy Roman Empire	
	1054: Great Schism between the Eastern Orthodox and the Roman Catholic Church
	1073–1085: Reign of Pope Gregory VII, who instituted a series of reforms to purify and strengthen the papacy
	1095: Pope Urban II calls Christians to fight in the First Crusade
	1198–1216: Reign of Pope Innocent III, under whom the papacy reaches the pinnacle of temporal power
	1204: Western Christians during the Fourth Crusade sack Constantinople and set up a Latin Kingdom, which lasts until it is reconquered by the Byzantine Empire in 1261
	1209: Francis of Assisi founds the Order of Friars Minor, commonly known as the Franciscans
Fourteenth century: Renaissance begins in Florence and spreads throughout Europe	

World history	Christian history
c. 1450: Invention of the printing press by Johannes Gutenberg	
	1453: Fall of Constantinople to the Turks
1492: Spain conquers Granada, the last remaining Muslim kingdom on the Iberian peninsula	
1492: Spain expels all its Jews	
1492: Columbus lands in the Americas	
	1517: Protestant Reformation begins when Martin Luther nails his 95 *Theses* to the door of the church in Wittenberg
	1531: Reformer Ulrich Zwingli killed in battle in Switzerland
	1531: Appearance of the Virgin Mary (Virgin of Guadalupe) to Juan Diego in Mexico
	1534: King Henry VIII of England breaks with the Roman Catholic Church, forming the Church of England
	1536: First edition of John Calvin's *Institutes of the Christian Religion*
	1536: Menno Simons, the founder of the Mennonites, leaves the Roman Catholic Church to join the Anabaptists
	1545–1563: Council of Trent (Nineteenth Ecumenical Council for Roman Catholics) meets to decide the response of the Roman Catholic Church to Protestantism
	1636: Roger Williams founds the colony of Providence (Rhode Island), the first American colony with complete religious liberty
1648: Peace of Westphalia brings internecine Christian wars over religion to an end in Europe	

World history	Christian history
	1672: Council of Jerusalem (Eastern Orthodox) meets to define Orthodox positions relative to Catholics and Protestants
	1738: John Wesley feels his heart "strangely warmed" and begins a movement that would result in the creation of the Methodist Church
1775: Beginning of American Revolution	
1789: Beginning of French Revolution	
1791: U.S. Bill of Rights adopted, enshrining religious liberty as the law of the land	
	1793: British missionary William Carey sails for India, beginning the Modern Missions movement
1807: William Wilberforce succeeds in abolishing the British slave trade	
1804–1822: Independence of Haiti and most Latin American nations from colonial rule	
1848: Year of Revolution in Europe	
1859: Charles Darwin publishes *On the Origin of Species*	
1861–1865: U.S. Civil war results in the abolition of slavery	1846–1878: Reign of Pope Pius IX
	1870: First Vatican Council (Twentieth Ecumenical Council for Roman Catholics) declares the infallibility of the pope
	1870: Rome annexed into the Kingdom of Italy, ending the temporal power of the papacy
1905: Albert Einstein publishes his paper on special relativity	
	1906: Azusa Street Revival begins the Pentecostal/Charismatic movement
1914–1918: World War I	

World history	Christian history
1939–1945: World War II, which includes the Holocaust and the detonation of atomic bombs over Hiroshima and Nagasaki	
	1948: First meeting of the World Council of Churches
1945–1989: Cold War between Soviet Union and Western democracies	
1951–1994: Independence of most African nations from colonial rule	
1953: James Watson and Francis Crick discover the structure of the DNA molecule	
	1955: Montgomery Bus Boycott marks start of U.S. Civil Rights Movement, led by several Christian pastors and other leaders
	1962–1965: Second Vatican Council (Twenty-first Ecumenical Council for Roman Catholics) institutes major changes in the Roman Catholic Church, sets the stage for dialogs with other Christians, Jews, and Muslims
	1978–2005: Reign of Pope John Paul II
1993: World enters the Internet age, as the World Wide Web becomes widely accessible	
2000: United Nations commits to Millennium Development Goals to work toward eliminating poverty, an initiative strongly supported by many Christians and people of other faiths	

Glossary

abbess   Head of a convent.

abbot   Head of a monastery.

acolyte   Lower level of clergy in some Christian traditions and historical periods who helps serve at the altar; often called an altar boy or altar girl.

adherent   Follower of a particular religion or system of belief and practice.

adoptionism   Belief that the divine Christ entered into the human Jesus at some point after his birth, such as at his baptism or at his resurrection.

adoration   Act of worshiping something or someone, such as an icon or Jesus Christ.

Advent   Season of the Christian year which anticipates the celebration of the birth of Christ at Christmas.

aeon   Divine or semi-divine emanation of God, common in many Gnostic systems of thought.

aisle   One of the walkways that run the length of a church, often parallel to one another.

altar call   Invitation offered by a minister to congregants at the end of a service to approach the altar (or front of the church) and make a public decision to follow God, for example, through baptism. *Also called* the invitation.

altar   Table on which the bread and wine of the Eucharist is laid before being served. In Catholic, Orthodox, and Anglican churches, the altar is typically in the middle of the transept, at the front of the church, often on a raised platform.

amillennial   View of the end times that sees the 1,000-year reign of peace as figurative rather than literal.

Anabaptist Reformation   *See* Radical Reformation.

Anatolia   Peninsula bordered on the north by the Black Sea, on the south by the Mediterranean Sea, and on the west by the Aegean Sea and the Bosporus Strait, the location of the Asian portion of the modern nation of Turkey.

anchorite *(m.)*, **anchoress** *(f.)*   A person whose pursuit of a religious life leads him or her to withdraw from society and live in isolation, for the purpose of engaging in a life focused on prayer or meditation.

annihilationism   Doctrine that human souls that are not destined to spend eternity with God are destroyed (rather than suffering eternal punishment).

anointing the sick   Rite in which a priest or other functionary anoints a sick person with consecrated oil. Anointing the sick is one of the seven sacraments of the Roman Catholic Church.

anoios   Greek term used to denote that Jesus was *dissimilar* to God the Father, a position associated with the Arian point of view.

antinomian   Characterized by a belief that since Christians are free from the law, they may sin with impunity.

antiphonal   Made up of two or more distinct voices; for example, a public scripture reading in which the priest, choir, and congregation are assigned different verses to read aloud in turn is an antiphonal reading.

antipope   Person claiming the title of pope but to whom later Roman Catholic authorities deny the title, because someone else living at the time is officially recognized as pope.

apocalypse   (1) Document that purports to reveal secrets about the end times, usually derived from an otherworldly mediator, often by means of elaborate symbolism. (2) (*Capitalized*) Another name for the book of Revelation.

Apocrypha   Books included in the Old Testament of Roman Catholic, Eastern Orthodox, and Anglican Christians but not in the Old Testament of most Protestants.

apologist   One of the early Christian authors who offered a written defense of Christianity.

apology   Reasoned defense of Christianity.

apostate   Person who has left the Church (or the orthodox Church) and adopted views that are outside the mainstream Christian tradition.

apostle   Term used in early Christian writings to refer to Jesus' original disciples (excluding Judas Iscariot) and to other prominent leaders, such as the Apostle Paul. The term is generally used today to refer to these historical figures, but in some Christian traditions it can also refer to contemporary leaders of the Church.

apostolic succession   Doctrine that all legitimate Christian bishops can trace the list of previous office-holders back through time to one of the original apostles.

archbishop   Bishop who leads a particularly important or large diocese, often centered around a large metropolitan area.

Arianism   Belief that Jesus was not divine but was God's first creation, associated with the fourth-century Alexandrian presbyter Arius.

atonement   Doctrine that concerns the manner in which Jesus' death reconciles sinful humanity to a holy God.

augustus   Title given to the chief emperor in the Eastern or Western Roman Empire. *See also* caesar.

B.C.E.   Dates Before the Common Era (equivalent to B.C., "Before Christ").

Babylonian Captivity of the papacy   Period of history (1309–1377) when the popes resided in Avignon, France, rather than Rome.

baptism   Initiation rite in which a person is either immersed in or sprinkled with water.

basilica   In Roman Catholicism, a church that has been granted certain privileges or recognition by the pope.

believer's baptism   Practice of baptizing only adults or children old enough to confess their faith in Christ on their own volition. *Also called* credobaptism.

benediction   Blessing given to the congregation, often at the end of a service.

biretta   Square, ecclesiastical headgear worn by Roman Catholic and some Anglican clergy.

bishop   Leader of a Christian church, or sometimes of several churches (a diocese), whose duties include oversight and preaching. In traditions with three levels of clergy, bishops are the highest level, above priests and deacons.

bodily assumption   Doctrine that Mary, the mother of Jesus, ascended directly to heaven without dying. This doctrine was proclaimed an official dogma of the Roman Catholic Church in 1950 by Pope Pius XII, but it is generally rejected by Orthodox and Protestant Christians.

Book of the Twelve   Twelve "Minor Prophets" (the books of Hosea through Malachi), considered a single book in the Jewish canon of scripture.

C.E.   Dates in the Common Era (equivalent to A.D., "Anno Domini" or "Year of the Lord").

caesar   Title given to the vice emperor in the Eastern or Western Roman Empire. *See also* augustus.

call to worship   Statement, scripture reading, or song inviting the congregants to worship God at the beginning of a service.

camp meeting   Service held outdoors, usually sponsored or supported by several different churches, often extending over a period of several days, made popular during the Second Great Awakening in the U.S. *See also* revival meeting.

canon law   Body of officially established laws governing a Church, used especially in the Roman Catholic Church.

canon   Fixed list of authoritative books. The Christian canon consists of the Old Testament and the New Testament.

canonize   To declare someone to be a saint. Roman Catholic, Eastern Orthodox, and Anglican Christians all recognize certain men and women after their deaths as saints.

cantor   Person whose duty is to lead the singing or chanting in a service. The term is primarily used in reference to liturgical (high-church) services.

catechism   (1) Document giving a detailed summary of the Christian faith, often in question and answer form. (2) Formal instruction in the Christian faith, based on the document described in (1).

catechumen   Person studying the Christian faith in preparation for baptism or confirmation.

cathedral   Official church of a bishop.

catholic   When not capitalized, refers to the universal Church.

cenobitic   Lifestyle or characteristics of a monastic who lives in a community within the walls of a monastery or convent.

charismatic movement   Emphasis on the work and transforming power of the Holy Spirit that began in the early twentieth century and spread throughout the Christian world. *Also called* Pentecostalism.

charismatic   Emphasizing or characterized by the work of the Holy Spirit, such as speaking in tongues and miracles.

chrismation   Anointing with consecrated oil, usually as part of a larger ceremony or sacrament.

Christendom   (1) Term that refers to those nations controlled by Christian rulers during the Middle Ages and during the early Modern period. (2) Term that encompasses all Christians everywhere.

Christian perfection   Doctrine that Christians can achieve sinlessness in their daily lives through discipline and the power of God.

Christmas   Celebration of Jesus' birth.

clergy   Those set apart by the Church for special Christian service, such as deacons, priests, bishops, or pastors. In some Christian traditions, deacons are considered lay leaders rather than clergy.

cloister   Enclosed, covered walkway surrounding a courtyard, attached to a church or monastery. The term is often used as a synonym for *monastery*.

commissioning service   *See* institution (2).

communicant   One who is eligible to receive communion, or who is actually receiving it.

communion   (1) Sacrament (or ordinance) observed by all Christian faith traditions that re-enacts Jesus' last supper with his disciples. (2) For a Church to be in *communion with* another implies that each of the two Churches recognizes the legitimacy of the other's clergy and sacraments.

confession (1) Admitting one's sin, either directly to God or through a priest or other intermediary, and asking for forgiveness. Confession is one of the seven sacraments of the Roman Catholic Church. *Also called the sacrament of* penance. (2) Statement of faith, especially one adopted by a religious body to define its beliefs.

confirmation Ceremony in which a person's commitment to Christ and the Church is celebrated. Confirmation is one of the seven sacraments of the Roman Catholic Church.

consubstantiation Lutheran doctrine that the bread and wine of communion retain their substance yet coexist with the body and blood of Christ.

convent House or compound where nuns live and work, usually led by an abbess or mother superior.

conversion experience Expression used to describe a conscious decision to change one's beliefs and/or lifestyle, particularly in reference to the initial decision to commit oneself to faith in God through Christ.

corporate worship Gathering together of a group of Christians for a shared worship experience.

cosmogony Story or explanation of the origin of the universe.

credobaptism *See* believer's baptism.

creed Formal statement of faith.

crisis conversion Experience of sorrow for sin and intense desire for forgiveness that often accompanies a decision to become a Christian in certain faith traditions.

Crusades Series of wars in the High and Late Middle Ages launched by various popes with the purpose of recapturing Christian lands that had fallen under the control of Muslims.

cult Worship practices associated with a religion.

deacon Leader of a Christian church, whose duties include ministry to members of the congregation. In traditions with two or three levels of clergy, deacons are the lowest level, below priests/pastors and bishops.

demiurge Creator god in Plato and in some Gnostic systems. In Gnosticism, the demiurge is distinct from the highest God.

denomination A group of Christian churches that have common beliefs and practices and that are associated with one another in some organized fashion.

deuterocanonical Another word to describe the books of the Apocrypha, emphasizing their status as canonical in some Christian traditions, but belonging to a second canon.

Diaspora Jews who lived outside the traditional Jewish homeland.

Diatessaron   Early gospel harmony created by Tatian in the second century.

disciple   Follower of Christ. The term is often used to refer specifically to Jesus' original twelve disciples.

dispensationalism   Method of interpreting the Bible that divides human history into several different dispensations, or periods in which God deals with people in different ways, usually based on a particular covenant (e.g. the Noahic covenant or the Mosaic covenant). Dispensationalists are typically premillennial futurists who accept the doctrine of the Rapture.

Docetic   (1) Member of a Christian group arising in the first century that denied the humanity of Jesus. (2) Of or pertaining to the beliefs of this group.

doctor of the church   Person identified by the Roman Catholic Church first as a saint, then as someone whose writings have proved especially beneficial to the Church as a whole. As of 2007, only 33 people have been named doctors of the Church: 30 men and 3 women.

doxology   Relatively brief refrain or hymn of praise.

Easter   Celebration of Jesus' resurrection from the dead.

ecstatic   Out of the body, conceived either literally or figuratively, as in "an ecstatic experience."

ecumenical council   Assembly of Church officials, called to address a specific set of issues. Only in historical retrospect is any particular meeting recognized as an ecumenical council, that is, one whose authority is recognized by the whole Church, or by major faith traditions within the Church.

ecumenical   Dealing with the worldwide Church, across lines of nationality, denomination, and faith tradition.

elder   Leader of a church. The word is associated with the wisdom that comes with age, though elders are not necessarily old. *Also called* presbyter.

elect   Those who are chosen by God to spend eternity with God in heaven, according to the teaching of some Christians.

election   Doctrine that God chooses those who will spend eternity in heaven (i.e., the elect).

encomendero   European owner or manager of an *encomiendo*.

encomiendo   Large estate in the New World owned by a European, or person of European descent, on which Native Americans or Native Caribbeans were forced to work.

entire sanctification   *See* Christian perfection.

Epiphany   January 6, the day on which Western Christians celebrate the visit of the Magi to the baby Jesus and on which Eastern Christians celebrate Jesus' baptism. In both Eastern and Western Churches, emphasis is placed on Christ's manifestation (Greek: *epiphania*) to the world.

episcopal   Form of church polity in which bishops – who exercise authority over the church, for example by selecting priests – are selected by other bishops.

eremitic   Lifestyle or characteristics of a hermit, characterized by a life of solitude.

eschatology   Study of the doctrine of the end times.

eschaton   The end times.

Essene   Member of a Jewish sect that originated in the late Second Temple period and separated itself from the other two main sects (Pharisees and Sadducees) because of disputes over doctrine and practice.

Eucharist   Another name for the sacrament (or ordinance) of communion.

evangelist   (1) Author of one of the four canonical gospels. (2) Christian minister whose primary focus is to convert non-Christians to Christianity, or to convert outsiders to his/her version of Christianity.

exclusivism   Belief that God's revelation through Jesus Christ is unique and that salvation can only be achieved through Christ. *See also* inclusivism *and* pluralism.

excommunication   Act of expelling a Christian from the Church for reasons of doctrine or behavior.

exilic   Pertaining to the period during which leading Jews and their descendants were required to remain in Babylonia, roughly 587 to 538 B.C.E.

exodus   Departure of the nation of Israel from Egypt under the leadership of Moses, described in the book of Exodus.

exorcism   Ritual in which evil spirits or demons are cast out of a possessed location or individual.

exorcist   Lower level of clergy in some Christian traditions and historical periods whose primary duty is to cast out demons from persons or places.

exposition   Explanation of a biblical text, usually accompanied by suggested applications of the truths of the text, as in a sermon or homily.

faith tradition   A group of Christian denominations that share a common historical ancestry, as well as certain beliefs and practices that distinguish them from other faith traditions.

Fall   Term referring to humankind's transition from a sinless state to a condition influenced or characterized by sin. The classic description of the Fall is in Genesis 3.

Father   First person of the divine Trinity, in traditional, Trinitarian Christianity. *See also* Son, Holy Spirit, *and* Trinity.

fief   Under the feudal system, land given by a lord to a vassal, in return for loyalty and tribute.

filioque   Latin term that means *and the Son*, added by the Western Church to the Niceno-Constantinopolitan Creed, over the objections of the Eastern Church. The

Western Church contended that the Holy Spirit proceeds from the Father *and the Son*, while the Eastern Church held to the original wording of the creed, which said the Holy Spirit proceeds (only) from the Father.

First Testament *See* Old Testament.

First Wave of the Spirit First movement of Pentecostalism, beginning in the early twentieth century, which resulted in the formation of many new, Pentecostal denominations.

formula quotation Quotation from the Hebrew Bible in the Gospel of Matthew that follows a specific pattern of citation, referring to the Hebrew Bible passage as having been "fulfilled" in the life of Jesus.

friar Member of a mendicant religious order.

futurist Method of interpreting biblical prophecy, especially the book of Revelation, that sees much of it as yet to be fulfilled.

general atonement *See* unlimited atonement.

Gentile Non-Jew.

glossolalia *See* speaking in tongues.

gnosis Knowledge, especially knowledge believed (by Gnostics) to be transmitted in secret by Jesus to one or more of his followers.

Gnostic One who believes that salvation comes through knowledge, usually some sort of esoteric knowledge not available to the general public.

Gnosticism System of thought that promotes the idea of salvation through esoteric knowledge. Many forms of Gnosticism in the early centuries of the Common Era incorporated various aspects of Christian thought into their systems.

Godhead Term denoting the totality of the deity, equated with the Trinity in most forms of Christianity (i.e., the Trinitarian forms).

Great Church Church in the second and third centuries whose views reflected those of the Apologists and which held positions later determined to be orthodox at the early ecumenical councils.

Great Schism Final, permanent division between the Eastern and Western branches of the Church, which occurred in 1054, occasioned by the rise of papal authority in the West and the *filioque* controversy.

Great Western Schism Period of history (1378–1417) when two or three rival popes – based in Rome, Avignon, and later Pisa – claimed the papacy at the same time.

heaven Destiny of those dead who were in a proper relationship with God, who lived their lives in accordance with God's will, or who received forgiveness from God prior to death. Christians differ in their understanding of the precise requirements for admission into heaven.

Hebrew Bible *See* Old Testament.

hell   Destiny of those dead who were not in a proper relationship with God, who lived evil lives, or who did not receive God's forgiveness prior to death; that is, all those not destined for heaven. Christian annihilationists and universalists reject the existence of hell.

Hellenism   Greek language and culture from the time of Alexander the Great through the next several centuries.

henotheism   Idea that only one God is worthy of worship and obedience.

heretic   Person who holds views outside the mainstream Christian tradition.

hermit   Ascetic religious who lives alone, apart from a community.

heteroousios   Greek term used to denote that Jesus was *of a different substance* from God the Father, a position associated with the Arian point of view.

Hexapla   Six-columned copy of the Old Testament developed by Origen, containing the text of the Bible in Hebrew, Greek transliteration of Hebrew, and several Greek versions.

high-church   Characterized by highly structured, liturgical worship.

historicist   Method of interpreting biblical prophecy, especially the book of Revelation, that sees many of the events described as being fulfilled throughout the history of the Church, with only a few events remaining to be fulfilled.

holy orders   Commissioning to one of the higher orders of clergy. Holy orders is one of the seven sacraments of the Roman Catholic Church.

Holy Spirit   Third person of the divine Trinity, in traditional, Trinitarian Christianity. *See also* Father, Son, *and* Trinity.

homily   Sermon or reflection on a biblical passage or a particular theme.

homoios   Greek term used to denote that Jesus was *similar* to God the Father, without further specificity, a position associated with the so-called semi-Arian point of view.

homoiousios   Greek term used to denote that Jesus was *of a similar substance* to God the Father, a position associated with the so-called semi-Arian point of view.

homoousios   Greek term used to denote that Jesus was *of the same substance* as God the Father, a position associated with Nicene orthodoxy.

host   Bread or wafer used during communion or Eucharistic service.

humanism   Intellectual movement that emphasized the study of Greek and Roman classical literature, as well as subjects such as grammar, rhetoric, and philosophy. The movement began in Florence in the fourteenth century and spread throughout Europe during an era called the Renaissance.

hymn   Song of praise to God.

hypostatic union   Union of the divine and the human in Jesus Christ in a single Person or essence (Greek: *hypostasis*), a position accepted as orthodox at the Council of Chalcedon in 451.

icon   Two-dimensional piece of religious art, often using stylized or traditional renderings of people and objects, used in religious devotion.

iconoclast   Opponent of the use of icons in worship.

iconodule   *See* iconophile.

iconophile   Supporter of the use of icons in worship. *Also called an* iconodule.

idealist   Method of interpreting biblical prophecy, especially the book of Revelation, that treats most or all of the events described, especially those described with elaborate symbols, as metaphorical, perhaps pointing to people and events contemporaneous with the composition of the books.

immaculate conception   Doctrine that Mary, the mother of Jesus, was conceived in her mother's womb without original sin (i.e., without the taint of sin). This doctrine was proclaimed an official dogma of the Roman Catholic Church by Pope Pius IX in 1854, but it is generally rejected by Orthodox and Protestant Christians.

incarnation   Doctrine that concerns God becoming a human being in the person of Jesus Christ.

inclusivism   Belief that God's revelation through Jesus Christ is normative but that God may offer paths to salvation through other religious traditions as well as Christianity. *See also exclusivism* and *pluralism*.

indulgence   Document that grants either full or partial remission of punishment for particular sins.

inerrant   Without error, a word applied by many conservative Christians to the Bible.

infant baptism   Practice of baptizing infants as an initiation into the church. *Also called* pedobaptism.

Inquisition   Office or institution of the Roman Catholic Church that sought to enforce the purity of the Christian faith.

institution   (1) Organization or group of people dedicated to a particular goal or type of work (e.g. the Church). (2) Service whose primary focus is the dedication or consecration of a person to a non-clerical office (e.g. an acolyte or missionary). *Also called* commissioning service.

introit   Hymn or psalm sung at the beginning of a service, often while the ministers are entering the sanctuary.

invitation   *See* altar call.

justification   Being made right with God or in God's sight.

lapse controversy   Disagreement over whether to allow Christians who had denied their faith during time of persecution back into the church, and if so, what was required of those who had "lapsed" in their faith. The two most important lapse controversies in early Christian history were the Novatian and Donatist controversies.

Law   *See* Torah *and* Pentateuch.

lay investiture   Practice whereby secular rulers would appoint leaders of the Church, such as bishops or abbots.

lay, laity   Christians who are not clergy.

lectionary   (1) Manuscript that contains the biblical text divided into sections that are to be read on certain dates throughout the Christian year. (2) List of scripture readings (without the texts themselves) for particular dates of the Christian year.

lector   Person designated to read the scripture during a service.

Lent   Season of the Christian year that anticipates Easter. Many Christians observe Lent, which begins on Ash Wednesday and ends on Holy Saturday, by renouncing certain pleasures or by undertaking spiritual disciplines.

Levant   Region bordering the eastern Mediterranean Sea.

libellus   Official letter from the Roman government, especially one issued during one of the persecutions of Christians during the late third and early fourth centuries stating that a person had offered sacrifice to the gods.

limited atonement   Doctrine that Christ's blood was shed only for the elect, not all of humanity. *Also called* particular atonement.

litany   Public prayer or other public reading, often accompanied by brief responses by the congregation (e.g. "Lord, hear our prayer").

liturgy   Prescribed order or form of worship, often involving prayers, scripture readings, congregational responses, etc. In the Eastern Orthodox Church, the primary service is called the Divine Liturgy.

Logos   Greek term that can be translated *word* or *reason*. The term was used in Greek philosophy by the Stoics and others to represent the rational principle of the universe, and it was applied to the preincarnate Christ in John 1.

low-church   Characterized by loosely structured, nonliturgical worship.

LXX   *See* Septuagint.

Major Prophets   Longer prophetic books: Isaiah, Jeremiah, Lamentations, Ezekiel, Daniel. Lamentations is a poetic book rather than a prophetic book, but it is listed among the Major Prophets because of its traditional association with Jeremiah.

martyr   One whose death bears witness to his or her faith in Christ, from the Greek word meaning *witness*.

Masoretic Text   Standard medieval Hebrew text of the Hebrew Bible, produced by Jewish scribes known as the Masoretes. *Abbreviated* MT.

mass   Roman Catholic term for the celebration of Christ's sacrificial death on the cross through the Eucharist. By extension, the term also means the service at which the Eucharist is celebrated.

matins   Morning prayers, or a morning prayer service.

megablocs　Large grouping of Christians based on faith traditions and denominational similarities, used, for example, in the *World Christian Encyclopedia*.

megachurch　Individual church with a membership of several thousand. The term is used primarily to refer to such churches that are in the Free Church tradition, especially Evangelical or Pentecostal churches.

mendicant order　Religious order whose members are dedicated to some sort of ministry outside the monastery or convent, such as preaching or ministering to the poor. Examples include the Franciscans and the Missionaries of Charity.

Mesopotamia　Geographic region in the Near East between the river valleys of the Euphrates and Tigris rivers, roughly coterminous with modern Iraq.

messianic secret　Idea that Jesus' warnings to his disciples and others not to proclaim his mighty deeds was a narrative device adopted by the author of Mark, the earliest gospel, in order to explain why Jesus' claims to be the Jewish messiah were not more widely known during his lifetime. This idea was originally developed by Wilhelm Wrede.

military order　Religious order whose members are dedicated both to devotion and to some aspect of military life, such as fighting battles against Christianity's enemies or caring for the sick or wounded. Examples include the Hospitallers and the Knights Templar. These orders first arose during the Crusades.

Minor Prophets　Shorter prophetic books: Hosea, Joel, Amos, Obadiah, Jonah, Micah, Nahum, Habakkuk, Zephaniah, Haggai, Zechariah, Malachi.

miter　Tall, pointed hat worn by bishops in some Churches.

modalism　View of God that understands the Father, Son, and Holy Spirit as different manifestations of the same God, with no substantive distinction.

monarchianism　Set of beliefs that emphasizes the unity of God. Historically, the two most prominent forms of monarchianism have been modalism and adoptionism.

monastery　House or compound where monks live and work, usually led by an abbot.

monenergist　Christian who believes that Christ had only one energy, or driving force, not separate divine and human energies.

monk　Man who is a Christian ascetic and/or is a member of a religious order.

monophysite　Christian who believes that Christ had only one nature, not separate divine and human natures.

monotheism　Idea that only one God exists.

monothelite　Christian who believes that Christ had only one will, not separate divine and human wills.

mortal sin　In the Roman Catholic tradition, a very serious sin for which the soul will suffer eternal damnation unless it is confessed and absolved.

mother superior   Leader of a convent.

MT   *See* Masoretic Text.

mystery   Term used by Orthodox Christians to refer to what Catholics and many Protestants call sacraments.

mystical   Concerned with or involving an encounter with the divine, usually an intense, possibly ecstatic, experience. *See also* spiritual.

myth   Narrative that recounts sacred history, usually related to (semi-)divine beings or cultural heroes.

nave   Central aisle in a church, especially a church laid out in a classic cruciform shape.

Neocharismatic   Relating to the movement originating in the late twentieth century that emphasized the work of the Holy Spirit. *Also called* the Third Wave of the Spirit.

nepotism   Favoritism shown to family members in clerical appointments. The term is derived from the Latin word *nepos* meaning "grandson." In medieval ecclesiastical Latin *nepos* could also mean "nephew."

New Testament   Collection of writings considered sacred by Christians and also written by Christians; the second part of the Christian canon.

nun   Woman who is a Christian ascetic and/or is a member of a religious order.

Old Testament   Collection of writings considered sacred by Christians, based on the sacred scripture of Judaism; the first part of the Christian canon. *Also called the* Hebrew Bible, Tanakh, *or* First Testament.

omnipotent   All powerful, a characteristic usually attributed to God.

omnipresent   Present everywhere at the same time, a characteristic usually attributed to God.

omniscient   All knowing, a characteristic usually attributed to God.

ontological argument   Argument for the existence of God, first proposed by Anselm of Canterbury in his *Proslogion*, that is based on the idea of God's supreme greatness and the notion of existence.

ordained   Person who has been dedicated or consecrated as a member of the clergy (or similar office).

ordinance   Name given by some Christian faith traditions to rituals believed to be ordained by Christ, such as baptism or communion; called sacraments by other Christians.

ordination   Service whose primary focus is the dedication or consecration of a person to become a member of the clergy (or similar office), or to move from one level of clergy to a higher level.

orthodox   When not capitalized, refers to doctrinal positions accepted by the dominant, historical Christian Church.

pacifism   Opposition to Christian involvement in war.

panentheism   Belief that all that is in the universe is contained in God, yet God at the same time transcends the universe.

pantheism   Belief that the entire universe is divine, so that God and the universe are equivalent.

papal bull   Formal proclamation issued by the pope.

papal encyclical   Letter sent by the pope to all Roman Catholic bishops, though often intended for a wider audience.

Papal States   Territories in the middle of the Italian peninsula, including Rome, ruled by the papacy. The Papal States in central Italy were ceded to the kingdom of Italy in 1861, and Rome and the surrounding region was annexed in 1870.

Paraclete   Name for the Holy Spirit, used in the Gospel of John.

Parousia   Greek term for the Second Coming of Christ.

particular atonement   *See* limited atonement.

Passover   Jewish festival associated with God's deliverance of the nation of Israel from bondage in Egypt. Jesus was crucified during Passover week, so Christians sometimes refer to Easter, the Christian celebration of the resurrection, as Passover.

pastor   Leader of a church in some denominations. The word comes from the Latin word *pastor* meaning *shepherd*.

Pastoral Epistles   The New Testament books of 1 Timothy, 2 Timothy, and Titus, ascribed to Paul.

patriarch   Term used by Eastern Christians to refer to the leader of a particular group of churches (e.g. the Patriarch of the Armenian Orthodox Church).

pedobaptism   *See* infant baptism.

penance   Punishment or discipline voluntarily undertaken as a means of (or in response to) obtaining forgiveness for specific sins. Penance is one of the seven sacraments of the Roman Catholic Church. *Also called* the sacrament of confession.

Pentateuch   The first five books of the Hebrew Bible: Genesis, Exodus, Leviticus, Numbers, Deuteronomy. *Also called* Law or Torah.

Pentecost   Jewish feast day on which the Holy Spirit descended with power on the early Church, according to Acts 2. This was the original Day of Pentecost, whose anniversary is celebrated in the Christian calendar seven weeks after Easter.

Pentecostal   Emphasizing or characterized by the work of the Holy Spirit, such as speaking in tongues and miracles.

Pentecostalism   *See* charismatic movement.

pericope   Distinct section of text.

perpetual virginity   Doctrine that Mary, the mother of Jesus, remained a virgin for her entire life. This doctrine is generally accepted by Catholic and Orthodox Christians but rejected by a majority of Protestants.

Pharisee   Member of a Jewish sect that originated in the late Second Temple period and provided the theological basis for the constitution of Rabbinic Judaism after the destruction of the Second Temple in 70 C.E.

pilgrimage   Journey undertaken to a sacred site or a place where an important event occurred.

plenary indulgence   Document that grants full remission of punishment for particular sins.

pleroma   Totality of divine (or semi-divine) *aeons* in Gnostic systems of thought.

pluralism   Belief that Christianity is God's revelation through Jesus Christ but that other paths of salvation also exist, particularly in other religious traditions. *See also* exclusivism *and* inclusivism.

pogrom   Organized persecution or massacre of a particular group, especially the Jews.

polity   Organization of a group, such as a church. The main forms of polity in Christian churches are episcopal, presbyterian, congregational, and societal.

Pontifex Maximus   Supreme Priest, a title originally assigned to the Roman emperor as leader of the imperial cult, but today given to the pope in the Roman Catholic Church.

pontiff   Another title that refers to the pope.

pope   Leader of the Roman Catholic Church, also known as the Bishop of Rome, the Vicar of Christ, etc.

postexilic   Pertaining to the period after Cyrus the Great allowed those Jews in Babylonia who so desired to return to their traditional homeland, after 538 B.C.E.

postmillennial   View of the end times that posits Christ's return after the 1,000 year reign of peace.

predestination   Doctrine that each person's eternal destination is predetermined before all time and that only the elect will spend eternity in heaven.

preexilic   Pertaining to the period before the exile of leading Jews to Babylonia in 587 or 586 B.C.E.

prelate   High-ranking member of the clergy, such as a bishop or abbot.

premillennial   View of the end times that posits Christ's return prior to the 1,000 year reign of peace.

presbyter   *See* elder.

presbyterian   Form of church polity in which leaders are elected to represent the individual church, synod, etc., in the next higher governing body.

preterist   Method of interpreting biblical prophecy, especially the book of Revelation, that sees most or all of it as having been fulfilled in the first Christian century.

priest   Leader of a Christian church, whose duties include preaching and pastoral care. In traditions with three levels of clergy, priests are the middle level, above deacons but below bishops.

primate   Bishop holding the highest rank in a particular country or region.

prophets   (1) (*Capitalized*) Second section of the Jewish canon of scripture. (2) People who feel themselves called by God to speak to their contemporaries.

Protestant Reformation   Sixteenth century reform movement within the Roman Catholic Church originally led by Martin Luther, which resulted in the formation of Churches outside the Catholic and Orthodox folds.

Protestant   Christian who is neither Roman Catholic nor Eastern (or Oriental) Orthodox, usually a member of a Church that traces its roots to the Protestant Reformation.

pulpit   Podium or stand at the front of a church, often on a raised platform, behind which a minister or other person stands when delivering the sermon or homily.

purgatory   In Roman Catholic theology, a place where the dead ultimately bound for heaven suffer punishment for sins from which they have not yet been fully purified. Orthodox and Protestant Christians do not accept the idea of purgatory.

Puritan   Protestant Christians in Britain or the British colonies who sought "purity" in worship, doctrine, and life.

Q   Hypothetical gospel that many scholars believe accounts for the similar passages in Matthew and Luke that have no parallel in Mark. The term comes from the German word *Quelle*, or "source."

Quran   Sacred text of Islam.

Rabbinic Judaism   Form of Judaism that survived the destruction of the Second Temple in 70 C.E. and the expulsion of the Jews from Jerusalem in 135 C.E., forming the basis for modern Judaism.

Radical Reformation   Sixteenth-century reform movement that urged more substantial changes from Roman Catholic doctrine and practice than most Protestants were prepared to follow. *Also called the* Anabaptist Reformation.

Rapture   Doctrine that living Christians will be suddenly removed from the earth to be with Christ, along with the righteous dead, at the beginning of the end times.

recant   To renounce one's belief in something.

Reconquista   Christian reconquest of the Iberian Peninsula from the Muslims, which culminated in the Spanish conquest of Granada in 1492.

religion   System of beliefs and practices, including some concept of a reality or realities beyond ordinary human experience, that is observed by adherents.

religious (*noun*)   Men and women who are members of a Christian religious order, also called monks and nuns.

religious order   Group of people, usually of the same sex, who have dedicated themselves to the religious life, who follow a particular rule or set of guidelines for living, and whose chief duty is to serve God. Roman Catholics, Eastern Orthodox, and Anglicans all have religious orders. Examples include Jesuits, Dominicans, and Carmelites.

revelation   Special communication of God with humans, sometimes through visions, auditions, or dreams.

revival meeting   Series of church services – originally held out of doors, primarily in frontier areas of the U.S. – which are aimed at producing crisis conversion experiences, often accompanied by manifestations of the divine (e.g. miraculous healings or speaking in tongues). *See also* camp meeting.

rogation days   Days in the Christian calendar, as observed by Anglicans and some Roman Catholics, in which Christians ask God's blessing and protection.

Sabbath   Day of rest prescribed in the Ten Commandments, traditionally identified as lasting from sundown Friday to sundown Saturday. Sunday, the day on which most Christians worship, is sometimes called the Christian Sabbath.

sacrament   Visible symbol of divine grace bestowed on Christians. Some Christian traditions have a fixed number of sacraments, while others do not, and still others do not use the term at all.

Sadducee   Member of a Jewish sect that originated in the late Second Temple period and was allied primarily with the high priests in Jerusalem during the first century C.E.

saint   Person of particular piety and closeness to God.

salvation   Deliverance from an evil situation or state, especially deliverance from sin.

sanctification   Being made holy before God.

sanctuary   Holy place, often a place of worship. In some church buildings, the sanctuary is the place immediately around the altar.

Sanhedrin   Jewish ruling council that wielded religious and political power.

Satan   Evil being who stands in opposition to God in the New Testament and in Christian theology.

schismatic   Someone who breaks away from the main group because of differences in doctrine or practice.

scholasticism   Method of teaching and learning, popular in late medieval universities, that emphasizes dialectical reasoning.

scripture   Sacred texts of a religious community.

Second Coming of Christ   Doctrine that Christ will return to earth at or near the end of time. *Also called the* Parousia.

Second Isaiah   Name given both to Chapters 40–55 of the book of Isaiah and to the anonymous sixth-century prophet responsible for delivering the message of these chapters.

Second Temple period   Period of Jewish history that spans the time from the building of the Second Temple (516 B.C.E.) to the destruction of the temple (70 C.E.).

Second Wave of the Spirit   Second movement of Pentecostalism, beginning in the mid-twentieth century, which resulted in the charismatic movement affecting many non-Pentecostal denominations, as well as swelling the ranks of existing Pentecostal churches.

Second Zechariah   Zechariah 9–14, often attributed to an individual or individuals other than the prophet whose words comprise Zechariah 1–8.

secular   (1) Of or pertaining to the world, especially as conceived as functioning apart from religion. (2) Related to ministry in the world rather than in a monastery or convent (e.g. a secular priest, who serves in a parish).

secularism   Trend toward excluding religion from public life.

see   Official seat, or center of authority, of a bishop.

seeker sensitive   Designed to attract the interest of people with little experience of Christianity.

seeker   (1) Person with little experience of Christianity who shows an interest in learning more about it. (2) (*Capitalized*) Member of a religious group, originating in seventeenth-century Britain, that rejected many of the prevalent Christian doctrines of the day, such as predestination.

semi-Arianism   Belief that Jesus was indeed divine but should not be described as being of the same substance (*homoousios*) as the Father. Semi-Arians preferred to use the terms *homoiousios* (of a similar substance) or *homoios* (similar) to describe Jesus' relationship with the Father.

semi-eremitic   Lifestyle or characteristics of an ascetic who lives in a skete.

Separatist   Christian in Britain or the British colonies belonging to a church that was independent of the Anglican Church.

Septuagint   Old Greek version of the Pentateuch. The term is often extended to include the oldest Greek version of the entire Hebrew Bible. *Abbreviated* LXX.

sermon   Reflection or exposition on a biblical passage or a particular theme.

Sheol   Place of the dead in most of the Hebrew Bible, the destiny of all humanity.

simony   Practice of buying or selling a sacred office or other ecclesiastical privilege.

sin   Deviating from the divine standard, resulting in separation from God.

sinner's prayer   Type of prayer spoken by new converts in certain Christian traditions, especially those that emphasize a crisis conversion experience.

skete   Settlement of monks or nuns, generally less organized than a monastery or convent.

slain in the Spirit   Manifestation of the Holy Spirit in which a person appears to lose consciousness.

Son   Second person of the divine Trinity, in traditional, Trinitarian Christianity. *See also* Father, Holy Spirit, *and* Trinity.

soul-sleep   Doctrine that when people die, their souls sleep until the final resurrection of the dead at the end of time, held by Seventh-day Adventists and some other Christian groups today.

speaking in tongues   Experience associated primarily with Pentecostal and Charismatic Christians, who utter words in no known language as praise to God. *Also called* glossolalia.

spiritual   Concerned with or involving an encounter with the divine in general or with the Holy Spirit in particular. *See also* mystical.

stigmata   The wounds of Christ that are said to have appeared on various Christian saints, such as Francis of Assisi, throughout history.

stole   Clerical sash worn around the neck (priests) or across the body (deacons), often with distinctive colors or patterns that reflect a particular day or season of the Christian calendar.

stylite   Ascetic who spends a great amount of his or her life on top of a pillar.

subdeacon   Lower level of clergy assigned certain tasks in some Christian traditions and historical periods.

superior general   Leader of a religious order.

symbol   (1) In general, an object or ritual that stands for or points to another, higher reality. (2) Another name for one of the traditional creeds of the Christian Church.

syncretism   Religious tradition that blends elements from two or more other religious traditions.

synod   Assembly of Church officials, called either to address a specific set of issues or to deal with regular Church business. Both the meeting and the group that meets can be called a synod.

Synoptic Gospels   The first three gospels – Matthew, Mark, Luke – which offer a similar outline of the life of Jesus, especially his public ministry.

Tanakh   Hebrew acronym referring to the Hebrew Bible or Old Testament, taken from the first letter for the three divisions of the Jewish canon: *Torah* (Law), *Neviim* (Prophets), *Ketuvim* (Writings). *Also called* Old Testament, Hebrew Bible, *or* First Testament.

targum   Aramaic translation of the Hebrew Bible, originally oral but committed to writing beginning in the late Second Temple period.

theodicy   Philosophical or theological explanation of God's goodness and justice in the light of the existence of evil in the world.

Theotokos   Greek term that means *one who gives birth to God*, or more simply, *God-bearer*, a reference to Mary, the mother of Jesus. The term, which was opposed by Nestorius, was accepted as orthodox at the Council of Ephesus in 431.

Third Isaiah   Isaiah 56–66, often attributed to a prophet living in Judah in the early Second Temple period.

Third Wave of the Spirit   Third movement of Pentecostalism, beginning in the late twentieth century, which gave rise to new, Neocharismatic denominations.

Tome of Leo   Document written by Pope Leo I in an effort to define the precise nature of the relationship between the divine and the human in Christ. It was accepted by the Council of Chalcedon in 451 as an official definition of the orthodox position.

Torah   (1) Jewish law or instruction. (2) First five books of the Hebrew Bible, the first section of the Jewish canon of scripture. *Also called* Law *or* Pentateuch.

transept   In a cruciform shaped church, the part of the church that runs perpendicular to the nave and the aisles.

Transjordan   Region east of the Jordan River.

transubstantiation   Roman Catholic doctrine that the bread and wine of Communion are transformed into the literal body and blood of Christ at the moment they are consecrated by the priest.

Trinity   Traditional Christian understanding of God as consisting of three separate Persons (Father, Son, and Holy Spirit) inseparably united to one another in a single Godhead.

universalism   Doctrine that all human souls will eventually be reconciled to God and spend eternity with God.

unlimited atonement   Doctrine that Christ's blood was shed for all humankind. *Also called* general atonement.

veneration   Act of giving honor to something or someone, such as an icon or Jesus Christ.

venial sin   In the Roman Catholic tradition, a sin that is of lesser magnitude than a mortal sin and for which the soul would not suffer eternal damnation, even if it remained unconfessed and not absolved.

vespers   Evening prayers, or an evening prayer service.

Vicar of Christ   Title of the pope, emphasizing his role as Christ's representative on earth.

virgin birth   Doctrine that Mary, the mother of Jesus, was a virgin when Jesus was conceived through the intervention of the Holy Spirit and that she remained a virgin until the time of his birth.

Writings   Third section of the Jewish canon of scripture.

Zealot   Member of a Jewish political group opposed to Rome and committed to ridding the Jewish homeland of Roman control.

Bibliography

Achebe, Chinua 1994. *Things Fall Apart*. New York: Anchor Books.

Ackroyd, P. E. and C. F. Evans, eds 1970. *The Cambridge History of the Bible*. Vol. 1: *From the Beginnings to Jerome*. Cambridge: Cambridge University Press.

Adamo, David Tuesday 2001. "The Use of Psalms in African Indigenous Churches in Nigeria." In *The Bible in Africa*, ed. Gerald O. West and Musa W. Duba, 336–49. Boston, MA: Brill.

Adherents.com. http://www.adherents.com.

Ahlström, Gösta W., and Gary O. Rollefson 1993. *The History of Ancient Palestine*. Edited by Diana Edelman. Minneapolis, MN: Fortress.

Altizer, Thomas J. J. and William Hamilton 1966. *Radical Theology and the Death of God*. Indianapolis, IN: Bobbs-Merrill.

Armstrong, Karen 1994. *A History of God: The 4000-Year Quest of Judaism, Christianity and Islam*. New York: Knopf.

Atwood, Margaret 1998. *The Handmaid's Tale*. New York: Anchor Books.

Bainton, Roland H. 1950. *Here I Stand: A Life of Martin Luther*. New York: Penguin.

Barbour, Ian G. 2000. *When Science Meets Religion*. New York: HarperSanFrancisco.

Barrett, David R. and Todd M. Johnson 2001. *World Christian Trends*. Pasadena, CA: William Carey Library.

Barrett, David R., Todd M. Johnson, and George T. Kurian 2001. *World Christian Encyclopedia: A Comparative Survey of Churches and Religions in the Modern World*. 2nd edn. New York: Oxford University Press.

Barth, Karl 1936–1977. *Church Dogmatics*. Translated by G. T. Thomson. Edinburgh: T&T Clark.

Barth, Karl 1968. *The Epistle to the Romans*. Translated from the sixth German edition by Edwyn C. Hoskyns. London: Oxford University Press.

Bauer, Walter 1971. *Orthodoxy and Heresy in Earliest Christianity*. Translated by Robert A. Kraft *et al.* Edited by Robert A. Kraft and Gerhard Krodel. Philadelphia, PA: Fortress. (http://ccat.sas.upenn.edu/rs/rak/publics/new/BAUER00.htm)

Bax, Douglas S. 1987. "From Constantine to Calvin: The Doctrine of the Just War." In *Theology and Violence: The South African Debate*, 147–71. Edited by Charles Villa-Vicencio. Johannesburg: Skotaville.

The Benedictine Monks of Santo Domingo de Silos 1994. *Chant*. New York: Angel Records.

Bettenson, Henry and Chris Maunder, eds 1999. *Documents of the Christian Church*. 3rd edn. New York: Oxford University Press.

Bonhoeffer, Dietrich 1959. *The Cost of Discipleship*. 2nd edn. New York: Collier.

Bonhoeffer, Dietrich 1967. *Letters and Papers from Prison*. Revised edn, edited by Eberhard Bethge. Translated by Reginald Fuller. New York: Macmillan.

Borg, Marcus J. 2003. *The Heart of Christianity: Rediscovering a Life of Faith*. New York: HarperSanFrancisco.

Borg, Marcus J. 2006. *Jesus: Uncovering the Life, Teachings, and Relevance of a Religious Revolutionary*. New York: HarperSanFrancisco.

Bradner, John 1977. *Symbols of Church Seasons and Days*. Harrisburg, PA: Morehouse.

Bruce, F. F. 1988. *The Canon of Scripture*. Downer's Grove, IL: InterVarsity.

Brunner, H. Emil 1931. *A Theology of Crisis*. New York: Scribner.

Bruyneel, Sally and Alan G. Padgett 2003. *Introducing Christianity*. Maryknoll, NY: Orbis.

Bultmann, Rudolf 1953. "The Case for Demythologizing: A Reply." In *Kerygma and Myth: A Theological Debate*, vol. 2, edited by Hans Werner Bartsch. London: SPCK.

Bunson, Matthew 1995. *The Pope Encyclopedia*. New York: Crown.

Calvin, John 1986. *Institutes of the Christian Religion*. Translated by Ford Lewis Battles. Grand Rapids, MI: Eerdmans.

Carroll, James 2001. *Constantine's Sword: The Church and the Jews*. Boston, MA: Houghton Mifflin.

Catechism of the Catholic Church 1997. 2nd edn. Vatican City: Libreria Editrice Vaticana.

Charlesworth, James H., ed. 1990. *Jews and Christians: Exploring the Past, Present, and Future*. New York: Crossroads.

Christianson, Eric S., Peter Francis, and William R. Teleford, eds 2005. *Cinéma Divinité: Religion, Theology and the Bible in Film*. London: SCM.

Church of England 1987. *The Book of Common Prayer*. Cambridge: Cambridge University Press.

Cobb, John B., ed. 2003. *Progressive Christians Speak*. Louisville, KY: Westminster John Knox.

Collins, Francis S. 2006. *The Language of God*. New York: Free Press.

Cone, James 1969. *Black Theology and Black Power*. New York: Seabury.

Cone, James 1970. *A Black Theology of Liberation*. Philadelphia, PA: Lippincott.

Cox, Harvey 1965. *The Secular City*. New York: Macmillan.

Cox, Harvey 1984. *Religion in the Secular City: Toward a Postmodern Theology*. New York: Simon and Schuster.

Crossan, John Dominic 1991. *The Historical Jesus: The Life of a Mediterranean Jewish Peasant*. New York: HarperSanFrancisco.

The Dalai Lama 1999. *Ethics for a New Millennium*. New York: Riverhead Books.

Darwin, Charles 2003. *The Origin of Species and the Voyage of the Beagle*. Everyman's Library. New York: Knopf.

Dawkins, Richard 2006. *The God Delusion*. Boston, MA: Houghton Mifflin.

Day, Peter 2003. *A Dictionary of Christian Denominations*. London: Continuum.

Dembski, William A. 1999. *Intelligent Design: The Bridge between Science and Theology*. Downer's Grove, IL: InterVarsity Press.

Dowe, Phil 2005. *Galileo, Darwin, and Hawking: The Interplay of Science, Reason, and Religion*. Grand Rapids, MI: Eerdmans.

Dowley, Tim 1990. *Introduction to the History of Christianity*. Revised edn. Minneapolis, MN: Fortress.

Durkheim, Émile 1915. *The Elementary Forms of Religious Life: A Study in Religious Sociology*. Translated by Joseph Ward Swain. London: Allen & Unwin.

Eddy, Mary Baker 1906. *Science and Health with a Key to the Scriptures*. Boston, MA: Published by the Trustees under the Will of Mary Baker G. Eddy.

Edwards, Jonathan 1741. *Sinners in the Hands of an Angry God*. Grand Rapids, MI: Christian Classics Ethereal Library. http://www.ccel.org/e/edwards/sermons/sinners.html.

Ehrman, Bart D. 2004. *The New Testament: A Historical Introduction to the Early Christian Writings*. 3rd edn. New York: Oxford University Press.

Eliade, Mircea 1959. *The Sacred and the Profane: The Nature of Religion*. Translated by Willard R. Trask. New York: Harcourt, Brace & World.

Eliade, Mircea 1963. *Myth and Reality*. Translated by Willard R. Trask. New York: Harper & Row.

Endo, Shusaku 1969. *Silence*. Translated by William Johnston. New York: Taplinger.

Erasmus, Desiderius 1989. *Discourse on Free Will*. Translated and edited by Ernst F. Winter. New York: Continuum.

Ferguson, George 1966. *Signs and Symbol in Christian Art*. London: Oxford University Press.

FitzGerald, Thomas E. 2004. *The Ecumenical Movement: An Introductory History*. Westport, CT: Praeger.

Fitzgerald, Timothy 2000. *The Ideology of Religious Studies*. Oxford: Oxford University Press.

Flannery, Austin, ed. 1996. *Vatican Council II*. Vol. 1: *The Conciliar and Post Conciliar Documents*. New revised edn. Northport, NY: Costello.

Foster, Richard J. 1998. *Celebration of Discipline: The Path to Spiritual Growth*. New York: HarperSanFrancisco.

Frend, W. H. C. 1984. *The Rise of Christianity*. Philadelphia, PA: Fortress.

The Fundamentals: A Testimony 1910. 12 vols. Chicago, IL: Testimony Publishing Co.

Funk, Robert W. 2001. "Milestones in the Quest for the Historical Jesus." *The Fourth R* 14: 9–11, 15–18. (http://www.westarinstitute.org/Periodicals/4R_Articles/ Milestones/milestones.html)

Garraty, John A. and Peter Gay, eds 1972. *The Columbia History of the World*. New York: Harper & Row.

Gingerich, Owen 2006. *God's Universe*. Cambridge, MA: Belknap Press.

González, Justo 1984–1985. *The Story of Christianity*. 2 vols. New York: HarperSanFrancisco.

González, Justo 1987. *A History of Christian Thought*. Revised edn, 3 vols. Nashville, TN: Abingdon.

Griffith-Dickson, Gwen 2005. *The Philosophy of Religion*. London: SCM.

Gutiérrez, Gustavo 1973. *A Theology of Liberation*. Translated and edited by Caridad Inda and John Eagleson. Maryknoll, NY: Orbis.

Gutiérrez, Gustavo 1993. *Las Casas: In Search of the Poor of Jesus Christ*. Translated by Robert R. Barr. Maryknoll, NY: Orbis.

Guyon, Jeanne 1975. *Experiencing the Depths of Jesus Christ*. Auburn, ME: Christian Books.

Hanson, Paul D. 1979. *The Dawn of Apocalyptic: The Historical and Sociological Roots of Jewish Apocalyptic Eschatology*. Revised edn. Philadelphia, PA: Fortress.

Harnack, Adolf von 1989. *Marcion: The Gospel of the Alien God*. Translated by John E. Steely and Lyle D. Bierma. Durham, NC: Labyrinth.

Hayes, John H. and J. Maxwell Miller, eds 1977. *Israelite and Judaean History*. London: SCM.

Holmes, Michael W., ed. 1999. *The Apostolic Fathers*. Revised edn. Grand Rapids, MI: Baker.

Hourani, Albert 1991. *A History of the Arab Peoples*. Cambridge, MA: Belknap (Harvard University Press).

Hudson, Winthrop S. 1981. *Religion in America*. 3rd edn. New York: Scribner.

Hurtado, Larry W. 2003. *Lord Jesus Christ: Devotion to Jesus in Earliest Christianity*. Grand Rapids, MI: Eerdmans.

Internet Encyclopedia of Philosophy. S.v. "Augustine." (http://www.iep.utm.edu/a/ augustin.htm)

James, William 1902. *The Varieties of Religious Experience*. New York: Longmans, Green.

Jenkins, Philip 2002. *The Next Christendom: The Coming of Global Christianity*. Oxford: Oxford University Press.

Johanson, Donald and Blake Edgar 2006. *From Lucy to Language*. Revised edn. New York: Simon and Schuster.

Johnson, Todd M. n.d. *Christianity in Global Context: Trends and Statistics*. Pew Forum on Religion and Public Life. http://pewforum.org/events/051805/global-christianity. pdf.

Johnston, Robert K. 2000. *Reel Spirituality: Theology and Film in Dialogue.* Grand Rapids, MI: Baker Academic.

Kairos Theologians 1986. *The Kairos Document: Challenge to the Church.* 2nd edn. Braamfontein, South Africa: Skotaville.

Kant, Immanuel 1952. *The Critique of Pure Reason; The Critique of Practical Reason, and Other Ethical Treatises; The Critique of Judgement.* Translated by J. M. D. Meiklejohn, T.K. Abbot, W. Hastie, and J. C. Meredith. Chicago, IL: Encyclopaedia Britannica.

Kelly, J. N. D. 1972. *Early Christian Creeds.* 3rd edn. New York: Longman.

Kerouac, Jack 1985. *On the Road.* New York: Penguin.

Kierkegaard, Søren 1954. *Fear and Trembling and Sickness unto Death.* Translated by Walter Lowrie. Princeton, NJ: Princeton University Press.

Kimball, Charles 2002. *When Religion Becomes Evil.* New York: HarperSanFrancisco.

King, Martin Luther, Jr. 1963. *Strength to Love.* Philadelphia, PA: Fortress.

Kingsolver, Barbara 1998. *The Poisonwood Bible.* New York: HarperPerennial.

Latourette, Kenneth Scott 1975. *A History of Christianity.* Revised edn, 2 vols. New York: Harper & Row.

Levine, Amy-Jill 2006. *The Misunderstood Jew: The Church and the Scandal of the Jewish Jesus.* New York: HarperSanFrancisco.

Lewis, John and Michael D'Orso 1998. *Walking with the Wind: A Memoir of the Movement.* San Diego, CA: Harcourt Brace & Company.

Lindsey, Hal and C. C. Carlson 1970. *The Late Great Planet Earth.* Grand Rapids, MI: Zondervan.

Lonsdale, John 2002. "Kikuyu Christianities: A History of Intimate Diversity." In *Christianity and the African Imagination.* Edited by David Maxwell, 157–97. Leiden: Brill.

Luther, Martin 1957. *Martin Luther on the Bondage of the Will.* Translated by J. I. Packer and O. R. Johnston. Westwood, NJ: Revell.

Lutheran World Federation and Roman Catholic Church 1999. "Joint Declaration on the Doctrine of Justification." http://www.vatican.va/roman_curia/pontifical_councils/chrstuni/documents/rc_pc_chrstuni_doc_31101999_cath-luth-joint-declaration_en.html.

Lyell, Charles 1997. *Principles of Geology.* Edited with an Introduction by James A. Secord. London: Penguin.

Margenau, Henry and Roy Abraham Varghese 1992. *Cosmos, Bios, Theos: Scientists Reflect on Science, God, and the Origins of the Universe, Life, and* Homo sapiens. La Salle, IL: Open Court.

Marx, Karl and Friedrich Engels 1990. *Capital* and *Manifesto of the Communist Party.* 2nd edn. Chicago, IL: Encyclopaedia Britannica.

Mathewes-Green, Frederica 1999. *At the Corner of East and Now: A Modern Life in Ancient Christian Orthodoxy.* New York: Tarcher/Putnam.

Maugham, Somerset 1944. *The Razor's Edge.* Garden City, NY: Doubleday.

Maxwell, David 1998. *Christianity and the African Imagination*. Leiden: Brill.

McBrien, Richard R. 1994. *Catholicism*. 2nd edn. New York: HarperSanFrancisco.

McBrien, Richard P. 1997. *Lives of the Popes*. New York: HarperSanFrancisco.

McClymond, Michael J. 2002. "Making Sense of the Census, or, What 1,999,563,838 Christians Might Mean for the Study of Religion." *Journal of the American Academy of Religion* 70: 875–90.

Meier, John P. 1991–2001. *A Marginal Jew: Rethinking the Historical Jesus*. 3 vols. Anchor Bible Reference Library. New York: Doubleday.

Merton, Thomas 1948. *The Seven Storey Mountain*. New York: Harcourt, Brace and Company.

Meyer, Marvin 1992. *The Gospel of Thomas*. New York: HarperSanFrancisco.

Miller, Kenneth R. 1999. *Finding Darwin's God*. New York: Cliff Street Books.

Mitchell, Donald W. and James Wiseman, eds 1998. *The Gethsemani Encounter: A Dialogue on the Spiritual Life by Buddhist and Christian Monastics*. New York: Continuum.

Moltmann, Jürgen 1967. *Theology of Hope*. London: SCM.

Mowinckel, Sigmund 1954. *He That Cometh: The Messiah Concept in the Old Testament and Later Judaism*. Translated by G. W. Anderson. New York: Abingdon.

Mowinckel, Sigmund 1953. *Religion und Kultus*. Translated by Albrecht Schauer. Göttingen: Vandenhoeck and Ruprecht.

Moynahan, Brian 2002. *The Faith: A History of Christianity*. New York: Doubleday.

Ndung'u, Nahason W. 2001. "The Role of the Bible in the Rise of African Instituted Churches: The Case of the Akurinu Churches in Kenya." In *The Bible in Africa*, ed. Gerald O. West and Musa W. Duba, 236–47. Boston, MA: Brill.

Neusner, Jacob 1988. *The Mishnah: A New Translation*. New Haven, CT: Yale University Press.

Niebuhr, Reinhold 1932. *Moral Man and Immoral Society*. New York: Scribner.

Niebuhr, H. Richard 1951. *Christ and Culture*. New York: Harper & Row.

Norris, Herbert 1950. *Church Vestments*. New York: Dutton.

Oleksa, Michael 1992. *Orthodox Alaska: A Theology of Mission*. Crestwood, NY: St. Vladimir's Seminary Press.

Olson, Steve 2003. *Mapping Human History*. Boston, MA: Houghton Mifflin.

Otto, Rudolf 1958. *The Idea of the Holy*. Translated by John W. Harvey. New York: Oxford University Press.

Palmer, G. E. H., Philip Sherrard, and Kallistos Ware, trans. and ed. 1979–1995. *The Philokalia*. 4 vols. London: Faber and Faber.

Papal Encyclicals Online. http://www.papalencyclicals.net.

Pelikan, Jaroslav 1971–1989. *The Christian Tradition: A History of the Development of Doctrine*. 5 vols. Chicago, IL: University of Chicago Press.

Pelikan, Jaroslav 1997. *The Illustrated Jesus through the Centuries*. New Haven, CT: Yale University Press.

Pelikan, Jaroslav 1999. *Jesus through the Centuries: His Place in the History of Culture*. 2nd edn. New Haven, CT: Yale University Press.

Pirsig, Robert M. 1974. *Zen and the Art of Motorcycle Maintenance: An Inquiry into Values*. New York: Quill.

Quasten, Johannes and Angelo Di Berardino. 1950–1986. *Patrology*. 4 vols. Vol. 4 translated by Placid Solari. Allen, TX: Christian Classics.

Raeburn, Michael 1973. *An Outline of World Architecture*. London: Octopus.

Rauschenbusch, Walter 1997. *A Theology for the Social Gospel*. Louisville, KY: Westminster John Knox.

Religion Past and Present 2007. S.v. "Art and Religion." Leiden: Brill.

Renan, Ernest n.d. *Vie de Jésus*. Paris: Calmann-Lévy.

Roberts, J. M. 1993. *History of the World*. New York: Oxford University Press.

Robinson, James M. 1996. *The Nag Hammadi Library in English*. 4th edn. Leiden: Brill.

Robinson, John A. T. 1963. *Honest to God*. Philadelphia, PA: Westminster.

Sanders, E. P. 1992. *Judaism: Practice and Belief 63* B.C.E.*–66* C.E. London: SCM.

Schell, Jonathan 2003. *The Unconquerable World: Power, Nonviolence, and the Will of the People*. New York: Metropolitan Books.

Schleiermacher, Friedrich 1958. *On Religion: Speeches to Its Cultured Despisers*. Translated by John Oman. New York: Harper & Row.

Schweitzer, Albert 1968. *The Quest of the Historical Jesus*. Translated by W. Montgomery, with an Introduction by James M. Robinson. New York: Macmillan.

Scofield, C. I. 1917. *The Scofield Reference Bible*. 2nd edn. New York: Oxford University Press.

Sider, Ronald J. 1977. *Rich Christians in an Age of Hunger*. Downer's Grove, IL: Inter-Varsity Press.

Smart, Ninian 1977. *The Long Search*. Boston, MA: Little, Brown.

Smith, Huston 1958. *The Religions of Man*. New York: Harper & Row.

Smolarski, Dennis Chester 2003. *The General Instruction of the Roman Missal*. Collegeville, MN: Liturgical Press.

Spong, John Shelby 1998. *Why Christianity Must Change or Die*. New York: HarperSanFrancisco.

Tattersall, Ian 1998. *Becoming Human*. San Diego, CA: Harcourt Brace & Company.

Taylor, Richard 2005. *How to Read a Church: A Guide to Symbols and Images in Churches and Cathedrals*. Mahwah, NJ: HiddenSpring.

Tillich, Paul 1951–1963. *Systematic Theology*. 3 vols. Chicago, IL: University of Chicago Press.

Tillich, Paul, 1952. *The Courage to Be*. New Haven, CT: Yale University Press.

Tillich, Paul 1968. *A History of Christian Thought*. Edited by Carl E. Braaten. New York: Simon and Schuster.

Thurber, James 1940. *Fables for Our Time*. New York: Harper & Row.

Trueblood, Elton 1946. *Foundations for Reconstruction*. New York: Harper & Brothers.

Vickers, Graham 1999. *Architecture: The Evolution of the City*. New York: Da Capo.

Villa-Vicencio, Charles, ed. 1987. *Theology and Violence: The South African Debate.* Johannesburg: Skotaville.

Ward, Benedicta, trans. 1975. *The Sayings of the Desert Fathers.* London: Mowbray.

Ware, Timothy 1997. *The Orthodox Church.* 2nd edn. New York: Penguin.

West, Gerald O. and Musa W. Duba, eds 2001. *The Bible in Africa.* Boston, MA: Brill.

Westcott, Brooke Foss 1896. *A General Survey of the History of the Canon of the New Testament.* London: Macmillan.

Whiston, William 1980. *The Works of Josephus.* Lynn, MA: Hendrickson.

Williams, George Huntston 1992. *The Radical Reformation.* 3rd edn. Kirksville, MO: Sixteenth Century Journal Publishers.

Williams, Roger 2001. *The Bloudy Tenent of Persecution for Cause of Conscience.* Macon, GA: Mercer University Press.

World Christian Database. Online database. http://worldchristiandatabase.org/wcd/.

Wright, N. T. 1996. "The Historical Jesus and Christian Theology." *Sewanee Theological Review* 39: 404–12. (http://www.ntwrightpage.com/Wright_Historical_Jesus. htm)

Index